The New York Public Library

African American
Desk Reference

SCHOMBURG CENTER
FOR RESEARCH IN BLACK CULTURE

The New York Public Library

African American
Desk Reference

A STONESONG PRESS BOOK

John Wiley & Sons, Inc.

New York • Chichester • Weinheim • Brisbane • Singapore • Toronto

This book is printed on acid-free paper. ⊚

Published by John Wiley & Sons, Inc.
Published simultaneously in Canada

A STONESONG PRESS BOOK

Illustration credits appear on page 565 and constitute an extension of this copyright page.

This publication is designed to provide accurate and authoritative information in regard to the subject matter covered. It is sold with the understanding that the publisher is not engaged in rendering professional services. If professional advice or other expert assistance is required, the services of a competent professional person should be sought.

ISBN 0-471-23924-0

Printed in the United States of America
10 9 8 7 6 5 4 3 2

The New York Public Library
Project Sponsors

A Note from the Editors

Every attempt has been made to ensure that this publication is as accurate as possible and as comprehensive as space would allow. We are grateful to the many friends, librarians, reference editors, researchers, teachers, and state and U.S. government employees who contributed facts, figures, time, energy, ideas, and opinions. Our choice of what to include was aided by their advice and their voices of experience. The contents, however, remain subjective to some extent, because we could not possibly cover everything that one needs to know about African American history, culture, and resources. If errors or omissions are discovered, we would appreciate hearing from you, the user, as we prepare future editions. Please address suggestions and comments to The Stonesong Press at 11 East 47th Street, New York, NY, 10017.

We hope you find our work useful.

Contents

6 *Religion* 147

7 *Education* 173

8 *Health* 211

9 *Business and Entrepreneurship* 237

10 *Science and Technology* 271

11 *The Military* 283

12   The Law   307

13   Literature and Language   335

14   Music   367

15   Performing Arts   403

16   Fine and Applied Arts   437

17   The Media   461

Foreword

People of African descent living in the United States at the beginning of the new century and the new millenium are a prominent part of the American social, cultural, political, and spiritual landscape. Wherever one looks in American society—in government, business, sports, the arts, and the military; on film, television, Wall Street, or the internet—African American men and women (and sometimes children) are involved in the affairs of this nation. They are mayors of some of the nation's largest and/or most significant cities. They have served as governors, state legislators, senators, members of the House of Representatives, members of presidential cabinets, ambassadors, Supreme Court justices, and more. They have become larger-than-life figures in the NBA, the WNBA, the NFL, and major league baseball. In Hollywood films and on prime-time television programs, they have assumed starring and leading production roles. African music, including jazz, rock, blues, gospel, and rap, essentially defines American music as a distinctive contribution to world culture. And African Americans, who have long been an established presence in American theater and dance, have also distinguished themselves in law and diplomacy, technology and inventions, and science and industry.

While events like Black History Month have begun to create a heightened public awareness of the African American presence in American society, most Americans (including African Americans) have limited knowledge of the breadth and depth of the black population's impact on American life. Most have not had access to basic information about their historical and cultural development. Nor have they been able to turn to a single reference source to answer basic questions that contemporary African American life is constantly raising. This *African American Desk Reference*, from the Schomburg Center for Research in Black Culture of The New York Public Library, is designed to provide such up-to-date information for the general public in a handy single-volume format.

The Schomburg Center is a logical place to turn for information on people of African descent in general and African Americans in particular. The world's leading research library devoted exclusively to documenting, preserving, and interpreting the global African diaspora and African experiences, the Schomburg Center for Research in Black Culture has been in the forefront of such initiatives since its inception in 1925 as the Division of Negro History, Literature and Prints in The New York Public Library's 135th Street branch. It won international acclaim a year later when it acquired the 10,000-item personal collection of the distinguished bibliophile and scholar Arturo Alfonso Schomburg. Over the past seventy-five years, the Center has evolved into the preeminent public research library in the world on black history and culture. With collections totaling more than five million items, it serves more than 50,000 researchers free of charge in its Harlem-based facilities annually and responds to another 40,000 to 50,000 mail and telephone reference inquiries.

The wide-ranging collections in the General Research and Reference Division include more than 150,000 books and 6,500 serial titles in English as well as other European and African languages. There are more than 400 black newspapers and 1,000 current periodicals from around the world. About 20 percent of the book collection deals with Afro-Hispanic and Afro-Caribbean history and culture.

The four Special Collections offer an enormous variety of primary source material. The Manuscripts, Archives and Rare Books Division, which began with rare treasures from Schomburg's personal holdings, today contains more than 3.5 million items including more than 3,900 rare books, 580 collections of personal and professional papers and organizational records, and 15,000 pieces of sheet music. Original manuscripts and correspondence by such diverse figures as Richard Wright, W. E. B. Du Bois, Langston Hughes, Booker T. Washington, Frederick Douglass, Zora Neal Hurston, and Toussaint L'Ouverture are included in the Division's holdings.

The Photographs and Prints Division includes more than 750,000 items from mid-eighteenth-century graphics to contemporary documentary and art photographs. The collection, which records black life throughout the United States, also includes scenes from Africa, Europe, the Caribbean, and the Americas. Stereographic views and cartes-de-visité depict scenes from slavery through the Civil War. Among the master photographers represented are James VanDerZee, Gordon Parks, Edward Steichen, Coreen Simpson, Bert Andrews, and Chester Higgins.

Often surprising to many visitors are the numerous nonbook or nonprint materials found in the Schomburg. Its Art and Artifacts Division houses one of the most comprehensive collections of black artists' works in a major research facility, including paintings, sculptures, works on paper, textiles, and artifacts, many of them from Africa and the African diaspora. The collection is particularly strong in art produced during the Harlem Renaissance and WPA periods. Yet another aspect of the Center's diverse collections is the Moving Image and Recorded Sound Division, which holds collections of early radio broadcasts and recordings of such personalities as Marcus Garvey, Booker T. Washington, and George Washington Carver. Its musical documentation ranges from African chants to American jazz. Today these assets are being complimented by an ongoing Oral History/Video Documentation Project that videotapes interviews with historically or culturally significant figures.

As we move into the 21st century, the Schomburg Center has begun an effort to make its collections freely available to a worldwide audience through its web site, where one can find more detailed information about its collections and services, online exhibitions, video clips from oral history interviews, and unique online databases of texts and images of African Americans. Launched in 1998, the Digital Schomburg (*http://www.digital.nypl.org/research/sc/sc.html*) provides access to the full text of the work of fifty-two 19th-century black writers and more than 500 images from the Schomburg materials relating to 19th-century African American history and culture. Slated for addition to the Digital Schomburg are additional 19th-century works by black Americans as well as books and images on African diaspora and African themes. The Digital Schomburg will continue to extend access to its holdings to users around the world.

The Schomburg Center complements its research services by regularly interpreting its collections for the general public through a variety of educational and cultural programs. *The New York Public Library African American Desk Reference* has been created with that general user or reader in mind. It is intended to provide a convenient and useful one-volume reference to important aspects of black life and culture, beginning with a chronology of African American history. It surveys the story of Africans in the Americas, including the Caribbean, from slavery through contemporary political and civil rights movements. Throughout it is filled with facts and data—frequently in easy-to-reference charts and lists—about African American life and culture at the close of the 20th-century from business, law, and education to literature, music, and sports. In essence it is an overview or introduction to a subject of enormous complexity and importance.

A project of this size represents the work of many people. In addition to the staff of The Stonesong Press who originated and developed this book with the Library, I would like to thank Karen Van Westering and Roberta Yancy for their invaluable assistance in preparing this text for publication. Thanks also to the list of advisors who reviewed and commented on various sections of the text and Theresa Martin and Marabel Pimentel for administrative assistance.

Howard Dodson
Director Schomburg Center
January 1999

The New York Public Library

African American
Desk Reference

1

The Saga of African American History

TIME LINE OF AFRICAN AMERICAN HISTORY

c. 1200 B.C.–700 B.C.	According to a number of scholars, black Africans from Egypt and Nubia sail west across the Atlantic Ocean and have extensive contact with native peoples of the Americas. (This theory is based on studies of ocean currents and navigation, reports of later European explorers, botanical research, oral traditions, Native American sculptures resembling black Africans, and other evidence—however, the subject of pre-Columbian contact has been extensively debated by historians and archeologists and remains highly controversial.)
c. 300 B.C.	Iron Age begins in sub-Saharan Africa; Nok culture flourishes in present-day Nigeria, producing works of art that rival the works of ancient Greece and Rome.
c. A.D. 750	Ancient Ghana (located in present-day Mali and Mauretania) emerges as the first great kingdom of sub-Saharan Africa and prospers by regulating the North African gold trade; West Africans begin to adopt Islam through contacts with Muslim traders.
c. 850	The Sefawa dynasty begins its thousand-year reign in the West African kingdom of Kanem.
c. 1000	Ancient Ghana reaches the height of its power; fortified city-states begin to emerge in Hausaland.
c. 1100	Feudal kingdoms arise in Ethiopia.
c. 1200	Swahili civilization, sustained by Indian Ocean trade, flourishes in East Africa.
1240	Sundiata Keita creates the unified kingdom of Mali in West Africa; Mali replaces ancient Ghana as the region's great power.
c. 1300	According to a 14th-century Arabic chronicle, African mariners from Mali cross the Atlantic Ocean in a fleet of 2,000 ships, seeking the mouth of the Amazon River in South America.
1312–1337	Mali attains the height of its power and wealth under Mansa Musa, whose fame spreads throughout the Middle East and Europe; Mali's immense gold supplies facilitate the economic development of Europe.
c. 1350	The great Zimbabwe culture thrives in the central grasslands, where African builders erect immense stone structures; Wolof kingdoms emerge in Senegambia; Yoruba artists in Ile Ife (central Nigeria) produce magnificent bronze sculptures.
1440s	Portuguese take the first captives from sub-Saharan Africa, transporting them to Portugal and Spain.
1464–1528	Under Sunni Ali and Askia Muhammad, the kingdom of Songhai emerges as the dominant power in West Africa, controlling most of the Niger River.
1492	Afro-Spaniard named Pedro Alonzo Niño accompanies Christopher Columbus on his first voyage to the Americas.
1502	Several Afro-Spaniards accompany Nicolás de Ovando when he becomes the first Spanish governor of Hispaniola; Portuguese bring enslaved Africans to the Americas for the first time.
1517	The first enslaved Africans reach the Caribbean islands on Spanish ships.
1522	Africans in Santo Domingo stage the first known slave revolt.

1526	First enslaved Africans arrive in continental United States in present-day South Carolina.
1520s–1530s	Africans take part in numerous Spanish expeditions in the New World, ranging from Florida to California.
1542	The Spanish monarchy outlaws the enslavement of Native Americans; as a result, the African slave trade increases in intensity.
1565	Africans take part in founding of St. Augustine, Florida, the first permanent city in present-day United States built by nonnative Americans.
c. 1590	Portuguese begin large-scale slave trade to Brazil, taking Africans mainly from Angola and coastal regions of the Congo.
1605	Rebellious slaves in northeastern Brazil found the kingdom of Palmares, which eventually contains 20,000 inhabitants. (See 1694.)
1606	The first recorded birth of a black child in North America occurs at St. Augustine, Florida.
1619	Twenty Africans having the status of indentured servants arrive in the English settlement of Jamestown aboard a Dutch ship—they are probably the first black people brought to the British North American colonies.
1623	The first known African child born in the English colonies—William Tucker of Jamestown, the son of indentured servants.
1624	Dutch bring enslaved Africans into New Amsterdam (later New York) for the first time.
1634	Enslaved Africans are brought to Massachusetts and Maryland for the first time.
1644	Eleven blacks in New Amsterdam successfully petition for their freedom.
1652	Rhode Island enacts the first antislavery law in the colonies, limiting the term of servitude to 10 years, for both blacks and whites.
c. 1660	The British and the Dutch begin to supplant the Spanish as the major colonial powers in the Caribbean and the leading slave traders; there are about 100,000 slaves in the West Indies and only about 5,000 in the American colonies.
1663	The first major slave conspiracy in the British North American colonies is uncovered in Virginia.
1688	Pennsylvania Quakers publish the first manifesto condemning slavery in the colonies.
1694	The Brazilian kingdom of Palmares, composed of escaped slaves, falls to Portuguese troops after repeated assaults—inhabitants are reenslaved and branded to show that they are escapees. (See 1605.)
1695	Reverend Samuel Thomas, a white cleric in Charleston, South Carolina, establishes the first known school for African Americans in the colonies.
1700	The enslaved population in the American colonies reaches 28,000 (23,000 in the South); Boston merchant Samuel Sewall and the Boston Committee of Massachusetts formally oppose the slave trade.
1708	Enslaved Africans outnumber European colonists in the Carolinas for the first time.
1712	Enslaved Africans revolt in New York City, burning buildings and killing 9 European colonists; 20 Africans involved in the revolt are killed or commit suicide.

c. 1725	The Fon kingdom of Dahomey (present-day Benin) becomes the dominant state in the area of West Africa the British call the "Slave Coast."
1730s	The First Maroon War in Jamaica leads to a treaty between British authorities and rebellious blacks, allowing many of the Maroon communities to exist free of enslavement.
1738	Africans escaping from bondage in the American colonies set up the first black settlement in North America, at Gracia Real de Santa Teresa de Mosé, in Florida. (The settlement is disbanded in 1763, when the Spanish cede Florida to Britain.)
1739	The Stono Uprising takes place in South Carolina as more than a hundred slaves revolt—all the rebels were either killed in battle or hanged.
1746	Lucy Terry writes "Bar's Fight" (a ballad about the conflict between Massachusetts colonists and Native Americans), the first known writing in English by an African American—the poem is not published until 1855.
1750	The enslaved African population in the American colonies reaches 236,000; the gold-rich Asante (Ashanti) Empire rises in West Africa.
1754	Self-taught scientist Benjamin Banneker constructs the first clock made entirely of American parts.
1770	Crispus Attucks, a black seafarer, is the first colonist killed in the Boston Massacre.
1772	Britain's highest court frees all slaves living in the United Kingdom.
1773	Phillis Wheatley becomes the first African American to publish a book (*Poems on Various Subjects, Religious and Moral*); the first black church (Baptist) is founded in Silver Bluff, South Carolina, by George Liele, then a slave of Henry Sharp, a Baptist deacon. (Liele was later freed by Sharp and moved to Jamaica, where he founded that island's first black Baptist church, as well as a free school.)
1774	Massachusetts is the first colony to pass a law forbidding the importation of slaves.
1775	Pennsylvania Quakers organize the first abolition society in the United States, the Pennsylvania Society for the Abolition of Slavery; African American minutemen engage in combat at Lexington and Concord.
1776	The Second Continental Congress adopts the Declaration of Independence, severing ties between the American colonies and Great Britain; a passage condemning slavery authored by slave owner Thomas Jefferson is dropped from the document at the insistence of Georgia and South Carolina delegates.
1777	In a petition to the Massachusetts legislature, enslaved Africans argue that slavery is in conflict with the principles of the American Revolution; Vermont is the first state to abolish slavery.
1778	Virginia abolishes the slave trade, although slavery itself is not outlawed; Jupiter Hammons publishes his poem "To Miss Phyllis Wheatley."
1778–1781	Five thousand African Americans serve as regular soldiers in the patriot armies during the American Revolution.
1779	Jean Baptiste Point du Sable, a black Canadian fur trader born in the West Indies, establishes a trading post that will eventually become the city of Chicago; George Liele begins preaching to blacks in British-occupied Savannah, Georgia.
1780	Pennsylvania adopts a policy of gradual emancipation; George Derham becomes the first black licensed to practice medicine in the United States.

1781	Twenty-six blacks are among the 44 settlers founding the city of Los Angeles.
1783	Massachusetts abolishes slavery.
1784	Rhode Island and Connecticut enact laws to gradually emancipate slaves.
1787	Delegates in Philadelphia approve the new U.S. Constitution, which contains three clauses protecting the institution of slavery; a colony for liberated slaves is established in Sierra Leone, Africa, with 377 settlers; Richard Allen and Absalom Jones form the Free African Society, the first U.S. civil rights organization; Richard Allen founds Bethel Church in Philadelphia, the first African American church in the North; the African Free School opens in New York.
1789	Olaudah Equiano publishes his autobiography, detailing his experiences under slavery.
1790	The first U.S. Census places the black population at 757,208 (19.3% of the total population), of whom 59,557 are free; slavery has been abolished in all the New England colonies.
1791	François-Dominique Toussaint-Louverture, a former slave, leads a successful slave revolt on the French-held Caribbean island of St. Domingue (the western half of which later becomes the nation of Haiti); Benjamin Banneker takes part in surveying the land chosen for the new national capital in the District of Columbia.
1792	Banneker publishes his first almanac, which proves remarkably accurate in calculating astronomical events; 1,200 African Americans living in Nova Scotia resettle in Sierra Leone.
1793	The invention of the cotton gin increases the size of the Southern cotton industry and creates a greater demand for slave labor; the first fugitive slave law is enacted by the U.S. Congress, making it a crime to harbor an escaped slave.
1794	Congress bans the exportation of slaves from the United States to any foreign country.
1795	The Second Maroon War erupts in Jamaica—many rebellious Maroons are deported to Nova Scotia and Sierra Leone after being tricked into laying down their arms; Richard Allen organizes a school for African American children in Philadelphia.
1796	African Americans in Boston establish the Boston African Society, a mutual aid organization; Joshua Johnson, the first widely recognized African American painter, opens a studio in Baltimore.
1800	The U.S. African American population tops 1 million; U.S. citizens are barred from taking part in the foreign slave trade; a planned rebellion by a thousand slaves in Virginia is thwarted by violent rainstorms.
1801	A new constitution outlaws slavery and declares independence for the whole island of St. Domingue; Toussaint-Louverture becomes St. Domingue's president.
1803	South Carolina reopens its ports to the slave trade from Latin America to satisfy the demand for labor in the newly acquired Louisiana Purchase; escaped slaves and members of the Cherokee, Creek, Choctaw, and other southeastern U.S. tribes that have been defeated by U.S. government troops begin moving into Indian Territory (present-day Oklahoma).
1804	Haiti, on the western part of St. Domingue, becomes an independent republic under Jean-Jacques Dessalines; Muslim reformers launch a series of holy wars in West Africa.

1808	Importation of slaves into the United States is officially outlawed, effective January 1, though illegal slaving continues; Britain abolishes the slave trade in Jamaica and other Caribbean colonies.
1810	Tom Molineaux achieves prominence as a boxer.
1812–1815	African Americans serve as sailors and militia members in the War of 1812 against Great Britain—they distinguish themselves in the battles of Lake Erie and New Orleans.
1813	Argentina adopts a gradual emancipation law.
1814	Colombia begins the emancipation process.
1815	France abolishes importation of slaves to its American colonies; Paul Cuffe transports 38 free blacks from the United States to Sierra Leone.
1816	Richard Allen and associates found the African Methodist Episcopal (A.M.E.) Church.
1820	The American Colonization Society launches efforts to resettle liberated slaves in Liberia on the coast of West Africa; 86 blacks sail to Africa on the *Mayflower of Liberia*; the Missouri Compromise goes into effect, banning slavery in the territories north of latitude 36°30'; the British Navy begins measures to suppress the slave trade.
1821	The first black acting troupe, the African Grove Theater, is established in New York City; Thomas L. Jennings is the first African American to obtain a patent (for a dry-cleaning process).
1822	Denmark Vesey organizes a plan to seize Charleston, South Carolina, for the purpose of freeing slaves—he and 47 others are executed after the plot is betrayed.
1823	Alexander Lucius Twilight earns a B.A. degree from Middlebury College in Vermont, becoming the first African American college graduate; Chile abolishes slavery; the African Grove Theater performs Brown's *Drama of King Shotaway*, the first produced play written by an African American author.
1824	Slavery is abolished throughout Central America; Ira Aldridge begins his triumphant acting career in Europe.
1827	Slavery is abolished in New York State, freeing 10,000 people; the first African American newspaper, *Freedom's Journal*, is published in New York City.
1829	African Americans are attacked by white mobs in Cincinnati, Ohio, during three-day race riot—1,000 flee the city and resettle in Canada; Mexico abolishes slavery; Sister Elizabeth Lange, a Haitian nun, founds the Oblate Sisters of Providence in Baltimore, the first black women's religious order in the United States; David Walker's *Appeal* calls on enslaved blacks to rise up against their oppressors.
1830	The First National Negro Convention meets in Philadelphia—38 delegates from eight states agree on self-help measures.
1831	Nat Turner's rebellion erupts in Virginia, leading to repressive measures throughout the South; the Female Literary Association of Philadelphia, the first society of its sort for African American women, is organized—the association seeks the education of its members and challenges racism and prejudice; Bolivia abolishes slavery; the Emancipation Rebellion erupts in Jamaica.
1832	Abolitionists led by William Lloyd Garrison form the New England Anti-Slavery Society in Boston.
1833	Black and white abolitionists organize the American Anti-Slavery Society in Philadelphia; Ira Aldridge debuts as Othello in London.

1834	Slavery is abolished in the British Empire, freeing more than 700,000 people; David Ruggles opens the first African American bookstore in the United States in New York City—he carries general and abolitionist literature, including his own abolitionist tract *Extinguisher . . .*, which he publishes on his own press, another African American first.
1835	New York City African Americans form a vigilance committee to assist fugitive slaves.
1836	Congress adopts a "gag rule" that prevents debate on any antislavery legislation (the rule remains in effect until 1845); Alexander Lucius Twilight wins a seat in the Vermont legislature, becoming the first African American elected to public office.
1837	The first Anti-Slavery Convention of American Women (membership 10% black) meets in New York City.
1838	The first African American periodical, *Mirror of Liberty*, is published in New York City.
1839	The Liberty Party (first U.S. antislavery party) organizes in Warsaw, New York.
1840	The U.S. African American population reaches 2,873,648.
1841	Frederick Douglass makes his first antislavery speech, in Nantucket, Massachusetts.
1843	Sojourner Truth begins abolition work; at the National Negro Convention in Buffalo, New York, Henry Highland Garnet advocates armed rebellion against slavery; blacks take part in a national political convention for the first time at a meeting of the Liberty Party in Buffalo; Norbert Rillieux patents an evaporator that eventually revolutionizes the sugar industry.
1844	William Henry Lane begins to achieve prominence as a tap dancer under the name Master Juba.
1845	Frederick Douglass lectures in Britain on the abolition of slavery and publishes *Narrative of the Life of Frederick Douglass*, the first of his three autobiographies; Macon B. Allen, the first African American admitted to the bar, begins practicing law in Massachusetts.
1847	Douglass is elected president of the New England Anti-Slavery Society and begins publishing the *North Star*; William Wells Brown publishes *Narrative of William Wells Brown, A Fugitive Slave*; Liberia declares itself an independent republic; David J. Peck is the first African American graduate of a U.S. medical school.
1848	Antislavery politicians organize the Free Soil Party, opposing the extension of slavery into western territories; democratic revolutions sweep Europe; slavery is ended in all French and Danish colonies; Robert Duncanson achieves recognition as a painter; Lewis Temple invents an improved harpoon, which revolutionizes the whaling industry.
1849	Harriet Tubman escapes slavery in Maryland and begins her legendary career as a conductor on the Underground Railroad; Benjamin Roberts, a black man, unsuccessfully files the first integration lawsuit after his daughter is denied admission to Boston public schools.
1850	The U.S. African American population stands at 3,636,808 (15.7% of the total); Congress enacts the Compromise of 1850, admitting California as a free state and decreeing that the status of Utah and New Mexico will be decided by local residents; the federal Fugitive Slave Law goes into effect, giving slave catchers broad

powers and imposing harsh penalties on anyone aiding escapees; African American mountaineer Jim Beckwourth discovers a pass through the Sierra Nevada, which later bears his name; Lucy Ann Stanton is the first African American woman to graduate from a four-year college, earning a bachelor of literature degree from Oberlin College in Ohio.

1851	Brazil outlaws the slave trade.
1852	Harriet Beecher Stowe's novel *Uncle Tom's Cabin* is published, arousing wide sympathy for the abolitionist cause.
1854	Boston abolitionists storm the federal courthouse in a futile attempt to rescue captured fugitive Anthony Burns; the Kansas-Nebraska Act nullifies the Missouri Compromise of 1820 by allowing residents of Kansas and Nebraska to determine the status of slavery in their territories; the newly formed Republican Party opposes the extension of slavery into the territories; Peru and Venezuela abolish slavery; James A. Healy becomes the first African American Catholic priest; Edward M. Bannister produces his first commissioned painting, *The Ship Outward Bound*; the Ashmun Institute (later renamed Lincoln University), the first historically African American college, is founded in Oxford, Pennsylvania.
1857	The U.S. Supreme Court rules in *Dred Scott v. Sanford* that escaped slaves cannot sue for freedom and that Congress has no authority to prohibit slavery in the territories—this ruling makes further compromise on slavery impossible.
1858	Abraham Lincoln gains national recognition as an antislavery candidate during his unsuccessful campaign for the U.S. Senate.
1859	White abolitionist John Brown and a band of 23, including 5 African Americans, raid the federal arsenal at Harpers Ferry, Virginia, hoping to capture arms and start a slave insurrection in the South—Lewis Leary and Dangerfield Newby are killed in the raid, while Brown, John Copeland, and Shields Green are captured, found guilty of murder and treason, and then hanged. Survivor Osborne Anderson writes *A Voice from Harper's Ferry*. Harriet E. Wilson publishes the first African American novel, *Our Nig, or Sketches from the Life of a Free Black*.
1860	Abraham Lincoln is elected president of the United States; South Carolina secedes from the Union in protest, followed by several other states; the U.S. African American population stands at 4,441,830 (14.1%), 4 million remain enslaved.
1861	Civil War begins on April 12 when Confederates fire on Union forces at Fort Sumter, South Carolina.
1862	Congress bans slavery in Washington, D.C., and the territories; enlistment of freed blacks into the Union armies begins; black troops see the first combat of the war in Missouri and South Carolina; the United States officially recognizes Liberia; Wilberforce University in Ohio (founded in 1856) becomes the first college run by African American educators; Cuba ends the slave trade.
1863	The Emancipation Proclamation takes effect on January 1, freeing all slaves in Confederate-held territories; black troops of the 54th Massachusetts regiment make a heroic charge on Fort Wagner in South Carolina; all-black 9th and 11th Louisiana regiments defeat Confederate forces at Milliken's Bend.
1864	Congress repeals the Fugitive Slave Laws and grants black Union troops equal pay with whites; the National Convention of Colored Citizens meets in Syracuse, New York, and issues an appeal for voting rights; Congress authorizes public

schools for African Americans in Washington, D.C.; Georgia Minstrels, the first all-black minstrel troupe, is formed.

1865   Civil War ends with the defeat of the South—250,000 African Americans served in Union armies, 38,000 died; Congress ratifies the Thirteenth Amendment to the Constitution, abolishing slavery in the United States; Congress creates the Freedman's Bank and the Freedmen's Bureau to aid former slaves; Lincoln is assassinated; President Andrew Johnson announces plans for Reconstruction in the South; Southern legislatures enact Black Codes, laws restricting the rights of former slaves; John S. Rock of Boston is the first African American admitted to practice before the U.S. Supreme Court, although he dies in 1866, before he has a chance to argue a case.

1866–1904   During the 35 years following the end of the Civil War, a number of colleges and universities for African Americans are founded in the South to educate successive generations of black leaders; among these are Howard University in Washington, D.C. (1866); Talladega College in Talladega, Alabama (1867); Clark College in Atlanta, Georgia (1869); Allen University in Columbia, South Carolina, and LeMoyne-Owen College in Memphis, Tennessee (1870); Stillman College in Tuscaloosa, Alabama, and Meharry Medical College (the first all-black medical school) in Nashville, Tennessee (1876); Jackson State University in Jackson, Mississippi, Howard University Medical School in Washington, D.C., and Hampton Institute in Hampton, Virginia (1877); Selma University in Selma, Alabama (1878); Spelman College for Women in Atlanta, Georgia, Tuskegee Institute (founded by Booker T. Washington) in Tuskegee, Alabama, Morris Brown College in Atlanta, Georgia, and Bishop College in Dallas, Texas (1881); Shorter College in Little Rock, Arkansas (1884); Kentucky State University in Frankfort and University of Maryland Eastern Shore in Princess Anne (1886); North Carolina A&T in Greensboro (1891); Texas College in Tyler, Texas (1894); and Daytona Normal Industrial School (founded by Mary McLeod Bethune and later renamed Bethune-Cookman College) in Daytona, Florida (1904).

1866   The Civil Rights Act decrees that all African Americans are full U.S. citizens; the Ku Klux Klan and other white supremacist groups begin a campaign of terror against emancipated blacks in the South; racial violence in Memphis, Tennessee, results in the death of 46 African Americans; African American jockey Abe Hawkins rides winners at Belmont and Saratoga.

1867   Congress passes the First Reconstruction Act, which includes voting rights for all citizens, and the Peonage Abolition Act, outlawing forced labor for discharge of debt; William Wells Brown publishes *Clotel*.

1868   The Fourteenth Amendment, granting African Americans full civil rights, wins approval in Congress; black candidates are elected to state legislatures in the South and fill other government posts, beginning a series of political advancements that continue until the end of Reconstruction in 1877; Edmonia Lewis completes her sculpture *Forever Free*, celebrating the Emancipation Proclamation.

1869   The Fifteenth Amendment forbids denial of the vote on the basis of "race, color, or previous condition of servitude"; four African American regiments are incorporated into the regular U.S. Army; Joseph Rainey of South Carolina is the first African American to take a seat in the U.S. House of Representatives.

1870   Hiram Rhoades Revels of Mississippi is the first African American to win election

	to the U.S. Senate; Congress passes the first of a series of measures to combat the Ku Klux Klan and other terrorist groups; Lewis Latimer makes technical drawings of Bell's newly invented telephone.
1871	Brazil begins gradual emancipation of slaves; Fisk Jubilee Singers tour the United States and Europe, popularizing black spirituals.
1872	Pinckney Benton Stewart Pinchback is appointed interim governor of Louisiana and is the first African American to serve as a state governor; the Ku Klux Klan temporarily disbands (it will be resurrected in 1915); John Conyers is the first African American admitted to the U.S. Naval Academy; Elijah McCoy patents an automatic lubricating device for steam engines.
1873	Slavery is abolished in Puerto Rico.
1875	The 44th U.S. Congress convenes with eight African American members, the greatest number to have served at that time; the Civil Rights Act prohibits discrimination in employment and establishes the right of African Americans to serve on juries; jockey Oliver Lewis, riding Aristide, wins the first Kentucky Derby, beginning an era when black jockeys dominate the Derby and other races.
1876	John Knowles Paine is the first African American to compose a symphonic work; Edward Alexander Bouchet is the first African American to obtain a doctorate (in physics).
1877	The U.S. government removes all federal troops from the South as Reconstruction comes to an end; Henry Ossian Flipper is the first African American to graduate from a U.S. military academy.
1878	Exodusters begin migrating from Southern states to Kansas to escape intensified oppression in the South—50,000 resettle by 1881; J. R. Winters patents a fire-escape ladder.
1881	Frederick Douglass becomes a recorder of deeds for Washington, D.C.; Henry Highland Garnet becomes U.S. minister to Liberia; Tennessee enacts its first Jim Crow law, enforcing segregation in railroad cars; William Wells Brown publishes *My Southern Home*.
1882	Lewis Latimer patents carbon filament for electric lamp.
1883	George Washington Williams publishes *History of the Negro Race in America from 1619 to 1880*; Jan E. Matzeliger patents a shoe-lasting machine; Lewis Latimer begins working with Thomas Edison; Eatonville, Florida, is the first all-black incorporated town.
1884	Granville Woods founds the Woods Electric Company, which produces 35 patented devices over the next 20 years; Moses Fleetwood Walker, a catcher with the Toledo, Ohio, team of the American Association, is the first African American to play major league baseball (black players are squeezed out of the major leagues during the 1890s); T. Thomas Fortune founds the *New York Age*.
1884–1885	European powers delineate colonial spheres of influence in Africa and press all-out military assault on African societies.
1885	Granville Woods patents a telegraphy device; the Cuban Giants, the first African American professional baseball team, is formed.
1886	Slavery is abolished in Cuba.
1888	Brazil abolishes slavery; transatlantic slave trade comes to an end.
1889	Frederick Douglass becomes U.S. minister to Haiti; 10,000 African Americans stake claims to land in the newly opened territory of Oklahoma.

1891	Provident Hospital, the first to be operated by African Americans, is founded in Chicago.
1892–1924	About 170,000 West Indians migrate to the United States.
1892	The first black college football game is played (Biddle vs. Livingstone); William Henry Lewis of Amherst becomes the first black all-American in football.
1893	African American surgeon Daniel Hale Williams performs the first successful heart operation at Chicago's Provident Hospital; Paul Laurence Dunbar publishes his first poetry collection, *Oak and Ivy*; Henry Ossawa Tanner begins painting scenes of black life.
1894	Congress repeals the Enforcement Act, making it easier for states to disfranchise black voters; the Church of God in Christ is founded in Memphis.
1895	Lynchings claim the lives of 113 African Americans in the South; Booker T. Washington delivers his Atlanta Compromise speech, accepting segregation in return for economic advancement; the National Baptist Convention, U.S.A., is organized in Atlanta; Bert Williams and George Walker form their legendary show business team.
1896	The National Federation of Afro-American Women is formed to help combat racism; in *Plessy v. Ferguson*, the U.S. Supreme Court rules that Tennessee's "separate but equal" facilities on railroad cars are constitutional, paving the way for additional Jim Crow laws throughout the South; Richard Henry Boyd founds the National Baptist Publishing Board in Nashville; *Oriental America* is the first African American play produced on Broadway.
1897	The Lott Carey Baptist Mission begins operations in Liberia.
1898	African American troops fight in the Spanish-American War; John Merrick and associates found the North Carolina Mutual Life Insurance Company, anchoring an African American business boom in Durham; *A Trip to Coontown* opens—the first musical comedy created and performed by African Americans.
1899	Scott Joplin publishes "Maple Leaf Rag."
1900	European colonization of Africa is virtually complete; the first Pan-African Congress is held in London, with its stated aim to promote the liberation of colonized people—W. E. B. Du Bois is elected vice president; Booker T. Washington publishes *Up from Slavery*; brothers James Weldon Johnson and J. Rosamond Johnson write "Lift Every Voice and Sing"; Henry Ossawa Tanner wins the French Medal of Honor for his paintings at the Paris Exposition.
1901	The Johnson brothers and Bob Cole are the first African Americans to sign a songwriting contract for the Broadway stage; Booker T. Washington organizes the National Negro Business League and dines at the White House with President Theodore Roosevelt.
1903	W. E. B. Du Bois publishes *The Souls of Black Folk*; Maggie Lena Walker founds the St. Luke Penny Savings Bank.
1905	Full-scale construction begins on the Panama Canal—in the course of the project, 30,000 black workers from the West Indies contribute their labor, and 4,500 lose their lives; the *Chicago Defender* begins publication as a champion of African American rights; the Niagara Movement begins to shape a more radical alternative to Booker T. Washington's policies.
1906	Black soldiers are accused of raiding Brownsville, Texas—167 men are court-martialed, deprived of a fair hearing, and dishonorably discharged (this ruling is

reversed in 1962); race riots break out in Atlanta, Georgia; Madame C. J. Walker begins her successful business career by establishing a hair-care company in Denver; the Azusa Street Revival in Los Angeles (1906–1909) inspires the creation of Holiness/Pentecostal/Apostolic churches.

1907   Alain Locke is the first African American to earn a Rhodes Scholarship.

1908   Alpha Kappa Alpha, the first African American sorority, is founded at Howard University; Jack Johnson becomes the first black heavyweight boxing champion in the United States; Vertner Tandy is the first African American architect licensed in New York State.

1909   W. E. B. Du Bois and others plan the creation of a new civil rights organization that will become the National Association for the Advancement of Colored People (NAACP); *Amsterdam News* begins publication in New York City.

1910   The NAACP is formally established and begins publishing *Crisis* magazine.

1911   The National Urban League is founded to assist African Americans newly resettled in northern cities; John E. Bruce, Arthur Schomburg, David Fulton, and William E. Braxton found the Negro Society for Historical Research; Scott Joplin's *Treemonisha* is performed for the first time.

1912   James Weldon Johnson's *Autobiography of an Ex-Colored Man* is published; W. C. Handy publishes the first blues composition ("Memphis Blues").

The Silent Protest Parade in July 1917, organized by the NAACP, where over 15,000 African American men, women, and children marched silently down Fifth Avenue to the beat of muffled drums to protest lynchings and other racial indignities.

1913	Noble Drew Ali founds the Moorish Holy Temple of Science in Newark, New Jersey.
1914	The NAACP institutes the Spingarn Medal to honor outstanding achievements by African Americans; Marcus Garvey founds the Universal Negro Improvement Association (UNIA) in Kingston, Jamaica; World War I breaks out in Europe.
1915	The Great Migration begins as Southern blacks move to the North—1.5 million relocate by 1930; the Ku Klux Klan is reborn in Georgia; Carter G. Woodson founds the Association for the Study of Negro Life and History; Father Divine (George Baker) establishes his first church in New York City.
1916	The first issue of *Journal of Negro History* appears, edited by Carter G. Woodson; Marcus Garvey relocates to New York with the UNIA; James Van Der Zee opens his photo studio in Harlem; the American Tennis Association is created to promote tennis among African Americans.
1917	United States enters World War I—300,000 African Americans serve in the armed forces during the war; 100 blacks are killed in a race riot in East St. Louis, Missouri; 10,000 blacks protest lynching and other violence against blacks in a silent march down New York City's Fifth Avenue.
1919	Race riots occur in many U.S. cities during Red Summer; Garvey establishes the Black Star (steamship) Line to link New World blacks with Africa; W. E. B. Du Bois organizes the second Pan-African Congress in Paris (see 1900); Oscar Micheaux releases his first film, *The Homesteader;* the Negro National Baseball League begins operation.
1920	The Harlem Renaissance begins a period of unprecedented artistic creative output by African Americans; Charles Gilpin stars in *The Emperor Jones;* Marcus Garvey holds the first International Convention of Negro Peoples at Madison Square Garden.
1921	Pace Phonograph Company is the first record company owned and operated by African Americans (Ethel Waters's "Down Home Blues/Oh Daddy," issued on the Black Swan label, is the company's first hit); Jesse Binga founds a successful bank in Chicago.
1922	The Black Star Line goes bankrupt as Garvey and three associates are indicted for mail fraud—many believe that Garvey was framed by opponents who feared his influence; Congress fails to pass the Dyer antilynching bill; William Leo Hansberry of Howard University offers the first course in African history at a U.S. university; Blake and Sissle's *Shuffle Along,* the first musical created entirely by African Americans, opens on Broadway; major publications include Claude McKay's *Harlem Shadows* and James Weldon Johnson's *Book of American Negro Poetry.*
1923	Bessie Smith's "Downhearted Blues/Gulf Coast Blues" is the first million-selling record by a black artist; the National Urban League begins publishing *Opportunity* magazine; Jean Toomer's novel *Cane* is published; Paul Robeson stars in *The Emperor Jones;* the Harlem Renaissance (Rens) basketball team is formed.
1924	The Immigration Act limits number of blacks and other ethnic groups allowed to enter the United States; important novels include Jesse Redmon Fauset's *There Is Confusion* and Walter White's *Fire in the Flint.*
1925	A. Philip Randolph founds the Brotherhood of Sleeping Car Porters; immigration from the West Indies drops to 308 (from 10,000 in 1924), primarily as a result of the 1924 Immigration Act; Clifton Reginald Wharton Sr. is the first African American to enter the U.S. Foreign Service; Countee Cullen publishes first volume of poetry, *Color;* the first *Opportunity* Awards banquet is held, honoring outstanding writers; singer Josephine Baker achieves stardom in Paris.

1926	Negro History Week, which later becomes Black History Month (February) (see Chapter 5), is celebrated for the first time; the personal collection of distinguished black scholar Arthur A. Schomburg is added to the New York Public Library Division of Negro Literature, History, and Prints at the 135th Street Branch—it would be renamed in his honor in 1940 and designated the Schomburg Center for Research in Black Culture in 1972; with Harlem Renaissance at its height, notable publications include Alain Locke's anthology *The New Negro*; Langston Hughes's first collection of poetry, *The Weary Blues*; and Eric Walrond's *Tropic Death*; Hughes, Zora Neale Hurston, and Wallace Thurman establish the literary magazine *Fire!*; Paul Revere Williams is the first African American fellow of the American Institute of Architects.
1927	Major poetry collections include Hughes's *Fine Clothes to the Jew*, Cullen's *Copper Sun*, and James Weldon Johnson's *God's Trombones*; the Harmon Foundation begins efforts to promote African American artists; the Harlem Globetrotters team is founded.
1928	Oscar DePriest is the first African American elected to Congress since Reconstruction; major novels include Nella Larsen's *Quicksand* and Claude McKay's *Home to Harlem*; Bill "Bojangles" Robinson stars on Broadway.
1929	A. Philip Randolph's Brotherhood of Sleeping Car Porters receives a charter from the American Federation of Labor; publications include Nella Larsen's *Passing*, Claude McKay's *Banjo*, and Countee Cullen's *Black Christ*; Augusta Savage creates award-winning sculpture *Gamin*; circulation of *Chicago Defender* reaches 250,000.
1930	The world enters the Great Depression, the effects of which are felt acutely by African Americans; James Weldon Johnson publishes *Black Manhattan*; Josh Gibson begins his legendary baseball career in the Negro Leagues.
1931	Nine young African Americans, soon to be known as the Scottsboro Boys, are falsely accused and convicted of rape in a controversial Alabama trial; Katherine Dunham founds her Negro Dance group in Chicago; Oscar Michaux's film *The Exile* is the first talkie released by a black-owned company; Duke Ellington records "Creole Rhapsody."
1932	The New York Rens defeat the Boston Celtics, becoming the first black sports team to win a world championship; publications include Rudolph Fisher's *Conjure Man Dies*, considered the first African American detective novel.
1933	Franklin D. Roosevelt takes office as president of the United States and institutes social programs of the New Deal; Jacob Lawrence, Aaron Douglas, and other black artists participate in federal arts projects; prominent African American officials form Roosevelt's "Black Cabinet," advising the president on social issues; NAACP begins to attack segregation through a series of lawsuits.
1934	Arthur Mitchell of Illinois is the first African American Democrat elected to the U.S. Congress; major publications include Hurston's *Jonah's Gourd Vine* and Hughes's *Ways of White Folks*; Aaron Douglas completes his mural series *Aspects of Negro Life*; Augusta Savage is the first black member of the National Association of Women Painters and Sculptors.
1935	A Harlem riot marks the symbolic end of the Harlem Renaissance; Italy invades Ethiopia, spurring protests by African Americans; numerous African Americans take part in the Federal Theater Project; Mary McLeod Bethune is named to head a division of the National Youth Administration, becoming the first African American woman to head a U.S. government office; chemist Percy Julian synthe-

	sizes a drug for treating glaucoma; African American artists form the Harlem Artists Guild.
1936	African American voters decisively shift to the Democrats as Roosevelt is re-elected; the National Negro Congress is established to fight for antilynching laws, desegregation, and unionization of black workers; track star Jesse Owens wins four gold medals at the Berlin Olympics, shattering Nazi myths of white racial superiority; Father Divine attains the height of his influence as an evangelist; Joe Louis wins the heavyweight boxing championship.
1937	William Hastie is the first African American appointed a federal judge; the Brotherhood of Sleeping Car Porters reaches a historic agreement with the Pullman Company; Adam Clayton Powell Jr. succeeds his father as pastor of the Abyssinian Baptist Church; Zora Neale Hurston publishes *Their Eyes Were Watching God*; Billie Holiday performs at the Apollo Theater in Harlem.
1938	NAACP establishes its Legal Defense Fund to fight segregation; Jacob Lawrence completes 41 panels of *Toussaint L'Ouverture*, his series of paintings about the Haitian revolutionary leader.
1939	Soprano Marian Anderson gives her historic concert at the Lincoln Memorial after being refused permission to sing at the Daughters of the American Revolution Hall in Washington, D.C.; the U.S. Department of Justice creates the Civil Liberties Unit.
1940	Charles Drew creates the first blood bank; Benjamin O. Davis Sr. becomes the first African American promoted to the rank of general in the U.S. armed forces; the National Negro Congress dissolves amid charges of Communist influence; Frederick M. Jones patents the first workable refrigeration unit for trucks and railway cars; Richard Wright's *Native Son* is published; Abram Hill founds the American Negro Theater; Hattie McDaniel becomes the first African American to win an Academy Award (for best supporting actress in *Gone with the Wind*).
1941	The United States enters World War II; President Roosevelt bans racial discrimination in defense industries, responding to pressure from A. Philip Randolph and other civil rights leaders, after Randolph forms the March on Washington Movement; more than 1 million African Americans will serve in the armed forces during the war; Tuskegee Airmen begin training in Alabama; Lena Horne is the first African American to sign a contract with a major movie studio.
1942	The F. D. Roosevelt Administration issues Executive Order 8802, creating the Fair Employment Practices Committee for war industries; the Congress of Racial Equality (CORE) is founded; Gordon Parks takes memorable photographs of rural life for the U.S. Farm Security Administration.
1943	CORE conducts its first sit-ins, protesting discrimination in Chicago restaurants; riot erupts in Harlem after a white police officer shoots a black soldier; Paul Robeson plays Othello on Broadway; Adam Clayton Powell Jr. wins election to the U.S. Congress; sculptor Selma Burke designs the portrait of Franklin Roosevelt that is used on the dime.
1944	The U.S. Navy integrates all vessels; Adam Clayton Powell Jr. takes his seat in Congress; the United Negro College Fund is founded; American Negro Theater production of *Anna Lucasta* begins record-setting run on Broadway.
1945	*Ebony* magazine begins publication; Gwendolyn Brooks publishes her first book of poems, *A Street in Bronzeville*; Katherine Dunham founds the Dunham School of

Dance and Theater; Richmond Barthé is the first black sculptor elected to the American Academy of Arts and Letters.

1947   Jackie Robinson makes his debut with the Brooklyn Dodgers, breaking baseball's long-standing color line and winning Rookie of the Year honors; the first Freedom Riders travel through the South, testing compliance with federal civil rights measures; historian John Hope Franklin publishes *From Slavery to Freedom: A History of Negro Americans*.

1948   President Harry Truman issues Executive Order 9981, integrating the armed forces, but his administration fails to obtain civil rights legislation from Congress; Edward R. Dudley is the first African American to be a U.S. ambassador; a system of apartheid, enforcing rigid racial segregation, begins in South Africa.

1949   Jackie Robinson wins the Most Valuable Player Award in the National League; Joe Louis retires from the ring after successfully defending his heavyweight boxing title 25 times; the Charlie Parker Quintet emerges as an innovative jazz ensemble; Gordon Parks is the first African American photographer on the staff of *Life* magazine.

1950   United Nations official Ralph J. Bunche receives the Nobel Peace Prize for his work in mediating the Palestine crisis; Gwendolyn Brooks is the first African American author to win a Pulitzer Prize (awarded for *Annie Allen*, a volume of poetry); Juanita Hall is the first African American to win a Tony Award (best supporting actress) for her performance in *South Pacific*; Chuck Cooper is the first black player drafted by a National Basketball Association (NBA) team (Boston Celtics).

1951   The 24th Infantry Regiment, the last all-black unit in the U.S. Army, is disbanded after seeing action in the Korean War; during the height of the McCarthy anti-Communist witch hunt, the U.S. government revokes W. E. B. Du Bois's passport because officials suspect him of being a Communist.

1952   For the first time in 71 years, no lynchings are reported in the United States; Ralph Ellison's novel *Invisible Man* wins the National Book Award; eight African Americans win gold medals at the Helsinki Olympics.

1954   In *Brown v. Board of Education*, the U.S. Supreme Court bans segregation in public schools, overturning the "separate but equal" doctrine; Norma Sklarek is the first African American woman to be licensed as an architect.

1955   African Americans in Montgomery, Alabama, begin a bus boycott under the leadership of the Reverend Martin Luther King Jr.; the U.S. Interstate Commerce Commission bans segregation in interstate travel facilities; Roy de Carava and Langston Hughes publish *The Sweet Flypaper of Life*, a tribute to Harlem; Chuck Berry and Fats Domino record rock 'n' roll hits; Sugar Ray Robinson wins the middleweight boxing championship.

1956   The Montgomery bus boycott ends as the city agrees to integrate public transportation; Autherine Lucy integrates the University of Alabama, but the reaction to her presence is so severe that the university expels her within the first month of her studies; Nat "King" Cole is the first African American to host a TV variety show; Harry Belafonte's *Calypso* is the first record album to sell 1 million copies.

1957   The Civil Rights Act of 1957 contains measures to protect African American voting rights; the Southern Christian Leadership Conference (SCLC) is founded to battle segregation; federal troops enforce the integration of public schools in Little Rock, Arkansas; sit-ins begin in Durham, North Carolina; Ghana becomes the first sub-Saharan African nation to gain independence from European colonial rule; Althea Gibson wins the women's tennis title at Forest Hills, New York, becoming the first African American U.S. tennis champion.

1958   The Nation of Islam, led by Elijah Muhammad and, later, Malcolm X, achieves national prominence with calls for black separatism; Alvin Ailey founds the Alvin Ailey American Dance Theater.

1959   Miles Davis releases *Kind of Blue*, considered by many to be the all-time greatest jazz album; Paule Marshall's novel *Brown Girl, Brownstones* is published; Lorraine Hansberry's *Raisin in the Sun* becomes a hit on Broadway; Berry Gordy founds Motown Records in Detroit; Ella Fitzgerald and Count Basie are the first African Americans to win Grammy Awards.

1960   Four African American students begin a sit-in protest at a segregated Woolworth's lunch counter in Greensboro, North Carolina, sparking a sit-in campaign across the South; the Student Nonviolent Coordinating Committee (SNCC) is founded to coordinate civil rights efforts in the South; Congress passes the Civil Rights Act of 1960, which imposes sanctions against antiblack terrorism and interference with court-ordered desegregation; black voters play a significant role in the election of John F. Kennedy to the presidency; Nigeria and 14 French colonies gain independence in Africa; Harry Belafonte is the first African American to win an Emmy Award, given for his television special, "Tonight with Harry Belafonte"; Wilma Rudolph wins three gold medals at the Rome Olympics.

1961   Atlanta, Georgia, peacefully integrates four high schools; congressional representative Adam Clayton Powell Jr. becomes chair of the Education and Labor Committee and spearheads legislation designed to correct racial and economic injustices; a new wave of Freedom Rides begins throughout the South, touching off antiblack violence; the Kennedy Administration calls for affirmative action in awarding of government contracts; Leontyne Price makes her Metropolitan Opera debut in *Il Trovatore*; Syracuse running back Ernie Davis becomes the first African American to win the Heisman Trophy.

1962   James Meredith becomes the first African American to enroll in the University of Mississippi, sparking riots on campus—12,000 federal troops are dispatched to ensure Meredith's safe admission; the U.S. government bans discrimination in public housing; Samuel L. Gravely is the first African American in modern times to command a U.S. Navy combat ship; Jamaica gains independence from British rule; Jackie Robinson is the first African American inducted into the Baseball Hall of Fame.

1963   Police attack civil rights marchers in Birmingham, Alabama, focusing nationwide attention on the civil rights struggle; civil rights activist Medgar Evers is murdered in Mississippi; four young African-American girls are killed when white supremacists bomb a Birmingham church; Southern members of Congress block civil rights legislation proposed by the Kennedy Administration; Martin Luther King Jr. leads a massive March on Washington, delivering his historic "I Have a Dream" speech; President Kennedy is assassinated in Dallas; James Baldwin publishes *The Fire Next Time*; Romare Bearden, Charles Alston, and others form the group Spiral to promote the interests of African American artists.

1964   The U.S. Congress passes the Civil Rights Act of 1964 and the Economic Opportunity Act, banning discrimination in public accommodations, employment, and education; Dr. King receives the Nobel Peace Prize; Freedom Summer is launched as students from the North volunteer for civil rights campaigns in the

South; three civil rights workers—James Earl Chaney, Andrew Goodman, and Michael Schwerner—are murdered in Mississippi; the U.S. Equal Employment Opportunity Commission (EEOC) is created; Fannie Lou Hamer of the Mississippi Freedom Democratic Party makes a bid to unseat the state's all-white delegation at the Democratic National Convention; riots break out in Harlem and Bedford-Stuyvesant in New York City; African National Congress leader Nelson Mandela is sentenced to life imprisonment by a South African court for his efforts to overturn apartheid; Sidney Poitier wins the Academy Award for Best Actor (in *Lilies of the Field*), the first African American so honored; *Dutchman*, by Leroi Jones (who later took the name Amiri Baraka) opens on Broadway, an opening salvo in the Black Arts Movement, which furthers black consciousness among writers, painters, and musicians; Cassius Clay wins the heavyweight boxing championship, adopts Islam, and changes his name to Muhammad Ali.

1965   Rev. King leads the Selma-to-Montgomery march in Alabama; Malcolm X is assassinated, allegedly by members of the Nation of Islam after he broke with the group; confrontation between police officers and black residents sparks unprecedented rioting in Watts section of Los Angeles, resulting in 34 deaths, hundreds of injuries, and more than $50 million in property damage; Congress passes the Voting Rights Act of 1965, leading to a massive surge in black registration; Lowndes County Freedom Organization in Alabama organizes black voters without the aid of white civil rights workers; major publications include *The Autobiography of Malcolm X* and Claude Brown's *Manchild in the Promised Land*; the Supremes top the pop-music charts.

1966   Rev. King carries his civil rights campaign to Chicago; SNCC chair Stokely Carmichael declares the advent of Black Power, rejecting the goal of integration; black troops represent 25 percent of total U.S. casualties in Vietnam; the Black Panther Party begins operations in Oakland, California; Robert C. Weaver is appointed secretary of housing and urban development, becoming the first African American to serve in a cabinet post; Edward L. Brooke of Massachusetts is the first African American elected to the U.S. Senate since Reconstruction; the First World Festival of Black Arts is held in Dakar, Senegal; Bill Cosby wins an Emmy Award for his role in *I Spy*; Bill Russell leads the Boston Celtics to an eighth consecutive NBA championship—appointed player-coach in 1966, he is the first African American to coach an NBA team.

1967   Rev. King declares his opposition to the Vietnam War; riots break out in black neighborhoods of 75 cities and towns, including Detroit, Chicago, Memphis, Cincinnati, and Newark; Thurgood Marshall becomes the first African American to sit on the U.S. Supreme Court; Carl B. Stokes becomes the first African American mayor of a major U.S. city (Cleveland); major publications include Nikki Giovanni's *Black Feeling, Black Thought*, John A. Williams's *Man Who Cried I Am*, and Ishmael Reed's *Free-lance Pallbearers*; Douglas Turner Ward founds the Negro Ensemble Company.

1968   Rev. King is assassinated in Memphis, Tennessee, sparking violent protests throughout the United States; Rev. Ralph Abernathy takes over the leadership of SCLC and the Poor People's Campaign; the Kerner Commission reports that white racism is the cause of urban rioting, which continues unabated; Congress passes the Civil Rights Act of 1968, offering guarantees of open housing and protection for blacks exercising their civil rights; Shirley Chisholm is the first African American woman elected to Congress; Eldridge Cleaver publishes *Soul on Ice*; the Studio Museum in Harlem opens; Henry Lewis is the first African American to direct a symphony orchestra (New Jersey Symphony); James Earl Jones wins a Tony Award (best actor in a drama) for *The Great White Hope*; Arthur Ashe wins the U.S. men's tennis championship at Forest Hills, New York; sprinters Tommie Lee Smith and John Carlos protest U.S. racism by giving the Black Power salute when accepting medals at the Olympics in Mexico City.

1969   James Earl Ray pleads guilty to the murder of Rev. King and receives a 99-year prison sentence; law-enforcement authorities in several localities begin a crackdown on the Black Panther Party; African American students at Brandeis and Cornell occupy administration buildings, demanding black-studies programs and greater voice on campus; the federal government establishes the Office of Minority Business Enterprise; Harvard University creates an Afro-American studies program; Arthur Mitchell and Karel Shook found the Dance Theater of Harlem; the "Harlem on My Mind" exhibition at the Metropolitan Museum features the photography of James Van Der Zee; Romare Bearden and other black artists found the Cinque Gallery.

1970   Coretta Scott King founds the Martin Luther King, Jr., Center for Nonviolent Social Change; 12 African Americans take seats in the 92nd Congress; African American students conduct demonstrations on a number of campuses; Charles Gordone is the first African American to win a Pulitzer Prize for drama (*No Place to Be Somebody*); Toni Morrison publishes her first novel, *The Bluest Eye*; *Black Enterprise* and *Essence* magazines begin publication; Clifton Wharton becomes president of Michigan State, the first black president of a predominantly white major university.

1971   African American members of Congress organize the Congressional Black Caucus to promote the interests of black Americans; the Reverend Jesse Jackson founds Operation PUSH; states and localities begin busing to achieve school integration; Ernest J. Gaines publishes *The Autobiography of Miss Jane Pittman*; the Whitney Museum of American Art presents a major exhibition of 20th-century black artists; Samuel L. Gravely Jr. becomes the first African American admiral in the U.S. Navy; Romare Bearden has a one-person show at New York's Museum of Modern Art; Johnson Products is the first black-owned company listed on a major U.S. stock exchange (Amex); the Baseball Hall of Fame begins inducting former Negro League stars, starting with pitcher Leroy "Satchel" Paige.

1972   The U.S. government reveals that hundreds of poor black men were denied proper treatment during the U.S. Public Health Service's 40-year Tuskegee syphilis experiment; Congress passes the Equal Employment Opportunity Act; Diana Ross stars in *Lady Sings the Blues*, a film biography of Billie Holiday; Wilt Chamberlain becomes the first NBA player to reach the 30,000-point total.

1973   Newly elected African American mayors include Tom Bradley (Los Angeles), Maynard Jackson (Atlanta), and Coleman Young (Detroit); Illinois is the first state to declare Rev. King's birthday a holiday; Marian Wright Edelman founds the Children's Defense Fund to champion the welfare of poor and minority youngsters; John Edgar Wideman publishes his novel *The Lynchers*.

1974   Whites riot in Boston in an attempt to block a court-ordered school-integration busing plan; nearly 500 delegates, half from the United States, attend the Sixth Pan-African Congress in Dar es Salaam, Tanzania; Toni Morrison's *Sula* is published; the soundtrack of the movie *The Sting* creates a nationwide revival of Scott Joplin's music; Stevie Wonder wins a Grammy Award for his album *Innervisions*; Henry Aaron becomes baseball's all-time home run king; Frank Robinson is the first African American hired to manage a major-league baseball team (Cleveland Indians); Muhammad Ali regains the heavyweight crown by knocking out George Foreman in Zaire.

1975   Daniel "Chappie" James is the first African American to achieve the four-star rank in the U.S. Army; Mozambique and Angola gain independence from Portuguese rule after lengthy guerrilla wars; Harvard establishes the W. E. B. Du Bois Institute for Afro-American Research; notable dramatic productions include *The Wiz* and Shange's *for colored girls who have considered suicide/when the rainbow is enuf*; Arthur Ashe wins the men's singles title at Wimbledon; Lee Elder is the first black golfer to play in the Masters Tournament.

1976   Barbara Jordan is the first African American to deliver the keynote address at the Democratic National Convention; African American voters play a key role in Jimmy Carter's election to the presidency; FBI COINTELPRO documents reveal that the agency waged a massive campaign against the civil rights movement during the 1960s; Alex Haley's *Roots*, reconstructing the history of an African American family, becomes a national best-seller and wins a special Pulitzer Prize; new Broadway productions include *Bubbling Brown Sugar* and *Your Arms Too Short to Box with God*; Aretha Franklin performs at New York's Lincoln Center; the Los Angeles County Museum of Art mounts its "Two Centuries of Black American Art" exhibit.

1977   Clifford Alexander becomes first black secretary of the Army; Patricia Roberts Harris is appointed secretary of Housing and Urban Development, becoming the first African American woman to attain cabinet rank; Andrew Young is appointed the first African American ambassador to the United Nations; a TV miniseries based on *Roots* draws record-setting audiences and sweeps the Emmy Awards; a Ku Klux Klan member is convicted in the 1963 bombing of a Birmingham church; the Second World Festival of Black and African Art is held in Lagos, Nigeria.

1978   The U.S. Supreme Court strikes down the University of California affirmative-action program as "reverse discrimination"; *Ain't Misbehavin'* opens on Broadway; Audre Lorde publishes *The Black Unicorn: Poems*; Max Robinson becomes the first black anchor on a network news program (ABC's *World News Tonight*).

1979   Jesse Jackson meets with heads of state in the Middle East, attempting to mediate Arab-Israeli conflict; five anti–Ku Klux Klan demonstrators are killed by gunfire in Greensboro, North Carolina; Maya Angelou publishes her collection of poems, *And Still I Rise*; *Roots: The Next Generation* (a miniseries) airs on ABC; rap emerges as a major genre on the pop music scene, as "Rapper's Delight" by the Sugar Hill Gang becomes the first top-40 rap single in America.

1980   The National Conference for a Black Agenda brings together a thousand African American leaders for discussion of political and social issues; riots erupt in Miami as a result of the shooting of an African American by a police officer; the Catholic church publicly recognizes the contributions of black Catholics and their struggle against racism within the church; Robert L. Johnson founds Black Entertainment Television (BET), the first black-owned company to be listed on the New York Stock Exchange.

1981   More than 300,000 demonstrators from labor and civil rights groups gather in Washington to protest the Reagan Administration's assault on affirmative action, school desegregation, and other civil rights programs; important works are published, written by Toni Morrison (*Tar Baby*), David Bradley (*The Chaneysville Incident*), and Maya Angelou (*The Heart of a Woman*); Broadway hits include

Dreamgirls, *Sophisticated Ladies*, and *Lena Horne: The Lady and Her Music*; Charles Fuller's *Soldier's Play* wins a New York Drama Critics Award and a Pulitzer Prize.

1982   Congress extends the Voting Rights Act of 1965 for an additional 25 years; Andrew Young becomes mayor of Atlanta; Quincy Jones wins five Grammy Awards for his album *The Dude*; James Earl Jones stars in *Othello* on Broadway; Michael Jackson releases the album *Thriller*, which will go on to sell 40 million copies around the world, the best-selling album in music history; Julius "Dr. J" Erving leads the Philadelphia 76ers to an NBA title.

1983   Harold Washington becomes Chicago's first black mayor; U.S. forces invade the Caribbean island of Grenada; an annual federal holiday honoring Rev. King is declared; Colonel Guion S. Bluford Jr. is the first African American astronaut to orbit the Earth in the space shuttle *Challenger*; Vanessa Williams is the first black Miss America; Alice Walker wins the Pulitzer Prize for her novel *The Color Purple*; Motown Records celebrates its 25th anniversary with a landmark prime-time TV special.

1984   Jesse Jackson makes a powerful bid for the Democratic presidential nomination—his candidacy draws unprecedented black participation in the primaries; Shirley Chisholm founds the National Political Caucus of Black Women; Wynton Marsalis wins Grammy Awards for both jazz and classical recordings; *The Cosby Show* premieres on NBC, and it will go on to be a critically praised and top-rated series; Carl Lewis wins four gold medals at the Los Angeles Olympics; Walter Payton becomes the leading rusher in pro football history.

1985   African American artists lead collaboration in producing the "We Are the World" record to raise funds for famine relief in Africa; Grambling's Eddie Robinson achieves the highest victory total of any coach in college football history; Gwendolyn Brooks is named U.S. poet laureate.

1986   Americans celebrate the first annual Martin Luther King, Jr., Day on the third Monday of January; Bishop Desmond Tutu of South Africa wins the Martin Luther King, Jr., Nonviolent Peace Prize; August Wilson's *Fences* wins acclaim on Broadway; Spike Lee emerges as a major new filmmaker with *She's Gotta Have It*; Oprah Winfrey is the first African American woman to host a nationally syndicated TV talk show; Mike Tyson becomes the youngest (at 20) heavyweight champion in history.

1987   Kurt Schmoke becomes Baltimore's first African American mayor; Johnnetta Cole becomes the first black female president of Spelman College; the Studio Museum in Harlem organizes an immensely popular traveling exhibition on the art of the Harlem Renaissance; Reginald Lewis acquires Beatrice International Foods, creating the largest black-owned U.S. company.

1988   Jesse Jackson makes a second bid for the Democratic nomination, once again energizing black voters and winning a substantial number of delegates; more than 60,000 marchers commemorate the 25th anniversary of the 1963 March on Washington; South Africa begins to feel the effects of black resistance and worldwide efforts directed against apartheid; Temple University becomes the first institution to offer a doctorate in African American studies; Bill and Camille Cosby donate $20 million to Spelman College; Carl Lewis, Florence Griffith-Joyner, and Jackie Joyner-Kersee dominate track and field events at the Seoul Olympics.

1989   General Colin L. Powell becomes the first African American chair of the Joint Chiefs of Staff; David Dinkins is elected as the first black mayor of New York City;

L. Douglas Wilder of Virginia is the first African American elected to govern a state; Barbara Harris becomes the first female bishop of the Episcopal church; Denzel Washington and Morgan Freeman star in the film *Glory*, portraying the Civil War exploits of the 54th Massachusetts Regiment; the Dallas Museum of Art presents "Black Art: Ancestral Legacy"; Bill White, chosen to head the National League, is the first African American league president in baseball history; Art Shell of the Oakland Raiders becomes the first African American head coach in the NFL.

1990   South African civil rights leader Nelson Mandela, freed from prison after 27 years, makes a triumphal tour of major U.S. cities and addresses Congress; Charles Johnson wins the National Book Award for his novel *The Middle Passage*; August Wilson's play *The Piano Lesson* opens on Broadway; Quincy Jones earns a record 76th Grammy Award nomination; Denzel Washington wins an Academy Award for Best Actor for *Glory*.

1991   Thurgood Marshall retires from the U.S. Supreme Court; Clarence Thomas is selected to replace Marshall despite the opposition of civil rights groups and allegations of sexual harassment brought by former colleague Anita Hill; African Americans compose nearly 25% of U.S. forces engaged in Operation Desert Storm; a videotape of Los Angeles police officers savagely beating African American motorist Rodney King sparks nationwide outrage; physicist Walter Massey is the first African American president of the National Science Foundation.

1992   Derek Walcott of St. Lucia becomes the first black writer from the Americas to win the Nobel Prize for Literature (for his works of poetry); acquittal of four police officers in the Rodney King case touches off Los Angeles riots that cost 58 lives; black voters play an important role in the election of Bill Clinton to the presidency; Clinton names four African Americans to hold Cabinet posts; Carol Moseley Braun of Illinois is the first African American woman elected to the U.S. Senate; Mae C. Jemison becomes the first African American woman to complete a successful space mission; Terry McMillan's novel *Waiting to Exhale* becomes a major best-seller; Spike Lee releases his epic film biography of Malcolm X.

1993   A U.S. Supreme Court ruling makes it more difficult to sue for job discrimination; Toni Morrison, a novelist, becomes the first African American woman to win the Nobel Prize for Literature; Martin Luther King, Jr., Day is celebrated in all 50 states; Maya Angelou reads a specially composed poem at the inauguration of President Bill Clinton; Rita Dove is named poet laureate of the United States; George C. Wolfe becomes head of the New York Public Theater; Michael Jordan leads the Chicago Bulls to a third straight NBA championship.

1994   African Americans retain 38 seats in Congress but lose three committee chairs in a Republican takeover; Marion Barry is elected to his fourth, nonconsecutive term as mayor of Washington, D.C.; Len Coleman is named president of baseball's National League.

1995   Former football star O. J. Simpson is acquitted of the murder of his ex-wife and a friend by a mostly black jury, following defense allegations of racism within the Los Angeles Police Department; more than one-million African American men gather in Washington for the Million Man March, organized by the Nation of Islam's Louis Farrakhan; Shirley Ann Jackson becomes head of the Nuclear Regulatory Commission.

1996   California voters approve Proposition 209, barring the state from pursuing affirmative-action policies; Texaco settles the largest discrimination case in U.S. history, agreeing to pay $176 million to 1,400 current and former African American employees; Kweisi Mfume is chosen to head the NAACP; Secretary of Commerce Ron Brown dies in a plane crash during a mission to Croatia; sprinter Michael Johnson is the first man to win both the 200-meter and the 400-meter events at the Olympics; *Bring in 'Da Noise, Bring in 'Da Funk,* a history of black America in tap dance created by George Wolfe and Savior Glover, wins four Tony Awards.

1997   President Clinton makes a formal apology for exploitation of black patients during the Tuskegee syphilis experiment; a Congressional Medal of Honor is belatedly awarded to seven African Americans for heroism during World War II; California implements Proposition 209, ending affirmative-action policies; hundreds of thousands of African American women gather in Philadelphia for the Million Woman March; Wynton Marsalis's *Blood on the Fields* is the first jazz composition to win the Pulitzer Prize for Music; Tiger Woods becomes the first African American (and Asian American) to win a major golf tournament with his record-breaking victory in the Masters; Eddie Robinson retires as coach of Grambling State football team after 57 seasons and a record 408 victories.

1998   The President's Commission on Race, led by John Hope Franklin, pursues a national dialogue on issues affecting African Americans; Julian Bond is appointed chair of the NAACP's board of directors; government statistics reveal that AIDS is taking a disproportionate toll on the African American community; the *Pittsburgh Courier* wins a special Polk Award as the top source of news geared to African American readers; BET announces plans to produce films for the African American market; Michael Jordan leads the Chicago Bulls to their sixth NBA championship in eight years.

SOURCES FOR ADDITIONAL INFORMATION

Asante, Molefi, and Mark T. Mattson. *The Historical and Cultural Atlas of African Americans.* New York: Macmillan, 1991.

Bennett, Lerone, Jr. *Before the Mayflower,* 6th ed. New York: Penguin, 1993.

Christian, Charles M. *Black Saga: The African-American Experience.* Boston: Houghton Mifflin, 1995.

Cowan, Tom, and Jack McGuire. *Timelines of African-American History.* New York: Roundtable, 1994.

Davidson, Basil. *Africa in History,* rev. ed. New York: Collier, 1991.

Franklin, John Hope. *From Slavery to Freedom: A History of Negro Americans,* 5th ed. New York: Knopf, 1980.

Harley, Sharon. *The Timetables of African-American History.* New York: Touchstone, 1996.

Hine, Darlene Clark, and Kathleen Thompson. *A Shining Thread of Hope: The History of Black Women in America.* New York: Broadway Books, 1997.

Hornsby, Alton, Jr. *Chronology of African-American History.* Detroit: Gale, 1991.

Ploski, Harry A., ed. *The Negro Almanac: A Reference Work on the African American,* 5th ed. Detroit: Gale, 1989.

Salzman, Jack, Cornel West, and David Lionel Smith, eds. *Encyclopedia of African-American Culture and History*, 5 vols. New York: Simon & Schuster, 1996.

Smith, Jesse Carney. *Black Firsts: 2,000 Years of Extraordinary Achievement*. Detroit: Visible Ink, 1994.

Stewart, Jeffrey C. *1001 Things Everyone Should Know about African-American History*. New York: Doubleday, 1996.

2

Slavery and Freedom

THE TRANSATLANTIC SLAVE TRADE

European enslavement of Africans began around 1300, when black Africans—supplied by Arab traders—were among the slaves raising sugarcane on the Mediterranean islands of Cyprus, Crete, and Sicily. These colonies were models for the sugar plantations later established in the West Indies. Enslaved Africans also found their way to Spain and Portugal via Muslim traders. By the 1480s, the Portuguese had established sugar plantations on the island of São Tomé, just off the African coast, as well as in Madeira and the Cape Verde Islands. The growth of these plantations created a demand for slave labor, and with the opening of the Western Hemisphere to Europeans during the 16th century, that demand increased enormously.

SLAVERY IN AFRICA

Slavery in Africa began in ancient times, as it did in every other part of the inhabited world. Throughout African history, there were three main ways in which an individual could be enslaved: (1) capture during warfare or raids; (2) punishment for specific crimes, principally murder, adultery, sorcery, and treason (in these cases, the offender was usually sold outside of the community); and (3) voluntary slavery, a rare and less severe form of servitude that usually occurred in times of famine, when those on the verge of starvation might sell themselves or their children to wealthier individuals, ensuring their survival. In most African societies, the laws forbade enslaving members of one's own ethnic group. On the whole, there was no slave class in African societies. Generally, slaves were not considered inferior beings but rather individuals who had suffered misfortune and were thus confined to a lower social role.

The Portuguese established their trading bases in west-central Africa, mainly the Congo-Angola area. Between 1500 and 1700, this was the predominant slave-exporting region in the Atlantic trade, accounting for nearly 2 million captives, or 75 percent of the Africans brought to the Americas. After 1700, when the English, French, Dutch, and other nationalities supplanted the Portuguese as the principal slave merchants, the focus of the trade moved progressively northward to encompass almost the entire coastal region of western Africa.

Table 2.1 Enslaved Africans Brought to the Americas

Period	Number of slaves accounted for	%
1450–1600	409,000	3.6
1601–1700	1,348,000	11.9
1701–1800	6,090,000	53.8
1801–1900	3,466,000	30.6
Total	11,313,000	100.0

Source: Du Bois database, 1999.

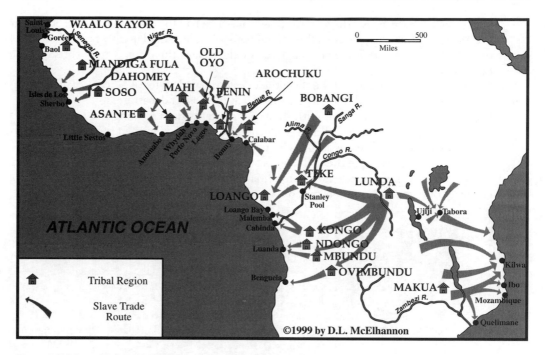

Figure 1.1 Map of Regions of Africa in the Atlantic Slave Trade

CAPTURE AND SALE

Captives were taken in a variety of ways, including organized slave raids on villages and kidnappings of isolated individuals. Following capture, transportation to the coast was often a brutal experience for captives. Slaves were transported in *coffles*, a term derived from the Arabic *qafila* (caravan). Typically, two captives marched abreast; they were chained together at the ankle, forcing them to walk slowly and to synchronize their movements. Groups of three or four were linked one behind the other by a stout rope twisted around their necks. When the coffle stopped for the night, the captives' hands were usually placed in shackles, as well. Captives on the coasts of western and eastern Africa had to march as much as 200 kilo-

Table 2.2 Sex and Age of Captives Taken from Africa, 1600–1800

Category	Number (in millions)
Young females (14–30)	2.40
Young males (14–30)	4.48
Children (under 14)	1.12
Adults over 30	0
Total	8.00

Source: Lovejoy, *Transformations in Slavery.*

meters to reach the coast; those in west-central Africa had to march as much as 500 kilometers (300 miles). When they reached the coastal ports, captives would usually be held in large structures known as *barracoons*. Some captives would remain there for two or three *years* before being sold.

At the deadly height of the slave trade, an estimated 10 to 14 percent of all captives died en route to the coast, and 6 to 10 percent died at the port of departure, usually as a result of being introduced to new diseases. With shipboard mortality rates running at 15 to 20 percent, this means that no more than two thirds of all captives ultimately reached the New World, and the proportion may have been as small as 55 percent.

The Portuguese were the only European slave traders who sometimes ventured inland and captured slaves themselves—merchants from other nations obtained their cargoes almost exclusively through African go-betweens.

> One day, when all our people were gone out to their works as usual, and only I and my dear sister were left to mind the house, two men and a woman got over our walls, and in a moment seized us both; and, without giving us time to cry out, or make resistance, they stopped our mouths, and ran off with us into the nearest wood. Here they tied our hands, and continued to carry us as far as they could, till night came on, when we reached a small house, where the robbers halted for refreshment, and spent the night. . . . The next day proved a day of greater sorrow than I had yet experienced; for my sister and I were then separated, while we lay clasped in each other's arms: it was in vain that we besought them not to part us: she was torn from me, and immediately carried away, while I was left in a state of distraction not to be described.
>
> Olaudah Equiano, taken from the Niger Delta region during the 1750s

WHAT AFRICA LOST

Though the slave trade provided short-term gains for some Africans, the ultimate effect on Africa was disastrous. Slave raiding by warlords and state-sponsored wars designed to gain captives created an atmosphere of violence and lawlessness that led to social disintegration. In addition, Africa suffered a devastating population decline and loss of productivity compared with the growing European and American populations and economies. On the west coast of Africa as a whole, the population declined from 25 million in 1700 to 20 million in 1850. The removal of captives, whose number exceeded 70,000 per year by the mid-18th century, was a major factor. Also, many of the captives, in fact one third of the total, were women in their childbearing years. And because most of the captives were males age 14 to 30, who would normally have been starting families, the effect was even more severe—in some areas, sex ratios fell to a level of 60 men to each 100 women. The loss of the skills and knowledge that went to America with those millions of captives was also keenly felt. Toward the end of the 19th century, Africa's relative weakness led to the onset of European colonialism.

THE MIDDLE PASSAGE

Many European merchants were engaged in a pattern of commerce called the "triangular trade." On the first leg of their journey, the ships brought manufactured goods to Africa; on the second leg, they transported captives from Africa to the Americas; and on the third leg, they brought

Table 2.3 Regional Origins of Africans in the Atlantic Trade, 1701–1867 (in thousands)

Years	Senegambia	Upper Guinea	Windward Coast	Gold Coast	Bight of Benin	Bight of Biafra	West-central Africa	South-east Africa	Total
1701–10	7,600	700	2,100	69,100	152,000	10,900	79,200	300	321,900
1711–20	17,100	3,800	300	76,300	173,400	22,000	96,900	12,200	402,000
1721–30	26,900	2,200	3,500	77,400	178,300	38,300	153,400	6,900	486,900
1731–40	41,500	3,800	4,600	73,000	111,100	34,100	244,800	0	512,900
1741–50	16,700	9,500	8,000	78,300	93,400	99,900	232,100	0	537,900
1751–60	47,600	28,400	30,900	97,200	89,200	98,000	230,500	700	622,500
1761–70	51,200	63,600	49,300	104,400	101,600	152,100	313,100	1,300	836,600
1771–80	50,600	20,400	30,000	103,300	113,200	119,000	296,800	3,800	737,100
1781–90	30,100	57,500	7,300	111,900	110,200	175,400	338,200	26,500	857,100
1791–1800	25,600	41,000	7,200	90,300	100,800	151,400	346,800	11,700	774,800
1801–10	38,000	26,400	7,000	68,600	125,000	100,600	296,300	21,700	683,600
1811–20	45,100	22,600	13,200	0	93,800	93,700	262,900	68,300	599,600
1821–30	13,200	32,200	8,900	0	114,700	127,300	292,800	101,300	694,400
1831–40	8,100	54,600	6,800	0	88,100	112,700	296,300	102,400	669,000
1841–50	9,500	24,300	2,700	0	98,700	12,100	309,900	87,000	435,300
1851–60	0	13,400	600	0	22,900	7,300	110,800	24,100	179,100
1861–67	0	2,700	0	0	3,000	0	44,200	2,700	52,600
Totals	428,800	407,100	182,400	949,800	1,769,400	1,354,800	3,945,000	470,900	9,403,300

Source: Du Bois database, as analyzed in Eltis, Behrendt and Richardson, 1999.

slave-produced sugar, rum, and molasses back to Europe. Traders referred to the second leg of the journey as the "middle passage," and the term has survived to denote the ordeal of the millions of Africans who were forcibly transported to the New World.

Cargo ships making the middle passage were generally midsized vessels of about 200 tons. British regulations specified that a ship could carry no more than five captives for every 3 tons of burden, thus the average ship carried about 350 individuals. However, this rule was often circumvented. Below decks, captured Africans were usually chained in twos, with little room to stretch out or move about. They were accorded about half the space normally granted to convicts, soldiers, and steerage passengers during the same era. Their provisions included boiled horsebeans, rice, corn, yams, palm oil, and a small amount of salted meat or fish.

Historians estimate that during the entire course of the slave trade, between 15 and 20 percent of all captives died during the middle passage. The voyage to the Americas took between 35 and 70 days; the longer the duration, the higher the death rate. Dehydration—brought on by vomiting from seasickness and diarrhea from dysentery spread by bad food and water—was the major cause of death among captives. An equally important cause of death was heat: When a slave ship cruised the African coast taking on cargo, captives were kept in the stifling hold to prevent escapes. (Often two months or more would elapse before a ship was ready to embark for the Americas.) Under these conditions, the daily ration of liquids—generally one pint of water and one quart of soup—would have been one quart less than the amount needed to replace the fluids an average person would lose in an extremely hot and humid environment. Finally, many of the captives fell into deep depression, which combined with dehydration, leaving them more open to diseases and leading to a high rate of suicide among Africans. Death rates declined during the course of the Atlantic trade, from nearly 25 percent in the early decades of the 18th century to 5 to 10 percent a century later, primarily due to the use of specialized slaving ships by traders eager to ensure the survival of their profitable cargo.

On top of these difficult conditions, and despite the fact that the slave traders' fortunes were tied to the survival of their cargo, the captives were often submitted to the worst atrocities, including sexual assaults and many cases of outright murder, as reported by former slave traders and enslaved captives. The worst known incident was the murder aboard the British slave ship *Zong*. The *Zong*'s captain, Luke Collingwood, observed that dozens of his captives and crew members were dying of disease, so he decided to throw overboard, and to their deaths, 132 Africans. He then made an insurance claim for the full value of each murdered slave but was defeated in court. This and other cases of drownings at sea became a rallying point for abolitionists.

Table 2.4 Nationality of Ships Engaged in the Atlantic Slave Trade, 1701–1800

National carrier	Number of slaves	%
English	2,468,000	40.5
Portuguese	1,888,000	31.0
French	1,104,000	18.1
Dutch	349,000	5.7
North American	206,000	3.4
Danish	66,000	1.0
Other (Swedish, Brandenburger)	10,000	0.2
Total	6,091,000	

Source: Du Bois database.

The enslaved captives often mutinied, most notably in the successful case of the *Amistad* mutiny (see "Major Slave Revolts," 1839, page 48).

IN MEMORIAM

Every year, during the last weekend in July, hundreds of African Americans gather on the beach at New York's Coney Island to conduct a memorial service for those lost during the middle passage. The rites are performed under the auspices of Yumanja, the Yoruba deity of the sea. Priests and priestesses make libations and carry offerings into the ocean so that Yumanja will watch over the spirits of the lost ancestors.

Table 2.5 Destinations of Enslaved Africans in the Transatlantic Trade, 1451–1870

Region	Captives bought	Region	Captives bought
BRITISH NORTH AMERICA	399,000	FRENCH CARIBBEAN	
SPANISH AMERICA		St. Domingue (Haiti)	864,300
Cuba	702,000	Martinique	365,000
Puerto Rico	77,000	Guadeloupe	290,000
Mexico	200,000	French Guiana	51,000
Venezuela	121,000	Louisiana (to 1803)	28,300
Peru	95,000	**Total for French Carribean**	1,600,200
La Plata and Bolivia	100,000	DUTCH CARIBBEAN	500,000

Table 2.5 (continued)

Region	Captives bought	Region	Captives bought
Chile	6,000	DANISH CARIBBEAN	28,000
Santo Domingo	30,000	BRAZIL	3,646,800
Colombia, Panama, Ecuador	200,000		
Central America	21,000	EUROPE	175,000
Total for Spanish America	1,522,000	**Total**	9,566,100
BRITISH CARIBBEAN			
Jamaica	747,500		
Barbados	387,000		
Leeward Islands	346,000		
Ceded or conquered islands	159,500		
Small possessions	25,000		
Total for British Carribbean	1,655,000		

Source: Curtin, *The Atlantic Slave Trade: A Census.*

LEADING SLAVE-TRADE CENTERS IN THE UNITED STATES

Following are the leading U.S. ports in the transatlantic slave trade, ranked according to the number of ships they dispatched to transport slaves from Africa to the Americas:

1. Newport, Rhode Island
2. Bristol, Rhode Island
3. Charleston, South Carolina
4. Providence, Rhode Island
5. Boston, Massachusetts
6. Salem, Massachusetts
7. New York City
8. Philadelphia, Pennsylvania
9. Savannah, Georgia
10 St. Mary's, Georgia
11. Virginia estuaries (Accomac, Hampton, York, Rappahannock, Potomac, Upper James)
12. St. Mary's, Maryland

Massachusetts ships were the first to enter the slave trade, beginning in 1638. Neighboring Rhode Island, though the smallest of the American colonies, began to surpass Massachusetts during the 18th century; by 1770, Rhode Island ships commanded 70 percent of the trade. Between 1709 and 1807, Rhode Island ships made 934 voyages to Africa, loaded mainly with rum, and returned to Rhode Island with 106,544 captives: About two thirds of these were sold in the West Indies. Though slaving was never a dominant part of New York's commerce, New York ships made 151 slaving voyages to Africa between 1715 and 1774, and by the end of the colonial period, blacks composed 12 percent of the city's population. In general, merchants in the ports below the Delaware River served as factors and agents rather than importers. Excluding a sudden spate of activity from Charleston during the final 15 years of the slave trade, southern ports sent only 16 ships to Africa during the entire duration of the trade.

Charleston was by far the largest slave entrepôt in the United States. Between 1717 and 1775, Charleston brought in nearly 75,000 captives from Africa and another 15,000 enslaved Africans from the West Indies. When Southern cotton production began to boom after the 1790s, the numbers rose dramatically. Between 1800 and 1820, Charleston supplied South Carolina with 112,324 additional captives, more than doubling the state's slave population. The demand was so great that Charleston merchants finally began dispatching their own vessels to Africa, sending out 110 ships between 1792 and 1807, a total exceeded only by Newport and Bristol.

 PROFITING FROM SLAVERY

Some of the most illustrious names in colonial history had financial interests in the slave trade at one time or another. In Massachusetts, the list included the legendary Cabot and Lowell clans; in Rhode Island, the Browns (instrumental in founding Brown University), William Ellery (father of the William Ellery who signed the Declaration of Independence), the Vernons, and the De Wolfs; in New York, the Livingstons, Van Cortlandts, Schuylers, and Beekmans; in Virginia, Benjamin Harrison (ancestor of two presidents) and William Byrd I; in South Carolina, Henry Laurens, who served as president of the Second Continental Congress. In at least one instance (in 1764), John Paul Jones, the future naval hero of the American Revolution, delivered a shipment of slaves to the West Indies on behalf of a Philadelphia merchant.

SLAVERY IN THE AMERICAS

ARRIVAL AND SALE

Upon arrival, after one to three months at sea in physically and emotionally arduous conditions, the slave captain would bring his frightened and exhausted captives ashore in small boats and immediately herd them to town. In town, the slaves would be fed and cleaned, then sold. The ship captains often retained the services of a broker, who would pick out the extremely ill or crippled among the captives and have them sold separately as "refuse" slaves. The remaining captives were then taken to the auction block, where they were roughly inspected and auctioned off as individuals or in lots. Another method of sale was the clamorous "scramble," where the prices for the captives were set, and buyers scrambled and fought to rope off or seize with their hands the best and healthiest men, women, and children among the captives. This process was terrifying for the newly arrived captives, some of whom were under the impression they had been brought to this new land to be devoured by cannibals.

GROWTH OF POPULATION

The enslaved population in the United States increased from close to 700,000 in 1790 to close to 4 million in 1860. As the importation of slaves was forbidden after 1808 and only about 250,000 captives were imported illegally up to 1865, these increases were due mainly to childbearing. Despite long-held beliefs that African American families were usually fragmented during the time of slavery, recent scholarship suggests that while many families were separated, others were remarkably stable and close knit, even under the most adverse conditions. As of 1850, 64 percent of those enslaved in the United States lived in nuclear families (this figure includes some childless couples) and 21 percent in one-parent families. By contrast, only 24 percent of the enslaved population in Trinidad and 37 percent of those in Jamaica lived in nuclear families. In the West Indies, men outnumbered women by a considerable margin, and most plantation workers lived in barracks; in the United States, African Americans on plantations were far more likely to live in one- or two-family cabins. Due to these and other factors (including a comparatively low death rate), the United States replaced Brazil as the predominant slaveholding society in the Americas during the early part of the 19th century—despite the vast disparity in the number of enslaved Africans brought to the two nations (see the preceding table, "Destinations of Enslaved Africans in the Transatlantic Trade, 1451–1870").

Table 2.6 Growth of the Enslaved Population of the United States, 1790–1860

Year	Population	Year	Population
1790	697,624	1830	2,009,043
1800	893,602	1840	2,487,355
1810	1,191,362	1850	3,204,313
1820	1,538,022	1860	3,953,760

Source: U.S. Census Bureau, *A Century of Population Growth.*

S ome [two-family cabins] had partitions, while others had none. Where there were not partitions each family would fit up his own part as he could, sometimes they got old boards and nailed them up, stuffing the cracks with old rags; when they could not get boards they hung up old clothes. When the family increased, the children all slept together, both boys and girls, until either got married, then a part of another cabin was assigned to the one that was married, but the rest would have to remain with their mother and father as they did when children unless they could get with some of their relatives or friends who had small families. . . . The young men slept in the apartment known as the kitchen and the young women slept in the room with their mother and father.

Jacob Stroyer, former slave from South Carolina

Table 2.7 Geographic Distribution of the Enslaved Population in the United States, 1790

State	Population	State	Population
Virginia	292,627	New Jersey	11,423
South Carolina	107,094	Delaware	8,887
Maryland	103,036	Pennsylvania	3,707
North Carolina	100,783	Tennessee	3,417
Georgia	29,264	Connecticut	2,648
New York	21,193	Rhode Island	958
Kentucky	12,430	New Hampshire	157

Source: U.S. Census Bureau, *A Century of Population Growth.*

Table 2.8 Geographic Distribution of the Enslaved Population in the United States, 1820

State	Population	State	Population
Virginia	426,987	New York	10,088
South Carolina	258,475	New Jersey	7,557
North Carolina	204,917	Delaware	4,509
Kentucky	126,732	Pennsylvania	211
Maryland/D.C.	111,056	Connecticut	97
Georgia	110,055	Rhode Island	48
Tennessee	80,107		

Source: U.S. Census Bureau, *A Century of Population Growth.*

Table 2.9 Geographic Distribution of the Enslaved Population in the United States, 1860

State	Population	State	Population
Virginia	490,865	Kentucky	225,483
Georgia	462,198	Texas	182,566
Mississippi	436,631	Missouri	114,931
Alabama	435,080	Arkansas	111,115
South Carolina	402,406	Maryland/D.C.	90,374
Louisiana	331,726	Florida	61,745
North Carolina	331,059	Delaware	1,798
Tennessee	275,719		

Source: U.S. Census Bureau, A Century of Population Growth.

THE PLANTATION SYSTEM

After the invention of the cotton gin in 1793, the geographic focus of the slave economy shifted away from the upper South, where the soil had been increasingly exhausted, to newly opened lands west of the Mississippi. As cotton became king, Southern agriculture was organized more and more around the plantation system, and slaveholding became increasingly concentrated. In 1790, approximately 17 percent of the white families in the United States owned slaves, and the average number of slaves per family was 7.3. In the South, 28 percent of families owned slaves, with an average of 7.5 slaves per family. In 1860, slaveholders numbered only 338,637 out of nearly 8 million whites in the South (4%). Of these, 2,292 were classified as large planters holding 100 slaves or more: Thus, a handful of Southerners (1 person of every 3,490) held at least 60 percent of the region's slaves in 1860.

The hands are required to be in the cotton fields as soon as it is light in the morning and, with the exception of ten or fifteen minutes, which is given them at noon to swallow their allowance of cold bacon, they are not permitted to be a moment idle until it is too dark to see, and when the moon is full, they often times labor till the middle of the night. They do not dare to stop even at dinner time, nor return to the quarters, however late it be, until the order to halt is given by the driver.

Solomon Northrup, a former field hand

Table 2.10 Employment of U.S. Slaves in Agriculture, 1850

Crop	Number employed
Hemp	60,000
Rice	125,000
Sugar	150,000
Tobacco	350,000
Cotton	1,815,000
Total	2,500,000

Source: Stampp, The Peculiar Institution, p. 50.

Table 2.11 Occupations of Slaves on a Typical U.S. Tobacco Plantation
(Belmead, in Virginia, 1854)

Category	Occupation	Category	Occupation
Field corps	8 plowmen	Domestics	1 butler
	10 male hoe hands		2 waiters
	12 female hoe hands		4 housemaids
	2 wagoners		1 nurse
	4 ox drivers		1 laundress
	2 cooks		1 seamstress
			1 dairy maid
Stable and pasture staff	1 carriage driver		1 gardener
	1 hostler		
	1 stable boy	Artisans	2 carpenters
	1 shepherd		5 stonemasons
	1 cow herd		1 miller
	1 hog herd		2 blacksmiths
			2 shoemakers
			5 spinners (female)
			1 weaver (female)

Note: Also enslaved were 45 children, 1 invalid, 1 elderly man and 2 elderly women
who were hired out, and one woman named Nancy with no listed occupation.
Source: Phillips, *American Negro Slavery.*

On the Caribbean sugar islands, the distribution of labor was somewhat different. On a typical Jamaican plantation, 60 percent of the workers labored in the fields; 10 percent were occupied with milling and refining the sugar; and barely 2 percent worked as domestics in the owner's household. Field workers were divided into three gangs, based on their relative capacity. On the French sugar islands, workers were organized in an atelier system. At the top was the grand atelier, made up of the most able-bodied men and women, followed by the second atelier, which might include those newly arrived from the slave ships or individuals recovering from illness or childbirth—these two gangs were responsible for all the plowing, planting, and cutting. Finally, the petit atelier was reserved for children, who had the task of weeding. Throughout the Americas, about 80 percent of the enslaved population were employed: Children typically began to work on weeding gangs at the age of eight, and elderly people cared for the youngest children or tended livestock. Throughout the Americas, women routinely worked in the fields alongside men and often made up a majority of the field hands. Away from the fields, there was a marked division of labor; craftspeople such as blacksmiths and carpenters were almost always male, while women filled most of the domestic positions.

Throughout the Americas, life on the plantations was an invariably cruel existence for the enslaved. By the dawn of the 18th century, in reaction to the increasing slave population and a rash of uprisings, slave codes had been enacted through the Americas, depriving slaves of almost every right and allowing planters almost unlimited freedom to discipline slaves. Slaves were not allowed to own anything, carry a weapon, or leave the plantation without a written pass—these offenses were commonly punished by whipping, maiming, branding, and sometimes with crueler forms of torture, including mutilation, amputation, and the use of torturing devices. Sexual abuse of enslaved women was also rampant. Throughout the slaveholding states, it was impossible for a white to be convicted for the murder of a slave.

URBAN AND RURAL SLAVERY

Jamaica was typical of the Caribbean sugar islands: Blacks outnumbered whites by nearly 10 to 1. In 1768, there were 167,000 enslaved workers on the island and 18,000 whites. Seventy-five percent of the enslaved were involved in sugar production, and 95 percent lived in rural areas. (Overall, about two thirds of all the Africans brought to the New World worked on sugar plantations—only in the 19th century did coffee begin to rival sugar as the major slave-produced export crop.) Leading cities on the sugar islands held less than 15,000 inhabitants, and urban slavery was never a factor in these societies.

In Latin America, by contrast, there were 21 cities with populations of 50,000 to 100,000, and many of these had sizable slave populations. Lima, Peru, had a slave population of 20,000 as early as 1640, and the city remained half black throughout the 17th century. In later years, urban slavery was especially significant in Havana, Cuba, and in the great cities of Brazil. Even in 1872, when slavery was on the decline in Brazil, 15 percent of those living in cities of 20,000 or more were slaves, a total of 118,000. Slaves represented 20 percent of the population in Rio de Janeiro, 17 percent in Recife, 12 percent in Bahia, and 10 percent in São Paulo. A significant proportion were *escravos de ganho* (employed slaves) who hired themselves out as vendors, porters, artisans, artists, and musicians, paying their owners a portion of their wages.

In the United States, about 10 percent of the enslaved were urban dwellers, and there were sizable slave populations in the major cities of the southern United States, such as Charleston, Richmond, Savannah, and Mobile. In each location, slaves made up around one third of the population. A breakdown of manual occupations in Charleston in 1848 shows the wide range of jobs filled by African Americans:

Table 2.12 Manual Occupations in Charleston, 1848

Occupations	Slaves		Free Negroes		Whites	
	Men	Women	Men	Women	Men	Women
Domestic servants	1,888	3,384	9	28	13	100
Cooks and confectioners	7	12	18	18	—	5
Nurses and midwives	—	2	—	10	—	5
Laundresses	—	33	—	45	—	—
Seamstresses and mantua makers	—	24	—	196	—	125
Milliners	—	—	—	7	—	44
Fruiterers, hucksters, and peddlers	—	18	6	5	46	18
Gardeners	3	—	—	—	5	1
Coachmen	15	—	4	—	2	—
Draymen	67	—	11	—	13	—
Porters	35	—	5	—	8	—
Wharfingers and stevedores	2	—	1	—	21	—
Pilots and sailors	50	—	1	—	176	—
Fishermen	11	—	14	—	10	—
Carpenters	120	—	27	—	119	—
Masons and bricklayers	68	—	10	—	60	—
Painters and plasterers	16	—	4	—	18	—
Tinners	3	—	1	—	10	—
Ship carpenters and joiners	51	—	6	—	52	—
Coopers	61	—	2	—	20	—
Coach makers and wheelwrights	3	—	1	—	26	—

Table 2.12 (continued)

Occupations	Slaves		Free Negroes		Whites	
	Men	Women	Men	Women	Men	Women
Cabinet makers	8	—	—	—	26	—
Upholsterers	1	—	1	—	10	—
Gun, copper, and locksmiths	2	—	1	—	16	—
Blacksmiths and horseshoers	40	—	4	—	51	—
Millwrights	—	—	5	—	4	—
Boot and shoemakers	6	—	17	—	30	—
Saddle and harness makers	2	—	1	—	29	—
Tailors and cap makers	36	—	42	6	68	6
Butchers	5	—	1	—	10	—
Millers	—	—	1	—	14	—
Bakers	39	—	1	—	35	1
Barbers and hairdressers	4	—	14	—	—	6
Cigarmakers	5	—	1	—	10	—
Bookbinders	3	—	—	—	10	—
Printers	5	—	—	—	65	—
Other mechanics	45	—	2	—	182	—
Apprentices	43	8	14	7	55	5
Unclassified, unskilled laborers	838	378	19	2	192	—
Superannuated	38	54	1	5	—	—

Source: Phillips, American Negro Slavery.

Though most slaves worked directly for those who had purchased them, a number were hired out to plantation owners or industrial enterprises such as ironworks. This was particularly common in the cities, where at least 30 percent of all enslaved workers were "on hire" in 1860. (In Richmond, the South's center of industry, the proportion surpassed 50%.) In rural areas, only about 6 percent of the slave force hired out. A small proportion of slaves had the privilege of "hiring their own time," making their own arrangements with employers and paying their owners a portion of their earnings. In this way, a number of individuals saved enough money to eventually purchase their freedom.

I remained with Mr. Covey one year . . . and during the first six months that I was there, I was whipped, either with sticks or cowskins, every week. Aching bones and a sore back were my constant companions. Frequent as the lash was used, Mr. Covey thought less of it, as a means of breaking down my spirit, than that of hard and long continued labor. He worked me steadily, up to the point of my powers of endurance. From the dawn of the day in the morning till the darkness was complete in the evening, I was kept at hard work, in the field or the woods.

Frederick Douglass's recollection of being hired out to a farmer notorious for "breaking" slaves

FREE BLACKS IN THE AMERICAS

Table 2.13 Free Blacks as a Percentage of Total Population in Selected Societies

Society	1764–1768	1773–1776	1784–1790	1800–1808	1812–1821	1827–1840
Puerto Rico	—	48.4 (1775)	—	43.8 (1802)	43.6 (1812)	—
Curaçao	—	—	—	—	32.0 (1817)	43.4 (1833)
Brazil						
Minas Gerais	—	—	35.0 (1786)	41.0 (1808)	40.3 (1821)	—
São Paulo	—	—	—	18.8 (1800)	22.7 (1815)	23.2 (1836)
Martinique	2.3 (1764)	3.3 (1776)	3.7 (1784)	7.1 (1802)	9.4 (1816)	24.9 (1835)
Saint Domingue	—	—	4.0 (1784)	—	—	—
Jamaica	1.7 (1768)	2.1 (1775)	—	2.9 (1800)	—	—
Barbados	0.5 (1768)	0.6 (1773)	1.0 (1786)	2.6 (1801)	3.3 (1815)	6.5 (1833)
United States						
Upper South	—	—	1.8 (1790)	2.7 (1800)	3.4 (1820)	3.7 (1840)
Lower South	—	—	0.6 (1790)	0.8 (1800)	1.7 (1820)	1.6 (1840)
Cuba	—	20.3 (1774)	—	—	—	15.1 (1827)

Sources: Cohen and Greene, *Neither Slave nor Free*. The data for the United States were taken from U.S. Census Office, *Population of the United States in 1860* (Washington, D.C., 1864), pp. 600–603.

FREE BLACKS IN THE UNITED STATES

Free blacks were never more than a small proportion of the total U.S. population before the Civil War and were always greatly outnumbered by their enslaved brethren, but their numbers grew steadily throughout the 19th century. Whereas in 1790 there were only 60,000 free blacks in the United States, their number had grown to nearly 500,000 by 1860. Approximately half lived in the slave states and half in the free states. The states with the largest populations of free blacks in 1860 were Maryland (83,942), Virginia (58,042), Pennsylvania (56,949), New York (49,005), Ohio (36,673), North Carolina (30,463), New Jersey (25,318), Delaware (19,829), and Louisiana (18,647).

Table 2.14 Growth of the Free Black Population in the United States, 1790–1860

Year	Population	Year	Population
1790	59,557	1830	319,599
1800	108,435	1840	386,293
1810	186,446	1850	434,495
1820	233,634	1860	488,070

Source: Cohen and Green, *Neither Slave nor Free*.

FREE BLACKS IN THE SOUTH

In the South, most free blacks lived in rural areas, where they continued to work in agriculture, but a sizable number also lived in major Southern cities: Baltimore's free black population numbered more than 25,000, and that of New Orleans exceeded 10,000. In the cities, free blacks often worked as barbers, carpenters, bricklayers, carters, and house servants. Beginning in the 1840s, however, they faced growing competition and hostility from recently arrived Irish and German laborers, and many were obliged to return to the land as agricultural workers and small-farm owners. Some free blacks even resided on the plantations where their relatives remained in bondage, hiring out their labor to the owner.

Free blacks in the South were obliged to adopt a more cautious approach to politics than their Northern counterparts. Acutely aware of their precarious position in a society dominated by slaveholders, they often felt it advisable to demonstrate their loyalty during slave rebellions by siding with whites. Despite these efforts, Southern whites generally distrusted free blacks, accusing them of aiding runaways and encouraging slaves to revolt. As a result, free blacks usually bore the brunt of white anger in the aftermath of slave revolts. Between 1830 and 1860, Southern states passed laws forbidding further manumission and took measures to expel free black residents: By 1860, Mississippi, Florida, Texas, and Arkansas each had fewer than 1,000 free blacks within their borders. Moreover, as slave prices rose sharply during the 1850s, free blacks were in constant danger of being kidnapped and sold back into slavery. They were also pressured to reenslave themselves voluntarily and often found it possible to maintain their freedom only by seeking the protection of a white guardian. Only in Delaware and Louisiana were free blacks permitted to testify against whites in court, and only Tennessee and North Carolina ever allowed free blacks to vote (the franchise in both states was withdrawn in 1835).

Southern free blacks were, however, allowed to own property, including slaves. In this way, a number of individuals were able to "purchase" and then liberate their wives, husbands, children, and other relatives. After 1830, however, free blacks living in the slave states were legally obliged to keep their loved ones in a condition of legal bondage, because antimanumission laws prevented any other course of action.

> I was in slavery until I was about eighteen years old. There were four uncles, myself and mother, and another sister of my uncles. My uncles paid fifteen hundred dollars apiece for themselves. They bought themselves three times. They got cheated out of their freedom in the first instance, and were put in jail at one time, and were going to be sold down South, right away; but parties who were well acquainted with us, and knew we had made desperate struggles for our freedom, came forward and advanced the money, and took us out of jail, and put us on a footing so that we could go ahead and earn money to pay the debt. We had an uncle in Pittsburgh, who had accumulated a good deal of property since he obtained his freedom. My uncles bought me and my mother, as well as themselves.
>
> Former slave quoted in S. G. Howe, *The Refugees from Slavery in Canada West* (1864)

FREE BLACKS IN THE NORTH

Free blacks in the North gravitated to cities such as Boston, New York, Philadelphia, and Cincinnati; there were also free black communities in Cass County, Michigan; Hammond County, Indiana; and Wilberforce, Ohio. In addition to following a wide variety of skilled trades, the free blacks also became teachers, ministers, lawyers, and dentists. Free blacks in Philadelphia owned nearly 100 houses and lots by 1800, and by 1837, New York City's free black population owned real estate valued at $1.4 million and had bank accounts totaling $600,000.

In virtually all the cities where they lived, free blacks created a variety of institutions. In addition to religious congregations (see Chapter 6, "Religion"), various fraternal organizations and mutual aid societies had a prominent role. Often regarded as the first of these was the African Union Society, founded in Newport, Rhode Island, in 1780. A second influential organization, the Free African Society of Philadelphia, was created by Richard Allen and Absalom Jones in 1787. By 1848, there were 106 known African American societies in Philadelphia, with a combined membership of 8,000. Typically, the associations demanded high standards of personal conduct from their members, as well as an initiation fee and monthly dues. In return, members received disability benefits and burial allowances.

A sizable number of free blacks also belonged to fraternal orders such as the Freemasons. In 1775, Prince Hall and 14 other African Americans joined a British lodge of Freemasons in Boston, and 12 years later, the group received their own charter, becoming African Lodge No. 459. A number of subordinate black lodges subsequently sprang up in other states, and their members—drawn mainly from the middle classes—came to be known as Prince Hall Masons. Other important antebellum black fraternal organizations were the Grand United Order of Odd Fellows, founded in New York in 1843, and the Grand United Order of Galilean Fishermen, which arose in Washington, D. C., in 1856.

The mutual aid societies and fraternal organizations were an important resource for free blacks, whose situation in the North was far from enviable. They may have been technically free, but they did not enjoy anything approaching equal status with whites. Following the Missouri Compromise of 1819, every newly admitted state (except Maine) barred African Americans from voting, with the full approval of the federal government. Beginning in 1830, states such as New York, Pennsylvania, Connecticut, and Indiana either abolished or restricted (via property requirements) the voting privileges previously extended to African Americans. By 1840, only about 7 percent of free blacks in the North—those living in Massachusetts, New Hampshire, Vermont, and Maine—had full access to the ballot box.

In addition, a number of states prohibited blacks from testifying in any legal case involving a white person. Thus any offense committed by a white against an African American was sure to go unpunished unless a white eyewitness came forward to give testimony. Not surprisingly, African Americans made up a disproportionate percentage of the prison population.

Beyond the legal sphere, discrimination and segregation in the North extended to virtually every aspect of life: railway cars, omnibuses, stagecoaches, steamboats, theaters, lecture halls, hotels, restaurants, churches, and schools all had restricted facilities for African Americans or barred them outright. Many states passed laws that denied residence to out-of-state African Americans; though these laws were rarely enforced, they provided an excuse for outbreaks of violence against free blacks, such as the 1829 riot in Cincinnati that drove hundreds of African Americans to flee the city for Canada. (See Chapter 4, "The Diaspora," for African American settlements in Canada.) After traveling throughout the United States in 1831–1832, Alexis de Tocqueville observed, "The prejudice of race appears to be stronger in the states that have abolished slavery than in those where it still exists; and nowhere is it so intolerant as in those states where servitude has never been known."

The federal government showed no more regard for equality than did the states. As early as 1790, the government decreed that only whites could become naturalized citizens. This exclusionary attitude culminated in the 1856 Dred Scott decision, in which the Supreme Court declared that African Americans, whether enslaved or free, were not citizens of the United States, had no right to sue in the federal courts, and "no rights the white man is bound to respect." Northern politicians, in their efforts to exclude slavery from the territories, were motivated not by concern for the freedom of African Americans but rather by the desire to ensure that the West would be the exclusive province of white farmers and laborers seeking land and economic opportunity.

The great majority of Northern free blacks were as restricted in their choice of occupation as they were in other areas. As of 1855, 87 percent of employed African Americans in New York City performed menial or unskilled labor—as laborers, mariners, servants, bootblacks, waiters, porters, and the like—and this pattern generally prevailed in other Northern cities. The one area in which segregation did not strictly apply was housing. Studies show that though many African Americans lived in poor neighborhoods with run-down housing, they generally shared these neighborhoods with whites in similar circumstances. Thus the concentration of African Americans in urban ghettos, so prevalent during most of the 20th century, was largely unknown in the 19th century.

FREE BLACKS IN LATIN AMERICA

Following the tradition of Roman law with regard to slaves, all Latin American colonial regimes permitted manumission, and small numbers of free blacks emerged in the region as early as the 16th century. By the late 18th century, free blacks outnumbered slaves in a number of Spanish-speaking areas: Among the most striking examples were the Viceroyalty of New Granada (Colombia and Ecuador), which was home to 420,000 free blacks and 80,000 slaves; Venezuela (198,000 free, 64,000 enslaved); and Santo Domingo (80,000 free, 15,000 enslaved). In Brazil, the free black population surged ahead of the slave population around 1850 and grew so rapidly that Brazil's first census (1872) listed 4.2 million free blacks to 1.5 million slaves and 3.8 million whites. Spanish and Portuguese regimes were traditionally more liberal in granting legal rights to persons of color than were their North American counterparts, but free blacks were often denied entry to educational institutions and a number of professions, and eventually laws were passed restricting manumission.

Unlike North Americans, who recognized only black and white, the Spanish and Portuguese developed an elaborate system of social gradations to acknowledge the extensive intermarriage among Europeans, Africans, and Native Americans in the New World. In addition to *negro* (the child of African parents) and *mestizo* (European and Indian), the categories included *zambo* (African and Indian), *mulatto* (African and European), *quadroon* (negro and mulatto), *mustee* (quadroon and European), *mustifino* (mustee and European), *quintroon* (mustifino and European), and *octoroon* (quintroon and European). (In the United States, the terms had different meanings: a *quadroon* had one fourth African ancestry, and an *octoroon* had one eighth African ancestry.) It was common for Latin American whites to acknowledge the children that resulted from their unions with enslaved women, and these children were commonly regarded as free. In North America, by contrast, few slaveholders acknowledged their mixed-race children even when physical resemblance was obvious; the children were sometimes allowed special privileges, but they customarily inherited the enslaved status of their mothers.

FREE BLACKS IN THE CARIBBEAN

Caribbean slave regimes were closer to North America than to Latin America in restricting the expansion of the free black population. In the 1780s, the French-held islands of Saint

Domingue, Martinique, and Guadeloupe had only 30,000 free blacks, compared to 575,000 slaves and 52,000 whites. In the entire British West Indies, the free black population was only 13,000, compared with 53,000 whites and 467,000 slaves.

Caribbean slave societies adopted the Iberian system of social gradations; mustifinos, quintroons, and octoroons were classed as whites, whereas all others were subject to varying forms of discrimination. In the British-held islands during the 18th century, free blacks were barred from political office and supervisory positions, and the laws forbade them to own or inherit property worth more than £2,000. The restrictive laws were reversed gradually during the 19th century as the vastly outnumbered whites became more pliant toward the black majority in the wake of the Haitian Revolution. At this point, a number of free blacks acquired extensive properties and joined the planter class.

ANTISLAVERY MOVEMENTS

SPANISH OPPONENTS OF SLAVERY

The first European opposition to slavery arose among a number of Spanish clerics during the middle of the 16th century. At that time, Fray Domingo de Soto condemned the practice of seizing men by violence and selling them into bondage. In 1571, the theologian Tomás de Mercado decried the cruelties of the slave trade and condemned the enslavement of human beings for economic gain. (However, Mercado claimed that parents had the right to sell their children, and he also sanctioned the enslavement of prisoners of war.) Two years later, Bartolomé de Albornoz, a law professor at the University of Mexico, went far beyond Mercado by refuting all philosophical justifications for slavery, including the argument that captives were achieving salvation through conversion to Christianity. The Vatican placed Albornoz's book on its index of forbidden works.

QUAKERS

In North America, the first whites to oppose slavery were members of the Religious Society of Friends, commonly known as Quakers. In 1688, a group of Pennsylvania Quakers issued the Germantown Petition, declaring that slavery was incompatible with Christian principles, and the 1696 Yearly Meeting urged Quakers to avoid the slave trade. During the 18th century, antislavery sentiments were expressed by such prominent Quakers as John Hepburn, Elihu Coleman, Ralph Sandiford, and Benjamin Lay.

The best known of the Quaker antislavery advocates, John Woolman (1720–1772) of New Jersey, traveled to the South in 1746 and 1757, urging Quaker brethren to free their slaves, either immediately or by a provision in their wills. In concert with Anthony Benezet, Woolman convinced the Society of Friends to take a definitive stance against slavery. In 1755, the society decreed that any member engaged in the importation of slaves would be expelled. In 1790, the Quakers petitioned Congress to end slavery.

UNDERGROUND RAILROAD

As early as the 1780s, an informal network sprang up to aid runaway slaves making their way to freedom in the North. The network was especially active in the western territories after the War of 1812, and by 1830, it had spread through 14 Northern states. The network derived its historic nickname from a Kentucky slave owner who pursued an escaped slave into Ohio and then lost track of him, remarking that the man "must have gone off an underground road."

> I hope you will remember me now just as same as you did when I was there with you because my mind are with you night and day the Love that I bear for you in my breast is greater than I thought it was if I had thought I had so much Love for you I dont think I ever left being I have escape and has fled into a land of freedom I can but stop and look over my past Life and say what a fool I was for staying in bondage as Long My dear wife I dont want you to get married before you send me some letters because I never shall get married until I see you again My mind dont deceive and it appears to me as if I shall see you again
>
> Samuel Washington Johnson, writing to his wife after escaping from bondage in Richmond

Scholars have identified 3,200 active workers in the Underground Railroad, including legendary "conductors" such as Harriet Tubman, William Wells Brown, and Josiah Henson, who boldly ventured into the slave states to lead runaways north. The network consisted of numerous safe houses, including that of the Quaker Levi Coffin, who sheltered many fugitives in the attic of his Indiana home (now a national historic landmark). Another important stop on the Underground Railroad was Oberlin College in Ohio, the first U.S. college to admit women and blacks and a bastion of the abolitionist movement. Between 1810 and 1860, perhaps as many as 100,000 enslaved African Americans—most were between 15 and 35 years of age—reached the free states and Canada by means of the Underground Railroad. Pursuit by slaveholders and their agents, sanctioned by the federal Fugitive Slave Laws of 1793 and 1850, was a major cause of friction between North and South.

The legendary Harriet Tubman delivered over 300 enslaved men, women, and children to freedom as a conductor on the Underground Railroad. She was said to have used her gun to "encourage" the tired and frightened to keep moving on the journey North.

*W*hen I had crossed that line, I looked at my hands to see if I was the same person. There was such a glory over everything.

Harriet Tubman, recalling her first escape from slavery in 1849

MANUMISSION MOVEMENTS

Between 1785 and 1792, opponents of slavery established manumission societies in New York, Virginia, and Massachusetts, urging the liberation of slaves by will or by deed. During this period, a number of states in the northeast passed laws mandating a gradual abolition of slavery. Antislavery sentiment was reflected in Article I, Section 9 of the U.S. Constitution, which decreed that the slave trade would be illegal after 1808. By 1826, there were 143 manumission societies in the United States, 103 of them in the South. Leading Southern journals advocating manumission included the *Manumission Intelligencer*, the *Emancipator*, and the *Patriot*, all founded between 1819 and 1821.

COLONIZATION PROJECTS

The idea of repatriating freed slaves to settlements in Africa was first proposed in 1714 but never acted upon. In 1777, Thomas Jefferson drew up a colonization plan and presented it to the Virginia legislature. (At that time, Jefferson advocated manumission but doubted that free blacks would be able to live harmoniously with whites.)

Paul Cuffe, ship owner and early advocate of black nationalism, put Jefferson's ideas into action in 1815, when he transported 38 free blacks to Sierra Leone, the West African colony created by British antislavery activists in 1787. Cuffe's action inspired the formation of the American Colonization Society, founded in Virginia in 1817 by Henry Clay, Andrew Jackson, and other slaveholding whites. Four years later, the society founded the settlement of Monrovia, just south of Sierra Leone. In 1847, Monrovia became Liberia, the first republic in Africa with a government modeled on that of the United States. Other projects included the Mississippi Colonization Society, founded in 1831; and Nashoba, a utopian community near Memphis, Tennessee, founded in 1826 by Fanny Wright in order to prepare freed slaves for eventual resettlement abroad. In the years before the Civil War, approximately 15,000 free blacks resettled in West Africa.

The issue of colonization caused considerable controversy among African American leaders. Leaders such as Cuffe and John Russwurm argued that African Americans would never be treated justly in the United States and should return to their ancestral homeland. Most antislavery leaders, however, agreed with Richard Allen, James Forten, and Frederick Douglass, who maintained that African Americans should remain in the United States and fight for justice in the nation they had done so much to create. Black leaders recognized that many who urged the repatriation of free blacks to Africa were more interested in removing free blacks from the Americas than in improving the African Americans' lot or making some sort of restitution for their enslavement.

RADICAL ABOLITIONISM

By the 1830s, many opponents of slavery turned from moderate appeals for manumission to demands for immediate and complete abolition. The spearhead of the movement was William

Lloyd Garrison's newspaper the *Liberator,* which published its first issue on January 1, 1831. The following year, Garrison founded the New England Anti-Slavery Society, and in 1833 he played a leading role in founding the American Anti-Slavery Society. During the years before the Civil War, about 200,000 Americans belonged to various abolition societies. In addition to Garrison, leading white abolitionists included Wendell Phillips, Lewis and Arthur Tappan, Theodore Weld, James G. Birney, and Angelina and Sarah Grimké. After suffering a crippling internal split during the 1840s over the inclusion of women's rights in its agenda, the abolitionist movement scored its greatest propaganda success with the 1852 publication of Harriet Beecher Stowe's antislavery novel *Uncle Tom's Cabin.* Stowe's book became a runaway best-seller and aroused antislavery sentiment among many readers who had previously not supported the abolitionist cause.

MAJOR SLAVE REVOLTS

There are no exact statistics on how many revolts took place during the centuries of slavery in the Americas, but historical records indicate that they were frequent and widespread. Herbert Aptheker, in *American Negro Slave Revolts,* concluded that at least 250 significant slave revolts occurred in the United States alone during the years before 1865, in addition to more localized acts of resistance. In addition, there were at least 155 recorded instances of mutinies aboard slave ships—some successful and some brutally suppressed. As early as 1522, slaves in Saint Domingue rose up in an attempt to create an African republic; in 1529, rebellious slaves destroyed the settlement of Santa Maria in present-day Colombia; and a serious slave conspiracy was uncovered in Mexico City in 1537. Throughout the 17th century, Latin American mining camps—where conditions were especially harsh and life expectancy short—were the scene of innumerable slave revolts. Following are the major revolts from the 17th century to the Civil War:

1653	The first serious U.S. slave conspiracy occurred in Gloucester, Virginia; the plot was betrayed by a man named Berkenhead (probably a white indentured servant), who was rewarded with his freedom and 5,000 pounds of tobacco.
1658	Black slaves, aided by Native Americans, burned their masters' homes in Hartford, Connecticut.
1663	A major slave conspiracy was uncovered in Fairfax County, Virginia, involving both black slaves and white indentured servants; the leaders were beheaded. Because much of the planning for the revolt had taken place at funerals attended by large numbers of slaves, such gatherings were banned by the colonial authorities.
1691	A Virginia slave named Mingoe escaped from his master, gathered a group of followers, and ravaged a number of plantations, mainly in Rappahannock County. The rebels took cattle and hogs and also acquired some guns. Their fate was never recorded.
1708	Slaves in Long Island, New York, killed seven whites.
1712	After several months of planning, 25 to 39 slaves in New York City set fire to a building in early April and attacked the whites who arrived at the scene, killing 9 and wounding 6. Within 24 hours, soldiers of the local militia arrested 70 persons, including all but 6 of the rebels; 21 were executed. The uprising inspired Pennsylvania to raise the import duties on slaves, effectively ending their transportation into the colony; in 1713, Massachusetts forbade the importation of slaves completely.

1739	In St. Paul's Parish, South Carolina, a group of 20 slaves broke into a store and seized guns and powder, killing the owners. They proceeded to raid neighboring properties, burning houses and killing about 20 inhabitants, and their numbers grew beyond 100. At the end of the day, a number of the rebels were killed in a skirmish with the local militia, but the rest escaped and began making their way toward Florida, which was then Spanish territory and a haven for runaways. Not until the following Saturday did the militia catch up with this group, defeating them in a pitched battle. A handful of rebels still remained at large, and one man was not captured until three years later. Because it began along the western branch of the Stono River, the revolt became known as the Stono Uprising.
1740	Between 150 and 200 slaves staged an uprising near Charleston. However, they had no arms and no food supplies and were soon captured. Fifty of the rebels were put to death.
1741	In New York City, a number of suspicious fires broke out during a particularly harsh winter, and rumors circulated that slaves were conspiring to poison the city's water supply. Acting on testimony—later discredited—from a white indentured servant named Mary Burton, the authorities arrested about 150 slaves and 25 whites. Four of the whites and 31 slaves were executed; 70 slaves were transported to the West Indies and other locations.
1781–1786	Slaves aiding the British in their defense of Savannah, Georgia, at the end of the American Revolution escaped with their weapons and set up a fortified village in the Belle Isle swamp. Calling themselves "Soldiers of the King of England," they carried on a guerrilla war for several years. They were finally subdued by the Georgia and South Carolina militias, aided by Native Americans.
1791	In the midst of turmoil created by the French Revolution, slaves on the island of St. Domingue—inspired by a voodoo priest named Boukman—launched a carefully orchestrated revolt. By 1793, after killing 2,000 whites and destroying 1,000 plantations, the rebels gained control of the northern part of the island. Under the leadership of Toussaint-Louverture (also spelled Toussaint L'Ouverture), the former slaves reorganized the colony and repelled invasions by Spanish, British, and French armed forces, finally establishing the independent republic of Haiti in 1804 and formally abolishing slavery. The Haitian Revolution—involving half the black population of the Caribbean and one sixth the slave population of the New World—galvanized the African American population. It also terrified slave owners, who made concessions in areas where blacks were in the majority and instituted repressive measures in areas where whites predominated.

rothers and Friends: I am Toussaint L'Ouverture. My name is perhaps known to you. I have undertaken to avenge you. I want liberty and equality to reign throughout St. Domingo. . . . Come and join me, brothers, and fight by our side for the same cause.

Toussaint-Louverture's appeal to his compatriots in 1793

1795	Slaves in the Coro district of Venezuela organized a 300-person army that launched several assaults on urban centers before being put down.
1800	Two Virginia slaves, Gabriel Prosser and Jack Bowler, devised a plan to lead more than 1,000 fellow slaves in an attack on Richmond, Virginia. On August 30, the rebels assembled, armed with an assortment of clubs, scythes, bayonets, and a few guns. However, torrential rains washed out roads and bridges, making it impossible for the rebels to advance on Richmond. When the plot was uncovered, 35 men were executed.
1808–1835	During this period, Bahia, Brazil, was the scene of eight separate revolts led by Muslim slaves

belonging to the Hausa, Yoruba, and Nago peoples. The uprising took place in both the city and the countryside, involving sugar-plantation workers, fishers, and others. During the 1830 uprising, a group of *escravos de ganho* attacked an urban slave market and freed 100 captives. Unrest culminated in 1835 when authorities uncovered a plot for a wide-ranging insurrection by urban and rural slaves. After considerable loss of life and destruction of property, the rebels were subdued; 100 were executed, and new repressive measures were put in place.

1811   Led by Charles Deslandes, 400 to 500 slaves revolted in the Louisiana parishes of St. Charles and St. John the Baptist; U.S. troops and local militia put down the revolt, killing 66 rebels and capturing 16 more.

1816   Runaway slaves used a Seminole Indian fort at Appalachicola Bay, Florida, as a base for raids against slaveholders. In July, U.S. troops aided by Native American mercenaries began a siege of the fort. After 10 days, a cannon shot hit the fort's magazine, causing a massive explosion that killed 270 defenders—the surviving 40 men then surrendered.

1819   Led by an African American named Coo (also known as "Coot"), slaves in Augusta, Georgia, devised a plan to burn the city but were betrayed before they could act.

1822   Denmark Vesey—one of the few free blacks to take an active antislavery stance in the South—organized a carefully designed plot to seize Charleston on the second Sunday in July. In all, there may have been as many as 9,000 slaves and free blacks involved in the plan, which called for attacks on the city to be launched from five different locations. The plot was betrayed in June, and 137 men were arrested. Thirty-seven were hanged, including Vesey, and strict measures were taken to keep tabs on slaves and to limit their contacts with outsiders.

> We are free, but the white people here won't let us be so; and the only way is to rise up and fight the whites.
>
> Denmark Vesey, testifying at his trial

1831   In Southampton County, Virginia, Nat Turner and 6 cohorts began an insurrection on August 21. Within 24 hours, their number had grown to 70, and they had killed 57 whites along a 20-mile line of march. Turner planned to seize arms from the county seat, Jerusalem, but allowed his men to pause and refresh themselves at a farm 3 miles from the city. This gave the local militia time to gather and attack, breaking the momentum of the insurrection. Two days later, most of Turner's followers had been killed, captured, or dispersed. As Turner went into hiding, thousands of troops unleashed a wave of terror against the slave population, killing as many as 120 people. Turner was finally captured on October 30 and hanged on November 11. African Americans often referred to Turner's revolt as the First War against Slavery.

> I heard a loud noise in the heavens, and the Spirit instantly appeared to me and said the Serpent was loosened, and Christ had laid down the yoke He had borne for the sins of men, and that I should take it on and fight against the Serpent, for the time was fast approaching when the first should be last and the last should be first.
>
> Nat Turner, shortly before his death

1831–1832   Led by Sam Sharpe, 20,000 slaves revolted in Jamaica's western parishes, destroying more than £1 million in property. After the "Emancipation Rebellion" was suppressed by British

1839   Led by Cinqué (also known as "Singbe"), Africans on the Spanish slave ship *Amistad* revolted while the ship was moored off Cuba, killing the captain and most of the crew. They then sailed the vessel up the Atlantic coast of the United States. Cinqué and his men were taken into custody off Montauk, New York, by U.S. officials, who were prepared to deliver them up to Spain. Before that could happen, however, the *Amistad* mutineers got strong support from antislavery groups, who brought the case before the U.S. Supreme Court. Former president John Quincy Adams, then a passionate antislavery advocate in the U.S. House of Representatives, argued on behalf of the Africans. In 1841, the Supreme Court ruled that Cinqué and his men, having been taken in the illegal slave trade, were not Spanish property and were entitled to go free. With funds provided by supporters, they chartered a boat and sailed to Sierra Leone.

1844   In Cuba, authorities uncovered a plot involving thousands of free blacks and slaves, similar to the Denmark Vesey conspiracy in South Carolina. Three thousand individuals were tried by military courts; 11 of them were executed, and as many as 400 may have been exiled. Among those executed was the black poet Gabriel de la Concepción Valdés, also known as Plácido—in his honor, the aborted uprising is sometimes known as the Plácido Revolt.

1859   Five African Americans—Dangerfield Newby, Lewis Sheridan Leary, John Anthony Copeland, Shields Green, and Osborn Perry Anderson—took part in the radical white abolitionist John Brown's raid on the federal armory at Harpers Ferry, Virginia. Newby and Leary died in the fighting; Copeland and Green (and Brown) were later hanged, and Anderson escaped.

> In the name of the young girl sold from the warm clasp of a mother's arms to the clutches of a libertine or a profligate, in the name of the slave mother, her heart rocked to and fro by the agony of her mournful separations, I thank you, that you have been brave enough to reach out your hands to the crushed and blighted of my race.
>
> African American woman from Indiana, writing to John Brown in December 1859

MAROON COMMUNITIES IN THE AMERICAS

The term *Maroon* derives from the Spanish word *cimarrón*, which was first applied to runaway livestock before it came to denote escaped African slaves. The first known Maroon was a slave who escaped from a boatload of captives transported to Hispaniola by Nicolás de Ovando in 1502. His example was followed by countless others over the centuries; all over the Americas, runaways joined together to create their own self-supporting communities, which often served as bases for raids on white settlements. In some instances, Maroons joined with local Native Americans and adopted their technologies. Maroon communities were usually located in remote areas and protected by mountains, jungles, or swamps. Many were guarded by palisades and elaborately constructed defenses, including disguised paths, false trials that sometimes led into quicksand, and booby traps. Recruits were often brought in by circuitous routes and were kept on probation until their loyalty was assured. Maroon communities were known by various Spanish and Portuguese terms, including *palenques*, *quilombos*, *mocambos*, *cumbes*, *ladeiras*, and *mambises*. Before 1700, Maroon communities were generally led by men who had been born in Africa; many claimed they had been kings in their homeland. After 1700, Maroon leaders were often Creoles familiar both with the ways of the whites and with African practices.

BRAZIL

The most powerful of all the Maroon communities in the Americas was Palmares, located in the Pernambuco region of Brazil. Founded in 1605, Palmares was actually a confederation of communities that extended over 1,200 square miles and contained 20,000 inhabitants. The communities of Palmares were strongly fortified and organized into a centralized political entity along the lines of contemporary African kingdoms, under the leadership of Ganga Zumba. Beginning in 1672, the Portuguese began to mount assaults on Palmares every 15 months. When it became clear that Ganga Zumba was negotiating with the colonial authorities, he was deposed by his nephew, Zumbi (or Zambi), who became Palmares's greatest leader. Palmares finally fell in 1694, but only after a 42-day campaign involving 6,000 Portuguese troops. Zumbi himself managed to escape and eluded the Portuguese for 18 months before being captured and beheaded. The colonial authorities displayed his head in public "to kill the legend of his immortality," but he remains a living presence for many Brazilians of African descent. The date of his death, November 20, was proclaimed the National Day of Black Consciousness in 1978 by Afro-Brazilian civil-rights leaders, and members of the religious sect known as Umbanda make regular pilgrimages to the site of Palmares.

Maroon communities persisted in Brazil throughout the 18th and 19th centuries. They included Quilombo Grande in the Minas Gerais region, the population of which reached 10,000; Pará along the Amazon River near Manaus, which developed extensive trade relations and exported crops to Dutch Guiana; and Campo Grande in Maranhão, which dispatched 3,000 soldiers to take part in an 1838–1841 republican revolution led by local whites, who turned on their black allies in 1840 and executed the black leaders.

COLOMBIA

In the Cartagena region during the 1690s, there were more than a dozen Maroon communities, four of them with more than 200 inhabitants.

THE GUIANAS

The most enduring Maroon communities of all sprang up in the Guianas, as thousands of enslaved men and women escaped from the coastal plantations of Dutch-controlled Surinam during the 17th and 18th centuries. Once free, they built villages along the interior rivers. For the next hundred years, the Guiana Maroons repelled Dutch attempts to dislodge them. During the 1760s, the Dutch authorities finally came to terms with the two major Maroon groups, the Saramaka and the Djuka. As in Jamaica, the Maroons were granted their freedom on condition that they agreed to return any slaves who escaped to their settlements. Though Maroon communities in other countries had all dissolved by the end of the 19th century, the Surinam Maroons—also known as Bush Negroes—survive to this day, maintaining their distinct culture and way of life. The Saramaka and the Djuka currently number approximately 20,000 apiece. In addition, there are the Matawai, Paramaka, Kwinti, and Aluku groups. The Guiana Maroons' struggle for independence has continued into the late 20th century. In 1986, Djuka rebels took up arms against the national government of Surinam, beginning an enduring conflict that dislocated about 6,000 Maroon refugees to French Guiana: 2,500 were repatriated in 1992 with assistance from the French government.

JAMAICA

In Jamaica, the Maroon tradition dates back to 1655, when enslaved blacks took advantage of a British invasion to escape from their Spanish masters. They then formed three distinct groups under elected leaders. The following 85 years were marked by running conflicts between Maroons and the British, who controlled the island at that time. During this period, there were two main groups of Maroons, whose total strength may have exceeded 5,000. The Leeward Maroons, led by Cudjoe, established themselves in the rugged Cockpit county of west-central Jamaica. The Leewards' major settlements included Accompong and Trelawny Town. The Windward Maroons, located in the east near the Blue Mountains, were originally led by an Obeah woman named Nanny; their main settlements were Nanny Town and Guy Town.

During the First Maroon War of the 1730s, the British launched major assaults against both groups of Maroons but failed to dislodge them from their strongholds. Finally, in 1739, the Leewards and Windwards signed a treaty that guaranteed them defined territory and hunting rights in return for a pledge to return runaways and suppress Maroons who did not accept the treaty. More than 50 years of peace ensued, but the Second Maroon War erupted in 1795 when the Trelawny Town Maroons resisted British infringements of their treaty rights. After signing a new peace treaty, the Maroons surrendered their arms, only to be treacherously put in irons; 800 were deported to hard labor in Nova Scotia. (Those who survived the first winter resettled in Sierra Leone.) Weakened by this blow, the Maroon communities gradually declined after emancipation in 1834.

MEXICO

Mexican Maroons established a number of settlements in the mountains around Vera Cruz. During the early 17th century, the Spanish authorities signed treaties with the Maroon communities of San Lorenzo de los Negros (founded by King Yanga in 1609) and San Lorenzo Cerralvo (founded 1635). A third community, Nuestra Señora de Guadelupe de los Morenos de Ampa, was founded in 1769.

PANAMA

A black leader known as King Bayano established a number of Maroon communities in Panama between 1553 and 1558, and the total Maroon population eventually exceeded 3,000. Like other coastal Maroons, the Panamanians sometimes engaged in piracy. The English buccaneer Francis Drake enlisted their aid for a 1573 attack on Spanish holdings in Panama and rewarded the Maroons' leader with a gilded scimitar that had once belonged to King Henry II of France.

UNITED STATES

Between 1672 and 1864, there were at least 50 Maroon communities in the southern United States, all located in mountainous or swampy areas. The largest, located in the Dismal Swamp spanning the Virginia–North Carolina border, may have been home to 2,000 individuals. Also significant was Gracia Real de Santa Teresa de Mosé, a haven for runaway slaves and dispossessed Native Americans; it flourished with official sanction between 1738 and 1763 in Spanish-controlled Florida, about 2 miles north of St. Augustine. The community was disbanded when Spain ceded Florida to Britain in return for control over Cuba.

BLACK TOWNS

Carrying on the legacy of the various Maroon communities were the numerous black towns founded in many parts of the United States during the 19th and early 20th centuries—estimates of the total number range from 90 to 200. (For black communities in Canada, see Chapter 4, "The Diaspora.") The first of these was New Philadelphia, Illinois, founded by Free Frank McWhorter, a former slave from Kentucky, in 1835. New Philadelphia soon dissolved, but following the Civil War—and especially after the end of Reconstruction—a host of other black communities sprang up as African Americans left the South in search of a better life. Among the most important were the following:

- **Nicodemus, Kansas,** was founded in the western part of the state (now Graham County) in the mid-1870s; had more than 300 residents by 1880 and soon supported three churches, a school, and two newspapers; began to decline in the late 1880s when the newly built railroads passed it by.

- **Eatonville, Florida,** became the first incorporated black town in the United States in 1886; located north of Orlando; birthplace of the writer Zora Neale Hurston (1903–1960), who captured its history and daily life in *Dust Tracks on a Road* and other works; 1990 population 2,170.

- **Langston, Oklahoma,** was founded by Edwin and Sarah McCabe in 1890; population stood at 600 in 1892; facilities included the Colored Agricultural and Normal School, later Langston College, which ensured the town's survival; 1990 population 1,471.

- **Boley, Oklahoma,** was founded in 1904; population grew to 1,000 by 1907 and supported churches, fraternal lodges, and a literary society; the town's fortunes declined after 1910, when Oklahoma's statehood brought Southern Democrats to power in the state capital.

- **Mound Bayou, Mississippi,** is regarded as the most successful of the black towns; founded by a railroad company in 1887 and populated by African Americans when fear of bayou-country diseases discouraged white settlement; population was 287 in 1900, with 1,500 African American farmers in the vicinity; economic development, aided by Booker T. Washington, included a bank, sawmills, cotton gins, and the nation's only black-owned cottonseed mill.

- **Allensworth, California,** was created in 1908 by a black-owned Los Angeles real-estate company; located in the fertile San Joaquin Valley, developed into an agricultural community with 3,000 acres of farmland.

VENEZUELA

Escaped slaves who had worked as pearl divers established a Maroon community in 1549 on the island of Margarita, off the Venezuelan coast. A number of large *palenques* existed on the mainland. The largest was established during the 1550s by King Miguel, who led a revolt of local gold miners; with a population of 800, this community appears to have been organized along Spanish administrative lines, rather than African patterns.

ANTISLAVERY LEADERS

Allen, Richard (1760–1831).   Born into slavery, Allen purchased his freedom while in his twenties and settled in Philadelphia. A convert to Methodism, he began preaching while serving as a wagon driver during the Revolutionary War. In 1786, Allen began to hold prayer meetings for blacks. The following year he and Absalom Jones, a fellow preacher, left the Methodist Church after experiencing discrimination and formed the Free African Society, the first African American civil-rights organization in the United States. The society advocated strict rules of morality and behavior for members and also agitated against slavery. After founding Bethel Church in 1794, Allen also opened a day school for 60 black pupils in 1795. When most of Bethel's congregation decided to follow Jones in abandoning Methodism for the Episcopal Church, Allen founded the African Methodist Episcopal (A.M.E.) Church. In his sermons and religious writings, Allen articulated a vision of Christianity that aided the oppressed and refuted religious doctrines justifying slavery. In 1830, he helped organize the American Society of Free Persons of Color and became the organization's first president. In 1833, he published his autobiography, *The Life, Experience, and Gospel Labors of the Rt. Rev. Richard Allen*.

Barbadoes, James G. (c. 1796–1841).   Possibly born in the West Indies, Barbadoes established himself as a free black barber in Boston during the 1830s. He helped found the American Anti-Slavery Society in 1833 and strongly supported the abolitionist leader William Lloyd Garrison and his newspaper, the *Liberator*. He died of a fever when he attempted to resettle his family in Jamaica.

Bibb, Henry Walton (1815–1854).   Born into slavery in Kentucky, Bibb escaped to Detroit in 1842, becoming an antislavery lecturer and a campaigner for the Liberty Party—along with Frederick Douglass and William Wells Brown, he was considered the most dynamic and effective of the antislavery orators. The passage of the Fugitive Slave Law in 1850 drove him north to Canada, where he and his wife, Mary Miles Bibb, became leaders of the black community, which numbered 30,000. Bibb established schools and churches and founded Canada's first black newspaper, *Voice of the Fugitive*. He actively encouraged fugitive slaves to follow his example and go north.

Brown, John (1800–1859).   Born in Connecticut, Brown was white, the son of an abolitionist and Underground Railroad agent. After working at a variety of occupations, Brown devoted himself completely to the antislavery cause as a militia leader in Kansas and Missouri. In 1856, Brown and six other men (four were his sons) killed five proslavery men in Ossawatomie County, Kansas. After proslavery forces drove him out of the territory, he began raising money to finance a slave insurrection in the South. Along with a group of 21 companions, Brown led a raid on the federal armory at Harpers Ferry, Virginia, on October 16, 1859, intending to capture weapons and distribute them to enslaved African Americans. Though they succeeded in taking the armory, Brown and his men were surrounded by federal troops and captured two days later. After defending his actions eloquently in court, Brown was hanged on December 2. He became the first great martyr to the abolitionist cause and remains a hero to many African Americans.

Brown, William Wells (c. 1814–1884).   Born into slavery in Kentucky, Brown escaped in 1834 and settled in upstate New York. He worked on Lake Erie steamers and became an expert conductor on the Underground Railroad. In 1842 alone, he conveyed 69 fugitives to Canada. Between 1843 and 1847, Brown lectured for the Western New York Anti-Slavery Society. In 1849 he traveled to Great Britain and remained there until 1854, covering more than 25,000 miles and delivering about 1,000 antislavery lectures. He returned to the United States after English friends purchased his freedom. He then studied medicine and began practicing as a physician after the Civil War. In addition to his antislavery activities and medical career, Brown was a pioneer in African American literature (see Chapter 13).

Cuffe, Paul (1759–1817).   The son of an African American father and a Native American mother, Cuffe became a prosperous entrepreneur in Massachusetts, engaging in farming, shipping, and milling. After making his first commercial voyage to Sierra Leone in 1810, he became an advocate of black nationalism and self-determination and supported efforts to resettle African Americans in Africa. In 1815, he transported 38 emigrants to Sierra Leone. He returned to the United States the following year because his wife refused to emigrate. Cuffe's *Brief Account of the Settlement and Present Situation of the Colony of Sierra Leone in Africa* (1812) remains a valuable source of information on Sierra Leone's early history.

Delany, Martin Robinson (1812–1885).   Delany was taken from Virginia to Pennsylvania by his mother, a free black, so that he could receive a proper education. He became an antislavery activist in Pittsburgh, coedited the *North Star* with Frederick Douglass, and rescued fugitive slaves from slave catchers. Having lost faith in the effectiveness of white abolitionists, Delany called for black separatism in his 1852 book, *The Condition, Elevation, Emigration, and Destiny of the Colored People of the United States*. Initially opposed to colonization schemes focused on Africa, he entertained the possibility of resettling African Americans in Central and South America. After moving to Ontario, he began scouting locations for possible black settlements in Canada. In 1859, Delany traveled to Africa. After exploring the Niger basin, he changed his mind about emigration and obtained permission from African rulers to found a colony in Abeokuta, in present-day Nigeria. He returned to the United States in 1863 and played a leading role in recruiting black troops for the Union Army during the Civil War. After the war, Delany was an important official in the Freedmen's Bureau and later worked at a variety of occupations, including lecturer, newspaper editor, and trade agent.

De Baptiste, George (1814–1875).   Born free in Virginia, De Baptiste spent several years as a valet for a professional gambler, set up a barbershop in Wisconsin, and then went to work for William Henry Harrison, who was elected president of the United States in 1840. De Baptiste accompanied Harrison to Washington, but when the new president died of pneumonia after only a month in office, De Baptiste returned to the Midwest and settled in Detroit. He became a primary leader of the Underground Railroad and on one occasion rescued Anthony Burns, a fugitive slave, by leading a mass assault on a courthouse. After the Civil War, he became a wealthy man, operating restaurants, steamship lines, and other businesses.

Douglass, Frederick (c. 1817–1885).   Born into slavery in Maryland, Douglass escaped in 1838 and made his way to New Bedford, Massachusetts, where he worked as a laborer. He soon revealed distinctive gifts as an orator and traveled throughout the North as a lecturer for the Massachusetts Anti-Slavery Society. His 1845 autobiography, *Narrative of the Life of Frederick Douglass, An American Slave*, became a runaway best-seller. In 1847, Douglass founded the *North Star*, an antislavery newspaper that was largely sustained by the African American community. He published his second autobiography, *My Bondage and My Freedom*, in 1855. In addition to freedom for blacks, he also advocated equal rights for women and overall reform of working conditions. In the late 1850s, Douglass was a friend and supporter of John Brown's but declined to support Brown's plan to spark a slave insurrection; nevertheless, Douglass was forced to flee to Canada for a time after the failure of Brown's 1859 raid on Harpers Ferry. When the Civil War erupted, Douglass played a leading role in convincing President Lincoln to recruit African Americans into the Union Army. During the Reconstruction period (1865–1877) that followed the Civil War, Douglass edited a newspaper called the *New National Era* and continued the fight for social justice, urging such measures as the extension of voting rights to liberated slaves. In 1872, Douglass moved to Washington, D.C., and held a number of government posts, including marshal of the District of Columbia (1877–1886) and minister to the Republic of Haiti (1889–1891). The final volume of Douglass's memoirs, *Life and Times of Frederick Douglass*, appeared in 1881.

Equiano, Olaudah (1745?–1797).   Born in what is now eastern Nigeria, Equiano was kidnapped by slave traders at the age of 10 and transported to the West Indies. There, he served a British army officer and a merchant, both of which enabled to him to travel widely and obtain an education. At the age of 21, Equiano (known as "Gustavus Vassa" in the New World) purchased his freedom and set up as a merchant. Widely respected because of his business success and intellectual achievements, Equiano petitioned the British government to end the slave trade and also helped organize the first efforts to settle liberated slaves in Sierra Leone in 1787. In 1789, he published his autobiography, *The Interesting Narrative of the Life of Olaudah Equiano, or Gustavus Vassa the African*, a classic of antislavery literature, which also contains valuable information on Igbo village life during the 18th century.

Forten, James, Sr. (1766–1842).   Born free in Philadelphia, Forten served as a teenage sailor during the Revolutionary War. After the war, he went to work for a sailmaker and eventually inherited the business. By 1832, he had amassed a large fortune, which he used to promote abolition, women's rights, temperance, and peace. He aided Richard Allen in his organizational efforts, petitioned Congress to repeal the Fugitive Slave Law of 1793, and gave financial support to William Lloyd Garrison. Forten denounced the celebration of July 4 as a national holiday, pointing out that the United States had not provided freedom for African Americans.

Garnet, Henry Highland (1815–1882).   Born into slavery in Maryland, Garnet escaped to New York with his father at age nine. Along with two other African American students, he enrolled in Noyes Academy in Hew Hampshire, but the school building was destroyed by a mob of angry whites. Garnet then studied for the ministry and settled in Troy, New York. Garnet's "Call to Rebellion" speech at the 1843 Negro National Convention advocated armed resistance as a last resort; though this proposal narrowly fell short of adoption by the delegates, it spurred abolition groups to take more militant action. After lecturing on slavery in Europe and doing missionary work in Jamaica, Garnet became the pastor of churches in New York City and Washington, D.C. During the Civil War, he helped recruit African Americans for the Union Army. After the war, he continued to campaign for civil rights. Keenly interested in African affairs, he was appointed the U.S. government's minister resident and consul general to Liberia and spent his last year there.

Garrison, William Lloyd (1805–1879).   Trained as a journalist, Garrison committed himself to the abolitionist cause in the late 1820s. In 1830 he joined with Isaac Knapp to launch the *Liberator,* which became known as the most uncompromising voice of the abolitionist movement, demanding immediate and complete emancipation of all enslaved African Americans. Garrison also helped found the New England Anti-Slavery Society and the American Anti-Slavery Society during the early 1830s. In 1835, he was set upon by a proslavery mob in Boston, dragged through the streets, and nearly killed. Undaunted, he continued to edit the *Liberator* until slavery was abolished in 1865.

Henson, Josiah (1789–1883).   After working for many years as a slave supervisor, Henson made a daring escape to Canada in 1830 with his wife and four children. He then became a sawmill operator and a conductor on the Underground Railroad, helping more than 100 African Americans escape from Kentucky to Canada. In the course of his Underground Railroad activities, Henson founded Dawn, a colony for escapees in Ontario. After Harriet Beecher Stowe acknowledged that she had drawn on Henson's 1849 autobiography when writing *Uncle Tom's Cabin*, there was a widespread public impression that Henson had been the model for the subservient Uncle Tom. Henson himself may have encouraged this idea, which gained him great celebrity but ultimately damaged his reputation in the African-American community.

Prosser, Gabriel (1775?–1800).   Prosser was serving as a coach driver in Henrico County, Virginia, when he began planning his rebellion for late August 1831, reasoning that the crops would be ripe in the fields, providing the slaves with ample food supplies. He intended to kill all slave owners in the Richmond area but to spare whites of French ancestry and also Quakers, both groups being known for their opposition to slavery. After the failure of the revolt, Prosser fled to Norfolk in the hold of a schooner but was captured there and returned for trial; he was hanged on October 7, 1800.

Ruggles, David (1810–1849).   Born free in Connecticut, Ruggles spent most of his life in New York City. In 1834, he became the first African American bookseller in the United States, publishing abolitionist tracts at his shop at 67 Lispenard Street in lower Manhattan. After a white mob burned the store in 1835, Ruggles continued his abolition work, writing articles and pamphlets and soliciting subscriptions to the *Emancipator,* a newspaper published by white abolitionists in the South. Ruggles was a highly effective conductor on the Underground Railroad and also represented fugitive slaves—including Frederick Douglass—in some 300 court cases. He later became a highly successful hydropathic therapist in Northampton, Massachusetts, and numbered Sojourner Truth and William Lloyd Garrison among his patients.

Russwurm, John Brown (1799–1851).   Russwurm was born in Jamaica, the son of a slave woman and a white planter. Acknowledged by his father and raised in freedom, he graduated from Maine's Bowdoin

College in 1826. The following year he went to New York and founded *Freedom's Journal*, the first African American newspaper in the United States. After coediting the paper with Samuel Cornish for two years, Russwurm moved to Liberia. There he became editor of the *Liberia Herald* and served as superintendent of education in Monrovia, Liberia's capital. He remained a leading advocate of African colonization projects, a stance that put him at odds with most members of the antislavery movement.

Still, William (1821–1902).   Born free in New Jersey, Still moved to Philadelphia and in 1847 went to work for the Pennsylvania Society for the Abolition of Slavery. After becoming chair of the organization in 1851, he played an active role in the work of the Underground Railroad. In the course of aiding fugitives, he conducted hundreds of interviews and collected a host of valuable documents. After the Civil War, Still collected all this material into a classic volume, *The Underground Railroad* (1872).

Toussaint-Louverture, François-Dominique (c. 1744–1803).   Born into slavery on the island of St. Domingue, Toussaint purchased his freedom in 1776 and was educated by French missionaries. When the slaves revolted in 1791, he soon rose to a position of leadership in their ranks. Supported by the revolutionary government in France, Toussaint led his armies against the Spanish and British and drove them from the island. He then reorganized the government and sought to institute reforms in the island's social system. When Napoleon Bonaparte came to power in France, he saw Toussaint as a dangerous rival and sent an army against him. When the French soldiers were unable to conquer the Haitians, Napoleon offered Toussaint a peace treaty but then had him seized by trickery and brought to France, where Toussaint died in a dungeon.

Truth, Sojourner (c. 1798–1883).   Born into slavery (under the name Isabella Van Wagener) in upstate New York, Truth gained her freedom when New York abolished slavery in 1827. Supporting herself as a maid, she also became an itinerant preacher. In 1843, Truth moved to Massachusetts, where she became involved in the abolitionist movement and began her career as a powerful antislavery orator. At this time, she also became a staunch advocate of women's rights; her fame as a feminist was ensured by her dynamic "Aren't I a Woman?" speech at the 1851 women's rights convention in Akron, Ohio. Truth's life story, *The Narrative of Sojourner Truth: A Bondswoman of Olden Time* (recorded by Olive Gilbert), was published in 1850.

> That man . . . says that women need to be helped into carriages, and lifted over ditches, and to have the best place everywhere. Nobody ever helps me into carriages, or over mud puddles, or gives me any best place, and aren't I a woman? . . . I have plowed, and planted, and gathered into barns, and no man could head me—and aren't I a woman? I could work as much and eat as much as a man (when I could get it), and bear the lash as well—and aren't I a woman? I have borne thirteen children and seen them most all sold off into slavery, and when I cried out with a mother's grief, none but Jesus heard—and aren't I a woman?
>
> Sojourner Truth, speaking at an Ohio women's rights convention, 1851

Tubman, Harriet (1820–1913).   Born in the Tidewater region of Virginia, Tubman endured a harsh childhood under slavery and escaped in 1849, using a series of safe houses provided by the Underground Railroad. After finding work in Philadelphia, Tubman resolved to return to the South and rescue other slaves, beginning with her family members. Armed with a revolver, she made 19 trips in all, rescuing more than 300 men and women. Though frail and unassuming, she became a legend on the Underground Railroad for her courage and determination, and she was known to the other workers as Moses. During the Civil War, Tubman served with Union troops in coastal South Carolina, where she aided the war effort as a nurse, launderer, and spy. After the war, she established a home for aged former slaves in Auburn, New York, and published an autobiography, *Scenes in the Life of Harriet Tubman* (1869).

Turner, Nat (1800–1831).   Turner apparently inherited his hatred of slavery from his African-born mother, who reportedly tried to kill him at birth rather than sees him grow up in bondage. A man of unusual abilities and great spiritual power, Turner became a preacher among the slaves of Southampton County, Virginia. Often experiencing mystical visions, he believed that he was destined to lead his people to freedom. Turner interpreted a solar eclipse that occurred in February 1831 as a sign of divine sanction and immediately began organizing his rebellion. At his trial, Turner was asked whether he regretted his deeds now that he faced the death penalty, and he replied, "Was not Christ crucified?"

Vesey, Denmark (1767–1822).   Vesey spent 20 years in bondage, often accompanying his owner, a slave trader, on voyages to the Caribbean. After winning a lottery, Vesey purchased his freedom for $600. As a freedman, he worked as a carpenter in Charleston, saving his money, buying some property, and becoming a Methodist minister. Determined to strike a blow for those in bondage, Vesey began recruiting followers in 1821. Placed on trial after the betrayal of the plot, Vesey defended himself with great skill but was convicted nonetheless; he was executed on July 2, 1822.

Walker, David (1785–1830).   Born free in North Carolina, Walker eventually settled in Boston and went into the clothing business. Before leaving the South, he had traveled widely and studied the evils of slavery; in the North, he wrote diligently in favor of abolition and generously aided escaped slaves. His best known contribution to the antislavery movement was the pamphlet entitled *David Walker's Appeal* (1829), which called for a worldwide black revolt against white oppression and is the first known expression of pan-African ideals. Walker's views aroused so much alarm in the South that slaveholders enacted protective measures, restricting publications, discouraging literacy, and limiting the activities of black preachers. When Walker died suddenly in 1830, many of his admirers believed that he had been poisoned.

SOURCES FOR ADDITIONAL INFORMATION

Aptheker, Herbert. *American Negro Slave Revolts*. New York: International Publishers, 1941.

Berlin, Ira. *Slaves without Masters: The Free Negro in the Antebellum South*. New York: Oxford University Press, 1981.

Blassingame, John W., ed. *Slave Testimony: Two Centuries of Letters, Speeches, Interviews, and Autobiographies*. Baton Rouge: Louisiana State University Press, 1977.

Campbell, Edward D. C., Jr., and Kym S. Rice, eds. *Before Freedom Came: African-American Life in the Antebellum South*. Richmond: Museum of the Confederacy; Charlottesville: University Press of Virginia, 1991.

Cohen, David W., and Jack P. Greene, eds. *Neither Slave nor Free: The Freedman of African Descent in the Slave Societies of the New World*. Baltimore: Johns Hopkins University Press, 1972.

Craton, Michael. *In Search of the Invisible Man: Slaves and Plantation Life in Jamaica*. Cambridge, MA: Harvard University Press, 1978.

Curtin, Philip. *The Atlantic Slave Trade: A Census*. Madison: University of Wisconsin Press, 1969.

Davidson, Basil. *The African Slave Trade*. New York: Little, Brown, 1988.

Davis, David Brion. *The Problem of Slavery in Western Culture*. New York: Oxford University Press, 1988.

Douglass, Frederick. *Narrative of the Life of Frederick Douglass, an American Slave, written by Himself*. New York: Norton, 1997.

Fogel, Robert W. *Without Consent or Contract: The Rise and Fall of American Slavery*. New York: Norton, 1989.

Fogel, Robert W., and Stanley L. Engerman. *Time on the Cross: The Economics of American Negro Slavery*. Boston: Little, Brown, 1974.

Genovese, Eugene. *Roll, Jordan, Roll: The World the Slaves Made*. New York: Random House, 1976.

Hart, Richard. *Blacks in Rebellion*. Kingston, Jamaica: Institute of Social and Economic Research, 1985.

Inikori, Joseph E., and Stanley L. Engerman, eds. *The Atlantic Slave Trade*. Durham, NC: Duke University Press, 1992.

Irwin, Graham W., ed. *Africans Abroad: A Documentary History of the Black Diaspora in Asia, Latin America, and the Caribbean during the Age of Slavery*. New York: Columbia University Press, 1977.

James, C. L. R. *The Black Jacobins: Toussaint L'Ouverture and the San Domingo Revolution*, 2nd ed. New York: Vintage, 1963.

Klein, Herbert S. *African Slavery in Latin America and the Caribbean*. New York: Oxford University Press, 1986.

————. *The Middle Passage: Comparative Studies in the Atlantic Slave Trade*. Princeton, NJ: Princeton University Press, 1978.

Litwack, Leon F. *North of Slavery: The Negro in the Free States, 1790–1860*. Chicago: University of Chicago Press, 1961.

Logan, Rayford, and Michael R. Winston, eds. *Dictionary of American Negro Biography*. New York: Norton, 1982.

Lovejoy, Paul E. *Transformations in Slavery: A History of Slavery in Africa*. New York: Cambridge University Press, 1983.

Miller, Randall M., and John David Smith. *Dictionary of Afro-American Slavery*, rev. ed. Westport, CT: Praeger, 1997.

Patterson, Orlando. *Slavery and Social Death: A Comparative Study*. Cambridge, MA: Harvard University Press, 1982.

Pescatello, Ann M., ed. *The African in Latin America*. New York: Knopf, 1975.

Phillips, Ulrich B. *American Negro Slavery*. New York: Appleton, 1918.

Price, Richard, ed. *Maroon Societies: Rebel Slave Communities in the Americas*, 2nd ed. Baltimore: Johns Hopkins University Press, 1979.

Quarles, Benjamin. *Black Abolitionists*. New York: Oxford University Press, 1969.

Rawick, George P., ed. *The American Slave: A Composite Autobiography*, 41 vols. Westport, CT: Greenwood, 1972–1979.

Rawley, James A. *The Transatlantic Slave Trade: A History*. New York: Norton, 1981.

Rose, Willie Lee, ed. *A Documentary History of Slavery in North America*. New York: Oxford University Press, 1976.

Stampp, Kenneth. *The Peculiar Institution: Slavery in the Ante-Bellum South*. New York: Vintage, 1956.

Tannenbaum, Frank. *Slave and Citizen*. Boston: Beacon, 1947, 1992.

Thomas, Hugh. *The Slave Trade: The Story of the Atlantic Slave Trade, 1440–1870*. New York: Simon & Schuster, 1997.

3

Politics and
Civil Rights

HISTORIC MOVEMENTS

The earliest political and civil rights movements took place before the Civil War and included slave insurrections, repatriation movements, and abolition struggles (see Chapter 2). This chapter presents brief histories of the major post–Civil War political and civil rights movements.

> *O*ur history in this country dates from the moment that restless men among us became restless under oppression and rose against it. . . . Agitation, contentions, ceaseless unrest, constant aspiring—a race so moved must prevail.
>
> T. Thomas Fortune, *New York Globe* (August 18, 1883)

THE CIVIL RIGHTS MOVEMENT

The Reconstruction and Jim Crow Eras

The modern civil rights movement began in the South during the years after the Civil War, when newly emancipated African Americans fought for their rightful place in society. The earliest civil rights demonstrations took place during the late 1860s and early 1870s, as African Americans forced an end to segregated public transport in cities such as Charleston, Richmond, New Orleans, and Savannah. These early victories were negated by the rising tide of Jim Crow laws in the South, and civil rights efforts were repressed throughout the latter part of the 19th century, when the accommodationist policies of Booker T. Washington held sway. A revival of civil rights activity was heralded by the emergence of the Niagara Movement and the rise of the NAACP during the first decade of the 20th century (see pp. 67, 65).

The Modern Civil Rights Movement

The modern civil rights movement matured after World War II, when many African Americans who had served with honor in the war were no longer willing to accept racial discrimination and injustice in the country they had fought so hard to defend. Further, many blacks had made economic gains in the wartime economy and used their newfound wealth to further their education. Membership in the NAACP flourished, and its increased financial support from both whites and blacks helped push through the passage of historic civil rights legislation. The NAACP had begun its concerted legal campaign against segregation in the 1930s. (See Chapter 12, "The Law.") In 1941, A. Philip Randolph's March on Washington Committee was a major step forward and led to the creation of a federal commission to promote integration in wartime defense industries.

The civil rights movement entered its major phase after the 1954 *Brown* decision outlawing segregation in public schools; at this point, African American leaders determined to break down all racial barriers, and European Americans in the South dug in for a last desperate stand. Events such as the Montgomery bus boycott (1955–1956), the formation of the Southern Christian Leadership Conference (SCLC) (1957) and the Student Nonviolent Coordinating Committee (SNCC) (1960), the Freedom Rides (1961), the March on Washington (1963), and Freedom Summer (1964) were milestones in the successful struggle to abolish Jim Crow.

The 1963 March on Washington was a signature moment in the modern civil rights movement.

ring on your tear gas, bring your grenades, your new supplies of Mace, your state troopers, and even your national guards. But let the record show, we ain't going to be turned around.

Reverend Ralph David Abernathy, SCLC

Following the passage of the Civil Rights Act of 1964 and the Voting Rights Act of 1965, when the attention of African Americans turned to racism and de facto segregation outside the South, there was widespread disagreement about the future direction of the civil rights movement. The younger generation of civil rights workers was impatient with the tactics of nonviolence and gradualism, while their elders maintained faith in the tactics that had produced landmark victories in the past. In 1968, the assassination of Dr. King unleashed the pent-up anger of younger African Americans and also deprived the civil rights movement of its most dynamic and influential leader. From the 1970s on, civil rights advocates found themselves increasingly on the defensive, as political conservatives and other groups contested government efforts to integrate schools and implement affirmative-action programs. However, the growth of the African American middle class during those decades, as well as the dramatic increase in African American voter participation and the number of African American officeholders on all levels, testifies to the fundamental achievements of the civil rights movement in the modern era.

BLACK NATIONALISM AND BLACK POWER

Although some post–Civil War black leaders believed that the American dream could and would include the African American people, many other African Americans, especially the poor, were dubious. They feared that African Americans would never be allowed to become equals either economically or politically in the bigoted political and social climate of the United States, and they espoused racial nationalism rather than integration. These "race first" advocates became known as black nationalists.

Philosophically, the black-nationalist movement and its offshoot, the Black Power movement, extended the black-nationalist principles that were first espoused during the 19th century by leaders such as Martin Delany, Henry Highland Garnet, and David Walker. In addition, these movements were given new impetus in the 20th century by Marcus Garvey's Universal Negro Improvement Association (see p. 69).

"Black Power," as first used by congressional representative Adam Clayton Powell Jr. and later by members of SNCC, meant a belief in economic and political self-help. The Black Power movement had its roots in the Lowndes County Freedom Organization (LCFO) of Alabama, which emerged in 1965 as an all-black political party that chose the image of a black panther as its emblem. Despite harassment from whites, the LCFO put up a number of candidates in the November 1966 county elections, vying for offices such as sheriff, tax collector, and coroner. Though the local Democratic Party used a variety of shady tactics to ensure the defeat of all the black candidates, the LCFO's success in galvanizing black voters had a powerful impact on other activists. SNCC chair Stokely Carmichael, a fervent supporter of the LCFO, formally proclaimed the advent of Black Power on June 17, 1966, when he addressed a rally in Greenwood, Mississippi, after being released from jail for an earlier confrontation with police. In his speech, Carmichael rejected the participation and direction of whites in the civil rights movement. He called upon African Americans to embrace their heritage, build their communities, and take over leadership of their own organizations. After the disappointments and frustrations of countless confrontations with hostile police and civilians in the segregated South, Carmichael was essentially espousing a more militant and confrontational approach to obtaining civil rights.

> To most whites, black power seems to mean that the Mau Mau are coming to the suburbs at night. . . . Black people do not want to "take over" this country. They don't want to "get whitey"; they just want to get him off their backs.
>
> Stokely Carmichael, *New York Review of Books* (1996)

Though condemned by mainstream civil rights leaders such as Martin Luther King Jr., Roy Wilkins, and Bayard Rustin, Carmichael's initiative had great resonance for younger African Americans frustrated by the entrenched nature of racism in American society. Black Power inspired Huey Newton and Bobby Seale to form the Black Panther Party the following October in Oakland, California (see p. 64). In July 1967, 1,000 delegates from all over the United States (as well as Bermuda and Nigeria) attended the National Conference on Black Power in Newark, New Jersey. Prominent participants included Maulana Karenga, Ossie Davis, Dick Gregory, James Farmer, H. Rap Brown, and Amiri Baraka. After conferring for three days, the delegates addressed numerous social and economic issues, advocating that African Americans secure a larger measure of control over their own communities and take greater pride in their heritage. Among the more radical proposals were calls for the formation of a black militia, affirmation of the right of African Americans to revolt, and for a national debate on partitioning the United States into separate black and white nations.

The Black Power ideology also had roots in the Nation of Islam (NOI), which had long rejected the goal of integration while maintaining its own educational system, military organization, and economic development program, under the leadership of Elijah Muhammad (see p. 66). In the late 1990s, Minister Louis Farrakhan of the NOI has been the most prominent proponent of the Black Power tradition.

PAN-AFRICANISM

As an intellectual and cultural movement, Pan-Africanism has two main goals: to foster unity among peoples of African descent across barriers of geography and language, and to celebrate the contributions of Africa to world history and civilization. Political ties between Africa and the Americas first developed through the colonization schemes of the early 19th century and developed further through the work of religious missionaries such as Alexander Crummell and early black nationalists such as Martin Delany and David Walker. Among the early organizations promoting Pan-African ideas was the U.S.–based African Civilization Society, founded in 1861 to promote Christianity, self-reliance, and self-government.

Pan-Africanism entered a new phase in 1897, when the Trinidad-born lawyer Henry Sylvester Williams founded the Pan-African Association in London and laid the groundwork for a series of influential Pan-African conferences. The first of these, the London Conference of 1900, marked the first occasion on which the actual term *Pan-Africanism* was used in an international context. During the early years of the century, the Tuskegee Institute, the student body of which included a number of Africans, played an important role in fostering Pan-African ideals; in 1912, for example, Tuskegee hosted the International Conference on the Negro, a forum for planning African American religious and economic projects in Africa. Subsequently, W. E. B. Du Bois organized Pan-African Congresses in 1919 (Paris), 1921 (Paris, London, and Brussels), and 1923 (London and Lisbon). Attended by delegates from the United States, the Caribbean, and Africa, the conferences coordinated efforts to end European colonialism in Africa and to champion black political rights worldwide. During this era, Pan-African ideas achieved their greatest popular impact through Marcus Garvey's Universal Negro Improvement Association (UNIA), founded in 1914 (see p. 69).

During the 1930s, blacks throughout the world supported Ethiopian resistance against Italian aggression, working mainly through the International Committee on Africa. After World War II, this organization, along with the Council on African Affairs, played an important role in the fight for African self-determination. To hasten the process, W. E. B. Du Bois organized the Fifth Pan-African Congress in Manchester, England, in 1945. The conference was notable for the participation of Kwame Nkrumah, Jomo Kenyatta, and other prominent Africans, who at this time assumed leadership of the Pan-African movement. During the 1960s, Pan-African ideas exerted a powerful influence on African Americans, prompting an upsurge in black nationalism and Afrocentric ideas, a rejection of mainstream U.S. culture, the adoption of African-related dress and hairstyles, and the demand for African and African American Studies programs. In the following decades, numerous cultural and political links have been forged between Africa and the Americas. This was dramatically manifested during the 1980s and early 1990s as African American organizations such as TransAfrica persuaded U.S. government and business leaders to isolate the white-supremacist regime in South Africa.

HISTORIC ORGANIZATIONS

BLACK PANTHER PARTY (BPP)

Originally called the Black Panther Party for Self-Defense, the organization was founded in Oakland, California, by Bobby Seale and Huey Newton in October 1966 and soon recruited members across the nation. Taking their name from the symbol of the LCFO, the Black Panthers combined Marxist socialism with black nationalism; the party's radical Ten-Point Program concluded with the demand, "We want land, bread, housing, clothing, justice, peace, and people's community control of modern technology." However, the Black Panthers became less known for their ideology than for their hands-on tactics.

Wearing trademark black leather jackets and often bearing arms, groups of Black Panthers began to monitor police activity in inner-city areas, seeking to ensure that African Americans were not subjected to police brutality. These patrols led to a number of clashes with police; in one of these, a police officer was killed, leading to Newton's arrest in 1967. A campaign mounted against the Panthers by the Federal Bureau of Investigation (FBI) and local law enforcement agencies took its toll on the party. By 1969, the Panthers had gradually shifted their focus from political confrontation to community organizing, which included free lunch programs for children, educational initiatives, and voter-registration drives.

During the 1970s, the Black Panthers became deeply involved in Oakland's electoral politics, playing an important role in the election of Lionel Wilson as the city's first African American mayor. Though the party has not garnered much nationwide attention for many years, it continues to operate in the Oakland area. Among its most visible activities are a speaker's bureau, the Dr. Huey P. Newton Foundation, and organized bus tours of the city, which explore the history of the organization.

BROTHERHOOD OF SLEEPING CAR PORTERS (BSCP)

The first successful African American labor union, the BSCP was organized in 1925 by A. Philip Randolph, to better the lot of the African American porters and maids employed by the Pullman Company. Having achieved only limited recognition from the American Federation of Labor (AFL) and finding that many Pullman porters—who belonged to a company-sponsored union—were reluctant to risk their jobs by joining an outside organization, the BSCP nearly collapsed in 1928. However, after the 1934 Railway Act outlawed company unions, the BSCP found itself in a more favorable environment. The following year, the union secured an international charter from the AFL. Finally, on August 25, 1937, the BSCP achieved an accord with the Pullman Company, securing improved wages and working conditions for the African American workers. In addition to bettering the lives of its members, the BSCP fought against racism within the organized labor movement, long known for its hostility to African American workers, and it worked to promote civil rights in society at large.

The BSCP was closely involved in Randolph's effort to ensure fair hiring practices in World War II defense industries and in numerous subsequent campaigns. These efforts were bolstered by the 1955 merger between the AFL and the more progressive Congress of Industrial Organizations (CIO). The newly formed AFL-CIO soon adopted civil rights as part of its political agenda and gave valuable support to the civil rights movement, the leaders of which included a number of former BSCP officials. During the 1960s and 1970s, however, the BSCP was severely affected by the growth of air travel and the steady decline of passenger railroads. In 1978, the union was obliged to merge with the Brotherhood of Railway and Airline Clerks, losing its distinct identity but retaining its rich historical legacy.

CONGRESS OF RACIAL EQUALITY (CORE)

CORE was founded in Chicago in 1942 by members of the Fellowship of Reconciliation, an interracial Christian pacifist group. The cornerstone of CORE's program was the use of nonviolent direct action to promote social justice and racial equality. CORE members—who included the future civil rights leaders James Farmer and Bayard Rustin—took part in the first sit-in demonstrations, which were directed against Chicago restaurants that discriminated against blacks. In 1947, CORE organized the first Freedom Ride, known as the Journey of Reconciliation; the organizers aimed to integrate interstate travel facilities in the upper South but were arrested before they could make much headway. CORE entered into a fresh burst of activity in the early 1960s, organizing a new round of Freedom Rides and picketing Northern chain stores having Southern affiliates that practiced segregation. By this time, CORE—deeply involved in the civil rights struggle—joined the Council of Federated Organizations (COFO), a united front of civil rights groups in Mississippi. In 1964, CORE members played a major role in organizing both Freedom Summer and the Mississippi Freedom Democratic Party.

In 1966, CORE followed SNCC in adopting a Black Power agenda. Under the leadership of Roy Innis, who became director in 1968, the organization has continued to follow that path, though Innis himself has often backed conservative Republican politicians such as Ronald Reagan.

NATIONAL ASSOCIATION FOR THE ADVANCEMENT OF COLORED PEOPLE (NAACP)

By 1909 the racial situation had aroused the concern of a number of white reformers, including William English Walling, Mary White Ovington, and Oswald Garrison Villard. They invited the members of the Niagara Movement to a 1909 conference. There, the National Association for the Advancement of Colored People was created to prevent racially motivated violence and job discrimination, and to promote equality in the legal system.

In 1910, the organization was formally organized with Du Bois as the director of publicity and research and the editor of *Crisis*, the official magazine of the NAACP. By 1918, the circulation of *Crisis* reached 100,000, and the NAACP had won three major victories in the U.S. Supreme Court (see Chapter 12). By 1921, the organization had more than 400 branches.

Between the world wars, the NAACP pressed its legal campaign against segregation, employing the legal talents of Charles Houston, William Hastie, and Thurgood Marshall. These efforts bore fruit in the decade after World War II, culminating in the landmark 1954 Supreme Court decision on school desegregation.

The NAACP's stature as the leading African American civil rights organization began to diminish somewhat after 1955, as the philosophy of nonviolent direct action, advocated by Martin Luther King Jr. and others, became the focus of the civil rights struggle. Following the 1977 retirement of Roy Wilkins as executive secretary, the NAACP struggled to maintain its effectiveness in a more conservative political climate and finally experienced a leadership crisis during the early 1990s. The appointment of former congressional representative Kweisi Mfume as executive director in 1996 was widely regarded as a new beginning for the organization. The NAACP currently has 1,800 branches and a total membership of more than 500,000.

NATIONAL URBAN LEAGUE

By the first decade of the 20th century, substantial numbers of Southern blacks had begun moving to the cities of the North. Three major organizations were helping the newcomers adjust to urban life: the Committee for Improving the Industrial Condition of Negroes in New York, the

National League for the Protection of Colored Women, and the Committee on Urban Conditions Among Negroes. In 1911, these organizations merged to form the National Urban League, which was led by George Haynes and Eugene Kinckle Jones. By the end of World War I, when the Great Migration was in full swing, the league had branches in all the major industrial cities. In addition to conducting extensive research and publishing the magazine *Opportunity* (1923–1948), the Urban League worked to end discrimination in labor unions, federal programs, and the armed forces. Under the leadership of Whitney Young, the organization took part in the civil rights movement of the 1960s, opening branches in a number of Southern cities. Responding to inner-city rioting during the late 1960s, the Urban League offered direct aid to African American communities, funding programs for school dropouts, voter-registration drives, job training, and health services. This approach—with an added emphasis on self-help organizing—has continued under the leadership of John Jacob, who became executive director in 1981, and Hugh B. Price, who succeeded Jacob as head of the organization in 1994.

NATION OF ISLAM (NOI)

Though it began in 1930 as an essentially religious organization (see Chapter 6, "Religion"), the NOI has achieved its greatest recognition as a leading exponent of black nationalism. Under the guiding principle of "Do for Self," the NOI pushed economic development within the African American community and promulgated an ethic of black pride while castigating whites and challenging white racism. By adopting a distinctive form of Islam and using an X in place of their original surnames, NOI members sought to create a new identity untainted by white racism and control. Under the leadership of Elijah Muhammad, which began in the mid-1930s, the NOI developed its own schools (the Clara Muhammad Schools), military organization (the Fruit of Islam), and a variety of properties and businesses.

The NOI, familiarly known as the Black Muslims, achieved its greatest influence during the 1950s and early 1960s, when Malcolm X emerged as Elijah Muhammad's chief aide and the national spokesperson for the organization. At this time, the NOI's membership reached approximately 500,000. Malcolm X's eloquent and biting rejection of nonviolence and of the very goal of integration (which the NOI considered a form of cultural suicide for African Americans) made the NOI a controversial force in the eyes of white society and provided the groundwork for the development of Black Power. Following Malcolm X's assassination in 1965, the NOI's membership began to decline, even as its economic activities grew more profitable.

After Elijah Muhammad died in 1975, his son Warith Dean Muhammad led the organization away from politics and formed the World Community Islam, a more traditional form of Islam. At this point, Elijah Muhammad's chief minister, Louis Farrakhan, became the head of an important breakaway faction, now known as the Nation of Islam, which sought to resurrect Elijah Muhammad's founding ideals. It has continued to maintain its headquarters in Chicago where it pursues a black-nationalist agenda. The NOI's current activities include a speaker's bureau, a student association, the Abundant Life Clinic (operated by the NOI's Ministry of Health and Human Services), and a newspaper entitled *The Final Call*.

In 1995, Farrakhan, working with Rev. Benjamin Chavis, former NAACP executive director, organized the Million Man March in Washington, D.C. Calling for "Atonement, Reconciliation and Responsibility," the men-only march served to send a message of unity to African Americans, while stressing the need for personal responsibility and economic empowerment. Speakers such as Rosa Parks and Rev. Jesse Jackson addressed huge crowds, drawing attention to policy issues that affect African Americans. In following years, Million Woman and Million Youth marches have continued to draw enthusiastic crowds.

THE NIAGARA MOVEMENT

The Niagara Movement arose at a time of deepening racism and antiblack violence in the United States. It addressed the concerns of African Americans dissatisfied with Booker T. Washington's policy (articulated in his Atlanta Compromise speech of 1895) of accepting segregation in return for economic benefits. Led by the scholar and writer W. E. B. Du Bois, a group of younger and more radical African American leaders, 29 in all, met at Niagara Falls, Canada, in June 1905 (no hotel on the American side of the falls would accept them). There, they drew up a manifesto calling for full voting rights, an end to discrimination, equal access to education, fair treatment in the courts, and other measures. The group's manifesto vigorously condemned racial discrimination as the cause of all the ills suffered by African Americans:

> The Negro race in America, stolen, ravished, and degraded, struggling up through difficulties and oppression, needs sympathy and receives criticism, needs help and is given hindrance, needs protection and is given mob-violence, needs justice and is given charity, needs leadership and is given cowardice and apology, needs bread and is given a stone.

In addition to Du Bois, attendees at the inaugural conference included William Monroe Trotter, Clement Garnett Morgan, Charles Bentley, William H. Hart, and Edwin Jourdain. Following their decision to convene annually at a place of historic significance, the Niagara Movement members met at Harpers Ferry in 1906, at Boston in 1907, and at Oberlin, Ohio, in 1908. Though the Niagara Movement never posed a serious threat to Booker T. Washington's position of leadership in the black community and had little impact on the average African American, it fostered a new consensus among black intellectuals that the times demanded a new approach to the struggle for equal rights, and its activities laid the groundwork for the founding of the NAACP (see the preceding section, p. 65).

OPERATION PUSH (PEOPLE UNITED TO SAVE HUMANITY)

Operation PUSH was founded in 1971 by the Reverend Jesse Jackson, who had gradually drifted away from the SCLC following the assassination of King. Based in Chicago and modeled on the SCLC's Operation Breadbasket, PUSH initially focused its energies on economic issues, supporting minority businesses and pressuring white-owned firms to hire a fair proportion of minority employees. The organization also developed educational initiatives under the PUSH/EXCEL program, attracting widespread support for its efforts to help minority schoolchildren. Operation PUSH scaled down its activities considerably during the 1980s as Rev. Jackson directed his efforts toward securing the Democratic presidential nomination. During the 1990s, however, PUSH has broadened the spectrum of its concerns to include AIDS, drugs, teenage pregnancy, and violence in the black community. The organization now has branches in 35 cities.

RAINBOW COALITION

Rev. Jesse Jackson also founded the Rainbow Coalition, a multiracial political organization, in 1984, when he made his first serious bid for the Democratic presidential nomination. The organization reached its highest level of political influence in 1988, when it won nine state primaries and garnered 7 million votes out of the 23 million cast. Though it has not been a major factor in subsequent nationwide campaigns, the Rainbow Coalition currently has about 13,000 active members and operates in all 50 states. It seeks to build a progressive consensus on both national and international political issues. In 1997, the Rainbow Coalition joined forces with Operation PUSH to monitor the hiring, promotion, and investment practices of Wall Street firms and other wealthy corporations. The new organization is called the Rainbow/PUSH Coalition.

SOUTHERN CHRISTIAN LEADERSHIP CONFERENCE (SCLC)

SCLC was founded in January 1957 at the Ebenezer Baptist Church in Atlanta, Georgia, by a group of 60 African American leaders representing cities throughout the South. Leading members of the group included Martin Luther King Jr., Ralph Abernathy, T. J. Jemison, Fred Shuttlesworth, and C. K. Steele. Most were Baptist ministers and NAACP members. Though they supported the NAACP strategy of battling segregation in the courts, they also believed that direct action—such as the 1955–1956 Montgomery bus boycott and subsequent campaigns in other cities—could be highly effective. SCLC began cautiously but began to hit its stride after 1959, when Rev. King, the organization's president, moved to Atlanta from Montgomery. The following year, SCLC gave support to sit-in participants and Freedom Riders and was a catalyst for the creation of SNCC. SCLC achieved a new level of effectiveness in 1962–1963, when it organized civil rights campaigns in Alabama, Virginia, and Florida. At this point, the organization had 50 full-time staff members and 85 chapters.

Following the emergence of the Black Power movement and the urban unrest of the late 1960s, SCLC broadened its efforts to include African American communities in the North. Following Rev. King's assassination in 1968, Rev. Abernathy assumed the presidency and served until 1977, when he was succeeded by Rev. Joseph E. Lowery. Under Lowery's leadership, SCLC focused its energies on apartheid in South Africa, U.S. voter registration, and social problems within African American communities. In 1997, SCLC chose Martin Luther King III, Rev. King's eldest son, to succeed Rev. Lowery as president.

STUDENT NONVIOLENT COORDINATING COMMITTEE (SNCC)

SNCC had its genesis in the sit-in movements that swept the South in 1960. The sit-ins began in Greensboro, North Carolina, in February, when four students from North Carolina A&T set out to integrate a Woolworth's lunch counter. The Greensboro sit-in sparked a wave of protest that spread to 31 cities in nine states within the following three months. Student leaders from nearly 60 colleges met at Shaw University in Raleigh, North Carolina, on April 15, receiving warm support from SCLC leaders. On that occasion they decided to coordinate their efforts and formed what was initially called the Temporary Student Nonviolent Coordinating Committee, with Marion Barry as chair. In 1961, when James Forman took over as executive secretary, SNCC offered decisive support to the Freedom Rides and decided to focus on two main areas: voter registration and direct action. SNCC was involved in all the major events of the following years, including the 1963 March on Washington, the formation of the Mississippi Freedom Democratic Party in 1964, the Selma-to-Montgomery March in 1965, and the creation of the Lowndes County Freedom Organization in 1965.

In 1966, when Stokely Carmichael became chair of SNCC, the organization moved decisively to embrace the principles of Black Power and to renounce previously held goals of integration and nonviolence. Carmichael resigned in 1967, and new leader H. Rap Brown changed the organization's name to the Student National Coordinating Committee. In 1968, SNCC merged with the Black Panther Party. Many SNCC members were uncomfortable with the Black Panther's militancy, and the union proved temporary. After Martin Luther King's assassination in 1968, SNCC lost membership and political impetus. By the early 1970s, SNCC had ceased to exist, although its political legacy continues today in voter-registration drives and grassroots political activism.

TRANSAFRICA

Founded in 1977, TransAfrica is a national African American organization that concentrates on influencing U.S. foreign policy toward Africa and the Caribbean. The organization grew out of an initiative by the Congressional Black Caucus, which convened a 1976 conference in Washington, D.C., attended by leaders from civil rights groups, churches, business groups, academia, and elsewhere. Concerned over U.S. support for white minority interests in Southern Rhodesia (now Zimbabwe), the conferees issued a manifesto and agreed to take further steps to support freedom and democracy in Africa. When TransAfrica was formed the following year, Randall Robinson was chosen as executive director. TransAfrica's major focus became the struggle against apartheid in South Africa. The organization's efforts to mobilize public opinion—including demonstrations outside the South African embassy throughout 1985—led to the passage of the 1986 Anti-Apartheid Act, which imposed sanctions on the South African government.

During the 1990s, TransAfrica exerted its influence on behalf of democracy and human rights in Haiti and the humane treatment of Haitian refugees. In addition to its political activities, the organization sponsors TransAfrica Forum (created in 1981), a research and educational division. TransAfrica Forum publishes *TransAfrica Forum* magazine, maintains a library, offers career programs for minority students seeking to enter the foreign service, and holds an annual conference on foreign policy issues at its Washington, D.C., headquarters.

UNIVERSAL NEGRO IMPROVEMENT ASSOCIATION (UNIA)

UNIA was founded in Kingston, Jamaica, in 1914 by Marcus Garvey, who brought the organization to New York in 1916 and incorporated it in 1918. UNIA was organized to promote the destruction of colonialism and the political unification of African peoples everywhere. UNIA had its own flag (a red, black, and green tricolor), medical organization (Black Cross Nurses), church (African Orthodox Church), and uniformed military forces (Universal African Legion, Universal African Motor Corps, Black Eagle Flying Corps). Through these organizations, an official newspaper (*The Negro World*), and a series of month-long conventions held in New York City between 1920 and 1924, UNIA had a profound political and cultural influence throughout the black diaspora and in Africa. Ideologically, UNIA advocated a pan-African, nationalistic, anticolonialist stance. Its first convention issued a document entitled the "Declaration of Rights of the Negro Peoples of the World," a protest against the wrongs and injustices suffered by blacks at the hands of whites. The declaration demanded basic civil rights, political and judicial equality, racial self-determination, and perhaps most important, a free Africa under black African government. UNIA's motto was proclaimed as, "One God! One Aim! One Destiny!"

I asked myself, *Where is the black man's Government? Where is his President, his country, and his ambassador, his army, his navy, his men of big affairs? I could not find them, and then I declared, "I will help to make them."*

Marcus Garvey, *The Philosophy and Opinions of Marcus Garvey* (1923)

By the mid-1920s, there were nearly 1,000 UNIA chapters throughout North America, the West Indies, South America, the United Kingdom, and Africa. With hundreds of thousands—perhaps millions—of members, UNIA may have been the largest global African political organization of all time. The most ambitious UNIA economic project was the Black Star Line. In addition to transporting the peoples of the diaspora back to Africa, the Black Star Line was intended to promote economic development fostering the commercial exchange of goods between the African peoples of Africa and the Americas.

UNIA suffered a near-fatal blow, however, when the Black Star Line collapsed in 1923 due to Garvey's imprisonment for mail fraud. This was followed by increasing factionalism within the organization. Back in Jamaica after his release, Garvey reincorporated UNIA and sought to reassert his leadership; he made a further attempt after moving to London in 1935, but by this point the Great Depression had severely reduced the ability of African Americans to support UNIA.

Despite all these obstacles, UNIA continued to operate on a reduced scale. Following Garvey's death in 1940, the organization moved its headquarters to Cleveland and later relocated to Liberia, although not as an effective organized force. Many former UNIA members were absorbed into the black-nationalist movements of the 1930s and 1940s. Garvey's legacy continued, however. Important leaders in the African independence movement, such as Jomo Kenyatta of Kenya, Kwame Nkrumah of Ghana, and Dr. Nnamdi Azikiwe of Nigeria, cited their indebtedness to Garvey's writings and his philosophy of black internationalism.

ACTIVE POLITICAL AND CIVIL RIGHTS ORGANIZATIONS

AFL-CIO
Department of Civil Rights
815 16th Street, NW
Washington, DC 20006
202-637-5270
Implements AFL-CIO policies on equal opportunity; deals with complaints of discrimination in unions; serves as liaison with other organizations and government agencies promoting equal opportunity.

American Association for Affirmative Action
200 N. Michigan Avenue
Chicago, IL 60601
312-541-1271
Coordinates monitoring of businesses and educational institutions.

The Black Agenda
P.O. Box 09726
Columbus, OH 43209
614-338-8384
Works to enhance the political, economic, social, and cultural status of African Americans.

Center for Democratic Renewal
P.O. Box 50469
Atlanta, GA 30302
404-221-0025
Helps communities combat groups, movements, and government practices that promote hatred and bigotry.

Coalition of Black Trade Unionists
P.O. Box 66268
Washington, DC 20035
202-429-1203
Promotes voter registration, economic development, and employment opportunities.

Congress of Racial Equality (CORE)
30 Cooper Square, 9th Floor
New York, NY 10003
212-598-4000
(See preceding description, p. 65.)

Congressional Black Caucus Foundation
1004 Pennsylvania Avenue, SE

Washington, DC 20003
202-675-6730
Seeks to advance the political participation
of African Americans and other minority
groups; sponsors a graduate internship
program and sponsors annual Congressional
Black Caucus Legislative Weekend, which
brings together black leaders from around
the country.

Institute for Black Leadership, Development, and
Research
1028 Dole Human Development Center
University of Kansas
Lawrence, KS 66045
913-864-3990

International Committee Against Racism
150 W. 28th Street, Room 301
New York, NY 10001
212-255-3959
Dedicated to fighting racism and building a
multiracial society.

Joint Center for Political and Economic Studies
1090 Vermont Avenue, NW, Suite 1100
Washington, DC 20005
202-789-3500
Conducts research on public policy issues
concerning African Americans; promotes
participation in the political process.

Klanwatch
400 Washington Avenue
Montgomery, AL 36104
334-264-0286
Created by the Southern Poverty Law Center (see
separate entry) in 1981, Klanwatch gathers and
disseminates information on hate groups,
including antigovernment militias.

Leadership Conference on Civil Rights
1629 K Street, NW, Suite 1010
Washington, DC 20036
202-667-1780
Coalition of 165 groups representing African
Americans, Asian Americans, Hispanic
Americans, women, the aged, and other groups.

Martin Luther King, Jr., Center for Nonviolent
Social Change

449 Auburn Avenue, NE
Atlanta, GA 30312
404-524-8969
Continues the work of Rev. King through
education, training, research, and constructive
action.

National Alliance of Black Organizations
3724 Airport Boulevard
Austin, TX 78722
512-478-9802
Coordinates voter-registration activities; serves as
a forum for the exchange of ideas.

National Association for the Advancement of
Colored People (NAACP)
4805 Mount Hope Drive
Baltimore, MD 21215
301-358-8900
(See preceding discussion, p. 65.)

National Association for the Advancement of
Colored People (NAACP) Legal Defense and
Education Fund
99 Hudson Street, 16th Floor
New York, NY 10021
212-310-9000
Operates independently of the NAACP; supports
litigation on behalf of minorities and women
with respect to discrimination in housing,
employment, education, and other areas.

National Black Caucus of Local Elected Officials
1301 Pennsylvania Avenue, NW, Suite 550
Washington, DC 20004
202-626-3000
Sponsors national education programs and
organizes conferences that promote strategies
and solutions to public policy issues facing
African Americans.

National Black Caucus of State Legislators
Hall of States
444 N. Capitol Street, NW, Suite 622
Washington, DC 20001
202-624-5457

National Black Leadership Roundtable
1424 Longworth House Building
Washington, DC 20515
202-331-2030
Brings together chief executive officers of

national African American organizations; aids in the development of strategies beneficial to the black community; seeks to ensure that black elected officials are responsive to their communities.

National Black United Front
700 E. Oakwood Boulevard
Chicago, IL 60653
312-268-7500
Works toward liberation and self-determination for African Americans; cooperates with African liberation movements throughout the world; combats racism and other forms of political oppression.

National Coalition of Blacks for Reparations in America
P.O. Box 62622
Washington, DC 20029
202-635-6272
Seeks to obtain reparations from the U.S. government, other governments, and corporations that profited from the enslavement of blacks.

National Rainbow Coalition
1700 K Street, NW
Washington, DC 20006
202-728-1192
(See preceding description, p. 67.)

National Urban League
500 E. 62nd Street
New York, NY 10021
212-310-9000
(See preceding description, p. 65.)

Operation PUSH (People United to Serve Humanity)
930 E. 50th Street
Chicago, IL 60615

312-373-3366
(See preceding description, p. 67.)

A. Philip Randolph Institute
1444 Eye Street, NW
Washington, DC 20005
202-289-2774
Prepares information and educational materials for all civil rights groups.

Scholarship, Education, and Defense Fund for Racial Equality
164 Madison Avenue
New York, NY 10016
212-532-8216
Develops community organization programs; assists with voter-registration and legal problems; provides scholarship assistance.

Southern Christian Leadership Conference (SCLC)
334 Auburn Avenue, NE
Atlanta, GA 30312
404-522-1420
(See preceding description, p. 68.)

Southern Poverty Law Center
400 Washington Avenue
Montgomery, AL 36104
205-264-0286
Seeks to protect and advance the civil rights of poor people of all ethnic groups; operates Klanwatch (see separate entry).

TransAfrica
545 8th Street, SE
Washington, DC 20003
202-547-2550
(See preceding description, p. 69.)

Voter Education Project
604 Beckwith Street, SW
Atlanta, GA 30314
404-522-7495
Provides financial and technical assistance to voter-registration projects in the former Confederate states.

THE AFRICAN AMERICAN VOTER

Table 3.1 Percentage of Reported Voting, by Age and Race, in November Elections, 1964–1996 (in thousands)

Year	Total		18 to 44 years		45⏋ years	
	White	Black	White	Black	White	Black
1996						
Number	162,779	22,483	88,301	14,266	74,477	8,217
Percentage voted	56.0	50.6	46.9	43.9	66.9	62.3
1994						
Number	160,317	21,799	88,671	14,066	71,647	7,734
Percentage voted	47.3	37.1	36.9	29.2	60.1	51.6
1992						
Number	157,837	21,039	87,966	13,353	69,871	7,686
Percentage voted	63.6	54.0	57.2	47.9	71.7	64.7
1990						
Number	155,587	20,371	88,320	13,030	67,267	7,341
Percentage voted	46.7	39.2	37.2	33.0	59.1	50.1
1988						
Number	152,848	19,692	87,145	12,607	65,703	7,084
Percentage voted	59.1	51.5	51.3	44.3	69.5	64.4
1986						
Number	149,899	19,020	85,839	12,186	64,059	6,834
Percentage voted	47.0	43.2	36.9	36.4	60.6	55.5
1984						
Number	146,761	18,432	83,752	11,952	63,009	6,479
Percentage voted	61.4	55.8	54.9	51.1	70.1	64.6
1982						
Number	143,607	17,624	81,458	11,284	62,149	6,340
Percentage voted	49.9	43.0	40.1	37.4	62.8	53.1
1980						
Number	137,676	16,423	77,225	10,224	60,451	6,198
Percentage voted	60.9	50.5	54.6	44.3	69.0	60.6
1978						
Number	133,370	15,636	73,827	9,634	59,543	6,002
Percentage voted	47.3	37.2	37.9	30.7	59.0	47.5
1976						
Number	129,316	14,927	70,600	9,101	58,717	5,826
Percentage voted	60.9	48.7	55.4	41.6	67.6	59.8
1974						
Number	125,132	14,175	67,491	8,556	57,641	5,620
Percentage voted	46.3	33.8	37.6	27.3	56.5	43.6
1972						
Number	121,243	13,493	64,733	8,124	56,508	5,370
Percentage voted	64.5	52.1	60.0	47.9	69.6	58.5
1970						
Number	107,997	11,472	52,923	6,423	55,074	5,049
Percentage voted	56.0	43.5	48.4	38.9	63.2	49.4

(continued)

Table 3.1 (continued)

Year	Total		18 to 44 years		45+ years	
	White	Black	White	Black	White	Black
1968						
Number	104,521	10,935	50,675	5,968	53,508	4,878
Percentage voted	69.1	57.6	64.8	55.8	73.3	60.4
1966						
Number	101,205	10,533	49,332	5,767	51,873	4,766
Percentage voted	57.1	41.8	50.3	39.3	63.6	44.8
1964						
Number	99,353	10,340	48,911	5,711	50,443	4,630
Percentage voted	70.7	58.5	66.9	58.1	74.3	58.9

Note: Prior to 1972, data are for persons of voting age, 21 years old and over, in most states.
Source: U.S. Census Bureau

Table 3.2 Percentage of African Americans Voting
Democratic in Presidential Elections, 1932–1996

Year	City	%	Year	%
1932*	Chicago	21.0	1944	NA
	Cincinnati	28.8	1948	70.0
	Cleveland	17.3	1952	83.0
	Detroit	31.0	1956	68.0
	Knoxville	29.8	1960	72.0
	New York	50.8	1964	99.0
	Philadelphia	26.7	1968	92.0
	Pittsburgh	41.3	1972	86.0
1936*	Chicago	48.8	1976	94.0
	Cincinnati	65.1	1980	93.0
	Cleveland	60.5	1984	89.0
	Detroit	66.2	1988	87.0
	Knoxville	56.2	1992	83.0
	New York	81.3	1996	84.0
	Philadelphia	68.7		
	Pittsburgh	74.7		
1940*	Chicago	52.5		
	Cincinnati	66.9		
	Cleveland	64.7		
	Detroit	74.8		
	New York	81.0		
	Philadelphia	68.4		
	Pittsburgh	82.0		

*National election figures not available.

Table 3.3 African American Voters in the South, 1940–1966 (in thousands)

State	1940		1947		1952		1956		1966	
	Registered	% of Voting-Age Blacks Registered	Registered	% of Voting-Age Blacks Registered	Registered	% of Voting-Age Blacks Registered	Registered	% of Voting-Age Blacks Registered	Registered	% of Voting-Age Blacks Registered
Alabama	1.5	0.30	6.0	1.2	50.0	9.68	53.366	11.0	246.396	51.2
Arkansas	8.0	3.00	47.0	17.3	60.0	25.84	69.677	36.0	115.00	59.7
Florida	10.0	3.20	49.0	15.4	150.0	40.89	148.703	32.0	286.446	60.9
Georgia	10.0	1.71	125.0	18.8	125.0	20.07	163.384	27.0	289.545	47.2
Louisiana	2.0	0.42	10.0	2.6	130.0	27.01	161.410	31.0	242.130	47.1
Mississippi	0.5	0.09	5.0	0.9	40.0	8.04	20.000	5.0	139.099	32.9
North Carolina	50.0	10.14	75.0	15.2	97.5	17.73	135.000	24.0	281.134	51.0
South Carolina	1.5	0.39	50.0	13.0	130.0	33.33	99.890	27.0	190.609	51.4
Tennessee	50.0	16.15	80.0	25.8	155.0	48.62	90.000	27.0	225.000	71.7
Texas	50.0	9.24	100.0	18.5	200.0	34.31	214.000	37.0	400.000	61.6
Virginia	20.0	5.29	48.0	13.2	70.0	16.56	82.603	19.0	205.000	46.9
Totals	203.5		595.0		1,207.5		1,238.033		2,620.359	

Source: Encyclopedia of African American Culture and History, V. p. 3017

AFRICAN AMERICANS IN GOVERNMENT

AFRICAN AMERICAN MEMBERS OF THE 105TH CONGRESS (1997–1999)

(with party affiliation, state and district, year first elected, and current committee membership)

House of Representatives

Bishop, Sanford D. (D). Georgia, 2nd Dist. (1992). Agriculture; Intelligence (Select).

Brown, Corrine (D). Florida, 3rd Dist. (1992). Transportation and Infrastructure; Veterans Affairs.

Carson, Julia (D). Indiana, 10th Dist. (1996). Banking and Financial Services; Veterans Affairs.

Christian-Green, Donna M. (D). Delegate, U.S. Virgin Islands (1996). Resources.

Clay, William (D). Missouri, 1st Dist. (1968). Education and the Workforce (ranking Democrat).

Clayton, Eva M. (D). North Carolina, 1st Dist. (1992). Agriculture; Budget.

Clyburn, James E. (D). South Carolina, 6th Dist. (1992). Transportation and Infrastructure; Veterans Affairs.

Conyers, John, Jr. (D). Michigan, 14th Dist. (1964). Judiciary (ranking Democrat).

Cummings, Elijah (D). Maryland, 7th Dist. (1996). Government Reform and Oversight; Transportation and Infrastructure.

Davis, Danny K. (D). Illinois, 7th Dist. (1996). Government Reform and Oversight; Small Business.

Dellums, Ronald V. (D). California, 9th Dist. (1970). National Security.

Dixon, Julian C. (D). California, 32nd Dist. (1978). Appropriations; Intelligence.

Fatta, Chaka (D). Pennsylvania, 2nd Dist. (1994). Education and the Workforce; Government Reform and Oversight.

Flake, Floyd H. (D). New York, 6th Dist. (1986). Banking and Financial Services; Small Business.

Hastings, Alcee (D). Florida, 23rd Dist. (1992). International Relations; Science.

Hilliard, Earl F. (D). Alabama, 7th Dist. (1992). Agriculture; International Relations.

Jackson, Jesse L., Jr. (D). Illinois, 2nd Dist. (1995). Banking and Financial Services; Small Business.

Jefferson, William J. (D). Louisiana, 2nd Dist. (1990). Ways and Means.

Johnson, Eddie Bernice (D). Texas, 30th Dist. (1992). Science; Transportation and Infrastructure.

Kilpatrick, Carolyn Cheeks (D). Michigan, 15th Dist. (1997). Banking and Financial Services; Government Reform and Oversight; Joint Committee on the Library of Congress.

Lee, Sheila Jackson (D). Texas, 18th Dist. (1994). Judiciary; Science.

Lewis, John (D). Georgia, 5th Dist. (1980). Chief Deputy Minority Whip; Ways and Means.

McKinney, Cynthia A. (D). Georgia, 4th Dist. (1992). Banking and Financial Services; International Relations.

Meek, Carrie (D). Florida, 17th Dist. (1992). Appropriations.

Millender-McDonald, Juanita (D). California, 37th Dist. (1996). Transportation and Infrastructure; Small Business.

(continued)

Table 3.4 Black Elected Officials, by Office, 1970–1993, and by Region and State, 1993

[As of January 1993, no black elected officials had been identified in Hawaii, Idaho, Montana, North Dakota, or Utah]

Region, Division, and State	Total	U.S. and State Legislatures[1]	City and County Offices[2]	Law Enforcement[3]	Education[4]
1970 (Feb.)	1,469	179	715	213	362
1980 (July)	4,890	326	2,832	526	1,206
1985 (Jan.)	6,016	407	3,517	661	1,431
1990 (Jan.)	7,335	436	4,485	769	1,645
1991 (Jan.)	7,445	473	4,496	847	1,629
1992 (Jan.)	7,517	499	4,557	847	1,614
1993 (Jan.)	7,984	561	4,819	922	1,682
NORTHEAST	777	96	291	126	264
N.E.	109	35	60	4	10
ME	1	—	1	—	—
NH	2	2	—	—	—
VT	2	2	—	—	—
MA	30	8	18	2	2
RI	12	9	3	—	—
CT	62	14	38	2	8
M.A.	668	61	231	122	254
NY	299	30	63	70	136
NJ	211	13	113	—	85
PA	158	18	55	52	33
MIDWEST	1,361	106	757	171	327
E.N.C	1,119	78	604	143	294
OH	219	16	124	30	49
IN	72	12	50	4	6
IL	465	25	282	37	121
MI	333	17	133	68	115
WI	30	8	15	4	3
W.N.C	242	28	153	28	33
MN	16	1	2	10	3
IA	11	1	6	1	3
MO	185	18	134	14	19
SD	3	1	2	—	—
NE	6	1	2	—	3
KS	21	6	7	3	5
SOUTH	5,492	328	3,675	518	971
S.A.	2,200	173	1,522	147	358
DE	23	3	14	—	6
MD	140	32	79	23	6
DC	198	4[5]	185	—	9
VA	155	14	126	15	—
WV	21	1	17	3	—
NC	468	28	328	31	81
SC	450	26	269	15	140
GA	545	43	371	32	99
FL	200	22	133	28	17
E.S.C.	1,681	85	1,175	175	246
KY	63	4	47	5	7
TN	168	16	104	24	24
AL	699	23	529	58	89
MS	751	42	495	88	126
W.S.C.	1,611	70	978	196	367
AR	380	13	214	51	102
LA	636	33	346	104	153
OK	123	6	95	1	21
TX	472	18	323	40	91
WEST	354	31	96	107	120
Mountain	49	11	11	16	11
WY	1	—	—	—	1
CO	20	4	4	10	2
NM	3	—	—	2	1
AZ	15	4	3	3	5
NV	10	3	4	1	2
Pacific	305	20	85	91	109
WA	19	2	9	5	3
OR	10	4	2	4	—
CA	273	13	72	82	106
AK	3	1	2	—	—

—Represents zero. [1]Includes elected state administrators. [2]County commissioners and councilmen, mayors, vice mayors, aldermen, regional officials, and other. [3]Judges, magistrates, constables, marshals, sheriffs, justices of the peace, and other. [4]Members of state education agencies, college boards, school boards, and other. [5]Includes two shadow senators and one shadow representative.

Source: Statistical Abstract of the U.S., No. 452.

Norton, Eleanor Holmes (D). Delegate, District of Columbia (1990). Government Reform and Oversight; Transportation and Infrastructure.

Owens, Major (D). New York, 11th Dist. (1982). Education and the Workforce; Government Reform and Oversight.

Payne, Donald M. (D). New Jersey, 10th Dist. (1988). Education and the Workforce; International Relations.

Rangel, Charles B. (D). New York, 15th Dist. (1970). Ways and Means (ranking Democrat); Joint Committee on Taxation.

Rush, Bobby (D). Illinois, 1st Dist. (1992). Commerce.

Scott, Robert C. (D). Virginia, 3rd Dist. (1992). Education and the Workforce; Judiciary.

Stokes, Louis (D). Ohio, 11th Dist. (1968). Appropriations.

Thompson, Bennie G. (D). Mississippi, 2nd Dist. (1993). Agriculture; Budget.

Towns, Edolphus (D). New York, 10th Dist. (1982). Government Reform and Oversight; Commerce.

Waters, Maxine (D). California, 35th Dist. (1990). Banking and Financial Services; Judiciary.

Watt, Melvin L. (D). North Carolina, 12th Dist. (1992). Banking and Financial Services; Judiciary.

Watts, J. C., Jr. (R). Oklahoma, 4th Dist. (1994). National Security; Transportation and Infrastructure.

Wynn, Albert R. (D). Maryland, 4th Dist. (1992). Commerce.

SENATE

Braun, Carol Moseley (D). Illinois (1992).   Banking, Housing, and Urban Affairs; Finance; Aging (Special).

POLITICAL AND CIVIL RIGHTS LEADERS

Abernathy, Ralph David, Sr. (1926–1990).   A Baptist minister and NAACP member since 1951, Abernathy was one of the main organizers of the Montgomery bus boycott in 1955 and helped Rev. Martin Luther King Jr. found the SCLC in 1957. He was arrested 19 times for civil rights activities during the 1950s and 1960s. Following the King assassination, Abernathy assumed leadership of SCLC and directed the Poor People's March on Washington. In 1977, he resigned from SCLC and made an unsuccessful bid for a congressional seat. He then devoted his energies to the Foundation for Economic Enterprises Development, which has worked to provide economic opportunities for African Americans. He also served as the pastor of Atlanta's West Hunter Street Baptist Church.

Alexander, Clifford, Jr. (1933–   ).   A graduate of Yale Law School, Alexander became an aide to President Lyndon B. Johnson in 1964. In 1967, he became the first African American chair of the Equal Opportunity Employment Commission (EEOC). During his three years at the helm, he shifted the agency's emphasis from antidiscrimination efforts to affirmative-action programs. In 1969, Alexander left the government and entered private law practice. He returned to public service during the Carter Administration as the first African American secretary of the army (1977–1980).

Baker, Ella Jo (1903–1986).   Often called the godmother of the civil rights movement, Baker was affiliated with all the major organizations and leaders. After graduating from Shaw University in Raleigh, North Carolina, she moved to New York, where she wrote for African American newspapers, worked for the Works Progress Administration (WPA), and helped found the Young Negroes Cooperative League. In 1940, Baker became a field secretary for the NAACP and traveled the country building the organization, with an emphasis on grassroots organization. Between 1947 and 1957, Baker worked for both the New York Cancer Society and the Urban League while fund-raising for the Southern civil rights movement. In 1957, she returned to the South as the first executive secretary of SCLC, and helped coordinate student sit-in activities for SCLC. After 1960, Baker continued to work with students through the Young Women's Christian Association (YWCA) and the Southern Conference Educational Fund, and she helped organize SNCC. In 1964 she helped to launch the Mississippi Freedom Democratic Party that challenged the all-white delegation to the 1964 presidential convention. In all her various activities, she worked to establish group-centered leadership, believing that this was more effective than hierarchical leadership structures.

Barry, Marion Shepilov (1936–   ).   Barry was a graduate student at Fisk University in the late 1950s when he joined the civil rights movement. In 1960 he became the first national chair of SNCC but resigned six months later to pursue a Ph.D. in chemistry. He continued to conduct civil rights workshops and returned to the movement in 1964, organizing campaigns against discrimination and police brutality in Washington, D.C. He was elected to the Washington City Council in 1974 and ran successfully for mayor in 1979. Though forced out in 1990 following a drug conviction, he resurrected his political career and was elected to a fourth term as mayor in 1994.

Bethune, Mary McLeod (1875–1955).   In 1904, Bethune founded the Daytona Normal and Industrial School, which later became Bethune-Cookman College. Beginning in 1914, she began to participate in health and child-welfare conferences, where she exchanged ideas with prominent social reformers. During the New Deal years, she formed a close alliance with Eleanor Roosevelt. She counseled President Franklin Roosevelt on African American issues and served as director of the Negro Division of the National Youth Administration. In 1974, a memorial to Bethune was unveiled in Lincoln Park in Washington, D.C.

Bond, Julian (1940–   ).   After achieving prominence as both a journalist and one of the founding members of SNCC (its first public affairs officer), Bond was elected to the Georgia State Legislature in 1965. He was denied his seat for a year, however, because of his opposition to the Vietnam War. At the Democratic Party convention of 1968, his name was placed in nomination for the vice-presidency, but he was too young to meet the constitutional age requirement and was obliged to withdraw. Bond served in the Georgia State Senate from 1974 to 1986, when he resigned to take up teaching positions at American University and the University of Virginia. In 1998, Bond returned to public life when he was named chair of NAACP.

Braun, Carol E. Moseley (1947–   ).   After earning a law degree from the University of Chicago, Braun served as an assistant U.S. attorney for the Northern District of Illinois from 1973 to 1977. In 1979 she won election to the state legislature and was elected recorder of deeds for Cook County in 1986. In 1992, Braun won election to the U.S. Senate, becoming the first African American woman to serve in that body. She lost her bid for reelection in 1998, in a close and politically charged campaign.

Brooke, Edward (1919–   ).   A moderate Republican, Brooke served as Massachusetts attorney general from 1962 to 1966, when he became the first African American since Reconstruction to be elected to the U.S. Senate. During his 12 years in Washington, he became an expert on housing legislation. Brooke supported measures to fight discrimination in housing and to create programs aiding low- and moderate-income home owners. After failing to win a third term in 1978, he returned to private law practice.

Bruce, Blanche Kelso (1841–1898).   Born into slavery in Virginia, Bruce escaped during the Civil War and opened a school in Kansas. In 1868 he went to Mississippi, where he joined the Republican Party and served as a sheriff and tax collector. After his election to the U.S. Senate in 1875, he worked to secure federal aid for rebuilding Mississippi's economy. He also championed the rights of Native Americans and Chinese immigrants. After his Senate term expired, Bruce held a number of government posts in Washington.

AN ERA OF ACHIEVEMENT

During the Reconstruction period (1865–1877), 1,510 African Americans are known to have held office on the national, state, and local levels. States with the largest number of black office-holders were South Carolina (316), Mississippi (226), Louisiana (210), North Carolina (187), Alabama (173), and Georgia (135). Nearly 700 African Americans served in state legislatures; 14 were elected to the U.S. House of Representatives; and 2 sat in the U.S. Senate. Apart from legislative service, the most commonly held positions for African Americans were justice of the peace/magistrate (232), city council member (146), registrar (116), county commissioner (113), and board of education member (79). Reconstruction governments in the South were responsible for significant social progress, creating the first state-supported public schools and establishing hospitals, orphanages, and asylums. The University of South Carolina was the only southern, white institution of higher learning to welcome black students; alternatively, the higher-education needs of African Americans were met by the creation of black colleges (see Chapter 7, "Education").

Bunche, Ralph Johnson (1904–1971).   Following graduate work at Harvard, Bunche headed the Department of Political Science at Howard University from 1928 to 1932, when he left to do independent research. During World War II he served in government intelligence posts and then took a position with the newly created United Nations. Bunche achieved international acclaim when he negotiated a cease-fire in the 1948 Arab-Israeli war, and his work was recognized with a Nobel Peace Prize in 1950. He later served as U.N. undersecretary for special political affairs (1957–1967) and then as undersecretary general (1968–1971).

Carmichael, Stokely (1941–1998).   Born in Trinidad, Carmichael came to the United States in 1952. He joined the civil rights movement while a student at Howard University. Heading a voter-registration project in Alabama in 1965, he boosted the number of black voters from 70 to 2,600 and built an all-black political organization, the Lowndes County Freedom Organization. Carmichael became director of SNCC in May 1966 and a month later made his famous Black Power speech, which changed the focus of the civil rights movement from nonviolence and integration to self-defense and black nationalism. Carmichael left SNCC in 1967 to join the Black Panther Party; in 1968, he became the Panther's prime minister. In 1973, he changed his name to Kwame Ture and took up residence in Ghana, becoming a vocal champion of Pan-Africanism. He moved to New Guinea in 1969, where he continued to champion Pan-Africanism until his death.

Chisholm, Shirley Anita St. Hill (1924–   ).   A New York native of Guyanese and Barbadian heritage, Chisholm worked as a teacher and educational consultant after graduating from Brooklyn College and Columbia University. She began her political career as a state assembly representative in 1964, and in 1968 she became the first African American woman to win election to the U.S. House of Representatives. Chisholm represented Brooklyn's Bedford-Stuyvesant district in Congress for the next 14 years, specializing in education, labor, veterans', and women's issues. She was a Democratic presidential candidate in 1972. After leaving Congress in 1983, she taught at Spelman and Mt. Holyoke colleges. In 1993, President Clinton offered Chisholm the post of ambassador to Jamaica, but she was forced to decline due to ill health.

Conyers, John (1929–   ).   Active in the Democratic Party since his student days at Wayne State University, Conyers was elected to the U.S. House of Representatives from Michigan in 1964. As a member of the House Judiciary Committee, Conyers has consistently worked for progress on civil rights, immigration, employment, and medical care. He was a major supporter of the Voting Rights Act of 1965, a founder of the Congressional Black Caucus, and a leading sponsor of the legislation that created the national holiday in honor of Rev. Martin Luther King Jr.

THE CONGRESSIONAL BLACK CAUCUS

In 1969, the nine African Americans serving in the U.S. House of Representatives began to hold informal meetings that were chaired by Representative Charles Diggs of Michigan. In January 1971, the group officially became the Congressional Black Caucus and established a legislative agenda addressing the needs of African Americans. The measures sponsored and championed by the caucus have included the Humphrey-Hawkins Full-Employment Act and the Public Works Employment Act (1977); the law establishing a Martin Luther King Jr. national holiday (1982); and the Anti-Apartheid Act (1986). In the 105th Congress, there were 38 members of the Congressional Black Caucus.

DePriest, Oscar Stanton (1871–1951).   A Chicago real-estate agent and Republican politician, DePriest became the first African American member of the Chicago City Council in 1915. He entered the U.S. Congress in 1929, the first black member of that body since Reconstruction and the first ever from outside the South. As a congressional representative, DePriest worked to get more federal jobs for African Americans and sponsored blacks for entry into the military academies. In 1934, he was unseated by Arthur A. Mitchell, a black Democrat.

Dinkins, David Norman (1927–   ).   After graduating from Howard University and Brooklyn Law School, Dinkins spent 20 years in private law practice in New York City. He became active in politics during the 1960s, eventually becoming the Democratic Party's district leader in Harlem. In 1972, Dinkins became the first African American president of the New York City Board of Elections; the following year, he was appointed deputy mayor for planning and development by Mayor Abraham Beame. In 1985, Dinkins was elected Manhattan borough president. Four years later, he was elected mayor, becoming the first African American in history to lead New York City. During his tenure in city hall, Dinkins was known as a conciliator; he earned widespread praise in 1992 for his successful effort to maintain civic calm in the wake of the Rodney King verdict in Los Angeles. After losing his bid for reelection in 1993, Dinkins accepted a professorship at Columbia University's School of International and Public Affairs.

Douglass, Frederick   (See Chapter 2, "Slavery and Freedom.")

Du Bois, William Edward Burghardt (1868–1963).   A sociologist by training, Du Bois was drawn into the political arena by his hatred of racism and his opposition to the accommodationist approach of Booker T. Washington. Rejecting Washington's Atlanta Compromise, he called for blacks to claim their rights, educate themselves, and assume positions of leadership within the community. In 1909, Du Bois was one of the principal founders of the Niagara Movement and the subsequent NAACP, and for the next 25 years, he edited NAACP's journal, *Crisis*. Between 1919 and 1945, Du Bois also organized five Pan-African congresses. A socialist since 1911, he joined the Communist Party in 1961. Harassed by the U.S. government, he moved to Ghana at the invitation of President Kwame Nkrumah to edit the *Encyclopedia Africana*, and died there two years later. His numerous publications include the classic studies *The Souls of Black Folk* (1903) and *Black Reconstruction in America* (1935).

Edelman, Marian Wright (1939–   ).   The daughter of a South Carolina minister and a graduate of Yale Law School, Edelman began her civil rights career working for the NAACP in Mississippi and also helped organize the Poor People's March on Washington in 1968. She headed Harvard University's Center for Law and Education from 1971 to 1973, when she founded and became president of the Children's Defense Fund. The author of *Families in Peril, The Measure of Our Success,* and other books, Edelman now ranks as the foremost advocate of children's rights and interests in the United States.

Evers, Medgar (1925–1963).   Evers was drawn into civil rights work while selling insurance in the impoverished Mississippi Delta region. He led economic boycotts to fight discrimination and became the NAACP field secretary for Mississippi in 1954. He was especially active in the state capital, Jackson, organizing numerous direct-action campaigns despite repeated beatings and jailings. On June 11, 1963, in the driveway of his own home, Evers was shot to death by a sniper. Thirty years later, Byron De La Beckwith, a member of a local white-supremacist organization, was convicted of the slaying, although he had been acquitted twice previously by all-white juries.

Farmer, James (1920–).   In 1942, Farmer and other Christian pacifists founded the Congress of Racial Equality (CORE) as an agency of nonviolent social change. Farmer organized the first sit-ins, directed against discrimination in Chicago restaurants, during 1947. He became CORE's national director in 1961 and took part in the first Freedom Rides. Farmer resigned from CORE in 1966 to head a national literacy project. From 1971 to 1981 he headed the Coalition of American Public Employees in Washington and also directed the Council on Minority Planning and Strategy. In 1981 he joined the faculty of Mary Washington College.

Farrakhan, Louis [né Louis Eugene Walcott] (1933–).   Born in New York City but raised in Boston in the Episcopal Church, Farrakhan spent two years at Winston-Salem Teachers College in North Carolina and then embarked on a successful career as a calypso singer. He joined the Nation of Islam in 1955 as Louis X and devoted himself to building the organization first with Malcolm X and then as Elijah Muhammad's principal aide. In 1978, after Muhammad's son directed the Nation of Islam away from black nationalism, renaming the organization the World Community of Al-Islam in the West, Farrakhan formed his own organization, also known as the Nation of Islam. Farrakhan's organization has undertaken numerous community development projects and has exerted an impact on the national scene, most notably in the Million Man March of 1995. At the same time, Farrakhan's effectiveness as a national leader of the African American community has often been marred by public controversy, mainly because of statements regarded as disparaging of Jews and of Judaism.

Forman, James (1928–).   After graduating from Roosevelt University in Chicago, Forman worked as a reporter for the *Chicago Defender* and began doing civil rights work in the South in 1960. After being beaten during a Freedom Ride, Forman joined SNCC and soon became executive secretary, guiding the organization during its formative years. In addition to organizing civil rights campaigns and protests, he was also an active opponent of U.S. military actions in Southeast Asia. After resigning his position at SNCC in 1966, Forman devoted his energies to black economic development. Among the organizations he founded were the National Black Economic Development Conference and Black Star Publications. Forman received a Ph.D. in 1982 and has published several books and articles, including an autobiography, *The Making of Black Revolutionaries* (1972).

Garvey, Marcus Mosiah (1887–1940).   Born in Jamaica, Garvey was a printer and trade unionist. In 1914, he founded the Universal Negro Improvement Association (UNIA) with the aim of promoting unity among peoples of African descent. In 1916, Garvey carried his message to the United States, and by 1919, the UNIA had 30 chapters and 2 million members. Garvey then announced the advent of a back-to-Africa movement and proposed to resettle African Americans in Liberia: To this end, UNIA purchased three ships and created the Black Star Line. When funds from subscribers vanished and the Black Star Line collapsed, the blame fell on Garvey. Though many people believed he was being framed, Garvey was convicted of mail fraud in 1925 and served two years in prison. Returning to Jamaica as a national hero, he concentrated on projects to benefit the Jamaican poor. In 1935, Garvey moved to England and continued to advocate Pan-African ideas until his death.

Hamer, Fannie Lou (1917–1977).   Hamer joined SNCC in 1962 as a Mississippi plantation worker and tried to register to vote. After losing her job—one she had held for almost 40 years—she became a SNCC field-worker in 1963. She helped found the Mississippi Freedom Democratic Party (MFDP), which challenged the all-white Mississippi delegation at the 1964 Democratic National Convention. Hamer left SNCC in 1966 when the organization embraced Black Power but remained active in the civil rights movement. In 1971, she helped found the National Women's Political Caucus.

Henry, Aaron (1922–1997).   The owner of a drugstore in Clarksdale, Mississippi, Henry was an active member of the NAACP and joined the fight against segregation in the 1950s. Known as Doc, he took part in many of the major civil rights struggles of the following decade, leading demonstrations, boycotts, and voter-registration drives. Henry served as president of the Mississippi NAACP from 1960 to 1993. He was also the founding chair of the MFDP in 1964 and later became a powerful force in the regular Democratic organization in Mississippi. In 1992, Henry was elected to the Mississippi State Legislature.

Houston, Charles   (See Chapter 12, "The Law.")

Jackson, Jesse Louis (1941–   ).   Jackson joined CORE while he was a student at North Carolina A&T. After graduating and becoming a Baptist minister, he took part in SCLC's 1965 voting-rights campaign and became an ally of Rev. Martin Luther King Jr. From 1966 to 1971, Jackson headed SCLC's Operation Breadbasket, pushing for greater economic opportunities for African Americans. Jackson founded People United to Save Humanity (PUSH) in 1971, fighting drugs, teenage pregnancy, and violence in the black community. He also worked for greater African American involvement in the political process. In both 1984 and 1988, Jackson made strong bids for the Democratic presidential nomination; his Rainbow Coalition won nine state primaries in 1988 and garnered 7 million votes. During the 1980s, Jackson began to play a prominent role on the world scene, negotiating the release of prisoners and hostages in the Middle East and in Cuba. In May 1999 he arranged the release of three U.S. soldiers held as prisoners of war in Yugoslavia.

> I was born in a slum, but the slum was not born in me. And it wasn't born in you, and you can make it. Wherever you are tonight, you can make it. Hold your head high, stick your chest out. You can make it. It gets dark sometimes, but the morning comes. Suffering breeds character. Character breeds faith. In the end, faith will not disappoint.
>
> Jesse Jackson, address at the Democratic National Convention (July 17, 1984)

Jackson, Maynard (1938–   ).   A graduate of Morehouse College and North Carolina College at Durham, Jackson began working as a lawyer with the National Labor Relations Board in Atlanta before moving to the Community Legal Services Center at Emory University, where he focused on representing the poor. Jackson was elected vice mayor of Atlanta in 1969, and four years later he became the city's first African American mayor. During his two terms in city hall, he worked to break down discrimination in hiring practices and the awarding of city contracts. Upon leaving office in 1982, Jackson went into private law practice and founded his own securities firm. He served a third term as mayor from 1989 to 1993, preparing Atlanta for the advent of the 1996 Olympic Games.

Jordan, Barbara Charline (1936–1996).   As a young lawyer in Houston, Jordan became the first African American women elected to the Texas State Senate (1966). She went on to become the first African American to serve as president pro tem of that body. In 1972, she was elected to the U.S. House of Representatives from Texas's 18th District, gaining nearly 85 percent of the vote. Jordan was the first black woman from the South to serve in the Congress. As a member of the House Judiciary Committee, Jordan gained wide recognition as an expert on constitutional issues and achieved national acclaim for her role in the committee's Watergate hearings. Diagnosed with multiple sclerosis, Jordan resigned from Congress in 1977 and accepted a teaching post at the University of Texas. She was awarded the Presidential Medal of Freedom in 1994.

Jordan, Vernon Eulion, Jr. (1935–   ).   Jordan served as field director for the Georgia branch of the NAACP from 1961 to 1963 and headed the Voter Education Project of the Southern Regional Council from 1964 to 1968, where he led the drive that registered over 2 million black voters. In 1970 he became executive director of the United Negro College Fund. As head of the Urban League from 1972 to 1981, Jordan emphasized issues such as full employment, voter registration, and national health coverage. In 1981 he went into private law practice but returned to public life in 1992–1993 as chair of

President-elect Clinton's transition team. He remained an advisor during both of President Clinton's terms.

Karenga, Maulana [née Ronald McKinley Everett] (1941–).   A graduate of UCLA, Karenga became involved in civil rights after the Watts riot of 1965, when he founded the cultural nationalist and social change organization, Us. Powerfully influenced by Pan-African ideas, he developed an Afrocentric philosophy called *Kawaida* and urged African Americans to embrace their ancestral heritage in all its aspects. Though best known for originating the yearly celebration of Kwanzaa in 1966 (see Chapter 5, "Family and Heritage"), which is based on the principles of Kawaida, Karenga also helped organize a number of Black Power conferences, most notably the 1967 conference in Newark, New Jersey, for which he wrote the mission statement. During the 1970s, Karenga earned the first of his two Ph.D. degrees. He currently chairs the Black Studies Department at California State University at Long Beach.

King, Martin Luther, Jr. (1929–1968).   Educated at Morehouse, Crozier Theological Seminary, and Boston University, Rev. King became pastor of the Dexter Avenue Baptist Church in Montgomery, Alabama, in 1954 and was chosen to lead the Montgomery bus boycott the following year. As the success of the boycott brought him national prominence, he formulated a strategy of nonviolent activism that he articulated in his book *Stride toward Freedom* (1958). In 1959, Rev. King moved to Atlanta to head the SCLC and also became copastor of the Ebenezer Baptist Church with his father, Rev. Martin Luther King Sr. During the early 1960s, the younger King emerged as the foremost leader of the civil rights movement and a figure of international stature. In 1963, after leading a massive campaign against segregation in Birmingham, Alabama, he delivered his historic "I Have a Dream" speech at the Lincoln Memorial in Washington. He was awarded the Nobel Peace Prize in 1964. Following up on the Civil Rights Act of 1964, Rev. King led civil rights campaigns in Selma, Alabama, and St. Augustine, Florida, and led the dramatic march from Selma to Montgomery. In 1966 he shifted his civil rights activities to the North, and the following year he denounced U.S. military activities in Vietnam. In 1968, Rev. King was assassinated in Memphis, Tennessee, where he had gone to support a strike by black sanitation workers.

> I have a dream that one day on the red hills of Georgia, sons of former slaves and the sons of former slaveowners will be able to sit down together at the table of brotherhood. I have a dream that my four little children will one day live in a nation where they will not be judged by the color of their skin, but by the content of their character. . . . And when that happens, and when we allow freedom to ring, when we let it ring from every state and every city, we will be able to speed up that day when all of God's children, black men and white men, Jews and Gentiles, Protestants and Catholics, will be able to join hands and sing the words of that old Negro spiritual: "Free at last! Free at last! Thank God almighty, we are free at last!"
>
> Reverend Martin Luther King Jr. speech during the March on Washington (August 28, 1963)

Lewis, John (1940–).   A leader of the Nashville Student Movement during the early 1960s, Lewis became a major ally of Rev. Martin Luther King Jr. and played a leading role in the Freedom Rides, the creation of SNCC, and the 1963 March on Washington. He served as chair of SNCC from 1963 to 1966. Lewis was elected to the Atlanta City Council in 1981. Since 1990, he has represented Georgia in the U.S. House of Representatives.

Lynch, John Roy (1847–1939).   Liberated from slavery in 1865, Lynch won election to the Mississippi House of Representatives in 1869 and became speaker of the house in 1872. In 1873 he began the first of three terms as a U.S. congressional representative. Lynch played an important role in the passage of the Civil Rights Act of 1875. In 1884, he delivered the keynote address at the Republican convention, marking the first time that an African American had filled that role for a major political party.

Marshall, Thurgood   (See Chapter 12, "The Law.")

Malcolm X (1925–1965).   While serving a prison term for burglary, Malcolm converted to Islam and changed his name from Malcolm Little to Malcolm X. Released in 1952, he began working with Elijah Muhammad and the Nation of Islam. By 1958, he was the organization's national spokesperson, condemning white society and advocating black nationalism. Growing friction with Elijah Muhammad prompted Malcolm to leave the Nation of Islam in 1964. He founded the Organization of Afro-American Unity and the Muslim Mosque, Inc., made a pilgrimage to Mecca, and took the name El-Hajj Malik El-Shabazz. By 1965, he had strengthened his ties with the World Islamic Community, the Organization of African Unity, and the Southern Civil Rights movement. He was shot and killed in February 1965 by assassins allegedly associated with the Nation of Islam.

Mays, Benjamin (1894–1984).   A Baptist minister and the sixth president of Morehouse College, Mays was an early opponent of segregation and a mentor to Martin Luther King Jr. He remained an unofficial senior advisor throughout Rev. King's career and delivered the eulogy at King's funeral. In 1970, Mays became the first African American president of the Atlanta school board.

McKissick, Floyd (1922–1991).   After desegregating the University of North Carolina Law School and receiving his degree in 1951, McKissick practiced law in Durham. He was named head of CORE's Durham chapter in 1962; four years later, he took over leadership of the organization and embraced Black Power. McKissick left CORE in 1968 to launch Soul City, a model town and industrial project near Raleigh.

Mfume, Kweisi (1948–   ).   Educated at Morgan State and Johns Hopkins, Mfume worked as an educator and broadcaster before his election to Congress from Maryland's 7th District in 1987. He served on the House Commission on Banking, Finance, and Urban Affairs and on the Joint Economic Commission. In 1993, when the 103rd Congress included 40 African American legislators (a record number), Mfume was chosen to chair the Congressional Black Caucus and emerged as an eloquent spokesperson for African American concerns. In 1996, he resigned from Congress to become president and CEO of the NAACP at a crucial time in the organization's history.

Moses, Robert Parris (1935–   ).   Though beaten and jailed several times, Moses carried on voter-registration work in Mississippi during the early 1960s and directed the Freedom Summer of 1964, when a thousand Northerners—mostly white college students—joined African American activists in Mississippi to help register black voters. In 1966 he left the United States to protest U.S. involvement in Vietnam. Moses lived and taught in Tanzania until 1977, when President Carter declared an amnesty for Vietnam-era draft resisters. Moses then founded the Algebra Project in Boston's public schools with the aid of a MacArthur Foundation grant. The innovative educational program is currently being used in a number of school systems throughout the country.

Muhammad, Elijah [né Robert Poole] (1897–1975).   The son of a Georgia sharecropper, Muhammad moved to Detroit in 1923 and worked for several years in an auto plant. In 1931, he adopted Islam and soon became the chief aide of Wallace Fard, the founder of the Nation of Islam. After Fard disappeared in 1934, Muhammad and his followers relocated to Chicago, where he established a temple and developed his own doctrine of black pride, solidarity, and self-help. In the fifties, with Malcolm's dedicated involvement, the Nation of Islam expanded to more than 100 temples. It created its own school system (the Clara Muhammad Schools, named after Elijah Muhammad's wife) and founded its newspaper, *Muhammad Speaks*. The organization also opened numerous businesses and acquired sizable assets. During the 1950s and 1960s, Muhammad's opposition to the civil rights movement and the goal of racial integration, which he regarded as "self-destruction, death, and nothing else," made the Nation of Islam a controversial and influential force on the national scene. He somewhat softened his antiwhite rhetoric in the late 1960s and early 1970s, while continuing to push his black-nationalist agenda.

Newton, Huey Percy (1942–1989).   In his teens, Newton moved from Louisiana to Oakland, California, where he earned a college degree, entered law school, and delved into community politics. Following an incident in 1964 he was convicted of assault with a deadly weapon and served six months in prison before being paroled. In concert with fellow student Bobby Seale, Newton developed a political stance that reflected the views of young, urban African Americans impatient with the slow progress of the civil rights movement and the failure of municipal authorities to deal with police misconduct in the black community. The Black Panther Party, founded by Newton and Seale in October 1966, advocated community control of key institutions, armed self-defense, and exemption of African Americans from military service. A crackdown on the Black Panthers by the FBI and local police departments led to several gun battles, and in 1967, Newton was jailed for killing a police officer. Two years later, he was granted a retrial and freed after two successive hung juries. Newton resumed studying and community organizing, earning a Ph.D. from the University of California, Santa Cruz, and spending time in Cuba. On August 22, 1989, Newton was found dead on an Oakland street, the victim of an unexplained shooting. In 1993, his widow, Fredrika Newton, and David Hilliard founded the Dr. Huey P. Newton Foundation to further his legacy.

Nixon, Edgar Daniel (1899–1987).   A Pullman porter by profession, Nixon headed the Alabama branch of the Brotherhood of Sleeping Car Porters during the 1920s and 1930s. He then served as president of the NAACP's Montgomery branch from 1939 to 1951. In that capacity he led the fight for voting rights and school desegregation in Alabama. In 1955, Nixon was instrumental in organizing the Montgomery bus boycott. His record of achievement earned him the nickname "Mr. Civil Rights."

Norton, Eleanor Holmes (1937–   ).   Norton became active in SNCC as a student at Yale and later founded the New Haven chapter of CORE. After graduating from Yale Law School in 1964, she worked for the American Civil Liberties Union until 1970, when she was appointed chair of the New York City Commission on Human Rights. In 1977, Norton joined the Equal Employment Opportunity Commission, reorganized that agency, and served as its head from 1979 to 1981. Since 1990, Norton has been the District of Columbia's delegate to the U.S. House of Representatives. She is also the president of the National Black Leadership Roundtable.

Powell, Adam Clayton, Jr. (1908–1972).   In 1937, Powell succeeded his father, Adam Clayton Powell Sr., as pastor of Harlem's Abyssinian Baptist Church. Carrying on the church's tradition of social activism, he pressured New York businesses to hire African Americans. Powell was elected to the city council in 1941 and went on to the U.S. House of Representatives in 1945. During his 11 terms in Congress, he desegregated the congressional dining facilities, secured the admission of African American journalists to the press galleries, fought racism in the armed forces, pushed for antilynching laws, and sponsored measures to deny federal funds to any organization practicing discrimination. As chair of the Education and Labor Committee from 1960 to 1967, Powell also championed antipoverty and minimum-wage legislation. Despite his contribution to the cause of civil rights, Powell's flamboyant lifestyle, absenteeism, and use of public funds for vacations gave his political enemies the excuse to expel him from Congress in 1967. He was elected to his seat in 1969 but was denied his 22 years of seniority. In 1972, after an unsuccessful re-election campaign, he died from cancer.

TAXATION WITHOUT REPRESENTATION

During the years 1870 to 1901, 22 African Americans served in the U.S. Congress—2 in the Senate and 20 in the House of Representatives. In the first half of the 20th century, however, as restrictions on black voters became more severe, only 4 African Americans were elected to Congress: William Dawson (Illinois), Adam Clayton Powell Jr. (New York), Charles Diggs (Michigan), and Robert N. C. Nix (Pennsylvania). Change came only after the Voting Rights Act of 1965 permitted a surge in black voter registration. The 1966 elections brought six black legislators to the U.S. House of Representatives; when the 103rd Congress convened in 1993, its members included 40 African Americans, the largest number in U.S. history.

Rainey, Joseph Hayne (1832–1887).   A former slave who deserted from the Confederate Navy during the Civil War, Rainey was elected to the U.S. House of Representatives in 1871. He was the first African American to serve as a U.S. congressional representative. During his eight years in the House, he presented petitions that called for equal rights for black citizens and the outlawing of segregation throughout the South. He also spoke out for the rights of Chinese immigrants in California and requested federal troops to protect African American voters who were being harassed.

Randolph, Asa Philip (1889–1979).   After graduating from New York's City College, Randolph organized black elevator operators in New York. A socialist, he was jailed during World War I for urging African Americans not to register for military service. Randolph then organized black railway porters, founding the Brotherhood of Sleeping Car Porters (BSCP) in 1925 and winning substantial raises and benefits for his members. As the United States prepared to enter World War II in 1941, Randolph vowed to lead 50,000 African Americans in a March on Washington unless the Roosevelt Administration acted to fight discrimination in war-related industries—his efforts brought about the creation of the Fair Employment Practices Commission. In 1955, Randolph joined the labor establishment as a vice president of the AFL-CIO, but he continued to pursue the struggle for civil rights. He was one of the main organizers of the 1963 March on Washington, and in 1965 he helped found the A. Philip Randolph Institute (APRI), which worked to bring more African Americans into the labor movement.

THE BLACK CABINET

In 1936, African American officials in the Roosevelt Administration formed an unofficial group variously known as the Black Cabinet, the Black Brain Trust, and the Federal Council on Negro Affairs. The members included Mary McLeod Bethune, Robert Weaver, Laurence Augustus Oxley, William Johnson Trent Jr., Eugene Kinckle Jones, and Frank S. Horne. The group did not hold regular meetings but convened when there was an issue on the table affecting the interests of African Americans. On the whole, the Black Cabinet had limited influence on the actions of the administration, and many of its members soon left the government in frustration. However, the Black Cabinet symbolized the emergence of African Americans on the national political scene and played a role in educating public officials on racial issues. It also laid the groundwork for future African American participation and influence in the Democratic Party.

Revels, Hiram Rhoades (1822–1901).   A minister and educator in Mississippi, Revels was appointed to fill a vacant U.S. Senate seat in 1870. As the first African American to serve in the Senate, he worked to integrate the District of Columbia schools and the naval shipyard in Baltimore. After his term expired, he became president of Alcorn State University and continued to advocate educational opportunities for African Americans.

Robeson, Paul   (See Chapter 15, "Performing Arts.")

Robinson, Randall (1941–   ).   After graduating from Harvard Law School in 1970, Robinson worked as a civil rights attorney in Boston and moved to Washington in 1975 to serve as a congressional staffer. His interest in Africa was sparked by a year in Tanzania on a Ford Fellowship and a fact-finding mission to South Africa with a congressional delegation. In 1977, Robinson was named executive director of TransAfrica, a political lobbying group focusing on human rights and democracy in Africa and the Caribbean. Under Robinson's leadership, TransAfrica played a pivotal role in the successful campaign to end apartheid in South Africa. In addition, Robinson has mobilized support for political freedom in Nicaragua, Grenada, and Angola, and he has vigorously lobbied for humane treatment of Haitian refugees.

Rustin, Bayard (1912–1987).   A revolutionary socialist in his early years, Rustin became an organizer for the Fellowship of Reconciliation in 1941 and helped recruit young people for A. Philip Randolph's March on Washington movement. The following year, Rustin assisted in founding CORE. A confirmed pacifist, he refused to register for military service during World War II and therefore spent three years in prison. During the 1950s and early 1960s, Rustin played a leading role in civil rights campaigns conducted by SCLC. He also helped found the A. Philip Randolph Institute. In addition to his civil rights activities, Rustin vigorously opposed U.S. military involvement in Southeast Asia during the late 1960s and played a major role organizing school boycotts in New York City.

Shuttlesworth, Fred Lee (1922–).   While serving as pastor of the Bethel Baptist Church in Birmingham, Alabama, Shuttlesworth organized the Christian Movement for Human Rights in 1956 and served as its president until 1969. He also helped create the SCLC, of which he was secretary from 1958 to 1970. Called "the most courageous civil rights fighter in the South" by Rev. King, Shuttlesworth took part in numerous civil rights battles, undaunted by beatings and firebomb attacks on his home. He later became pastor of a church in Cincinnati and director of the Shuttlesworth Housing Fund, which assists poor people in purchasing homes.

Stokes, Carl (1927–1996).   As a Cleveland lawyer during the 1950s, Stokes joined the NAACP and played an active role in the civil rights movement and local community affairs. In 1962 he was elected to the Ohio State Legislature, and five years later, he ran successfully for the mayoralty of Cleveland, becoming the first African American mayor of a major U.S. city. After leaving office in 1972, Stokes spent eight years as an anchor and correspondent for NBC News. In 1983, he was appointed to a judgeship on the Cleveland Municipal Court and remained in that post until 1995, when he became U.S. ambassador to the Seychelles.

Terrell, Mary Eliza Church (1863–1954).   A graduate of Oberlin College, Terrell began her civil rights activities in Washington, D.C., where her husband was a municipal judge. In 1892, she helped organize the National League for the Protection of Colored Women, and in 1896, she served as the first president of the National Association of Colored Women. Active in the women's suffrage movement, Terrell addressed numerous conferences in the United States and Europe. She also played a role in the founding of the NAACP and served as head of the organization's Washington chapter for many years. In 1949, when she was in her eighties, Terrell began taking part in sit-ins in Washington, and she witnessed the integration of the city's public facilities in 1953. She wrote numerous magazine articles, as well as an autobiography, *A Colored Woman in a White World* (1940).

Trotter, William Monroe (1872–1934).   After graduating magna cum laude from Harvard in 1895, Trotter started a real-estate firm in Boston. Concerned about the growth of racism in the United States and opposed to the accommodationist strategy of Booker T. Washington, Trotter became active in politics and civil rights activities. Along with George W. Forbes, he founded the Boston *Guardian*, which published its first issue in 1901. Known for his uncompromising attitude, Trotter was jailed for a month in 1903 after disrupting one of Washington's speeches. After taking part in the creation of the Niagara Movement in 1905, Trotter again went his own way, forming the National Equal Rights League as an alternative to the NAACP, then dominated by whites. Trotter was a highly visible public figure during the first two decades of the 20th century, leading protests against the racist film *The Birth of a Nation*, visiting the White House to criticize the racial policies of presidents Wilson and Coolidge, and opposing the Treaty of Versailles because it had no provision for racial equality. By the 1920s, his influence began to wane, but he continued to publish the *Guardian*, draining his personal assets to keep the paper going.

Washington, Booker Taliaferro (1856–1915).   Born into slavery, Washington graduated from Hampton Institute in 1875 and became a teacher. In 1881, he founded the Tuskegee Normal and Industrial Institute (now Tuskegee University) and assumed a leading role in African American education. Washington achieved national prominence in 1895 with his Atlanta Compromise speech, proposing that African Americans accept segregation in return for guarantees of economic progress. For the next 12 years, Washington was the officially recognized spokesperson for the African American community, dining in the White House with President Theodore Roosevelt and approving all black appointees to federal jobs. Nevertheless, Washington secretly financed court battles against segregation. His failure to protest

Roosevelt's harsh treatment of black soldiers in the Brownsville Affair of 1906 (see Chapter 12) severely damaged his standing in the African American community, however, and the rise of the NAACP significantly challenged his political influence.

Washington, Harold (1922–1987).   The son of a Chicago stockyard worker and Democratic Party precinct captain, Washington served in the army during World War II and then earned a degree from Roosevelt University. When his father died in 1953, Washington took over as captain of the Third Ward and proved to be a gifted organizer. As a member of the Illinois House of Representatives (1965–1976) and State Senate (1976–1980), he broke with the Democratic leadership, advocating a civilian review board for the Chicago police, organizing the Illinois Black Legislative Caucus, and supporting a number of civil rights measures. After serving in the U.S. House of Representatives from 1980 to 1982, Washington entered the Democratic mayoral primary in Chicago, upset two white candidates, and went on to become Chicago's first black mayor. Despite fierce opposition from the white-dominated Chicago city council, Washington was able to appoint a black police chief, increase minority hiring and business opportunities, outlaw political patronage, institute campaign-finance reform, and provide better services to black communities. A year after winning reelection to a second term, Washington suffered a fatal heart attack while working at his desk.

Weaver, Robert C. (1907–1997).   After earning a Ph.D. in economics from Harvard, Weaver became an aide to Secretary of the Interior Harold Ickes in the early days of the New Deal, served in the U.S. Housing Authority, and was a prominent member of Roosevelt's Black Cabinet. During World War II, he worked for a number of government agencies, specializing in housing, employment, and urban affairs. In 1966 he was appointed to head the Department of Housing and Urban Development, becoming the first African American to hold a cabinet post.

Wells-Barnett, Ida B. (1862–1931).   Following an impoverished childhood in Mississippi, Wells-Barnett attended Rust College and became a teacher and journalist in Memphis. Her attacks on segregation in the *Memphis Free Speech*, of which she was part owner, caused her to lose her teaching job. She then became an antilynching campaigner, writing for the *New York Age* and organizing antilynching organizations in New York, Boston, Washington, and other cities. Wells-Barnett also founded the first African American women's suffrage group and helped found the NAACP.

Wilder, Lawrence Douglas (1931–   ).   After earning a law degree from Howard University in 1959, Wilder practiced law in Richmond, Virginia, for 10 years and then ran successfully for the Virginia State Senate, becoming the first African American to serve in that body. During his 16 years as a senator, he supported numerous civil rights initiatives. Wilder was elected lieutenant governor in 1985 and governor in 1989, becoming the first elected black governor in U.S. history. He retired from Virginia politics after serving one term and returned to private law practice.

Wilkins, Roy Ottaway (1901–1981).   A native of Minnesota, Wilkins embarked on a career as a journalist and soon became involved in NAACP activities. He served as an assistant secretary of the organization in 1931 and in 1934 succeeded W. E. B. Du Bois as editor of *Crisis*. In 1955 he became executive secretary of the NAACP and guided the organization through the most eventful years of the civil rights movement, retiring in 1977. Throughout the civil rights era, Wilkins opposed direct action, a stance that put him at odds with Rev. Martin Luther King Jr. and a number of other civil rights leaders. He believed that more progress could be made through legislation, court action, and persuasion.

Williams, Hosea (1926–   ).   While working as a research chemist for the U.S. Department of Agriculture in the 1950s, Williams joined the NAACP in Savannah, Georgia. During the early 1960s, he organized voter-registration drives and joined SCLC's board of directors. As a result of his leadership during 1963 civil rights demonstrations, Savannah officials agreed to desegregate a number of public facilities. Williams then moved to Atlanta as a member of the SCLC staff and was involved in the major civil rights campaigns of the mid and late 1960s. In 1974 he was elected to the Georgia State Legislature and won a seat on the Atlanta city council in 1985. Still dedicated to civil rights, he led a 1987 march protesting racism and Ku Klux Klan activity in Georgia's Forsyth County.

Young, Andrew Jackson (1932–   ).   After becoming an ordained minister in the United Church of Christ, Young joined the SCLC in 1961 and became its executive director in 1964. He remained with the organization until 1970, when he resigned to enter politics. In 1972, Young won election to the U.S. House of Representatives, where he focused on civil rights and environmental issues. After playing an active role in President Jimmy Carter's 1976 election campaign, Young became the nation's first African American ambassador to the United Nations. In 1981 he ran successfully for the mayoralty of Atlanta and served two terms as the city's chief executive.

Young, Whitney Moore, Jr. (1921–1971).   Trained as a social worker, Young went to work for the Urban League in 1948. During the 1950s, he also served as dean of the School of Social Work at Atlanta University and studied at Harvard as a Rockefeller Foundation scholar. Young became executive director of the Urban League in 1961 and guided the organization for the next 10 years. A proponent of massive federal aid for social ills afflicting African American communities, he had a powerful influence in shaping the Johnson Administration's War on Poverty programs.

SOURCES FOR ADDITIONAL INFORMATION

Barnes, Catherine A. *Journey from Jim Crow: The Desegregation of Southern Transportation*. New York: Columbia University Press, 1983.

Branch, Taylor. *Parting the Waters: America in the King Years, 1954–1963*. New York: Simon & Schuster, 1988.

———. *Pillar of Fire: America in the King Years, 1963–1965*. New York: Simon & Schuster, 1997.

Du Bois, W. E. B. *Black Reconstruction in America, 1860–1880* (reprint). New York: Touchstone, 1992 (original 1935).

Foner, Eric. *Freedom's Lawmakers: A Directory of Black Officeholders during Reconstruction*, rev. ed. Baton Rouge: Louisiana State University Press, 1996.

———. *Reconstruction: America's Unfinished Revolution, 1863–1877*. New York: Harper & Row, 1988.

Garrow, David J. *Bearing the Cross: Martin Luther King, Jr., and the Southern Christian Leadership Conference, a Personal Portrait*. New York: Morrow, 1986.

Haines, Herbert H. *Black Radicals and the Civil Rights Movement, 1954–1970*. Knoxville: University of Tennessee Press, 1988.

Hampton, Henry, and Steve Fayer, with Sarah Flynn. *Voices of Freedom: An Oral History of the Civil Rights Movement from the 1950s through the 1980s*. New York: Bantam, 1990.

Kellogg, Charles F. *NAACP: A History of the National Association for the Advancement of Colored People*. Baltimore: Johns Hopkins University Press, 1967.

Lawson, Steven F. *Running for Freedom: Civil Rights and Black Politics in America Since 1941*. Philadelphia: Temple University Press, 1990.

Levy, Peter B., ed. *Documentary History of the Modern Civil Rights Movement*. Westport, CT: Greenwood, 1992.

Lewis, David Levering. *King: A Critical Biography*. New York: Praeger, 1970.

———. *W.E.B. DuBois: Biography of a Race*. New York: Holt, 1993.

Lowery, Charles D., and John F. Marszalek, eds. *Encyclopedia of the African-American Civil Rights Movement*. Westport, CT: Greenwood, 1992.

Luker, Ralph E., ed. *Historical Dictionary of the Civil Rights Movement*. Lanham, MD: Scarecrow, 1997.

McCartney, John T. *Black Power Ideologies: An Essay in African-American Political Thought*. Philadelphia: Temple University Press, 1992.

Myrdal, Gunnar. *An American Dilemma: The Negro Problem and American Democracy*. New York: Harper & Brothers, 1944.

Salmond, John A. *My Mind Set on Freedom: A History of the Civil Rights Movement, 1954–1968*. Lanham, MD: Ivan R. Dee, 1997.

Weisbrodt, Robert. *Freedom Bound: A History of America's Civil Rights Movement*. New York: Norton, 1990.

Wirt, Frederick M. *"We Ain't What We Was": Civil Rights in the New South*. Durham, NC: Duke University Press, 1997.

4

The Diaspora

The movement of Africans to the Americas brought on by the slave trade was one of the greatest forced migrations in human history. This dispersal of black peoples from their homes in Africa is also one of the grandest sagas of world history. This chapter offers a brief history of the many roles African Americans played in the exploration and settlement of what Europeans called "the New World," as well as statistics on immigration and population of the countries that make up the Americas, including the Caribbean.

AFRICANS AND THE MAKING OF THE AMERICAS

The greatest majority of Africans of the diaspora are in the Western Hemisphere, scattered among the Spanish-, French-, and English-speaking countries of the Americas. The role played by the peoples of African descent in the building of the Americas was not merely substantial but indispensable, prompting the historian Frank Tannenbaum, in his classic 1947 study *Slave and Citizen,* to describe the creation of contemporary American culture as a "joint Afro-European enterprise."

EXPLORATION

Africans traveled with some of the first European explorers of the Americas—an African man was Christopher Columbus's navigator on his first voyage of discovery—and some became famed explorers themselves. Although Spanish chronicles indicate that numerous Africans accompanied the conquistadors on their expeditions throughout the Americas, the Africans' names were rarely recorded. Among the exceptions was Estéban (also known as Estevanico or Little Stephen), a black African who been captured by North African slave traders and lived in Morocco before reaching Spain. Estéban played an important part in Pánfilo de Narváez's unsuccessful 1528 expedition to conquer Florida and was then shipwrecked off the Texas coast. After four years of captivity by local American Indians, only 4 of the party of 80 had survived, Estéban included. He was reunited with Álvar Núñez Cabeza de Vaca and 2 other survivors of the Narváez group. The 4 men began a long westward journey through what is now the southwestern United States; Estéban, who was gifted at languages and spoke more than a dozen Native American tongues, often served as an advance scout. In 1536, eight years after leaving Florida, the explorers finally reached the Pacific and the Spanish settlement of Culiacán. Three years later, the viceroy of New Spain dispatched Estéban and a Franciscan friar named Fray Marcos to explore California in search of the fabled Seven Cities of Cíbola. Estéban went ahead as an advance scout, erecting crosses along his route as a guide for Marcos. Most of the natives he encountered welcomed him, except for the Zuñi, who identified Estéban with a hostile neighboring tribe and put him to death.

Many other black pioneers followed in Estéban's footsteps as Spain established its presence in California. Of the 44 settlers who founded the pueblo of Nuestra Señora de Los Angeles (the precursor of present-day Los Angeles) in 1781, at least 26 were of African descent. By the end of the 18th century, nearly 20 percent of California's residents were black.

As the United States began pushing westward during the 19th century, African Americans were in the vanguard. In 1824, the African American trapper Peter Ranne was a member of the first U.S. party to reach California by an overland route, and the following year, Moses Harris became the first non–Native American to explore the Great Salt Lake. Legendary mountaineers

James Beckwourth and Edward Rose traversed much of what are now Montana, Idaho, Wyoming, and Colorado. In 1850, Beckwourth—an adopted member of the Crow people—located a pass through the Sierra Nevada, just north of present-day Reno, and led the first wagon train through it. The pass now bears his name.

MINING

The first great sources of wealth in the Americas were the gold, silver, and diamond mines of Mexico, Peru, and Brazil—their products, when shipped to Europe, fueled the growth of a mercantile capitalist economy. Many of the Africans coming to the Americas had lived in gold-mining areas such as Bambuk, Buré, or the Akan country of the Gold Coast, and they had considerable experience in shaft mining and panning for gold in waterways. Though they were usually outnumbered by Native Americans in the mines of Mexico and Bolivia, African miners were in great demand and were often granted special privileges. In the Minas Gerais region of Brazil, the opening of gold and diamond mines caused the enslaved population to rise from 20,000 in 1710 to 100,000 in 1735—in the 1750s, about 60 percent of the Africans arriving in the port of Salvador de Bahia were assigned to work in the mines of the interior. Work in the mines was brutally hard, and few men survived more than a dozen years. On the other hand, miners were often allowed to prospect on their own after meeting a specified quota; in this way, many black miners were able to accumulate enough capital to purchase their freedom.

In the United States, coal from eastern Virginia became an essential commodity during the late 18th century, and much of the mining was done by African Americans. A French traveler who visited a Virginia mine in 1796 reported that the owner knew little of the operation and depended on 500 enslaved miners to make the venture work. The Black Heath Pits, which produced the highest-quality coal in the region, employed large numbers of black men, who were often entrusted with the most difficult and complex tasks, such as operating the steam engines at the pitheads.

In 1858, a company of 600 African American gold miners made some successful strikes in California, only to find that new legislation deprived them of the right to own property or to give evidence in a court of law against whites, while requiring them to wear special badges that identified them as "coloreds." These newly wealthy miners organized an emigration society and moved to British Columbia, Canada, where the governor guaranteed them the rights and protections of all other citizens. (For more about African Canadians, see the following section on North America.)

HERDING

Residents of the vast savanna region of West Africa—notably the Mandinka, Wolof, Fulani, Hausa, and Nupe—began raising cattle at least as early as 4000 B.C. Those who came to the Americas played a crucial role in the development of livestock industries. Their expertise was essential because Europeans had no experience with the conditions presented by the Americas, where there was abundant land and a small labor force. Africans, on the other hand, were adept at managing large numbers of cattle with a limited number of herders. (The Fulani in particular have long been legendary for their ability to identify every member of a large herd and to know immediately whether an animal is missing.) Not surprisingly, Africans were in great demand in all areas of the Americas where ranching was a major activity, and they introduced the patterns of open grazing now practiced throughout the Americas. Both the harvesting of cattle and the cattle drive were adapted from African practices. In addition, Africans were the first to use artificial insemination in cattle breeding and to use cow's milk for human consumption.

Africans had tended cattle as slaves in the South, and slave owners brought them to Texas from other Southern states. In 1845, Texas had an estimated 100,000 whites and 35,000 slaves. By 1861, the state had 430,000 whites and 182,000 slaves.

After the Civil War, African Americans played a major though seldom acknowledged role in the American expansion into the West. After the Civil War, 5,000 black cowhands took part in the great cattle drives along the Chisholm Trail. Among them were Nat Love (also known as Deadwood Dick), Bronco Sam, Bill Pickett, One Horse Charley, George Glenn, and Bose Ikard, whose exploits matched those of the white cowhands and gunslingers so familiar to the general public. In addition, a number of familiar western terms have been traced back to African origins. *Bronco*, which means "rough" or "crude" in contemporary Spanish, derives from an African-language term and was first used to denote African cattle hands. *Dogie*, the cowpuncher's term for a motherless calf, derives from the Kimbundu words *kidogo* (a little something) and *dodo* (small). Some Texas ranches had all-black crews, and as many as 25 percent of the cowhands working trail drives north were African American. There are many African American cowhands today, and some 20,000 are members of The National Black Cowboys Association.

AGRICULTURE

From the establishment of the various American colonies, there was a pressing need for African agricultural skills. Africans from the coastal regions were especially adept at clearing and cultivating large tracts of forest land, an expertise unknown to Europeans. (A time-honored African technique involved burning carefully delineated sections of forest and then using the ash as fertilizer.) Africans also knew how to raise crops in tropical and semitropical soils, where high temperatures and heavy rains cause nutrients to leach out far more quickly than they do in temperate climates.

A prime example of African technology was the complex art of rice cultivation, practiced for centuries by many West African peoples but unknown to Europeans outside of southern Italy. As they tried to sustain themselves in areas such as Florida, Louisiana, and South Carolina, European settlers specifically sought out Africans with rice-growing skills. Rice cultivation was also among the most difficult kinds of work to do, with many of the enslaved workers forced to work in knee-deep water every day. South Carolina soon became the rice-growing center of North America, and by 1750, rice was the colony's major export. The African American tradition of rice cultivation still prevails in parts of the South Carolina lowlands, where many growers use tools and techniques derived from Africa.

Other familiar American crops introduced by Africans include peanuts, black-eyed peas, pumpkins, sesame seeds, kola nuts, cotton, yams, sorghum, muskmelons, and watermelons. In more general terms, agricultural staples produced mainly by African and African American labor—sugar, tobacco, cotton, coffee, and others—added incalculably to the wealth and economic development of both the Americas and Europe.

BOATBUILDING AND SEAFARING

Africans living near the water built a variety of canoes for fishing, shipping, and travel, ranging from one-person boats to larger vessels that could hold 100 passengers. Carved from massive tree trunks, these canoes could easily navigate shallow waterways and were highly stable and maneuverable in heavy surf. In the Americas, vessels known as *periaugas*, or *pettiaugers*, were essential to short-range water transportation throughout the southern United States and the Caribbean. These essential crafts were an amalgam of African, Native American, and European skills, combining carved-out hulls with European-style rigging and sails.

As the economies of the Americas developed, local water travel often became the province of African Americans, who hauled produce and supplies up and down the U.S. coast and from island to island in the West Indies. On some of the Caribbean islands, a significant portion of the enslaved workforce followed the sea—16 percent in the Bahamas and 14 percent on Nevis. In South Carolina, during the 18th century, about 9 percent of enslaved African Americans were mariners, and a full 25 percent of those who escaped bondage were seafarers by trade. This trend carried over into the early part of the 19th century. During the 1820s, about 2,500 black seafarers shipped out of New York City each year, and during the 1840s, there were about 700 African American officers and harpooners in the crews of New England whaling ships. These men played an important role in the African American community, carrying ideas and news from one part of the Americas to another.

NORTH AMERICA

UNITED STATES

Population: 267,839,000

Approximately 12 percent of the U.S. population, or about 32 million people, is African American.

Since the arrival of the first Africans in Virginia in 1619 and throughout colonial and U.S. history, the black population has never been static. Migrations, wars, and social change have been reflected in changing African American demographics. The following statistics reflect the dramatic changes in the black population of the United States over time, as well as its relationship to other parts of American society.

Table 4.1 U.S. African American Population, 1790–1998

Decade	Total Black	Enslaved Population	Free Population	Total U.S. Population	% Black
1790	757,208	697,624	59,557	3,929,214	19.27
1800	1,002,037	893,602	108,435	5,308,483	18.88
1810	1,377,808	1,191,362	186,446	7,239,881	19.03
1820	1,771,656	1,538,022	233,634	9,638,453	18.38
1830	2,328,612	2,009,043	319,599	12,866,020	18.10
1840	2,873,648	2,487,355	386,293	17,069,453	16.84
1850	3,638,808	3,204,313	434,495	23,191,846	15.69
1860	4,441,830	3,953,760	488,070	31,443,321	14.13
1870	4,880,009			38,558,371	12.66
1880	6,580,793			50,155,783	13.12
1890	7,488,676			62,947,714	11.90
1900	8,833,994			75,991,575	11.62
1910	9,827,763			91,972,266	10.69
1920	10,463,131			105,710,620	9.90
1930	11,891,143			122,775,046	9.69
1940	12,865,518			131,669,275	9.77
1950	15,042,286			150,697,361	9.98
1960	18,871,831			179,323,175	10.52
1970	22,580,289			203,211,920	11.11
1980	26,495,000			226,546,000	11.70
1990	29,986,000			248,710,000	12.06
1998	31,912,000			265,284,000	12.02

Source: Encyclopedia of African American Culture and History, V, pp. 3019–20.

Table 4.2 Top Ten Cities in African American Population, 1820–1990

City	Black Population	Total Population	% Black
1820			
1. Baltimore	14,192	62,738	22.62
2. Charleston	14,127	24,780	57.01
3. District of Columbia	10,425	33,039	31.55
4. New York	10,086	123,706	8.15
5. Philadelphia	8,785	63,802	13.77
6. New Orleans	8,515	14,175	60.07
7. Richmond	5,622	12,067	46.59
8. Savannah	3,657	7,523	48.61
9. St. Louis	2,035	10,049	20.25
10. Boston	1,737	42,536	4.08
1860			
1. Baltimore	27,898	212,418	13.13
2. New Orleans	24,074	168,675	14.27
3. Philadelphia	22,185	562,529	3.94
4. Charleston	17,146	40,522	42.31
5. District of Columbia	14,316	75,080	19.07
6. Richmond	14,275	37,910	37.65
7. New York	12,472	805,658	1.55
8. Savannah	8,417	22,292	37.76
9. Mobile	8,404	29,258	28.72
10. Donaldsonville, LA	7,544	11,484	65.69
1900			
1. District of Columbia	86,702	278,718	31.11
2. Baltimore	79,258	508,957	15.57
3. New Orleans	77,714	287,104	27.07
4. Philadelphia	62,613	1,293,697	4.84
5. New York	60,666	3,437,202	1.76
6. Memphis	49,910	102,320	48.78
7. Louisville	39,139	204,731	19.12
8. Atlanta	35,727	89,872	39.75
9. St. Louis	35,516	575,238	6.17
10. Richmond	32,230	85,050	37.90
1920			
1. New York	152,467	5,620,048	2.71
2. Philadelphia	134,229	1,823,799	7.30
3. District of Columbia	109,966	437,571	25.13
4. Chicago	109,458	2,701,705	4.05
5. Baltimore	103,322	733,826	14.08
6. New Orleans	100,930	387,219	26.07
7. Birmingham	70,230	178,806	39.28
8. St. Louis	69,854	772,897	9.04
9. Atlanta	62,796	200,616	31.30
10. Memphis	61,181	162,351	37.68
1940			
1. New York	458,444	7,454,995	6.15
2. Chicago	277,731	3,396,808	8.18

Table 4.2 (continued)

City	Black Population	Total Population	% Black
1940			
3. Philadelphia	251,880	1,931,334	13.04
4. District of Columbia	187,226	663,091	28.24
5. Baltimore	165,843	859,100	19.30
6. Detroit	149,119	1,623,452	9.19
7. New Orleans	149,034	494,537	30.14
8. Memphis	121,498	292,942	41.48
9. Birmingham	108,938	267,583	40.71
10. St. Louis	108,765	816,048	13.33
1960			
1. New York	1,087,931	7,781,984	13.98
2. Chicago	812,637	3,550,404	22.89
3. Philadelphia	529,240	2,002,512	26.43
4. Detroit	482,223	1,670,144	28.87
5. District of Columbia	411,737	763,956	53.90
6. Los Angeles	334,916	2,479,015	13.51
7. Baltimore	325,589	939,024	34.67
8. New Orleans	233,514	627,525	37.21
9. Houston	215,037	938,219	22.92
10. St. Louis	214,377	750,026	28.58
1990			
1. New York	2,102,512	7,322,564	28.71
2. Chicago	1,087,711	2,783,726	39.07
3. Detroit	777,916	1,027,974	75.67
4. Philadelphia	631,936	1,585,577	39.86
5. Los Angeles	487,674	3,485,398	13.99
6. Houston	457,990	1,630,553	28.09
7. Baltimore	435,768	736,014	59.21
8. District of Columbia	399,604	606,900	65.84
9. Memphis	334,737	610,337	54.84
10. New Orleans	307,728	496,938	61.92

Source: Encyclopedia of African American Culture and History, V,
pp. 3019–20.

SAMPLING AND THE CENSUS

In reviewing the national census of 1990, the U.S. Census Bureau concluded that it had missed more than 10 million people and significantly undercounted the minority population. (The largest single group affected were black and Hispanic men age 30 to 34, who were undercounted by an estimated 14%.) Such errors can have serious political consequences, affecting the boundaries of legislative districts and the apportionment of seats in the U.S. House of Representatives. In order to obtain a more accurate count in the 2000 Census, the bureau proposed to use sophisticated sampling techniques similar to those used in opinion polls.

Table 4.3 African American Population by Region, 1790–1990

Year	Region	Black Population in Region	Total Population of Region	% of U.S. Black Population in Region	% of Regional Population Black
1790	Northeast	67,120	1,968,040	8.86	3.41
	Midwest	0	0	0.00	0.00
	Southeast	690,061	1,961,174	91.13	35.19
	South Central	0	0	0	0
	Mountain	0	0	0	0
	Pacific	0	0	0	0
1810	Northeast	102,237	3,486,675	7.42	2.93
	Midwest	7,072	292,107	0.51	2.42
	Southeast	1,226,254	3,383,481	89.00	36.24
	South Central	42,245	77,618	3.07	54.43
	Mountain	0	0	0	0
	Pacific	0	0	0	0
1830	Northeast	125,214	5,542,381	5.38	2.26
	Midwest	41,543	1,610,473	1.78	2.58
	Southeast	2,030,870	5,461,721	87.21	37.18
	South Central	131,015	246,127	5.63	53.23
	Mountain	0	0	0	0
	Pacific	0	0	0	0
1850	Northeast	149,762	8,626,851	4.12	1.74
	Midwest	135,607	5,403,595	3.73	2.51
	Southeast	2,983,661	8,042,361	82.00	37.10
	South Central	368,537	940,251	10.13	39.20
	Mountain	72	72,927	0.00	0.10
	Pacific	1,169	105,891	0.03	1.10
1870	Northeast	179,738	12,298,730	3.68	1.46
	Midwest	273,080	12,981,111	5.60	2.10
	Southeast	3,680,957	10,258,055	75.43	35.88
	South Central	739,854	2,029,965	15.16	36.45
	Mountain	1,555	315,385	0.03	0.49
	Pacific	4,825	675,125	0.10	0.71
1890	Northeast	269,906	17,406,969	3.60	1.55
	Midwest	431,112	22,410,417	5.76	1.92
	Southeast	5,382,487	15,287,076	71.88	35.21
	South Central	1,378,090	4,740,983	18.40	29.07
	Mountain	12,971	1,213,935	0.17	1.07
	Pacific	14,110	1,920,334	0.19	0.73
1910	Northeast	484,176	25,868,573	4.93	1.87
	Midwest	543,498	29,888,542	5.53	1.82
	Southeast	6,765,001	20,604,796	68.84	32.83
	South Central	1,984,426	8,784,534	20.19	22.59
	Mountain	21,467	2,633,517	0.22	0.82
	Pacific	30,195	4,448,304	0.31	0.68
1930	Northeast	1,146,985	34,427,091	9.65	3.33
	Midwest	1,262,234	38,594,100	10.62	3.27
	Southeast	7,079,626	25,680,803	59.54	27.57
	South Central	2,281,951	12,176,830	19.19	18.74

Table 4.3 (continued)

Year	Region	Black Population in Region	Total Population of Region	% of U.S. Black Population in Region	% of Regional Population Black
	Mountain	30,225	3,701,789	0.25	0.82
	Pacific	90,122	8,622,047	0.76	1.05
1950	Northeast	2,018,182	39,477,986	13.42	5.11
	Midwest	2,227,876	44,460,762	14.81	5.01
	Southeast	7,793,379	32,659,516	51.81	23.86
	South Central	2,432,028	14,537,572	16.17	16.73
	Mountain	66,429	5,074,998	0.44	1.31
	Pacific	507,043	15,114,964	3.37	3.35
1970	Northeast	4,344,153	49,040,703	19.24	8.86
	Midwest	4,571,550	56,571,633	20.25	8.08
	Southeast	8,959,787	43,474,807	39.68	20.61
	South Central	3,010,174	19,320,560	13.33	15.58
	Mountain	180,382	8,281,562	0.80	2.18
	Pacific	1,514,243	26,522,631	6.71	5.71
1990	Northeast	5,613,222	50,809,229	18.72	11.05
	Midwest	5,715,940	59,668,632	19.06	9.58
	Southeast	11,900,363	58,725,137	39.69	20.26
	South Central	3,718,126	26,702,793	12.40	13.92
	Mountain	373,584	13,658,776	1.25	2.74
	Pacific	2,454,426	39,127,306	8.19	6.27

Sources: U.S. Bureau of the Census Release, 1991; and *Statistical Abstract,* 1990.

THE GREAT MIGRATION

Tens of thousands of African Americans seeking a better life left the South in the decades following the Civil War—including 50,000 "Exodusters" who settled in Kansas between 1878 and 1881. This movement reached epic proportions around 1915, when the escalation of World War I in Europe spurred an economic boom in the United States, creating a host of industrial jobs in the Northern cities. Between 1915 and 1930, at least 1.25 million African Americans relocated to the North. Settling in cities such as New York, Chicago, Cleveland, and Detroit, they opened a new chapter in African American history and transformed the social landscape of urban America. The Great Migration slowed during the 1930s as the nation's economy sank into depression, but African Americans started moving north again during World War II and continued to do so during the 1950s and 1960s. In 1910, 75 percent of African Americans had lived in rural areas, and nearly 90 percent had lived in the South; by 1960, more than 75 percent lived in cities, and only 60 percent remained in the South. As of 1994, the percentage of African Americans in the South had dropped to 55 percent; 17 percent of the black population lived in the Northeast, 20 percent in the Midwest, and 8 percent in the West.

POPULATION TRENDS

In 1998, 12 percent of the U.S. population was African American, numbering more than 31 million. The African American population increased an average of 1.5 percent per year between 1980 and 1998, compared with 0.9 percent for both the white population and the total population. Projections indicate that in the year 2025, there will be nearly 48 million African Americans, 14 percent of a total U.S. population of 335 million.

Table 4.4 Projections of U.S. Population, by Age, Sex, and Race, 2000–2025 (in thousands)

Age, Sex, and Race	Population				% Distribution			
	2000	2005	2010	2025	2000	2005	2010	2025
TOTAL	274,634	285,981	297,716	335,050	100.0	100.0	100.0	100.0
Under 5 years old	18,987	19,127	20,012	22,498	6.9	6.7	6.7	6
5 to 13 years old	36,043	35,850	35,605	40,413	13.1	12.5	12.0	12
14 to 17 years old	15,752	16,986	16,894	17,872	5.7	5.9	5.7	5
18 to 24 years old	26,258	28,268	30,138	30,372	9.6	9.9	10.1	9
25 to 34 years old	37,233	36,306	38,292	43,119	13.6	12.7	12.9	12
35 to 44 years old	44,659	42,165	38,521	42,391	16.3	14.7	12.9	12
45 to 54 years old	37,030	41,507	43,564	36,890	13.5	14.5	14.6	11
55 to 64 years old	23,962	29,606	35,283	39,542	8.7	10.4	11.9	11
65 to 74 years old	18,136	18,369	21,057	35,425	6.6	6.4	7.1	10
75 to 84 years old	12,315	12,898	12,680	19,481	4.5	4.5	4.3	5
85+ years old	4,259	4,899	5,671	7,046	1.6	1.7	1.9	2
Male	134,181	139,785	145,584	164,119	48.9	48.9	48.9	49
Female	140,453	146,196	152,132	170,931	51.1	51.1	51.1	51
BLACK, TOTAL	35,454	37,734	40,109	47,539	100.0	100.0	100.0	100.0
Under 5 years old	3,127	3,244	3,454	3,964	8.8	8.6	8.6	8
5 to 13 years old	5,727	5,813	5,962	6,990	16.2	15.4	14.9	14
14 to 17 years old	2,414	2,735	2,737	3,104	6.8	7.2	6.8	6
18 to 24 years old	3,966	4,233	4,674	5,053	11.2	11.2	11.7	10
25 to 34 years old	5,172	5,212	5,489	6,514	14.6	13.8	13.7	13
35 to 44 years old	5,649	5,499	5,236	6,017	15.9	14.6	13.1	12
45 to 54 years old	4,111	4,909	5,326	5,007	11.6	13.0	13.3	10
55 to 64 years old	2,406	2,995	3,801	4,865	6.8	7.9	9.5	10
65 to 74 years old	1,675	1,781	2,033	3,901	4.7	4.7	5.1	8
75 to 84 years old	890	959	1,002	1,582	2.5	2.5	2.5	3
85+ years old	317	354	396	541	0.9	0.9	1.0	1
Male	16,811	17,874	18,981	22,473	47.4	47.4	47.3	47
Female	18,643	19,860	21,129	25,066	52.6	52.6	52.7	52

Source: U.S. Bureau of the Census, Current Population Reports, P25-1130.

CANADA

Population: 30,287,000

As of 1993, there were only 460,000 Canadians of African descent, but the peoples of the diaspora have a long historical association with Canada.

Enslaved Africans first arrived in New France in 1628, but slavery was never widespread. When the British wrested control of Canada from France in 1763, there were only about 1,000 black slaves in the country. The black population increased dramatically during the American Revolution, when tens of thousands of Loyalists fled the colonies to Canada, bringing their slaves with them. By 1800, Canadian authorities began to discourage slaveholding, and the practice effectively came to an end by 1820. As a result, Canada became a haven for many U.S. blacks, and perhaps as many as 30,000 African Americans who escaped via the Underground Railroad eventually migrated to Ontario (then known as Upper Canada, or Canada West).

CANADIAN AFRICAN AMERICAN COLONIES

Because slavery was essentially nonexistent in Canada by 1820, the region became home to a number of well-known communities created to provide security and economic advancement for blacks, many of whom had escaped from bondage in the United States.

Wilberforce

Founded in 1829 as a refuge for free blacks seeking respite from racial strife in Cincinnati, Wilberforce occupied 800 acres on the shores of Lake Huron. The colony's population numbered only 200 at its highest point, with another 800 free blacks settled nearby in the Lucan-Biddulph area. Lacking sufficient financing and support, Wilberforce disbanded in 1836.

Dawn

Hiram Wilson and a group of white trustees founded Dawn (officially known as the British-American Institute) at Chatham, Ontario, in 1842. The institute began modestly as a vocational school for escaped slaves and had only 12 students in its first class. With the encouragement of black abolitionists such as Josiah Henson, 500 free blacks eventually settled around the institute, occupying 1,500 acres and operating sawmills, a brickyard, and other businesses. The cohesion of the colony was fatally damaged by factionalism, poor management, and religious disputes, and by 1861, Dawn was in disarray.

Elgin

In 1849, William King freed the 14 slaves he had inherited from his late wife's estate and founded the Elgin colony near Chatham. Comprising 9,000 acres, Elgin grew to contain 300 families and had schools, a variety of businesses (including a shingle factory), a hotel, and a post office. The community had 5,000 acres of land under cultivation and 800 head of livestock. Though it was carefully planned out and well financed by means of a stock company, Elgin began to decline with the onset of the Civil War and issued its last report in 1873.

Refugee Home Society

This colony was founded near Amherstburg, Ontario, in 1851 by a black Methodist cleric, T. Willis, and a group of Detroit backers. At its height, the colony had 150 inhabitants, but it dissolved around 1860 due to factional disputes.

The largest wave of black refugees came to Canada during the 1850s. This coincided with the passage of the Fugitive Slave Act in the United States, which required that escaped slaves be captured and returned to their Southern masters. Between the years 1850 and 1852, 5,000 to 6,000 fugitive slaves made their way to Canada, and it was estimated in 1851 that some 30,000 runaways had settled there. The Canadian reaction to these refugees was generally positive. Efforts were made to integrate schools, churches, and other institutions, and when The North American Convention of Colored Freemen met in 1851 in Toronto, they declared "that the British government was the most favorable in the civilized world to the people of color." Black-owned businesses flourished in Canadian cities, as did black newspapers, debating societies, chorales, and other associations. Mixed audiences welcomed the talents of such singers as "The Black Swan," Miss Eloise Greenfield. Blacks were among the first class enrolled in the University of Toronto, and one of the most distinguished young men of the period was Dr. Anderson Ruffin Abbott, a second-generation black Canadian, who was acting resident physician of Toronto General Hospital and, later, county coroner.

After the end of the U.S. Civil War, about 75 percent of Ontario's black settlers returned to the United States, and Canada's black population remained small. This did not, however, prevent the growth of virulent discrimination. As early as the middle of the 19th century, both

Nova Scotia and Ontario had created segregated school systems, and segregation was enforced in various public facilities throughout the country. During the early 20th century, the Ku Klux Klan moved north and achieved a solid foothold in many Canadian communities, creating 119 separate chapters. The situation did not improve until World War II, when the Canadian Army—after some initial reluctance—began to accept black recruits. A number of African Americans from the United States went north to enlist, believing they would be treated more fairly in the Canadian forces. Ontario promulgated its first civil-rights law in 1944, and in the following years other provinces—as well as the national government—followed suit with similar legislation.

Despite these moves toward racial equality, the Canadian government had made it nearly impossible for black immigrants to gain admission to the country. A tiny breach in this wall of exclusion opened in 1955, when Canada agreed to admit 100 female domestics each year from Jamaica and Barbados. The quota was raised to 300 in 1960, and a few years later, Canada began admitting immigrants on a merit system, without racial restrictions. At this point, large-scale immigration from the West Indies began. According to 1990 immigration figures, 74 percent of Canada's Caribbean immigrants reside in Ontario (mainly in the Toronto-London-Kingston area), 9.1 percent in Quebec, and 15.9 percent in other provinces, notably New Brunswick and Nova Scotia. In addition, census figures for the first five months of 1991 list 166,200 continental Africans as legal residents of Canada.

In Toronto, West Indian newcomers (along with immigrants from Asia and Latin America) have helped to transform a staid, predominantly Anglo-Saxon city into a vibrant cosmopolitan center.

Table 4.5 Caribbean-Born Population
of Canada, 1992

Jamaica	102,440
Guyana	66,055
Trinidad and Tobago	49,385
Haiti	39,880
Barbados	14,820
All others	37,005
Total	309,585

Source: Henry, *The Caribbean Diaspora in Toronto.*

THE CARIBBEAN

(Note: Population figures are for 1997 and were taken from the *1998 Encyclopædia Britannica Book of the Year.*)

ANGUILLA

Population: 10,424

In 1967, Anguilla joined with St. Kitts and Nevis to form a self-governing entity but quickly withdrew after claiming political and economic discrimination. The island attempted to become an independent republic in 1969, leading to an invasion by British troops. Anguilla became a British dependency in 1971, but the constitution of 1980 gave Anguillans substantial control over their internal affairs. Fishing, livestock, and salt mining are currently mainstays of Anguilla's economy, along with a growing tourist trade.

ANTIGUA AND BARBUDA

Population: 64,500

The English colonized Antigua in 1632, importing African slaves to tobacco and sugar-cane plantations. Barbuda was colonized by the English in 1678; the colonizers had intended to set up a slave-breeding colony, but, instead, Barbuda's slaves became self-reliant sailors, hunters, and fishers who owned the land on Barbuda communally. In 1834 the slaves of Antigua were emancipated. Antigua (with Barbuda) was administratively a part of the British colony of the Leeward Islands from 1871 until 1958, when Antigua joined the West Indies Federation. After that federation was dissolved in 1962, Antigua entered into free association with Great Britain in 1967, a relation under which Antigua received the right of self-government in all its internal affairs. Antigua and Barbuda achieved independence from Great Britain in 1981. The sugar industry declined steadily after the abolition of slavery, and no sugar has been produced on the island since the mid-1980s. Tourism is now the major industry.

THE BAHAMAS

Population: 287,000

Many Bahamians are descended from slaves who accompanied British Loyalists fleeing the Mid-Atlantic states during the American Revolution. Many of the newcomers labored on cotton plantations, but cotton cultivation died out soon after the abolition of slavery. The islands have enjoyed internal self-government since 1964. In the 1967 elections, black Bahamians gained control of their nation for the first time, as the Progressive Liberal Party ousted the white-dominated United Bahamian Party. The Bahamas' first black prime minister, Lynden Oscar Pindling, remained in office from 1967 to 1992; during his tenure the Bahamas achieved independence within the British Commonwealth and prospered through the promotion of tourism and offshore banking services.

BARBADOS

Population: 265,000

During the slave-trade era, Barbados had a population with the highest concentration of enslaved persons in the Americas. Conditions changed little for black Barbadians ("Bajans") after emancipation, as the island's white planter elite kept wages at the lowest level of any British Caribbean island. Beginning in 1905, about 20,000 Bajans migrated to Panama to work on the Panama Canal; many of those who returned used their earnings to buy land or start small businesses. Electoral reforms in 1943 and 1950 greatly increased the number of black voters, and the island slowly moved toward self-government. Full independence came in 1966, and the government of Prime Minister Errol Barrow developed the economy by promoting tourism, which is now the island's main employer. Barbados instituted universal free education shortly after independence, an achievement in which Bajans take considerable pride. They also pride themselves on having produced some of the West Indies' finest cricketers.

BERMUDA

Population: 62,099

About three fifths of Bermuda's population is descended from African slaves brought to Bermuda before Britain outlawed the slave trade in 1807. Whites include the British and the descendants of Portuguese laborers who migrated in the mid-19th century. The Spanish were the first Europeans to reach Bermuda, around 1503, but it was chartered by the Virginia Company in 1612, when 60 English settlers were sent to colonize the islands. Native American and African slaves were transported to Bermuda beginning in 1616, and by 1834, when slavery was abolished in Bermuda, the slave population outnumbered the white settlers. Before becoming a tourist destination in the 20th century, Bermuda was a warehouse port for Confederate blockade-runners during the Civil War, and for American rumrunners during Prohibition. The first Bermudan political party, the Progressive Labor Party, organized in 1963, claimed to represent the nonwhite citizens and advocated total independence from Britain. Despite the Progressives' efforts and the island's black majority, however, the white-led United Bermuda Party has been able to maintain control over the government. This situation led to considerable unrest, particularly in 1973 when the governor, Sir Richard Sharples, was assassinated. Extensive rioting in 1977 ended in official efforts to end racial discrimination and to begin independence talks, but a majority of Bermudans have continued to oppose independence. Despite problems relating to overpopulation and a growing drug trade, tourism and financial services have brought Bermudans one of the highest per-capita incomes in the world.

BRITISH VIRGIN ISLANDS

Population: 13,195

The British Virgin Islands are made up of more than 30 separate islands, only half of them inhabited. Tortola, Anegada, Virgin Gorda, and Jost Van Dyke are the principal islands, and they were acquired by the British from the Dutch in 1666. The great majority of British Virgin Islanders are the descendants of African slaves. In the 17th century, the islands were a popular destination for pirates, and Dutch buccaneers held Tortola until 1666, when English planters took possession and set up slave-based sugar plantations. Tortola was later made one of the British Leeward Islands in 1672. From 1872 to 1956, the islands were members of the Colony of the Leeward Islands, and then became the colony of the British Virgin Islands. The colony was given a ministerial form of government in 1967, which was continued under the new constitution of 1977. Tourism and offshore banking dominate the economy.

CAYMAN ISLANDS

Population: 34,646

The islands of Grand Cayman, Little Cayman, and Cayman Brac compose the Cayman Islands. One quarter of Caymanians are descended from enslaved Africans, another quarter are descendants of the British, and the other half of the population is of mixed ancestry. Named for the *caimánes*, or alligators that used to roam the islands, the Caymans were first settled in the 17th century by enslaved Africans, British sailors, pirates, and the unfortunate victims of shipwrecks. By the end of the 18th century, uncontrolled fishing had eliminated the native turtle population, virtually the only resource of the island. For some time the Cayman Islands were a dependency of Jamaica, becoming internally self-governing in July 1959. When Jamaica declared its independence from Britain in 1962 the Caymans reverted to British rule. In 1972 a new constitution provided for domestic autonomy. Tourism accounts for approximately 75 percent of the islands' economy, with offshore financial services ranking as the second most important industry, owing to the lack of taxes and banking laws. More than 500 banks and trust companies, including the world's 50 largest banks, are registered in the Caymans.

CUBA

Population: 11,190,000

Twelve percent of Cuba's population is classified as black and 17 percent as mulatto, but at least 50 percent of the island's people are believed to have some degree of African ancestry. During the 19th century, when its sugar economy expanded, Cuba was one of the major destinations for enslaved Africans: In 1872 the island's population numbered 107,000 free blacks and mulattos, 287,000 enslaved blacks, and 306,000 whites. Discrimination against blacks remained in force from emancipation (1886) until well into the 20th century. Afro-Cubans' first organized response to racism came in 1907 with the formation of the Cuban Independent Party of Color, which was brutally suppressed in 1912 after sparking a revolt. The Batista regime, which came to power in 1933, officially endorsed racial equality, but Afro-Cubans were still treated as second-class citizens. For this reason, many black Cubans supported Fidel Castro's 1958 revolution. The Castro regime brought significant benefits to the poorest Cubans, raising income levels and providing universal education and health care without drawing any distinctions based on race or gender. Though the top political leadership has always remained white and culturally Hispanic, Afro-Cubans have risen to high posts in the military and in the Communist Party. On the other hand, the Cuban government has cracked down on efforts to promote Afro-Cuban religion and culture. Of the 125,000 Cubans who left the island for the United States in the 1980 Mariel boat lift, an estimated 25 percent were black.

DOMINICA

Population: 74,400

Even before formal emancipation, the so-called Brown Privilege Bill of 1831 conferred political and social rights on Dominica's black population. After emancipation, blacks gained control of the legislature; as a result, the British authorities changed the rules in 1865, appointing half the legislators and gradually curtailing the rights of blacks. Dominica finally gained its independence in 1978, but the island's economic development was disrupted by a severe hurricane in 1979. Bananas remain the major export crop.

DOMINICAN REPUBLIC

Population: 7,802,000

The black population of the Dominican Republic is officially 15 percent, but it is estimated that 80 percent of Dominicans are of African descent. The nation's racial politics have long been complicated by proximity to Haiti, as a succession of Dominican governments sought to create a distinctive identity by emphasizing the Hispanic heritage of the population and denigrating all things African. As a result, Afro-Dominicans have been treated as outsiders throughout most of the nation's history, especially during the brutal dictatorship of Rafael Trujillo Molina, which lasted from 1930 to 1961. Among the most lurid acts of the Trujillo regime was a 1937 massacre of at least 10,000 to 15,000 Haitians who had entered the Dominican Republic seeking work on sugar plantations.

GRENADA

Population: 98,400

Once known as the Isle of Spice, Grenada is populated by people of African descent, East Indians, and a small minority of Europeans. Formerly the site of British-owned sugar plantations, Grenada achieved complete independence in 1974. The government of Prime Minister Maurice Bishop, which came to power in 1978, antagonized the United States with its pro-Cuban and pro-Soviet stance, resulting in the U.S. invasion of 1983. (United States troops were joined by a small military force made up of contingents from Barbados, Dominica, Jamaica, St. Lucia, and St. Vincent.) United States and Caribbean peacekeeping forces were gradually withdrawn from Grenada between 1983 and 1985. A 1984 election led to the reestablishment of democratic self-government on the island. Since that time, Grenada has been led by more centrist governments and has sought to promote tourism as well as agricultural development.

GUADELOUPE

Population: 433,000

Guadeloupe was a major sugar producer as early as the 17th century. Following a slave revolt against the British and a decree of emancipation by the revolutionary government in France, Guadeloupe enjoyed a respite from slavery between 1794 and 1802. During this period, free blacks and mulattos played a leading role in the economy and society. In 1802, however, Napoleon Bonaparte reinstituted slavery by force of arms, and it remained in force until 1831. Though Guadeloupe now benefits financially from its status as a French department, all the high administrative posts on the island are held by whites, and there is considerable sentiment in favor of independence.

HAITI

Population: 6,611,000

The world's oldest black republic, Haiti has been independent since 1801 but endured turmoil throughout the 19th century because of conflicts with the Spanish-controlled government of neighboring Santo Domingo (later the Dominican Republic) and friction between the black masses and the ruling mulatto elite. Economic disarray led to a much-resented U.S. military intervention and direct control by the United States from 1915 to 1934. The brutal dictatorship of the Duvaliers lasted from 1957 to 1986. United States troops, followed by a UN peacekeeping force, returned to Haiti in 1994 to suppress the Haitian police and military and enforce the restoration of democratic government under Jean-Bertrand Aristide. Enduring an unemployment rate of 50 percent, Haitians have by far the lowest standard of living and the lowest life expectancy in the region: age 43 for men, 47 for women (the Caribbean average is 63.7 for men, 68.2 for women).

JAMAICA

Population: 2,536,000

Following the abolition of slavery, many Jamaicans moved off the large estates and settled on small farms in the countryside, supplementing their farming income with occasional labor on the sugar plantations. Though the tiny white minority continued to dominate the island's political system, the power of the sugar planters declined during the second half of the 19th century with the growth of the banana industry (controlled largely by U.S. interests). During this time, tens of thousands of Jamaicans left the island to work on the sugar plantations in Cuba or to work on construction projects in Panama and Costa Rica. The withering of these outside sources of employment during the early 20th century led to considerable hardship for Jamaicans.

Economic discontent and the growth of black nationalism culminated in the general strike of 1938, which was accompanied by severe rioting. Political reforms followed, and the legislative elections of 1944 were the first conducted under full adult suffrage. During this era, political power shifted from whites to the Afro-European middle class, as the People's National Party and the Jamaica Labor Party vied—often violently—for ascendancy. Jamaica achieved independence from Britain in 1962, but the country did not have a black prime minister until P. J. Patterson replaced Michael Manley in 1992. In cultural terms, Jamaica's presence in the world has grown substantially in the latter half of the 20th century, due to a thriving tradition in visual arts and the widespread popularity of reggae music.

MARTINIQUE

Population: 399,000

After slavery was abolished in 1848, sugar production remained the focus of Martinique's economy for many years. It is still a major factor in the island's agricultural output, along with bananas and pineapples. Long the jewel of the French Caribbean empire, Martinique remains an overseas department of France. The island is outwardly prosperous, but imports far exceed exports, and some analysts believe that substantial subsidies from the French government have inhibited economic development. Nevertheless, Martinique enjoys a vibrant cultural life centered in Fort-de-France and administered by the official umbrella agency known as SERMAC (*Service municipale d'action culturelle*).

MONTSERRAT

Population: Formerly 12,771, now about 4,000

By the early 1990s, tourism accounted for 25 percent of Montserrat's economy, along with the manufacture of electrical components and rum. Since 1995, the island's life has been severely disrupted by the activity of the Soufrière Hills volcano at the southern end of the island; many communities, including the former capital of Plymouth, have been buried under volcanic ash. As of 1997, two thirds of the population had been evacuated, either to Great Britain or to neighboring islands such as St. Kitts and Antigua.

NETHERLANDS ANTILLES

Population: 208,968

Most of the islands that make up the Netherlands Antilles have a majority of citizens descended from African slaves. Dutch is the official language, but Papiamento—a local Spanish-based creole that includes Portuguese, Dutch, and some African words—is widely used in the southern islands and is taught in elementary schools. The largest of the islands, Curaçao, was settled in 1527 and was a major center of the Caribbean slave trade until the 1860s. Its economy declined after the abolition of slavery, but it is now a major oil-refining center, handling a substantial portion of Venezuela's crude oil output. Tourism and shipbuilding have also become major industries.

PUERTO RICO

Population: 3,809,000

Though Puerto Rico's ethnic identity is classified as Hispanic, an estimated 25 to 30 percent of Puerto Ricans are of African descent. Though Africans first came to Puerto Rico in 1513, the island's black population remained small until the 19th century, when sugar production became a major industry. Even at its highest point in 1834, Puerto Rico's enslaved population was only 42,000, a relatively small number by Caribbean standards. In the 1930s, Puerto Rico's political parties divided over the island's future status, one supporting independence and the other advocating U.S. statehood. In 1946, U.S. President Harry Truman appointed the first native Puerto Rican governor of the island, and, from 1948, governors have been chosen by general election. The Commonwealth of Puerto Rico was established in 1952. In the period from the 1940s to the late 1960s, Puerto Rico's farm-based economy became manufacturing based. Workers left the sugarcane fields and coffee plantations and moved into the cities, and a Puerto Rican independence movement sponsored such terrorist acts in the United States as an attempted assassination of President Truman. Currently, one of the major political issues facing Puerto Ricans is not independence, but whether to remain a commonwealth or to become a state with full state's rights within the United States.

ST. KITTS AND NEVIS

Population: 41,800

St. Kitts and Nevis are part of a chain of volcanic islands. They were first inhabited by the Arawak tribe, which was driven away by the Caribs, who were, in turn, annihilated by European settlers. Today the islands are mostly inhabited by the descendants of African slaves who were brought to the islands to work on sugar plantations. The economy of St. Kitts still relies on its sugar plantations; Nevis's mountainous terrain made sugarcane unprofitable there. In the 19th century, sharecroppers grew sea-island cotton, but by the 1970s, much of the land had reverted to scrub. St. Kitts and Nevis gained independence from Britain in 1983. Tourism, sugar processing, and salt extraction are the islands' major industries.

ST. LUCIA

Population: 148,000

Nearly 90 percent of the inhabitants of St. Lucia are black. English is the official language, but French patois, a Creole dialect, is also spoken. During the slave-trade era, possession of St. Lucia was hotly contested between Britain and France, and the island changed hands more than a dozen times before Britain gained undisputed control in 1814. St. Lucia became one of the Windward Islands in 1871. In the 19th century, prosperity was impeded by the effects of wars, epidemics, and a decline in the sugarcane industry. Although sugarcane revived later, with an increase in banana and cacao cultivation, its production finally ceased in 1964. Its major industries are now agriculture, oil refining, and shipping—the banana crop accounts for two thirds of St. Lucia's yearly exports.

Representative government was granted by the constitution of 1924, and that of 1936 provided for an unofficial majority of elected representatives in the legislative council. St. Lucia was a member of the Federation of the West Indies (1958–1962), and in 1967, under the West Indies Act, it became fully self-governing in internal affairs, while the United Kingdom remained responsible for defense and external matters. The island gained full independence on

February 22, 1979. The United Workers Party (UWP), then in power, called for new elections and was defeated by the Saint Lucia Labor Party (SLP). The struggle for power continued, however, and the UWP was returned in the elections of 1982 and again by a narrow margin in 1987.

ST. VINCENT AND THE GRENADINES

Population: 112,000

The majority of these islands' populations are descendants of African slaves, with a small minority made up of Europeans and East Indians. Independence was achieved on October 27, 1979, when a constitutional monarchy was formed. The Saint Vincent Labor Party came to power in 1979, and Milton Cato became the first prime minister. Cato was critical of the revolution in Grenada, preferring closer ties with the centrist governments of Trinidad and Tobago and of Barbados. In 1979 the Soufrière volcano erupted once again, damaging agriculture and the tourist trade. Hurricane Allen virtually wiped out the all-important banana crop in 1980. Agriculture has continued to be the focus of the economy, with bananas, arrowroot, copra, and sea-island cotton ranking as the major export crops.

TRINIDAD AND TOBAGO

Population: 1,276,000

Following the abolition of slavery in 1831, Trinidad experienced a massive influx of East Indian workers. By the 20th century, East Indians predominated on the sugar estates, while black Trinidadians held most of the jobs in the developing oil industry. Differences between the two communities were often exploited by politicians throughout the 19th and 20th centuries; the dominant People's National Movement (PNM), which led Trinidad to independence in 1962, was closely identified with the black population; the mainly East Indian United National Congress represented the opposition. The PNM's leader, Eric Williams (1911–1981), who served as Trinidad's first prime minister, was also a renowned historian and political analyst. In 1985, black and East Indian Trinidadians joined in creating a multiethnic third party, National Alliance for Reconstruction, and since then, race has been a less volatile factor in politics. Economically, Trinidad remains heavily dependent on oil and petrochemicals. Trinidadians have long enjoyed a rich and distinctive cultural life; in addition to producing world-class intellectuals such as Eric Williams, C. L. R. James, and the novelist V. S. Naipaul, Trinidad is credited with inventing calypso music and the steel drum.

TURKS AND CAICOS ISLANDS

Population: 14,302

More than 30 cays and islands make up the Turks and Caicos Islands, but only six islands are inhabited. The "Turks" were named after a native scarlet cactus, the flowers of which resemble a Turkish fez; "Caicos" may be derived from *cay icoco*, a coco palm tree. More than 90 percent of the population is descended from slaves, and natives are called "Belongers." In 1799 the islands were annexed by the Bahama Islands government, but in 1848 they were granted a separate charter. In the meantime, slavery had been abolished, and the plantation owners left the islands and the plantations to the former slaves. For a time in the 1960s and 1970s, the islands were again under the control of the Bahama Islands, but with Bahamian independence (1973), the Turks and Caicos were placed under a British governor at Grand Turk. As preparation for independence, a commission was appointed in the 1980s to make recommendations on a new constitution and to consider the future economic direction of the islands. Offshore banking and tourism play a large role in the economy, and major exports include lobster and conch.

U.S. VIRGIN ISLANDS

Population: 97,120

The people of the U.S. Virgin Islands (the islands of St. Croix, St. Thomas, St. John) are U.S. citizens, but they are not allowed to vote in U.S. elections, although they do elect a non-voting representative to the U.S. House of Representatives. There are three political parties: the Democratic and the Republican, affiliated with the U.S. counterparts, and the Independent Citizens Movement. The Virgin Islands were probably first inhabited by the Arawak, but the Carib tribe had driven them away by 1493, the year when Christopher Columbus first landed on St. Croix. In 1555 the Caribs were defeated by a Spanish expedition, and by 1625, English and French settlers were farming on St. Croix. In 1671 the Danish West India Company acquired St. Croix, St. Thomas, and St. John. At first convicted criminals, then (after 1673) African slaves, worked sugar plantations there. The triangular trade made many Europeans wealthy before emancipation; slaves were brought from Africa to a major slave market in St. Thomas, rum and molasses were sent to Europe, and European goods were shipped back to the island. The sugar plantations began to fail after slave revolts in the early 19th century, and emancipation put an end to the industry.

In 1917, the United States bought the islands for their strategic position along the approaches to the Panama Canal. Virgin Islanders became U.S. citizens in 1927. In 1970 the first popularly elected governor took office, and in 1976, the islands were given the right to draft a constitution, subject to approval by the U.S. Congress and president. Completed in 1978, the islands' constitution was rejected in a referendum (1979) and again rejected after amendment (1981). Tourism now accounts for 70 percent of the jobs in the Virgin Islands, with more than 2 million vacationers a year visiting St. Croix, St. Thomas, and St. John.

CENTRAL AND SOUTH AMERICA

BELIZE

Population: 228,000

Twenty-nine percent of Belize's population is classified as Creole (predominantly black), and 7 percent as Black Carib. The Black Caribs (also known as Garifunas) are descendants of a group of Africans who survived the wreckage of a slave ship during the 17th century and took refuge on the island of St. Vincent, a stronghold of the Carib Indians. The Africans adopted the Caribs' language and many of their customs, though the two groups remained separate and eventually became antagonistic. When the British gained control of St. Vincent in 1763, they came into conflict with the Black Caribs, who controlled most of the island's arable land. After British troops repressed a Black Carib uprising in 1795 to 1796, 5,000 Black Caribs were deported to the island of Roatán off the coast of Honduras. In 1802, Spanish authorities persuaded the Black Caribs to settle along the coast of Central America, in what are now Belize, Honduras, and Guatemala. There are now six Black Carib settlements in southern Belize, with a combined population of about 10,000; each village is governed by a board of locally elected officials. A number of Black Caribs have emigrated to North America, settling in New York City, Chicago, Los Angeles, and New Orleans. On Settlement Day, November 19, Black Caribs throughout the Americas commemorate the first arrival of their ancestors on the mainland.

BRAZIL

Population: 159,691,000

Brazil now has the largest African-descent population in the world outside Africa itself: Afro-Brazilians constitute about one third of the country's population, with mulattos and mestizos constituting another one third. Despite their strong numerical presence, Afro-Brazilians have had to struggle for equality since the abolition of slavery in 1888. Beginning in the late 19th century, successive Brazilian governments sought immigrants from Europe in the hope of "whitening" the population, even as they professed to be creating a racial democracy and decried the practice of segregation in the United States. By the 1920s, Afro-Brazilian societies (descendants of the famous religious brotherhoods of the colonial era) began publishing journals that advocated racial equality and disseminated political ideas from other parts of the diaspora. The first national civil-rights organization, the Frente Negra Brasiliera, was founded in 1931. Following World War II, Afro-Brazilian groups began publishing politically oriented journals such as *Senzala* and *Alvorada*.

In addition, black music and dance groups such as the *escolas de samba* exerted a growing influence, transforming the Afro-Brazilian carnival tradition into a major component of Brazil's national culture. During this period, theater groups such as Abidas do Nascimento's Teatro Experimental do Negro became a major forum for the exploration of racial issues. Following a military coup in 1964, the Brazilian government began a crackdown on Afro-Brazilian journals and activists, but the push for equality was revived in the 1970s with the emergence of the Movimento Negro Unificado.

Currently, many Afro-Brazilians who live in the major cities are relegated to outlying slums known as *favelas*, where they eke out a living through peddling and other pursuits; in recent years, systematic police killings of homeless youths in favelas have been publicized by human-rights groups in Brazil and abroad. Middle-class Afro-Brazilians have also reported various forms of discrimination, such as being asked to use the service elevator in apartment buildings and being denied tables in restaurants. Contemporary organizations fighting for racial equality include the Institute for the Study of Black Culture (IPCN) and local groups seeking to improve conditions in the favelas.

COLOMBIA

Population: 36,200,000

Colombia's population is classified as 14 percent mulatto, 4 percent black, 58 percent mestizo, and 4 percent other. Colombians of African descent are concentrated in the Buenaventura region along the Pacific Ocean and in the Chocó region south of Panama. They make up a significant proportion of the population in seaports such as Buenaventura, Barranquilla, Cartagena, and Cali, often dominating municipal politics despite widespread social discrimination.

COSTA RICA

Population: 3,468,000

Three percent of Costa Rica's population is classified as black or mulatto. Among the largest African-descent groups are the approximately 30,000 Costa Ricans of Jamaican origin who live in Puerto Limón. They are descendants of workers who came to Costa Rica during the 19th century to build railroads linking the developing banana plantations with the coast. When the railroads were completed, many of these workers stayed on and took jobs with the United

Fruit Company. For several generations, they continued to speak English and to worship in Protestant churches. However, present-day black Costa Ricans have generally assimilated into the predominantly Hispanic culture of the nation.

ECUADOR

Population: 11,937,000

Six percent of Ecuador's population is classified as either mulatto or black. Afro-Ecuadorians are concentrated north of Quito, especially in the Esmereldas district along the northwest coast. They are mostly descendants of former Maroon communities and have generally remained isolated from Ecuador's majority population.

FRENCH GUIANA

Population: 151,187

During the slave-trade era, French Guiana's port of Cayenne was one of the leading points of entry for enslaved Africans. French Guiana is now an overseas department of France, and 66 percent of its population is classified as black or Afro-European. Timber, rum, and shrimp are the country's leading exports.

GUYANA

Population: 773,000

The majority of Guyana's people are of East Indian ancestry, and another 35 percent are classified as black. When slavery was abolished in British Guiana in 1837, the liberated blacks either settled as peasants on the land they had worked or migrated to the towns. Indentured servants from India were then imported to work the sugar plantations; as a result, Indians now predominate among the rural population, and town dwellers are mostly black. Conflicts between the two groups led to violent clashes during the early 1960s. Guyana's first black prime minister, Forbes Burnham, took office in 1964, and two years later, Guyana gained its independence. Burnham nationalized a number of industries and was credited with fostering interest in Guyana's African heritage. At the same time, he was condemned (by blacks and Indians alike) as a dictator who rigged elections and rode roughshod over opponents. Burnham's 21-year rule ended with his death in 1985. At this point the sugar industry had declined considerably, leading to the emigration of many Guyanese. In 1992, Cheddi Jagan, who had served as prime minister of Guyana's first provisional government during the 1950s, was elected president of the nation. Of Indian descent, Jagan set about healing the nation's racial divisions. He confronted a complex situation in which black Guyanese owned little property but essentially controlled the civil service and the armed forces.

HONDURAS

Population: 5,666,000

Honduras's population is classified as only 2 percent black, but the country has the largest population of Black Caribs in the Western Hemisphere—some 70,000 in all, living in 43 villages and towns along the eastern coast. (See Belize.)

MEXICO

Population: 94,275,000

About 3 percent of Mexico's population is of African ancestry, classified as Afro-mestizo because of considerable intermarriage with Native Americans. Their existing communities were once Maroon settlements. There are 16 independent Afro-mestizo towns in the states of Guerrero and Oaxaca along the Pacific Coast; on the Gulf Coast, there are two towns, Mata Clara and Coyolillo, near Veracruz. In general, Mexico's Afro-mestizos have identified closely with Native Americans.

NICARAGUA

Population: 4,632,000

Nicaraguans of African descent compose approximately 9 percent of the population; they are largely of Jamaican origin and are concentrated along the Mosquito Coast.

PANAMA

Population: 2,719,000

Approximately 14 percent of Panama's population is classified as black or mulatto. Many are descendants of the approximately 30,000 West Indians who migrated to Panama early in the 20th century to take part in the building of the Panama Canal. Others, who call themselves colonial blacks, trace their roots in Panama back to the Maroons of the 16th century. The two groups have tended to remain distinct, as colonial blacks have long been Spanish-speaking and Catholic, while West Indian groups have tended to cluster in the Canal Zone, attending Protestant churches and often speaking English. Neither group has managed to gain much influence in national politics.

SURINAM

Population: 424,000

Bush Negroes, the descendants of Surinam's dynamic Maroons (see Chapter 2) make up approximately 10 percent of the population. Due to their long tradition of autonomy, they have maintained a unique culture that preserves many African elements, drawn from a variety of traditions and blended into a new synthesis. African influences are particularly evident in the elaborate artwork of the Bush Negroes—which includes complex embroidery and cloth making, jewelry making, and wood carving—and in their rich oral traditions.

VENEZUELA

Population: 22,777,000

Ten percent of Venezuela's population is currently classified as of African descent. During the 16th and 17th centuries, Caracas was a major port of entry for slave ships, and in 1810 the region had an enslaved population of 64,000, about 60 percent of whom worked on cacao plantations. At the time, blacks and mulattos made up half of Venezuela's total population. After emancipation, many groups of liberated slaves settled in fishing or farming villages along the Pacific Coast. During the 19th century, the black population was augmented by an influx of West Indians seeking work in mining, agriculture, and oil industries. The black population was concentrated in the Barlovento region east of Caracas. Discrimination against Afro-Venezuelans remained in force until the 1930s, when the rise of the Acción Democrática (AD) Party brought a move for multiracial democracy. Since the 1950s, Afro-Venezuelans have been far more visible in schools, universities, local police forces, and all levels of government. Venezuelans often use the phrase *café con leche* (coffee with milk) to describe their society.

DIASPORA POPULATION AND MIGRATION

Table 4.6 African and African-Descent Populations

SUB-SAHARAN AFRICA*	
Central Africa	82,467,000
East Africa	220,884,000
Southern Africa	47,628,000
West Africa	190,952,000
Total	541,931,000
CENTRAL AND SOUTH AMERICA	
Belize	77,500
Brazil	51,420,000
Colombia	7,360,000
Costa Rica	100,300
Ecuador	688,000
French Guiana	92,000
Guyana	270,000
Honduras	110,000
Mexico	2,735,000
Nicaragua	390,000
Panama	368,000
Surinam	43,000
Venezuela	2,000,000
Total	65,653,000
CARIBBEAN	
Anguilla	10,000
Antigua and Barbuda	58,000
Bahamas	235,000
Barbados	212,000
Bermuda	37,200
British Virgin Islands	11,300
Cayman Islands	22,000
Cuba	5,500,000
Dominica	74,000
Dominican Republic	5,800,000
Grenada	80,700
Guadeloupe	377,000
Haiti	6,600,000
Jamaica	1,900,000
Martinique	365,000
Netherlands Antilles	177,600
Puerto Rico	950,000
St. Kitts and Nevis	37,400
St. Lucia	128,700
St. Vincent Islands	95,000
Trinidad Islands	505,000

Table 4.6 (continued)

Turks and Caicos Islands	14,000
U.S. Virgin Islands	80,000
Total	23,168,000
CANADA	460,000
UNITED STATES	33,140,000
TOTAL IN THE AMERICAS	122,361,000

Source: Figures are from 1996 and were compiled by the author from *1997 Encyclopædia Britannica Book of the Year*, *The CIA World Factbook*, and *The Information Please Almanac, 1997*.
*According to a 1994 United Nations world-population study, the population of sub-Saharan Africa is the fastest-growing in the world and is expected to double by the year 2025.

Table 4.7 U.S. Immigration: Immigrants Admitted by Region and Selected Country of Birth, 1981–1996*

Region and Country of Birth	1981	1983	1985	1987	1989	1991	1993	1995
Sub-Saharan Africa								
Cameroon	69	92	123	132	187	452	262	506
Cape Verde	849	594	627	657	1,118	973	936	968
Ethiopia	1,749	2,643	3,362	2,156	3,389	5,127	5,191	5,960
Ghana	951	976	1,041	1,120	2,045	3,330	1,604	3,152
Ivory Coast	28	54	57	63	98	347	250	289
Kenya	657	710	735	698	910	1,185	1,065	1,419
Liberia	556	518	618	622	1,175	1,292	1,050	1,929
Nigeria	1,918	2,354	2,846	3,278	5,213	7,912	4,448	6,818
Senegal	65	71	91	92	141	869	178	506
Sierra Leone	277	319	371	453	939	951	690	919
Somalia	61	83	139	197	228	458	1,088	3,487
South Africa	1,559	1,261	1,210	2,741	1,899	1,854	2,197	2,560
Sudan	65	128	271	198	272	679	714	1,645
Tanzania	423	364	395	385	507	500	426	524
Uganda	410	332	301	357	393	538	415	383
Non-Hispanic Caribbean								
Antigua and Barbuda	929	2,008	957	874	979	944	554	374
Bahamas	546	505	533	556	861	1,062	686	585
Barbados	2,394	1,849	1,625	1,665	1,616	1,460	1,184	734
Dominica	721	546	540	740	748	982	683	591
Grenada	1,120	1,154	934	1,098	1,045	979	827	583
Haiti	6,683	8,424	10,165	14,819	13,658	47,527	10,094	14,021
Jamaica	23,569	19,535	18,923	23,148	24,523	23,828	17,241	16,398
St. Kitts and Nevis	867	2,773	769	589	795	830	544	360
St. Lucia	733	662	499	496	709	766	634	403
St. Vincent and Grenadines	799	767	693	746	892	808	657	349
Trinidad and Tobago	4,599	3,156	2,831	3,543	5,394	8,407	6,577	5,424
Non-Hispanic Central America								
Belize	1,289	1,585	1,353	1,354	2,217	2,377	1,035	644
Panama	4,613	2,546	2,611	2,084	3,482	4,204	2,679	2,247
Non-Hispanic South America								
Guyana	6,743	8,990	8,531	11,384	10,789	11,666	8,384	7,362

Source: U.S. Immigration and Naturalization Service.
* Figures represent total immigration from countries, including nonblacks.

Table 4.8 Top Five Predominantly Black Immigrant Groups to the United States, by Selected Country of Birth, 1972–1992, 1994–1996

	1972	1973	1974	1975	1976	1977	1978
Jamaica	13,427	9,963	12,408	11,076	11,100	11,501	19,265
Haiti	5,809	4,786	3,946	5,145	6,691	5,441	6,470
Guyana	2,826	2,969	3,241	3,169	4,497	5,718	7,614
Trinidad and Tobago	6,615	7,035	6,516	5,982	6,040	6,106	5,973
Nigeria	738	738	670	653	907	653	1,007

	1979	1980	1981	1982	1983	1984	1985
Jamaica	19,714	18,970	23,569	18,711	19,535	19,822	18,923
Haiti	6,433	6,540	6,683	8,779	8,424	9,839	10,165
Guyana	7,001	8,381	6,743	10,059	8,990	8,412	8,531
Trinidad and Tobago	5,225	5,154	4,599	3,532	3,156	2,900	2,831
Nigeria	1,054	1,896	1,918	2,257	2,354	2,337	2,846

	1986	1987	1988	1989	1990	1991	1992
Jamaica	19,595	23,148	20,966	24,523	25,013	23,828	18,915
Haiti	12,666	14,819	34,806	13,658	20,324	47,527	11,002
Guyana	10,367	11,384	8,747	10,789	11,362	11,666	9,064
Trinidad and Tobago	2,891	3,543	3,947	5,394	6,740	8,407	7,008
Nigeria	2,976	3,278	3,343	5,213	8,843	7,912	4,551

	1994	1995	1996
Jamaica	14,349	16,398	19,089
Haiti	13,333	14,021	18,386
Guyana	7,662	7,362	9,489
Trinidad and Tobago	6,292	5,424	7,344
Nigeria	3,950	6,818	10,221

Source: U.S. Immigration and Naturalization Service.

SOURCES FOR ADDITIONAL INFORMATION

Cohen, Robin, ed. *The Cambridge Survey of World Migration.* Cambridge, England: Cambridge University Press, 1995.

Conniff, Michael L., and Thomas J. Davis. *Africans in the Americas: A History of the Black Diaspora.* New York: St. Martin's, 1994.

Henry, Frances. *The Caribbean Diaspora in Toronto: Learning to Live with Racism.* Toronto: University of Toronto Press, 1994.

Higgins, Chester, Jr. *Feeling the Spirit: Searching the World for the People of Africa.* New York: Bantam, 1994.

Núñez, Benjamin. *Dictionary of Afro-Latin American Civilization.* Westport, CT: Greenwood, 1980.

———. *Dictionary of Afro-Portuguese Civilization,* 2 vols. London, NJ: Zell, 1995–1996.

Palmer, Ransford W. *Pilgrims from the Sun: West Indian Migration to America.* New York: Twayne, 1995.

Parker, Philip M. *Ethnic Cultures of the World.* Westport, CT: Greenwood, 1997.

Pescatello, Ann M., ed. *Old Roots in New Lands: Historical and Anthropological Perspectives on Black Experiences in the Americas*. Westport, CT: Greenwood, 1977.

Segal, Ronald. *The Black Diaspora*. New York: Farrar, Straus & Giroux, 1995.

Tenenbaum, Barbara A., ed. *Encyclopedia of Latin American History and Culture*, 5 vols. New York: Scribner, 1996.

Thornton, John. *Africa and Africans in the Making of the Atlantic World, 1400–1680*. Cambridge, England: Cambridge University Press, 1992.

Williams, Eric. *From Columbus to Castro: The History of the Caribbean, 1492–1969*. New York: Harper & Row, 1969.

Winks, Robin W. *The Blacks in Canada: A History*. New Haven, CT: Yale University Press, 1971.

5

Family and Heritage

HOLIDAYS AND OBSERVANCES

There are a variety of uniquely African American holidays and commemorations observed throughout the United States.

BLACK HISTORY MONTH

In 1926, scholar and author Carter G. Woodson established Negro History Week to highlight African American contributions to the United States. What was once a week's recognition has blossomed into a full month, celebrated in February, in order to include the birthdays of the great antislavery activist Frederick Douglass and of President Abraham Lincoln. Black History Month is especially important because many school curriculums do not address the range and diversity of African American achievements, contributions, struggles, and triumphs. This annual observance thus provides an opportunity to spotlight all aspects of the African American experience. Many schools and cultural organizations hold special exhibitions, lectures, concerts, poetry readings, movies, and panel discussions. Children can be encouraged to pay tribute to the past by reading books about inspiring historical figures and achievements in black history.

JUNETEENTH

On June 19, 1865, enslaved African Americans in Texas belatedly learned that the Emancipation Proclamation of January 1, 1863, had declared them free. The Texans were the last in the nation to receive this news, and the day became a celebration for black folks in Texas and neighboring states, including Oklahoma, Arkansas, Louisiana, and Alabama. In 1972, the Texas State Legislature recognized Juneteenth as an official state holiday. Currently, Juneteenth is celebrated in more than 200 cities throughout the United States with parades, picnics, parties, and other cultural and spiritual gatherings. In 1997, Juneteenth was chosen as the annual starting date for National Black Bookstore Week, a celebration of black bookstores and their cultural connections to their communities. These community bookstores not only highlight African cuisine, music, and literature, but they also collect used books for the Soweto Book Project, which was established to encourage literacy and support local bookstores in Soweto, South Africa.

KWANZAA

Kwanzaa is a family-oriented holiday created in 1966 by Maulana Karenga, Black Studies Department Chair at the California State University, Long Beach. Karenga has believed that in order to prevail against racism, black people in this country have needed a distinctive way of honoring their heritage and reinforcing a sense of community and family solidarity. The increasingly popular holiday, often celebrated in conjunction with—or instead of—Christmas, focuses on enhancing people's pride in community and connection with African traditions, customs, symbols, and language. Kwanzaa is a spiritual, festive, and joyous celebration of the oneness and goodness of life, which claims no ties with any religion. It is, instead, a week of remembering, reassessing, and rejoicing.

The term *Kwanzaa* derives from a Swahili word meaning "first" and relates to the practice of gathering the first fruits of the soil each year. The seven-day observance starts the day after Christmas, December 26, extends through January 1, and is devoted to the *nguzo saba*, or seven principles of blackness: *umoja* (unity), *kujichangulia* (self-determination), *ujima* (collective work and responsibility), *ujamma* (economic cooperation), *nia* (purpose), *kuumba* (creativity), and *imani* (faith). Families celebrating Kwanzaa devote each of the holiday's seven nights to the discussion of one of these principles, until all seven have been addressed. The ceremony begins with the lighting of a candle displayed in a seven-branched candleholder called a *kinara*, a gesture of tribute to African ancestors. There are three green candles, symbolizing hope and the green earth; three red ones, symbolizing the blood of the African diaspora; and one black candle, symbolizing solidarity among black people. The kinara is then placed on a straw mat (*mkeka*), which symbolizes traditional African culture, alongside other objects, including the *akikomba*, a cup representing the unity of all African peoples. Other ceremonial objects included in Kwanzaa include *mazao* (fruits and vegetables, representing unified effort); *vibunzi* (an ear of corn for each child in the family); and *zawadi* (simple gifts, preferably related to education or to African or African American themes).

Kwanzaa concludes with *karamu*, a community festival that welcomes the new year with music, dancing, and traditional dishes derived from the cuisine of Africa and the African diaspora. The karamu meal begins with the Kaukaribisha (welcoming), which may take the form of songs, dance, and poetry. Next comes the Kukumbuka, or remembering, where family members and guests offer reflections of the past year. During the Kushangilia, there is a remembrance of ancestors followed by the festive meal. The karamu is concluded with the farewell statement or Tamshi la Tutaonana.

Many people blend Christmas and Kwanzaa celebrations. Because the traditional Christmas colors of red and green and the Afrocentric colors of red, black, green, and yellow overlap, there are many ways to incorporate both holidays into home decor, gifts, and holiday fashions. A growing tradition in many parts of the United States is for families to celebrate one night of Kwanzaa at home and some or all of the other nights at community gatherings sponsored by various families or groups. This brings the community together in larger celebrations of family, unity, and pride.

MALCOLM X DAY

Although this is not an official holiday, many honor the late Malcolm X on May 19, the day of his birth in 1925, by recounting and discussing his philosophical writings and his lifelong battles against injustice and religious intolerance.

MARTIN LUTHER KING DAY

The United States honors the Reverend Martin Luther King, Jr., on the third Monday of January, the first and only national holiday to celebrate the life and achievements of an African American. Legislation creating the holiday was adopted by the U.S. Congress in 1983, and the holiday was observed nationwide for the first time in 1986. Although there is no universally agreed-upon way to celebrate King's birthday, many people use it as a time of reflection or an opportunity to perform community service in his memory.

UMOJA KARAMU (UNITY FEAST)

Held the fourth Sunday in November, this celebration was originated in 1971 by Edward Simms, Jr., with the purpose of bringing black families together. This increasingly popular observance centers on the five major historical passages, each of which is represented by a symbolic color: black (the strength of the African family prior to slavery); white (the black family under slavery); red (the black family's emancipation); green (the black family's struggle for equal rights), gold or orange (the black family's hopes for the future). Umoja Karamu observances can include a prayer, a libation poured to honor the ancestors, historical readings, and the passing and eventual sharing of foods in the five colors. These foods may represent different passages in African American history.

FAMILY AND WEDDING CELEBRATIONS AND TRADITIONS

Increasing numbers of communities, families, and individuals are adding elements of African and African American traditions to common celebrations in order to reclaim their cultural heritage. Some of these rituals are based in African culture, others on family or religious traditions, but all seek to infuse these common celebrations with greater cultural significance.

PREBIRTH CELEBRATIONS

There are numerous ways to incorporate African traditions, decor, and delicacies into the traditional baby shower. One tradition is the *mamatoto* (mother and child) ritual that includes empowering music, affirmations, candles, carefully chosen scents, and healing embraces to communicate positive feelings to the mother and baby. In her book *For Every Season*, Barbara Eklof tells how women in the Sudan encourage an expectant mother and allay her fears by braiding her hair "in a comfortable, yet elegant style, then crown it with earth fragrances. They drape a knotted twine of leather around her waist and place a ceremonial bracelet on her wrist as symbolic shields of protection." This tradition can be incorporated into a contemporary shower by giving the expectant mother a manicure or pedicure and reading poetry and affirmations aloud. Whether traditional, contemporary, or a bit of both, baby showers are meant to prepare the mother-to-be for her transition and lay the welcome mat for a new arrival. Eklof recommends gifts that lead to "decorating the baby's room with enchantment," such as woven baskets, African carved masks, toys (e.g., stuffed forest animals or small drums), Afrocentric children's books, live or silk plants, and music boxes or wind chimes.

NAMING CEREMONIES

In many traditional cultures of Africa, naming ceremonies are a must for every child, celebrating a child's entry into the community and affirming deep religious principles such as reverence for a family's ancestors. Following the depiction of this custom in Alex Haley's *Roots*, many people have been celebrating this early rite of passage in which newborn babies are announced to the ancestors and the earthly family. The event can be combined with a christening or other religious welcoming ceremony or can stand alone. Either way, it is an opportunity to invite family and friends to a theme ceremony with decorations, food, and symbolic words of welcome. Some examples of themes are nature, such as a tree planting or a flower theme; light, including the lighting of candles or holiday strings of lights; and water, perhaps taking place at the seashore or a lake. The significance or meaning of the child's name is explained, and those present communicate their understanding of the name's particular significance. Thus, the naming ceremony is a positive link among past, present, and future.

COMING-OF-AGE CEREMONIES AND RITE-OF-PASSAGE PROGRAMS

Many African communities signal the transition from childhood to young adulthood with rite-of-passage rituals. Often, the community elders require the initiate to study certain traditions or to meet a prescribed set of challenges to earn the status of young adult and become independent of her or his parents.

In recent years, parents, teachers, and community leaders have come to recognize the value of African rituals for the transition into adulthood. Afrocentric rite-of-passage programs are flourishing in schools, communities, churches, and social groups throughout the United States. Growing numbers of adolescents and preadolescents gather in classes or group retreats where they learn about themselves, their history, and their culture, and they participate in coming-of-age ceremonies. These programs have proved so effective that they are being adapted for toddlers and preadolescent children as well. The following examples show the range and diversity of programs that are at work.

THE AFRICAN SON-RISE RITES OF PASSAGE MANHOOD TRAINING PROGRAM

Run by the Washington, D.C., chapter of Concerned Black Men, this program meets twice monthly to teach boys (ages 8–13) economic intuition, leadership, health and physical fitness, cultural awareness, and academic competence. Instruction on the culture and history of Africans worldwide includes lectures, films, and visits to museums. (202-783-5414)

SOJOURNER TRUTH ADOLESCENT RITES SOCIETY (STARS)

This New York City–based 10-month program teaches girls spirituality, cooking, and quilting, along with confidence, responsibility, self-love, and self-esteem. At the final ceremony, the young women don African garb and share insights with their families and others at New York City's famed Abyssinian Baptist Church. (212-928-5165)

BALTIMORE RITES OF PASSAGE KOLLECTIVE

This program employs a "positive, preventive, and practice" curriculum to help boys and girls ages 7 to 18 grow into strong, responsible adults. The 20-week program has five phases: family orientation, rites of separation, curriculum, retreat and naming ceremony, and the transformation ceremony. (410-462-1494)

HAWK (HIGH ACHIEVEMENT, WISDOM AND KNOWLEDGE) FEDERATION OF OAKLAND

HAWK began as an African-based manhood training program and added the Asset Society, a similar program, for girls. Each child must pass a series of tests to build courage, character, and consciousness. Both programs are open to those between ages 5 and 18, but HAWK targets adolescent boys. (410-836-3245)

WEST DALLAS COMMUNITY CENTERS, INC.

This is a program for youths who have been in the correctional system or involved in family intervention. Based on the *nguzo saba* (seven principles of Kwanzaa), boys and girls ages 9 to 17 receive counseling while learning language skills, karate, and African American history. (214-634-7691)

KABAZ (BLACK JEWELS) CULTURAL CENTER

Based in Detroit, Kabaz has been training youths for adulthood for 30 years. Their 12-step plan for boys and girls, beginning at age five, is designed to instill positive Afrocentric values. For example, they use trips to the woods to put children in closer touch with nature and employ precision drills to teach discipline. (313-924-1140)

AFRICAN AMERICAN WOMEN ON TOUR

This organization holds five conferences around the country each year. Included is a three-day workshop where 12- to 19-year-old girls learn about self-empowerment, teen sexuality, and African culture and history. (300-560-AAWT)

PREWEDDING CELEBRATIONS

Many couples are combining their African pasts with their American presents to establish rituals that bring more spirituality and ceremony to their engagements and marriages. Some couples have added Afrocentric flavor to their wedding showers by incorporating customs from throughout the diaspora. In the *queh-queh*, a Guyanese custom based on African tradition, anyone (whether or not they are invited to the wedding) may come and share in prewedding festivities that include sensual music and dancing. Because Guyanese parents traditionally did not speak to their children about sex, the bawdy song lyrics were devised to provide instruction in the carnal arts. Ingrid Sturgis, in *The Nubian Wedding Book*, writes, "The dancers may perform only two or three days before the wedding, with the biggest bash the night before. Family elders or kinsmen who hold the knowledge of the celebration are invited to bring the songs they remember and lead the crowd in singing them to the bride and groom."

Many African villages observe a ritual called "loading the bride," in which the bride-to-be is given advice and gifts to prepare her for married life and help her set up housekeeping. Modern-day showers adopting this theme can employ food, fun, and games.

Sturgis suggests a "jumping-the-broom luncheon" in which guests bring "home-related" gifts and ribbons inscribed with advice, observations, old wives' tales, or other words of wisdom and place them in a basket. The bride then draws out each ribbon and reads it to the guests, after which the ribbons are tied to a decorative broom. The bride can use the broom at her wedding if she chooses.

Another possibility is a Kwanzaa shower where guests bring gifts related to the seven principles of *nguzo saba*. Instead, guests can commit to performing community service in honor of the bride.

AFROCENTRIC WEDDINGS

A growing number of couples are finding ways to embrace, honor, and include African traditions in their wedding ceremonies. Afrocentric accents, such as kinte colors and Adrinke symbols, can be added to the invitations; prewedding ceremonies (such as showers and rehearsal dinners); the attire of the bride, groom, and wedding party; the decorations; the ceremony or reception; and the wedding favors. Many couples include a literal or symbolic jumping of the broom in the ceremony in recognition of the fact that enslaved men and women jumped over a broomstick to symbolize commitment when the law of the land forbade them from marrying.

The blending of African, Afrocentric, and religious or spiritual touches provides a wide range of options. Growing numbers of couples are writing their own vows and incorporating the

A group picnic in South Carolina, on the Fourth of July, 1874.

African tradition of thanking the ancestors with a libation at the beginning of the ceremony. In *The Nubian Wedding Book*, Ingrid Sturgis describes a Yoruba wedding that begins with a traditional spiritual reading before the wedding by a *babalawo* or high priest. The reading determines whether the future surrounding the couple is in harmony. It also advises them how to eliminate all possible negatives to ensure harmony for their marriage. Sometimes an *ebo* (offering) is made to Sun—the governing *orisha* or spirit of love, money, and conception—before the wedding ceremony to rid the couple of family conflicts. At the ceremony, an altar is filled with baskets of food and fruit to welcome the ancestors. The delicacies might include honey, pumpkin, or yams as a gift to Sun. The bride, groom, families, and wedding guests then share in the tasting of spices: kola nut, as a symbol of the bitterness that life can bring; water, symbolizing life's abundance and blessings; honey, representing sweetness in the marriage and the home; pepper, for life's challenges and a spicy marriage; and salt, to help preserve what is good in the marriage. After declaring, "We are standing on the shoulders of our ancestors," the *babalawo* brings out two white doves to symbolize love and happiness, touches the couple with the doves, then releases the birds into the sky.

A popular theme for a December wedding is a Kwanzaa wedding, which features the lighting of the seven candles and the inclusion of the seven principles of *nguzo saba* in the wedding vows.

FAMILY REUNIONS

In recent years, the popularity of reunions has grown, and they are often held in the Southern hometowns of beloved parents, grandparents, and great-grandparents. Sometimes the reunions rotate among cities where family members reside, giving relations a chance to enjoy different environments while reaffirming their familial bonds.

M y grandmother, who was one of the greatest human beings I've ever known, used to say, "I am a child of God and nobody's creature." That to me defined the Black woman through the centuries.

Maya Angelou, quoted in *Essence* (December 1992)

In *For Every Season*, Barbara Eklof suggests that reunion planners "consider scheduling your reunion to coincide with special family occasions, such as birthdays, anniversaries, and births, or on holidays like Thanksgiving, Kwanzaa, or Christmas." By forming committees and delegating responsibilities, organizers are able to bring their loved ones together during the planning process, as well as at the actual event. Some families use reunions as an opportunity for family or community service: feeding the homeless or raising funds to aid those in need or giving scholarships to younger members. Eklof suggests creating a fund to care and provide security for elderly family members.

Reunions can also be a time for gathering family history, via interviews with elders, which are recorded on video- or audiotape or written down. This preserves memories that would otherwise be forgotten so that they can be shared with present and future generations. Some families combine reunions with the development of a family tree, accompanied by important historical notes. In any event, documentation provides warm memories and valuable information for relatives and others to enjoy.

TRACING GENEALOGY

Tracing family history has become an increasingly popular pursuit, due in large part to the impact of Alex Haley's *Roots*. In addition to interviewing relatives and examining family records, there are many avenues of research available. General resources include the extensive genealogical collections at the Library of Congress, The New York Public Library, the Los Angeles Public Library, the Newberry Library in Chicago, and the Genealogical Library of the Church of Jesus Christ of Latter-Day Saints in Salt Lake City, Utah. Links to genealogical resources on the Internet can be accessed at www.internetdatabase.com/geneal.htm. Sources of particular relevance to African American genealogical research include the following books, organizations, and collections.

BOOKS

Beasley, Donna. *Family Pride: The Complete Guide to Tracing African-American Genealogy*. New York: Macmillan, 1997.

Blockson, Charles, and Ron Fry. *Black Genealogy*. Baltimore: Black Classic Press, 1977.

Smith, Jesse Carney, ed. *Ethnic Genealogy: A Research Guide*. Westport, CT: Greenwood, 1983.

Willard, Jim, and Terry Willard, with Jane Wilson. *Ancestors: A Beginner's Guide to Family History and Genealogy*. Boston: Houghton Mifflin, 1997.

ORGANIZATIONS AND COLLECTIONS

The following organizations offer guidance and resources (e.g., archives, pamphlets, or software) for genealogical research.

African-American History Association
P.O. Box 115268
Atlanta, GA 30310
404-344-7405

African Heritage Foundation of the Americas
P.O. Box 2964
Pittsburgh, PA 15230
412-361-8425

Afro-American Cultural and Historical Society
  Museum
1765 Crawford Road
Cleveland, OH 44106
216-791-1700

Afro-American Genealogical and Historical
  Society of Chicago
740 E. 56th Place

Chicago, IL 60637
312-947-0600

Afro-American Historical and Genealogical
  Society
P.O. Box 73086
Washington, DC 20056
202-234-5350

Atlanta-Fulton Public Library
Special Collections Department
1 Margaret Mitchell Square
Atlanta, GA 30303
404-730-1700

Bienville Historical Society
Center for Gulf Studies
600 Government Street
Mobile, AL 36602
205-457-5242

Birmingham Public Library
Linn-Henley Library for Southern Historical
  Research

2100 Park Place
Birmingham, AL 35203
205-226-3645

Black Resources Information Coordinating
  Services
614 Howard Avenue
Tallahassee, FL 32304
904-576-7522

Cleveland Public Library
Fine Arts and Special Collections Department
325 Superior Avenue
Cleveland, OH 44414
216-623-2818

Tarrant County Black Historical and Genealogical
  Society
1020 E. Humboldt
Fort Worth, TX 76104
817-332-6049

STATISTICAL PROFILE OF THE AFRICAN AMERICAN FAMILY

Table 5.1 Marital Status, 1980–1996 (in millions)

Marital status	Total				Male				Female			
	1980	1990	1995	1996	1980	1990	1995	1996	1980	1990	1995	1996
TOTAL, U.S.	159.5	181.8	191.6	193.2	75.7	86.9	92.0	92.7	83.8	95.0	99.6	100.4
Never married	32.3	40.4	43.9	44.9	18.0	22.4	24.6	24.9	14.3	17.9	19.3	20.0
Married	104.6	112.6	116.7	116.4	51.8	55.8	57.7	57.6	52.8	56.7	58.9	58.8
Widowed	12.7	13.8	13.4	13.5	2.0	2.3	2.3	2.5	10.8	11.5	11.1	11.1
Divorced	9.9	15.1	17.6	18.2	3.9	6.3	7.4	7.8	6.0	8.8	10.3	10.5
PERCENT OF TOTAL	100.0	100.0	100.0	100.0	100.0	100.0	100.0	100.0	100.0	100.0	100.0	100.0
Never married	20.3	22.2	22.9	23.3	23.8	25.8	26.8	26.8	17.1	18.9	19.4	19.9
Married	65.5	61.9	60.9	60.3	38.4	64.3	62.7	62.1	63.0	59.7	59.2	58.6
Widowed	8.0	7.6	7.0	7.0	2.6	2.7	2.5	2.7	12.8	12.1	11.1	11.0
Divorced	6.2	8.3	9.2	9.5	5.2	7.2	8.0	8.4	7.1	9.3	10.3	10.5
BLACK, TOTAL	16.6	20.3	22.1	22.3	7.4	9.1	9.9	10.0	9.2	11.2	12.2	12.4
Never married	5.1	7.1	8.5	8.8	2.5	3.5	4.1	4.2	2.5	3.6	4.4	4.6
Married	8.5	9.3	9.6	9.4	4.1	4.5	4.6	4.5	4.5	4.8	4.9	4.9
Widowed	1.6	1.7	1.7	1.6	0.3	0.3	0.3	0.3	1.3	1.4	1.4	1.3
Divorced	1.4	2.1	2.4	2.6	0.5	0.8	0.8	1.0	0.9	1.3	1.5	1.6
PERCENT OF TOTAL	100.0	100.0	100.0	100.0	100.0	100.0	100.0	100.0	100.0	100.0	100.0	100.0
Never married	30.5	35.1	38.4	39.2	34.3	38.4	41.7	42.1	27.4	32.5	35.8	36.8
Married	51.4	45.8	43.2	42.2	54.6	49.2	46.7	45.0	48.7	43.0	40.4	39.9
Widowed	9.8	8.5	7.6	7.2	4.2	3.7	3.1	2.8	14.3	12.4	11.3	10.7
Divorced	8.4	10.6	10.7	11.5	7.0	8.8	8.5	10.2	9.5	12.0	12.5	12.6

Sources: U.S. Bureau of the Census, 1970 Census of Population Vol. I, part 1; and Current Population Reports,
P20-450, and earlier reports; and unpublished data.

Table 5.2 Family Groups with Children under 18 Years Old, 1980–1996

Household	Number (in thousands)			Percentage Distribution		
	1980	1990	1996	1980	1990	1996
U.S., TOTAL	32,150	34,670	37,077	100	100	100
Two-parent family groups	25,231	24,921	25,361	79	72	68
One-parent family groups	6,920	9,749	11,717	22	28	32
Maintained by mother	6,230	8,398	9,855	19	24	27
Maintained by father	690	1,351	1,862	2	4	5
BLACK, TOTAL	4,074	5,087	5,434	100	100	100
Two-parent family groups	1,961	2,006	1,942	48	39	36
One-parent family groups	2,114	3,081	3,493	52	61	64
Maintained by mother	1,984	2,860	3,171	49	56	58
Maintained by father	129	221	322	3	4	6

Source: U.S. Bureau of the Census, Current Population Reports, P20-447, and earlier reports; and unpublished data.

CUISINE AND RECIPES

Traditional African American and Caribbean cuisine has its roots in Africa. Across the middle passage, many Africans brought with them the seedlings for traditional crops—including okra (which they called gombo), peanuts (which they called groundnuts or goobers), cowpeas or black-eyed peas, and sesame seeds (which they called benne)—along with techniques for growing, seasoning, and cooking them. Once on plantations, the enslaved were often supplied with discarded animal parts, such as hog maw, hog jowl, pig's feet, and ham hocks. They also grew their own vegetables and spices on small gardens they were sometimes allowed; there, they cultivated traditional crops brought from Africa, as well as other available items, such as collard and dandelion greens. The improvisatory artisanship of these pioneering cooks led to the creation of a new cuisine, now known almost universally as soul food.

In the Caribbean, enslaved Africans combined African spices and cooking techniques with a wide variety of influences, including French, Spanish, and English cooking, as well as the spices and curries that East Indian residents of the Caribbean brought from their Asian homeland. The resulting combinations form the unique cuisine of the Caribbean islands.

In addition, a number of classic Southern and Creole dishes were directly imported from Africa: gumbo, jambalaya, calaloo, fufu, hoppin' Johns, and jollof rice, to name a few. The dishes listed in this section include traditional Southern and Creole favorites (some updated for healthier dining), as well as some well-known and much-loved treats from various parts of the Caribbean.

> I n Black American ghettos the hero is that man who is offered only the crumbs from his country's table but by ingenuity and courage is able to take for himself a Lucullan feast.
>
> Maya Angelou, I Know Why the Caged Bird Sings

SOUTHERN FAVORITES

Hoppin' John—Peas and Plenty   (from Nash's Celebrating Our Mothers' Kitchens)

2 tablespoons oil

1 smoked ham hock (or use 1 pound mild or hot Italian sausage, chopped)

1 medium onion, chopped

10 cups water, divided

1 package (16 ounces) dry black eye peas, rinsed

2 teaspoons salt

1 teaspoon dried parsley leaves

1 teaspoon dried thyme leaves

2 cups long-grain rice, uncooked

1. Heat oil in large saucepan on medium-high heat. Add ham hocks and onion; cook and stir until browned. Add 8 cups of the water, peas, salt, parsley and thyme; bring to boil. Reduce

heat to low; cover and simmer $2\frac{1}{2}$ hours or until tender. Remove ham hocks; cool slightly. Remove ham from bone. Shred ham. Return to pot; discard bone.

2. Add remaining 2 cups water; bring to boil. Stir in rice. Reduce heat to low; cover. Simmer 20 minutes or until rice is tender, adding additional water for moister consistency, if desired.

Makes 8 servings

Onions, Okra, Corn, and Tomatoes   (from Nash's *Celebrating Our Mothers' Kitchens*)

$\frac{1}{2}$ pound bacon

1 large onion, sliced

3 large tomatoes, sliced

2 cans (16 ounces each) whole kernel corn, drained

1 package (10 ounces) frozen cut okra

$\frac{3}{4}$ teaspoon salt

$\frac{1}{4}$ teaspoon pepper

1. Cook bacon in large saucepan on medium heat until crisp, turning frequently. Drain, reserving 2 tablespoons drippings in saucepan.

2. Heat reserved drippings in saucepan on medium heat. Add onion; cook and stir until tender. Add tomatoes, corn, okra, salt and pepper; cover and simmer 30 minutes, stirring occasionally. Crumble bacon; sprinkle over top just before serving.

Makes 10 servings

Nola's Cheesy Macaroni and Cheese   (from Nash's *Celebrating Our Mothers' Kitchens*)

1 package (16 ounces) small shell or elbow macaroni, cooked and drained

3 tablespoons Parkay spread, stick or butter

1 tablespoon flour

3 cups milk, divided

6 cups (24 ounces) shredded Kraft natural cheddar cheese, divided

2 eggs

1. Heat oven to 350 degrees. Place macaroni in 4-quart shallow baking dish.

2. Melt spread in medium saucepan on medium-low heat. Stir in flour. Gradually stir in 2 cups of the milk; cook until smooth. Add 3 cups of the cheese; cook, stirring constantly until sauce is thickened. Pour over macaroni. Add remaining cheese; stir gently until thoroughly mixed.

3. Beat eggs in small bowl; stir in remaining 1 cup of milk. Slowly pour over top of casserole. Let stand 5 minutes.

4. Bake 40 minutes or until set and lightly browned. Cool 10 minutes. Cut into squares.

Makes 12 servings

Creole Red Beans and Rice   (from Nash's *Celebrating Our Mothers' Kitchens*)

1 package (16 ounces) dry red beans

2 small smoked ham hocks (or use smoked beef sausages, cut into 1-inch pieces)

1 large onion, chopped

4 bay leaves

5 cloves garlic, minced

1 teaspoon dried thyme leaves

1 teaspoon crushed red pepper

1 tablespoon salt

$\frac{1}{2}$ teaspoon black pepper

1 pound shrimp, cleaned

Hot cooked rice

1. Rinse and soak beans as directed on package.

2. Bring beans, ham, water to cover, and

seasonings to boil in large saucepan. Reduce heat to low; cover and simmer 1 to 1½ hours or until ham and beans are tender, adding water if necessary. Add shrimp; cook 10 minutes. Serves over rice.

Makes 8½ cups

Southern Fried Chicken   (from Nash's *Celebrating Our Mothers' Kitchens*)

3½ pounds chicken pieces

1½ teaspoons salt

¼ teaspoon pepper

1 cup flour

1½ cups shortening

1. Sprinkle chicken with salt and pepper. Refrigerate 30 minutes. Place flour in paper or plastic bag. Add chicken pieces, 1 or 2 at a time; shake to coat.

2. Melt shortening in large cast-iron skillet on high heat. Add chicken, skin side down, a few pieces at a time; cook 15 minutes on each side or until cooked through and golden brown. Drain on paper towels; keep warm. Repeat with remaining chicken.

Makes 8 servings

Bless My Soul Chops   (from Nash's *Celebrating Our Mothers' Kitchens*)

6 tablespoons margarine or butter, divided

1 medium onion, chopped

1 stalk celery, chopped

1 clove garlic, minced

2 cups crumbled cornbread

1 cup fresh bread crumbs

⅓ cup chopped fresh parsley

1 tablespoon poultry seasoning

¼ teaspoon salt

dash pepper

1 egg, beaten

6 pork chops with pockets, about 1½ inches thick

1 cup apple juice

½ teaspoon dried basil leaves

1. Melt 4 tablespoons of the margarine in large skillet on medium-high heat. Add onion, celery, and garlic; cook and stir until tender. Mix cornbread, bread crumbs, parsley, poultry seasoning, salt, and pepper in large bowl. Stir in egg and vegetable mixture. Stuff chops, securing with toothpicks, if necessary. Sprinkle with additional salt and pepper.

2. Melt remaining 2 tablespoons margarine in large skillet with cover or Dutch oven on medium-high heat. Add 3 of the chops, cook 5 minutes on each side or until browned. Repeat with remaining chops. Return chops to skillet. Add apple juice and basil; bring to boil. Reduce heat to low; cover and simmer 40 minutes or until chops are cooked through, turning once.

Makes 6 servings

Billy's Ribs   (from Nash's *Celebrating Our Mothers' Kitchens*)

Ribs

10 pounds pork baby back ribs

2 quarts water

2 medium onions, chopped

¼ cup liquid hickory smoke

2 tablespoons salt

1 tablespoon pepper

1 teaspoon onion salt

1 clove garlic, sliced

dash paprika

Sauce

8 cups assorted purchased barbecue sauces

1 bottle (14 ounces) catsup

1 bottle (12 ounces) beer

1 onion, chopped

2 hot chili peppers

1 tablespoon firmly packed brown sugar

1 clove garlic, sliced

1 teaspoon seasoning salt

1. For ribs: mix ribs, onions, liquid smoke, salt, pepper, onion salt, garlic, and paprika in large saucepan; cover. Refrigerate overnight to marinate.
2. For sauce: mix barbecue sauces, ketchup, beer, onion, peppers, brown sugar, garlic, and seasoning salt in large saucepan. Simmer on low heat 1 hour.
3. Heat grill.
4. Drain ribs. Discard any remaining marinade. Brush ribs thoroughly with sauce.
5. Place ribs in grill over hot coals. Grill 1 to $1\frac{1}{2}$ hours or until cooked through, turning and basting frequently with sauce.

Makes 8 servings

Fried Catfish   (from Nash's *Celebrating Our Mothers' Kitchens*)

1 cup cornmeal

$\frac{1}{2}$ cup flour

1 teaspoon salt

$\frac{1}{2}$ teaspoon garlic salt

$\frac{1}{4}$ teaspoon onion powder

$\frac{1}{4}$ teaspoon pepper

1 pound boneless catfish fillets, cut into serving pieces

$\frac{3}{4}$ cup shortening

Lemon Wedges

1. Mix cornmeal, flour, salt, garlic salt, onion powder, and pepper in paper or plastic bag. Add fish pieces, 3 or 4 at a time; shake to coat.
2. Melt shortening in large skillet on medium-high heat. Add fish, 2 or 3 pieces at a time; cook 5 minutes on each side or until golden brown and fish flakes easily with fork. Remove from skillet. Drain on paper towels; keep warm. Repeat with remaining fish. Garnish with lemon wedges.

Makes 4 servings

Baking-Powder Biscuits   (from Nash's *Celebrating Our Mothers' Kitchens*)

$1\frac{3}{4}$ cups flour

1 tablespoon baking powder

$\frac{1}{2}$ teaspoon salt

$\frac{1}{3}$ cup shortening or margarine

$\frac{3}{4}$ cup milk

1. Heat oven to 450 degrees.
2. Mix flour, baking powder, and salt in large bowl. Cut in margarine until mixture resembles coarse crumbs. Add milk to flour mixture; stir until soft dough forms.
3. Knead dough on lightly floured surface until smooth. Pat or roll lightly until dough is $\frac{1}{2}$ inch thick. Cut with floured 2-inch cookie cutter. Place on ungreased cookie sheet.
4. Bake 10 minutes or until golden brown.

Makes 16 servings

Southern-Style Corn Bread   (from Nash's *Celebrating Our Mothers' Kitchens*)

1 cup flour

1 cup white or yellow cornmeal

2 tablespoons sugar

2 teaspoons baking powder

1 teaspoon baking soda

1 teaspoon salt

2 eggs

$1\frac{1}{2}$ cups buttermilk

$\frac{1}{3}$ cup shortening or butter, melted

1. Heat oven to 425 degrees. Grease 9-inch square baking pan.
2. Mix flour, cornmeal, sugar, baking powder, baking soda, and salt in large bowl. Beat eggs in medium bowl; stir in buttermilk and shortening. Add to flour mixture. Stir just until moistened. Pour into prepared pan.
3. Bake 25 minutes or until golden brown.

Makes 10 servings

Sour Cream Pound Cake   (from Nash's *Celebrating Our Mothers' Kitchens*)

2 cups flour

1 teaspoon baking powder

$\frac{1}{2}$ teaspoon salt

1 cup (2 sticks) butter, softened

$1\frac{2}{3}$ cups sugar

5 eggs

$1\frac{1}{2}$ teaspoons vanilla

$\frac{1}{2}$ cup sour cream

1. Heat oven to 325 degrees. Grease 9-by-5-inch loaf pan.

2. Mix flour, baking powder, and salt in small bowl. Beat butter and sugar in large bowl with electric mixer on medium speed until light and fluffy. Add eggs, 1 at a time, beating well after each addition. Beat in vanilla. Add flour mixture alternately with sour cream, stirring after each addition until smooth. Pour into prepared pan.

3. Bake 1 hour and 10 minutes or until toothpick inserted in center comes out clean. Cool 10 minutes; remove from pan. Cool completely on wire rack.

Makes 12 servings

Mary McLeod Bethune's Sweet Potato Pie   (from Nash's *Celebrating Our Mothers' Kitchens*)

1 cup (2 sticks) margarine or butter, softened

$\frac{1}{2}$ cup refined sugar

$\frac{1}{2}$ cup firmly packed brown sugar

$\frac{1}{2}$ teaspoon salt

$\frac{1}{4}$ teaspoon ground nutmeg

9 medium sweet potatoes or yams (4 pounds), cooked, peeled, and mashed

3 eggs, beaten

2 cups milk

1 tablespoon vanilla

3 unbaked pastry shells (9 inch)

1. Heat oven to 350 degrees.

2. Beat margarine, sugars, salt, and nutmeg in large bowl with electric mixer on medium speed until creamy. Add sweet potatoes; beat until well blended. Beat in eggs. Gradually beat in milk and vanilla. Pour filling into pastry shells, using about 4 cups in each shell.

3. Bake 50 to 60 minutes or until set. Cool completely on wire racks. Refrigerate until ready to serve. Store leftover pie in refrigerator.

Makes 3 (9-inch) pies

Southern Banana Pudding   (from Nash's *Celebrating Our Mothers' Kitchens*)

2 packages (4-serving size) Jell-O vanilla or banana cream flavor cook and serve pudding & pie filling

$4\frac{1}{2}$ cups milk

3 egg yolks, beaten

42 round vanilla wafer cookies ($\frac{1}{2}$ of a 12-ounce package)

2 large bananas, sliced

3 egg whites

Dash salt

$\frac{1}{3}$ cup sugar

1. Heat oven to 350 degrees.

2. Stir pudding mix into milk in medium saucepan. Add egg yolks. Stirring constantly, cook on medium heat until mixture comes to full boil. Remove from heat.

3. Arrange layer of cookies on bottom and up sides of 2-quart baking dish. Top with $\frac{1}{2}$ of the banana slices; top with $\frac{1}{3}$ of the pudding. Repeat layers, ending with pudding.

4. Beat egg whites and salt in medium bowl with electric mixer on high speed until foamy. Gradually add sugar, beating until stiff peaks form. Spoon lightly onto pudding, sealing edges well.

5. Bake 10 to 15 minutes or until meringue is lightly browned. Cool on wire rack. Serve warm or refrigerate, if desired. Before serving, garnish with additional banana slices dipped in lemon juice to prevent darkening if desired.

CHILDREN'S GAMES

Here are some contemporary and historical games played by black children in rural and urban areas around the United States.

DOUBLE DUTCH

The classic jump-rope game that girls have been playing for years needs at least three participants—two to turn the two jump ropes, one to jump. In her memoir *Mama's Girl*, Veronica Chambers describes her own experience of double dutch: "While the ropes are turning, jumpers rock back and forth before springing into the middle to jump without stepping on the rope. The challenge comes in the longevity of jumping and performing tricks, like pop-ups, mambos and around the world. [When doing a pop-up], you drop down and then you jump up again and you do it over and over until the rope catches on your foot. . . . You keep your arms to your sides, out of the way, so they don't get tangled in the rope. . . . When you mambo back and forth, it's like dancing. When you do around the world, it's like a ballet dancer's pirouette."

JUBA THIS AND JUBA THAT

This game was created in the 19th century in reference to the mixture of leftover food—"a little of this and a little of that"—that enslaved and freed Southern blacks used to make meals. This version also evokes Juba, a traditional African American dance form that became popular during the early 19th century. Words were added later.

In this game, one player is chosen as the caller, and the others follow the caller's movements. The caller continues as long as possible, continuing to invent rhymes; when the caller runs out of ideas, she or he is replaced by another player. A traditional set of rhymes accompanying the game goes as follows (players clap once after the first line of each couplet, twice after the second line):

> Juba this and Juba that,
> And Juba killed a yellow cat.
>
> You sift a meal, you give me husk,
> You cook the bread, you give me the crust.
>
> You fry the meat, you give me the skin
> And that's where my mama's troubles begin.
>
> Juba up, Juba down.
> Juba all around the town.
>
> Juba for ma, Juba for pa,
> Juba for your brother-in-law.
>
> Juba that and Juba this.
> I'll keep rhyming, I won't miss.

MY MAMA'S CALLING ME

In this game, players hold hands, forming a circle, with one youngster in the middle. As the player in the center sings each verse of the song, the others sing the second verse in a call-and-response pattern. During the song, the player in the center tries to leave the circle, and whoever lets that player through takes the place inside the circle.

Song

My mama's calling me.
    You can't get out of here.
My mama's calling me.
    You can't get out here.
What shall I do?
    Pat your ones to your knees.
What shall I do?
    Pat your twos to your knees.
(Repeat until the center player escapes.)

LITTLE SALLY WALKER

Little Sally Walker, created in the United States, goes with the song "Shake It to the One That You Love the Best." The players form a circle around one youngster, who is called Sally. Sally kneels and sings the song, acting out its words. As she (or he) does this, the other players hold hands and move in a circle as they sing along. As Sally sings the lines beginning with "Shake it to the east . . . ," he or she moves toward the edge of the circle, feinting and retreating, and at the song's end, this player picks another player to take the place in the middle.

Song

Little Sally Walker sitting in a saucer,
Ride, Sally, ride.
Wipe your weeping eyes,
Put your hands on your hips,
And let your backbone slip.
Shake it to the east,
Shake it to the west,
Shake it to the one you love the best!
Little Sally Walker sitting in a saucer,
Crying for the old man to come for the dollar.
Ride, Sally, ride.
Put your hands on your hips,
And let your backbone slip.

MARY MACK

This clapping rhyme combines the song "Mary Mack" with various clapping hand formations. As explained in Warren-Maddox's *Shake It to the One That You Love*, participants "clap" individually or with a partner. The claps come on the last three words of each verse, or on the last three words of each verse, clap your knees, clap your hands, clap your partner's hands. Alternatively, pantomime actions as suggested by the words.

Song

Oh, Mary Mack, Mack, Mack
All dressed in black, black, black
With silver buttons, buttons, buttons
All down her back, back, back.
She asked her mother, mother, mother

For fifteen cents, cents, cents
To see the elephant, elephant, elephant
Jump the fence, fence, fence.
He jumped so high, high, high
He reached the sky, sky, sky
And he didn't come back, back, back
'till the Fourth of July, 'ly, 'ly.

HERE COMES SALLY

The players form two facing lines, each player matched with a partner. During the first part of the song, the players dance whatever steps they choose and clap their hands. They then take three steps back to create an aisle ("Step back Sally") so that each set of partners can sashay down the middle on "Struttin down the alley." Players then pantomime the actions described in the rest of the song.

Song

Here comes Sally, Sally, Sally
Here comes Sally all night long.
So step back Sally, Sally, Sally
Step back Sally, all night long.
Struttin down the alley, alley, alley
Struttin down the alley all night long.
Here comes another one just like the other one
A little bit bigger, but that's all right.
I looked over there and what did I see?
A big, fat lady from Tennessee.
I bet you five dollars I can beat that man.
To the front, to the back, to the side, side, side.
To the front, to the back, to the side, side, side.
Sing! Um be-bop, bop
Um um, be-bop, bop
Um be-bop, bop
All night long.

MUSEUMS AND HISTORIC SITES

The historic sites listed in this section are just a sampling of the hundreds of significant African American historical places in the United States. Complete listings can be found in George Cantor, *Historic Black Landmarks: A Traveler's Guide* (Detroit: Visible Ink, 1991) and *African American Historic Places* (Washington, DC: Preservation Press, 1994). The sites are listed alphabetically by state, then by city, then by site. (See also "Galleries and Museums Specializing in African and African American Art" on p. 447.)

ALABAMA

Sixteenth Street Baptist Church
Sixth Avenue and N. 16th Street
Birmingham

Site of the 1963 bombing that claimed the lives of four African American children.

Birmingham Civil Rights Institute
Sixth Avenue and N. 16th Street
Birmingham (205-328-9696)
Exhibits encompass segregation, African American culture, and the civil rights movement.

Alabama Department of Archives and History
1 Dexter Drive
Montgomery (205-262-0013)
Complex housing eight museums devoted to various aspects of the African American experience.

Civil Rights Memorial
Washington Street, near Hull Street
Montgomery
Erected in 1989 by the Southern Poverty Law Center.

Dexter Avenue–King Memorial Baptist Church
454 Dexter Avenue
Montgomery
Reverend King's home church; served as the headquarters of the Montgomery bus boycott.

Old Depot Museum
Foot of Water Avenue
Selma (205-875-9918)
Materials on Selma's black community.

Tuskegee Institute National Historic Site
Carver Museum
Tuskegee (205-727-6390)
Exhibits highlight the achievements of George Washington Carver and Booker T. Washington.

ARIZONA

Fort Huachuca Museum
Fort Huachuca Military Base
Fort Huachuca (602-533-5736)
Former headquarters of the 10th Cavalry and 24th Infantry (Buffalo Soldiers) during the 19th century; largest African American military base during World War II.

ARKANSAS

Kiblah School
Route 1
Doddridge
Built in 1926; associated with the historic African American town of Kiblah, founded in 1866 by freed blacks.

Central High School
Park Avenue and 14th Street
Little Rock
Scene of the epic desegregation battle in 1957.

Ethnic Minorities Memorabilia Association Museum
Franklin Street
Washington (501-983-2891)

CALIFORNIA

California Afro-American Museum
600 State Drive, Exposition Park
Los Angeles (213-744-7432)

Northern California Center for Afro-American History and Life
5606 San Pablo Avenue
Oakland (510-658-3158)
Collections illuminate African American life in California.

African-American Historical and Cultural Society
Fort Mason Center, Building C-165
San Francisco (415-441-0640)
Facilities include a museum and gallery.

COLORADO

Black American West Museum and Heritage Center
3091 California Street
Denver (303-292-2566)

CONNECTICUT

Amistad Foundation at the Wadsworth Atheneum
600 Main Street
Hartford (860-270-2670)
Collection of more than 6,000 objects documenting African American Art and History.

Connecticut Afro-American Historical Society
444 Orchard Street
New Haven (203-776-4907)
Museum highlights the contributions of African Americans in New England.

DISTRICT OF COLUMBIA

Bethune Museum and Archives
1318 Vermont Avenue, NW (202-332-1233)

Contains memorabilia of Mary McLeod Bethune and exhibits on African American women.

Frederick A. Douglass National Historical Site
1411 W. Street, SE (202-426-5960)
Known as Cedar Hill, this house was Douglass's home from 1877 until his death in 1895.

Lincoln Memorial
West Potomac Park
Scene of Marian Anderson's 1939 concert and the 1963 March on Washington.

Moorland-Springarn Research Center
Howard University (202-636-6108)
Houses a museum of African American history.

Smithsonian Institution Center for African American History and Culture
900 Jefferson Drive, SW (202-357-2700)

FLORIDA

American Beach
Amelia Island
Located 40 miles northeast of Jacksonville; developed as a black resort colony by the Afro-American Life Insurance Company; many properties are still in the hands of the original owners and their heirs.

Zora Neale Hurston Memorial Park and Marker
11 People Street
Eatonville (407-647-3307)
Eatonville, America's first black incorporated town, is often celebrated in the work of its most famous citizen, born here in 1891; every January, the town holds a festival celebrating Hurston's life and achievements.

Kingsley Plantation
Ft. George Island, 25 miles northwest of Jacksonville

Black Archives History and Research Foundation
Joseph Caleb Community Center
Miami (305-638-6375)
Contains materials illustrating the variety of diaspora cultures represented in South Florida.

Olustee State Historical Site
3 miles east of Olustee
Site of the 1864 battle in which the 54th Massachusetts distinguished itself.

Castillo de San Marcos National Monument
St. Augustine
This fort was once a beacon to African Americans who escaped from bondage; they usually settled in nearby Fort Mose.

Black Archives, Research Center, and Museum
Carnegie Library
Tallahassee (904-599-3020)

GEORGIA

Apex Museum
135 Auburn Avenue
Atlanta (404-521-2739)

Atlanta University Center District
West of downtown via Martin Luther King, Jr. Drive
Comprises the campuses of Atlanta, Clark, Morris Brown, Morehouse, and Spelman universities.

Martin Luther King, Jr. National Historic Site and Preservation District
Bounded roughly by Courtland, Randolph, and Chamberlain Streets and Irwin Avenue
Atlanta (404-331-3919)
Includes Reverend King's birthplace and gravesite, as well as Ebenezer Baptist Church and the Martin Luther King, Jr., Center for Nonviolent Social Change.

Ma Rainey House
805 Fifth Avenue
Columbus (706-571-4700)
Restored home of the renowned blues singer.

Michael C. Carlos Museum
Emory University
571 Kilgo Street
Atlanta (404-727-4282)

Harriet Tubman Historical and Cultural Museum
340 Walnut Street
Macon (912-743-8544)

ILLINOIS

Black History Tours
1721 W. 85th Street
Chicago (312-233-8907)

DuSable Museum of African-American History and Art

740 E. 56th Street
Chicago (312-947-0600)

Ida B. Wells-Barnett House
3624 S. Martin Luther King, Jr. Drive
Chicago
Memorabilia of the outstanding civil rights
    activist and antilynching crusader.

African American Hall of Fame Museum
309 S. DuSable Street
Peoria (309-673-2206)

INDIANA

Levi Coffin House
115 Main Street
Fountain City
Major stop on the Underground Railroad.

Freetown Village
202 N. Alabama Street
Indianapolis (317-232-1637)
Re-creation of the life of black settlers in
    Indiana after the Civil War.

Madame Walker Urban Life Center
617 Indiana Avenue
Indianapolis (317-236-2099)
Built in 1927 as the headquarters of Madame
    C. J. Walker's business enterprises; now a
    cultural center for the African American
    community.

IOWA

Buxton Heritage Museum
1226 Second Avenue
Des Moines (515-276-2252)
Commemorates the African American coal-
    mining communities of the region.

Carver Museum
Warren County Fairgrounds
Indianola (515-961-6031)
Housed in the shack in which Carver did much
    of his work.

KANSAS

Nicodemus Historic District
Located along Route 24 in Graham County, 2

miles west of the Graham-Rooks county line.
Site of once-prosperous African American
town founded in 1877 by a group of
Exodusters.

John Brown Memorial Park
10th and Main Streets
Ossawatomie (913-755-4384)
Site includes the John Brown Cabin, used as a
    headquarters for Brown's antislavery activities
    in Kansas.

Brown v. Board of Education National
    Historic Site
330 Western Avenue (Sumner School)
1515 Monroe Street (Monroe School)
Topeka
The Sumner and Monroe schools were involved
    in the lawsuits leading up to the historic 1954
    Supreme Court decision ending school
    segregation.

KENTUCKY

Whitney M. Young, Jr. House and Historical
    Marker
U.S. 60 W
Simpsonville (502-585-4733)
Birthplace of the civil rights leader.

Old Slave Market
5 miles south of Mayville off Route 68
Washington (606-759-7411)

LOUISIANA

Melrose Plantation
Highway 119, off Louisiana 493
Melrose (318-379-0171)

Chalmette Battlefield, Jean Lafitte National
    Historic Park
New Orleans
Site of the Battle of New Orleans, where free
    black militia fighters distinguished themselves
    in 1815.

Congo Square
Intersection of Rampart and St. Peter Streets
New Orleans
Site of weekly African American festivals during
    the first half of the 19th century.

MARYLAND

Banneker-Douglass Museum
84 Franklin Street
Annapolis (410-974-2893)

Cab Calloway Jazz Institute Museum
Coppin State College
Baltimore (410-383-5926)

Eubie Blake National Museum
409 N. Charles Street
Baltimore (301-396-3181)

Harriet Tubman Birthplace
Near Cambridge on Maryland 397 (301-228-0401)

MASSACHUSETTS

African Meeting House
8 Smith Street
Boston
Built in 1806; oldest known extant church
    building in the United States built by African
    Americans.

Black Heritage Trail (617-742-5415)
Includes 14 sites in Boston, including those
    listed herein.

Crispus Attucks Monument
Boston Common
Erected in 1888; honors Attucks and the four
    other Americans killed in the Boston
    Massacre (see Chapter 11 for a biography of
    Attucks).

Museum of Afro-American History
46 Joy Street
Boston (617-742-1854)

Robert Gould Shaw and 54th Regiment
    Memorial
Boston Common
Erected in 1897; bronze sculpture by Augustus
    Saint-Gaudens honors the illustrious African
    American Civil War regiment (a gilded
    plaster bas-relief of the same subject,
    completed in the following year, currently
    resides at the National Gallery of Art in
    Washington, D.C.).

MICHIGAN

Sojourner Truth Memorial
Oak Hill Cemetery
Battle Creek

Motown Museum
2648 W. Grand Boulevard
Detroit (313-867-0991)
Commemorates the achievements of the
    illustrious black-owned music and
    entertainment empire.

Museum of African-American History
315 East Warren Avenue
Detroit (313-494-5800)
Largest museum of African American history in
    the United States; exhibits include a model of
    a slave ship with 40 life-size figures.

National Museum of Tuskegee Airmen
6325 W. Jefferson
Detroit (313-843-8849)
Preserves the history of the legendary African
    American aviators of World War II.

Malcolm X Homesite Historical Marker
4705 S. Logan Street
Lansing

MISSISSIPPI

Delta Blues Museum
114 Delta Avenue
Clarksdale (601-624-4461)

Booker-Thomas Museum
Highway 12 (Tchula Road)
Lexington (601-834-2672)
Preserves the history of African Americans in
    rural Mississippi during the early 20th century.

Mound Bayou
On U.S. 61, 25 miles south of Clarksdale
Largest African American town in the United
    States (population c. 3,000), self-governing
    since 1898.

Natchez Museum of Afro-American History and
    Culture
307A Marker Street
Natchez (601-445-0278)

MISSOURI

George Washington Carver National Monument
Diamond (417-325-4151)
Site includes the farm where the great scientist
was born and raised.

Lincoln University Hilltop Campus Historic
District
Jefferson City (573-681-5000)
Historically black university founded with
donations from African American soldiers in
1866.

Black Archives of Mid-America
3022 Vine Street
Kansas City (816-483-1300)

Scott Joplin House
2658 Delmar Boulevard
St. Louis (314-533-1003)

NEBRASKA

Great Plains Black Museum
2213 Lake Street
Omaha (402-345-2212)

NEW JERSEY

Afro-American Historical Society Museum
1841 Kennedy Boulevard
Jersey City (201-547-5262)

Newark Museum
43–49 Washington Street
Newark (201-596-6550)

NEW YORK

Harriet Tubman House
180 South Street
Auburn (315-252-2081)
The renowned abolitionist moved into this
house after the Civil War and occupied it
until her death in 1913.

African American Museum
110 N. Franklin Street
Hempstead (516-485-0470)

Preserves the history of African Americans on
Long Island.

Abyssinian Baptist Church
132 W. 138th Street
New York City (212-862-7474)
Contains a museum of memorabilia relating to
the careers of Adam Clayton Powell Sr. and
Adam Clayton Powell Jr.

African Burial Ground
Near intersection of Broadway and Reade Street
New York City (212-432-5707)
Largest known African American burial ground
in the United States, dating from the 17th
century; discovered in 1991 during
excavations for a construction project; as
many as 20,000 African Americans may have
been buried here.

Audubon Ballroom and Malcolm X Memorial
165th Street and Broadway
New York City
Site of Malcolm's assassination.

Fraunces Tavern
Pearl and Broad Streets
New York City (212-269-0144)
Scene of Washington's farewell speech to his
officers in 1783; owned at the time by Samuel
Fraunces, a West Indian who had staunchly
supported the patriot cause and who ran the
Executive Mansion when Washington became
president.

Museum of the City of New York
Fifth Avenue at 103rd Street
New York City (212-534-1672)
Exhibits on the history of African Americans in
New York.

Schomburg Center for Research in Black
Culture
515 Malcolm X Boulevard
New York City (800-261-8783)
Internationally renowned collections of more
than 5 million books, photographs, films,
documents, video and sound recordings, art
objects, and international resources dedicated
to the documentation of the historical and
cultural development of African peoples.

NORTH CAROLINA

Diggs Gallery
Winston-Salem University
Winston-Salem (910-750-2468)

OHIO

African American Museum
1765 Crawford Road
Cleveland (216-791-1700)

Harriet Tubman Museum
9250 Miles Park
Cleveland (216-341-1202)

Paul Laurence Dunbar House
219 N. Summit Street
Dayton (513-224-7061)
The house is furnished as it was at the time of
the poet's death.

National Afro-American Museum and Cultural
Center
Wilberforce University
1350 Brush Row Road
Wilberforce (513-376-4944)

OKLAHOMA

Boley National Historic District
Okfuskee County, 60 miles east of Oklahoma
City on U.S. 62 (Boley Chamber of
Commerce: 918-667-3341)
Built by African American railway workers in
1903; historic district bounded roughly by
Seward Avenue, Walnut and Cedar Streets,
and the southern city limits; site of annual
Black Rodeo held Memorial Day weekend.

PENNSYLVANIA

African American Museum in Philadelphia
701 Arch Street
Philadelphia (215-574-0380)

All-Wars Memorial to Black Soldiers
42nd Street and Parkside Avenue
Philadelphia (215-685-0001)

John W. Coltrane Home and Historical Marker
1511 N. 33rd Street
Philadelphia (215-763-1118)
Contains a museum honoring African American
musicians in Philadelphia.

Mother Bethel A.M.E. Church
419 Sixth Street
Philadelphia (215-925-0616)
The present building, built in 1859, stands on
the site of the original church founded by
Richard Allen in 1794; the plot is the oldest
piece of real estate in the United States
continuously owned by African Americans;
the church houses a museum and Allen's
tomb.

SOUTH CAROLINA

Denmark Vesey House
56 Bull Street
Charleston
Vesey settled in the house after purchasing his
freedom and set up his carpenter's shop on the
ground floor; the aborted 1822 insurrection
was planned in meetings on the premises.

Old Slave Mart Museum
6 Chalmers Street
Charleston

Stono River Slave Rebellion Site
Rantowles, 12 miles west of Charleston on
U.S. 17
Historic marker on the site of the 1739 uprising.

TENNESSEE

Alex Haley House Museum
200 S. Church Street
Henning (901-738-2240)
Contains memorabilia of the author of *Roots*.

Fort Pillow State Park
17 miles west of Henning, on Tennessee 87
Site of the 1864 massacre of black and white
Union soldiers.

Beale Street Historic District
Beale Street from Second to Fourth Streets
Memphis (901-526-0110)
Site of the saloons, clubs, and theaters where the
blues was developed during the early 20th
century.

National Civil Rights Museum
450 Mulberry Street
Memphis (901-521-9699)
Incorporates the Lorraine Motel, where
Rev. King was assassinated.

Fisk University Historic District
Nashville
Roughly bounded by 16th and 18th Avenues and
Hermosa, Herman, and Jefferson Streets.

TEXAS

African American Museum of History
and Culture
35-36 Grand Avenue
Dallas (214-565-9026)

George Washington Carver Museum
1165 Angelina Street
Austin (512-472-4809)

Taylor-Stevenson Ranch
11822 Alameda Street
Houston (713-433-4441)
Long-established black-owned cattle ranch.

VIRGINIA

Fredericksburg Area Museum and Cultural
Center
904 Princess Anne Street
Fredericksburg (703-371-3037)
Explores the influence of African culture in the
United States.

Jamestown Settlement
Colonial Parkway
Jamestown (804-229-1607)
Historic re-creation of North America's first
English settlement; exhibits stress African

American contributions to the first 100 years
of Virginia's history.

Lynchburg Museum
901 Court Street
Lynchburg (804-846-1459)
Highlights 20th-century African American
history.

Black History Museum and Cultural Center of
Virginia
Clay Street
Richmond (804-780-9093)

Jackson Ward National Historic Site
Bounded by Fourth, Marshall, and Smith Streets
and I-95
Richmond
Commercial center of Richmond's African
American community at the turn of the 20th
century.

Maggie Walker House
110 Leigh Street
Richmond (804-780-1380)
Commemorates the influential bank president
and community leader.

Booker T. Washington National Monument
22 miles southeast of Roanoke on Virginia 122
(703-721-2094)
Historic restoration of the farm on which
Washington spent his first nine years;
illustrates the operation of a small farm during
slavery days.

WEST VIRGINIA

Harpers Ferry National Historic Park
Harpers Ferry (304-535-6223)
Site of John Brown's 1859 raid.

WISCONSIN

America's Black Holocaust Museum
2233 N. Fourth Street
Milwaukee (414-264-2500)

SOURCES FOR ADDITIONAL INFORMATION

Asante, Molefi Kete. *The Book of African Names*. Trenton, NJ: Africa World, 1991.

Beasley, Donna. *The Family Reunion Planner*. New York: Macmillan, 1997.

Chambers, Veronica. *Mama's Girl*. New York: Riverhead, 1996.

Cole, Harriette. *Jumping the Broom: The African-American Wedding Planner*. New York: Holt, 1993.

Courlander, Harold. *A Treasury of African Folklore*. New York: Marlowe, 1996.

———. *A Treasury of Afro-American Folklore*. New York: Marlowe, 1996.

Crockett, Norman L. *The Black Towns*. Lawrence: Regents Press of Kansas, 1979.

Dinwiddie-Boyd, Elza. *Proud Heritage: 11,001 Names for Your African-American Baby*. New York: Avon, 1994.

Dolkart, Andrew S., and Gretchen S. Sorin. *Touring Historic Harlem*. New York: New York Landmarks Conservancy, 1977.

Eklof, Barbara. *For Every Season: The Complete Guide to African American Celebrations, Traditional to Contemporary*. New York: HarperCollins, 1997.

Grigsby Bates, Karen, and Karen Elyse Hudson. *Basic Black: Home Training for Modern Times*. New York: Doubleday, 1996.

Gutman, Herbert G. *The Black Family in Slavery and Freedom, 1750–1925*. New York: Vintage, 1976.

Hare, Nathan, and Julia Hare. *Bringing the Black Boy to Manhood: The Passage*. San Francisco: Black Think Tank, 1985.

Hausman, Gerald, and Kelvin Rodriques. *African-American Alphabet: A Celebration of African-American and West Indian Culture, Custom, Myth, and Symbol*. New York: St. Martin's, 1996.

Hopson, Darlene Powell, and Derek S. Hopson, with Thomas Calvin. *Juba This & Juba That: 100 African-American Games for Children*. New York: Simon & Schuster, 1996.

LeBat, Carla. *Satisfy Your Soul: A Nationwide Listing of African American, African and Caribbean Restaurants*. McLean, VA: Impressions, 1997.

Moore, Mafori. *Transformation: A Rites of Passage Manual for African American Girls*. New York: STARS Press, 1987.

Nash, Jonell. *Celebrating Our Mothers' Kitchens: Treasured Memories and Tasted Recipes*. Washington, DC: National Council of Negro Women, 1994.

Puckett, Newbell N. *Black Names in America: Origin and Usage*. Boston: G. K. Hall, 1975.

Spaulding, Henry D. *Encyclopedia of Black Folklore and Humor*. New York: Johnathan David, 1972.

Sturgis, Ingrid. *The Nubian Wedding Book: Words and Rituals to Celebrate and Plan an African-American Wedding*. New York: Crown, 1997.

Warren-Maddox, Cheryl. *Shake It to the One That You Love: The Best Play Songs and Lullabies from Black Musical Traditions*. Nashville, TN: JTG of Nashville, 1996.

6
Religion

RELIGIOUS AFFILIATIONS

Listed here are the major religious groups with the largest numbers of black adherents in the United States. They are listed according to their approximate number of African American adherents.

CHRISTIAN AND CHRISTIAN-BASED DENOMINATIONS

Christianity has served a pivotal and complex role in African American history. Upon their arrival in the United States, enslaved Africans were denied the right to practice their own African faiths, while also being turned away from joining whites in their worship. They therefore found their own way to worship, incorporating mysticism and dynamic physical and oral expression, while developing their own perspectives on Christian faith. In the years before the Civil War, many Protestant clerics supported slavery from their pulpits, while others denounced it. After the Civil War, white churches often rejected black parishioners, leading black clergy and worshipers to form their own churches, which quickly became the backbone of black communities across the country. During the 1950s and 1960s, many of those churches and their clerics spearheaded the civil rights movement.

BAPTIST

The Baptist faith was established by 17th-century English Puritans who held that only believers should be admitted to church membership. They therefore rejected the Anglican practice of infant baptism; in their view, the rite of baptism could be performed only as a conscious testimony to religious faith. The Baptist faith was established in New England in 1620 but embraced African Americans only in the 1750s, when slaveholders became more lenient in allowing evangelists to preach to slaves. The first African American church in the United States was a Baptist congregation founded around 1773 in Silver Bluff, South Carolina. The church was disbanded during the Revolutionary War and revived by Reverend Jesse Peters in 1781. By 1822, there were some 37 African American Baptist churches in the United States. During the 1840s, a split developed between black and white Baptists over the vigor with which the church should pursue the cause of abolition. Black Baptists have gone their own way ever since, and there are now seven major African American Baptist groups, representing more than 40,000 churches and 13 million congregants. (In addition, nearly 500,000 African Americans still adhere to the racially mixed American Baptist Convention, which had a total membership of 1.5 million as of 1990.)

Baptists still adhere to the practice of baptizing (by immersion) those who profess their belief. There are many currents of thought within the Baptist faith but, in general, Baptists are equally concerned with theology and with religious experience and the expression of faith. Baptist worship centers on sermons that illuminate Scripture, often accompanied—most notably in the black church—by enthusiastic prayers and hymn singing. The governance of Baptist churches is decentralized; authority rests with local congregations, who are linked voluntarily in larger organizations. Separation between church and state has long been a cherished tenet of Baptist organizations.

National Baptist Convention, U.S.A., Inc.
  (NBCUSA)
915 Spain Street
Baton Rouge, LA 71103
225-383-5401
30,000 churches; 7.5 million members
Organized in 1895 in Atlanta; auxiliaries include
  the National Baptist Laymen's Movement, the
  National Baptist Congress of Christian
  Education, and the Women's Convention;
  active in Central America, the Caribbean, and
  Africa; supports a number of educational
  institutions, including Morehouse School of
  Religion, Shaw University, and the American
  Baptist Theological Seminary.

National Baptist Convention of America, Inc.
  (NBCA)
1450 Pierre Avenue
Shreveport, LA 71103
318-221-2629
7,000-plus churches; 3.5–5 million members
  (estimated)
Organized in 1915 after a dispute over control of
  the National Baptist Publishing Board.

National Missionary Baptist Convention of
  America
719 Crosby Street
San Diego, CA 92113
619-233-6487
14,281 churches; 2,142,150 members
Organized in 1988 with the aim of restoring the
  original structure of the Baptist organization
  and organizing a separate Sunday school
  congress.

Progressive National Baptist Convention, Inc.
  (PNBC)
601 50th Street, NE
Washington, DC 20019
202-396-0558
1,800 churches; 1.8 million members
Organized in 1961 by Baptists who believed that
  the NBCUSA was undemocratic and overly
  conservative on civil rights issues; PNBC took
  an active role in the fight against apartheid in
  South Africa and has supported the NAACP,

Urban League, SCLC, and Martin Luther King,
  Jr., Center for Nonviolent Social Change;
  contributes to a number of educational
  institutions, including the Howard School of
  Divinity and the Central Baptist Theological
  Seminary.

National Primitive Baptist Convention of the
  U.S.A.
P.O. Box 2355
Tallahassee, FL 32301
904-222-5218 or 5549
606 churches; 250,000 members
Organized in 1907 in opposition to the growing
  trend among Baptists to embrace missionary
  activity, which Primitive Baptists regarded as
  having no divine sanction; Primitive Baptists
  strive to maintain the original ("primitive")
  characteristics of the faith.

United American Free Will Baptist
  Denomination, Inc.
1011 University Street
P.O. Box 3303
Kinston, NC 28501
252-527-0120
836 churches; 100,000 members (1952 figures,
  latest available)
Branched off from Free Will Baptist movement in
  1901 in response to discrimination within
  parent body; observes Arminian rites, such as
  foot washing and anointing the sick with oil;
  local churches are autonomous in all but
  doctrinal matters.

Lott Carey Baptist Foreign Missionary
  Convention
1501 11th Street, NW
Washington, DC 20001
202-667-8493
Founded in 1897 and named in honor of the
  Reverend Lott Carey, a former slave who
  became the first U.S. missionary to Africa in
  1821; supports more than 130 missionaries in
  Guyana, India, and West Africa, providing
  health care and food supplies, in addition to
  religious and secular instruction.

METHODIST

Methodism, a reform movement within the Church of England, was introduced to North America in 1766 by Charles and John Wesley. Because the early evangelists made no distinctions based on skin color, Methodism attracted African Americans from the start: The pioneering John Street Methodist Episcopal Church in New York City counted 211 black members, one third of the total congregation, at the end of the century. Before long, African Americans grew disenchanted as the Methodist Church began to pull back from its vigorous opposition to slavery, and some congregations began to practice various forms of discrimination. Many African American Methodists began to establish their own congregations while still adhering to Methodist doctrine.

Methodists place great emphasis on the power of the Holy Spirit to bolster the faith of believers and transform their lives. Their services and church activities are characterized by simplicity of worship. Though the general administration of Methodist denominations is centralized, Methodists strive for a genuine partnership between ministers and laity. Methodist churches have historically been known for their social and educational concerns.

African Methodist Episcopal (A.M.E.) Church
1134 11th Street, NW
Washington, DC 20001
202-371-8700
8,000 churches; 3.5 million members (1 million in Africa and the Caribbean)
Founded by Richard Allen, Absalom Jones, and others in 1787 in Philadelphia as the Free African Society; severed its ties with the Methodist Episcopal Church in 1816; membership is open to all, though the church recognizes its special mission in African American communities; represented in more than 20 African nations, as well as Canada, England, the Caribbean, Suriname, and Guyana; supports Wilberforce University, Allen University, Paul Quinn College, Payne Theological Seminary, and others; maintains Monrovia College and Industrial Training School in Liberia and the School of Religion in Johannesburg, South Africa; publications include *The Voice of Missions*, *A.M.E. Church Review*, and *The Christian Recorder*, the oldest continuously published black paper in America.

African Methodist Episcopal Zion (A.M.E.Z.) Church
1200 Windermere Drive
Pittsburgh, PA 15218
412-242-5842
6,000 churches; 3 million members
Founded in New York in 1796 by James Varick and others dissatisfied with conditions in the John Street Church; severed its ties with the Methodist Episcopal Church in 1821; added "Zion" in 1848 to distinguish itself from Allen's A.M.E. Church; enjoyed explosive growth after the Civil War, increasing membership from 25,000 in 1860 to 200,000 in 1870; ordained women to preach in 1894; supports a number of educational institutions, including Livingstone College and Hood Theological Seminary; publishes *Star of Zion*, *Quarterly Review*, and other periodicals, as well as school literature; maintains a strong presence in the Caribbean, Liberia, and England.

Christian Methodist Episcopal Church
National Headquarters
2323 W. Illinois Avenue
Dallas, TX 75224
214-339-5129
3,000 churches; 800,000 members
Split from the mother church in 1866, in response to the drive for African American independence in the South; concentrates on evangelism; many leaders played a prominent role in the civil rights movement; at one time supported 22 educational institutions, including Miles, Lane, and Paine colleges; congregations in Nigeria, Ghana, Liberia, Haiti, and Jamaica, as well as the United States.

United Methodist Church
P.O. Box 320
Nashville, TN 37202
615-742-5410
257,000 African Americans (out of 8.8 million
congregants)

Though the vast majority of African American
Methodists now belong to predominantly black
congregations, a substantial number have
remained in the United Methodist Church. In
recent times, the United Methodist Church has
made efforts to increase the participation of
African American parishioners in all aspects of
church affairs. More than 100 sacred-music
selections in the liturgy are drawn from the
African American tradition. In addition, a
number of African Americans have been
chosen to lead predominantly white
congregations; others—most notably Leontine
Kelly (see "African American Religious
Leaders," at the end of this chapter)—have
played important roles in church administration
and in Methodist-affiliated colleges and
seminaries. The church has also created
specialized organizations such as Black
Methodists for Church Renewal, Inc. (BMCR),
which includes clergy and laypersons of all ages.
BMCR's headquarters is located at 601 W.
Riverview Avenue, Suite 325, Dayton, OH
45406 (513-227-9460).

Union American Methodist Episcopal Church,
Inc.
772–74 Pine Street
Camden, NJ 08103
609-962-4530
609-963-0434
55 churches; 15,000 members

Organized by Peter Spencer, William Anderson,
and others who withdrew from the Asbury
Methodist Church in Wilmington, Delaware, in
1805; maintains long-standing policy of
licensing women to preach; concentrated in
New England, the Mid-Atlantic states, and
Jamaica.

African Union First Colored Methodist Episcopal
Church, Inc.
602 Spruce Street
Wilmington, DE 19801
33 churches; 5,000 members (1957 figures, the
latest available)

Formed in 1865 by a merger of the African Union
Church and the First Colored Methodist
Church.

Reformed Methodist Union Episcopal Church
1136 Brody Avenue
Charleston, SC 29407
803-776-3534
18 churches; 3,800 members (1980s figures)

Founded in 1885 by worshipers splitting from the
A.M.E. Church; follows traditional Methodist
practices, such as class meetings and *love feasts*
(members-only services that include the Lord's
Supper and an informal time of prayer, singing,
and witness).

United Wesleyan Methodist Church of America
270 W. 126th Street
New York, NY 10027
4 churches

Founded in 1905 by West Indian immigrants
wishing to preserve the practices followed by
the Methodist Church in the Caribbean;
adheres to the doctrines of British Methodism
rather than American modifications; does not
have a governing episcopacy; engages in joint
projects in the Caribbean with the United
Methodist Church.

HOLINESS/PENTECOSTAL/APOSTOLIC

The Holiness/Pentecostal/Apostolic churches grew out of the African American Baptist and
Methodist churches at the end of the 19th century, typically emerging from informal prayer
meetings that were marked by a special intensity and emotion. The seminal event in the movement was the Azusa Street Revival, a series of religious meetings held in Los Angeles from 1906
to 1909 under the direction of William J. Seymour. The Azusa Street meetings inspired both

Baptism by immersion is one of the pivotal expressions of the Baptist faith.

black and white Pentecostal groups to form their own congregations. Core beliefs shared by the various Holiness churches include the active manifestation of the Holy Spirit and spirit baptism, often evidenced through the phenomenon of speaking in tongues. From the beginning, music has played a pivotal role in the so-called folk-church tradition, and Holiness churches pioneered the use of gospel music in their services, introducing instruments and polyphonic textures. Currently, Holiness/Pentecostal/Apostolic denominations support more than 17,000 churches, with a total membership that exceeds 6.5 million.

Church of God in Christ, Inc.
272 S. Main Street
P.O. Box 320
Memphis, TN 38103
901-578-3838
15,300 churches; 6 million members
Founded in Memphis in 1894 by Charles Price Jones and Charles Harrison Mason; the first U.S. Holiness church to receive a charter; currently the second-largest black denomination in the United States, with additional congregations in Africa, Canada, the West Indies, and Europe; publishes *The Whole Truth* and *The Voice of Missions*. The 1980 publication of *Yes, Lord!*, the church's hymnal, was a major landmark in the development of African American religious music.

Pentecostal Assemblies of the World
3939 Meadows Drive
Indianapolis, IN 46205
317-547-9541

1,000 churches; 450,000 members (1980 figures)
Began in 1906 as a loosely organized fellowship of those inspired by the Azusa Street Revival; oldest of the Apostolic ("Jesus Only") Pentecostal churches, which reject the Trinity and embrace the doctrine of Jesus as God the Father; initially attracted an interracial following, but whites began to withdraw during the 1920s due to pressure from segregationists; African Americans gradually developed a cohesive church with a presiding bishop and 30 regional bishops; missions in Egypt, Ghana, Nigeria, Jamaica, and the United Kingdom.

United Holy Church of America
312 Umstead Street
Durham, NC 27707
919-682-1819
470 churches; 50,000 members
Founded in 1900 in Durham as the Holy Church of North Carolina; adopted its present name in 1916; added a northern district in 1920 and a

northwestern district in 1924; emphasizes spirit baptism and speaking in tongues; publishes *Holiness Union*.

Church of Christ (Holiness), U.S.A.
329 E. Monument Street
Jackson, MS 39202
601-353-4033
170 churches; 10,000 members
Founded by Charles Price Jones in 1907, when he refused to accept the teachings of the Azusa Street movement (notably the experience of speaking in tongues) and split with Charles Harrison Mason; follows Methodist doctrine but emphasizes the second work of grace in the life of believers.

Fire-Baptized Holiness Church of God in the Americas
556 Houston Street
Atlanta, GA 30312
775 churches
Began in the 1890s as the Fire-Baptized Holiness Association, a predominantly white group that embraced the doctrine of a third blessing—the baptism of fire—in addition to justification and sanctification; attracted large numbers of African Americans; Jim Crow laws prompted black congregants to form their own church in 1908; adopted present name in 1922; centered mainly in Georgia and South Carolina.

ROMAN CATHOLICISM

Throughout the slavery era, the Catholic Church actively baptized enslaved African Americans in all areas where it held sway, principally South America and the French- and Spanish-held islands of the Caribbean. In the United States, the principal areas of Catholic influence were Louisiana, Maryland, and the Gulf Coast regions. Though it embraced African Americans, the church was slow to oppose slavery, and many Catholic orders were themselves slaveholders. Nevertheless, an order of African American nuns (mostly Haitian), the Oblate Sisters of Providence, was established in Baltimore in 1829; it included five women from Haiti. A second order, the Sisters of the Holy Family, arose in New Orleans in 1842. The first black priest, James Augustine Healy, was ordained in 1854 and became a bishop. (Because Healy's father did not minister to a predominantly black congregation, many consider Augustus Tolton—ordained in 1886—the first true African American priest.)

After the Civil War, the church launched a concerted effort to convert African Americans, working through such bodies as St. Joseph's Society of the Sacred Heart, the Society of the Divine Word, the Sisters of the Blessed Sacrament, the Catholic Afro-American Congress Movement, and the Federated Colored Catholics of the United States. The first black Catholic university, Xavier University, was founded in New Orleans in 1931. With the growth of the civil rights movement, black Catholics began to voice their unique concerns, and the National Office for Black Catholics was founded in 1970. In 1979, the American bishops officially condemned racism as a sin. There are currently about 2 million African American Catholics in the United States, along with 300 clergy and nearly 600 sisters.

In addition to the traditional liturgy, the Catholic Church has commissioned a number of jazz masses and other compositions by African American composers, beginning with Edward V. Bonnemère's *Missa Hodierna* (1966). Other important pieces in this genre include Clarence Rivers's *Brother of Man* (1967); David Baker's *The Beatitudes* (1968); and several works by the jazz pianist Mary Lou Williams, who contributed three jazz masses between 1970 and 1972, as well as "Black Christ of the Andes" (1963), a hymn celebrating the deeds of the Afro-Peruvian priest St. Martin de Porres (1579–1639).

In 1989, Reverend George Augustus Stallings broke with the Roman Catholic Church, saying it was racist and failed to meet the needs of black parishioners. He formed the African-

American Catholic Congregation, which combines Catholic rites with African-based music and customs. He went on to launch churches in seven cities across the United States, with membership reported to be 7,000.

The following organizations are nationwide groups of African American Catholics.

African-American Catholic Congregation
1015 I Street, NE
Washington, DC 20002
202-398-2499

Independent African-American Catholic Rite
Church of St. Martin de Porres
Washington, DC 20018
202-544-5234

National Black Catholic Clergy Caucus
1419 V Street, Suite 400

Washington, DC 20009
202-328-0718

Oblate Sisters of Providence
701 Gun Road
Baltimore, MD 21227
410-242-8500

Sisters of the Holy Family
6901 Chef Menteur Highway
New Orleans, LA 70126
504-241-5400

JEHOVAH'S WITNESSES

The group that became the Jehovah's Witnesses was founded by Charles Taze Russell in the 1880s. A former Presbyterian and Seventh Day Adventist, Russell founded his own Bible study group after the Second Coming of Christ predicted by the Adventists failed to occur. He began publishing *Zion's Watch Tower and Hearald of Christ's Prescence* in 1879; by 1884 the group he led was established as a corporation. The primary texts are the Bible and Russell's *Studies in the Scriptures*. In 1931, the Watch Tower group officially adopted the name Jehovah's Witnesses. Missionary activity and very active proselytizing and distribution of church literature ensured the rapid expansion of the group among African Americans, as well as others. Members, divided into Pioneers (full-time missionaries) and Publishers (also obligated to proselytize), are expected to participate in congregations, attend five meetings per week, and be baptized. Their places of worship are called Kingdom Halls. They do not vote, accept military duty, or salute any national flag; nor do they accept blood transfusions or celebrate any holidays other than Christ's death. About 400,000 of the approximately 1 million Jehovah's Witnesses in the United States are African American, and it is among the leading religions in several Caribbean and African nations. Their membership totals about 5.5 million worldwide.

Watch Tower Bible and Tract Society
Main Headquarters
25 Columbia Heights
Brooklyn, NY 11201-2483
718-625-3600

SEVENTH-DAY ADVENTIST

The Seventh-Day Adventists, who trace their origins back to the Great Awakening of the 19th century, adopted a firm antislavery stance during the years before the Civil War and actively evangelized among African Americans in the South. The first Seventh-Day Adventist congregation including blacks was organized in 1881 in Edgefield Junction, Tennessee, and churches sprang up in Kentucky and Louisiana, as well, during the ensuing years. These efforts were enhanced by the creation of the Southern Missionary Society in 1898 and the 1896 founding of a school in Hunstville, Alabama, which became Oakwood College. During the early 20th century, the Seventh-Day Adventists became active among African Americans in the North, founding churches in Harlem and other communities. However, black leaders in the church did not begin to emerge until the 1920s, and there were many complaints about unequal treatment. This began to change in 1943, when regional conferences were created to assist the General Conference in the governance of the church. These regional groups afforded black parishioners greater influence, and the number of African American Seventh-Day Adventists grew dramatically. All church institutions were desegregated in 1965; in 1979, Charles Bradford became the first black president of the church's North American Division. Seventh-Day Adventist congregations currently include about 280,000 African Americans, out of a total membership of 717,000.

Seventh-Day Adventist doctrine includes the observance of the Sabbath on Saturday and the reliance on the Bible as the sole source of religious inspiration. Seventh-Day Adventists believe in the imminent return of Christ—this event will herald a final judgment in which the wicked will be slain and the righteous taken to heaven for 1,000 years before finally returning with Christ to a cleansed Earth. Parishioners enter the church through the rite of baptism by immersion.

General Conference of Seventh-Day Adventists
World Headquarters
12501 Old Columbia Pike
Silver Spring, MD 20904
301-680-6000

EPISCOPAL

African Americans have belonged to the Episcopal Church since 1624, when the Church of England first baptized colonial slaves, though serious evangelic work did not begin until the end of the 17th century. When the Protestant Episcopal Church separated from the Church of England during the American Revolution, most blacks drifted away, though a black Episcopalian parish was founded in Philadelphia in 1794. Within the next half century, other Episcopalian congregations took root in New York, Baltimore, New Haven, Detroit, Newark, and other locations. Northern churches played an active role in the antislavery and emigrationist movements. In the South, by contrast, most black Episcopalians were enslaved, and their worship was directed by white clerics; following the Civil War, blacks in the South deserted the Episcopal Church. During this period, Northern black Episcopalians often concentrated on the international sphere, launching religious efforts in Haiti and Africa.

During the first half of the 20th century, Episcopal ranks were swelled by immigrants from the West Indies who had been Anglicans in their homelands. (This trend continues today.) Black Episcopalians also responded actively to the call of the civil rights movement. Their impact on the church as a whole has been significant; it was a black parish, the Church of the Advocate in Philadelphia, that witnessed the first ordination (in 1974) of female clergy. As of 1992, there were approximately 250,000 African American members of the Episcopal Church. African Americans among the clerical ranks include more than 450 priests, 33 deacons, and 24 bishops.

Episcopal Commission for Black Ministries—Episcopal Church
815 Second Avenue
New York, NY 10017
212-867-8400

PRESBYTERIAN

The first African American Presbyterians were slaves converted by Scotch-Irish immigrants living in Virginia during the 1730s. Because of the Presbyterian emphasis on learning, these converts were often taught to read, a practice normally forbidden by slaveholders. The first black Presbyterian preacher was John Chavis, who served as a missionary to slaves from 1800 into the 1830s and founded several schools. The First African Presbyterian Church of Philadelphia was founded in 1807, with John Gloucester as its pastor. Other African American congregations sprang up in New York; Charleston; Washington, D.C., and Reading, Pennsylvania. The Presbyterian Church split over the issue of slavery in 1861, and many blacks in the South shifted their allegiance to the Northern branch of the church. The black congregations in the South formed an independent church in 1898, but this movement dissolved in 1916. In 1983, the competing branches reunited to form the Presbyterian Church (U.S.A.), which claimed 64,841 African American adherents in 1990, about 2.5 percent of the total membership. The National Black Presbyterian Caucus has been created to monitor race relations and support the development of African American congregations.

National Black Presbyterian Caucus
2923 Hawthorne Avenue
Richmond, VA 32222
804-321-9250

Presbyterian Church (U.S.A.)
100 Witherspoon Street
Louisville, KY 40202
502-569-5000

UNITED CHURCH OF CHRIST

The United Church of Christ (UCC) was formed in 1957 when the Congregational Christian Church merged with the Evangelical and Reformed Church. The roots of the Congregational Church extend back to the earliest days of European settlement in New England; the first recorded conversion of an African American, an unidentified woman held in bondage by a Congregational minister, took place in 1641. The early church, adhering to the strict Puritan worldview, showed little concern for the plight of enslaved blacks. In 1780 the Congregationalists ordained their first African American minister, the Rev. Lemuel Haynes. During the 19th century, the church intensified its involvement with African Americans through the American Missionary Association (AMA) and its support of the American Anti-Slavery Society. During this period, there were a number of African American Congregational parishes in New England and Ohio. Following the Civil War, the AMA launched a massive evangelical and educational effort in the South, founding numerous churches and educational institutions, including Fisk University and LeMoyne-Owen College. Nonetheless, the church maintained a policy of segregation throughout its facilities in the South. For this and other reasons,

Congregationalism never achieved a mass appeal among African Americans, and its influence was largely limited to urban areas.

Segregation within the church was abolished only in 1961, following the merger that created the UCC. At this point, a number of African Americans, including Andrew Young, had risen to prominence within the church. They were instrumental in forming church organizations such as the Commission for Racial Justice (1967) and the Council for Racial/Ethnic Minorities (1983). The Commission for Racial Justice currently sponsors the annual Amistad Awards in race relations and the annual Fisk University Institutes on Race Relations. Currently, the UCC has about 62,000 African American members (attending some 280 predominantly black churches) out of a total membership of 1.6 million. Following the traditional practice of the Congregational Church, the UCC has no bishops or presbyteries. Each congregation is self-governing and is considered to be under the leadership of Christ, though a general synod meets biannually to plan and coordinate UCC activities. The sacraments are limited to baptism and communion.

Commission for Racial Justice—United Church
    of Christ, Inc.
700 Prospect Avenue
Cleveland, OH 44115
216-736-2100

Ministers for Racial and Social Justice—United
    Church of Christ, Inc.
10723 Magnolia Drive
Cleveland, OH 44106
216-736-2160

United Black Christians—United Church of
    Christ, Inc.
5118-B Gary Avenue
Fairfield, AL 35064
205-781-4700

United Church of Christ
Office of Communication
700 Prospect Avenue
Cleveland, OH 44115
216-736-2222

DISCIPLES OF CHRIST (CHRISTIAN CHURCH)

Founded in Kentucky in 1832, the church numbered free blacks from both North and South among its earliest adherents. The first African American congregation was founded in 1834, and black membership in the church reached 7,000 by 1860. After the Civil War, black Disciples increasingly developed their own organizations, such as the National Convention of Churches of Christ, founded by Preston Taylor. At the same time, the church leadership addressed the needs of African American Disciples by creating agencies such as the Board of Negro Education and Evangelization, with the principal aim of training black ministers.

During the early 20th century, African American Disciples played an increasingly important role through the National Convention of Disciples in Christ, founded in Nashville in 1917. Under the leadership of Preston Taylor and Rosa Brown Bracy, the convention vastly increased the church's involvement in the black community and developed a cooperative effort with white missionary groups. By 1969, the Disciples of Christ had merged the National Convention into the newly created National Convocation of the Christian Church, thereby moving African American leaders into the highest levels of the church. The merger also spawned the creation of the Fund for Reconciliation, an agency concerned with developing black entrepreneurship and church leadership.

The Disciples of Christ Church now numbers about 61,000 African Americans among its adherents, out of a total membership of more than 1 million. The church's doctrine holds that the Bible is the exclusive guide to faith and conduct, allowing each believer to interpret Scripture in his or her own way.

National Convocation of the Christian Church (Disciples of Christ)
P.O. Box 1986
222 S. Downey Avenue
Indianapolis, IN 46206
317-353-1491

RASTAFARIAN

The Rastafarian movement has its roots in Jamaica and drew its first impetus from the preaching of Native Baptist ministers during the late 18th and early 19th centuries. Though these ministers advocated Christianity, they infused it with elements from West African religions, including the importance of dreams and visions induced by long nights of praying in the woods. By the 1860s, the movement was seen as a source of competition by orthodox Christian churches dominated by whites. These religious traditions combined with the powerful legacy of the Jamaican Maroons (see Chapter 2, "Slavery and Freedom") and were echoed in the writings of the black-nationalist Marcus Garvey, some of whose followers proclaimed during the 1920s that the advent of a black prince in Africa would begin the liberation of blacks around the world.

Garvey's prophecy was recalled in 1930 when Ras Tafari Makkonen succeeded to the throne of Ethiopa, taking the royal title Hailie Selassie I and claiming descent from the biblical King David. Finding support in the Bible for Selassie's claim to divinity, a number of Jamaican groups adopted the belief that he was destined to be the Messiah of black people. Rastafarian men began to grow dreadlocks during the 1940s, following a biblical injunction against the cutting of one's hair, and were often the target of crackdowns by the authorities. The movement received its greatest impetus on April 21, 1966, when Emperor Haile Selassie visited Jamaica, and that date is celebrated as a holy day by Rastafarians. Though the world believes that the emperor died in 1975, Rastafarians maintain that he is still alive, referring to him by titles such as the Living God and Jah (Jehovah). Jah's kingdom, Ethiopia, represents the whole of Africa, which will be restored to its former glory when the children of Jah return home.

In their religious practices, Rastafarians rely as much on oral tradition and interpretation as they do on strict reference to the text of the Bible, which they honor as the history of the African race. They contend that the Bible was stolen by Europeans and distorted to bolster myths of white supremacy; however, Rastafarians are able to see through these falsifications and recapture the true meaning of Scripture. Historically, Rastafarianism has been a diverse movement—some followers have concentrated exclusively on religious observance, whereas others have focused on racial pride, condemnation of whites, and political protest. The intimate connection between Rastafarianism and reggae music has given the religion worldwide exposure and far-reaching cultural impact. There are currently between 3,000 and 5,000 Rastafarians in the United States, but there is no accurate estimate for membership in Jamaica and other areas. (On the island of Dominica, Rastafarians are known as Dreads.) Jamaican Rastafarians have also established settlements in Ethiopia and Ghana. There are two major Rastafarian publications:

Arise
Creative Publishers, Ltd.
8 Waterloo Avenue
Kingston, Jamaica, West Indies

Jahugligman
c/o Carl Gayle
19C Annette Crescent
Kingston 10, Jamaica, West Indies

ISLAM

Islam was first introduced to North America by enslaved Africans from Muslim regions of West Africa, though there is no indication that their beliefs were perpetuated into the succeeding generation of African Americans. The religion did not have a significant impact on the African American community until the early 20th century. In 1913, Noble Drew Ali (1886–1929) founded the Moorish Science Temple of America in Baltimore, arguing that African Americans were in fact Moors from Morocco who had been stripped of their identity (and religion) by whites. Following Ali's death, his teachings were expanded by one of his followers, Wallace Fard Muhammad, who founded the Nation of Islam during the 1930s. After Wallace Fard Muhammad mysteriously disappeared, the movement was headed by Elijah Muhammad, who eventually moved its headquarters to Chicago. As the Nation of Islam was growing, other African Americans were drawn to Islam through the Muslim Mission of America, established in 1920 by Sheikh Daa'wud Faisal, a Bermudan immigrant to New York. Still others joined groups of Ahmadiyya Muslims, inspired by immigrants from East Asia entering North America via West Africa.

During the civil rights era, the Nation of Islam (NOI) became a powerful and controversial presence in the black community under the leadership of Elijah Muhammad and Malcolm X. By the time of Elijah Muhammad's death in 1967, NOI membership exceeded 100,000. As the NOI drew closer to orthodox Islam, several dissident groups split off and formed smaller, alternative organizations under the NOI banner. The group headed by Louis Farrakhan remains the most publicized because of its espousal of black nationalism. The original organization, now directed by Warith Deen Muhammad, remains the largest by far and is now known as the American Muslim Mission. The American Muslim Mission operates about 200 centers, with locations in the Caribbean, Guyana, and Belize, as well as the United States and Canada.

Ahmadiyya Movement in Islam
2141 Leroy Place, NW
Washington, DC 20008
202-232-3737

American Muslim Mission
7351 S. Stony Island Avenue
Chicago, IL 60649
312-667-7200

Moorish Science Temple Divine and National
  Movement of North America, Inc.
P.O. Box 21218
Baltimore, MD 21218
301-366-3591

The Nation of Islam (Louis Farrakhan)
734 W. 79th Street
P.O. Box 20083
Chicago, IL 60620
312-602-1230

Nation of Islam (John Muhammad)
c/o Muhammad Temple #1
16187 Hamilton Avenue
Highland Park, MI 48203

Nation of Islam (Silas Muhammad)
P.O. Box 50559
Atlanta, GA 30302

JUDAISM

Black Judaism in the United States emerged during the 19th century, when a number of African American preachers identified black people with the Jews of the Old Testament. Early groups espousing this belief included the Church of the Living God, the Church of God (Black Jews), and the Church of God and Saints in Christ. In 1924, Arnold Josiah Ford, a West Indian living in New York, founded Beth B'Nai Abraham, a black congregation combining Judaism with the black-nationalist ideology of Marcus Garvey. Several additional groups of Black Jews emerged during the following decades, among them three congregations—the Original Hebrew Israelite Nation, the House of Judah, and the Nation of Yahweh (Hebrew Israelites)—founded during the 1960s. In addition, the New York City area is home to several congregations comprising African Americans who have formally converted to Judaism; these have been officially sanctioned by the Jewish community at large. In addition, the Pan African Orthodox Christian Church has incorporated a number of Black Jewish themes into its doctrines.

Church of God and Saints in Christ
3927 Bridge Road
Suffolk, VA 23435
804-484-1161

Commandment Keepers Congregation of the
   Living God
1 E. 123rd Street
New York, NY 10035

Nation of Yahweh
Temple of Love
2766 62nd Street
Miami, FL 33147

Original Hebrew Israelite Nation
Communicators Press
P.O. Box 19504
Chicago, IL 60649

AFRICAN-INSPIRED RELIGIONS IN THE AMERICAS

Religious movements based on African forms of worship have historically been far more common in South America and the Caribbean than in the United States. This phenomenon resulted from a number of factors peculiar to the great sugar-growing regions: Their population was overwhelmingly black during the slave-trade era; the number of African-born blacks far exceeded those born in the Americas; and black populations had far less exposure to European culture there than they did in the United States. Even in areas where there were many Catholic converts, the Catholic Church encouraged the formation of African brotherhoods and religious societies, and these groups tended to perpetuate ancestral beliefs. Today, all the Caribbean islands and several South American nations have one or more religious groups with practices derived in part from African religions. During the second half of the 20th century, however, many of these groups have experienced a decline in membership, largely a result of the advances made by Pentecostal churches.

BATUQUE

Batuque has been centered in Belém, in northern Brazil, since the end of the 19th century, but its roots go further back into the slave-trade era. It combines Yoruban and Dahomean beliefs with indigenous South American Indian shamanism, folk Catholicism, Iberian folklore, and elements of Umbanda (described later in this section). Though most followers of Batuque consider themselves Catholics, they worship at cult centers rather than churches, and they organize street processions in honor of saints without inviting priests to take part. In addition to worshiping Catholic saints, followers of Batuque venerate spirits known as *encantados* (enchanted ones). *Encantados* are related to Catholic saints and are sometimes represented by saints' images or honored on saints' days, but they are separate beings in the eyes of believers. In return for prayers and offerings, *encantados* are expected to look out for the well-being of worshipers.

BONI

Practiced in French Guiana by members of the black population—both Creoles and descendants of Maroons (including Djuka exiles from Surinam)—Boni combines religious rites of African peoples such as the Akan, Agni, Mina, Fon, and Naga. Boni belief incorporates worship of a Supreme Being, called Nana or Masu Gadu, with the cult of Odun, who forbids witchcraft, violence, and unsanctioned communion with the spirits of the dead. Secondary deities—known as Kumenti, Djadja, Opete, and Bunsuki—take the form of animals or Native American women. The Kumenti are regarded as especially benevolent, with the power to protect against wounds through a charm known as *obia*.

CANDOMBLÉ

Based in Bahia, Brazil, Candomblé traces its origins to the beginning of the 18th century. In this form of worship, the Supreme Being is known as Olorun (the chief Yoruba deity) or Zaniapombo (the chief deity in the Congo-Angola region). Secondary deities (*orisas, vodun, inkices*) are identified with Catholic saints: Shango (god of lightning) is identified with St. Jerome, St. Barbara, St. Peter, or St. Jerome the Younger; Ogun (god of iron and guardian of the roads) with St. Anthony; Omolu (god of smallpox and other contagious diseases) with St. Lazarus, St. Sebastian, and St. Roque. Yemanjá, a leading water goddess, corresponds to Our Lady of the Conception. As of the mid-20th century, there were an estimated 100 individual centers of worship, known as *candomblés*, in Bahia.

MARÍA LIONZA

In Venezuela, where enslaved Africans were relatively few in number and readily mixed with European, Creole, and Native American populations, Africanisms have survived in the cult of María Lionza, which flourishes among the urban poor, crossing racial lines. The cult originated in the mountains of Sorte, near the Caribbean coast, during the colonial era. It combined veneration of the Virgin of Coromoto with worship of María Lionza, a Native American princess who assumed supernatural powers after being abducted by a snake. The figure of María Lionza, usually portrayed as a white woman with long black hair, has been surrounded in the liturgy by Native American nature spirits and seven Yoruba deities that were introduced by immigrants from Cuba and Trinidad. Among the chiefs of María Lionza's court are Negro Felipe, an Afro-Cuban figure, and Negro Miguel, the leader of an 18th-century slave rebellion. Thousands of pilgrims, most of whom consider themselves practicing Catholics, come to Sorte every year to worship at the many shrines to María Lionza and to bathe in the healing waters of the Yaracuy River.

SANTERÍA

Santería originated in Cuba among Fon and Yoruba peoples. Santería deities (*orisa*) bear the names of the ancient Yoruba gods: Olodumare (the Creator), Ogun (the god of war and iron), Yemaya (goddess of the rivers), Eshu/Elegba (the divine messenger), Obaluaiye (the god of pestilence), and numerous others. As in Brazilian Candomblé, these deities share many of the attributes of Catholic saints and are often embodied in the saints' images. Santería worship traditionally includes animal sacrifice, drumming, and the use of special herbs. An important role is assigned to Ifá, often identified with St. Francis of Assisi. Ifá is the Yoruba god of divination, and a supplicant can obtain his guidance by consulting a priest known as a *babalawo*. In Africa, babalawos perform a complex procedure that involves the casting of 16 palm nuts on a divination board; each of the 256 possible figures described by the nuts relates to a verse or parable that applies to the supplicant's situation. In the Americas, where babalawos have not had the same opportunities for training as in Africa, Ifá divination has evolved into a simplified form that employes cowrie shells or a divining chain and a smaller number of possible combinations. Scholars estimate that Santería now has hundreds of thousands of followers in North America, representing all social classes and ethnic groups. Herbs and oils used in Santería rituals are sold at shops known as *botánicas*, which are found in many urban black and Hispanic neighborhoods.

SHANGO

Shango—now practiced in Trinidad, Grenada, and Recife, Brazil (where it is known as Xangó)—developed during the 19th century among Yoruba descendants in Trinidad. Shango worship centers on the *chapelle*, a small cult house, and the *palais*, a tent where ceremonies and healing take place. The *chepelle* houses objects of worship, which include crucifixes and images of Catholic saints alongside African ceremonial objects such as *thunderstones* (axe-shaped stones said to be hurled from the sky by Shango), swords, and rattles. Each year, the *palais* is the scene of a major festival that ranges from recitation of the Lord's Prayer to manifestations of spirit possession to animal sacrifice.

UMBANDA

Umbanda is a form of spiritualism that began to flourish in the Brazilian cities of Rio de Janeiro and São Paulo during the late 19th century. The majority of adherents are Afro-Brazilians, though other ethnic groups are well represented. Among the five major types of spirits worshiped by Umbandans are the *prêto velho*, spirits of dead African slaves, and various *orisas* combining Yoruba and Catholic attributes. Many black Umbandans make regular pilgrimages to the former site of Palmares, the great 17th-century Maroon stronghold in the Pernambuco region. Dressed completely in white garments, they light votive candles and leave offerings of flowers and food to the spirits of the departed African Americans who fought and died for the cause of freedom.

VAUDOU

Perhaps the most famous of all African-derived faiths, Vaudou (also known as Voodoo) arose in Haiti during the 18th century. Many elements of Vaudou derive from the religious practices of the Fon people of Dahomey (present-day Benin), who had themselves been influenced over hundreds of years by the neighboring Yoruba. The Fon deities (*vodun*), closely resembling the *orisas* of the Yoruba, were transformed by Haitians into hundreds of *loa*. Olorun became Mawu in Dahomey and Bondieu in Haiti; Eshu/Elegba became Legba in Dahomey and Papa Legba in Haiti. As in other Caribbean cults, the *loa* are often identified with Catholic saints. A distinctively African element of Vaudou is the emphasis on multiple souls: the *Gros-bon-ange*, which animates the body, and the *Ti-bon-ange*, which protects a person against danger. The dreaded zombies of Haitian lore are deceased individuals whose *Gros-bon-ange* has been captured by a *bocor* (sorcerer) and used for evil purposes. (In Jamaica, where similar beliefs prevail, conjuring is known as *obeah*, and the spirits of the dead are called *duppies*.) The evil work of *bocors* can be averted through the intercession of Vaudou priests, or *houngans*, who pursue their calling in temples known as *houmforts*.

AFRICAN AMERICAN RELIGIOUS ORGANIZATIONS

RELIGIOUS COUNCILS

African American Religious Connection
c/o Fellowship Baptist Church
4534 Princeton Avenue
Chicago, IL 60609
312-924-3232
Promotes interdenominational fellowship and encourages the use of mass communications media.

African-American Women's Clergy Association and Male Auxiliary
P.O. Box 1493
Washington, DC 20013
202-797-7460
Group of lay ministers; operates House of Imagene, a 24-hour homeless shelter in northwest Washington, D.C.

Black National Religious Broadcasters
Information Center
6930 Belvedere Drive
Newport News, VA 23607
804-928-0018
Division of National Religious Broadcasters; focuses on reaching local religious communities throughout the United States and providing assistance to local broadcasters.

Hampton University Ministers Conference
Office of the Chaplain

Hampton University
P.O. Box 6177
Hampton, VA 23668
804-727-5340
Brings together ministers and church music professionals belonging to the Choir Directors and Organists Guild Workshop; semiannual sessions in February and June include lectures and worship services.

Interdenominational Women's Ministerial Alliance
716 Charing Cross Road
Baltimore, MD 21229
410-744-1997
Promotes networking among female ministers and works to advance the acceptance of women in the ministry.

National Black Evangelical Association
5736 North Alibina Avenue
Portland, OR 97217
503-289-0143
Works to facilitate communication among different denominations; publishes a monthly newsletter, *NBEA Outreach*; sponsors the Institute of Black Evangelical Thought and Action.

ECUMENICAL/NONDENOMINATIONAL ORGANIZATIONS

African Peoples' Christian Association
415 Atlantic Avenue
Brooklyn, NY 11217
718-596-1991
Affirms biblical Christianity and African American heritage; promotes human rights and African nationhood; sponsors educational and cultural programs, a prison ministry, and other community activities; publishes quarterly newsletter, *The Horizon*.

Black Light Fellowship
P.O. Box 5369
Chicago, IL 60680
312-563-0081
Sponsors seminars in the Chicago area and publishes a variety of religious materials.

Campus Crusade for Christ, International
Arrowhead Springs
San Bernardino, CA 92414
714-886-5224

Sponsors the Here's Life Black America program, based in Union City, Georgia, and the Intercultural Resources Ministry, which maintains programs on college campuses and in foreign nations.

Clergy Interracial Forum—GRACE
38 West Fulton Street
Grand Rapids, MI 49503
616-774-2042
Sponsors congregational combination, pulpit exchanges, and an annual multiracial service, among other activities; conducts monthly meetings.

Coalition for Christian Outreach—Black Campus Ministry
6740 Fifth Avenue
Pittsburgh, PA 15208
412-363-3303
Serves 45 campuses with 400,000 students; seeks to inspire future leaders of the African American community and to break down cultural and racial barriers; publishes *Focus on Black Campus Ministry*.

Congress of National Black Churches
1225 I Street, NW, Suite 750
Washington, DC 20005
202-371-1091
Represents six major African American denominations, with 15 million members and 50,000 participating churches; sponsors a wide variety of initiatives in fields ranging from education to communications; sponsors the National Fellowship Program for Black Pastors to develop future leaders.

The Information Services Clearinghouse
Howard University School of Divinity

1400 Shepherd Street, NE
Washington, DC 20017
202-806-0750
Provides guidelines and technical support for the creation of educational and community-based programs; publishes *Interlock*; hosts an annual conference for African American clergy and community leaders.

Interreligious Foundation for Community Organization (IFCO)
402 W. 145th Street
New York, NY 10031
212-926-5757
Supports and funds initiatives in the struggle for human and civil rights; assists more than 100 community organizations and public-policy groups; sponsors Central America Information Week and the Church Partnership Program; publishes *IFCO News*.

National Black Christian Students Conference
P.O. Box 4311
Chicago, IL 60680
312-722-0236
Seeks to guide and inspire African American students in spiritual and cultural matters; awards scholarships to students of black theology.

United Black Church Appeal
c/o Christ Church
860 Forest Avenue
Bronx, NY 10456
718-665-6688
Seeks to provide leadership for the African American church through economic development, political empowerment, and institution building.

SERVICE AGENCIES AND ORGANIZATIONS

Apostolic Community Organization, Inc.
1572 E. 66th Street
Cleveland, OH 44103
216-361-0960
Provides services to children in the Cleveland area by facilitating adoption, foster care, health care, and Sunday-school activities.

Association of Black Directors of Christian Education
1439 W. 103rd Street
Chicago, IL 60643
312-275-1430
Provides a support network for directors of Christian education, focusing on areas such as

drug abuse, evangelism, black history, and the black family.

Black Church Project—American Association for the Advancement of Science
Directorate for Education and Human Resource Programs
1333 H Street, NW
Washington, DC 20005
202-326-6670
Helps churches to incorporate science-related activities into their educational programs, providing workshops, manuals, videos, and volunteer programs; participating organizations include museums, science centers, and universities throughout the nation.

Knights of Peter Claver
National Headquarters
1825 Orleans Avenue
New Orleans, LA 70116
504-821-4225
Interracial lay Catholic organization founded in 1909; supports programs in education, recreation, and athletics and has long contributed to civil rights organizations; operates a sickle-cell program and maintains a development fund for Xavier University.

Martin Luther King, Jr., Center for Nonviolent Social Change
449 Auburn Avenue, NE
Atlanta, GA 30312
404-524-1956
Supports numerous programs to continue the life work of Rev. King, including the Annual Summer Workshop on Nonviolence, the Early Learning Center, the Scholars Internship Program, and the Cultural Affairs Program.

National Baptist Publishing Board, Inc.
6717 Centennial Boulevard
Nashville, TN 37209
615-350-8000
Established in 1896; ranks as the oldest and largest minority-owned and -operated religious publisher in the world.

National Office for Black Catholics
3025 Fourth Street, NE

Washington, DC 20017
202-635-1778
Comprises both clergy and laypeople; serves as an advocate for African Americans in the Catholic Church and society at large.

Operation PUSH
930 E. 50th Street
Chicago, IL 60615
312-373-3363
Founded in 1971 by Rev. Jesse Jackson; seeks to promote economic development and political empowerment in the African American community, as well as international peace and justice; publishes *Operation PUSH Magazine.*

Opportunities Industrialization Centers of America, Inc.
100 W. Coulter Street
Philadelphia, PA 19144
215-915-2200
Founded in 1964 by Rev. Leon H. Sullivan; now has 70 centers in the United States, Africa, the Caribbean, and England; provides training, employment, and remedial education programs seeking to meet the specific needs of businesses.

Southern Christian Leadership Conference
334 Auburn Avenue, NE
Atlanta, GA 30312
404-522-1420
Founded in 1957 as a spearhead of the civil rights movement; operates chapters in cities and states across the country, fighting injustice on national and local levels.

Successful Stewardship for Life Ministries, Inc.
1526 E. Capitol Street, NE
Washington, DC 20003
202-547-8782
Assists Christians in using financial and material resources in accordance with Christian principles; offers debt counseling, consumer education, business establishment, and retirement planning; church-based programs combine economic guidance with personal development counseling; publishes *The Christian's Financial Clinic,* a monthly newsletter.

Tom Skinner Associates (TSA)
5875 Solomon's Island Road
Tracy's Landing, MD 20779
301-261-9800
Works with African American leaders in politics, business, sports, and entertainment to enhance leadership skills; operates TSA Learning Center in Newark, New Jersey, to provide job training and prepare students for the SAT exams; publishes quarterly magazine, *The News in Black and White.*

United Outreach for Christ Mission Team, Inc.
P.O. Box 56035
Washington, DC 20011
202-829-7837
Provides services for prisoners and their families; operates a residence for female ex-offenders, as part of a six-month reentry program; publishes quarterly newspaper, *Good News from Prison Cells.*

Urban Ministries, Inc.
1350 W. 103rd Street
Chicago, IL 60643
312-233-4499
Publishes Sunday-school and vacation Bible-school literature; provides training and educational videos; operates Urban Outreach, a leadership-development organization.

Women's International Religious Fellowship (WIRF)
6458 32nd Street, NW
Washington, DC 20012
202-686-0312
Works for human rights around the world, with more than 50 countries participating in its programs; publishes the *WIRF Newsletter.*

AFRICAN AMERICAN RELIGIOUS LEADERS

Allen, Richard   (See Chapter 2, "Slavery and Freedom.")

Boyd, Richard Henry (1843–1922).   Born into slavery on a Mississippi plantation, Boyd—then known as Dick Gray—moved to Texas with the Gray family in 1849. After the plantation owner and two of his sons were killed in action during the Civil War, Dick took over the management of the plantation. When slavery came to an end, he worked as a cotton trader, cowboy, and sawmill hand while teaching himself to read and write. He changed his name in 1867. Boyd entered Bishop College in 1869 and became a Baptist minister. He then began to organize churches throughout Texas and held a number of posts in the Baptist hierarchy. In 1896 he moved to Nashville and founded the National Baptist Publishing Board, which issued 128 million pieces of literature during its first 18 years of operation. In addition to other prominent business ventures, Boyd also founded the Negro Doll Company, which in 1911 began marketing the first black dolls. One of his nine children, Henry Allen Boyd (1876–1959), succeeded him as the head of the Publishing Board and as a leader of the African American community in Tennessee.

Brown, Leo C., Jr. (1942–   ).   A native of Washington State, Brown became a minister in the Church of God in Christ after obtaining a divinity degree from Hardy Theological Institute in Seattle. Between 1972 and 1975, he founded Progress House and Dorcas House to provide services for ex-offenders and established the True Vine Community Church of God in Christ. Following on the success of his social-service initiatives, Brown created the Youthful Offender Program in 1983. In addition to being president of the Tacoma Ministerial Alliance and superintendent of the Puget Sound District Church of God in Christ, he is a member of the state's Housing Finance Commission.

Brown, Morris (1770–1849).   Born free in South Carolina, Brown became a Methodist in his youth while working as a cobbler. After obtaining a license to preach, Brown formed a church and tried to help enslaved African Americans. In 1816, when Brown's church became part of the officially established

A.M.E. Church, his congregation numbered 1,400. Suspected of taking part in Denmark Vesey's 1822 conspiracy, Brown was harassed by the authorities and decided to leave South Carolina. He settled in Philadelphia and in 1831 succeeded Richard Allen as bishop of the A.M.E. Church. During Brown's tenure, the church established branches in 13 states. He traveled extensively to preside over church conferences until suffering a stroke in 1844, after which he presided over church affairs from his home in Philadelphia.

Burroughs, Nannie Helen (1879–1961).   Born in Virginia, Burroughs moved with her family to Washington, D.C., in 1883. From 1900 to 1909, she worked as a bookkeeper and editorial secretary for the Foreign Mission Board of the National Baptist Convention in Louisville, Kentucky. At the same time, she was among the founders of the Women's Convention, an auxiliary to the National Baptist Convention. Burroughs served as the recording secretary of the Women's Convention from 1900 to 1947 and was the organization's president, serving in that role from 1948 to 1961. In 1909 she founded the National Training School for Women and Girls in Washington (later renamed the National Trades and Professional School for Women). In its first 25 years, the school trained more than 2,000 women from the United States, Africa, and the Caribbean. During her career, Burroughs wrote numerous articles on religion and on African American self-reliance.

Cone, James (1938–).   Born in Arkansas, Cone received his education at Philander Smith College, Garret Evangelical Seminary, and Northwestern University. He joined the faculty of New York's Union Theological Seminary in 1969 and is currently Charles A. Briggs Professor of Systematic Theology. Throughout his career, he has articulated a theological framework for the cause of black liberation and is credited with inaugurating the movement known as "black theology." Cone's publications include *Black Theology and Black Power* (1969), *The Spirituals and the Blues* (1972), and *Martin and Malcolm and America: A Dream or a Nightmare?* (1991).

BLACK THEOLOGY

The movement known as "black theology" drew its inspiration from the civil rights movement of the 1950s and 1960s and the contemporaneous emergence of Black Power. (See Chapter 3, "Politics and Civil Rights.") Though mainstream white church groups rejected attempts to ground the black liberation struggle in Christian theology, many African American religious thinkers believed that this was essential. Following the groundbreaking publication of James H. Cone's *Black Theology and Black Power*, theologians such as J. Deotis Roberts (*Liberation and Reconciliation*, 1971) and Gayraud S. Whitmore (*Black Religion and Black Radicalism*, 1972) made other important contributions. Though they disagreed on some points, these theologians placed the struggle for liberation as the essence of the Gospel and the ministry of Jesus. In their view, the Exodus was spiritually linked to Nat Turner's rebellion, Harriet Tubman's work on the Underground Railroad, and other actions in pursuit of liberation. During the 1970s, black theology was enriched by an infusion of feminist principles, articulated by womanist theologians such as Delores Williams, Jacquelyn Grant, and Katie D. Brown.

Costen, James Hutton.   After graduating from Southwestern Baptist Theological Seminary, Costen began a 10-year tenure at Mount Pisgah Presbyterian Church in Rocky Mount, North Carolina, and headed an interracial congress at the Presbyterian Church of the Master in Atlanta. In 1969 he became the first dean of the newly created Interdenominational Theological Center and held that post until 1983, when he became the institution's president. In 1992 he was elected president of the Atlanta Theological Association.

Crummell, Alexander(1819–1898).   Born free in New York City, Crummell was educated at the Oneida Institute in Whitesboro, New York (an academy run by white abolitionists), and decided to become a minister in the Protestant Episcopal Church. After the General Theological Seminary in New York rejected him as a student, on racial grounds, he studied privately for the ministry. Though ordained as a priest in Philadelphia in 1844, he was denied admission to the Diocese of Pennsylvania on equal terms. Crummell returned to New York, where he organized a congregation of black working people and played a leading role in the antislavery cause. He spent the years 1848 to 1853 in England, lecturing, raising money for his church, and studying at Queen's College, Cambridge. Crummell then traveled to the newly established African republic of Liberia as an Episcopal missionary and decided to become a Liberian citizen. There, he established several churches, served as master of a high school, and taught at Liberia College in Monrovia. Crummell left Liberia in 1872 after becoming embroiled in a political conflict between the ruling mulatto elite and so-called pure Africans. He settled in Washington, D.C., founded St. Luke's Church, and ranked as the senior African American priest in the Episcopal clergy until his retirement in 1894. His books include *The Relations and Duties of Free Colored Men in America to Africa* (1861) and *The Greatness of Christ* (1882).

Father Divine [né George Baker] (1880?–1965).   Born on a sharecropper's farm in Georgia, Baker moved to Baltimore in 1899 and worked as a garden laborer. He became involved in religious activity, and in 1914 he moved to Valdosta, Georgia, with a small group of followers. The rousing street-corner services of Baker and his group upset the city authorities, and they were soon driven out. Baker then went North and established a church on Myrtle Avenue in Brooklyn. He soon had so many supporters that in 1918 he was able to build a house in Sayville, Long Island. Credited with possessing mystical powers, Baker took the name Father Divine in 1930. In the following years, his Peace Mission movement attracted both blacks and whites from all social classes. Utilizing the substantial financial support of his wealthier devotees, Father Divine became one of the largest landlords in Harlem and owned property in several other cities. During the Depression of the 1930s, Father Divine's organization provided meals for the unemployed and the working poor, and his influence in Harlem was such that political candidates (including New York's Fiorello La Guardia) eagerly sought his endorsement. Father Divine's influence began to decline in the 1940s amid accusations of financial impropriety and controversy over his marriage to a white Canadian following the death of his first wife.

Farrakhan, Louis   (See Chapter 3, "Politics and Civil Rights.")

Flake, Floyd H. (1945–   ).   A native of Houston, Flake was educated at Wilberforce, Payne Theological Seminary, and Northeastern University. He was employed as a social worker and a marketing analyst while serving as pastor of the Bethel A.M.E. Church in Miami. From 1973 to 1976, Flake was chaplain of Marsh Chapel at Boston University and director of the Martin Luther King Jr., African American Center. He became pastor of the Allen A.M.E. Church in Jamaica, Queens, in 1976 and guided the church through a period of tremendous growth and community involvement, increasing membership from 1,400 to 8,600. In 1986, Reverend Flake was elected to the U.S. House of Representatives, where he led the fight against drugs and advocated new legislation to promote housing and education. In 1997, as the Allen A.M.E. Church celebrated the opening of a new $23 million cathedral, Rev. Flake announced that he would not run for reelection to Congress in 1998, choosing instead to devote himself full-time to his pastoral duties.

Harris, Barbara Clementine (1930–   ).   A native of Philadelphia, Harris was involved in Episcopal Church activities as a youngster. After graduating from Philadelphia High School for Girls in 1948, Harris worked in the public-relations field, eventually rising to a senior executive post at the Sun Oil Company. At the same time, she pursued a career of social activism, counseling prisoners and taking part in the civil rights movement. In 1976, when the Episcopal Church opened its clerical ranks to women, Harris began studying for the priesthood at Villanova University and Hobart and William Smith colleges. She was ordained in 1980 and immediately made it clear that she would be deeply involved in social causes, including women's rights. In addition to her clerical duties, she served as executive director of the Episcopal Church Publishing Company and contributed articles on social issues to *The Witness*, a leading church publication. In 1988, Harris was elected suffragan bishop of the 110,000-member Diocese of Massachusetts, becoming the first woman to hold such a post in the history of the Episcopal Church.

Healy, James Augustine (1830–1900).   Born in Georgia, Healy was the son of an Irish immigrant and a mulatto slave woman. In 1837, his father took him (and his younger brothers, Michael and Patrick) to Flushing, New York, and enrolled them in a Quaker school. James Healy went on to the Jesuit College of the Holy Cross in Worcester, Massachusetts, receiving his B.A. in 1849 and his M.A. in 1851. Ordained as a priest in Paris in 1852, he served as the pastor of Boston's Cathedral of the Holy Cross during the Civil War. In 1866, Healy became pastor of St. James, the largest church in Boston, and served in that post until 1875. Renowned as an orator, he devoted himself to numerous social causes, including aid for immigrants and those confined to public institutions. Healy was appointed bishop of Portland, Maine, in 1875 by Pope Pius IX. During his 25 years as head of the diocese, he built 60 churches and ministered to the needs of 96,000 Catholics in Maine and New Hampshire. Because of his initiative in building orphanages and his concern for the families of soldiers killed in the Civil War, he was known as the children's bishop. (His brother Patrick Francis [1834–1910] became the first African American Jesuit and, as president of Georgetown University from 1874 to 1882, the first African American to head a Catholic university.)

Jackson, Jesse Louis   (See Chapter 3, "Politics and Civil Rights.")

Kelly, Leontine (1920–   ).   Kelly grew up in Cincinnati as the daughter of a prominent Methodist Episcopal minister, David DeWitt Turpeau Sr., and was early imbued with a belief in social activism and racial justice. After attending West Virginia State, she married and raised three children. During the 1950s, her second husband, Methodist minister James David Kelly, persuaded her to complete her college education. Obtaining her degree in 1960, she became a social-studies teacher and a lay speaker in the church. Following her husband's death in 1969, Kelly—at the request of the congregation—succeeded him as pastor of the Galilee United Methodist Church in Edwardsville, Virginia. A year later she began her theological studies and was ordained an elder in 1977. She then held a number of ecclesiastical posts and in 1984 was elected the first black woman bishop of a major denomination in the United States. She served as bishop of the San Francisco area until 1988, when she retired at the age of 68 to become a part-time teacher and the first president of the AIDS National Interfaith Network.

King, Martin Luther, Jr.   (See Chapter 3, "Politics and Civil Rights.")

King, Martin Luther, Sr. (1899–1984).   Born in Stockbridge, Georgia, King was the son of a sharecropper and grew up with close ties to the church, becoming a licensed Baptist minister at age 15. Three years later he moved to Atlanta, where he became the pastor of the East Point Baptist Church and also founded the Second Baptist Church of College Park. While working at a variety of jobs and serving his parishioners, he was also determined to continue his education. A year after receiving his bachelor's degree in theology from Morehouse College in 1930, he succeeded his father-in-law, A. D. Williams, as pastor of Atlanta's prestigious Ebenezer Baptist Church. In this new and influential post, King became a community leader, joining the NAACP and taking part in numerous efforts to achieve fair treatment for African Americans. During the 1950s, King had the satisfaction of seeing his son Martin Jr. rise to prominence as a Baptist minister and a leader of the civil rights movement. Following his son's assassination, the elder King continued his leadership role and traveled widely, carrying his message of faith to diverse groups. In 1975, King became the first African American to address the Alabama State Legislature, and in 1980 he delivered the benediction at the Democratic National Convention.

Lee, Jarena (1783–?).   Lee was born in Cape May, New Jersey, and went to work as a maid at age seven. She converted to Christianity in 1801. She joined the A.M.E. Church, and in 1818, the recently widowed Lee determined to become a preacher. Bishop Richard Allen accepted her petition, and she became an itinerant minister, preaching to whites, blacks, and Native Americans wherever she found them. When the rigors of this life took their toll on Lee's health, Allen appointed her to a post in Bethel A.M.E. Church in Philadelphia. This proved to be a frustrating experience, however, as the congregation was not ready to accept a female preacher. During this period, Lee began to write of her experiences, publishing *The Life and Religious Experiences of Jarena Lee* in 1836 and *Religious Experiences and Journal of Jarena Lee* in 1849.

Liele, George (c. 1750–1820).   Said to be the first ordained African American preacher, Liele (also known as Lisle) was born into slavery in Virginia. Around 1770 he came to live in Georgia, where he was initiated into the Baptist faith by a white preacher and subsequently emancipated. During the American Revolution, Liele lived in British-occupied Savannah, preaching to African American Baptists and founding the second black church in the United States. After the war, he accompanied British forces to Jamaica. There he gained a large following, built a church and school, and earned a living as a farmer and hauler. While in the West Indies, Liele preserved his ties with the African American community in Savannah, founding the African Baptist Church in that city.

Lyke, James P. (1939–1992).   A native of Chicago who grew up in an inner-city housing project, Lyke converted to Catholicism while attending parochial school and joined the Franciscan order at age 20. He then earned a Master of Divinity degree from St. Joseph's Seminary in Illinois and a Ph.D. from Union Institute in Cincinnati. During the 1970s he served as pastor of St. Thomas's Church in Memphis, emphasizing youth programs and African American culture. He became a bishop in 1979, and in 1991, Pope John Paul II appointed Lyke archbishop of Atlanta. As the highest-ranking African American in the Roman Catholic Church, he presided over a diocese of 180,000 worshipers and served as the spokesperson for 1 million African American Roman Catholics.

Michaux, (Elder) Solomon Lightfoot (c. 1885–1968).   Born into a devout Baptist family, Michaux was educated in Newport News, Virginia, and went to work in his family's seafood business. In 1917, Michaux established the first black Church of God in Hopewell, Virginia, and created a branch in Newport News two years later. At this time, he began to employ the growing medium of radio to broadcast his services. After he founded a Church of God branch in Washington, D.C., in 1928, his radio broadcasts earned him a huge following in the area. Known as the Happy Am I Evangelist and the Colored Billy Sunday, Michaux often baptized followers in the Potomac River and in a huge tank erected in Griffith Stadium. These ceremonies were preceded by parades that attracted huge crowds. Michaux's newspaper, *Happy News*, had 8,000 subscribers, and a number of prominent officials—including President Franklin Roosevelt's private secretary—were honorary deacons in his church.

Muhammad, Elijah   (See Chapter 3, "Politics and Civil Rights.")

Payne, Daniel Alexander (1811–1893).   Born of free parents in South Carolina, Payne moved to Philadelphia as a young man and joined the Lutheran Church. He was licensed to preach in 1837 and also opened a school. In 1841 he joined the African Methodist Episcopal Church and was ordained as a preacher. Elected a bishop in 1952, he traveled widely for the next 11 years, setting up schools and training institutes. In 1862 he purchased Wilberforce University from its white founders for $10,000 and began to build it into a leading African American institution before retiring in 1876. Payne Theological Seminary was named in his honor.

Powell, Adam Clayton, Jr.   (See Chapter 3, "Politics and Civil Rights.")

Powell, Adam Clayton, Sr. (1865–1953).   Born in a log cabin in Virginia, Powell graduated from Wayland Seminary in Washington, D.C., in 1892 and continued his training at Yale Divinity School. Between 1893 and 1908, Powell served as pastor of the Immanuel Baptist Church in New Haven, Connecticut. He then moved to New York and took the helm of the newly founded Abyssinian Baptist Church, then located on West 40th Street. (The church moved to its present site on West 138th Street in 1923.) Among the many programs Powell sponsored in Harlem were the community's first recreation center and a home for the aged. Throughout the Great Depression, Powell helped feed the poor and campaigned for jobs and improved city services. By the mid-1930s, Abyssinian Baptist Church had 14,000 members, making it the largest Protestant congregation in the United States. In 1937, Powell became pastor emeritus and was succeeded in the pulpit by his son, Adam Jr. (See Chapter 3, "Politics and Civil Rights.")

Smith, Amanda Berry (1837–1915).   Smith was born into slavery in Maryland, but her father was able to purchase his family's freedom and move them to Pennsylvania before the Civil War. Smith began to work as a domestic at age 17 and joined the A.M.E. Church soon afterward. In 1870 she experienced a religious revelation and determined to join the ministry. Smith began preaching in New Jersey, and in 1876 she evangelized in Europe before moving on to India. In 1881 she began eight years of service in Africa, where she worked closely with Methodist missionaries. After her return to the United States, Smith continued preaching and published an autobiography in 1893. After settling in Chicago, Smith purchased a house in Harvey, Illinois, and opened the Amanda Smith Industrial Home for orphans. In 1912, she moved to Sebring, Florida, where she enjoyed a comfortable retirement during her final years.

Sullivan, Leon H. (1922–   ).   Ordained as a Baptist minister at age 17, Sullivan earned a bachelor's degree in 1943 from West Virginia State, where he starred in football and basketball before a knee injury ended his athletic career. He then studied at Union Theological Seminary while assisting at the Abyssinian Baptist Church in New York. Between 1950 and 1988 he served as pastor of Zion Baptist Church in north Philadelphia and boosted church membership from 600 to 6,000. In 1964, Sullivan founded the Industrialization Opportunities Center (IOC), a retraining program that now operates in 130 U.S. cities and 7 African nations. Since its inception, IOC has trained more than 1 million men and women for a variety of occupations. Other projects founded by Sullivan include Progress Investment Associates, which has financed housing developments and shopping centers, and Progress Human Service Center, which provides health care and human services to African Americans in Philadelphia. In 1977, Sullivan established the Sullivan Principles, a set of guidelines for companies operating in South Africa and other areas where human rights have been in jeopardy. He also served as president of the International Foundation for Education and Self-Help, which trains workers, farmers, and health-care professionals in Africa. Among many other honors, Sullivan holds the Presidential Medal of Freedom and Ivory Coast's Distinguished Service Award.

Thurman, Howard (1900–1981).   Born in Daytona, Florida, Thurman was the first African American in the city's history to complete the eighth grade. He went on to graduate from Morehouse College (1923) and the Rochester Theological Seminary (1926). He then became pastor of Mt. Zion Baptist Church in Oberlin, Ohio (1926–1928), before accepting a professorship at Morehouse and Spelman colleges, where he also served as director of religious life. In 1932, Thurman became professor of religion and director of Rankin Chapel at Howard University, remaining in that post until 1944, when he cofounded the Fellowship Church for All Peoples, an interfaith, interracial congregation in San Francisco. In 1953, Thurman accepted a professorship at Boston University and also became the director of the university's Marsh Chapel. After retiring in 1965, he devoted himself to running the Howard Thurman Educational Trust, which he had created in 1961. Adopting the "search for common ground" as the guiding principle of his career, Thurman had a profound influence on many national leaders, including Martin Luther King Jr., Mary McLeod Bethune, A. Philip Randolph, Arthur Ashe, and Eleanor Roosevelt. He is the author of several major works of social theology, including the seminal *Jesus and the Dispossessed*.

Turner, Henry McNeal (1834–1915).   Born to free parents in South Carolina, Turner taught himself to read and found a job in a law firm. He joined the Methodist Episcopal Church, became a licensed preacher in 1853, and then embarked on a career as an itinerant minister. After moving to St. Louis, he joined the A.M.E. Church in 1858. In 1863, President Lincoln appointed Turner a chaplain in the Union Army, attached to the 1st Regiment, U.S. Colored Troops. Assigned to a post in the Freedmen's Bureau in 1865, Turner played a leading role in implementing Reconstruction policies in the South. In 1876, he began a 12-year tenure as president of Morris Brown College (see earlier biography). At this time he became convinced that African Americans could not achieve justice in the United States and advocated African colonization projects, traveling to Europe and Africa to promote this initiative.

Varick, James (1750–1827).   Raised in New York City, Varick learned the trade of shoemaking while in his teens. At age 16, he joined the John Street Methodist Episcopal Church and was licensed to preach. In 1796, reacting to growing discrimination within the church, he resigned with a group of 30 followers and founded the first African American church in New York—Zion Church at the corner of Liberty and Leonard streets. Varick served as the first chaplain of the New York African Society for Mutual Relief (founded in 1810) and helped start *Freedom's Journal,* the first African American newspaper in the United States. In 1822, he was elected the first bishop of the African Methodist Episcopal Zion Church.

X, Malcolm   (See Chapter 3, "Politics and Civil Rights.")

SOURCES FOR ADDITIONAL INFORMATION

Baer, Hans, and Merrill Singer. *African-American Religion in the Twentieth Century: Varieties of Protest and Accommodation.* Knoxville: University of Tennessee Press, 1992.

Barrett, Leonard E. *Soul-Force: African Heritage in Afro-American Religion.* Garden City, NY: Doubleday, 1974.

Bascom, W. R. *Sixteen Cowries: Yoruba in Africa and the New World.* Bloomington: Indiana University Press, 1980.

Carter, Harold A., Wyatt T. Walker, and William A. Jones. *The African-American Church: Past, Present, and Future.* Morristown, NJ: Aaron Press, 1991.

Frazier, E. Franklin. *The Negro Church in America.* New York: Schocken, 1963.

Lincoln, C. Eric, and Lawrence H. Mamiya. *The Black Church in the American Experience.* Durham, NC: Duke University Press, 1990.

Murphy, Larry G., J. Melton, and Gary Ward, eds. *Encyclopedia of African-American Religions.* New York: Garland, 1993.

Payne, Wardell, ed. *Directory of African-American Religious Bodies.* Washington, DC: Howard University Press, 1995.

Simpson, George Eaton. *Black Religions in the New World.* New York: Columbia University Press, 1978.

Thompson, Robert Farris. *Flash of the Spirit: African and Afro-American Art and Philosophy.* New York: Vintage, 1983.

Wood, Forrest G. *The Arrogance of Faith: Christianity and Race in America from the Colonial Era to the Twentieth Century.* New York: Knopf, 1990.

7

Education

MILESTONES IN EDUCATION

1695   First known school for blacks is established in Charleston, South Carolina, by Samuel Thomas, a white cleric.

1704   French immigrant Elias Neau opens a school for blacks in New York City.

1740   South Carolina makes it illegal to teach slaves to write.

1758   Schools for African American children are opened in Philadelphia.

1770   Quakers open a school for blacks in Philadelphia.

1787   Manumission Society establishes the New York African Free School.

1789   Free blacks in Massachusetts organize a school.

1802   African Americans in Ohio's Western Reserve organize the Ohio School Fund Society.

1804   Richard Allen and Absalom Jones found schools in Philadelphia.

1806   New York City opens its first schools for black children.

1807   Free blacks establish the Bell School in Washington, D.C.

1820   The city of Boston opens an elementary school for black children.

1823   Alexander Twilight receives B.A. from Middlebury College, Vermont, becoming the first African American to earn a degree at a U.S. college.

1829   Blacks from Santo Domingo open St. Francis Academy, a girls' school in Baltimore; a school for blacks is established in Charleston.

1830   Southern states move to curb black education in the wake of slave insurrections.

1833   Oberlin College is founded in Ohio, a coeducational and interracial school that plays a leading role in the abolitionist movement.

1835   The black-led Ohio School Fund Society opens schools in Columbus, Cleveland, Cincinnati, and Springfield.

1849   Charles Lewis Reason is appointed professor of mathematics, belles lettres, and French at Central College in McGrawville, New York, becoming the first African American faculty member at a predominantly white (though integrated) college.

1850   Lucy Ann Stanton (later Mrs. Levi Sessions) receives a bachelor of literature degree from Oberlin, becoming the first African American woman to earn a college degree.

1854   Lincoln University, the first historically black college in the United States, is founded in Pennsylvania.

1856   Wilberforce University opens in Ohio.

1859   Sarah Jane Woodson becomes the first black woman to serve on the faculty of a U.S. university when she takes a teaching post at Wilberforce.

1862   Wilberforce University is purchased by the A.M.E. (African Methodist Episcopal) Church, making it the first U.S. university controlled by African Americans; LeMoyne-Owen College is founded in Memphis.

1863   Historian, educator, and A.M.E. minister Daniel A. Payne takes the helm at Wilberforce, becoming the first African American college president.

1865   Shaw, Atlanta, and Virginia State universities are founded, as is Bowie State College.

1866   Lincoln University is founded in Missouri with a $5,000 donation from the officers and men of the 65th Colored Infantry; Barber-Scotia and St. Augustine's colleges are founded in North Carolina.

1867   Howard University is founded in Washington, D.C., by act of Congress, as a coeducational and multiracial institution; created to train ministers and teachers as guides for newly freed blacks, it grows to become a top-level research institution and the leading historically black university in the United States.

1870–1875   Several historically black institutions are founded, including Benedict, Allen, Alcorn, Wiley, Simmons Bible College, Alabama State, and Alabama A&M.

1876   Meharry Medical College (first all-black U.S. medical school) is founded.

1881   The Atlanta Baptist Female Seminary (later Spelman College) is founded, the first institution of higher learning dedicated to the education of African American women; Booker T. Washington founds Tuskegee Normal and Industrial Institute (later Tuskegee University) in Alabama.

1895   W. E. B. Du Bois becomes the first African American to earn a doctorate from Harvard.

1896   In the infamous *Plessy v. Ferguson* case, the Supreme Court upholds the policy of "separate but equal" accommodations for blacks, asserting that the Fourteenth Amendment was not meant "to enforce social as distinguished from political equality."

1901   Grambling State University is founded in Louisiana.

1902   Industrialist John D. Rockefeller founds the General Education Board, designed to aid black education and to train teachers for Southern schools.

1907   Alain Locke graduates from Harvard and becomes the first African American to win a Rhodes Scholarship.

1922   William Leo Hansberry of Howard offers the first course in African civilization at a U.S. university.

1932   *Journal of Negro Education* begins publication at Howard.

1933   NAACP begins its campaign to eliminate segregation and discrimination in U.S. educational institutions.

1944   Frederick D. Patterson, president of Tuskegee Institute, founds the United Negro College Fund, dedicated to coordinating the fund-raising efforts of historically black colleges.

1954   In *Brown v. Board of Education* the Supreme Court rules that segregation in public schools is unconstitutional, overturning the "separate but equal" policy that legalized school segregation since the *Plessy v. Ferguson* decision in 1896; Washington, D.C., and Baltimore begin to integrate their schools.

1955   Willa B. Player becomes president of Bennett College, the first African American woman to head a four-year institution.

1956   Autherine Lucy becomes the first black student to enroll at the University of Alabama.

1957   Nine black students who attempted to register at Central High School in Little Rock, Arkansas, are denied access by Governor Orval Faubus; after attempts to negotiate, President Eisenhower sends federal troops to protect the students and ensure state compliance with desegregation orders.

> Y*ou just realize that survival is day to day and you start to grasp your own spirit, you start to grasp the depth of the human spirit, and you start to understand the ability to cope no matter what.*
>
> Melba Pattillo Beals, recalling her experience as one of the students who integrated Little Rock's Central High School

1961   Atlanta peacefully desegregates four high schools.

1962   Riots erupt at the University of Mississippi when James Meredith tries to enroll as its first black student. Federal troops are sent to ensure Meredith's admission and to maintain order.

1968   Only 20.3 percent of black schoolchildren in the South are in integrated schools when the U.S. Supreme Court rules that all public schools must prepare realistic desegregation plans without delay. Two years later, more than 90 percent of public schools in the South are classified as desegregrated.

1968   Students at Howard demand stronger emphasis on African American studies in the curriculum, inspiring demonstrations and sit-ins by black students at other universities, including Brandeis, Cornell, and Jackson State.

1969   Harvard establishes an Afro-American Studies Program; Clifton Wharton becomes the first African American to head a predominantly white public university (Michigan State).

1970   Governor John Williams announces that he will help build a Mississippi private-school system as an alternative to public-school desegregation. John S. Martin resigns as superintendent of public schools in Jackson, Mississippi, citing the pressures of school desegregation as the cause.

1977   Mary Frances Berry, African American activist and educator, is appointed assistant secretary for education in the Department of Health, Education, and Welfare.

1980   First annual Black College Day is celebrated by more than 18,000 students in Washington, D.C.

1983   U.S. Supreme Court rules that private schools practicing racial discrimination cannot receive tax exemptions.

1988   Temple University becomes the first institution to offer a doctorate in African American studies.

1989   A USA Today report critiques the Scholastic Aptitude Test (SAT) for being biased against blacks and other minorities because of the language and situations used.

1990   Walter H. Annenberg, a white businessperson, promises $50 million to the United Negro College Fund, the largest donation pledged to the fund.

1992   U.S. Supreme Court ruled that "race-neutral policies" did not relieve Mississippi's responsibility to end segregation in the public university system, including historically black public colleges.

HISTORICALLY BLACK COLLEGES AND UNIVERSITIES (HBCUs)

Historically black colleges and universities account for 3 percent of all institutions of higher learning in the United States, but they enroll 16 percent of all African American students in higher education and graduate nearly 30 percent of all African Americans earning bachelor's degrees. On the professional level, HBCUs have trained 75 percent of black Ph.D.s, 85 percent of black physicians, 46 percent of black business executives, 50 percent of black engineers, 50 percent of black attorneys, 40 percent of black dentists, 50 percent of black pharmacists, and 75 percent of black veterinarians. In addition, 53.4 percent of African American public-school teachers in 1993–1994 received their undergraduate degrees from HBCUs.

PUBLIC INSTITUTIONS

(Year of founding in parentheses; includes four-year course of study unless otherwise indicated.)

Alabama A&M University (1875)   205-851-5000
P.O. Box 908   800-533-0816
Normal, AL 35762   state supported; 5,215 students

Alabama State University (1874)
915 S. Jackson Street
Montgomery, AL 36101
205-293-4100
5,490 students

Albany State College (1903)
504 College Drive
Albany, GA 31705
912-430-4600
3,106 students

Alcorn State University (1871)
New Administration Building
Lorman, MS 39096
601-877-6147
3,256 students

Atlanta Metropolitan College (1974)
Atlanta, GA 30310
404-756-4004
state-supported two-year college; 1,785 students

Bishop State Community College (1965)
351 N. Broad Street
Mobile, AL 36603
205-690-6419
state-supported junior college; 2,144 students

Bluefield State College (1895)
219 Rock Street
Bluefield, WV 24701
304-327-7747
2,907 students

Bowie State University (1865)
1400 Jericho Park Road
Bowie, MD 20715
301-464-3000
4,437 students

Central State University (1887)
Norman Ward University Center
Wilberforce, OH 45384
513-376-6348
3,266 students

Cheyney University of Pennsylvania (1837)
Cheyney, PA 19319
215-399-2275
state supported; 1,607 students

Chicago State University
95th Street at King Drive
Chicago, IL 60628
312-995-2516
8,004 students

City University of New York—Medgar Evers
    College (1969)
1650 Bedford Avenue
Brooklyn, NY 11225
718-270-6024
state supported; 4,400 students

Coahoma Community College (1949)
Route 1, Box 616
Clarksdale, MS 38614
601-627-2571
state- and locally supported two-year college;
    1,500 students

Coppin State College (1900)
2500 W. North Avenue
Baltimore, MD 21216
410-383-3400
2,800 students

Delaware State University (1891)
1200 N. Dupont Highway
Dover, DE 19901
302-739-4917
2,880 students

Denmark Technical College (1948)
Solomon Blatt Boulevard
Denmark, SC 29042
803-793-3301
state-supported two-year college; 725 students

Elizabeth City State University (1891)
P.O. Box 901 ECSU
Elizabeth City, NC 27909
919-335-3400
1,760 students

Fayetteville State University (1867)
1200 Murchison Road
Fayetteville, NC 28301
919-486-1371
800-222-2594
part of the University of North Carolina system;
    3,786 students

Florida A&M University (1887)
1500 Wahnish Way
Tallahassee, FL 32307
904-599-3796
state supported; 9,196 students

Fort Valley State College (1895)
1005 State College Drive
Fort Valley, GA 31030
912-825-6307
2,368 students

Grambling State University (1901)
100 Main Street
Grambling, LA 71245
318-274-6000
6,485 students

Harris-Stowe State College (1857)
3026 Laclede Avenue
St. Louis, MO 63103
314-533-3366
1,850 students

Hinds Community College—Utica Campus
   (1903)
Utica, MS 39715
601-885-6062
state-supported two-year college; 1,030 students

Jackson State University (1877)
1400 John R. Lynch Street
Jackson, MS 39217
601-968-2911
800-848-6817
6,200 students

J. F. Drake State Technical College (1961)
3421 Meridian Street, N
Hunstville, AL 35811
205-539-8161
953 students

Kentucky State University (1886)
P.O. Box PG-92
Frankfort, KY 40601
502-227-6000
2,518 students

Langston University (1897)
Langston, OK 73050
405-466-2231
state supported; 2,030 students

Lawson State Community College (1965)
3060 Wilson Road, SW
Birmingham, AL 35221
205-925-2515
two-year college; 1,960 students

Lincoln University, Missouri (1866)
820 Chestnut Street
Jefferson City, MO 65102
314-681-5000
state supported; 4,100 students

Lincoln University, Pennsylvania (1854)
Lincoln University, PA 19352
215-932-8300
state supported; 1,458 students

Mississippi Valley State University (1946)
Itta Bena, MS 38941
601-254-9041
1,675 students

Morgan State University (1867)
Cold Spring Lane and Hillen Road
Baltimore, MD 21239
443-885-3333
800-332-6674
5,034 students

Norfolk State University (1935)
2401 Corprew Avenue
Norfolk, VA 23504
757-683-8600
8,300 students

North Carolina A&T State University (1891)
1601 E. Market Street
Greensboro, NC 27411
919-334-7946
7,100 students

North Carolina Central University (1910)
P.O. Box 19717
Durham, NC 27707
919-560-6326
state supported; 5,400 students

Prairie View A&M University (1878)
P.O. Box 2610
Prairie View, TX 77446
409-857-2626
800-334-1807
state supported; 5,600 students

Roxbury Community College (1973)
1234 Columbus Avenue
Roxbury Crossing, MA 02120
617-541-5310
state-supported two-year college; 2,500 students

Savannah State College (1890)
James A. Colston Administration Building
Savannah, GA 31404
912-356-2181
2,656 students

South Carolina State College (1896)
300 College Street, NE
Orangeburg, SC 29117
803-536-7185
5,145 students

Southern University and A&M University, Baton
  Rouge (1880)
T. H. Harris Hall
Baton Rouge, LA 70813
504-771-2430
state supported; 10,000 students

Southern University at New Orleans (1956)
6400 Press Drive
New Orleans, LA 70126
504-286-5000
state supported; 2,180 students

Southern University at Shreveport (1964)
3050 Martin Luther King Jr. Drive
Shreveport, LA 71107
318-674-3342
state-supported two-year college; 930 students

Tennessee State University (1912)
3500 John Merritt Boulevard
Nashville, TN 37209
613-230-3420
7,400 students

*Howard University, founded in 1867, is
the largest of the private historically
black colleges and universities.*

Texas Southern University (1947)
3100 Cleburne Avenue
Houston, TX 77004
713-527-7474
state supported; 10,270 students

Trenholm State Technical College
1225 Air Base Boulevard
Montgomery, AL 36108
205-832-9000
823 students

University of Arkansas at Pine Bluff (1873)
P.O. Box 31
University Drive
Pine Bluff, AR 71601
501-541-6500
state supported; 3,625 students

University of the District of Columbia (1976)
4200 Connecticut Avenue, NW
Washington, DC 20008
202-282-7300
state and locally supported; 12,000 students

University of Maryland Eastern Shore (1886)
Princess Anne, MD 21853
410-651-2200
state supported; 2,400 students

Virginia State University (1882)
20708 Fourth Avenue
Petersburg, VA 23806
804-524-5695
4,600 students

West Virginia State College (1891)
Farrell Hall, Room 106
Institute, WV 25112
304-766-3221
5,000 students

Winston-Salem State University (1892)
601 Martin Luther King Jr. Drive
Winston-Salem, NC 27110
919-750-2070
2,600 students

PRIVATE INSTITUTIONS

Allen University (1870)
1530 Harden Street
Columbia, SC 29204
803-254-4165
independent; 223 students

Arkansas Baptist College (1884)
1600 Bishop Street
Little Rock, AR 72202
501-374-7856
independent; 408 students

Barber-Scotia College (1867)
145 Cabarrus Avenue, W
Concord, NC 28025
704-786-5171
independent, affiliated with the Presbyterian
    Church; 708 students

Benedict College (1870)
1600 Harden Street
Columbia, SC 29204
803-253-5143
private Baptist college; 1,422 students

Bennett College (1873)
900 E. Washington Street
Greensboro, NC 27401
919-370-8624
800-838-BENN
private undergraduate women's college; 568 students

Bethune-Cookman College (1904)
640 Second Avenue
Daytona Beach, FL 32115
904-255-1401
independent Methodist college; 2,301 students

I f our people are to fight their way out of bondage, we must arm them with the sword and the shield and the buckler of pride—belief in themselves and their possibilities based upon a sure knowledge of the past. That knowledge and pride we must give them—if it breaks every back in the kingdom.

Mary McLeod Bethune, *Journal of Negro History* (January 1938)

Charles R. Drew University of Medicine and
   Science (1978)
1621 E. 120th Street
Los Angeles, CA 90059
213-563-4960
federally funded private university; 140 students

Claflin College (1869)
700 College Street, NE
Orangeburg, SC 29115
803-534-2710
independent Methodist college; 885 students

Clark Atlanta University (1869)
240 James P. Brawley Drive, SW
Atlanta, GA 30314
404-880-8784
independent; affiliated with the United Methodist
   Church; 3,996 students

Clinton Junior College (1894)
1020 Crawford Road
P.O. Box 968
Rock Hill, SC 29730
803-327-5587
private two-year college; 76 students

Concordia College (1922)
1804 N. Green Street
Selma, AL 36701
205-874-5700
private two-year college; 385 students

Dillard University (1869)
2601 Gentilly Boulevard
New Orleans, LA 70122
504-283-8822
independent, interdenominational; 1,650 students

Edward Waters College (1866)
1658 Kings Road
Jacksonville, FL 32209
904-353-3030
independent; 635 students

Fisk University (1866)
1000 17th Avenue, N
Nashville, TN 37208
615-329-8665
independent, affiliated with the United Church of
   Christ; 857 students

Florida Memorial College (1879)
15800 Florida Memorial College Avenue
Miami, FL 33054
305-625-4141
independent, affiliated with the Baptist Church;
   2,000 students

Hampton University (1868)
Hampton, VA 23668
804-727-5238
independent; 5,704 students

Howard University (1867)
2400 Sixth Street, NW
Washington, DC 20059
202-806-6100
800-822-6363
independent; 11,222 students

Huston-Tillotson College (1875)
1820 E. Eighth Street
Austin, TX 78702
512-476-7421
independent religious college; 653 students

Interdenominational Theological Center (1958)
671 Beckwith Street, SW
Atlanta, GA 30314
404-527-7700
private graduate center; 383 students

Jarvis Christian College (1912)
Highway 80 West
Hawkins, TX 75765
independent, affiliated with the Christian Church;
   543 students

Johnson C. Smith University (1867)
100–152 Beatties Ford Road
Charlotte, NC 28216
704-378-1010
independent; 1,256 students

Knoxville College (1875)
901 College Street, NW
Knoxville, TN 37921
615-524-6525
private undergraduate college; 1,266 students

Lane College (1882)
545 Lane Avenue

Jackson, TN 38301
901-426-7532
private; 562 students

LeMoyne-Owen College (1870)
807 Walker Avenue
Memphis, TN 38126
901-942-7302
private; 1,064 students

Lewis College of Business (1929)
17370 Meyers Road
Detroit, MI 48235
313-862-6300
independent two-year college; 386 students

Livingstone College (1879)
Salisbury, NC 28144
704-638-5502
private; 683 students

Mary Holmes College (1892)
Highway 50 West
West Point, MS 39773
601-494-6820
private two-year college; 742 students

Meharry Medical College (1876)
1005 D. B. Todd Boulevard
Nashville, TN 37208
615-327-6223
private; 562 students

Miles College (1905)
Bell Building
Birmingham, AL 35208
205-923-2771
independent Christian Methodist Episcopal
   college; 750 students

Morehouse College (1867)
830 Westview Drive, SW
Atlanta, GA 30314
404-681-2800
independent; 3,000 students

Morehouse School of Medicine (1975)
720 Westview Drive
Atlanta, GA 30310
404-752-1651
145 students

Morris Brown College (1881)
643 Martin Luther King Jr. Drive, NW
Atlanta, GA 30314
404-220-0270
private; 2,000 students

Morris College (1908)
100 W. College Street
Sumter, NC 29150
910-692-6185
private; 700 students

Natchez College (1885)
1010 N. Union Street
Natchez, MS 39120
601-445-9702
private two-year college; 100 students

Oakwood College (1896)
Oakwood Road, NW
Hunstville, AL 35896
private; 1,335 students

Paine College (1882)
1235 15th Street
Augusta, GA 30910
404-821-8200
800-746-7703
private; 790 students

Paul Quinn College (1872)
1020 Elm Avenue
Waco, TX 76704
817-753-6415
independent African Methodist Episcopal college;
   587 students

Philander-Smith College (1877)
812 W. 13th Street
Little Rock, AR 72202
501-375-9845
independent United Methodist college;
   620 students

Rust College (1866)
150 Rust Avenue
Holly Springs, MS 38635
601-252-8000
private; 1,075 students

St. Augustine's College (1867)
1315 Oakwood Avenue
Raleigh, NC 27610
919-828-4451
independent Episcopal college; 1,900 students

St. Paul's College (1888)
406 Windsor Avenue
Lawrenceville, VA 23868
804-848-3984
800-678-7071
independent Episcopal college; 700 students

Selma University (1878)
1501 Lapsley Street
Selma, AL 36701
334-872-2533
independent Baptist college; 207 students

Shaw University (1865)
118 E. South Street
Raleigh, NC 27611
919-546-8275
independent Baptist college; 2,150 students

Shorter College (1886)
604 Locust Street
North Little Rock, AR 72114
501-374-6305
private two-year college; 120 students

Simmons Bible College (1879)
1811 Dumesnil Street
Louisville, KY 40210
502-776-1443
denomination supported; 115 students

Sojourner-Douglass College (1980)
500 N. Caroline Street
Baltimore, MD 21205
401-276-0306
independent; 441 students

Southwestern Christian College (1949)
Jack Evans Administration Building
Terrell, TX 75160
214-563-3341
private; 245 students

Spelman College (1881)
350 Spelman Lane, SW

Atlanta, GA 30314
404-681-3643
800-241-3421
private women's college; 1,850 students

Stillman College (1876)
P.O. Box 1430
Tuscaloosa, AL 35403
205-349-4240
private; 820 students

Talladega College (1867)
627 W. Battle Street
Talladega, AL 35160
205-362-0206
private; 750 students

Texas College (1894)
2404 N. Grand Avenue
Tyler, TX 75202
903-593-8311
independent, affiliated with the Christian
    Methodist Episcopalian Church; 355 students

Tougaloo College
Tougaloo, MS 39174
601-977-7764
private; 1,000 students

Tuskegee University (1881)
Carnegie Hall, 4th Floor
Tuskegee, AL 36088
independent; 3,690 students

Virginia Union University (1865)
1500 N. Lombardy Street
Richmond, VA 23220
804-257-5600
private Baptist university; 1,360 students

Voorhees College (1897)
1411 Voorhees Road
Denmark, SC 29042
803-793-3351
private; 615 students

Wilberforce University (1856)
Xenia, OH 45384
937-376-2911
independent, affiliated with the African
    Methodist Episcopal Church; 760 students

Wiley College (1873)
711 Wiley Avenue
Marshall, TX 75670
214-938-8341
private; 400 students

Xavier University of Louisiana (1925)
7325 Palmetto Street
New Orleans, LA 70125
504-483-7651
private; 3,100 students

THE UNITED NEGRO COLLEGE FUND

In response to an initiative by Frederick D. Patterson, the president of Tuskegee University, the United Negro College Fund (UNCF) was formed in 1944 with 27 member colleges. Since its founding, the UNCF has raised more than $1 billion for its member institutions, which now number 41 HBCUs, with a combined enrollment of more than 54,000. Non–African American enrollment at UNCF schools is nearly 15 percent, and non–African American faculty is approximately 35 percent. In addition to offering financial aid to students, the UNCF provides more than 450 separate services to member colleges, including summer programs, internships, faculty training, and administrative assistance. In 1997, the UNCF's Frederick D. Patterson Research Institute published the *African-American Education Data Book*, the most comprehensive study of African American education ever undertaken.

AFRICAN AMERICAN STUDIES PROGRAMS

Early advocates for what came to be known as black studies included Alexander Crummell, who founded the American Negro Academy in 1897, and Carter G. Woodson, who organized the Association for the Study of Negro Life and History in 1915. The first black-studies department was established in 1969 at Harvard University, an addition to the preexisting African Studies Department. An African and African-American Studies Program was also established at Stanford University that year; the program was to serve as a model for others across the nation. Black-studies departments proliferated in the late 1960s and early 1970s in response to the demands of black students across the country for programs that reflected the African American experience.

AFROCENTRICITY

Afrocentricity is a black-studies movement that seeks to understand American and world history from an African-centered perspective. It emerged in the early 1970s, led by scholars such as Molefi Asante, a professor at Temple University and author of *Afrocentricity* (1980), and Maulana Karenga, a professor at the University of California, Los Angeles, and author of *Introduction to Black Studies* (1993). According to Karenga, "The afrocentric vision . . . demands that black studies root itself in the African experience and in the world view which evolved from and informs that experience. Having rooted itself in the African experience, which is the source and substance of its raison d'être, black studies as a mode of grasping reality expands outward, to the acquisition of other relevant human knowledge and the knowledge of other humans. . . . for even as there are lessons for humanity in African particularity, there are lessons for Africans in human commonality and African humanity is enriched and expanded by mutually beneficial exchanges with others. Moreover, in understanding human history as a whole, Africans can even more critically appreciate their fundamental role in the origins of humanity and human civilization and in the forward flow of human history." The Afrocentric movement has met with strong dissent within certain precincts of academia, but with its focus on the proud achievements of African classical civilizations, it has gained popularity among primary and secondary teachers seeking an alternative to Eurocentric education.

Following is a listing of colleges and universities that include African American studies programs.

Amherst College
Department of Black Studies
Amherst, MA 01002

Antioch College
African-American Studies
Yellow Springs, OH

Ball State University
Afro-American Studies
Muncie, IN 47306

Bowdoin College
African-American Studies Program
Brunswick, ME 04011

Bowling Green State University
Ethnic Studies Department
Bowling Green, OH 43403

Brandeis University
Department of African and African-American
  Studies
Waltham, MA 02254

Brown University
Afro-American Studies Program
Providence, RI 02912

Bryn Mawr College
Africana Studies
Bryn Mawr, PA 19010

California State University Dominguez Hills
African-American Studies Program
Carson, CA 90747

> The final test of Afro-American studies will be the extent to which they rid the minds of whites and blacks alike of false learning, and the extent to which they promote for blacks and whites alike a completely rewarding participation in American life.
>
> J. Saunders Redding, "The Black Youth Movement" (1989)

California State University Fullerton
Department of Afro-Ethnic Studies
Fullerton, CA 92634

California State University Hayward
Afro-American Studies Program
Hayward, CA 94542

California State University Long Beach
Department of Black Studies
Long Beach, CA 90840

California State University Los Angeles
Department of Pan-African Studies
Los Angeles, CA 90032

California State University Northridge
Pan-African Studies Department
Northridge, CA 91330

California State University Sacramento
Pan-African Studies Program
Sacramento, CA 95819

Central State University
Department of Political Science
African and African-American Studies
Wilberforce, OH 45384

Chatham College
African-American Studies
Pittsburgh, PA 15232

City College of City University of New York
Department of African and Afro-American
   Studies
New York, NY 10031

Claremont-McKenna College
Black Studies Department
Claremont, CA 91711

Clark Atlanta University
Afro-American Studies
Atlanta, GA 30314

Coe College
Afro-American Studies
Cedar Rapids, IA 52404

Colgate University
Africana Studies
Hamilton, NY 13346

College of the Holy Cross
African-American Studies
Worcester, MA 01601

College of Staten Island of City University of
   New York
Institute for African-American Studies
Staten Island, NY 10301

College of Wooster
Black Studies Program
Wooster, OH 44691

Columbia University
Institute of African Studies
New York, NY 10027

Cornell University
African Studies and Research Center
Ithaca, NY 14853

Dartmouth College
African and Afro-American Studies Program
Hanover, NH 03755

Denison University
Center for Black Studies
Granville, OH 43023

DePaul University
African-American Studies
Chicago, IL 60604

Duke University
Black Studies
Durham, NC 27706

Earlham College
African and African-American Studies
Richmond, IN 47374

Eastern Illinois University
Afro-American Studies
Charleston, IL 61920

Eastern Michigan University
Department of Afro-American Studies
Ypsilanti, MI 48197

Edinboro University of Pennsylvania
History Department
African History
Edinboro, PA 16444

Emory University
African American and African Studies Program
Atlanta, GA 30322

Florida A&M University
Afro-American Studies
Tallahassee, FL 32307

Fordham University
Afro-American Studies Department
Bronx, NY 10458

Friends World College
African Studies
Huntington, NY 11743

Grinnell College
Afro-American Studies
Grinnell, IA 50112

Hamilton College
African-American Studies Program
Clinton, NY 13323

Hampshire College
Social Science Department
Amherst, MA 01002

Harvard University
Afro-American Studies Department
Cambridge, MA 02138

Hobart College
African & Latin Studies
Geneva, NY 14456

Hofstra University
Africana Studies
Hempstead, NY 11550

Hunter College of City University of New York
Black and Puerto Rican Studies Department
New York, NY 10021

Indiana State University
Center for Afro-American Studies
Terre Haute, IN 47809

Indiana University Bloomington
Afro-American Studies Department
Bloomington, IN 47405

Indiana University Northwest
Department of Minority Studies
Gary, IN 46408

Kent State University
Institute of African American Affairs
Kent, OH 44242

Kenyon College
African and African-American Studies
    Concentration
Gambier, OH 43022

Knox College
Black Studies Department
Galesburg, IL 61401

Lehigh University
African-American Studies
Bethlehem, PA 18015

Lehman College of City University of New York
Black Studies Department
Bronx, NY 10468

Loyola Marymount University
Department of Afro-American Studies
Los Angeles, CA 90045

Loyola University of Chicago
Afro-American Studies Program
Chicago, IL 60626

Luther College
African-American Studies
Decorah, IA 52101

Martin University
African-American Studies
Indianapolis, IN 46218

Mercer University Macon
Afro-American Studies
Macon, GA 31207

Metropolitan State College
Department of Afro-American Studies
Denver, CO 80204

Miami University
Afro-American Studies
Oxford, OH 45056

Mount Holyoke College
African-American Studies
South Hadley, MA 01075

New York University
Africana Studies
New York, NY 10012

Northeastern University
Department of African and Afro-American
   Studies
Boston, MA 02115

Northwestern University
African American Studies Department
Evanston, IL 60201

Oakland University
African and African-American Studies Program
Rochester, MI 48309

Oberlin College
Black Studies Department
Oberlin, OH 44074

Occidental College
Department of History
Los Angeles, CA 90041

Ohio State University
Department of Black Studies
Columbus, OH 43210

Ohio University Athens
Afro-American Studies
Athens, OH 45701

Ohio Wesleyan University
Black World Studies
Delaware, OH 43015

Pomona College
Black Studies
Claremont, CA 91711

Princeton University
African-American Studies Program
Princeton, NJ 08544

Purdue University
Afro-American Studies Center
West Lafayette, IN 47907

Rhode Island College
African and African-American Studies Program
Providence, RI 02908

Roosevelt University
African, Afro-American, and Black Studies
Chicago, IL 60605

Rutgers State University of New Jersey
Camden College of Arts and Sciences
African-American Studies
Camden, NJ 08102

Rutgers State University of New Jersey
Douglas College
Africana Studies
New Brunswick, NJ 08903

Rutgers State University of New Jersey
Newark College of Arts and Sciences
Afro-American and African Studies Department
Newark, NJ 07102

St. Olaf College
American Minority Studies Program
Northfield, MN 55057

San Diego State University
African-American Studies Department
San Diego, CA 92182

San Jose State University
Afro-American Studies Department
San Jose, CA 95192

Scripps College
African Studies Department
Claremont, CA 91711

Seton Hall University
African-American Studies
South Orange, NJ 07079

Shaw University
Afro-American Studies
Raleigh, NC 27611

Simmons College
Afro-American Studies Program
Boston, MA 02115

Smith College
Department of Afro-American Studies
Northampton, MA 01063

Sonoma State University
American Multi-Cultural Studies
Rohnert Park, CA 94928

Southern Illinois University Carbondale
Black American Studies Program
Carbondale, IL 60091

Southern Methodist University
Department of Anthropology
Dallas, TX 75275

Stanford University
African and Afro-American Studies Program
Stanford, CA 94305

State University of New York at Albany
African and Afro-American Studies
Albany, NY 12222

State University of New York at Binghamton
Afro-American and Asian Studies Department
Binghamton, NY 13901

State University of New York at Brockport
Department of African and Afro-American
    Studies
Brockport, NY 14420

State University of New York at Cortland
Black Studies Program
Cortland, NY 13045

State University of New York at Geneseo
Black Studies Program
Geneseo, NY 14454

State University of New York at New Paltz
Black Studies Department
New Paltz, NY 12561

State University of New York at Oneonta
Department of Black and Hispanic Studies
Oneonta, NY 13820

Syracuse University
Afro-American Studies Department
Syracuse, NY 13244

Temple University
Pan-African Studies
Philadelphia, PA 19122

Towson State University
African-American Studies
Towson, MD 21204

Trenton State College
African-American Studies
Trenton, NJ 08625

University of California Berkeley
Afro-American Studies Department
Berkeley, CA 94720

University of California Davis
African-American Studies Program
Davis, CA 95616

University of California Los Angeles
Center for Afro-American Studies
Los Angeles, CA 90024

University of California Santa Barbara
Department of Black Studies
Santa Barbara, CA 93106

University of Chicago
African and Afro-American Studies
Chicago, IL 60637

University of Cincinnati
Afro-American Studies
Cincinnati, OH 45221

University of Colorado at Boulder
Black Studies Program
Boulder, CO 80309

University of Colorado at Boulder
Center for Studies of Ethnicity and Race in
    America
Boulder, CO 80309

University of Delaware
Black American Studies
Newark, DE 19716

University of Hartford
African-American Studies
Hartford, CT 06117

University of Illinois at Chicago
Black Studies Program
Chicago, IL 60680

University of Illinois at Urbana-Champaign
Afro-American Studies and Research Center
Urbana, IL 61801

University of Iowa
African-American World Studies Program
Iowa City, IA 52242

University of Kansas
African and African American Studies
    Department
Lawrence, KS 66045

University of Maryland Baltimore County
Department of African-American Studies
Catonsville, MD 21228

University of Maryland College Park
Afro-American Studies
College Park, MD 20742

University of Massachusetts at Amherst
W. E. B. Du Bois Department of Afro-American
    Studies
Amherst, MA 01003

University of Massachusetts at Boston
Black Studies
Boston, MA 02125

University of Michigan Ann Arbor
Center for Afro-American and African Studies
Ann Arbor, MI 48109

University of Michigan Flint
Afro-American and African Studies Program
Flint, MI 48502

University of Minnesota, Twin Cities Campus
Afro-American and African Studies Program
Minneapolis, MN 55455

University of Missouri Columbia
Black Studies Program
Columbia, MO 65211

University of Nebraska Lincoln
Ethnic Studies Program
Lincoln, NE 68588

University of Nevada Las Vegas
Ethnic Studies Program
Las Vegas, NV 89154

University of New Mexico
African-American Studies Department
Albuquerque, NM 87131

University of North Carolina at Chapel Hill
Afro-American Studies
Chapel Hill, NC 27514

University of North Carolina at Charlotte
Afro-American and African Studies
Charlotte, NC 28223

University of North Carolina at Greensboro
Anthropology Department
Black Studies Department
Greensboro, NC 27412

University of Northern Colorado
Afro-American Studies
Greeley, CO 80639

University of Notre Dame
African-American Studies Program
Notre Dame, IN 46556

University of the Pacific
Department of Black Studies
Stockton, CA 95211

University of Pennsylvania
Afro-American Studies Program
Philadelphia, PA 19104

University of Pittsburgh
Department of Black Studies
Pittsburgh, PA 15260

University of South Carolina Columbia
Afro-American Studies
Columbia, SC 29208

University of South Florida
Department of African and Afro-American
   Studies
Tampa, FL 33620

University of Tennessee Knoxville
Afro-American Studies Program
Knoxville, TN 37996

University of Texas at Austin
Center for African and Afro-American Studies
Austin, TX 78712

University of Toledo
Minority Affairs
Toledo, OH 43606

University of Virginia
Carter G. Woodson Institute for Afro-American
   and African Studies
Charlottesville, VA 22903

University of Washington
Afro-American Studies Program
Seattle, WA 98195

University of Wisconsin Milwaukee
Afro-American Studies Department
Milwaukee, WI 53201

Upsala College
Black Studies
East Orange, NJ 07019

Vanderbilt University
African American Studies Department
Nashville, TN 37240

Virginia Polytechnic Institute and State
   University
Black Studies Program
Blacksburg, VA 24061

Washington State University
Heritage House
Pullman, WA 99164

Washington University
Black Studies
St. Louis, MO 63130

Wayne State University
Black Americana Studies Center
Detroit, MI 48202

Wellesley College
African Studies Department
Wellesley, MA 02181

Wesleyan University
Center for Afro-American Studies
Middletown, CT 06457

Western Illinois University
African-American Studies Program
Macomb, IL 61455

Western Michigan University
Black Americana Studies
Kalamazoo, MI 49008

William Patterson College of New Jersey
Department of African and Afro-American
   Studies
Wayne, NJ 07470

Williams College
African-American Studies Program
Williamstown, MA 10267

Yale University
African-American Studies Department
New Haven, CT 06520

York College of City University of
    New York

Afro-American Studies
Jamaica, NY 11451

Youngstown State University
Black Studies Program
Youngstown, OH 44555

FRATERNITIES AND SORORITIES

Alpha Kappa Alpha Sorority, Inc.
5656 S. Stony Island Avenue
Chicago, IL 60637
312-684-1282
Founded at Howard University in 1908; more
    than 120,000 members in 820 chapters,
    including Germany, the Virgin Islands, and
    Korea; service to African American
    communities around the world; has published
    Ivy Leaf weekly since 1921.

Alpha Phi Alpha Fraternity, Inc.
2313 St. Paul Street
Baltimore, MD 21218
410-544-0054
Founded at Cornell University; more than 650
    chapters worldwide, including Africa; involved
    in voter registration and community
    development; provides scholarships.

Chi Eta Phi Sorority, Inc.
3029 13th Street, NW
Washington, DC 20009
202-232-3858
International professional nursing organization
    with 6,000 members in 60 graduate and 18
    undergraduate chapters, including the Virgin
    Islands and the Republic of Liberia.

Delta Sigma Theta Sorority, Inc.
1701 New Hampshire Avenue, NW
Washington, DC 20009
202-986-2400
Founded at Howard University; more than
    185,000 members in 850 chapters worldwide;
    provides scholarships and endowments for
    professorships.

Groove Phi Groove Social Fellowship, Inc.
P.O. Box 8337
Silver Springs, MD 20907
Founded at Morgan State University; promotes
    academic awareness and moral standards;
    supports community programs and educational
    projects.

Iota Phi Lambda Sorority, Inc.
P. O. Box 11609
Montgomery, AL 36111
205-284-0203
Organization of business and professional women;
    activities include promoting interest in business
    education among young women.

Kappa Alpha Psi Fraternity, Inc.
2322–24 N. Broad Street
Philadelphia, PA 19132
215-228-7184
Nearly 700 undergraduate and graduate chapters;
    promotes tutorial aid for students and services
    to the elderly.

National Pan-Hellenic Council Inc.
Suite 30, IMU
Bloomington, IN 47405
812-855-8820
Coordinating agency for eight African American
    fraternities and sororities with a total
    membership of 1.5 million; assists with
    development of graduate and undergraduate
    councils.

National Sorority of Phi Delta Kappa, Inc.
8233 S. King Drive

Chicago, IL 60619
312-783-7379
Professional organization of educators with more
than 5,000 members; provides scholarships.

Omega Phi Psi Fraternity, Inc.
2714 Georgia Avenue, NW
Washington, DC 20001
202-667-7158
Organized at Howard University; 661 chapters;
focuses on community services and youth; offers
scholarships for undergraduate and graduate
study.

Phi Beta Sigma Fraternity, Inc.
145 Kennedy Street, NW

Washington, DC 20011
202-726-5434
Founded at Howard University; 90,000
members, including academia, business, and
the professions; support for education,
business development, and social
welfare.

Sigma Gamma Rho Sorority, Inc.
8800 S. Stony Island Avenue
Chicago, IL 60617
312-873-9000
Founded at Butler University; more than
70,000 members in the United States
and the Caribbean; supports community
service and education; publishes
The Aurora.

TOP 10 HISTORICALLY BLACK COLLEGES AND UNIVERSITIES

Black Exel, a college admissions and scholarship service for African American students provided
this list of the top academic HBCUs.

1. Clark Atlanta University
2. Fisk University
3. Florida A&M University
4. Hampton University
5. Howard University
6. Morehouse College
7. North Carolina A&T State University
8. Spelman College
9. Tuskegee University
10. Xavier University of Louisiana

STATISTICAL OVERVIEW OF AFRICAN AMERICAN EDUCATION

Table 7.1 Years of School Completed by Persons Age 25 and Over, by Race and Sex, 1940 to 1994

Sex and Year	All Races				Black and Other Races			
	Percent, by Years of School Completed				Percent, by Years of School Completed			
	Less Than 5 Years of Elementary School	4 or More Years of High School	4 or More Years of College	Median Years of School Completed	Less Than 5 Years of Elementary School	4 or More Years of High School	4 or More Years of College	Median Years of School Completed
TOTALS								
1940	13.7	24.5	4.6	8.6	41.8	7.7	1.3	5.7
1950	11.1	34.3	6.2	9.3	32.6	13.7	2.2	6.9
1960	8.3	41.1	7.7	10.5	23.5	21.7	3.5	8.2
1970	5.3	55.2	11.0	12.2	14.7	36.1	6.1	10.1
1980	3.4	68.6	17.0	12.5	8.8	54.6	11.1	12.2
1990	2.4	77.6	21.3	12.7	5.4	68.7	16.5	12.5
1994	1.9	80.9	22.2	—	3.3	74.5	18.1	—
MALES								
1940	15.1	22.7	5.5	8.6	46.2	6.9	1.4	5.4
1950	12.2	32.6	7.3	9.0	36.9	12.6	2.1	6.4
1960	9.4	39.5	9.7	10.3	27.7	20.0	3.5	7.9
1970	5.9	55.0	14.1	12.2	17.9	35.4	6.8	9.9
1980	3.6	69.2	20.9	12.6	10.3	55.3	11.9	12.2
1990	2.7	77.7	24.4	12.8	5.9	69.1	18.3	12.6
1994	2.1	81.0	25.1	—	4.5	74.5	19.0	—
FEMALES								
1940	12.4	26.3	3.8	8.7	37.5	8.4	1.2	6.1
1950	10.0	36.0	5.2	9.6	28.6	14.7	2.4	7.2
1960	7.4	42.5	5.8	10.7	19.7	23.1	3.6	8.5
1970	4.7	55.4	8.2	12.1	11.9	36.6	5.6	10.3
1980	3.2	68.1	13.6	12.4	7.6	54.1	10.4	12.1
1990	2.2	77.5	18.4	12.7	5.0	68.4	15.1	12.5
1994	1.7	80.7	19.6	—	2.8	74.6	17.4	—

Source: U.S. Department of Commerce, Bureau of the Census, U.S. Census of Population, 1960, Vol. 1, Part 1; Current Population Reports, Series P-20, Series P-19, No. 4; 1960 Census Monograph, "Education of the American Population," by John K. Folger and Charles B. Nam; and unpublished data from the Current Population Survey; and U.S. Department of Labor, Bureau of Labor Statistics, Office of Employment and Unemployment Statistics, "Educational Attainment of Workers, March 1991," and unpublished data. (This table was prepared June 1995.)

Table 7.2 Highest Level of Education Attained by Persons Age 18 and Over, by Age and Race, 1994 (in thousands)

Age and Race	Total Population	Elementary Level		High School			Some College	College				
		Less Than 7 Years	7 or 8 Years	1 to 3 Years	4 Years	Graduate		Associate Degree	Bachelor's Degree	Master's Degree	First Professional	Doctorate
TOTAL												
25 and over	164,512	6,778	7,737	15,028	1,896	56,515	28,554	11,460	24,256	8,398	2,267	1,623
25 to 34	41,946	987	677	3,527	530	14,483	8,337	3,578	7,627	1,519	410	273
35 to 49	59,811	1,632	1,146	3,709	462	19,118	11,085	3,240	10,193	3,979	1,071	655
50 to 64	33,697	1,531	1,684	5,222	446	12,406	5,317	1,807	4,013	2,039	340	328
65 and over	30,779	2,628	4,229	4,255	458	10,508	3,814	1,037	2,423	862	320	246
BLACK												
25 and over	17,807	918	869	2,604	419	6,447	3,128	1,125	1,684	484	69	59
25 to 34	5,396	37	50	638	139	2,242	1,207	398	576	93	13	2
35 to 49	6,644	110	183	797	106	2,542	1,328	519	783	216	32	28
50 to 64	3,282	222	204	649	120	1,091	422	170	243	132	15	13
65 and over	2,483	550	431	520	54	572	171	37	81	44	10	14

Source: U.S. Department of Commerce, Bureau of the Census, Current Population Survey, unpublished data. (This table was prepared August 1995.)

HIGHER EDUCATION

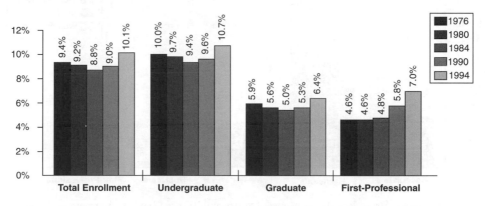

Figure 7.1 Percentage of African American Students Enrolled in U.S. Colleges and Universities

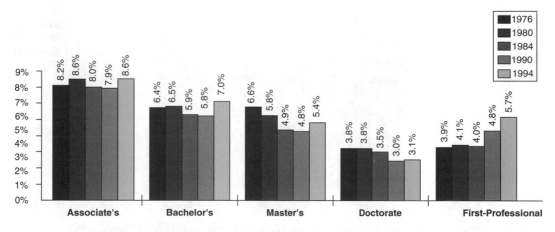

Figure 7.2 Percentage of African American Degree Recipients Nationwide

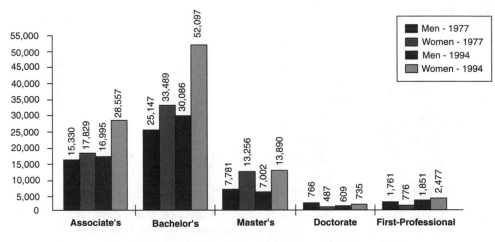

Figure 7.3 Degrees Awarded to African American Men and Women

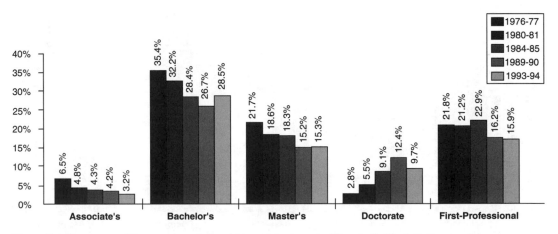

Figure 7.4 Percentage of Degrees Awarded to African Americans by Historically Black Colleges and Universities

Table 7.3 Major Field of Study of 1992–93 Bachelor's Degree Recipients, by Race and Sex

Major Field	Total			Black		
	Total	Male	Female	Total	Male	Female
Total	100.0	100.0	100.0	100.0	100.0	100.0
Business and management	21.9	26.1	18.4	27.3	31.8	24.9
Education	13.0	6.2	18.6	7.8	3.7	9.9
Engineering	6.1	11.7	1.6	3.6	8.9	0.8
Health professions	7.4	4.1	10.1	7.9	3.6	10.1
Public affairs/social services	3.5	3.1	3.8	6.1	6.1	6.1
Biological sciences	4.5	5.2	4.0	4.9	3.5	5.6
Mathematics and science	5.7	7.5	4.2	6.1	5.2	6.6
Social science	9.6	10.4	8.9	10.5	12.5	9.4
History	1.8	2.5	1.3	0.8	1.3	0.5
Humanities	9.2	8.4	9.9	7.1	6.9	7.2
Psychology	3.6	2.2	4.7	4.3	1.9	5.6
Other	13.7	12.7	14.6	13.7	14.7	13.2

Source: Baccalaureate and Beyond Longitudinal Study, First Follow-up (B&B: 93/94).

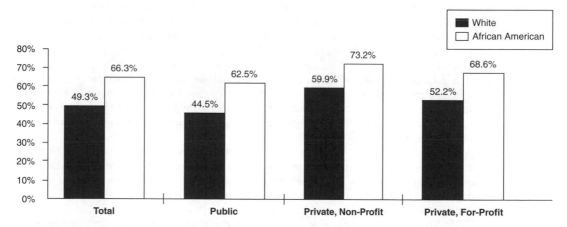

Figure 7.5 Percentage of Undergraduates Attending Four-Year Colleges and Universities Who Received Financial Aid, by Institutional Control: Fall 1992

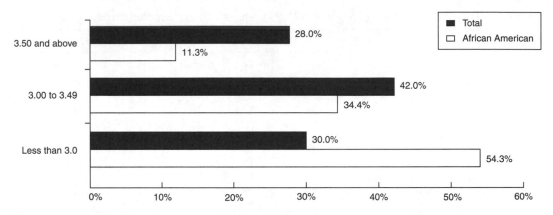

Figure 7.6 Cumulative Undergraduate Grade Point Averages of 1992–1993 Bachelor's Degree Recipients, by Race

- Though African American presence in the U.S. college population increased from 8.8 to 10.1 percent between 1984 and 1994, the numbers still fell short of blacks' share of the total college-age population, which stood at 14.3 percent.
- Women greatly outnumber men among African American college students, representing 6.3 percent of the total higher-education enrollment in 1994, as compared to 3.8 percent for males. Women's overall rate of enrollment is 24 percent higher than that of African American males; by contrast, white women have a 10 percent edge in enrollment rates over white males.
- A smaller proportion of African Americans are now receiving degrees from HBCUs than in the past, but black enrollment at these institutions has remained constant. HBCUs continue to play an important role in conferring undergraduate degrees on African American students who go on to receive doctorates in education, biological sciences, and professional fields. Predominantly white universities now play a larger role in educating African American undergraduates who later obtain doctorates in the physical sciences.
- A study of 1992–1993 graduates revealed that nearly twice as many African Americans (9.4%) as European Americans (5.5%) were neither employed nor doing postgraduate work one year after graduation. Of those who were employed, salaries for both groups were roughly the same; however, a smaller percentage of African Americans owned an automobile (67.4% compared with 84.6%) or a house or condominium (18.1% compared with 27.2%).
- In 1992, African Americans accounted for 4.9 percent of the faculty in higher education, far below the African American share of total enrollment in higher education (9.6%). Nearly half of all African American faculty members were employed in the Southeast.

PRIMARY AND SECONDARY EDUCATION

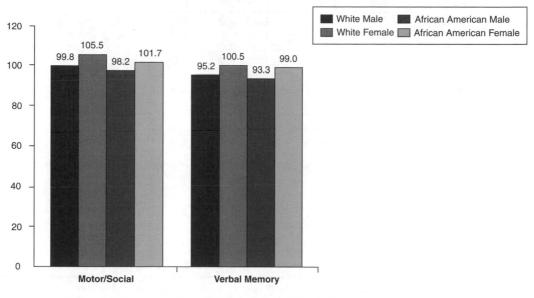

Figure 7.7 Test Scores of Preschoolers

Table 7.4 Proficiency Test Scores for Selected Subjects, 1977–1992

Test and Year	Total	Black	Test and Year	Total	Black
READING			1989–1990	257	239
9 year olds			1991–1992	274	258
1979–1980	215	189	11th graders		
1987–1988	212	189	1983–1984	290	270
1991–1992	211	185	1989–1990	287	268
13 year olds			1991–1992	287	263
1979–1980	259	233			
1987–1988	258	243	MATHEMATICS		
1991–1992	260	238	9 year olds		
17 year olds			1977–1978	219	192
1979–1980	286	243	1989–1990	230	208
1987–1988	290	274	1991–1992	230	208
1991–1992	290	261	13 year olds		
WRITING			1977–1978	264	230
4th graders			1989–1990	270	249
1983–1984	204	182	1991–1992	273	250
1989–1990	202	171	17 years olds		
1991–1992	274	258	1977–1978	300	268
8th graders			1989–1990	305	289
1983–1984	267	247	1991–1992	307	286

Table 7.4 (continued)

Test and Year	Total	Black	Test and Year	Total	Black
SCIENCE			1989–1990	255	226
9 year olds			1991–1992	258	224
1976–1977	220	175	17 year olds		
1989–1990	229	196	1976–1977	290	240
1991–1992	231	200	1989–1990	290	253
13 year olds			1991–1992	294	256
1976–1977	247	208			

Source: U.S. National Center for Education Statistics, *NAEP Trends in Academic Progress*, Report No. 23-TR01, July 1994.

Table 7.5 Scholastic Aptitude Test (SAT) Score Averages, by Race, 1975–1976 to 1993–1994

Racial Background	1975–1976	1980–1981	1984–1985	1989–1990	1993–1994
SAT—VERBAL					
All students	431	424	431	424	423
Black	332	332	346	352	352
SAT—MATHEMATICAL					
All students	472	466	475	476	479
Black	354	362	376	385	388

Source: College Entrance Examination Board, *National Report on College Bound Seniors*, various years.

Table 7.6 High-School Dropouts by Age, 1970 to 1994

Age	Number of Dropouts (1,000)					Percentage of Population				
	1970	1980	1985	1990	1994	1970	1980	1985	1990	1994
Total dropouts	4,670	5,212	4,456	3,854	3,820	12.2	12.0	10.6	10.1	9.5
Black	1,047	934	748	611	629	22.2	16.0	12.6	10.9	10.3

Source: U.S. Bureau of the Census, *Current Population Reports*, P20–487; and earlier reports.

Table 7.7 Enrollment Status, by Race and Sex, 1975 and 1994

	Total Persons		Percentage Distribution							
	18 to 21 (1,000)		Enrolled in High School		High-school Graduates				Not High School Graduates	
					Total		In College			
Characteristic	1975	1994	1975	1994	1975	1994	1975	1994	1975	1994
Total	15,693	13,927	5.7	8.7	78.0	77.5	33.5	43.6	16.3	13.7
Black total	1,997	2,081	12.5	12.4	60.4	69.7	24.9	31.6	27.0	17.6
Total male	7,584	6,923	7.4	10.5	76.6	74.5	35.4	40.9	15.9	14.8
Black male	911	1,009	15.9	14.1	55.0	65.3	23.9	29.0	29.0	20.2
Total female	8,109	7,003	4.2	6.9	79.2	80.4	31.8	46.4	16.6	12.5
Black female	1,085	1,072	9.7	10.8	65.0	73.9	25.8	34.0	25.4	15.2

Source: U.S. Bureau of the Census, Current Population Reports, P20–487, and earlier reports.

Table 7.8 Unemployment Rates of High-School Graduates and School Dropouts, by Race, 1980 to 1993

| | Graduates[1] | | | | Dropouts[2] | | | |
Race	1980	1985	1990	1993	1980	1985	1990	1993
Unemployment rate, total	12.5	12.7	11.7	12.1	25.3	25.9	20.5	20.4
Unemployment rate, black	26.1	29.4	26.0	21.1	43.9	41.5	43.3	34.4

[1]For persons not enrolled in college who have completed 4 years of high school only.
[2]For persons not in regular school and who have neither completed the 12th grade nor received a general equivalency degree.
Source: U.S. Bureau of Labor Statistics, Bulletin 2307, News, USDL 94-252, May 20, 1994; and unpublished data.

- United Negro College Fund data show that African American students start their education with significant socioeconomic disadvantages, compared with European American students. Twice the percentage of African American babies (10.4 vs. 5.1) weigh less than 5 pounds at birth. Nearly 44 percent of African American preschoolers live in households with less than $10,000 annual income, compared with only 9.5 percent of European American preschoolers in similar circumstances. Sixty-six percent of African American children live in single-parent homes, compared with 15.8 percent of European American children. Statistics on general education levels (see Tables 7.1 and 7.2) show that African American children generally grow up in families in which the experience of higher education is less common than in European American families.

- African American children outstrip European American children in preschool enrollment (52.5% vs. 43.5%). They score equally well on tests of motor and social development and verbal memory, scoring less well only in the area of vocabulary (Peabody Picture test). As indicated by Table 7.4, African American students begin to lag behind during grade school, and the gap remains consistent from then on.

- As of 1993–1994, African Americans represented 16.5 percent of all students enrolled in public elementary and secondary schools and only 9.3 percent of private-school students. African American public-school students were generally concentrated in the South and in large central cities. Twenty-eight percent attended special-education schools, 29.8 percent attended vocational schools, and 23 percent attended alternative or other schools—considerably higher ratios than their representation among all public-school students.

- African Americans composed only 12.5 percent of all students who received regular high-school diplomas in 1993–1994.

MAJOR SCHOLARSHIPS AND FINANCIAL AID

Like other students, African Americans qualifying for financial aid rely mainly on Pell Grants, Supplemental Education Opportunity Grants (SEOG), federally funded student loans, grants provided by state and local governments, and aid offered by the institutions they attend. In addition to these resources, there are hundreds of privately funded programs designed to aid African American students. A selection of major awards for undergraduate and graduate study is listed in this section. In addition, there are numerous scholarships, fellowships, grants, and internships applicable to minority students attending particular institutions, seeking degrees in specific fields, and belonging to sponsoring organizations or religious denominations. A full up-to-date listing can be consulted in specialized publications available in many public libraries. (See "Sources for Additional Information.")

AAUW Focus Professions Fellowships
American Association of University Women
Educational Foundation
1111 16th Street, NW
Washington, DC 20006
202-728-7603
Awarded to minority women for graduate study in business, law, or medicine.

Agnes Jones Jackson Scholarships
National Association for the Advancement of Colored People
4805 Mt. Hope Drive
Baltimore, MD 21215
410-358-8900
Cash awards to undergraduates and graduates who are NAACP members.

Alphonso Deal Scholarship Awards
National Black Police Association
3251 Mt. Pleasant Street, NW
Washington, DC 20010
202-986-2070
Cash awards of $500 to high-school seniors entering college.

APSA Graduate Fellowships for African American Students
American Political Science Association
1527 New Hampshire Avenue, NW
Washington, DC 20036
Stipends for one year of graduate study in political science; fellows usually receive exemption from tuition and fees.

AT&T Bell Laboratories Cooperative Research Fellowships for Minorities

AT&T Bell Laboratories
Special Programs
Crawfords Corner Road
Holmdel, NJ 07733
908-949-6800
Twelve fellowships awarded annually for graduate study in the sciences and engineering; includes a stipend, full tuition, and travel expenses.

Big Apple Engineering Scholarship Program
National Action Council for Minorities in Engineering
3 W. 35th Street
New York, NY 10001
212-279-2626
Supplemental awards for undergraduates in New York State.

Corporate Sponsored Scholarships for Minority Undergraduate Physics Majors
American Physical Society
335 E. 45th Street
New York, NY 10017
212-682-7341
For high-school seniors and college freshmen and sophomores.

Earl Warren Legal Training Program Scholarships
Earl Warren Legal Training Program, Inc.
99 Hudson Street, Suite 1600
New York, NY 10013
212-219-1900
150 yearly grants for African American law students.

Ford Foundation Predoctoral Fellowships for Minorities

National Academy of Sciences
National Research Council
2101 Constitution Avenue
Washington, DC 20418
202-334-2860
Fifty-five fellowships awarded annually to
minority students beginning graduate study and
planning to work toward a Ph.D. or Sc.D.
degree; can be renewed for a second and a
third year if progress toward a doctorate
is evident.

Herbert Lehman Scholarships
Herbert Lehman Education Fund
99 Hudson Street
New York, NY 10013
212-219-1900
Assistance for undergraduates at recently
desegregated, publicly supported colleges and
universities in the deep South.

IBM Minority Fellowships
International Business Machines
T. J. Watson Research Center
Yorktown Heights, NY 10598
Fellowships for minority graduate students in
computer science, physics, chemistry, and
engineering.

Lorraine Hansberry Playwrighting Awards
Kennedy Center American College Theatre
Festival
Attn: Producing Director/Education Department
Kennedy Center
Washington, DC 20566
202-416-8850
First- and second-place awards for a student play
dealing with the African American experience
in the United States.

NAACP Willems Scholarships
National Association for the Advancement of
Colored People
4805 Mt. Hope Drive
Baltimore, MD 21215
410-358-8900
For graduate and undergraduate study in
engineering and science.

NABJ Scholarship Awards
National Association of Black Journalists

11600 Sunrise Valley Drive
Reston, VA 22091
703-648-1270
For undergraduates majoring in or planning a
career in journalism or mass communications.

National Achievement Scholarship Program for
Outstanding Negro Students
National Merit Scholarship Corporation
1560 Sherman Avenue, Suite 200
Evanston, IL 60201
About 750 scholarships awarded annually to high-
school seniors; winners are often recommended
for further aid through the agency's College-
Sponsored Awards and Corporate-Sponsored
Awards.

New York Philharmonic Music Assistance Fund
Scholarships
New York Philharmonic
Avery Fisher Hall
10 Lincoln Center Plaza
New York, NY 10023
Merit scholarships for high-school students,
undergraduates, and graduates wishing to
attend schools of music and summer
institutes.

NIH Postdoctoral Fellowships for Minority
Students
National Institute of General Medical Sciences
Bethesda, MD 20892
301-496-7137
Thirty fellowships for minority students in Ph.D.
or M.D./Ph.D. programs in the biological
sciences.

Nuclear Energy Scholarships at Historically Black
Colleges and Universities
Oak Ridge Institute for Science and Education
Attn: Science/Engineering Education Division
P.O. Box 117
Oak Ridge, TN 37831
615-576-5300
For students interested in careers in nuclear
energy–related technologies.

Roy Wilkins Scholarship Program
National Association for the Advancement of
Colored People
4805 Mt. Hope Drive
Baltimore, MD 21215

410-358-8900

For high-school seniors who are NAACP members.

Smithsonian Institution Minority Fellowships
Smithsonian Institution
Office of Fellowships and Grants
955 L'Enfant Plaza, Suite 7300
Washington, DC 20560
202-287-3271

Internships, including cash stipends and travel allowances, for undergraduates and graduate students.

Thurgood Marshall Scholarships
Thurgood Marshall Black Education Fund

One Dupont Circle, Suite 710
Washington, DC 20036
202-778-0894

For study at 37 historically black colleges and universities.

United Negro College Fund Scholarships
United Negro College Fund
Attn: Director, Educational Services
500 E. 62nd Street
New York, NY 10021
212-326-1238

Grants ranging from $500 to $7,500 a year for study at any of the 41 institutions belonging to the UNCF.

NOTABLE ACADEMIC LEADERS

Asante, Molefi Kete (1942–   ).   Educated at Oklahoma Christian (B.A. 1964), Pepperdine (M.A. 1965), and UCLA (Ph.D. 1968). Director of the Center for Afro-American Studies at UCLA, 1970–1973; currently Director of African-American Studies at Temple University; editor of the *Journal of Black Studies*. Publications include *The Afrocentric Idea* (1987); *Kemet: Afrocentricity and Knowledge* (1990); *Historical and Cultural Atlas of African Americans* (with Mark T. Mattson, 1991).

Bethune, Mary McLeod   (See Chapter 3, "Politics and Civil Rights.")

Brown, Roscoe C., Jr. (1922–   ).   Degrees from Springfield College (B.S.) and New York University (M.A., Ph.D.). Currently president of Bronx Community College. Host of weekly TV series *Black Arts* and radio series *Soul of Reason*; cohost of *Black Letters* on CBS-TV and *A Black Perspective* on NBC-TV. Author of numerous articles on education, black studies, sports, and physical fitness.

Cole, Johnnetta Betsch (1936–   ).   Degrees from Oberlin (B.A. 1957) and Northwestern (M.A. 1959, Ph.D. 1967): specialist in anthropology. Appointed president of Spelman College in 1987, the first African American woman to hold the post. Publications include *Anthropology for the Eighties* (1982); *All American Women* (1986); *Anthropology for the Nineties* (1988); *Conversations: Straight Talk with America's Sister President* (1993).

Cook, Samuel DuBois (1928–   ).   Educated at Morehouse (A.B. 1948) and Ohio State (M.A. 1950, Ph.D. 1954). First African American to hold a professorship at Duke University (1966–1974, winner of Outstanding Professor Award) and the first to hold a regular faculty position at a white-run university in the South. President of Dillard University since 1975. Author of numerous articles in professional journals and anthologies.

Franklin, John Hope (1915–   ).   Educated at Fisk (B.A. 1935) and Harvard (M.A. 1936, Ph.D. 1941). Professor of history at St. Augustine's, North Carolina Central, and Howard, 1939–1956. Chair of the History Department at Brooklyn College, 1956–1964. President of the United Chapters of Phi Beta Kappa, 1937–1976. Professor of American history at the University of Chicago, 1964–1982. James B. Duke Professor of History at Duke, 1982–1985; professor emeritus since 1985. Recipient of numerous awards and honors; ranks as one of the most eminent historians in the United States. Appointed head of President Clinton's special committee on race. Publications include *The Free Negro in North Carolina*,

1790–1860 (1943); *From Slavery to Freedom: A History of Negro Americans* (1947); *The Militant South, 1800–1860* (1956); *The Emancipation Proclamation* (1963); *A Southern Odyssey* (1976).

Gates, Henry Louis, Jr. (1950–).   Educated at Yale (B.A. 1973) and Cambridge, England (M.A. 1974, Ph.D. 1979). Taught English and African American studies at Yale, Cornell, and Duke from 1976 to 1990. W. E. B. Du Bois Professor of the Humanities and chair of the Department of Afro-American Studies at Harvard since 1990. Publications include *Black Literature and Literary Theory* (1984); *The Classic Slave Narratives* (1987); *Colored People* (1994); *Thirteen Ways of Looking at a Black Man* (1997); *The Norton Anthology of African-American Literature* (1997, editor).

Gordon, Vivian V. (1934–).   Degrees from Virginia State (B.A. 1955), University of Pennsylvania (M.A. 1957), and University of Virginia (Ph.D. 1974); specialist in sociology. Held posts with the Library of Congress and the U.S. House of Representatives Committee on Education and Labor while earning her Ph.D. First African American to come through the ranks and gain tenure at the University of Virginia. Chairperson of the African Studies Department from 1975 to 1980. Professor at State University of New York at Albany since 1992. Publications include *Black Women, Feminism, Black Liberation: Which Way?* (1985); *Kemet and Other Ancient African Civilizations* (1991).

Gray, William H. III (1941–).   Pursued graduate study at Temple University, University of Pennsylvania, and Oxford University. Earned graduate degrees from Drew Seminary (1966) and Princeton Theological Seminary (1970). Pastor of Union Baptist Church in Montclair, New Jersey, from 1964 to 1972. Served as U.S. congressional representative from Pennsylvania, 1978–1991; vice chair of the Congressional Black Caucus. President of the United Negro College Fund since 1991. Recipient of more than 50 honorary degrees. Served as special envoy to Haiti in 1994.

Harris, William H. (1944–).   Educated at Paine College (B.A. 1966) and Indiana University (M.A. 1967, Ph.D. 1973). Professor of History at Indiana, 1972–1982; director of Minorities Fellowship Pprogram, 1977–1982. President of Paine College, 1982–1988; president of Texas Southern University, 1988–1994; president of Alabama State since 1994. Publications include *The Harder We Run* (1982).

Hine, Darlene Clark (1947–).   Educated at Roosevelt University of Chicago (B.A. 1968) and Kent State (M.A. 1970, Ph.D. 1975). John A. Hannah Professor of History at Michigan State since 1987. Publications include *Black Victory: The Rise and Fall of the White Primary in Texas* (1979); *Black Women in White: Social Conflict and Cooperation in the Nursing Profession 1890–1950* (1989); *Black Women in America* (1993, editor).

hooks, bell (1952–).   Degrees from Stanford (B.A. 1973), Wisconsin (M.A. 1976), and University of California Santa Cruz (Ph.D. 1987). Taught African and African American Studies at Yale, 1980–1985. Associate professor of Women's Studies and American Literature at Oberlin, 1985–1994. Distinguished Professor of English at City College of New York (CCNY) since 1994. Publications include *Ain't I a Woman: Black Women and Feminism* (1981); *Talking Back: Thinking Feminist, Thinking Black* (1989); *Breaking Bread* (with Cornel West, 1991); *Teaching to Transgress: Education as the Practice of Freedom* (1995); *Bone Black: Memories of Girlhood* (1996); *Wounds of Passion: A Writing Life* (1997).

Jenifer, Franklin Green (1939–).   Educated at Howard (B.S. 1962, M.S. 1965) and Maryland (M.D. 1970). Chair of the Biology Department at Rutgers, 1974–1977. Chancellor, Massachusetts Board of Regents, 1986–1990; president of Howard University, 1990–1994; president of the University of Texas at Dallas since 1994.

Johnson, Charles Spurgeon (1893–1956).   Educated at Virginia Union University (B.A.) and the University of Chicago (Ph.D.), Johnson went on to serve as assistant executive secretary of the Chicago Commission on Race Relations and as research director of the National Urban League, where he founded *Opportunity* magazine. In 1928, Johnson became chair of Fisk University's Department of Social Science and established the Fisk Institute of Race Relations. In 1946, he was appointed Fisk's first black president.

Lewis, David Levering (1936–   ).   Educated at Fisk (B.A. 1956), Columbia (M.A. 1959), and the London School of Economics (Ph.D. 1962). Held teaching posts at University of Ghana, Howard University, Morgan State, University of the District of Columbia, and University of California San Diego, 1963–1985. Martin Luther King, Jr., University Professor of History at Rutgers University since 1985. Publications include *King: A Biography* (1970); *When Harlem Was in Vogue* (1981); *W. E. B. Du Bois: Biography of a Race 1868–1919* (1993), which won the Pulitzer and Bancroft prizes for biography.

Mays, Benjamin E. (1894–1984).   Educated at Bates College (B.A.) and the University of Chicago (M.A., Ph.D.). Acting dean of Howard University's School of Religion (1934–1940). President of Morehouse College (1940–1967).

Patterson, Frederick Douglass (1901–1988).   Educated at Iowa State University (M.S.) and Cornell University (Ph.D.). Joined the faculty of Tuskegee Institute in 1928, eventually serving as its president. Organized the United Negro College Fund in 1944.

Payton, Benjamin Franklin (1932–   ).   Educated at South Carolina State (B.A. 1955), Harvard (B.D. 1958), Columbia (M.A. 1960), and Yale (Ph.D. 1963). President of Tuskegee University since 1981. Director of the National Association for Equal Opportunity in Higher Education.

Ponder, Henry (1928–   ).   Educated at Langston (B.S. 1951), Oklahoma State (M.S. 1958), and Ohio State (Ph.D. 1963). Chair of the Department of Agriculture and Business at Virginia State, 1963–1964. Dean at Alabama A&M, 1966–1969, and vice president for academic affairs, 1969–1973. President of Benedict College, 1973–1984. President of Fisk University since 1984. Named one of the 100 Most Effective College Presidents in the United States, 1986.

Poussaint, Alvin Francis (1934–   ).   Degrees from Columbia (B.A. 1956), Cornell Medical College (M.D. 1960), and UCLA (M.S. 1964). Clinical professor of Psychiatry and associate dean of students at Harvard Medical School since 1969. Senior associate psychiatrist at Judge Baker Children's Center since 1978. Publications include *Raising Black Children: Questions and Answers for Parents and Teachers* (1992).

Rampersad, Arnold (1941–   ).   Born in Trinidad, educated at Bowling Green (B.A., M.A.) and Harvard (Ph.D.). Began his career as a Melville scholar, teaching literature at Stanford, Rutgers, and Columbia. Woodrow Wilson Professor of Literature at Princeton since 1990. Recipient of a National Book Award and a MacArthur Foundation Fellowship. Publications include *Melville's Israel Potter* (1969); *The Art and Imagination of W. E. B. Du Bois* (1976); *The Life of Langston Hughes* (1986–1988); *Jackie Robinson: A Biography* (1977).

Rice, Condoleeza (1954–   ).   Educated at the University of Denver (B.A. 1974, Ph.D. 1981) and Notre Dame (M.A. 1975); specialist in arms control and eastern European affairs. Assistant and then associate professor of political science at Stanford (1981–1993), professor and provost since 1993. Served as presidential advisor and member of National Security Council during the Bush Administration. Publications include *The Gorbachev Era* (with Alexander Dallin) and *The Soviet Union and the Czechoslovak Army*.

Schomburg, Arthur A.   (See Chapter 13, "Literature and Language.")

Simmons, Ruth J. (1946–   ).   Educated at Dillard University (B.S. 1967), studied for a year at the University of Lyon in France as a Fulbright Scholar, and earned a doctorate in Romance Languages at Harvard University (Ph.D. 1983). Served as director of Black Studies at Princeton and vice provost of the university, 1992–1995. President of Smith College since 1995, the first African American to lead a Seven Sisters school.

Thompson, Robert Ferris (1932–   ).   Educated at Yale University (B.A. 1995, M.A. 1961, Ph.D. 1965). Professor of African and Afro-American History of Art, master of Timothy Dwight College at Yale since 1964. Publications include *African Influence on the Art of the United States* (1969); *The Four Movements of the Sun* (1981); *Flash of the Spirit* (1982).

Van Sertima, Ivan (1935–   ).   Guyanese-born educator, currently a professor of African Studies at Rutgers University. Publications include *They Came Before Columbus: The African Presence in Ancient America* (1977) and *Caribbean Writers*, a collection of essays. Also the founder of *The Journal of African Civilizations*.

West, Cornel (1953–   ).   Educated at Harvard and Princeton, where he served as professor of Religion and director of the Department of Afro-American Studies before joining the Harvard University faculty in 1995 as professor of Afro-American Studies and the Philosophy of Religion. Publications include *Breaking Bread: Insurgent Black Intellectual Life* (with bell hooks, 1992); *Race Matters* (1993); *The Future of the Race* (with Henry Louis Gates Jr., 1996).

Wharton, Clifton R., Jr. (1926–   ).   Educated at Harvard (B.A. 1947), Johns Hopkins (M.A. 1948), and the University of Chicago (M.A. 1956, Ph.D. 1958). President of Michigan State, 1970–1978. Chancellor of the State University of New York system, 1978–1987. Chair and CEO, Teachers Insurance and Annuity Association and College Retirement Equities Fund, 1987–1993. Deputy Secretary of State since 1993.

Wilson, William Julius (1935–   ).   Degrees from Wilberforce (B.A. 1958), Bowling Green (M.A. 1961), and Washington State (Ph.D. 1966). Joined the faculty of the University of Chicago in 1975 as Professor of Sociology. Chair of the Sociology Department, 1978–1981; Lucy Flower University Professor of Sociology and Public Policy, 1990–1996. Became Malcolm Wiener Professor of Social Policy at Harvard's John F. Kennedy School of Government in 1996 and also joined the W. E. B. Du Bois Institute board of directors. Recipient of a MacArthur Foundation Fellowship, 1987–1992. Fellow of the American Academy of Arts and Sciences. Publications include *Through Different Eyes* (1973), *The Truly Disadvantaged* (1987), and *When Work Disappears* (1996).

Woodson, Carter G.   (See Chapter 13, "Literature and Language.")

SOURCES FOR ADDITIONAL INFORMATION

The African American Education Data Book, 3 vols. Fairfax, VA: Frederick D. Patterson Research Institute of the College Fund/UNCF, 1997.

Allen, Walter R., Edgar Epps, and Nesha Z. Haniff, eds. *College in Black and White: African-American Students in Predominantly White and Historically Black Public Universities*. Albany: State University of New York Press, 1991.

Encyclopedia of African-American Education. Westport, CT: Greenwood, 1996.

Hill, Livern, ed. *Black American Colleges and Universities*. Detroit: Gale, 1994.

Mitchell, Robert. *The Multicultural Student's Guide to Colleges*, rev. ed. New York: Noonday, 1996.

National Center for Educational Statistics. *Historically Black Colleges and Universities, 1976–1994*. Washington, DC: U.S. Department of Education, 1996.

Schlachter, Gail Ann, and R. David Weber. *Directory of Financial Aid for Minorities, 1995–1997*. San Carlos, CA: Reference Service Press, 1995.

Willie, Charles, V., Antoine M. Garibaldi, and Wornie L. Reed, eds. *The Education of African Americans*. Westport, CT: Auburn House/Greenwood, 1991.

Wilson, Erlene B. *The 100 Best Colleges for African-American Students*. New York: Plume, 1993.

———. *Money for College: A Guide to Financial Aid for African-American Students*. New York: Plume, 1996.

Woodson, Carter G. *The Education of the Negro Prior to 1861*. New York: Arno, 1919, (reprint) 1968.

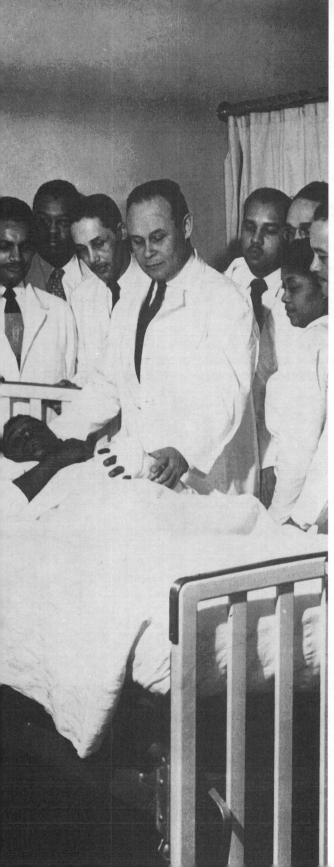

8

Health

The good news is that African Americans are living longer than ever before; nonetheless, statistics show that African Americans are still not living as long as the rest of the American population. In fact, the life expectancy for white men is some eight years higher than for black men, while white women live almost six years longer than black women.

Statistics from the National Center for Health Statistics (NCHS) describe unacceptably high mortality rates. For instance, AIDS is five times as deadly for young African Americans ages 25 to 44 as for their European American counterparts. African Americans are almost three times as likely to die of kidney disease, septicemia, and diabetes, and almost twice as many African Americans as European Americans die of stroke and heart disease. African American men have the highest rate of prostate cancer in the world.

Although some of this poor health is related to lifestyle—higher incidence of drug use, smoking, and obesity—there is another culprit: the inequities of medical treatment. The legacy of racism in the medical community and the lack of adequate medical care for poor and lower-middle-class African Americans greatly increases the number of deaths by disease.

The situation is not beyond control, however. Regular check-ups and good preventive care could greatly reduce the death rates for stroke, cancer, diabetes, asthma, and other diseases. As Fred Daniels, a Chicago internist whose patients are 99% African American, told *Ebony* magazine, "Most patients still feel that to go to the doctor, something has to be wrong. . . . But I want to see them when they're healthy."

TOP HEALTH CONCERNS

Here are the most common diseases among African Americans, as well as current treatments, risk factors, and some tips on prevention.

HEART DISEASE
FACTS ABOUT HEART DISEASE

The most common form of heart disease is atherosclerosis, or coronary heart disease (CHD), which is caused by a narrowing and hardening of the arteries that supply blood to the heart. CHD occurs when fatty deposits accumulate along the walls of an artery, restricting the amount of blood that can flow through the vessel, a condition known as *ischemia*. When ischemia occurs, symptoms of heart disease, such as chest pains (angina pectoris), are likely to appear. When an artery becomes blocked and the heart is deprived of oxygen, a heart attack may occur. CHD is the leading cause of death among all Americans, regardless of race or ethnicity. Although it was once thought that heart disease was rare among African Americans, the death rate for those suffering from heart disease is one of the highest in the world. In 1995, one and a half times as many African Americans died of heart disease, as compared with European Americans.

RISK FACTORS

Gender and Age   Men suffer a higher incidence of heart disease than women. It is, however, the number one cause of death among postmenopausal women. During this stage of life, women produce less estrogen, a hormone that protects younger women from heart disease.

Family History   Heart disease is more prevalent among men and women whose parents or siblings suffered a heart attack before age 50.

Smoking   Smoking doubles the risk of developing heart disease and contributes to 30 to 40 percent of all CHD deaths. Forty percent of African Americans smoke, 8 percent more than European Americans, and they are thus more vulnerable to the disease.

Obesity   A weight 20 percent or higher than the average recommended weight range doubles the chance of developing heart disease. Obesity is more common among African American women than European American women. A 1997 study of 166 overweight women (44 black and 122 white) revealed that the black women had lower resting metabolic rates and burned about 100 fewer calories per day than did the white women. This difference is probably due to their more sedentary lifestyles because regular exercise increases metabolic rates.

Hypertension   A person is considered hypertensive if his or her blood pressure is higher than 140/90. Hypertension, or high blood pressure, is the number one CHD risk factor in men and women above the age of 45. According to NCHS surveys for 1988 to 1991, 33.5 percent of black men and 27.5 percent of black women suffered from hypertension, compared to 24.7 percent of white men and 19.7 percent of white women. On a more positive note, the incidence of hypertension among African Americans has been decreasing—in 1960 to 1962, half of all African American adults were defined as hypertensive.

Diabetes and CHD   Diabetes is a significant factor in CHD because excess sugar in the blood damages the walls of blood vessels. For more information on this condition, see the section on "Diabetes" later in this chapter.

High Cholesterol and Blood Fats   Medical experts have found that a high level of cholesterol is a leading risk factor in developing heart disease. A blood-cholesterol level of 240 or greater doubles the risk of heart disease. Studies show that the incidence of high cholesterol levels is relatively the same among black and white Americans. On the other hand, African Americans have higher levels of HDL, a form of cholesterol that is believed to be more beneficial to the heart. Experts have not yet been able to determine whether higher HDL levels protect African Americans from an even higher rate of death from heart disease.

PREVENTION

A low-fat diet high in vegetables and fruits, combined with a regimen of regular exercise, can do a lot toward lowering the risk of CHD. Other major factors in the prevention of this disease include cessation of cigarette smoking and cutting down on alcohol and salt intake. Additional information about heart disease can be obtained from the American Heart Association. Toll-free number: 800-MY-HEART.

CANCER
FACTS ABOUT CANCER

Cancer is the second leading cause of death in the United States—1 million Americans are stricken with cancer every year, and 500,000 die from it each year. Cancer's inroads in the African American community have far outstripped the national average. Since 1950, cancer deaths have increased by 10 percent for the total population, but they have increased by 50 percent for black Americans. The five-year survival rate for cancer diagnosed in African Americans between 1986 and 1991 was 42 percent, considerably lower than European Americans' 58 percent survival rate. Medical experts attribute such disparities mainly to African Americans' lower rate of participation in cancer-screening programs that can increase the likelihood of early diagnosis and intervention. The relatively high proportion of low-income households in the black community is another contributing factor, as members of low-income groups are less likely to enjoy the balanced, nutritious diet that can be instrumental in preventing cancer.

TYPES OF CANCER

Lung Cancer   Lung cancer is the number one cause of cancer deaths among African Americans. In 1994, lung cancer claimed 10,555 African American men (a death rate of 68.1 per 100,000 population) and 5,115 African American women (29.8 per 100,000 population).

Breast Cancer   Breast cancer is the second leading cause of cancer-related deaths among African American women. In 1994 alone, 5,083 black women died of the disease. Although the age-adjusted death rates for breast cancer declined 8 percent for all women between 1990 and 1994, there was only a 2 percent decline for African American women.

Prostate Cancer   African American men are two to three times more likely to die of prostate cancer than are European American men, and doctors today are powerless to explain why or to reduce the risks. An estimated one out of every four black men will be diagnosed with the disease in his lifetime—a rate 33 percent higher than the incidence of the disease among whites. In 1994, the prostate-cancer death rate for blacks was 36.5 per 100,000 population, compared to 27.2 per 100,000 for whites. More than 5,000 black men die of the disease each year.

RISK FACTORS

Smoking   Cancer of the throat, mouth, and lung are directly linked to cigarette smoking. Among African Americans 20 years of age and older, more than 40 percent smoke cigarettes, compared to 32 percent of European Americans.

High-Fat Diet   A diet composed mostly of high-fat foods is a major contributor to colon, breast, and prostate cancer. Animal fats, found in meats and in dairy products such as butter, are considered to be less healthy than plant and fish oils. Medical experts do not yet know why high-fat foods are linked to cancer, but sticking to a low-fat diet is a highly recommended way to prevent the disease.

Nitrates/Smoked Foods   The nitrates used to preserve certain foods have been linked to cancer. Smoked and preserved foods such as bacon, sausage, luncheon meats, and salted, smoked, or cured foods should be eaten in moderation.

Prevention   About one third of cancer deaths, according to the American Cancer Society, are caused by improper diets. Eating a low-fat, low-salt diet, including high proportions of fruit, vegetables, and fiber, is highly recommended. Studies have found that avoidance of nitrates, cigarettes, and alcohol can aid the fight against cancer.

Additional information can be obtained from the American Cancer Society. Toll-free number: 800-ACS-2345.

STROKE
FACTS ABOUT STROKE

In 1994, nearly 18,000 African Americans suffered a stroke, also known as a cerebrovascular accident. The age-adjusted death rate for stroke among black men is more than 95 percent higher than the death rate for white men—52.4 per 100,000 black men, compared to 26.6 per 100,000 white men. The age-adjusted death rate for black women is more than 75 percent higher than that for white women—40.1 per 100,000 black women, compared to 22.8 per 100,000 white women.

A stroke is the result of an interruption in the flow of blood to the brain. The interruption is usually caused by a blood clot or a buildup of foreign matter in the arteries. The onset of a stroke is often sudden, although the event can unfold over the span of several hours. The symptoms of stroke range from dizziness or a sudden weakness in the limbs to a loss of speech or vision. Stroke can also result in temporary paralysis, memory loss, or even death.

RISK FACTORS

Smoking and high blood pressure are leading contributors to the onset of a stroke, by constricting the arteries and reducing the amount of blood that can reach the heart. This forces the heart to work harder, increasing the pressure on the cerebral arteries that carry blood to the brain.

PREVENTION

A low-cholesterol diet is fundamental in the fight against strokes, as is a routine of regular exercise, the moderate use of alcohol, and avoidance of cigarettes.

Additional information can be obtained from the National Stroke Association. Toll-free number: 800-STROKES.

HIV INFECTION/AIDS
FACTS ABOUT HIV/AIDS

Acquired immunodeficiency syndrome (AIDS) is the number one cause of death among African Americans ages 25 to 44 years. In 1997, the Centers for Disease Control and Prevention announced a significant shift in AIDS epidemiology—for the first time, African Americans accounted for a higher proportion of AIDS cases than European Americans throughout the nation (41% of all cases, compared with 38%). In New York City, the Health Department announced that the death rate of black men from AIDS was twice that for white men and 30 percent greater than that of Hispanic men; among women, the death rate for black women was six times that of white women and 46 percent greater than that of Hispanic women.

AIDS is caused when HIV (human immunodeficiency virus) attacks the body's CD4 cells (also known as T cells) and impairs the immune system's natural ability to protect the body from disease. HIV destroys the CD4 cell and transforms it into a production site for the virus. The production of HIV within the body creates a vicious cycle that eventually cripples the entire immune system. The body deteriorates when it is finally besieged by other diseases and infections that it is unable to fight off.

Biologically, African Americans are no more likely to contract AIDS than any other racial or ethnic group. Medical experts believe the disproportionate number of reported AIDS cases in the black community is due to a lack of information about the disease and to socioeconomic factors that lead to increased intravenous drug use among African Americans.

RISK FACTORS

Intravenous Drug Use   The intravenous injection of cocaine and heroin accounted for more than 2,500 transmissions of HIV in African American adolescent females from July 1995 to June 1996. For black adolescent males, more than 6,500 cases were reported to have been transmitted in this way. The virus is transmitted when needles are shared and HIV-infected blood is transmitted from one person to another.

Unprotected Sexual Intercourse   Heterosexual or homosexual intercourse without the use of a condom or dental or vaginal dams increases the risk of HIV transmission.

Multiple Partners   Frequent sexual intercourse with multiple partners greatly increases the risk of HIV transmission, as well as other sexually transmitted diseases.

Birth to an HIV-Infected Mother   Studies show that from 7 to 40 percent of women who are infected with HIV may pass the virus to the fetus during pregnancy or delivery. There is also some risk of transmission through breastfeeding.

Blood Transfusions   All donated blood has been tested for HIV since 1985. However, anyone who received a blood transfusion or used blood products between 1977 and 1985 may be at risk for HIV infection.

TESTING AND TREATMENT

There is no test for AIDS, but an antibody test, which is used for checking blood donations, exposes the HIV infection. Tests are available at doctors' offices and clinics. Counseling is recommended for those scheduling a test, and for persons who test positive for HIV. Counselors can explain treatments and recommend procedures, as well as offer emotional support. Clinics will also contact the local health departments, which routinely notify clients' sexual partners of an HIV-positive diagnosis.

Home HIV tests, which can be bought in stores or ordered over the phone or Internet, are also available. Most are FDA (Food and Drug Administration) approved and 99 percent accurate but are more expensive than clinic tests. In a home test kit, a person is given a test ID card that is used to identify the blood sample by number. After taking the test, the person sends in the specimen, then contacts the company by phone for the results. The down side of these home tests is that getting a positive result over the phone can be emotionally devastating, and no counseling is offered, nor do these companies notify the client's sexual partners. Consumers should also beware of HIV tests that are not FDA approved and should look for the appropriate FDA stamp of approval on the packaging. Early detection is crucial in the treatment of HIV and AIDS. Many people who have been diagnosed HIV-positive are living healthy and happy lives today.

PREVENTION

AIDS is not curable but it is preventable. Practicing safe sex—that is, using condoms and vaginal dams for penetration, and plastic wrap or dental dams for oral sex—can prevent the spread of HIV. These are not foolproof methods, however. Because condoms can come off and tear, withdrawal before ejaculation is recommended, as is the use of nonoxynol-9 spermicide with a condom (although some women are allergic to this). The best protection is to choose sexual activities that do not allow semen, blood (including menstrual blood), or vaginal fluids to enter the mouth, vagina, or anus, or to touch any open cuts, scratches, or sores. Similarly, it is crucial to avoid drug use, particularly the sharing of intravenous needles during drug use, and to avoid sex with any known drug users. Taking an HIV-test is an important part of prevention. Early treatment can make the difference between life and death for those infected with HIV.

Additional information is available from the Centers for Disease Control and Prevention, National HIV/AIDS Hotline. Toll-free number: 800-342-AIDS.

DIABETES
FACTS ABOUT DIABETES

Diabetes mellitus is the third leading cause of death among African Americans. Black men accounted for 3,834 deaths from diabetes in 1994, while black women accounted for 6,015 deaths. Diabetes can also greatly contribute to other causes of death such as heart disease and stroke. The age-adjusted death rate for black men was 27.1 per 100,000 population, more than 45 percent higher than the 12.7 percent age-adjusted death rate for white men. Overall, diabetes-related deaths increased by 7 percent for African Americans between 1988 and 1993, compared to 5 percent for all other groups. Overall, African Americans are nearly twice as likely to suffer from diabetes as are European Americans.

Diabetes occurs when the body has difficulty making or using *insulin*, a hormone that enables cells to absorb sugar from food. Normally, the pancreas produces the needed amount of insulin, helping sugar pass into the bloodstream to the cells. As the sugar is transmitted, the amount of insulin in the blood decreases. However, if the pancreas fails to produce enough insulin, or if the insulin does not process sugar correctly, the body's cells will become malnourished, and sugar will build up in the bloodstream.

There are many kinds of diabetes. Type 1 is called juvenile onset or insulin-dependent diabetes mellitus (IDDM). Ten percent of Americans are afflicted with Type 1 diabetes; the rate is slightly lower among African Americans. This form of diabetes occurs suddenly in childhood or adolescence and sometimes appears in adults under age 40. With Type 1 diabetes, the body stops producing insulin and uses fat and protein for energy. This process can result in rapid weight loss and damage to the heart, nerves, eyes, and blood vessels. Type 1 diabetes can lead to coma or death if it is not properly treated. Patients with Type 1 must inject themselves with insulin daily to balance their sugar levels, and they must follow a regimen of regular exercise and a diet of regular meals that balance carbohydrates, fats, and proteins.

Type 2 diabetes is called adult-onset or non-insulin-dependent diabetes (NIDDM); it accounts for more than 90 percent of all diabetes cases among African Americans. Type 2 diabetics produce normal levels of insulin, but their bodies cannot use it. This form of diabetes develops more slowly; unfortunately, Type 2 diabetes is often diagnosed only after it has caused severe damage to the heart, eyes, kidney, or nerves. Type 2 diabetes is commonly treated through exercise, weight loss, and oral medication. A third form of diabetes, called gestational diabetes, occurs in 3 percent of pregnant women and disappears after delivery. At increased risk for gestational diabetes are women who are more than 20 pounds overweight prior to conception, are over age 30, have a family history of diabetes, or have had a baby who was especially large (over $9\frac{1}{2}$ pounds) or stillborn. Most pregnant women with gestational diabetes have no symptoms, though some may experience extreme thirst, hunger, or fatigue. Black diabetic women are three times more likely to lose their babies due to gestational diabetes than are white diabetic women because they are less likely to receive proper prenatal care.

RISK FACTORS

Medical researchers have found that Type 2 diabetes often occurs in succeeding generations of families. In addition to family history, these additional factors define those at higher-than-average risk for the disease:

Age 40 and older

Weight 20 pounds or more over the medical ideal

Insufficient exercise

Stress

Female gender

Pregnancy

PREVENTION

Diabetes can be controlled through such factors as food intake, exercise, body weight, blood-sugar monitoring, and medication. All of these methods affect the blood-sugar level. Preventive care necessitates a healthy low-fat, low-cholesterol, and high-fiber diet; regular exercise such as jogging, walking, or yoga; and frequent medical checkups.

Additional information can be obtained from the American Diabetes Association. Toll-free number: 800-342-2383.

PNEUMONIA AND INFLUENZA

Pneumonia and influenza accounted for 7,472 deaths among African Americans in 1994. Yearly influenza vaccinations are recommended for all members of the population over the age of 65, and for people whose immune systems are weak, such as chemotherapy patients. However, only 15 percent of African Americans received influenza vaccinations covered by Medicare in 1993, compared to more than 35 percent of eligible European Americans. Members of low-income groups who may not have adequate diet and heat during the winter months are at greater risk of contracting influenza and developing complications such as pneumonia.

PREVENTION

Annual flu inoculations, frequent medical checkups, and, if possible, clean air and healthful surroundings are important in the prevention of pneumonia and influenza.

CHRONIC OBSTRUCTIVE PULMONARY DISEASE (COPD)

COPD is one of the few ailments for which African American death rates are lower than the national average. Nevertheless, COPD claimed 3,857 black men and 2,654 black women in 1994. The age-adjusted death rate for African Americans of both sexes was 17.7 per 100,000 population, compared to 21.6 per 100,000 population for European Americans.

Chronic obstructive pulmonary diseases include emphysema, chronic bronchitis, and asthma, all of which narrow the airways in the lungs. Smoking is the main contributor to COPD, causing between 80 and 90 percent of reported cases. In 1993, 26 percent of African Americans were smokers.

The American Heart and Lung Institute estimates that 15 million Americans suffer from asthma, one third of them children under age 18. As of 1993, black children and young adults were three to four times more likely than white children and young adults to be hospitalized for asthma. African American youngsters were also four to six times more likely to die from asthma. In 1997, the National Institute of Allergy and Infectious Diseases revealed that allergic reactions to cockroaches were a major factor in the disease, causing about 25 percent of all asthma cases in inner-city areas.

PREVENTION

Many factors contribute to COPDs. The strongest is the lack of prenatal care, which increases the risk of childhood asthma and other COPDs by more than four times. Breast-feeding seems to offer some prevention for the onset of asthma in children, as does protecting children from passive smoking. Ultimately, early detection and consistent treatment; a clean, healthful surrounding; and avoidance of smoking can all help in the prevention or management of COPDs.

Additional information can be obtained from the American Heart and Lung Association. Toll-free number: 800-LUNG-USA.

INFANT MORTALITY

African American infants are more than twice as likely to die before reaching their first birthday as are European American infants. In 1994, the mortality rate for black infants was 15.8 per 1,000 live births, compared to a rate of 6.6 per 1,000 for white infants. However, the 1994 mortality rate for black infants did represent a decline from the 1987 level of 18.8 black infant deaths per 1,000 live births.

Low birth weight—defined as weighing less than 5 pounds at birth—is the most significant contributor to infant mortality. In 1992, a Harvard Medical School study found that among infants born in Boston, St. Louis, and rural east-central Mississippi, black infants were two to three times more likely than white infants to weigh less than 3 pounds at birth. Major factors in low birth weight include smoking and drinking during pregnancy, insufficient prenatal care, poor nutrition, and anemia. In addition, nearly 90 percent of African American mothers experience complications in pregnancy, such as infection or rupture of the amniotic membrane, premature labor, high blood pressure, and hemorrhaging. These problems are three times more likely to occur among blacks than whites.

PREVENTION

Regularly scheduled and comprehensive prenatal care can greatly reduce the likelihood of infant mortality. It is also recommended that expectant mothers limit their alcohol and caffeine intake, stop smoking and using other drugs, eat a healthy diet, and follow a moderate course of exercise.

SICKLE-CELL DISEASE

Although it is not a leading cause of death, sickle-cell disease in the United States (and elsewhere in the Americas) occurs disproportionately in people of African descent. The disorder can be traced back to the coastal regions of Africa, where some individuals developed the sickle-cell gene mutation as a biological defense—sickle cells destroy malaria parasites invading the bloodstream. (The sickle-cell mutation also occurs in malaria-infested regions of Italy, Greece, and India.) Those inheriting the sickle-cell trait from one parent rarely suffer any ill effects. However, individuals inheriting the trait from both parents may produce an excessive number of sickle cells. These cells cannot carry oxygen the way that normal red blood cells do, and their unusual shape often causes them to clog blood vessels, restricting the flow of blood to vital tissues and organs. Symptoms of sickle-cell disease range from fatigue, shortness of breath, and bouts of pain to complete circulatory collapse. About 1 in every 400 African Americans suffers from the disorder, which usually appears after the age of 6 months. Medical researchers are now working on a synthetic molecule capable of correcting the gene mutation in sickle-cell patients.

STATISTICAL OVERVIEW OF HEALTH ISSUES

Table 8.1 Expectation of Life and Expected Deaths of African Americans, by Sex and Age, 1993

Age in 1990 (years)	Expectation of Life in Years			Expected Deaths per 1,00 Alive at Specified Age[1]		
	Total	Male	Female	Total	Male	Female
At birth	75.5	64.6	73.7	8.35	18.27	14.64
1	75.2	64.8	73.8	0.63	1.24	0.87
2	74.2	63.9	72.9	0.47	0.87	0.73
3	73.3	62.9	71.9	0.36	0.63	0.61
4	72.3	62.0	71.0	0.30	0.50	0.50
5	71.3	61.0	70.0	0.26	0.43	0.42
6	70.3	60.0	69.0	0.23	0.38	0.35
7	69.3	59.0	68.0	0.21	0.34	0.30
8	68.4	58.1	67.1	0.19	0.29	0.27
9	67.4	57.1	66.1	0.16	0.21	0.24
10	66.4	56.1	65.1	0.14	0.16	0.23
11	65.4	55.1	64.1	0.15	0.17	0.23
12	64.4	54.1	63.1	0.20	0.31	0.24
13	63.4	53.1	62.1	0.31	0.61	0.28
14	62.4	52.2	61.2	0.45	1.03	0.33
15	61.5	51.2	60.2	0.62	1.50	0.39
16	60.5	50.3	59.2	0.77	1.95	0.45
17	59.5	49.4	58.2	0.90	2.33	0.52
18	58.6	48.5	57.3	0.97	2.63	0.59
19	57.7	47.7	56.3	1.00	2.85	0.66
20	56.7	46.8	55.3	1.02	3.07	0.74
21	55.8	45.9	54.4	1.05	3.30	0.83
22	54.8	45.1	53.4	1.08	3.44	0.91
23	53.9	44.3	52.5	1.10	3.49	0.99
24	52.9	43.4	51.5	1.11	3.47	1.06
25	52.1	42.6	50.6	1.13	3.42	1.15
26	51.1	41.7	49.6	1.14	3.39	1.23
27	50.1	40.9	48.7	1.18	3.43	1.32
28	49.2	40.0	47.8	1.23	3.56	1.41
29	48.3	39.2	46.8	1.31	3.78	1.51
30	47.3	38.3	45.9	1.39	4.01	1.61
31	46.4	37.5	45.0	1.47	4.24	1.72
32	45.5	36.7	44.1	1.55	4.47	1.84
33	44.5	35.8	43.2	1.63	4.68	1.99
34	43.6	35.0	42.2	1.71	4.90	2.14
35	42.7	34.2	41.3	1.80	5.11	2.32
36	41.8	33.4	40.4	1.89	5.35	2.49
37	40.8	32.6	39.5	1.99	5.62	2.66
38	39.9	31.8	38.6	2.08	5.94	2.80
39	39.0	31.0	37.8	2.18	6.29	2.93
40	38.1	30.2	36.9	2.30	6.67	3.06
41	37.2	29.5	36.0	2.43	7.05	3.22
42	36.3	28.7	35.1	2.56	7.39	3.40

(continued)

Table 8.1 (continued)

Age in 1990 (years)	Expectation of Life in Years			Expected Deaths per 1,00 Alive at Specified Age[1]		
	Total	Male	Female	Total	Male	Female
43	35.4	27.9	34.2	2.69	7.68	3.63
44	34.5	27.2	33.4	2.84	7.93	3.90
45	33.6	26.4	32.5	3.01	8.18	4.19
46	32.7	25.7	31.7	3.20	8.47	4.49
47	31.8	24.9	30.8	3.43	8.82	4.81
48	30.9	24.2	30.0	3.70	9.26	5.15
49	30.0	23.5	29.1	4.00	9.77	5.50
50	29.2	22.8	28.3	4.35	10.31	5.87
51	28.3	22.0	27.5	4.73	10.86	6.27
52	27.4	21.4	26.7	5.14	11.46	6.71
53	26.6	20.7	25.9	5.61	12.12	7.20
54	25.7	20.0	25.1	6.12	12.83	7.73
55	24.9	19.3	24.3	6.66	13.57	8.29
56	24.1	18.7	23.5	7.24	14.30	8.87
57	23.3	18.0	22.8	7.88	15.03	9.47
58	22.5	17.4	22.0	8.59	15.72	10.09
59	21.7	16.8	21.3	9.34	16.39	10.74
60	20.9	16.2	20.6	10.14	17.07	11.41
61	20.2	15.6	19.8	10.96	17.74	12.11
62	19.5	15.1	19.1	11.80	18.36	12.84
63	18.7	14.5	18.4	12.64	18.93	13.61
64	18.0	13.9	17.8	13.48	19.45	14.41
65	17.3	13.4	17.1	14.35	19.90	15.21
70	14.0	10.8	13.9	19.21	23.18	19.91
75	10.9	8.7	11.1	24.52	23.31	23.41
80	8.3	6.7	8.5	29.38	21.69	26.60
85 and over	6.0	5.0	6.3	324.28	131.98	300.96

[1] Based on the proportion of the group who are alive at the beginning of an indicated age interval who will die before reaching the end of that interval. For example, out of every 1,000 people alive and exactly 50 years old at the beginning of the period, between 4 and 5 (4.86) will die before reaching their 51st birthdays.
Source: U.S. National Center for Health Statistics, Vital Statistics of the United States, annual; and unpublished data.

Table 8.2 Deaths, by Selected Causes and Age and Race, 1993 (in thousands)

Age and Race	Total[1]	Heart Disease	Cancer	Accidents and Adverse Effects	Cerebrovascular Diseases	Chronic Obstructive Pulmonary Diseases[2]	Pneumonia, Flu	Suicide	Chronic Liver Disease, Cirrhosis	Diabetes Mellitus	Homicide and Legal Intervention
ALL RACES											
Total	2,268.6	743.5	529.9	90.5	150.1	101.1	82.8	31.1	25.2	53.9	26.0
Under 1	33.5	0.7	0.1	0.9	0.2	0.1	0.5	0	(Z)	(Z)	0.3
1 to 4	7.1	0.3	0.5	2.6	(Z)	0.1	0.2	0	(Z)	(Z)	0.5
5 to 14	6.7	0.3	1.1	3.5	0.1	0.1	0.1	0.3	(Z)	(Z)	0.7
15 to 24	35.5	1.0	1.7	14.0	0.2	0.2	0.3	4.8	(Z)	0.1	8.4
25 to 34	59.6	3.5	5.1	14.0	0.8	0.3	0.7	6.3	0.7	0.6	7.3
35 to 44	96.0	13.1	16.8	13.3	2.5	0.7	1.6	6.2	3.8	1.7	4.5
45 to 54	131.8	32.7	42.4	8.0	5.1	2.5	1.9	4.2	4.7	3.4	2.1
55 to 64	241.6	72.0	90.7	6.4	9.6	10.7	3.7	3.1	5.6	7.5	1.0
65 to 74	487.8	158.1	163.3	8.1	25.3	31.3	10.8	3.0	6.1	15.0	0.7
75 to 84	638.0	234.0	146.5	10.7	51.4	38.3	25.9	2.4	3.5	16.3	0.4
85+	528.4	227.6	61.7	9.0	54.9	16.9	37.2	0.8	0.7	9.2	0.1
BLACK											
Total[3]	282.2	79.0	59.9	12.7	17.6	6.4	7.7	2.3	3.2	9.4	12.9
Under 1	10.9	0.2	(Z)	0.3	(Z)	(Z)	0.2	0	(Z)	0	0.1
1 to 4	2.0	0.1	0.1	0.7	(Z)	(Z)	0.1	0	(Z)	(Z)	0.2
5 to 14	2.0	0.1	0.2	0.8	(Z)	0.1	(Z)	(Z)	(Z)	(Z)	0.3
15 to 24	9.7	0.3	0.3	1.9	(Z)	0.1	0.1	0.6	(Z)	(Z)	5.1
25 to 34	15.9	1.1	0.9	2.1	0.2	0.1	0.2	0.6	0.1	0.2	3.8
35 to 44	24.9	3.5	3.0	2.4	0.8	0.3	0.5	0.4	0.8	0.5	2.1
45 to 54	26.9	6.7	7.0	1.3	1.5	0.4	0.5	0.2	0.8	0.9	0.7
55 to 64	38.6	12.2	12.3	1.0	2.3	1.0	0.7	0.1	0.7	1.7	0.3
65 to 74	57.9	19.4	17.8	1.0	4.0	1.9	1.4	0.1	0.5	2.8	0.2
75 to 84	56.3	20.3	13.1	0.8	5.0	1.8	2.1	0.1	0.2	2.3	0.1
85+	37.0	15.2	5.2	0.6	3.7	0.7	2.0	(Z)	(Z)	1.1	(Z)

(Z) represents fewer than 50.
[1] Includes other causes not shown separately.
[2] Includes related conditions.
[3] Includes those deaths with age not stated.
Source: U.S. National Center for Health Statistics; Vital Statistics of the United States, annual.

Table 8.3 Personal Health Practices, by Race, 1990 (in percent, except total persons; for persons 18 years of age and over)

Race	Total Persons (1,000)	Eats Breakfast	Rarely Snacks	Exercised Regularly in Past Year	Had Two or More Drinks on Any Day in the Past Year	Currently Smokes	20% or More Above Ideal Weight
All persons	181,447	56.4	25.5	40.7	5.5	25.5	27.5
Black	20,248	46.9	22.7	34.3	4.3	26.2	38.0

Source: U.S. National Center for Health Statistics, *Health Promotion and Disease Prevention; United States, 1990, Vital and Health Statistics*, series 10, No. 185.

Table 8.4 Visits to Physicians and Dentists, by Patient's Race, 1970 to 1994

Type of Visit and Year	Total Visits (million)		Visit per Person per Year	
	Black	White	Black	White
PHYSICIANS				
1970	87	832	3.9	4.8
1980	115	903	4.5	4.8
1983	126	1,018	4.6	5.2
1986	131	1,110	4.6	5.5
1989	140	1,148	4.7	5.6
1990	148	1,178	4.9	5.7
1994	179	1,350	5.4	6.3
DENTISTS				
1970	17	283	0.8	1.6
1980	26	333	1.0	1.8
1983	31	382	1.1	1.9
1986	37	416	1.4	2.1
1989	34	441	1.2	2.2

Source: U.S. National Center for Health Statistics, *Vital and Health Statistics*, series 10, No. 193, and earlier reports; and unpublished data.

Table 8.5 Pregnancies, by Age of Woman, Outcome, and Race, 1991

Item	Total (1,000)	Under 15 Years Old	15 to 19 Years Old	20 to 24 Years Old	25 to 29 Years Old	30 to 34 Years Old	35 to 39 Years Old	40 Years Old and Over
PREGNANCIES								
Non-Hispanic								
White, pregnancies	3,964	8	489	1,007	1,145	884	368	63
Live births	2,635	3	250	637	834	640	235	36
Induced abortions	774	4	164	264	163	106	58	16
Miscarriages	556	1	75	107	148	138	76	11
Black, pregnancies	1,344	14	272	439	320	202	81	15
Live births	673	6	149	216	160	98	37	6
Induced abortions	507	7	101	178	119	67	29	7
Miscarriages	164	1	22	45	41	37	15	3
Hispanic								
Pregnancies	965	5	177	306	250	149	64	14
Live births	623	2	105	199	170	100	39	8
Induced abortions	208	1	40	73	50	28	13	4
Miscarriages	134	1	32	33	30	22	12	2
RATE PER 1,000 WOMEN								
Non-Hispanic								
White, pregnancies	91.8	1.3	84.7	151.4	154.7	107.6	47.3	8.6
Live births	61.0	0.5	43.4	95.7	112.7	77.9	30.2	4.8
Induced abortions	17.9	0.7	28.4	39.6	22.0	12.9	7.4	2.2
Miscarriages	12.9	0.2	13.0	16.0	20.0	16.8	9.7	1.6
Black, pregnancies	174.8	11.0	216.7	337.2	232.3	142.7	63.9	14.4
Live births	87.6	4.9	118.9	166.1	116.3	69.3	28.9	5.7
Induced abortions	65.9	5.1	80.5	136.4	86.3	47.1	23.0	6.2
Miscarriages	21.3	0.9	17.2	34.7	29.7	26.3	12.1	2.4
Hispanic								
Pregnancies	167.4	4.8	180.2	285.6	224.3	143.9	74.8	19.8
Live births	108.1	2.4	106.7	186.3	152.8	96.1	44.9	11.1
Induced abortions	36.2	1.4	40.4	68.1	44.4	27.1	15.5	5.2
Miscarriages	23.2	1.0	33.1	31.2	27.1	20.7	14.4	3.6

Source: U.S. National Center for Health Statistics, Monthly Vital Statistics Report, vol. 43, No. 12.

Table 8.6 Infant Mortality Rates, by Race and State, 1990 and 1993 (deaths per 1,000 live births; represents deaths of infants under 1 year old, excluding fetal deaths)

Region and State	Total 1990	Total 1993	Black 1990	Black 1993
United States	9.2	8.4	18.0	16.5
Northeast	7.2	6.5	14.0	13.1
ME	6.5	6.8	(NA)	(NA)
NH	7.1	5.6	(NA)[1]	(NA)
VT	6.4	6.7	(NA)	(NA)
MA	7.0	6.2	11.9	11.4
RI	8.1	7.3	(NA)[1]	(NA)
CT	7.9	7.1	17.6	15.6
Middle Atlantic	9.5	8.4	18.7	16.8
NY	9.6	8.4	18.1	15.4
NJ	9.0	8.3	18.4	17.5
PA	9.6	8.6	20.5	19.7
East North Central	10.1	9.3	21.0	18.7
OH	9.8	9.2	19.5	17.9
IN	9.6	9.2	17.4	18.3
IL	10.7	9.9	22.4	19.6
MI	10.7	9.5	21.6	18.8
WI	8.2	7.9	19.0	16.0
West North Central	8.4	8.1	18.9	17.1
MN	7.3	7.5	23.7	14.1
IA	8.1	6.9	21.9	22.9
MO	9.4	8.4	18.2	14.8
ND	8.0	7.9	(NA)[1]	(NA)
SD	10.1	9.5	(NA)	(NA)
NE	8.3	9.1	18.9	26.2
KS	8.4	8.8	17.7	23.5
South Atlantic	10.7	9.6	17.9	16.4
DE	10.1	8.8	20.1	19.9
MD	9.5	9.8	17.1	17.6
DC	20.7	17.4	24.6	20.6
VA	10.2	8.7	19.5	14.9
WV	9.9	8.6	(NA)	(NA)
NC	10.6	10.5	16.5	17.1
SC	11.7	10.1	17.3	15.7
GA	12.4	10.4	18.3	16.3
FL	9.6	8.6	16.8	15.3
East South Central	10.4	9.7	16.4	15.7
KY	8.5	8.2	14.3	14.3
TN	10.3	9.4	17.9	17.9
AL	10.8	10.3	16.0	15.1
MS	12.1	11.5	16.2	14.7
West South Central	8.7	8.3	15.3	14.9
AR	9.2	10.0	13.9	13.4
LA	11.1	10.8	16.7	15.6
OK	9.2	8.8	14.3	16.4
TX	8.1	7.5	14.7	14.6

Table 8.6 (continued)

Region and State	Total 1990	Total 1993	Black 1990	Black 1993
Mountain	8.6	7.4	18.5	18.0
MT	9.0	7.4	(NA)	(NA)
ID	8.7	7.2	(NA)	(NA)
WY	8.6	7.9	(NA)[1]	(NA)
CO	8.8	7.9	19.4	17.0
NM	9.0	8.4	(NA)[1]	(NA)
AZ	8.8	7.6	20.6	22.1
UT	7.5	6.0	(NA)[1]	(NA)
NV	8.4	6.7	14.2	14.0
Pacific	7.9	6.8	17.1	15.8
WA	7.8	6.4	20.6	17.8
OR	8.3	7.2	(NA)[1]	(NA)
CA	7.9	6.8	16.8	15.6
AK	10.5	8.2	(NA)[1]	(NA)
HI	6.7	7.2	(NA)[1]	(NA)

(NA) not available.

[1]Based on a frequency of less than 20 infant deaths.

Source: U.S. National Center for Health Statistics, *Vital Statistics of the United States*, annual; and unpublished data.

Table 8.7 Deaths and Death Rates for Drug-Induced Causes, by Race and Sex, 1980 to 1993 (rates per 100,000)

Year	All Races Both Sexes	All Races Male	All Races Female	Black Both Sexes	Black Male	Black Female
TOTAL NUMBER						
1980	6,900	3,771	3,129	1,006	648	358
1985	8,663	5,342	3,321	1,600	1,107	493
1990	9,463	5,897	3,566	1,703	1,155	548
1991	10,388	6,593	3,795	2,037	1,385	652
1992	11,703	7,766	3,937	2,148	1,533	615
1993	13,275	9,052	4,223	2,688	1,924	764
AGE-ADJUSTED RATE						
1980	3.0	3.4	2.6	4.1	5.8	2.7
1985	3.5	4.5	2.6	5.9	8.9	3.3
1990	3.8	5.0	2.7	6.6	9.7	3.9
1991	3.8	5.0	2.7	6.6	9.7	3.9
1992	4.3	5.9	2.8	6.8	10.6	3.6
1993	4.8	6.8	3.0	8.3	13.0	4.4

Source: U.S. National Center for Health Statistics, *Monthly Vital Statistics Report,* vol. 43, No. 12.

Table 8.8 Deaths and Death Rates for Alcohol-Induced Causes, by Race and Sex, 1980 to 1993

	All Races			Black		
Year	Both Sexes	Male	Female	Both Sexes	Male	Female
NUMBER						
1980	19,765	14,447	5,318	4,451	3,170	1,281
1985	17,741	13,216	4,525	4,114	3,030	1,084
1990	19,757	14,842	4,915	4,337	3,172	1,165
1991	19,233	14,467	4,766	3,883	2,816	1,067
1992	19,568	14,926	4,642	3,809	2,800	1,009
1993	19,557	14,873	4,684	3,663	2,759	904
AGE-ADJUSTED RATE						
1980	8.4	13.0	4.3	20.4	32.4	10.6
1985	7.0	11.0	3.4	16.8	27.7	8.0
1990	7.2	11.4	3.4	16.1	26.6	7.7
1991	6.8	10.9	3.2	13.9	22.9	6.8
1992	6.8	11.0	3.1	13.4	22.3	6.3
1993	6.7	10.8	3.0	12.5	21.3	5.5

Source: U.S. National Center for Health Statistics, Monthly Vital Statistics Reports.

Table 8.9 African Americans in the Health Professions, 1983 and 1995

	1983		1995	
Occupation	Total (1,000)	% Black	Total (1,000)	% Black
Physicians	519	3.2	693	4.9
Dentists	126	2.4	155	1.9
Registered nurses	1,372	6.7	1,977	8.4
Pharmacists	158	3.8	170	4.3
Dietitians	71	21.0	94	18.4
Therapists	247	7.6	466	9.2
Physicians' assistants	51	7.7	55	7.6

Source: U.S. Bureau of Labor Statistics.

NATIONAL MEDICAL ASSOCIATION

The National Medical Association (NMA), the oldest organization of African American physicians in the United States, was founded in 1895. At that time, African Americans were excluded from the American Medical Association, which had adopted an official policy of segregation in 1872. By the 1920s, African American physicians had organized 50 local and state medical associations under the NMA umbrella. The NMA played a crucial role in maintaining the accreditation and financing of African American medical schools and their allied hospitals and clinics. The organization also worked in conjunction with the NAACP, the Urban League, and other groups in combating segregation. Throughout its history, the NMA has supported progressive health-care legislation and has worked to promote the recruitment of African Americans into the medical professions.

HEALTH-ADVOCACY ORGANIZATIONS

African American Donor Task Force
P.O. Box 51315
East Palo Alto, CA 94303
415-322-9418

African American Hospital Foundation
1635 Campbellton Road, SW
Atlanta, GA 30311
404-755-2979

African American Natural Foods Association
c/o Cheryl A. Sims
7058 S. Clyde Avenue
Chicago, IL 60649
312-363-3939
Organizes workshops and seminars on health-maintenance techniques and health foods.

African Medical and Research Foundation, Inc.
19 W. 44th Street, Room 1708
New York, NY 10036
212-768-2440
Seeks to improve health care in Africa through service, training, and research.

Association of Black Psychologists
P.O. Box 55999
Washington, DC 20040
202-722-0808
Professional organization.

Black Health Research Foundation
14 E. 60th Street
New York, NY 10022
212-408-3485

Boston Sickle Cell Center
Boston City Hospital
818 Harrison Avenue, FGH 2
Boston, MA 02118
617-534-5727
Conducts scientific research on sickle-cell disease.

Center for Sickle Cell Disease
Howard University

2121 Georgia Avenue, NW
Washington, DC 20059
202-806-7950
Conducts scientific research on sickle-cell disease.

Charles R. Drew University of Medicine and Science
Hypertension Research Center
1621 E. 120th Street, MP 11
Los Angeles, CA 90059
213-563-5927
Conducts scientific research on hypertension.

Haitian Coalition on AIDS
50 Court Street, Suite 605
Brooklyn, NY 11201
718-855-0972
Provides counseling and care for immigrants in the New York area suffering from AIDS.

Minority Health Education Development
325 W. 26th Street
Erie, PA 16508
814-453-6229

Minority Health Professionals Foundation
20 Executive Park Drive, NE
Atlanta, GA 30329
404-634-1993
Promotes research for minority institutions on public and private health-care issues.

Narcotics Education League
1315 Fruitvale Avenue
Oakland, CA 94601
510-261-7120
Provides drug counseling for groups and individuals.

National Association of Health Services Executives
10320 Little Patuxent Parkway, Suite 1106
Columbia, MD 21044
202-628-3953
Professional organization.

National Black Alcoholism Council
1629 K Street, NW, Suite 802
Washington, DC 20006
202-296-2696
Provides counseling services and education on
    alcohol abuse.

National Black Child Development Institute
1023 15th Street, NW, Suite 600
Washington, DC 20005
202-387-1281
Provides educational information on health,
    cultural, and public-policy issues affecting black
    children and families.

National Black Nurses' Association
1012 10th Street, NW
Washington, DC 20001
202-393-6870
Professional organization.

National Black Women's Health Project
1237 Ralph David Abernathy Boulevard, SW
Atlanta, GA 30310
404-758-9590

National Medical Association
1012 10th Street, NW
Washington, DC 20001
202-347-1895
Professional association that sponsors clinical
    research.

National Minority AIDS Council
300 I Street, NE, Suite 400
Washington, DC 20002
202-483-6622
Sponsors workshops, forums, education,
    and training on AIDS treatment and
    legislation.

THE TUSKEGEE STUDY

The Tuskegee Study, entitled "Untreated Syphilis in the Negro Male," began in 1932 under the auspices of the U.S. Public Health Service and the Tuskegee Institute. The study was conducted in Macon County, Alabama, and involved 600 poor black men, 399 who had contracted syphilis and 201 who had no symptoms of the disease. The men were given free meals, free medical exams, and burial insurance. The study was originally slated to last six months, but it continued for 40 years. Though the purpose of the study was to justify the creation of a public treatment program for African Americans, the researchers essentially sacrificed the well-being of the patients to the quest for scientific knowledge. The men who had syphilis were never informed of their condition but were told only that they had "bad blood." When penicillin became available as a treatment for syphilis in the 1940s, the drug was not administered to the Tuskegee patients. They were allowed to suffer all the ravages of the disease so that the doctors could study their symptoms to the point of death. The study was finally halted in 1972 when the public learned of its existence. In the years that followed, the federal government has paid more than $10 million in compensation to the participants in the study, their families, and their heirs.

On May 16, 1997, in a special ceremony at the White House, President Bill Clinton made a formal apology on behalf of the U.S. government for the abuses committed during the Tuskegee study. Attending the ceremony were five of the eight surviving men who took part in the experiment. The president also announced a $200,000 federal grant to Tuskegee University for the creation of a Center for Bioethics in Research and Health Care and discussed plans to involve minority communities in the design and delivery of health-care programs.

The Tuskegee Study and other incidents have had a powerful impact on the way many African Americans view the medical profession and the integrity of federal programs. This is evident from a February 1997 survey conducted for the Institute of Minority Health Research at Emory University's Rollins School of Public Health. In the survey, 1,000 people were polled on medical-ethics issues—500 in African American households and 500 in general-population households, 84 percent of which were European American. Of the black respondents, 36 percent said they were "very likely" to be used as human guinea pigs without their consent, and 38 percent said they were "somewhat likely" to be used in that capacity. In contrast, only 16 percent of the other group gave the "very likely" response to the question, while 34 percent said "somewhat likely." Eighteen percent of the African Americans said they believed that AIDS was a human-made virus, and 9 percent said that AIDS was "definitely" part of a plot to kill African Americans. Of the other respondents, 9 percent believed that AIDS was human-made, and only 1 percent believed it was part of an antiblack conspiracy.

NOTABLE PHYSICIANS AND SURGEONS

(For biographies of scientists, biologists, chemists, and other prominent researchers, see Chapter 10, "Science and Technology.")

Adams, Numa Pompilius Garfield (1885–1940).   Under the guidance of his grandmother (an experienced midwife), young Numa Adams learned about medicinal herbs. Raised by a single mother, he received his early education in a Virginia country school run by his uncle. Adams attended high school in Pennsylvania, where he was befriended by Reverend Henry Howard Summers, a Howard University graduate, who encouraged the boy in his studies. After graduating from high school with honors in 1905, Adams taught school before enrolling in Howard University. He received his B.A. degree, summa cum laude, in 1911 and earned an M.A. in Chemistry from Columbia University the following year. Adams then joined the Howard faculty, attaining the position of associate professor and head of the Chemistry Department. In 1920 he entered Rush Medical College in Chicago. After receiving his M.D. in 1924, Adams began practicing medicine in Chicago. In 1929, Adams was appointed dean of the College of Medicine at Howard, the first African American to fill the post. At this point in its history, Howard's medical school was struggling to secure adequate funding and to establish itself as a first-rate institution. Adams played a leading role in this endeavor. He oversaw the reorganization of the curriculum; strengthened the medical school's role in the teaching programs at Freedmen's Hospital; supervised the recruitment of capable young physicians, putting together the first ever all–African American medical faculty; improved the salaries and professional opportunities of physicians affiliated with Howard; and generally encouraged a higher level of instruction and morale throughout the institution. The strain of this enormous undertaking gradually undermined Adams's own health, and he died of pneumonia following an operation at age 55.

Augusta, Alexander Thomas (1825–1890).   Born free in Virginia, Augustus moved to Philadelphia as a young man in the hope of studying medicine. Though he was denied admission to the University of Pennsylvania Medical School, he attracted the attention of Professor William Gibson, who allowed Augusta to study in his office. In 1850, Augusta was accepted as a student at Trinity Medical College in the University of Toronto and earned his medical degree in 1856. He then began to practice medicine in Toronto, also spending time in Baltimore and in the West Indies. In 1863, Augusta was commissioned as a major in the U.S. Army and assigned as a surgeon to newly recruited African American troops. He was the first of eight African American military surgeons and the highest-ranking black officer in the army. Augusta left the army in 1866 with the rank of lieutenant colonel and joined the faculty of Howard University Medical School. After nine years at Howard, he devoted himself to private practice in Washington, D.C.

Callender, Clive O. (1936–   ).   Callender earned degrees in chemistry and psychology from New York's Hunter College in 1959. He then entered Meharry Medical College in Nashville, Tennessee, and graduated first in his class in 1963. Callender interned at the University of Cincinnati and then became a surgeon at Fort Harcourt General Hospital in Nigeria during the Biafran Civil War. After studying transplant surgery for two years, he become the first African American transplant surgeon at the University of Minnesota Hospital. Callender joined the faculty of the Howard University Medical School in 1973 and established Howard's transplant center. He currently serves as director of the center, as well as professor and vice chair of the Department of Surgery.

Cardozo, William Warrick (1905–1962).   Born in Washington, D.C., Cardozo studied at Ohio State University, earning his A.B. in 1929 and his M.D. in 1933. After completing his internship and residency in pediatrics, he took up a two-year fellowship at Children's Memorial Hospital and Provident Hospital in Chicago. During this time, Cardozo conducted research on sickle-cell disease. His groundbreaking paper, "Immunologic Studies in Sickle Cell Anemia," appeared in the *Archives of Internal Medicine* in October 1937. In the same year, Cardozo returned to Washington, where he began private practice and also joined the staff of Freedmen's Hospital and the Howard University College of Medicine. He eventually attained the post of clinical associate professor of pediatrics and specialized in gastrointestinal disorders in children. Cardozo also served for 26 years as a school medical inspector for the District of Columbia Board of Health.

Carson, Benjamin (1951–   ).   Raised in Detroit's inner city, Carson credited his mother with inspiring him to become an outstanding student. He attended Yale University on a scholarship, earning a B.A. in 1973, and went on to earn his medical degree from the University of Michigan in 1977. Carson completed his internship in general surgery and residency in neurosurgery at Baltimore's Johns Hopkins Hospital, becoming the hospital's first-ever black neurosurgical resident. In 1983, he moved to Perth, Australia, to become senior neurosurgical resident at the Sir Charles Gardiner Hospital. In 1985, at age 34, Carson returned home to become director of pediatric neurosurgery at Johns Hopkins. He gained international acclaim in 1987 when he successfully separated a pair of Siamese twins who were joined at the back of the head. In the landmark operation, which lasted 22 hours, Carson led a surgical team comprising 70 doctors, nurses, and technicians.

Comer, James Pierpont (1934–   ).   One of the leading child psychiatrists in the United States, Comer was born in East Chicago, Indiana. Educated at Howard University and the University of Michigan, he trained in psychiatry at Yale from 1964 to 1968. It was while working at Yale's Child Study Center that he began to explore a new approach to education, one that stresses fulfilling the child's social and psychological needs as much as academic ones. In 1968, at the height of political and social upheaval in the United States, Comer began carrying out his program in two elementary schools in New Haven, greatly improving the scholastic performance of children from low-income and minority backgrounds. Unlike most education-reform programs that focus on academic concerns, such as improving a teacher's credentials, the Comer Method emphasizes the development of children's social skills and self-esteem. Based on his belief that any child can learn, his program has changed the lives of thousands of schoolchildren, many from broken homes and poor backgrounds. A professor of child psychiatry at Yale, and the author of *Maggie's American Dream,* a combination memoir and biography of his mother, Comer continues to promote his School Development Program.

Cooper, Edward Sawyer (1926–   ).   A native of South Carolina, Cooper received his B.A. from Lincoln University in Pennsylvania and graduated with highest honors from Meharry Medical College. In 1954 he joined the U.S. Air Force (USAF) and served as chief of the medical service at the USAF Hospital in the Philippines. In 1956, Cooper began private practice in the field of internal medicine and stroke prevention, and in 1958 he joined the faculty of the University of Pennsylvania School of Medicine. In 1972, Cooper became a tenured physician professor, the first African American to achieve that distinction at the medical school. He was also cofounder and codirector of the Stroke Research Center at Philadelphia General Hospital. In 1992, Cooper became the first African American president of the American Heart Association. He has also worked with a number of organizations promoting medical education and professional advancement for African Americans.

Dickens, Helen Octavia (1909–   ).   Born in Dayton, Ohio, Dickens decided to become a medical professional at age 12. She received her bachelor of science degree in 1930 from the University of Illinois and her medical degree from the University of Illinois College of Medicine in 1934. Dickens completed a residency in obstetrics at Provident Hospital in Chicago. She then became associate clinical professor in the Obstetrics and Gynecology Department at the Medical College of Pennsylvania and chief of service at Women's Hospital. From 1948 to 1967, Dickens served as director of the Department of Obstetrics and

Gynecology at Mercy-Douglass Hospital in Philadelphia. The first African American woman to be admitted as a fellow of the American College of Surgeons, Dickens is especially noted for her extensive research in psychological, educational, and social services for disadvantaged teenagers.

Drew, Charles Richard (1904–1950).   After receiving his medical degree from McGill University in Montreal, Drew held posts at Howard, Columbia, and Harvard universities. His pioneering work in the preservation of blood plasma saved the lives of countless soliders and civilians during World War II. In 1940, he traveled to Britain and set up the first blood bank there, and the following year, he was appointed head of the American Red Cross Blood Bank in New York. Drew resigned his post after a year to protest the practice of separating blood according to racial categories, but he later advised the U.S. Army on hospital care in occupied Europe. In 1942 he became head of the Department of Surgery at Howard University and chief of staff at Freedmen's Hospital. Throughout his career—cut short by a fatal automobile accident—Drew wrote many articles for scientific journals and trained numerous African American physicians.

Elders, Jocelyn (1933–   ).   Born in Arkansas, Elders graduated from Philander Smith College in 1952. Between 1953 and 1956, she served in the U.S. Army, attaining the rank of first lieutenant at the Brooke Army Medical Center. Elders then enrolled in the University of Arkansas Medical School. She obtained her M.D. in 1960 and completed her internship and residency in pediatrics. From 1967 to 1987, Elders was professor of pediatrics at the University of Arkansas Medical Center, publishing more than 200 articles and papers in her specialty. In 1987, Elders was appointed director of the Arkansas State Department of Health, and in 1992, President Clinton nominated her for the post of U.S. surgeon general. Elders was confirmed in 1993, but her outspoken support for sex education and her criticism of antiabortion groups soon angered conservatives, who demanded her dismissal. In 1994, Elders resigned her post under pressure from the White House and returned to the University of Arkansas as professor of pediatrics.

Fuller, Solomon Carter (1872–1953).   Fuller was born in Liberia and came to the United States at age 17 to attend Livingstone College in North Carolina. He received his bachelor's degree in 1893 and obtained a medical degree from the Boston University School of Medicine in 1897. In 1899, he joined the Boston University faculty and taught pathology, neurology, and psychiatry for the next 40 years. One of the first African American psychiatrists in the United States, Fuller contributed numerous articles to books and medical journals. His work on Alzheimer's disease was a major contribution to the early research on that ailment.

Hinton, William Augustus (1883–1959).   Though he earned a degree from Harvard Medical School in only three years, Hinton could not get an internship in a Boston hospital because of his skin color. He went to work for the Massachusetts Department of Public Health and spent 25 years as an instructor in bacteriology and immunology at Harvard. In 1949, Hinton was awarded a clinical professorship, becoming the first African American professor in Harvard's history. In the course of his career, Hinton did ground breaking work on syphilis; his book *Syphilis and Its Treatment*, published in 1936, has remained a classic in the field.

Kountz, Samuel Lee, Jr. (1930–1981).   A kidney specialist with a medical degree from the University of Arkansas, Kountz took part in the first West Coast kidney transplant while at the University of California. He developed a technique for monitoring the blood supply to a transplanted kidney, making it possible for doctors to detect early signs of rejection and to intervene with drug therapy. Prior to Kountz's innovations, only 5 percent of kidney-transplant patients survived more than two years. Subsequent to his work in California, Kountz was professor of surgery at the Downstate Medical Center in Brooklyn, New York, and surgeon-in-chief at Kings County Hospital.

Long, Irene Duhart (1952–   ).   Long received her B.A. from Northwestern University in 1973 and her M.D. from the St. Louis University School of Medicine in 1977. She spent the next five years completing a residency in general surgery and a residency in aerospace medicine. In 1982, Long joined the National Aeronautics and Space Administration (NASA). She is currently chief of NASA's Medical and

Environmental Health Office at the John F. Kennedy Space Center in Cape Canaveral, Florida, responsible for assessing and maintaining the health of astronauts and all other personnel.

Major, Benjamin (1924–   ).   Born in New Jersey, Major earned his B.A. at Fisk University and received his M.D. from Meharry Medical College in 1946. After completing his internship and residency in obstetrics and gynecology in St. Louis's municipal hospital system, Major served as a captain in the U.S. Air Force Medical Corps. In 1953 he began private practice in Berkeley and Oakland, California. From 1965 to 1966 and from 1970 to 1972, Major took time out from his practice and traveled to Africa, developing medical programs in Kenya, Ghana, and other nations. Upon returning to the United States each time, he directed maternity and infant-care programs and family-planning programs for the Berkeley Public Health Department. During the 1980s, Major was chief of obstetrics and gynecology at Highland General Hospital in Oakland and served as a consultant to family-planning organizations. He retired from private practice in 1987 and joined the faculty of the University of California School of Public Health in Berkeley.

Murray, Peter Marshall (1888–1969).   Murray graduated from New Orleans University in 1910. He then enrolled in the College of Medicine at Howard University and graduated in 1914 with honors in surgery and obstetrics. After practicing medicine in Washington for several years, Murray moved to New York City and took up a post at Harlem Hospital. He eventually became director of the hospital's gynecological service, retiring in 1953. He then served as vice president of the Hospital Council of Greater New York and served on a variety of city, state, and federal advisory boards. In addition to publishing a number of important articles in medical journals, Murray also fought to increase opportunities for African Americans in medicine. He was an important official of the National Medical Association for many years and in 1950 became the first black member of the American Medical Association's (AMA's) House of Delegates. During his 12 years with the AMA, Murray was instrumental in desegregating the organization's chapters, including those in the deep South.

Purvis, Charles Burleigh (1842–1929).   Born in Philadelphia, Purvis graduated from Oberlin College in Ohio and from Wooster Medical College (now Case Western Reserve Medical School). He joined the U.S. Army as a surgeon in 1865 and served in Washington for four years, providing health care for the thousands of freed former slaves who moved to the nation's capital after the Civil War. In 1869, Purvis became an assistant surgeon at Freedmen's Hospital. In 1873, Purvis was appointed professor of obstetrics and the diseases of women and children. In 1881, when President James A. Garfield was shot by a disappointed office seeker, Purvis was the first physician to aid the wounded chief executive. In recognition of his service, Purvis was appointed surgeon-in-chief at Freedman's Hospital, becoming the first African American to run a civilian hospital. For more than 50 years, Purvis also played a crucial role in the development of the College of Medicine at Howard University. He taught without compensation when the school was unable to pay faculty salaries and thus helped maintain the major source of medical education for African Americans.

Satcher, David (1941–   ).   Born in rural Alabama, Satcher graduated from Morehouse College in 1963. He went on to Case Western Reserve Medical School, receiving his M.D. and Ph.D. in 1970. Specializing in genetics and sickle-cell disease, Satcher became chair of the Department of Community Medicine and Family Medicine at Atlanta's Morehouse Medical School in 1975. He remained in that post until 1982, when he was appointed president of Meharry Medical College. In 1993, Satcher became director of the Centers for Disease Control and Prevention (CDC). During his tenure, the CDC launched a number of successful initiatives. Among other accomplishments, the agency increased childhood immunization rates to 78 percent (up from 55% in 1992) and expanded screening programs for breast and cervical cancer to all 50 states. Satcher also created programs to permit early detection of infectious diseases and food-borne illnesses. During his tenure at CDC, vaccine-preventable childhood illnesses fell to their lowest level in U.S. history. In September 1997, President Clinton recognized Satcher's achievements in the public-health field by nominating him for the post of U.S. surgeon general. At his confirmation ceremony, this doctor asserted, "It is a privilege to have this opportunity to give back to America what America has given me."

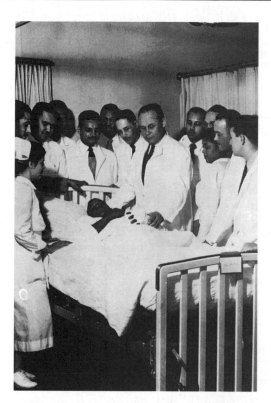

Pioneering blood researcher Charles Richard Drew was the head of the Department of Surgery at Howard University and chief of staff at the Freemen's Hospital.

Sullivan, Louis W. (1933–   ).   A native of Georgia, Sullivan graduated from Morehouse College in 1954 and earned his M.D. from Boston University in 1958. He completed his internship and residency at New York Hospital–Cornell Medical Center and went on to hold teaching posts at Harvard Medical School and the New Jersey College of Medicine. In 1974, Sullivan was appointed president of the newly created Morehouse School of Medicine, also serving as professor of biology and medicine. He served in that post until 1989, when President George Bush named him to head the U.S. Department of Health and Human Services. Throughout his career, Sullivan has been active in numerous medical and health organizations and was founding president of the Association of Minority Health Professions Schools.

Williams, Daniel Hale (1856–1931).   Born in Hollidaysburg, Pennsylvania, Williams received an M.D. from Chicago Medical College of Northwestern Medical School in 1883. In 1891 he founded the Provident Hospital and Medical Center in Chicago, the oldest independent black-owned hospital in the United States. Williams's most notable contribution to medicine came in 1893, when he performed the first open-heart surgery. In that instance, he removed a knife from the heart of a stabbing victim and sutured the pericardium, enabling the patient to survive for several years. When the American College of Surgeons was formed in 1913, Williams was the only African American among the 100 charter members. He also founded the National Medical Association and served as its first vice president. In 1970, the U.S. Congress authorized a commemorative postage stamp in Williams's honor.

Wright, Louis Tompkins (1891–1952).   A trailblazing researcher and physician, Wright was the first black physician to be appointed to the staff of a New York municipal hospital, the first black surgeon in the New York City police department, the first to experiment with chlortetracycline (Aureomycin; an antibiotic) on humans, the first African American surgeon to be admitted to the American College of Surgeons, and the first African American physician in America to head a public interracial hospital. The son of a prominent Georgia physician, Wright graduated cum laude from Harvard Medical School in 1915.

During World War I, Wright trained at the first training camp for African American officers and served as a first lieutenant in the U.S. Army's Medical Corps, working in triage hospitals. He was exposed to phosgene gas and suffered permanent lung damage. Despite his disability he spent the next 33 years as a practicing physician.

He returned to the United States in 1919 and became clinical assistant and visiting surgeon at the ailing Harlem Hospital in New York. There, Wright introduced a number of new medical techniques, such as the intradermal method of smallpox vaccination, a splint for cervical fractures, and a plate for the repair of recurrent hernias. As an administrator, Wright was highly regarded for his ability to create a spirit of harmony and mutual respect among the white and black members of the Harlem Hospital staff. Wright remained at Harlem Hospital for more than 30 years, publishing a total of 91 papers on medical research and spearheading much-needed hospital reforms.

In 1945, Wright became the only African American member of the American College of Surgeons, and he was elected president of Harlem Hospital's board in 1948. Scorning the "separate but equal" racial philosophy, Wright battled fiercely against discrimination. He was an active member of the NAACP and was awarded the organization's Spingarn Medal in 1940.

SOURCES FOR ADDITIONAL INFORMATION

Bailey, A. Peter. *The Harlem Hospital Story: 100 Years of Struggle against Illness*. Richmond, VA: Native Sun, 1991.

Bailey, Eric J. *Urban African American Health Care*. Lantham, MD: University Press of America, 1990.

Dixon, Barbara. *Good Health for African Americans*. New York: Crown, 1994.

Health of Black Americans from Post Reconstruction to Integration, 1871–1960: An Annotated Bibliography of Contemporary Sources. Westport, CT: Greenwood, 1990.

Journal of the National Medical Association. Monthly.

McBride, David. *From TB to AIDS: Epidemics among Urban Blacks Since 1900*. Albany: State University of New York Press, 1991.

National Black Health Leadership Directory. Washington, DC: NRW Associates. Published annually.

Villarosa, Linda. *Body and Soul*. New York: Harper Perennial, 1994.

White, Evelyn C. *The Black Women's Health Book*. New York: Seal, 1990.

9

Business and Entrepreneurship

THE DUNBAR NATIONAL BANK of NEW YORK

LEADING AFRICAN AMERICAN COMPANIES

Black Enterprise—a magazine that provides news analysis, business and financial advice, and career counseling—has compiled a yearly list of the top 100 industrial and service companies, the top 100 auto dealers, the top 25 ad agencies, the top 25 financial companies, the top 10 insurance companies, and the top 15 investment companies owned by African Americans. To be eligible for these lists, a company must have been fully operational in the previous calendar year and must be at least 51 percent black owned. Businesses are ranked by largest amount of gross sales, and *Black Enterprise* consults industry analysts and other sources to verify the information, which is then reviewed by the accounting firm of Mitchell & Titus, L.L.P.

Through *Black Enterprise*'s survey, the magazine determined that the auto industry is responsible for a disproportionate amount of African American wealth, making up 42.1 percent of gross sales of black-owned businesses. The next largest source of wealth is the food and beverage industry, at 21.3 percent. Other groups include manufacturing (8.1%), media (7.0%), technology (6.7%), construction (2.2%), and health and beauty aids (2.1%). The following lists contain companies consistently ranked at the top of *Black Enterprise*'s annual lists for at least 5 years or more during the 1990s, including 1998. Sales figures are from the 1998 list.

Table 9.1 Black Enterprise's Top 50 Industrial/Service Companies, 1999

Company	*Sales**
1. The Philadelphia Coca Cola Bottling Co.	389.000
2. Johnson Publishing Co.	371.945
3. TLC Beatrice International Holdings Inc.	322.000
4. Active Transportation	250.000
5. The Bing Group	232.000
6. World Wide Technology Inc.	201.000
7. Fuci Metal USA Inc.	200.000
8. Granite Broadcasting Corporation	193.934
9. H. J. Russell & Co.	184.436
10. BET Holdings 11 Inc.	178.000
11. Siméus Foods International Inc.	150.000
12. Anderson-Dubose Co.	143.665
13. Barden Companies Inc.	143.500
14. Midwest Stamping Inc.	135.000
15. Exemplar Manufacturing Co.	132.363
16. Mays Chemical Co.	130.000
17. Hawkins Food Group	129.703
18. Digital Systems International Corp.	116.102
19. Sayers Computer Source	110.000
19. Thomas Madison Inc.	110.000
21. Essence Communications Inc.	105.931
22. Spiral Inc.	104.000
23. Dallas & Mavis Specialized Carrier Co.	102.500
24. Belle of Orleans DBA Bally's Casino Lakeshore Resort	100.000
25. Wesley Industries Inc.	95.000
26. Pulsar Data Systems Inc.	90.000

Table 9.1 (continued)

Company	Sales*
27. Olajuwon Holdings	85.000
28. Calhoun Enterprises	81.752
29. The Holland Group L.L.C. DBA Workplace Integrators	80.798
30. The Bartech Group Inc.	76.500
31. Washington Cable Supply Inc.	74.300
32. V and J Holding Companies Inc.	74.000
33. Reliant Industries Inc.	73.151
34. Bridgeman Foods	72.000
35. Specialized Packaging Group	71.310
36. Rush Communications	70.000
36. Stop Shop Save Food Markets	70.000
38. Automotive Carrier Services	65.379
39. Pro-Line Corporation	65.119
40. Karl Kani Infinity Inc.	65.000
40. Luster Products Co.	65.000
40. Radio One Inc./Radio One of Atlanta Inc.	65.000
43. Regal Plastics Co.	62.531
44. Baldwin Richardson Foods Co.	62.000
45. Pepsi Cola of Washington, D.C., L.P.	61.756
46. Surface Protection Industries Inc.	59.000
47. Health Resources Inc.	56.400
48. Specialized Services Inc.	55.020
49. Wilson Office Interiors	55.000
50. Drew Pearson Co.	52.000

* In millions of dollars, to the nearest thousand. As of Dec. 31, 1998. Prepared by B.E. Research. Reviewed by Mitchell & Titus, L.L.P.

Table 9.2 Black Enterprise's Top 50 Auto Dealerships, 1999

Company	Sales*
1. Mel Farr Automotive Group	596.600
2. Chicago Truck Center	224.000
3. Family Automotive Group	192.000
4. March/Hodge Holding Company	184.000
5. Martin Automotive Group	159.259
6. S & J Enterprises	158.000
7. Southgate Automotive Group	136.325
8. 32 Ford Lincoln Mercury	122.012
9. Armstrong Holdings	116.000
10. Avis Ford	109.437
11. B & G Associates	108.977
12. Pavilion Lincoln-Mercury/JMC Auto Group	105.667
13. Brandon Dodge Inc.	105.195
14. Hubbard Investments L.L.C.	103.322
15. Legacy Automotive Inc.	101.000
16. Village Auto Plaza Inc.	91.000

Table 9.2 (continued)

Company	Sales*
17. Ray Wilkinson Buick-Cadillac Inc.	89.921
18. Baranco Automotive Group	83.634
19. Tropical Ford Inc.	80.456
20. Prestige Automotive Group	79.846
21. Davis Automotive Inc.	76.226
22. Bob Johnson Chevrolet	73.186
23. Bob Ross Buick Inc.	72.384
24. University Automotive Group	71.584
25. Long Automotive Group/ Vicksburg Chrysler-Plymouth Dodge Inc.	71.345
26. Mike Pruitt Ford	70.000
27. Briarwood Ford Inc.	69.272
28. Jim Mitchell Auto Group	67.700
29. Northwood Lincoln-Mercury/JMC Auto Group	67.311
30. Superstition Springs Toyota	67.000
31. Barnett Auto Group	66.450
32. Tyson Auto Group	65.531
33. Winston Pittman Enterprises	65.301
34. Simi Valley Pontiac GMC Buick Inc.	65.063
35. Fitzpatrick Dealership Group	65.000
36. Panhandle Automotive Inc.	64.000
37. Brookdale Dodge Inc.	62.000
38. Midfield Dodge Inc.	61.634
39. Spalding Automotive Group	59.602
40. Village Ford of Lewisville Inc.	57.100
41. Prestige Ford Inc.	56.652
42. Bradley Automotive Group	54.018
43. Mission Boulevard Lincoln Mercury Inc.	53.517
44. Taylor Companies	52.961
45. Bill Perkins Automotive Group	51.069
46. Chino Hills Ford	51.000
47. R. H. Peters Chevrolet Inc.	47.500
48. Rodgers Chevrolet	46.786
49. Wilson Auto Mall	45.893
50. Alan Young Buick-GMC Truck Inc.	44.118

* In millions of dollars, to the nearest thousand. As of Dec. 31, 1998. Prepared by B.E. Research. Reviewed by Mitchell & Titus, L.L.P.

America doesn't respect anything but money. . . . What our people need is a few million-aires.

Madame C. J. Walker

Table 9.3 Black Enterprise's Top 25 Banks, 1999

Company	Loans*
1. Carver Bancorp Inc.	251.005
2. Highland Community Bank	129.700
3. Industrial Bank N.A.	109.169
4. Independence Federal Savings Bank	212.681
5. Seaway National Bank of Chicago	121.606
6. Citizens Trust Bank	118.063
7. The Harbor Bank of Maryland	85.097
8. Liberty Bank and Trust Company	98.650
9. Family Savings Bank FSB	134.800
10. City National Bank of New Jersey	71.400
11. Mechanics and Farmers Bank	95.804
12. Broadway Federal Bank	113.500
13. First Independence National Bank	39.263
14. United Bank of Philadelphia	57.950
15. Illinois Service Federal S&L Association	26.553
16. Consolidated Bank and Trust Company	48.583
17. Tri-State Bank of Memphis	53.800
18. Boston Bank of Commerce	34.687
19. Founders National Bank of Los Angeles	70.000
20. Citizens Federal Savings Bank	76.586
21. Dryades Savings Bank FSB	68.098
22. Douglass National Bank	37.700
23. First Tuskegee Bank	40.540
24. Mutual Community Savings Bank Inc. SSB	48.597
25. Berean Federal Savings Bank	37.900

* In millions of dollars, to the nearest thousand. Ranked by total assets as of Dec. 31, 1998. Prepared by B.E. Research. Reviewed by Mitchell & Titus, L.L.P.

The Dunbar National Bank, established in 1926, was Harlem's first bank managed and staffed by African Americans.

Table 9.4 Black Enterprise's Top Insurance Companies, 1999

Company	Assets (in millions)
1. North Carolina Mutual Life Insurance Co.	215.208
2. Atlanta Life Insurance Co.	201.976
3. Golden State Mutual Life Insurance Co.	102.699
4. Universal Life Insurance Co.	59.503
5. Booker T. Washington Insurance Co.	58.366
6. Protective Industrial Insurance Co.	18.258
7. Winnfield Life Insurance Co.	11.445
8. Williams-Progressive Life & Accident Insurance Co.	8.270
9. Golden Circle Life Insurance Co.	6.924
10. Reliable Life Insurance Co.	6.034

Table 9.5 Black Enterprise's Top 15 Investment Banks, 1999

Company	Senior-Managed Issues (in millions)
1. Siebert Brandford Shank & Co. L.L.C.	2,503.375
2. Utendahl Capital Partners L.P.	1,640.000
3. The Williams Capital Group L.P.	1,541.279
4. Apex Securities, a Division of Rice Financial Products Co.	976.000
5. SBK-Brooks Investment Corp.	826.079
6. Jackson Securities Inc.	749.000
7. Blaylock & Partners, L.P.	678.440
8. M. R. Beal & Co.	530.000
9. Pryor, McClendon, Counts & Co. Inc.*	427.200
10. Walton Johnson & Co.	360.380
11. Powell Capital Markets Inc.	169.785
12. Smith Whiley & Co.	137.935
13. The Chapman Co.	115.000
14. Loop Capital Markets L.L.C.	9.380
15. Harvestons Securities Inc.	5.000

* *Source:* Securities Data/Thomson Financial.
Prepared by B.E. Research. Reviewed by Mitchell & Titus, L.L.P.

 ## ON THE RISE

An August 11, 1998, article in the *New York Times* indicated that black-owned companies begun in storefronts and basements in the 1950s and 1960s, which grew into thriving enterprises in the 1970s and 1980s, are more and more being taken over by large multinational companies. One reason cited was the steadily gaining purchasing power of black consumers.

Table 9.6 Black Enterprise's Top 20 Advertising Agencies, 1999 Billings*

Company	1998 Billings*
1. Burrell Communications Group Inc.	173.872
2. Uniworld Group Inc.	160.355
3. Don Coleman Advertising	137.000
4. The Chisholm-Mingo Group Inc.	78.014
5. Carol H. Williams Advertising	61.000
6. Muse Cordero Chen & Partners Inc.	55.000
7. The Wimbley Group Inc.	45.000
8. Sykes Communications Inc.	24.883
9. R. J. Dale Advertising & Public Relations	24.500
10. E. Morris Communications Inc.	18.200
11. Spike DDB	18.000
12. Anderson Communications	16.300
13. Vince Cullers Advertising	16.000
14. Circulation Experti Ltd.	13.800
15. Caroline Jones Inc.	12.000
16. The King Group Inc.	11.500
17. Jesse Lewis & Associates Inc.	6.800
18. Crawley Haskins & Rodgers Public Relations & Advertising	5.415
19. Images USA	5.000
20. George Beach Inc. T/A Beach Advertising	3.875

* In millions of dollars, to the nearest thousand. As of Dec. 31, 1998.
Prepared by B.E. Research. Reviewed by Mitchell & Titus, L.L.P.

TOP COMPANIES FOR MINORITIES

Source: Lawrence Otis Graham, *The Best Companies for Minorities.* New York: Plume, 1993.

American Telephone and Telegraph (AT&T)
550 Madison Avenue
New York, NY 10022
212-605-5500
Employees: 238,535
Percentage black employees: 15 percent
AT&T's primary business is providing basic telephone service to residential and business customers, but it also provides a wide range of products, systems, and services combining computers, telecommunications, and financing. Under the leadership of CEO Robert Allen, AT&T has actively sought to attract and develop talented minority managers and offers positions in such fields as sales and marketing, business applications/systems programming, manufacturing/operations engineering, and research and development.

Avon Products
9 W. 57th Street
New York, NY 10019
Employees: 6,809

Percentage black employees: 11 percent

One of the largest cosmetic companies in the world, Avon creates and markets lines of cosmetics, fragrances, toiletries, and jewelry throughout the United States and abroad. There are minorities in many high positions throughout the company. Aside from its work in recruiting minorities on college campuses, at job fairs, and from professional organizations, Avon is also well known for its minority employee organizations, such as the Black Professionals of Avon, which offers networking, mentoring, and cultural activities.

 ## EMPOWERMENT ZONES

In 1993, the Clinton Administration secured passage of the Omnibus Budget Reconciliation Act. The measure was designed to promote economic development in less affluent communities. Administered by the Department of Housing and Urban Development, the empowerment zone and enterprise community (EZ/EC) program was designed to operate in both rural and urban areas. Its main functions are to provide technical assistance, loans, grants, and tax credits to qualified businesses and organizations. As of 1997, EZ/ECs were operating in 43 states. In New York City, the Upper Manhattan Empowerment Zone, with a total budget of $300 million in loans and grants and $250 million in tax credits, had approved $15.2 million for 12 projects—ranging from a retail and entertainment complex to a geriatric center—that were expected to provide 1,300 jobs. Information about the program is available from the EZ/EC website (www.ezec.gov) or

USDA EZ/EC
Reporters Building, Room 701
300 Seventh Street, SW
Washington, DC 20004
202-619-7980
800-645-4712

Federal Express Corporation
P.O. Box 727
Memphis, TN 38194
901-369-3600
Employees: 72,048
Percentage black employees: 24.7 percent

Federal Express is an international package- and letter-delivery service that transports cargo across the United States and in more than 130 other countries. There are many minorities in positions of authority at Federal Express, which may partly be explained by their Leadership Effectiveness and Awareness Program (LEAP), designed to help nonmanagement employees work through a leadership-qualification process while being coached by their current manager. It also provides mandatory courses in cultural diversity, teaching cultural sensitivity.

General Mills, Inc.
One General Mills Boulevard
P.O. Box 1113
Minneapolis, MN 55440
612-540-2311
Employees: 96,488
Percentage black employees: 14.2 percent

A packaged-foods company that also owns and operates restaurant chains, General Mills is best known for its "Big G" ready-to-eat cereal division, featuring Cheerios, Wheaties, Total, Trix, and Lucky Charms. General Mills has an impressive record of promoting minorities and working with the minority community in Minneapolis, supporting black entrepreneurship through the Minneapolis Economic Development Association, the Minneapolis YMCA's Black Achievers Program, and an annual Martin Luther King Breakfast. In addition to an aggressive minority-recruitment program, the company has programs such as "Managing a Diverse Workforce" and "Understanding and Managing Diversity" to help support and promote minority employees.

General Motors Corporation
3044 W. Grand Boulevard
Detroit, MI 48202
313-556-5000
Employees: 403,000
Percentage of black employees: 16.8 percent
Through its Chevrolet, Pontiac, Buick, Oldsmobile, Cadillac, and Saturn car divisions and the GMC Truck Division, as well as its General Motors Europe (which includes 50% ownership of Saab and shares of various other auto manufacturers), GMC produces cars, trucks, buses, and aviation equipment. Emblematic of its commitment to minorities is the fact that General Motors is the only one of the Big Three auto manufacturers that has kept its corporate headquarters in Detroit, with its largely black population, and despite the downsizing it has undergone at both management and nonmanagement levels, minority representation has not been reduced; rather, it has increased. Some of the initiatives that GM has undertaken with an eye toward improving minority business relations are the Corporate Minority Dealer Development Department, which helps recruit and train new minority dealers; the General Motors Engineering Excellence Awards Program, which provides scholarships to eight historically black colleges; an Annual Black Collegian Conference in Detroit; and the Black Executives Forum.

Marriott Corporation
Marriott Drive
Washington, DC 20058
301-380-9000
Employees: 188,562
Percentage black employees: 21.6 percent
Marriott Corporation, which runs 698 hotels worldwide, and manages food facilities in office buildings, hospitals, and schools, is one of the world's leading hospitality companies. Not only does the company target minority recruitment as one of the factors of its large percentage of minorities in top positions, but it also runs a program through its Affirmative Action Compliance Department, in which many of the company's managers are rated on their affirmative-action goal-attainment efforts, the outcome of which affects their annual compensation.

Polaroid Corporation
549 Technology Square
Cambridge, MA 02139
617-577-2000
Employees: 8,056
Percentage black employees: 14 percent
Polaroid designs, manufactures, and markets cameras, films, electronic imaging recording devices, filters, and lenses to the consumer, professional, medical, and scientific markets. In the 1970s, Polaroid started both the Black Salaried Women and the Senior Black Managers groups in an effort to

structure a more diverse and improved work environment. Other such groups include Polaroid's Diversity Network Alliance, Affirmative Action Committees, the Team for the Improvement of the Environment for Women and Minorities ("the I Team"), and a companywide Buddy/Mentor Program.

The Prudential Insurance Company of America
751 Broad Street
Newark, NJ 07101
201-802-6000
Employees: 74,637
Percentage black employees: 10.4 percent
Besides offering insurance, annuities, IRAs, and mutual funds, Prudential provides residential real-estate services through a network of credit-card services, real-estate offices, and secured personal loans. Prudential has been actively seeking to increase minority participation within the company since 1966, when it instigated a program called Plans for Progress. It has continued this quest with its Managing Diversity program, a Managing Diversity Training Program, a group called the Minority Interchange, and through its sponsorship of the annual Future Leaders Conference.

Sara Lee Corporation
Three First National Plaza
Chicago, IL 60602
Employees: 62,783
Percentage black employees: 22.2 percent
Best known for its baked goods, Sara Lee is an international manufacturer and marketer of consumer packaged goods and also sells packaged meats under the Hillshire Farm, Jimmy Dean, and Ball Park labels, as well as coffee under the Omnia and Karavan brands, shoe-care products under the Kiwi label, Hanes underwear for men, and hosiery under the L'Eggs, Hanes, Liz Claiborne, and Donna Karan labels. Due to Sara Lee's heavy recruitment at black universities and extensive programs including scholarships, diversity training, and contributions to NAACP, Operation PUSH, the Jackie Robinson Foundation, and the National Urban League, many minorities are in management positions.

The Washington Post Company
1150 15th Street, NW
Washington, DC 20071
202-334-6600
Employees: 6,625
Percentage black employees: 18.6 percent
An international media company, The Washington Post Company owns the paper of the same name, as well as the *Herald* (in Everett, Washington), *Newsweek* magazine, several television stations, cable systems, a syndicated news service, the Stanley H. Kaplan Educational Center, and Legi-Slate, Inc., an online informational service for government-related matters. The treasurer of the corporation, Leonade Jones, is one of the highest-ranking African Americans in corporate America. Her progression to that place of power was made possible, in part, by the commitment the Washington Post has made to minority recruitment, participation in INROADS (the national internship program for minority students), work with the National Association of Black Journalists and the National Association of Minority Media Executives, and its diversity training program called "Valuing Diversity in the Workplace."

OPPORTUNITY ON WALL STREET

The number of African Americans in securities and financial services and sales positions tripled in just over a decade, going from 6,000 in 1984 to 18,000 in 1996. In 1996, African Americans comprised about 6 percent of all professionals in the New York securities industry.

BUSINESS SCHOOLS AT HISTORICALLY BLACK COLLEGES AND UNIVERSITIES

Of the 116 historically black colleges and universities, the following 6 provide Masters of Business Administration degrees.

Alabama A&M University
P.O. Box 1027
Normal, AL 35762
205-851-5000
David B. Henson, President
Ames Heyward, Director of Admissions

Clark Atlanta University
111 James P. Brawley Drive
Atlanta, GA 30314
404-880-8000
Thomas W. Cole, Jr., President
Peggy D. Wade, Associate Director of Admissions

Fayetteville State University
1200 Murchison Road
Fayetteville, NC 28301-4298
910-486-1111
Lloyd V. Hackley, Chancellor
Charles Darlington, Director of Admissions

Grambling State University
Grambling, LA 71245
314-247-2211
Harold W. Lundy, President

Jackson State University
1400 Jon R. Lynch Street
Jackson, MS 39217
601-968-2121
James E. Lyons, Sr., President
Barbara J. Luckett, Director of Admissions & Recruitment

Lincoln University
Jefferson City, MO 65102-0029
314-681-5000
Wendell Rayburn, President

BUSINESS AND TRADE ASSOCIATIONS

Whether curious about starting a new business or career or seeking growth within their current career, many people find the following groups to be helpful and supportive. The listings are alphabetical by state, by city, and then by association name.

ALABAMA

Alabama Minority Supplier Development
   Council, Inc.
3100 Cottage Hill Road, Suite 218
Mobile, AL 36606
205-471-6380

ALASKA

African American Business Council
1577 C Street
Anchorage, AK 99501
907-263-9885
907-263-9886

ARIZONA

African-American Summit (AAS)
5040 E. Shea Boulevard, Suite 260
Phoenix, AZ 85254
602-443-1800
The AAS was formed to encourage closer
cooperation between African Americans and
friends of Africa to strategize and create
meaningful programs to assist with the
development of sub-Saharan African
countries.

CALIFORNIA

Minority Business Development Center
1000 Wilshire Boulevard
Los Angeles, CA 90017
213-892-1632

Southern California Regional Purchasing Council
3325 Wilshire Boulevard, Suite 604
Los Angeles, CA 90010
213-380-7114

African Business Referral Association
1212 Broadway
Oakland, CA 94612
510-238-5170

National Black Chamber of Commerce
117 Broadway
Oakland, CA 94609
510-215-5410

Northern California Purchasing Council
1970 Broadway, Suite 710
Oakland, CA 94612
510-763-8162

Minority Business Development Center
1779 Tribute Road
Sacramento, CA 95815
916-649-2551

Minority Assistance Service
3004 16th Street
San Francisco, CA 94103
415-552-5466

COLORADO

Rocky Mountain Minority Supplier and
    Development Council
Minority Enterprises Inc.
940 Speer Boulevard
Denver, CO 80204
303-595-9638

CONNECTICUT

Minority Entrepreneur Network Association
955 Connecticut Avenue
Bridgeport, CT 06607
203-335-7599

DISTRICT OF COLUMBIA

African American Union
3048 Stanton Road, SE
Washington, DC 20020
202-610-0529

Minority Business Development Agency
14th Street and Constitution Avenue, NW
Washington, DC 20230
202-482-5741
Assists the 100 regional minority business-
development centers nationwide in starting up
and expanding competitive minority-owned
firms by providing managerial counseling,
marketing information, and technical
assistance.

Minority Business Enterprise Legal Defense and
    Education Fund
900 Second Street, Suite 8
Washington, DC 20002
202-289-1700

National Black Leadership Roundtable
1424 Longworth House Building
Washington, DC 20515

National Business League
1511 K Street, NW, Suite 432
Washington, DC 20005
202-737-4430

Group for minority businesspeople, which promotes economic development of minority-owned and -managed businesses, as well as full minority participation within the free-enterprise system. Maintains a file of minority vendors and corporate procurement and purchasing agents.

FLORIDA

Black Business Investment Fund—Central Florida
315 E. Robinson Street
Orlando, FL 32801
407-649-4780

Black Business Investment Corporation
2001 Broadway
West Palm Beach, FL 33404
407-845-8055

GEORGIA

Minority Business Development Agency
1371 Peachtree Street, NE
Atlanta, GA 30367
404-347-3438

Minority Business Referral Service
4336 Covington Highway
Decatur, GA 30035
404-286-4830

ILLINOIS

Chicago Regional Purchasing Council
36 S. Wabash Avenue, Suite 725
Chicago, IL 60603
312-263-0105

Minority Enterprise Development Information Association
7046 S. Crandon Avenue
Chicago, IL 60649
312-324-2927

INDIANA

Minority Business Development Center
4755 Kingsway Drive

Indianapolis, IN 46205
317-257-0327

National Association of African American Enterpreneurs
P.O. Box 1191
Indianapolis, IN 46206
317-466-9556
Provides business planning and marketing support, as well as technical and financial assistance to minority-owned businesses. Other services include matching small businesses with major corporations, setting up major networking events on the local, state, and national level, providing discounts on travel, and other such benefits. Membership is available on an individual, small business, organization, or corporate level.

KENTUCKY

Kentuckiana Minority Supplier Development Council
One Riverfront Plaza
Louisville, KY 40202
502-625-0000

LOUISIANA

Gulf South Minority Purchasing Council
935 Gravier Street, Suite 1710
New Orleans, LA 70112
504-523-7110

MASSACHUSETTS

Minority Business Development Agency
10 Causeway Street
Boston, MA 02110
617-565-6850

MISSISSIPPI

Mississippi Minority Supplier Development Council
P.O. Box 20092
Jackson, MS 39209
601-948-2253

MISSOURI

St. Louis Metropolitan Minority Supplier
    Development Council
4144 Lindell Boulevard
St. Louis, MO 63108
314-534-8916

NEW JERSEY

African Business to Business Program
55 Washington Street
Orange, NJ 07052
201-672-6666

NEW YORK

Upstate New York Regional Minority Purchasing
    Program
4455 Genessee Street
Buffalo, NY 14225
716-632-8422

Interracial Council for Business Opportunity
51 Madison Avenue, Suite 2212
New York, NY 10010
212-779-4360
800-252-4226
Provides business planning and marketing support,
    as well as technical and financial assistance to
    minority-owned businesses. Other services
    include matching small businesses with major
    corporations, setting up major networking events
    on the local, state, and national level, providing
    discounts on travel, and other such benefits.
    Membership is available on an individual, small
    business, organization, or corporate level.

National Minority Business Council, Inc.
235 E. 42nd Street
New York, NY 10017
212-573-2385

National Minority Supplier Development Council
15 W. 39th Street, 9th Floor
New York, NY 10018
212-944-2430
A group of members of regional purchasing
    council, the goal of which is to increase

business opportunities for minority businesses of
all sizes by providing networking, consultations,
advice, information, and technical resources to
all regional and local purchasing councils.

NORTH CAROLINA

Carolinas Minority Supplier Development
    Council
700 E. Stonewall Street, Suite 340
Charlotte, NC 28202
704-373-8731

OHIO

Cincinnati Minority Supplier Development
    Council
300 Carew Tower
441 Vine Street
Cincinnati, OH 45202
513-579-3102

Cleveland Regional Minority Purchasing Council
200 Tower City Center
50 Public Square
Cleveland, OH 44113
216-621-3300

PENNSYLVANIA

New Jersey-Pennsylvania-Delaware Minority
    Purchasing Regional Council
One Winding Drive, Suite 210
Philadelphia, PA 19131
215-578-0964

TENNESSEE

Minority Business Bureau
1828 McCalla Avenue
Knoxville, TN 37915
615-525-7550

Minority Business Development
5 N. Third Street
Memphis, TN 38103
901-527-2298

TEXAS

Dallas–Fort Worth Minority Business
   Development Council
2720 Stemmons Freeway, Suite 1000
Dallas, TX 75207
214-630-0747

VIRGINIA

Virginia Regional Minority Supplier and
   Development Council
201 E. Franklin Street
Richmond, VA 23219
804-780-2322

WASHINGTON

Northwest Minority Supplier Development
   Council
660 S. W. 39th Street
Renton, WA 98055
206-657-6721

WISCONSIN

Minority Business Development
1442 N. Farwell Avenue
Milwaukee, WI 53202
414-289-3422

PROFESSIONAL ASSOCIATIONS

In addition to the assistance given by business and trade associations, some people find the networking opportunities provided by the following professional associations to be invaluable.

> M any times I wondered whether my achievement was worth the loneliness I experienced, but now I realized the price was small. . . . There is nothing ignoble about a black man climbing from the troubled darkness on a white man's ladder, providing he doesn't forsake the others who, subsequently, must escape that same darkness.
>
> Gordon Parks, Sr., "What Their Cry Means to Me," *Life* (May 31, 1963)

Association of African-American Women
   Business Owners
c/o Brenda Alford, Brasman Research
P.O. Box 13933
Silver Spring, MD 20911
301-585-5081

Association of Black Foundation Executives
1828 L Street, NW
Washington, DC 20036
202-466-6512

Black Data Processing Associates
1250 Connecticut Avenue, NW, Suite 700
Washington, DC 20036
202-775-4301

Black Women in Publishing
10 E. 87th Street
New York, NY 10128
212-427-8100

Coalition of Black Tade Unionists
P.O. Box 62268
Washington, DC 20035
202-429-1203
Includes members of 76 labor unions, whose
   goal is to maximize the strength and impact
   of black and other minority workers in
   organized labor through voter registration,
   education, economic development,
   and improvement of employment
   opportunities.

Conference of Minority Public Administrators
1120 G Street, NW
Washington, DC 20005
202-393-7878

Council on Career Development for Minorities
1341 Mockingbird Lane, Suite 412E
Dallas, TX 75247
214-631-3677

Executive Leadership Council
1010 Wisconsin Avenue, NW, Suite 520
Washington, DC 20007
202-298-8226

Inter-American Travel Agents Society
c/o Almeda Travel
1020 Holcombe Boulevard, Suite 1306
Houston, TX 77030
713-799-1001

International Association of Black Business
    Educators
915 S. Jackson
Montgomery, AL 36195
205-293-4124
An organization of deans and directors of business
    departments on historically African American
    college campuses, dedicated to promoting
    development of business-related academic
    programs in order to increase participation of
    minorities in business.

International Association of Black Professional
    Fire Fighters
8700 Central Avenue, Suite 306
Landover, MD 20785
301-808-0804

International Black Writers and Artists
P.O. Box 43576
Los Angeles, CA 90043
213-964-3721

National Association of Black Accountants
7249A Hanover Parkway
Greenbelt, MD 20770
301-474-6222

National Association of Black Hospitality
    Professionals

P.O. Box 8132
Columbus, GA 31908
334-298-4802

National Association of Black-Owned
    Broadcasters
1333 New Hampshire Avenue, Suite 100
Washington, DC 20036
202-463-8970

National Association of Black Women Attorneys
724 Ninth Street, NW, Suite 206
Washington, DC 20001
202-637-3570
Formed to advance jurisprudence and the
    administration of justice through increasing
    opportunities for African American women.
    Also serves as a source of professional
    information for those in law-related fields.

National Association of Black Women
    Entrepreneurs
P.O. Box 1375
Detroit, MI 48231
313-341-7400

National Association of Health Services
    Executives
10230 Little Patuxent Parkway, Suite 1106
Columbia, MD 21044
202-682-3953

National Association of Management Consultants
4200 Wisconsin Avenue, NW, Suite 106
Washington, DC 20016
202-466-1601

National Association of Minority Contractors
1333 F Street, NW, Suite 500
Washington, DC 20004
202-347-8259
A nonprofit advocacy and educational organization
    representing minority contractors throughout the
    contiguous states and the Virgin Islands.

National Association of Minority Media
    Executives
P.O. Box 9806
Arlington, VA 22219
703-556-4119

National Association of Securities Professionals
700 13th Street, NW, Suite 950
Washington, DC 20005
202-434-4535

National Black MBA Association
180 N. Michigan Avenue, Suite 1820
Chicago, IL 60601
312-236-2622
Created to encourage and promote minorities seeking business advancement, membership in this organization comprises MBA graduates and students pursuing the advanced degree.

National Black Police Association
3251 Mt. Pleasant Street, NW
Washington, DC 20010
202-986-2070
Founded as a national voice for African American police officers, the goals of this nonprofit organization are fighting racism and job discrimination while encouraging minorities to join the police force. Programs include minority-recruitment seminars and crime-prevention projects.

National Black Public Relations Society
30 W. Washington, Room 503
Chicago, IL 60602
312-782-7703
Provides a forum for discussion of public-relations topics and concerns for professionals in the advertising, radio, television, business, or nonprofit industries.

National Conference of Black Lawyers
2 W. 125th Street
New York, NY 10027
212-864-4000

National Organization of Minority Architects (NOMA)
NOMA Office Archives
Howard University
School of Architecture and Planning
2366 Sixth Street
Washington, DC 20059
804-788-0338
In cooperation with other associations, professionals, and architectural firms, NOMA seeks to increase the number and influence of minority architects through youth programs and education.

Organization of Black Designers
300 M Street, SW, Suite N-110
Washington, DC 20024
202-488-3838
Promoting the value of diverse design perspectives, this national nonprofit organization encourages the increased visibility, education, empowerment, and interaction of its membership within the community.

CAREER DEVELOPMENT

The following is a list of career-development groups that can both help you prepare for your job search and educate you about the opportunities available.

CALIFORNIA

The Hawkins Company
5455 Wilshire Boulevard, Suite 1406
Los Angeles, CA 90036
213-933-3337
Executive search firm.

Minority Employment Journal
110 S. La Brea Avenue
Inglewood, CA 90301-1768
310-330-3670

Montgomery West
220 Montgomery Street
San Francisco, CA 94104

415-956-6010
Executive search firm.

CONNECTICUT

Minority Placement Services
1229 Albany Avenue
Hartford, CT 06112-2156
203-278-6611

DISTRICT OF COLUMBIA

Black Human Resources Network
1900 L Street, NW
Washington, DC 20036-5002
202-331-7398 or 202-775-1669

GEORGIA

Black Employment & Education
2625 Piedmont Road, NE
Atlanta, GA 30324-3012
404-469-5891

Excel Executive Recruiters
140 Wynchase Lane
Fayetteville, GA 30214
404-719-9745
Executive search firm.

ILLINOIS

Carrington & Carrington Ltd.
39 S. LaSalle Street, Suite 1125
Chicago, IL 60603
312-606-0015
Executive search firm.

MARYLAND

Career Communications Group
729 E. Pratt Street, Suite 504
Baltimore, MD 21202
410-244-7101
The country's largest minority-owned media-
   services company producing information
   about education and careers for African
   American and Hispanic American
   professionals.

MASSACHUSETTS

Minority Employment Program
2345 Main Street
Springfield, MA 01107-1907
413-736-8470
Job training and educational services.

OSA Partners Inc.
2 Park Plaza, Suite 600
Boston, MA 02116
617-357-7333
Executive search firm.

MICHIGAN

Benford & Associates Inc.
300 Town Center, Suite 1333
Southfield, MI 48034
810-351-0250
Executive search firm.

Joe L. Giles & Associates
18105 Parkside Street, Suite 14
Detroit, MI 48221
313-864-0022
Executive search firm.

Wing-Tips & Pumps Inc.
P.O. Box 99580
Troy, MI 48099
810-641-0980
Temporary agency.

MINNESOTA

S.E. Heifner & Associates
3954 Portland Avenue, S, Suite 2
Minneapolis, MN 55407
612-827-0267
Executive search firm.

MISSOURI

INROADS
1221 Locust Street, Suite 410
St. Louis, MO 63103
314-241-7330

Prepares African American, Hispanic American, and Native American high-school and college students for leadership positions within major American corporations in their own communities.

NEW JERSEY

Aces Employment Consultants
P.O. Box 1513
Linden, NJ 07036
908-925-8836
Executive search firm.

Howard Clark Associates
231 S. White Horse Pike
Audubon, NJ 08106
609-467-3725
Executive search firm.

NEW YORK

Milo Research
60 E. 42nd Street, Suite 1762
New York, NY 10017
212-972-2780
Executive search firm.

Minority Temporary Agency Inc.
41 E. 42nd Street
New York, NY 10017-5301
212-697-7500
Temporary agency.

National Minority Business Council Inc.
235 E. 42nd Street
New York, NY 10017
212-573-2385
Education and training in international trade.

P.S.P. Agency
188 Montague Street
Brooklyn, NY 11201

718-596-3786
Executive search firm.

OHIO

Minority Executive Search
6001 Landerhaven Drive
Cleveland, OH 44124-4190
216-449-8034
Executive search firm.

PENNSYLVANIA

Minority Personnel Service
5424 N. Fifth Street
Philadelphia, PA 19120-2802
215-457-5660

Minority Workforce Cooperative
339 Boulevard of the Allies
Pittsburgh, PA 15222-1917
412-281-6321

TENNESSEE

The African American Apprenticeship School
1011 S. Willett Street
Memphis, TN 38114-1846
901-725-5494

WISCONSIN

Minority Employment Recruiting
101 W. Pleasant Street
Milwaukee, WI 53212-3963
414-271-6376

Minority Training Project
6815 W. Capitol Drive
Milwaukee, WI 53216-2056
414-353-7240

FILING A CHARGE WITH THE EQUAL EMPLOYMENT OPPORTUNITY COMMISSION

The Equal Employment Opportunity Commission (EEOC) was established by Title VII of the Civil Rights Act of 1964 for the purpose of enforcing federal laws against employment discrimination. If you believe you have been discriminated against by an employer, labor union, or employment agency when applying for a job or while on the job, because of your race, color, sex, religion, national origin, age, or disability, or you believe that you have been discriminated against because of opposing a prohibited practice or participating in an equal employment opportunity matter, you may file a charge of discrimination with the EEOC. You can file a charge in person, by mail, or by telephone. If there is not an EEOC office in your immediate area, call 800-669-4000 or 800-669-6820 (TDD, telecommunications device for the deaf) for more information. There are strict time frames within which charges of employment discrimination must be filed. To preserve the ability of the EEOC to act on your behalf and to protect your right to file a private lawsuit, you should file your charge with the EEOC within 180 days of the alleged discriminatory act. However, in states or localities where there is an antidiscrimination law, a charge must be presented to that state or local agency. Furthermore, in such jurisdictions, you may file charges with the EEOC within 300 days of the discriminatory act, or 30 days after receiving notice that the state or local agency has terminated its processing of the charge, whichever is earlier. It is best to contact the EEOC promptly when discrimination is suspected. When charges or complaints are filed beyond these time frames, you may not be able to obtain any remedy.

ECONOMIC PROFILE OF AFRICAN AMERICANS

INCOME VERSUS WEALTH

Black gains in income doubled the size of the black middle class between 1982 and 1990 and continue to narrow the chronic income gap between blacks and whites. The greatest gains have been made by dual-income black families, which earned 87 percent of the income of similar white families. However, a stuy by Melvin Oliver and Thomas Shapiro (*Black Wealth/White Wealth*, 1997), sociologists from UCLA and Northeastern University, respectively, indicates that the wealth of black families—measured mainly by real estate, business ownership, stocks and bonds, and savings accounts—has not increased at a comparable pace. Oliver and Shapiro estimated that as of 1984, dual-income African American families possessed only 19 cents of mean financial assets for every dollar possessed by comparable European American families. They attributed this disparity to such factors as continuing discrimination by mortgage lenders and the historic restrictions that prevented African Americans from acquiring assets (such as businesses and homes) that they could pass on to their heirs.

Table 9.7 Household Income, 1970–1995

Year	Number of Households (1,000s)	Percentage Distribution							Median Income (dollars)
		Under $10,000	$10,000– $14,999	$15,000– $24,999	$25,000– $34,999	$35,000– $49,999	$50,000– $74,999	$75,000 and Over	
ALL HOUSEHOLDS									
1970	64,778	14.3	8.0	15.8	16.9	21.3	16.3	7.5	32,229
1980	82,368	13.3	8.7	16.5	14.6	19.3	17.4	10.3	32,795
1990	94,312	12.5	8.1	15.5	14.4	17.7	17.6	14.2	34,914
1995	99,627	12.3	8.7	15.9	14.2	16.9	17.1	14.8	34,076
BLACK									
1970	6,180	25.8	12.7	21.4	15.2	14.2	8.3	2.4	20,432
1980	8,847	26.7	13.2	20.3	12.9	13.9	9.8	3.4	19,932
1990	10,671	26.8	11.2	17.4	13.5	14.1	10.7	6.2	21,777
1995	11,577	24.0	11.5	18.8	13.6	14.6	11.2	6.2	22,393

Table 9.8 Poverty, 1979–1995

Race and Family Status	Number Below Poverty Level (millions)					Percentage Below Poverty Level				
	1979	1990	1993	1994	1995	1979	1990	1993	1994	1995
ALL PERSONS	26.1	33.6	39.3	38.1	36.4	11.7	13.5	15.1	14.5	13.8
In families	20.0	25.2	30.0	29.0	27.5	10.2	12.0	13.6	13.1	12.3
Head of family	5.5	7.1	8.4	8.1	7.5	9.2	10.7	12.3	11.6	10.8
Related children under 18 yrs.	10.0	12.7	15.0	14.6	14.0	16.0	19.9	22.0	21.2	20.2
Singles	5.7	7.4	8.4	8.3	8.2	21.9	20.7	22.1	21.5	20.9
Male	2.0	2.9	3.3	3.3	3.4	16.9	16.9	18.1	17.8	18.0
Female	3.8	4.6	5.1	5.0	4.9	26.0	24.0	25.7	24.9	23.5
BLACK	8.1	9.8	10.9	10.2	9.9	31.0	31.9	33.1	30.6	29.3
In families	6.8	8.2	9.2	8.4	8.2	30.0	31.0	32.9	29.6	28.5
Head of family	1.7	2.2	2.5	2.2	2.1	27.8	29.3	31.3	27.3	26.4
Related children under 18 yrs.	3.7	4.4	5.0	4.8	4.6	40.8	44.2	45.9	43.3	41.5
Singles	1.2	1.5	1.5	1.6	1.6	37.3	35.1	33.4	34.8	32.6

Table 9.9 Recipients of Government Assistance Programs, 1992

	Number of Participants (thousands)					Percentage of Population Participating				
	Major Means-tested Assistance Programs*	AFDC or General Assistance	Food Stamps	Medicaid	Housing Assistance	Major Means-tested Assistance Programs	AFDC or General Assistance	Food Stamps	Medicaid	Housing Assistance
Total, U.S.	33,954	11,862	20,700	23,924	10,878	13.4	4.7	8.2	9.4	4.3
Black	10,507	4,723	7,072	7,683	4,094	33.0	14.8	22.2	24.2	12.9

AFDC = Aid to Families with Dependent Children.
* Covers AFDC, General Assistance, food stamps, Medicaid, and housing assistance.

Table 9.10 Employment, 1996

Age and Race	Total (thousands)	Male (thousands)			Female (thousands)			Percentage of Labor Force			
								Employed		Unemployed	
		Total	Employed	Unemployed	Total	Employed	Unemployed	Male	Female	Male	Female
ALL WORKERS	133,943	72,087	68,207	3,880	61,857	58,501	3,356	94.6	94.6	5.4	5.4
16–19 years	7,806	4,043	3,310	733	3,763	3,190	573	81.9	84.8	18.1	15.2
20–24 years	13,377	7,104	6,429	675	6,273	5,709	564	90.5	91.0	9.5	9.0
25–34 years	33,833	18,430	17,527	903	15,403	14,549	854	95.1	94.5	4.9	5.5
35–44 years	36,556	19,602	18,816	786	16,954	16,235	720	96.0	95.8	4.0	4.2
45–54 years	26,397	13,967	13,483	484	12,430	12,031	399	96.5	96.8	3.5	3.2
55–64 years	12,146	6,693	6,470	223	5,452	5,269	183	96.7	96.6	3.3	3.4
65 years and over	3,828	2,247	2,172	76	1,581	1,518	63	96.6	96.0	3.4	4.0
BLACK	15,134	7,264	6,456	808	7,869	7,086	784	88.9	90.0	11.1	10.0
16–19 years	923	458	289	163	464	324	141	63.1	69.7	36.9	30.3
20–24 years	1,738	848	685	163	890	726	164	80.8	81.6	19.2	18.4
25–34 years	4,305	2,077	1,867	210	2,228	1,984	244	89.9	89.0	10.1	11.0
35–44 years	4,287	2,036	1,878	158	2,251	2,096	155	92.2	93.1	7.8	6.9
45–54 years	2,553	1,204	1,129	75	1,349	1,297	52	93.8	96.1	6.3	3.8
55–64 years	1,073	509	482	26	565	543	21	94.9	96.3	5.1	3.8
65 years and over	255	132	126	7	122	115	7	94.7	94.3	5.0	5.6

Table 9.11 Percentage of African Americans in Selected Occupations, 1983 and 1995

	1983		1995	
Occupation	Total Employed (thousands)	% of Total Black	Total Employed (thousands)	% of Total Black
TOTAL	100,834	9.3	126,708	10.7
Managerial and professional specialty	23,595	5.6	36,497	7.4
Executive, administrative, and managerial	10,722	4.7	17,746	6.9
Officials and administrators, public	417	8.3	636	12.9
Financial managers	357	3.5	621	6.5
Personnel and labor relations managers	106	4.9	122	12.9
Purchasing managers	82	5.1	121	4.6
Managers, marketing, advertising, and public relations	396	2.7	655	2.9
Administrators, education and related fields	415	11.3	668	10.2
Managers, medicine and health	91	5.0	713	8.5
Managers, properties and real estate	305	5.5	530	7.7
Management-related occupations	2,966	5.8	4,374	9.2
Accountants and auditors	1,105	5.5	1,538	8.8
Professional specialty	12,820	6.4	18,752	7.9
Architects	103	1.6	160	2.7
Engineers	1,572	2.7	1,960	4.2
Physicians	519	3.2	667	4.5
Dentists	1,226	2.4	137	1.2
Health assessment and treating occupations	1,900	7.1	2,812	8.7
Teachers, college and university	606	4.4	889	6.5
Teachers, except college and university	3,365	9.1	4,724	9.8
Counselors, educational and vocational	184	13.9	275	15.0
Librarians, archivists, and curators	213	7.8	202	8.0
Social scientists and urban planners	261	7.1	438	9.0
Lawyers and judges	651	2.7	911	3.4
Writers, entertainers, and athletes	1,544	4.8	2,188	6.0
Technical, sales, and administrative support	31,265	7.6	37,683	10.3
Technicians and related support	3,053	8.2	3,926	9.4
Health technologies and technicians	1,111	12.7	1,605	12.2
Engineering and related technologies	8,222	6.1	919	8.5
Science technicians	202	6.6	245	10.6
Technicians, except health, engineering, and science	917	5.0	1,157	5.8
Sales occupations	11,818	4.7	15,404	7.9
Supervisors and proprietors	2,958	3.6	4,501	5.4
Sales reps, finance and business services	1,853	2.7	2,529	6.1
Sales reps, commodities, except retail	1,442	2.1	1,559	3.1
Sales workers, retail and personal services	5,511	6.7	6,728	11.4
Sales-related occupations	54	2.8	87	5.3
Administrative support	16,395	9.6	18,353	12.5
Supervisors	676	9.3	670	13.6
Computer equipment operators	605	12.5	402	13.8
Secretaries, stenographers, and typists	4,681	7.3	3,868	10.3
Information clerks	1,174	8.5	1,927	10.2
Records processing occupations, except financial	866	13.9	911	16.0
Financial records processing	2,457	4.6	2,272	6.8
Duplicating, mail, and other office machine operators	68	16.0	75	13.2
Communications equipment operators	256	27.0	177	21.8
Mail and message-distributing occupations	799	18.1	998	21.3

(continued)

Table 9.II (continued)

Occupation	1983 Total Employed (thousands)	1983 % of Total Black	1995 Total Employed (thousands)	1995 % of Total Black
Material recording, scheduling, and distributing	1,562	10.9	1,922	14.7
Adjusters and investigators	675	11.1	1,598	13.4
Miscellaneous administrative support	2,397	12.5	3,533	13.8
Service occupations	13,857	16.6	17,177	17.2
Private household	980	27.8	804	17.2
Child-care workers	408	7.9	276	13.1
Cleaners and servants	512	42.4	504	18.5
Protective services	1,672	13.6	2,187	17.8
Supervisors, protective service	127	7.7	184	13.1
Firefighting and fire prevention	189	6.7	231	13.5
Police and detectives	645	13.1	960	16.0
Guards	711	17.0	811	22.1
Service, except private households and protective	11,205	16.0	14,186	17.2
Food preparation and service occupations	4,860	10.5	5,906	11.4
Health service occupations	1,739	2.5	2,398	29.4
Cleaning and building service occupations	2,736	24.4	3,125	22.8
Personal service occupations	1,870	11.1	2,756	12.4
Precision, productions, craft, and repair	12,328	6.7	13,587	7.9
Mechanics and repairers, except supervisors	4,158	6.8	4,521	7.4
Construction trades	4,289	6.6	5,108	7.5
Construction trades, except supervisors	3,784	7.1	4,443	7.9
Extractive occupations	196	3.3	130	6.0
Precision production occupations	3,685	7.3	3,828	9.0
Operators, fabricators, and laborers	16,091	14.0	18,197	15.3
Machine operators, assemblers, and inspectors	7,744	14.0	7,874	15.2
Textile, apparel, and furnishings machine operators	1,414	18.7	1,071	19.7
Fabricators, assemblers, and hand working	1,714	11.3	2,071	14.3
Production inspectors, testers, samplers, and weighers	794	13.0	771	12.6
Transportation and material moving occupations	212	6.7	184	11.4
Motor vehicle operators	2,978	13.5	4,025	14.8
Transportation and material moving occupations	212	6.7	184	11.4
Material moving equipment operators	1,011	12.9	1,093	14.4
Handlers, equipment cleaners, helpers, and laborers	4,147	15.1	5,021	16.4
Freight, stock, and material handlers	1,488	15.3	1,929	16.4
Laborers, except construction	1,024	16.0	1,334	17.8
Farming, forestry, and fishing	3,700	7.5	3,566	3.9
Farm operators and managers	1,450	1.3	1,314	0.5
Other agricultural and related occupations	2,072	11.7	2,096	6.0
Farm workers	1,149	11.6	840	3.4
Forestry and logging occupations	126	12.8	108	5.2

Table 9.12 Top 10 Jobs for African Americans, by Percentage of Total Employment within Each Field, 1996

Barber	30.3
Private business mail clerk	29.8
Health-services worker (dental assistant, nursing aide, hospital orderly)	29.4
Welfare aide	28.4
U.S. postal clerk	28.3
Cleaning and building maintenance worker	22.8
Correctional-institution officer	21.1
Private guard	21.1
Social or religious worker	17.1
Factory worker	15.3

Table 9.13 Top 10 Jobs for African Americans, by Number Employed, 1996

Factory worker	1,177,088
Sales representative	933,022
Cleaning and building maintenance worker	712,500
Health-services worker (dental assistant, nursing aide, hospital orderly)	702,012
Administrative clerk	487,554
Teacher	462,952
Secretary	398,404
Mechanics-machine-repair worker	316,000
Social or religious worker	142,101
Private guard	179,231

Table 9.14 Housing Trends, 1990 and 1996

	Number (thousands)				Percentage Distribution			
	Black		White		Black		White	
Housing	1990	1996	1990	1996	1990	1996	1990	1996
Total occupied units	10,486	11,577	80,163	84,511	100.0	100.0	100.0	100.0
Owner occupied	4,445	5,085	54,094	58,282	42.4	43.9	67.5	69.0
Renter occupied	5,862	6,290	24,685	24,798	55.9	54.3	30.8	29.3
No cash rent	178	201	1,384	1,430	1.7	1.7	1.7	1.7

ENTREPRENEURS AND BUSINESS LEADERS

Amos, Wally (1937–). Amos began his business career in the early 1960s as the first African American talent agent for the William Morris Agency, where he handled Simon and Garfunkel, Marvin Gaye, and the Supremes, among others. He founded Famous Amos Chocolate Chip Cookies in Atlanta in 1975, after friends persuaded him to market the treats he baked for clients. Within five years, Amos was selling more than $5 million worth of cookies a year. He sold Famous Amos in 1980 but stayed on as the company's vice chair. Amos has also served as a spokesperson for national literacy campaigns and has written a children's book and an autobiography.

Berry, Edwin C. (1854–1931).   An innovator in the hotel business, Berry began in 1878 with a restaurant in Athens, Ohio. In 1892 he built a 20-room hotel on an adjoining property. Berry eventually expanded his hotel to 55 rooms and became the most successful small-city hotel owner in the United States. He was renowned for serving fine food and attending to all the needs of his patrons. Berry was the first known hotel keeper to provide each room with a clothes closet and with amenities such as needle and thread and cologne.

CINCINNATI

During the early 19th century, Cincinnati emerged as a center of business enterprise among free blacks, who had acquired more than $500,000 worth of property by 1852.

Bing, Dave (1943–   ).   After a successful basketball career with the Detroit Pistons and other teams, Bing entered the business world in 1980 and achieved success by manufacturing steel components for the automobile industry. His firm, the Bing Group, employs 500 men and women and achieved nearly $130 million in sales during 1996.

Binga, Jesse (1865–1950).   Binga began working as a Pullman porter and used some of his savings to invest in Chicago real estate. His investments proved so lucrative that by 1907 he was one of the top black Realtors in the city, opening a number of white neighborhoods to black settlement. In 1921, he created Binga State Bank and made a point of serving black customers, who were largely neglected by white-owned banks. Like so many other institutions, Binga's bank failed after the 1929 stock market crash, and he lost $400,000 of his own money. Charged with embezzlement, Binga was jailed in 1933. He remained a hero to Chicago's African Americans, who petitioned the state government on his behalf, and he was released from prison in 1938. Binga subsequently took a job as a repairperson and lived quietly until his death.

Blaylock, Ronald (1960–   ).   After beginning his business career with Citibank, Blaylock joined Paine Webber in 1986 and became the firm's top salesperson. In 1990 he joined Utendahl Capital Partners as a founding partner; after 18 months at Utendahl, he left to form his own firm. In 1996, Blaylock and Partners became the first minority-owned firm to manage a corporate bond underwriting when it supervised a $150 million issue for the Tennessee Valley Authority.

Bush, George Washington (1790?–1863).   After fighting under Andrew Jackson at the Battle of New Orleans in the War of 1812, Bush worked for the Hudson's Bay Company on the Pacific Coast and then settled in Missouri, where he became wealthy through farming and cattle raising. In 1844, he led a party of settlers to the Oregon Territory, but racism forced him to settle with his family in British-held areas north of the Columbia River. He created a 640-acre farm near present-day Olympia, Washington, and prospered once again. When new settlers entered the territory, Bush supplied them with fruits and vegetables at fair prices, even though he was in a position to charge whatever he wished.

Chenault, Kenneth (1952–   ).   A graduate of Harvard Law School, Chenault began as a Wall Street attorney with Rogers and Wells and moved on to become a management consultant before joining American Express. He became head of the Division of Green Cards in 1981 and has been president of the entire Consumer Card Group since 1993.

Collins, Bert (1934–   ).   After earning business and law degrees, Collins began his career as an accountant. In 1967 he joined North Carolina Mutual Life Insurance, and in 1990 he became the company's president and CEO. The largest black-owned insurance firm in the nation, North Carolina Mutual had more than $213 million in assets in 1996.

Downing, George Thomas (1819–1903).   In addition to serving as a conductor on the Underground Railroad and fighting for civil-rights laws in New York and Rhode Island, Downing became a leading caterer and hotel operator in both New York and Newport during the 1840s. In addition, he ran the restaurant in the U.S. House of Representatives from 1865 to 1877. Over the years, Downing became a significant real-estate owner in Newport and contributed substantial sums for the architectural improvement of the city.

Farr, Mel, Sr. (1944–   ).   A graduate of the University of Detroit, Farr played professional football with the Detroit Lions from 1967 to 1973. He started a Ford dealership in 1975, and the Mel Farr Automotive Group is now the largest black-owned auto dealership in the United States, with annual sales of more than $500 million. Farr also owns a Michigan 7-Up franchise, the first major soft-drink franchise to be completely black owned.

Graves, Earl G.   (See Chapter 17, "The Media.")

Johnson, George E. (1927–   ).   Working as a production chemist for a Chicago cosmetics firm during the early 1950s, Johnson developed a hair preparation for African American men. In 1957 he started his own company to market the Ultra-Sheen line of products. In 1971, the stock of Johnson Products was being sold on the American Stock Exchange, marking the first time that an African American company was listed on a major U.S. stock exchange. In 1993, Johnson Products merged with IVAX Corporation, a white-owned cosmetics and pharmaceutical firm. Johnson now serves as a consultant to IVAX and directs the George E. Johnson Foundation.

Johnson, John H.   (See Chapter 17, "The Media.")

Johnson, Robert L.   (See Chapter 17, "The Media.")

Lafon, Thomy (1810–1893).   Born in New Orleans, the son of free persons of color, Lafon began his career as a teacher. In 1850 he opened a small store and used his profits to make loans and real-estate investments. When New Orleans began rapidly expanding, Lafon emerged as one of the city's leading African American real-estate brokers, amassing a fortune estimated at $500,000. He donated large sums to orphanages and antislavery causes and bequeathed most of his money to charitable institutions. In 1895, the Louisiana legislature voted to commission a bust of Lafon and put the sculpture on permanent display in New Orleans. It was the first time the state had conferred such an honor on an African American.

Lewis, Reginald (1942–1993).   A Harvard-trained lawyer, Lewis practiced corporate law until the 1980s, when he formed his own investment company, the TLC Group. TLC had its first great success in July 1987, when it sold the McCall Pattern Co. for a 90-to-1 return on its initial investment (made three years earlier). Later in the year, Lewis made headlines by engineering a leveraged buyout of Beatrice International Foods for $985 million, creating the largest black-owned company in the United States. In 1992, Lewis was named among *Fortune* magazine's 400 richest Americans, with a net worth estimated at $400 million. After donating $3 million to Harvard in 1992 for the creation of an international law center, he became the first African American to have a building named after him at the university. Lewis was also involved with several other charitable and public-interest organizations until his sudden death from a brain hemorrhage at age 50.

Llewelyn, J. Bruce (1927–   ).   After earning degrees in business, law, and public administration, Llewelyn pursued a varied career in both the public and private sectors, including administrative posts in the Small Business Administration and the New York City Department of Housing and Development. From 1969 to 1982, he served as president of Fedco Food Stores. Llewelyn is currently CEO of Queen City Broadcasting and chair of the Coca-Cola Bottler of Philadelphia.

Merrick, John (1859–1919).   Merrick began working as a barber in Durham, North Carolina, around 1880. He became known for devising a dandruff cure and prospered sufficiently to invest in real estate. In 1898, he founded the North Carolina Mutual Life Insurance Company, along with six other men, who invested $50 apiece. In 1899, the new company's income was only $840, but by 1919 it had risen to $1.6 million, and it remains the nation's largest African American insurance company. During the 20 years he was building his insurance firm, Merrick was the leader of the black business community in Durham. Among the companies he helped develop were the Mechanics and Farmers Bank, the Bull City Drug Company, Merrick-Moore-Spaulding Real Estate, and the Durham Textile Mill.

BLACK BUSINESS CENTERS

The founding of the North Carolina Mutual Life Insurance Company in 1898 stimulated African American entrepreneurship in Durham. By 1949, there were more than 300 black-owned businesses in the city, concentrated in a downtown district nicknamed Hayti. Though urban-renewal projects displaced about one third of the business section during the 1960s, Hayti still thrives today. Other historic centers of post–Civil War black enterprise, such as Wilmington, North Carolina, and Tulsa, Oklahoma, were less fortunate—in 1898, white mobs destroyed the African American business district in Wilmington, and similar atrocities occurred in Tulsa in 1921.

Nail, John E. (1883–1947).   The son of a successful tavern owner, Nail joined with Henry G. Parker to spearhead the movement of African Americans into Harlem at the time of World War I. By 1925, his real-estate firm, Nail and Parker, was managing 50 apartment complexes and had $1 million in income. Nail became the first African American to sit on the Real Estate Board of New York, and he also served on President Herbert Hoover's Commission on Housing. He envisioned building Harlem into a middle-class community of African American home owners, but his dream was shattered by the Great Depression and the subsequent economic decline of the community.

Parsons, Richard (1949–   ).   After attending the University of Hawaii and Union University Law School, Parsons began his career as a Wall Street lawyer and later entered public life as counsel to Governor Nelson Rockefeller of New York and President Gerald R. Ford. In 1988, he became the chief executive of the Dime Savings Bank and is now president of Time Warner. He has also served as chair of the New York City Economic Development Corporation, chair of the New York City Chamber of Commerce, and chair of the Upper Manhattan Empowerment Zone.

Procope, Ernesta Gertrude.   The daughter of West Indian immigrants, Procope trained to be a classical pianist. She ultimately found herself managing E. G. Bowman & Co., an insurance firm started by her first husband, who died in 1952. The company took off during the 1960s, when urban rioting caused many large insurance firms to pull out of the inner cities. Working with New York State, Procope helped set up the FAIR plan to provide insurance in black communities, and E. G. Bowman is now the leading insurance broker for independent churches. In 1979, Procope's company became the first black-owned brokerage to acquire Fortune 500 clients.

Sims, Naomi (1949–   ).   A trailblazing fashion model who was also the first African American woman to appear in a television commercial, Sims went on to establish her own fashion line, the Naomi Sims Collection, in 1973. She has also written a number of books on modeling careers, business ventures, and personal care, all directed at African American women. She is currently head of Naomi Sims Beauty Products Limited.

Smith, Stephen (1779?–1873).   Smith became an indentured servant at age five, and by his teens, he was managing the lumber holdings of his wealthy employer. By 1816 he was able to purchase his freedom, and he subsequently began a lumber and real-estate business in Columbia, Pennsylvania. In 1834, a white mob attacked his office, but he refused to be forced out of business. Smith moved his operations to Philadelphia in 1842, joining forces with William Whipper to open a large coal yard and lumberyard at the corner of Broad and Willow Streets. Before long, Smith owned 52 houses in Philadelphia, in addition to properties in other towns and stock in various companies, prompting the antislavery activist Martin Delany to call him "the most wealthy colored man in the United States." Smith was also a dedicated abolitionist, an official in the African Methodist Episcopal Church, and a benefactor of such charities as Philadelphia's House for Aged and Infirm Colored Persons.

Spraggins, Marianne.   After teaching at New York Law School from 1977 to 1979, Spraggins moved to Wall Street, and by 1988 she was a first vice president at Prudential Bache. In 1990, she joined Smith Barney, Harris Upham & Co. as the first female African American managing director on Wall Street.

Utendahl, John O. (1956–   ).   After receiving an M.B.A. from Columbia, Utendahl began his Wall Street career with Salomon Brothers and moved on to become a successful corporate bond trader at Merrill Lynch. In 1992, he founded Utendahl Capital Partners, which is currently the largest black-owned U.S. investment firm. Utendahl's company has been involved in the structuring, placing, and underwriting of more than $250 billion in securities; an affiliated company, Utendahl Capital Management, has managed more than $500 million in assets for a variety of blue-chip clients.

Walker, Madame C. J. (1867–1919).   Born Sarah Breedlove in Louisiana, Walker moved to St. Louis with her baby daughter in 1887, following the death of her first husband. For many years she worked as a launderer, while developing a number of hair preparations. In 1906, she moved to Denver, married journalist Charles J. Walker, and began marketing her products. By 1910, Walker was able to build a manufacturing plant in Indianapolis and was soon a millionaire. She employed 3,000 workers and inspired numerous other entrepreneurs. Walker lived in grand style, building a town house on 136th Street in New York and a country home, Villa Lewaro, in Irvington-on-Hudson. At the same time, she was devoted to social causes, founding numerous charities, an industrial school, and a mission in West Africa. She organized her sales representatives into Walker Clubs and gave cash prizes to those who performed community service.

Walker, Maggie Lena (1867–1934).   Growing up in Richmond, Walker became an advocate of civil rights and feminism while still in her teens. At age 14, she joined the Independent Order of St. Luke (IOSL), a black mutual-aid society formed after the Civil War. In 1890, when Walker became the grand secretary of the society, IOSL's funds totaled $31; by 1924, she built the organization's assets up to $3.5 million. Walker founded the St. Luke Penny Savings Bank in 1903 and became the first female bank president in the United States. By 1920, the bank had financed 645 black-owned homes. Walker's management was so effective that the Penny Savings Bank survived the Great Depression and still exists today, although it has changed its name, following a merger.

Wright, Deborah C. (1958–   ).   After graduating from Harvard Business School, Wright spent three years in corporate finance at First Boston before moving into the public sphere. In 1992, Mayor David E. Dinkins appointed Wright to the board of the New York Housing Authority, and in 1994 she became Commissioner of Housing, Preservation, and Development in the Giuliani Administration. Two years later, she was recruited by Richard Parsons to become president of the Upper Manhattan Empowerment Zone and take charge of allocating $550 million in grants, loans, and tax credits. In June 1999, she was named president and CEO of Carver Bank.

SOURCES FOR ADDITIONAL INFORMATION

Amos, Wally. *The Famous Amos Story.* Garden City, NY: Doubleday, 1983.

Bailey, Ronald W., ed. *Black Business Enterprise: Historical and Contemporary Perspectives.* New York: Basic Books, 1971.

Biddle, Stanton F., ed. *The African-American Yellow Pages: A Comprehensive Resource Guide and Directory.* New York: Holt, 1996.

Black Americans Information Directory, 3rd ed. Detroit: Gale, 1993.

Broadnax, Derek. *The Black Entrepreneur's Guide to Million-Dollar Business Opportunities.* Austin, TX: Black Entrepreneurs Press, 1990.

———. *The Black Entrepreneur's Guide to Money Sources.* Austin, TX: Black Entrepreneurs Press, 1990.

Butler, John Sibley. *Entrepreneurship and Self-help among Black Americans.* Albany: SUNY Press, 1991.

Fraser, George C. *Success Runs in Our Race: The Complete Guide to Networking in the African American Community.* New York: Morrow, 1994.

Graham, Lawrence Otis. *The Best Companies for Minorities.* New York: Plume, 1993.

Graves, Earl G. *How to Succeed in Business without Being White.* New York: HarperBusiness, 1997.

Green, Shelley, and Paul Pride. *Black Entrepreneurship in America.* New Brunswick, NJ: Transaction, 1990.

Harris, Abram L. *The Negro as Capitalist.* College Park, MD: McGrath, 1936.

Lewis, Reginald F. *"Why Should White Guys Have All the Fun?"* New York: Wiley, 1995.

"The New Black Power." *Fortune,* August 4, 1997.

Oliver, Melvin L., and Thomas M. Shapiro. *Black Wealth/White Wealth: A New Perspective on Racial Inequality.* New York: Routledge, 1997.

Pierce, Joseph A. *Negro Business and Business Education.* New York: Harper & Row, 1947.

10

Science and Technology

SCIENCE TIME LINE

1773   James Durham becomes the first recognized black physician in the United States when he is hired by a New Orleans doctor to perform medical services.

1821   Thomas L. Jennings is the first African American to obtain a patent, for a dry-cleaning process.

1837   James McCune Smith receives a medical degree from the University of Glasgow, in Scotland, becoming the first African American M.D.

1847   David J. Peck becomes the first black to graduate from a U.S. medical school (Rush Medical College, Chicago).

1863   Alexander Thomas Augusta becomes the first black surgeon in the U.S. Army.

1864   Rebecca Lee becomes the first African American woman to earn a medical degree when she graduates from the New England Female Medical College in Boston.

1867   Robert Tanner Freeman earns a degree in dentistry from Harvard University, an African American first.

1876   Edward Alexander Bouchet earns a Ph.D. in physics from Yale, the first African American to receive that degree. (Because of his race, Bouchet could not pursue a scientific career; he taught physics and chemistry for 26 years at the Institute for Colored Youth in Philadelphia.)

1881   Charles Burleigh Purvis becomes the first black physician to head a hospital under civilian auspices when he takes over Fredmen's Hospital in Washington, D.C.

1891   Provident Hospital in Chicago, founded by Daniel Hale Williams, is the first hospital operated by African Americans.

1913   Henry Edwin Baker, a black assistant examiner in the U.S. Patent Office, publishes the first list of African American inventors, *The Black Inventor*; 400 names were on the list.

1915   Julian Herman Lewis is the first African American to gain a Ph.D. in physiology (University of Chicago).

1916   The first African American to gain a Ph.D. in chemistry is St. Elmo Brady of the University of Illinois.

1925   Elbert Frank Cox becomes the first African American to achieve a doctorate in pure mathematics, earning a Ph.D. from Cornell University.

1932   Robert Stewart Jason (University of Chicago) is the first African American to gain a Ph.D. in pathology.

1935   Jesse Jarue Mark becomes the first African American to receive a doctorate in botany (Iowa State University).

1936   Roscoe Lewis McKinney is the first African American to earn a Ph.D. in anatomy (University of Chicago).

1940   Samuel M. Nabrit is the first African American appointed to the Atomic Energy Commission.

1948   The first African American Ph.D. in pharmacology is Ray Clifford Darlington of Ohio State University.

1949   William Augustus Hinton becomes the first black professor at Harvard Medical School.

1961   Harvey Washington Banks earns a Ph.D. in astronomy from Georgetown University, the first African American to obtain a doctorate in that field.

NASA astronauts (clockwise from top left) Colonel Guion (Guy) S. Bluford, Dr. Ronald McNair (who died in the Challenger disaster), and Colonel Fredrick D. Gregory.

1980   Physicist John B. Slaughter was named director of the National Science Foundation, the first African American to hold the post. He occupied the directorship from 1980 to 1982.

1983   Guion S. Bluford Jr. becomes the first African American to orbit the Earth.

1987   Mae C. Jemison becomes the first black female astronaut.

1993   David Satcher becomes the first black director of the Centers for Disease Control.

NOTABLE INVENTIONS AND INNOVATIONS

Ashbourne, A. P.	Biscuit cutter (1875)
Bailey, L. C.	Folding bed (1899)
Beard, A. J.	Rotary engine (1892), car coupler (1897)
Becket, G. E.	Letter box (1892)
Bell, L.	Locomotive smokestack (1871)
Binga, M. W.	Street-sprinkling apparatus (1879)
Blackburn, A. B.	Railway signal (1888)
Blackwell, David H.	Contribution to mathematical probability and decision theory (1950–1965)
Blair, Henry	Corn planter (1834), cotton planter (1836)
Boone, Sarah	Ironing board (1892)
Bramwell, Fitzgerald	Carbon-based superconductor development (1975–1985)
Brooks, C. B.	Street sweepers (1896)

Brown, L. E.	Bridle bit (1892)
Brown, O. E.	Horseshoe (1892)
Burr, J. A.	Lawnmower (1899)
Burr, W. F.	Railway switching device (1899)
Butts, J. W.	Luggage carrier (1899)
Campbell, W. S.	Self-setting animal trap (1881)
Cook, G.	Automatic fishing device (1899)
Cooper, J.	Elevator device (1895)
Cornwell, P. W.	Draft regulator (1888)
Cralle, A. L.	Ice cream mold (1895)
Darkins, J. T.	Ventilation aid (1895)
Davis, W. D.	Riding saddles (1896)
Davis, W. R., Jr.	Library table (1878)
Dickinson, J. H.	Pianola (1899)
Dorsey, O.	Door-holding device (1878)
Dorticus, C. J.	Photo-embossing machine (1895), photographic-print wash (1895)
Downing, P. B.	Electric switch for railroad (1890)
Elkins, T.	Refrigerating apparatus (1879)
Faulkner, H.	Ventilated shoe (1890)
Ferrel, F. J.	Apparatus for melting snow (1890)
Fleming, R. F., Jr.	Guitar variant (1886)
Fuller, A. Oveta	AIDS and virus cell research (1979–1990)
Grant, George F.	Golf tee (1899)
Grant, W.	Curtain rod support (1896)
Gray, R. H.	Baling press (1894)
Grenon, H.	Razor-stropping device (1896)
Griffith, F. W.	Pool-table attachment (1899)
Haines, J. H.	Portable basin (1897)
Hall, Lloyd A.	Asphalt emulsion (1932), puncture-sealing composition (1944), stable dry papain ingredient used in meat tenderizer (1949)
Harding, F. H.	Extension banquet table (1898)
Harper, Solomon	Electric hair treatment (1930), thermostatically controlled hair curlers (1953)
Headen, M.	Foot-power hammer (1886)
Hunter, J. H.	Portable weighing scales (1895)
Jackson, B. F.	Gas burner (1899)
Jackson, Shirley Ann	Electrical ceramic superconductors (1982)
Jackson, W. H.	Railway switch (1897)
Johnson, I. R.	Bicycle frame (1899)
Johnson, W.	Eggbeater (1884)
Jones, Frederick M.	Ticket-dispensing machine (1939), air-conditioning unit (1949), thermostat and temperature-control system (1960)
Julian, Percy L.	Preparation of cortisone (1954)
Latimer, Lewis H.	Carbon filament for electric lamp (1882)
Latimer & Tregoning	Globe support for electric lamps (1882)
Lavalette, W. A.	Printing press (1878)
Lewis, A. L.	Window cleaner (1892)
Love, L. J.	Pencil sharpener (1897)
Marshall, T. J.	Fire extinguisher (1872)
Matzeliger, Jan Ernst	Lasting machine (1883), nailing machine (1896)

McCoy, Elijah	Lubricator for steam engines (1872), ironing table (1874), steam-cylinder lubricator (1876), lubricator for safety valves (1887), lawn-sprinkler design (1899)
McCree, D.	Portable fire escape (1890)
Miles, A.	Elevator (1887)
Morgan, Garrett A.	Gas mask and helmet (1914), traffic signal (1923)
Murray, George W.	Fertilizer distributor (1894), planter (1894)
Newson, S.	Oil heater or cooker (1894)
O'Conner & Turner	Alarm for boilers (1896), steam gauge (1896)
Perry, John	Electrochemical fuel cell (1962–1970)
Phelps, W. H.	Apparatus for washing vehicles (1897)
Pickering, J. F.	Airship (1900)
Pinn, T. B.	File holder (1880)
Prather, A. G. B.	Human-powered glider aircraft (1973)
Purdy, W.	Tool-sharpening device (1896)
Purvis, William B.	Fountain pen (1890), electric railway (1894), electric railway switch (1897)
Reed, J. W.	Dustpan (1897)
Reynolds, Humpfrey H.	Safety gate for bridges (1890)
Richardson, A. C.	Churn (1891), casket-lowering device (1894), insect destroyer (1899)
Richardson, W. H.	Cotton chopper (1896), child's carriage (1889)
Richey, C. V.	Railroad switch (1897), fire-escape bracket (1897)
Rickman, A. L.	Overshoe (1898)
Ricks, J.	Overshoe for horses (1899)
Robinson, E. R.	Electric railway trolley (1893)
Robinson, J.	Dinner pail (1887)
Robinson, J. H.	Lifesaving guard for locomotives (1899), lifesaving guard for streetcars (1899)
Ross, Archia L.	Trousers support (1899)
Rouse, Carl A.	Material for shielding nuclear-power plants (1978)
Sampson, G. T.	Clothes drier (1892)
Scottron, S. R.	Adjustable window cornice (1880), curtain rod (1892)
Shorter, D. W.	Feed rack (1887)
Smith, J. W.	Lawn sprinkler (1897)
Snow & Johns	Liniment (1890)
Spears, H.	Portable shield for infantry (1870)
Spikes, R. B.	Automatic gear shift (1932), multiple-barrel machine gun (1940)
Standard, J.	Oil stove (1889), refrigerator (1891)
Stewart & Johnson	Metal-bending machine (1887)
Stewart, E. W.	Punching machine (1887), machine for forming vehicle seat bars (1887)
Stewart, T. W.	Station indicator for railways (1893)
Sutton, R. H.	Cotton cultivator (1874)
Taylor, B. H.	Rotary engine (1878)
Thomas, S. E.	Waste trap (1883)
Toliver, G.	Propeller for vessels (1891)
Walker, P.	Machine for cleaning seed cotton (1897)
Waller, J. N.	Shoemaker's cabinet or bench (1880)
Washington, W.	Corn-husking machine (1883)
Watts, J. R.	Bracket for miner's lamp (1893)
West, E. H.	Weather shield (1899)
West, J. W.	Wagon (1870)

Willams, C.	Canopy frame (1892)
Winn, F.	Direct-acting steam engine (1888)
Woods, Granville T.	Steam-boiler furnace (1884), telephone transmitter (1884), electromagnetic brake (1887), railway telegraph (1887), overhead conducting system for electric railway (1888), tunnel construction for electric railway (1888), galvanic battery (1888), automatic safety cutout (1889)
Wormley, J.	Lifesaving apparatus (1881)
Wright, Jane C.	Cancer-treatment therapy (1968–1980)

SCIENTIFIC AND TECHNICAL ORGANIZATIONS

American Association of Blacks in Energy
927 15th Street, NW, Suite 200
Washington, DC 20005
202-371-9530
Open to energy professionals, consultants, educators, and students.

Association of Black Sociologists
Howard University
P.O. Box 302
Washington, DC 20059
202-806-6853
Presents an annual award to an African American graduate student who has excelled in the field; conducts research programs; publishes the ABS Newsletter.

National Association of Black Geologists and Geophysicists
P.O. Box 720157
Houston, TX 77272
713-778-7128

National Network of Minority Women in Science
c/o American Association for the Advancement of Science
Directorate for Education and Human Resource Programs
1333 H Street, NW
Washington, DC 20005
202-326-6670

National Organization for Professional Advancement of Black Chemists and Chemical Engineers
525 College Street, NW
Washington, DC 20059
202-667-1699

National Society of Black Engineers
P.O. Box 25588
Alexandria, VA 22313
703-549-2207
Seeks to promote scholastic achievement, encourage the attainment of degrees, and enhance the standing of black students; offers tutorial and counseling services and assists with job placement.

National Society of Black Physicists
c/o North Carolina A & T State University
1610 E. Market Street
101 Martena Hall
Greensboro, NC 27411
919-334-7646
Open to professional physicists, holders of Ph.D.s in physics, and physics Ph.D. candidates.

Young Black Programmers Coalition
P.O. Box 1051
Vicksburg, MS 39181
601-631-7191

SCIENTISTS AND INVENTORS

Banneker, Benjamin (1731–1806).   Born free on a hundred-acre Maryland tobacco farm owned by his parents, Banneker taught himself mathematics, astronomy, and surveying. In 1791, he assisted Major Andrew Elicott in surveying the site for the new national capital in the District of Columbia. The following year he published his first almanac. The book sold in great numbers, and Banneker brought out a new edition every year until 1797. Though he had no formal training, his calculations of celestial bodies compared favorably to those compiled by the leading scientists of the day.

Bluford, Guion Stewart, Jr. (1942–   ).   After graduating from Penn State, Bluford enlisted in the Air Force and flew 144 combat missions in Vietnam, attaining the rank of lieutenant colonel. He earned an M.S. degree from the Air Force Institute of Technology in 1974 and a Ph.D. in 1978. In 1979, Bluford joined NASA's astronaut program. As a member of the crew on the *Challenger* space shuttle flight launched on August 30, 1983, he became the first African American to orbit the Earth. Bluford took part in two subsequent space missions (1985 and 1991), logging a total of 314 hours in space. After earning numerous medals and awards, he retired as an astronaut in 1993 to pursue a career in industry.

Boykin, Otis (1920–1982).   Educated at Fisk University and Illinois Institute of Technology, Boykin began his career as a laboratory assistant and quickly showed his brilliance as an innovator. Among the devices he invented were various resistors used in guided missiles, computers, radios, and televisions; a burglar-proof cash register; a chemical air filter; and a control unit for cardiac pacemakers. From 1964 until his death, Boykin worked as a consultant to a number of American and European firms.

Carruthers, George R. (1939–   ).   A native of Cincinnati, Carruthers was educated at the University of Illinois, where he earned degrees in physics (B.A. 1961, M.A. 1962) and astronomical engineering (Ph.D. 1964). Between 1964 and 1982, he held the post of Rocket Astronomy Research Physicist at NASA. In addition to conducting research on atomic nitrogen recombination, Carruthers played a leading role in the design of lunar-surface ultraviolet cameras. Since 1983, he has been editor of the *Journal of the National Technical Association* and chair of its Editing and Review Committee.

Carver, George Washington (1864–1943).   After earning bachelor's and master's degrees at Iowa State College, Carver joined the staff of the Tuskegee Institute as director of the Department of Agricultural Research. Embarking on a mission to improve the economy of the South and better the lot of African Americans, Carver produced more than 400 different products from the peanut, sweet potato, and pecan. On weekends, he visited poor farmers and taught them to diversify their crops, conserve soil, and improve their yields. He also derived useful products from cotton waste and discovered a method of extracting pigments from local clay. In 1953, Congress recognized his contributions by declaring his Diamond, Missouri, birthplace a national monument.

> I wanted to know the name of every stone and flower and insect and bird and beast. I wanted to know where it got its color, where it got its life—but there was no one to tell me.
>
> George Washington Carver, quoted in *American Life* (November 1923)

Chappelle, Emmett W. (1925–   ).   After attending the University of California and the University of Washington, Chappelle conducted research at Stanford from 1958 to 1963. He spent the next 10 years at Hazelton Laboratories as a biochemist, exobiologist, and astrochemist. In 1977, Chappelle took up a post at NASA's Goddard Space Flight Center, where he studied the effects of acid rain on chlorophyll. Along with Grace Piccolo, Chappelle developed a method for the immediate detection of bacteria in water, leading to valuable research on urinary infections and their treatment.

Coleman, John William (1929–   ).   After graduating from Howard University with a B.S. in 1950, Coleman joined the National Bureau of Standards as a physicist. He obtained an M.S. from the University of Illinois in 1957 and then served as an instructor in physics at Howard before joining RCA as an engineer in 1958. He earned a Ph.D. from the University of Pennsylvania in 1963, after writing a dissertation on the physics of electrons. His work at RCA contributed substantially to the development of the electron microscope.

Drew, Charles Richard　(See Chapter 8, "Health.")

Fuller, Solomon Carter　(See Chapter 8, "Health.")

Gourdine, Meredith C. (1929–).　After studying engineering physics at Cornell (B.S. 1953) and the California Institute of Technology (Ph.D. 1960), Gourdine undertook pioneering research in the field of gas dynamics. His work produced new techniques for removing smoke from buildings and dispersing fog on airport runways. Gourdine also invented the focus-flow heat sink, which is used for cooling computer chips. After working for a number of companies in the field of jet propulsion, he established Gourdine Laboratories in 1964, employing 150 staff members. Gourdine is currently president of Energy Innovation, Inc., in Houston. He was inducted into the Engineering and Science Hall of Fame in 1994.

Hall, Lloyd Augustus (1894–1971).　After earning a Ph.D. at Northwestern University in 1914, Hall worked as a chemist in industry for 45 years and served in U.S. government posts during both world wars. He held more than a hundred patents for meat-curing products, emulsions, bakery products, and other inventions. Most of the food preservatives in use today have derived from Hall's work. After retiring as technical director of Griffith's Laboratories in Chicago, Hall served as a consultant to the United Nations Food and Agriculture Organization.

Harris, James Andrew (1932–).　After earning a B.S. in chemistry in 1953, Harris went to work at the Lawrence Berkeley Laboratory in California. Specializing in nuclear chemistry research, he was a member of the team that identified two new elements: unnilquadium (104) and unnilpentium (105), in 1969 and 1970, respectively. In 1977, Harris became head of Lawrence Berkeley's Engineering and Technical Services Division.

Hinton, William Augustus　(See Chapter 8, "Health.")

Jackson, Shirley Ann (1946–).　A native of Washington, D.C., Jackson earned a Ph.D. in theoretical solid-state physics from the Massachusetts Institute of Technology in 1973, the first African American woman to achieve that distinction. After holding a number of prestigious research posts, she was appointed professor of physics at Rutgers University in 1976. Between 1991 and 1995, she also served as a consultant to AT&T Bell Laboratories. In 1995, Jackson returned to Washington as head of the Nuclear Regulatory Commission.

Jemison, Mae C. (1956–).　After obtaining a B.S. in chemistry and a B.A. in Afro-American studies from Stanford University, Jemison graduated from Cornell Medical College in 1981. After two years in private practice, she joined the Peace Corps and served as a medical officer in West Africa for two years. Seeking new challenges, Jemison joined NASA's astronaut program in 1987. When the space shuttle *Endeavour* was launched on September 12, 1992, Jemison was on board as a science specialist and the first African American woman in space. After earning a Ph.D. from Lincoln University, Jemison retired from NASA in 1993 to pursue a career in technology and science education. She is currently head of the Houston-based Jemison Group, Inc. Projects sponsored by the firm include both a satellite-based telecommunications system for delivery of health-care services in West Africa and The Earth We Share, an international science camp for teenagers. Jemison is also a professor of environmental studies at Dartmouth College and directs Dartmouth's Jemison Institute for Advancing Technology in Developing Countries.

Jones, Frederick McKinley (1893–1961).　McKinley began his working life as an auto mechanic, branched out into farm machinery, and mastered electronics on his own. In 1930, he took a job with a Minneapolis firm that manufactured sound equipment for movie theaters. In 1939, Jones was granted a patent for an automatic ticket-dispensing machine, and the following year he won another patent for the first practical air-conditioning unit suitable for trucks and railway cars. His employer, Joseph A. Numero, promptly sold the sound equipment company and formed the U.S. Thermal Control Company in partnership with Jones. As Jones's cooling units revolutionized the food industry, the company's business boomed to an annual volume of $3 million by 1949. During World War II, Jones designed portable cooling units for supplies in U.S. Army hospitals. In all, he held more than 60 patents, 40 of them for refrigeration devices.

Julian, Percy Lavon (1899–1975).   Educated at DePauw University, Harvard University, and the University of Vienna, Julian chaired the Chemistry Department at Howard University before joining the Glidden Company in 1936 as director of research. In 1953 he founded his own company, Julian Laboratories, Inc. Specializing in the adaptation of soybean products to commercial and medical uses, Julian held more than 100 patents. His work led to advances in the manufacture of drugs, hormones, vitamins, paint, and paper. Especially notable was his work on a synthetic cortisone, Compound S, which was used in treating glaucoma and led to synthesizing the hormones progesterone and testosterone. During World War II, Julian also isolated a protein that became the essential ingredient in a firefighting compound employed by the U.S. Navy. In private life, Julian struck a blow for racial equality when he became one of the first blacks to live in the city of Oak Park, Illinois, refusing to be intimidated even after his home was firebombed on two occasions. In 1973, he was elected to the National Academy of Sciences and the American Academy of Arts and Sciences.

Just, Ernest Everett (1883–1941).   Born in South Carolina, Just went north at age 17 and then graduated magna cum laude from Dartmouth College in 1907. He began teaching English at Harvard, but then he switched to biology and earned a Ph.D. in zoology from the University of Chicago in 1916. Supported by research grants during the 1920s, he produced 38 research papers on fertilization, embryology, and cellular physiology. Just was elected vice president of the American Society of Zoologists in 1930 and was invited to join the editorial boards of the leading zoological journals. Weary of racial restrictions in the United States, he took up a series of research posts in Europe and remained there until World War II broke out. Shortly after returning home, Just died in Washington, D.C. His image has been featured on a $0.32 U.S. postage stamp.

Kountz, Samuel Lee, Jr.   (See Chapter 8, "Health.")

Latimer, Lewis Howard (1848–1928).   Born in Massachusetts, Latimer enlisted in the Union Navy at age 15 and saw action on the James River. After the war, he worked as an office boy in a patent office and taught himself to be a patent drafter. He became acquainted with Alexander Graham Bell, then teaching at a nearby school, and drew the blueprints for the components of Bell's telephone, patented in 1876. Latimer was then hired as a drafter by the U.S. Electric Lighting Company in Bridgeport, Connecticut, and began to learn about electricity. In 1881, Latimer invented a carbon filament for the Maxim incandescent lamp and was assigned to supervise the installation of electric lighting in New York, Philadelphia, Montreal, and London. He began working with Thomas Edison in 1883 and joined the prestigious group of scientists and inventors known as the Edison Pioneers in 1918. Latimer's modest frame house in Flushing, New York, was designated a New York City landmark in 1995.

Massey, Walter E. (1938–   ).   After earning a Ph.D. in physics from Washington University in 1966, Massey spent seven years doing research at the University of Chicago's Argonne National Laboratory, investigating the behavior of various substances at extremely low temperatures. After serving as a professor of physics at Brown University from 1973 to 1979, Massey was appointed director of the Argonne Laboratory, where he manages a staff of 5,000 and an annual budget of nearly $250 million. In 1991, Massey was named director of the National Science Foundation, the first African American to hold the post.

SCIENCE CAREERS

A 1992 survey by the National Science Foundation indicated the following representation of African Americans in the U.S. science and engineering labor force:

Natural scientists	12,060	(3%)
Math and computer scientists	60,270	(7%)
Engineers	63,760	(4%)

Matzeliger, Jan Ernst (1852–1889).   Born in Surinam, Matzeliger apprenticed in machine shops run by his father, a Dutch engineer. He went to sea as a young man, settled in Massachusetts, and got a job in a shoe factory. Working on his own, he designed a lasting machine (for shaping the top of the shoe), secured a patent in 1883, and demonstrated his invention two years later. Matzeliger's machine could produce between 150 and 700 pairs of shoes a day, compared to a maximum output of 50 pairs by a skilled handworker. Marketed by the United Shoe Machinery Company, Matzeliger's shoe laster revolutionized the shoe industry. Unfortunately, Matzeliger died of tuberculosis before the impact of the machine could be felt, and he made little money from his invention.

McCoy, Elijah (1843–1929).   McCoy was born in Ontario, Canada, the son of escaped slaves from Kentucky. He learned mechanical engineering as a young man but could not find work in that field because of racial discrimination. While working as a firefighter on the Michigan Central Railroad, he invented a number of lubricators for steam engines. By selling the patents for these devices, McCoy was able to open his own machine shop. By the end of his career, his inventions—which included a folding iron table and a buggy-top support—had earned a total of 42 patents. His products were held in such esteem that customers were known to ask, "Is this the real McCoy?", giving rise to a popular metaphor for undisputed quality.

Morgan, Garrett A. (1875–1963).   Morgan first employed his mechanical talents in 1907, when he began repairing and selling sewing machines. While operating a successful tailor shop in Cleveland, he invented a gas mask and helmet that could be used in underground rescue work and in chemical spraying. The device was patented in 1914 and was used during World War I. In 1923, Morgan secured a patent for an automated traffic signal and sold the patent to General Electric. While pursuing his career as an inventor and entrepreneur, he was also a newspaper publisher and a civic leader in Cleveland.

Rillieux, Norbert (1806–1884).   Born in New Orleans, Rillieux was the son of a French planter and a black woman. His father sent him to be educated in France. At age 24, he became an instructor in applied mechanics at the École Centrale in Paris, the youngest man ever to join the faculty. After returning to New Orleans, Rillieux patented a vacuum-pan evaporator for sugar refining in 1843. Rillieux's invention revolutionized the sugar industry in Louisiana and the West Indies, vastly speeding production and helping transform sugar from a luxury into an affordable household item. Rillieux's evaporating process is now crucial to the chemical industry and is also used for waste recycling and the manufacture of soap, gelatin, and glue. In 1854, Rillieux tired of the racism he encountered in New Orleans and returned to Paris, where he became a leading Egyptologist.

Temple, Lewis (1800–1854).   Born in Richmond, Virginia, Temple moved to New Bedford, Massachusetts, where he operated a whalecraft shop and a blacksmithing business and took part in the abolition movement. He invented a new type of whaling harpoon with a pivoting barbed head, designed not to come loose (as ordinary harpoons often did). The device—known as Temple's Toggle or the Temple Iron—had a tremendous impact on the whaling industry during the mid-19th century. Though Temple never obtained a patent, he prospered by manufacturing the new harpoon.

Wilkins, J. Ernest, Jr. (1923–   ).   After receiving a Ph.D. in physics from the University of Chicago at age 19, Wilkins studied mechanical engineering at New York University, taught mathematics at Tuskegee University, and took part in the research that led to the development of the atomic bomb during World

War II. From 1946 to 1970 he was a senior mathematician for the Nuclear Development Corporation of America and a physicist with the General Dynamics Corporation. In 1970, Wilkins was appointed Distinguished Professor of Applied Mathematical Physics at Howard University. He is known for developing techniques for measuring the absorption of gamma radiation emitted by the sun and other nuclear sources.

Williams, Daniel Hale   (See Chapter 8, "Health.")

Williams, O. S. "Ozzie" (1921–   ).   During World War II, Williams became the first African American to be hired as an aeronautical engineer by Republic Aircraft. After the war he joined Greer Hydraulics, where he helped develop the first airborne radar beacon, an aid in the location of downed aircraft. He joined Grumman International in 1961 and developed rocket-control systems that were used during the Apollo moon landings. Williams is currently a Grumman vice president, in charge of trade and industrial relations with Africa. In that post, he has assisted African nations in developing energy resources from solar and wind power. He has also encouraged students at black colleges to embark on careers in business and technology.

Woods, Granville T. (1856–1910).   Born in Ohio, Woods worked at a variety of manual jobs while studying electrical and mechanical engineering in the evenings. In 1884, he was able to start his own machine shop, the Woods Electric Company, in Cincinnati. In 1890, he moved the company to New York and remained there for the rest of his life. In all, Woods patented 35 devices, including a steam-boiler furnace, a telephone transmitter, a railway telegraph, a galvanic battery, an overhead conducting system for electric railways, an automatic safety cutout for electrical circuits, and an automatic circuit-breaking apparatus. He also patented an automatic air brake that was purchased by Westinghouse in 1902.

Wright, Louis Tompkins   (See Chapter 8, "Health.")

Young, Roger Arliner (1889–1964).   A graduate of Howard University and the University of Chicago, Young was the first African American woman to conduct and publish research in the field of marine biology. In 1924, she published important findings on the structures that control salt concentration in *Paramecium*, and in 1928 she contributed to the understanding of how radiation effects the eggs of sea urchins. In 1940, Young was awarded a Ph.D. in zoology by the University of Pennsylvania, becoming the first African American woman to achieve that distinction. She then held teaching posts at a number of historically black colleges and universities.

SOURCES FOR ADDITIONAL INFORMATION

Carwell, Hattie. *Blacks in Science: Astrophysicist to Zoologist.* Hicksville, NY: Exposition Press, 1977.

Harber, Louis. *Black Pioneers of Science and Invention.* New York: Harcourt, Brace & World, 1970.

Klein, Aaron E. *The Hidden Contributors: Black Scientists and Inventors in America.* Garden City, NY: Doubleday, 1971.

Pearson, Willie, Jr. *Black Scientists, White Society, and Colorless Science: A Study of Universalism in American Science.* Millwood, NY: Associated Faculties Press, 1985.

————, and Alan Fechter, eds. *Who Will Do Science? Educating the Next Generation.* Baltimore: Johns Hopkins University Press, 1994.

Sammons, Vivian O. *Blacks in Science Education.* Washington, DC: Hemisphere, 1989.

U.S. Department of Energy. *Black Contributors to Science and Energy Technology.* Washington, DC: Office of Public Affairs, 1979.

Van Sertima, Ivan, ed. *Blacks in Science: Ancient and Modern.* New Brunswick, NJ: Transaction, 1983.

11

Military

PARTICIPATION IN MAJOR U.S. MILITARY CONFLICTS

REVOLUTIONARY WAR (1775–1781)

Washington and other American leaders were at first reluctant to recruit black soldiers into the Continental Army, fearing the consequences of arming an oppressed people. They changed their minds after the British promised to free all slaves who defended the Crown—large numbers went over to the British lines, and a contingent of African Americans formed the Ethiopian Regiment within the British Army. In order to counteract British enticements, many slaveholders offered to free all those who enlisted in the Continental Army. Approximately 8,000 to 10,000 black soldiers served the American cause during the Revolutionary War, about 5,000 of them in combat roles—about 2.5 percent of the total. (The total number of U.S. troops in the conflict is officially estimated at 184,000–250,000.)

Black soldiers fought or provided labor in virtually every major action of the war, from the first exchange of fire at Lexington and Concord to the decisive victory at Yorktown. A considerable number of African Americans served at sea: aboard privateers, in the ships of the Continental Navy, or in various state naval forces (especially those of Connecticut and Massachusetts). The proportion of black soldiers among the estimated 4,435 dead and 6,188 wounded is not known.

The promise of freedom in return for fighting drew many enslaved blacks into the war. Many earned their freedom this way, although often a slaveholder would refuse to honor the promise upon completion of the enlistment. Another route for thousands of fugitives, perhaps as many as 20,000 or more, was to fight for the British Army. Hundreds more were captured as prisoners of war by the British and later freed. In general, the upheaval of the American Revolution improved the situation of many African Americans. By the end of the conflict, about 60,000 individuals had gained their freedom, and the antislavery movement throughout the nation gained new impetus.

WAR OF 1812

War between Great Britain and America arose again over territory disputes in Canada, Florida, the West, and because of British and French attacks on the U.S. Navy. During the War of 1812, blacks were neither encouraged to enlist nor discouraged from doing so. New York raised two 1,000-man black regiments, and many white units included black soldiers. In Philadelphia, 2,500 African Americans volunteered to erect fortifications on the outskirts of the city. In addition, an estimated 10 percent of those serving on U.S. Navy ships in the Great Lakes were black, and these men took part as seamen in Captain Oliver Hazard Perry's victory over the British on Lake Erie in 1813 and earned his praise. A black soldier, Cyrus Tiffany, used his body as a shield to protect Perry during the battle. Perry wrote, "I have yet to learn that the colour of a man's skin . . . can affect a man's qualifications or usefulness." Perhaps the most notable black contribution to the war effort was the performance of the Free Men of Color, which were two all-black battalions of freed men at the Battle of New Orleans. They fought heroically January 8, 1815, killing many British soldiers from fortified positions; though unbeknownst to both sides in the fighting, a formal peace treaty had already been concluded two weeks before.

CIVIL WAR (1861–1865)

At the outset of the war, President Lincoln would not permit the recruiting of black troops for the Union Army, due in large part to the fear of alienating the slaveholding border states, which he wanted to remain loyal to the Union. He was also confident of a quick victory with his existing white army. At first, blacks trying to enlist were rejected. However, numerous slaves from the Confederacy quickly escaped to the Union lines and volunteered to serve in various capacities, eager to help destroy slavery. At the same time, regiments of black volunteers were organized in Kansas and in the Southern territories that fell under Union military control, such as coastal South Carolina and the New Orleans region.

The Emancipation Proclamation, which went into effect on January 1, 1863, opened the way for African Americans to join the Union Army as fighting men. A total of 186,000 African Americans—140,000 from the South and the border states—served in combat units, composing 120 infantry regiments, 7 cavalry regiments, 12 heavy artillery regiments, 10 companies of light artillery, and 5 regiments of engineers. Many also served as chaplains, hospital stewards, and spies. Particularly adept as spies were those who had recently been freed, who sometimes even volunteered to return to servitude so they could spy from inside. Two famous spies for the Union Army were Sojourner Truth and Harriet Tubman, whose experience of the Underground Railroad routes in their prewar years was useful in guiding Union forces along escape routes in hostile territories.

Together, blacks made up somewhat less than 10 percent of the Union Army. The black troops participated in some 200 battles and skirmishes during the course of the war. In addition, more than 29,000 black sailors served in the Union Navy, accounting for one fourth of the total forces. A total of 2,700 African Americans were killed in action; estimates of the number who died of wounds, disease, and accidents vary considerably, ranging from 38,000 to 68,000. President Lincoln was sure that black participation ensured Northern victory. Though the Union Army was racially segregated, and the pay scales between black and white soldiers were far apart, because the Union acted decisively to recruit and train so many black soldiers, the blacks' contribution was an important factor in the Union's success. The South not only feared arming slaves, who might turn against their masters, but also was forced to devote significant white labor to controlling and maintaining slavery.

FORT PILLOW MASSACRE

The presence of African American troops in the Union Army infuriated many Confederates. (The Confederate Army even established a death penalty for white officers who led black troops.) There is also ample evidence that they executed large numbers of black prisoners, regarding them as rebellious slaves, rather than prisoners of war. The most glaring atrocity took place on April 13, 1864, when Confederate forces led by General Nathan Bedford Forrest, later organizer of the Ku Klux Klan, overran Fort Pillow, Kentucky, which was defended by a white cavalry regiment and a black artillery battery. According to eyewitnesses, the Confederates systematically executed the captured Union soldiers who were trying to surrender, killing an estimated 360 blacks—including women and children at the fort—and 200 whites.

SPANISH-AMERICAN WAR (1898)

In April 1989, the U.S. Congress declared war on Spain to liberate Cuba from Spanish occupation. By then, the infamous "Jim Crow" laws enforcing racial segregation were widely in place, so the black community was divided over whether to support the cause with black troops.

African American participation in the brief and often controversial conflict was essentially limited to the four black regiments—two cavalry and two infantry—that had been created in the regular army and which had been serving in the West during the decades following the Civil War. These battle-hardened soldiers of the 9th and 10th Cavalry and the 24th and 25th Infantry were subjected to countless indignities upon their arrivals in Georgia and Florida, feeling the full force of racial segregation for the first time, despite their army uniforms.

Nevertheless, they performed heroically during the fighting against Spanish forces in Cuba and were a key factor in a speedy victory. One black sailor and five black soldiers received the Congressional Medal of Honor. (See the following section, "Historic Military Units.") In addition to these soldiers, there were black regiments from five states, sent to help fight. Also formed were two "Black Immune" regiments who were volunteers from places where tropical diseases prevailed, the army having the racist assumption that these blacks had natural immunity to such diseases. In fact, 50 percent of those who fought in these units contracted tropical diseases.

WORLD WAR I (1917–1918)

A total of 380,000 African Americans served in World War I, but only 42,000 were in combat units. White commanders were convinced that black troops would not perform well in battle, and most were used as laborers in segregated engineer, quartermaster, and other service battalions. This belief was disproved when black troops did get the chance to fight, most notably in the case of the New York–based 369th Infantry Regiment, which spent the highest number of consecutive days at the front lines during a major offensive, earning 71 battle awards among their company. African American battle casualties for the war were 750 dead and 7,500 wounded. Five hundred and fifty black officers and enlisted soldiers were decorated for gallantry by the U.S. and French military authorities.

WORLD WAR II (1941–1945)

More than 1 million African Americans served in World War II: 700,000 in the U.S. Army, 165,000 in the U.S. Navy, 17,000 in the Marine Corps, and 5,000 in the Coast Guard. During the training and in service, segregation was strictly practiced by the army, with separate barracks and mess halls, a condition that led to pressure and protests from the NAACP, the National Urban League, and others, including Eleanor Roosevelt. Approximately half the African American personnel served overseas, and about 5,000 were commissioned officers.

As in World War I, however, the majority were assigned to support duties, such as transportation, cargo handling, ordnance, and construction. There were only 22 black ground-combat units in the European theater, in addition to the four fighter squadrons collectively known as the Tuskegee Airmen. Blacks in the navy were strictly segregated and largely confined to the rank of messman, though 500 served as seamen and 12,500 as Seabees (construction battalions) in the Pacific. Black Marines were used exclusively as occupation forces on captured Pacific islands. In addition, about 25,000 African Americans served in the merchant marine, where there was little discrimination—as a result, they were able to serve in many different roles, and four attained command of Liberty ships.

For the first time, African American women became a significant presence in the military, with more than 4,000 enlisting in the Women's Army Corps (WAC) during the course of the war. This represented 4 percent of the total corps but fell short of the WAC goal of 10.6 percent, due to a shortage of skilled applicants. Most were relegated to menial jobs. Even in the exceptional case of the 688th Central Postal Directory Battalion, which was one of the few black WAC units that served in Europe during 1945, 40 percent were unskilled workers (vs. 10 percent of white units). As a result, low morale was a common problem for black WAC units, even for those with black commanding officers. African American nurses numbered only 512 by the end of the war, less than 1 percent of the total. Barely more than 100 of these nurses were posted overseas, but they served in all-black hospital units in the South Pacific, Africa, and Europe.

KOREAN CONFLICT (1950–1953)

In July 1948, President Harry Truman issued Executive Order No. 9981, directing that there be "equality of treatment or opportunity" in the armed forces, and in 1949 the services began moving gradually toward integration. The army was still segregated at the outbreak of hostilities in Korea, but by the end of 1951, 30 percent of U.S. troops in the field were serving in integrated units. By the end of fighting in 1953, that proportion had risen to 95 percent. Pockets of segregation survived only among troops stationed in Europe and the United States. In the course of the Korean conflict, 3,123 African Americans were either killed or wounded.

VIETNAM CONFLICT (1960–1972)

Whereas African Americans had been underrepresented among combat troops in previous wars, their deployment in Vietnam evoked charges that black soldiers were bearing an unfairly large share of the burden. At the time, African Americans represented 9.3 percent of U.S. armed forces personnel, but 15 percent of the infantrymen serving in Vietnam were black. Moreover, between 1965 and 1967, African American soldiers suffered 20 percent of all battlefield casualties in Vietnam. Most glaring was the discrepancy in rates of conscription: In 1967, 64 percent of eligible blacks were drafted, compared with only 31 percent of eligible whites. At the time, 98.5 percent of the officials serving on local draft boards were white. At the end of the war, 7,115 African American troops had died in the conflict, representing 12.2 percent of the total U.S. war dead.

PERSIAN GULF WAR (1991)

Of the 500,000 U.S. troops dispatched to evict Iraqi forces from Kuwait, 24 percent were African Americans—in the army, that proportion stood at 30 percent. Twenty-eight African Americans lost their lives in the conflict, 15.4 percent of the 182 battle deaths suffered by U.S. forces.

FIRST IN AFRICA

Operation Restore Hope, the United Nations peacekeeping mission in Somalia (1992–1993), marked the first major deployment of African American troops to an African country. The U.S. troops were the only multiracial units in the U.N. force and the only contingent to include women. Of the 29 U.S. soldiers killed in the course of the operation, 2 were African American.

HISTORIC MILITARY UNITS

1ST RHODE ISLAND REGIMENT (REVOLUTIONARY WAR)

The 1st Rhode Island, the only all-black unit in the Continental Army, consisted of 125 men, 95 of them enslaved. They took part in the Battle of Rhode Island on August 10, 1778. When the American forces were obliged to break off their attack on Newport due to lack of naval support, the First Rhode Island was among the units that held off counterattacking British troops while the bulk of the Americans pulled back.

FREE MEN OF COLOR (WAR OF 1812)

In 1814, General Andrew Jackson recruited 350 free blacks into this militia unit, the senior black officer of which was Major Vincent Populus. A second battalion, 250 strong, was later formed; it consisted mainly of blacks from Haiti, and its senior African American officer was Major Joseph Savary. Both battalions of the Free Men of Color played a prominent role in the rout of the British at the Battle of New Orleans in 1815; their heroism is commemorated at the Chalmette Battlefield historic site.

1ST KANSAS VOLUNTEER COLORED INFANTRY (CIVIL WAR)

This regiment was created in the spring of 1862 by James H. Lane as the U.S. government began to relax its opposition to the recruitment of African Americans for the Union Army. On October 28, 1862, the 1st Kansas defeated a Confederate force at Island Mound in Missouri, losing 10 men in the fight. On July 17, 1863, the 1st Kansas was part of a multiracial force (including Native Americans) that defeated the Confederate Army at Honey Springs in Indian Territory. The regiment then advanced into Arkansas and was stationed at Fort Smith until the end of the war.

1ST SOUTH CAROLINA COLORED VOLUNTEERS (CIVIL WAR)

This regiment was commissioned in 1862 by Thomas Wentworth Higginson, an abolitionist cleric from Massachusetts. The 1st South Carolina entered combat in November, taking part in raids along the Georgia-Florida coastline before being disbanded. Higginson later recounted the exploits of the 1st South Carolina in his 1869 memoir, *Army Life in a Black Regiment*.

54TH MASSACHUSETTS INFANTRY REGIMENT (CIVIL WAR)

The 54th Massachusetts was organized in 1863 by Colonel Robert Gould Shaw, with the aid of Frederick Douglass. The soldiers were drawn not only from the Northern states but also from those areas of the South under Union occupation. One thousand strong, the freshly trained black troops paraded triumphantly through the streets of Boston on May 28. The 54th Massachusetts achieved its greatest fame in the attack on Fort Wagner in South Carolina on July 18, 1863. Assaulting virtually impregnable Confederate fortifications, the 54th achieved the deepest penetration of any Union contingent, losing half its men in the process. The 282 dead, who included Colonel Shaw, were buried in a mass grave by the Confederates. A bronze memorial to the 54th, sculpted by Augustus Saint-Gaudens has stood on the Boston Common since 1897. The exploits of the 54th Massachusetts were also celebrated in the film *Glory* (1992).

CORPS D'AFRIQUE (CIVIL WAR)

The Corps d'Afrique consisted of black Louisiana regiments that originated in 1862 and were bolstered by further recruiting. The 1st, 2nd, and 3rd Louisiana Infantry Regiments saw action on May 27, 1863, at Port Hudson, where they made several charges into the teeth of Confederate artillery and rifle fire, losing one fifth of their men. Another all-black unit, the 1st Regiment of Engineers, attempted to undermine the Confederate fortifications with picks and shovels while coming under heavy fire. On June 7, the 9th and 11th Louisiana repulsed a force of 2,000 to 3,000 Confederates at Milliken's Bend in Mississippi, achieving the first major victory won by African American troops during the war.

9TH CAVALRY REGIMENT (INDIAN WARS/SPANISH-AMERICAN WAR/ WORLD WAR II)

The 9th Cavalry was one of the four all-black regiments incorporated into the regular U.S. Army in 1869. Throughout the Indian Wars (roughly 1866–1890), they served in the Central Plains, Texas, and the New Mexico and Arizona territories. Along with the 10th Cavalry and the 24th and 25th Infantry Regiments, the men of the 9th were known to their foes as the Buffalo Soldiers because their short, tightly curled hair reminded Native Americans of the buffalo's mane.

During the Spanish-American War, the Buffalo Soldiers distinguished themselves at the Battles of Las Guásimas, San Juan Hill, and Kettle Hill. (Colonel Theodore Roosevelt, commander of the Rough Riders, gave the black troops high praise while in Cuba; back in the United States, however, he downplayed their exploits and inflated his own in order to boost his political career.) They served in World War I, and during World War II, the 9th was part of the 2nd Cavalry Division and served as a support unit in North Africa during the Italian campaign. In 1950, the 9th Cavalry became the 509th Tank Battalion, which was integrated three years later.

10TH CAVALRY REGIMENT (INDIAN WARS/SPANISH-AMERICAN WAR/ WORLD WAR I/WORLD WAR II)

The history of the 10th Cavalry closely parallels that of the 9th. In addition to its service in the Indian Wars, the Spanish-American War, and both world wars, the 10th also took part in the Punitive Expedition, which unsuccessfully pursued Pancho Villa through northern Mexico in 1915–1916. (The expedition's commander-in-chief, General John J. Pershing—later head of the American Expeditionary Forces in World War I—earned the nickname Black Jack because of his service with African American regiments: As a captain during the Spanish-American War, he was the 10th Cavalry's quartermaster.) The 10th Cavalry became the 510th Tank Battalion in 1950 and was integrated in 1952.

24TH INFANTRY REGIMENT (INDIAN WARS/SPANISH-AMERICAN WAR/WORLD WAR I/WORLD WAR II/KOREAN CONFLICT)

The 24th was created in 1869, incorporating the 38th and 41st Regiments. During the Indian Wars, the 24th did most of its service in the Southwest. In the Spanish-American War, the 24th played a prominent part in the famous charge up San Juan Hill. During the early part of World War II, the 24th was restricted to support duty (mainly cargo handling) in Trinidad and the New

Hebrides. In 1944, however, the regiment saw action on Bougainville and performed mop-up duties on Saipan and Tinian. After the war, the 24th Regiment was stationed in Japan, where it helped guard the docks at Kōbe.

During the early days of the Korean conflict, when U.S. and South Korean forces were reeling in the face of a massive Chinese invasion, the 24th suffered a blow to its reputation when some of its units reportedly abandoned their foxholes. The 24th regrouped and fought valiantly in later actions—two of its members were posthumously awarded the Congressional Medal of Honor—but the army disbanded the regiment on October 1, 1951. In 1995, a study commissioned by the army attributed the 24th's problems in 1950 to inadequate training and subpar leadership by openly racist white officers. The study (published as *Black Soldier, White Army*) concluded that the men of the 24th deserved high praise for performing as well as they did under adverse conditions.

25TH INFANTRY REGIMENT (INDIAN WARS/SPANISH-AMERICAN WAR/ WORLD WAR I/WORLD WAR II)

Created (from the 39th and 40th Regiments) at the same time as the 24th, the 25th Infantry was the fourth contingent of Buffalo Soldiers who served in the West during the late 19th century. In the Spanish-American War, the 25th distinguished itself by capturing the village of El Caney on July 1, 1898, suffering 7 dead and 25 wounded. The regiment saw action on Bougainville in 1944, though its World War II activity was mostly restricted to occupation duty and cargo handling. The 25th was deactivated in 1952 as the army completed its integration process.

THE BROWNSVILLE AFFAIR

In August 1906, three companies of men from the 25th Infantry, stationed at Fort Brown, Texas, were enmeshed in a shooting spree at the fort one night. One citizen was killed, and two (including the chief of police) were injured. On the basis of a report that cartridges from army rifles had been found and the that the black troops had "shot up the town," President Theodore Roosevelt, with only circumstantial evidence, ordered a dishonorable discharge for the entire battalion, though their officers could find no one who would admit knowing who did it. A storm of protest by both blacks and whites ensued; Booker. T. Washington's failure to confront Roosevelt on the issue damaged his standing in the black community and helped spark the more radical Niagara Movement (see Chapter 3, "Politics and Civil Rights"). Two army reports had decided that the black troops had entered into "a conspiracy of silence." In 1909, an act of Congress (championed by Senator Joseph B. Foraker of Ohio, who uncovered forensic evidence indicating that the blacks had been framed) allowed 14 of the 167 discharged soldiers to reenlist with back pay. Not until 1972, however, when most of the men involved were dead, did Congress officially rescind the dishonorable discharge and grant the one surviving soldier $25,000. The suspension of charges came based on a likelihood of prejudgment and an absence of a verifiable precedent.

92ND INFANTRY DIVISION (WORLD WAR I/WORLD WAR II)

The 92nd Division was created in 1917, comprising the 365th, 366th, 367th, and 368th Infantry Regiments. In August 1918, the 92nd took over the St.-Dié position (in France) from the 6th Infantry, but these soldiers were hampered in their performance by lack of training. Nevertheless, the 367th and 368th performed well in the final stages of the war. The 367th was especially effective in the Allied drive against Metz on November 10–11, 1918, an operation ended by the armistice. In World War II, the 92nd Division took part in the July 1944 assault on the Gothic Line in Italy. One of the 366th Regiment's officers, Lieutenant John R. Fox, sacrificed his life by calling in artillery fire on his own position as it was being overrun by German troops. Fox was later awarded the Congressional Medal of Honor.

93RD INFANTRY DIVISION (WORLD WAR I/WORLD WAR II)

The 93rd Division (also formed in 1917) comprised the 369th, 370th, 371st, and 372nd Regiments. The most illustrious of the four, the 369th, evolved from the 15th New York, a National Guard unit. Known as the Men of Bronze and the Black Battlers, the 369th covered themselves in glory during World War I, when they served as a component of the French Army. Entering the trenches in July 1918, the 369th spent 191 consecutive days in the front lines, the highest total of any American unit. In addition, they never had a single man captured by the enemy and never surrendered an inch of ground. Joined by the 371st and 372nd, 369th played a major role in the Meuse-Argonne offensive—together, the three regiments took 2,500 casualties. The 369th was singled out for its performance at Maison-en-Champagne, winning a regimental croix de guerre. In addition, 71 men received either the individual croix de guerre or the Legion of Merit. The 370th Regiment, for its part, joined French forces in the Oise-Aisne offensive, suffering 665 casualties. During World War II, the 93rd Division was deployed both on the West Coast and in the Pacific Theater, where it served on Guadalcanal, Banika, and the New Georgia Islands.

969TH FIELD ARTILLERY (WORLD WAR II)

In World War II, the 969th supported the defense of Bastogne during the Battle of the Bulge, earning a Distinguished Unit Citation.

452ND ANTI-AIRCRAFT ARTILLERY BATTALION (WORLD WAR II)

The 452nd played an integral role in supporting the Allied advance across western Europe during World War II.

614TH TANK DESTROYER BATTALION (WORLD WAR II)

Near Climbach, France, in 1944, the 614th stopped one of the last German tank attacks. The 614th earned a total of 8 Silver Stars, 28 Bronze Stars, and 79 Purple Hearts.

761ST TANK BATTALION (WORLD WAR II)

The 761st supported the Allied advance into Germany in 1945 and fought in 30 major engagements during 183 days of continuous combat. The battalion received six separate nominations for the Presidential Unit Citation, but because of the racism prevalent in the army at that time, the award was not actually bestowed until 1978.

The first class of Tuskegee Airmen, standing by a fighter plane, 1942.

99TH PURSUIT SQUADRON AND 332ND FIGHTER GROUP (WORLD WAR II)

Under pressure from the NAACP and other groups, the army reluctantly created the 99th Pursuit Squadron in January 1941, with the proviso that black pilots would be strictly segregated from the rest of the Army Air Force. The airfield at Tuskegee, Alabama, was chosen as their training site, and the men were thereafter dubbed "The Tuskegee Airmen." The first black cadets, 13 in number, reported in August. Five cadets made it through the training period, and they received their wings in March 1942. During the course of the war, Tuskegee turned out 600 African American pilots and trained an additional 145,000 support personnel. Though the Tuskegee Airmen were ready for combat by October 1942, the army had no intention of deploying them. Only in April 1943, after pressure was applied from the Roosevelt Administration, was the 99th posted to North Africa. Flying P-40 fighters, the men of the 99th undertook their first combat mission in June and recorded their first kill in July. In January 1944, the 99th supported the invasion of Anzio, Italy, and shot down eight German planes, leading all U.S. squadrons in that category.

The 332nd Fighter Group was formed in May 1942, combining the all-black 100th, 301st, and 302nd Fighter Squadrons. After rigorous training, the 332nd was posted to Italy in February 1944; in July, the 99th Squadron was incorporated into the 332nd, making it the only four-squadron fighter group in the Army Air Force. Known as the Red Tails because they painted the tails of their planes bright red, the men of the 332nd flew bomber-escort missions for the duration of the war. According to reports, this group was the only escort group that never had a single bomber shot down by enemy fighters. Throughout World War II, the Tuskegee Airmen flew 1,578 missions, destroying 261 enemy aircraft and damaging 148. They earned 95 Distinguished

Flying Cross awards; the 99th Squadron received 3 Distinguished Unit Citations, and the 332nd Fighter Group earned 1. Sixty-six Tuskegee Airmen were killed in action.

USS MASON

The *Mason*, an escort destroyer commissioned in March 1944, was the first ship of the U.S. Navy to be staffed by African American sailors, who had previously been confined to the role of messmen or assigned to manual labor ashore. The *Mason*'s personnel consisted of 6 white officers, 38 white petty officers, and 160 black crew members. On its first Atlantic crossing, which took place in October, the *Mason* was charged with helping to protect Convoy NY-119 on its way from New York to Portsmouth, England. The men quickly proved their worth when they encountered a violent storm off the English coast. Braving 40-foot waves, the *Mason* guided half the scattered convoy into the harbor at Falmouth and then returned to the open sea to gather the rest of the ships and barges. Officers recommended the entire crew for commendations, but the navy took no action. In all, the *Mason* made six Atlantic crossings during the war.

USS PC-1268

The submarine chaser *PC-1268* was launched a month after the commissioning of the *Mason*. After an initial training period, the white petty officers were replaced by African Americans, resulting in a crew of 5 white officers, 8 black petty officers, and 50 black sailors. The *PC-1268* was assigned to antisubmarine duty along the East Coast of the United States and was preparing for transfer to the Pacific when the war ended. Like the *Mason*, the *PC-1268* was quickly decommissioned by navy officials, who had agreed to employ black sailors in combat roles only after intense pressure from the Roosevelt Administration.

RECIPIENTS OF THE CONGRESSIONAL MEDAL OF HONOR

CIVIL WAR

The Medal of Honor, approved by President Lincoln on December 21, 1861 (Navy), and July 12, 1862 (Army), is the highest American award for military valor. Typical descriptions of their actions cite black soldiers as acting "gallantly" and "bravely."

ARMY

William H. Barnes, Private, Company C, 38th United States Colored Troops

Powhatan Beaty, First Sergeant, Company G, 5th United States Colored Troops

James H. Bronson, First Sergeant, Company D, 5th United States Colored Troops

William H. Carney, Sergeant, Company C, 54th Massachusetts Infantry, United States Colored Troops

Decatur Dorsey, Sergeant, Company B, 39th United States Colored Troops

Christian A. Fleetwood, Sergeant Major, 4th United States Colored Troops

James Gardiner, Private, Company J, 36th United States Colored Troops

James H. Harris, Sergeant, Company B, 38th United States Colored Troops

Thomas R. Hawkins, Sergeant Major, 6th United States Colored Troops

Alfred B. Hilton, Sergeant, Company H, 4th United States Colored Troops

Milton M. Holland, Sergeant, 5th United States Colored Troops

Alexander Kelly, First Sergeant, Company F, 6th United States Colored Troops

Robert Pinn, First Sergeant, Company I, 5th United States Colored Troops

Edward Radcliff, First Sergeant, Company C, 38th United States Colored Troops

Charles Veal, Private, Company D, 4th United States Colored Troops

NAVY

Aaron Anderson, Landsman, USS *Wyandank*

Robert Blake, Landsman, USS *Marblehead*

William H. Brown, Landsman, USS *Brooklyn*

Wilson Brown, Landsman, USS *Hartford*

Clement Dees, Seaman, USS *Pontoosuc*

John Lawson, Landsman, USS *Hartford*

James Mifflin, Engineer's Cook, USS *Brooklyn*

Joachim Pease, Seaman, USS *Kearsarge*

NAVAL SERVICE RECIPIENTS 1865–1898

Daniel Atkins, Ship's Cook, First Class, USS *Cushing*

John Davis, Seaman, USS *Trenton*

Alphonse Girandy, Seaman, USS *Tetrel*

John Johnson, Seaman, USS *Kansas*

William Johnson, Cooper, USS *Adams*

Joseph B. Noil, Seaman, USS *Powhatan*

John Smith, Seaman, USS *Shenandoah*

Robert Sweeney, Seaman, USS *Kearsage*, USS *Jamestown*

WESTERN CAMPAIGNS

Thomas Boyne, Sergeant, Troop C, 9th United States Cavalry

Benjamin Brown, Sergeant, Company C, 24th United States Infantry

John Denny, Sergeant, Troop C, 9th United States Cavalry

Pompey Factor, Private, Seminole Negro Indian Scouts

Clinton Greaves, Corporal, Troop C, 9th United States Cavalry

Henry Johnson, Sergeant, Troop D, 9th United States Cavalry

George Jordan, Sergeant, Troop K, 9th United States Cavalry

Isaiah Mays, Corporal, Company B, 24th United States Infantry

William McBreyar, Sergeant, Troop K, 10th United States Cavalry

Isaac Payne, Private (Trumpeter), Seminole Negro Indian Scouts

Thomas Shaw, Sergeant, Troop K, 9th United States Cavalry

Emanuel Stance, Sergeant, Troop K, 9th United States Cavalry

Augustus Walley, Private, Troop 1, 9th United States Cavalry

John Ward, Sergeant, Seminole Negro Indian Scouts

Moses Williams, First Sergeant, Troop 1, 9th United States Cavalry

William O. Wilson, Corporal, Troop 1, 9th United States Cavalry

Brent Woods, Sergeant, Troop B, 9th United States Cavalry

SPANISH-AMERICAN WAR
ARMY

Edward L. Baker, Sergeant Major, 10th United States Cavalry

Dennis Bell, Private, Troop H, 10th United States Cavalry

Fitz Lee, Private, Troop M, 10th United States Cavalry

William H. Tompkins, Private, Troop G, 10th United States Cavalry

George H. Wanton, Sergeant, Troop M, 10th United States Cavalry

NAVY

Robert Penn, Fireman, First Class, USS *Iowa*

WORLD WAR I

Freddie Stowers, Corporal, Company C, 371st Infantry Regiment, 93rd Infantry Division (medal awarded in 1991)

WORLD WAR II

Vernon Baker, First Lieutenant, Company C, 370th Infantry Regiment, 92nd Division

Edward Carter, Jr., Staff Sergeant, Company No. 1 (Provisional), 56th Armored Infantry, 12th Armored Division

John R. Fox, First Lieutenant, Cannon Company, 366th Infantry, 92nd Division

Willy F. James, Private First Class, Company G, 413th Infantry Regiment, 92nd Division

Ruben Rivers, Staff Sergeant, Company A, 761st Tank Battalion, 3rd Army

Charles L. Thomas, Major, Company C, 614th Tank Destroyer Battalion, 103rd Division

George Watson, Private, 29th Quartermaster Regiment

NO TIME FOR HEROES

The seven Medals of Honor earned by African American soldiers for their actions in World War II were not awarded until 1997, when only one of the seven—Vernon Baker—was still alive. (Four of the men were killed in action.) Due to the relatively small percentage of African American troops assigned to combat duty in World War II, as well as the pervasive racism in the segregated armed forces during that era, not 1 black soldier was recommended for any of the 433 Medals of Honor awarded during the war years. In 1992, the U.S. Army finally decided to review the records and search for deserving African American candidates. An ensuing study, conducted under the auspices of Shaw University, recommended 10 names for consideration. Out of these candidates, 7 were chosen. The recipients were honored at a White House ceremony on January 13, 1997, during which Vernon Baker personally received his medal from President William J. Clinton. Relatives and former comrades-in-arms of the other honorees were also present.

VIETNAM CONFLICT
ARMY

Webster Anderson, Sergeant, Battery A, 2nd Battalion, 320th Artillery, 101st Airborne Division

Eugene Ashley Jr., Sergeant, Company C, 5th Special Forces Group (Airborne), 1st Special Forces

William M. Bryant, Sergeant First Class, Company A, 5th Special Forces Group, 1st Special Forces

Lawrence Joel, Specialist Sixth Class, Headquarters and Headquarters Company, 1st Battalion, 173rd Airborne Brigade

Dwight H. Johnson, Specialist Fifth Class, Company B, 1st Battalion, 69th Armor, 4th Infantry Division

Garfield M. Langhorn, Private First Class, Troop C, 7th Squadron, 17th Cavalry, 1st Aviation Brigade

Matthew Leonard, Platoon Sergeant, Company B, 1st Battalion, 16th Infantry, 1st Infantry Division

Donald R. Long, Sergeant, Troop C, 1st Squadron, 4th Cavalry, 1st Infantry Division

Milton L. Olive III, Private First Class, Company B, 2nd Battalion, 503rd Infantry, 173rd Airborne Brigade

Riley R. Pitts, Captain, Company C, 2nd Battalion, 27th Infantry, 25th Infantry Division

Charles C. Rogers, Lieutenant Colonel, 1st Battalion, 5th Infantry, 1st Infantry Division

Rupert L. Sargent, First Lieutenant, Company B, 4th Battalion, 9th Infantry, 25th Infantry Division

Clarence E. Sasser, Specialist Fifth Class, Headquarters Company, 3rd Battalion, 60th Infantry, 90th Infantry Division

Clifford C. Sims, Staff Sergeant, Company D, 2nd Battalion, 501st Infantry, 101st Airborne Division

John E. Warren Jr., First Lieutenant, Company C, 2nd Battalion, 22nd Infantry, 25th Infantry Division

MARINES

James A. Anderson Jr., Private First Class, Company F, 2nd Battalion, 3rd Marine Division

Oscar P. Austin, Private First Class, Company E, 7th Marines, 1st Marine Division

Rodney M. Davis, Sergeant, Company B, 1st Battalion, 5th Marines, 1st Marine Division

Robert H. Jenkins Jr., Private First Class, 3rd Reconnaissance Battalion, 3rd Marine Division

Ralph H. Johnson, Private First Class, Company A, 1st Reconnaissance Battalion, 1st Marine Division

AFRICAN AMERICANS IN THE CONTEMPORARY ARMED FORCES

Following the end of the draft in 1970, the U.S. armed forces made a concerted effort to attract black recruits and to increase the opportunities for African American personnel. Between 1975 and 1995, African Americans composed 19.1 percent of all active-duty personnel in the armed forces, considerably higher than their proportion of the 20- to 34-year-old U.S. population (13.1% in 1990). Opportunities for advancement also increased during this period. Whereas African Americans had composed 14 percent of senior noncommissioned officers in 1970, by 1995 the proportion had risen to 31 percent. During the same period, the proportion of African Americans in the officer corps rose from 3 percent to 11 percent.

Table 11.1 African American Armed Forces Personnel, 1997

	Total	Black	Percentage
ARMY	476,163	127,732	26.8
Officer	78,344	9,061	11.6
Enlisted	397,819	118,671	29.8
AIR FORCE	378,233	56,741	15.0
Officer	74,551	4,327	5.8
Enlisted	303,682	52,414	17.3
NAVY	396,614	68,967	17.4
Officer	56,076	3,313	5.9
Enlisted	340,538	65,654	19.3
MARINES	171,912	27,024	15.7
Officer	17,968	1,161	6.5
Enlisted	153,944	25,863	16.8
ALL SERVICES			
Officer*			
O-11	0	0	0.0
O-10	35	2	5.7
O-9	111	5	4.5
O-8	292	12	4.1
O-7	445	24	5.4
O-6	11,482	415	3.6
O-5	28,385	1,845	6.5
O-4	42,729	3,242	7.6
O-3	77,488	5,938	7.7
O-2	24,286	2,054	8.4
O-1	25,624	2,119	8.3
Unknown	341	21	3.9
Total	211,418	15,668	7.4
Warrant			
W-5	432	35	8.1
W-4	3,965	195	9.9
W-3	4,337	555	12.8
W-2	6,586	940	14.3
W-1	2,201	469	21.3
Total	15,521	2,194	14.1
OFFICER TOTAL	226,939	17,862	7.9
ENLISTED†			
E-9	10,724	2,134	19.9
E-8	27,392	6,513	23.8
E-7	107,039	27,079	25.3
E-6	172,391	43,965	25.5
E-5	253,909	60,834	24.0
E-4	272,160	53,779	19.8

(continued)

Table II.I (continued)

	Total	Black	Percentage
E-3	195,286	37,227	19.1
E-2	99,687	19,495	19.6
E-1	57,157	11,555	20.2
Unknown	238	1	0.4
Total	1,195,983	262,602	22.0
GRAND TOTAL	1,442,922	280,464	19.7

*O-7 and above = general or flag officer.
†E-4 and above = noncommissioned officer.
Source: U.S. Department of Defense.

BLACK WOMEN IN THE MILITARY

By 1996, blacks made up half of all enlisted women or 6.5 percent of the total armed forces (women accounted for 13% of enlisted personnel overall). Of the 280,464 African Americans serving in the U.S. armed forces in 1997, 59,784 were women. African American women officers numbered 4,200 (13.7% of all officers in the military), and the enlisted ranks included 55,584 African American women (34.3% of all blacks enlisted).

AFRICAN-AMERICAN GENERALS AND ADMIRALS: 1997
ARMY

Gen. Johnnie E. Wilson, Commanding General, U.S. Army Europe and 7th Army

Lt. Gen. Joe N. Ballard, Chief of Engineers/Commanding General, U.S. Army Corps of Engineers

Lt. Gen. Larry R. Jordan, Inspector General, Office of the Secretary of the Army

Maj. Gen. John S. Cowings, Commandant, Industrial College of the Armed Forces, National Defense University

Maj. Gen. Arthur T. Dean, Director of Military Personnel Management, Office of the Deputy Chief of Staff for Personnel

Maj. Gen. Larry R. Ellis, Commanding General, 1st Armored Division, U.S. Army Europe and 7th Army

Maj. Gen. Milton Hunter, Director of Military Programs, U.S. Army Corps of Engineers

Maj. Gen. James W. Monroe, Commanding General, U.S. Army Industrial Operations Command

Maj. Gen. Gregory A. Rountree, Deputy Commanding General, V Corps, Army Europe and 7th Army

Maj. Gen. Michael B. Sherfield, Commanding General, 2nd Infantry Division, 8th Army

Maj. Gen. Billy K. Solomon, Director for Logistics and Security Assistance, J-4/J-7, U.S. Central Command

Maj. Gen. Ralph G. Wooten, Commanding General, U.S. Army Chemical and Military Police Centers

Brig. Gen. George J. Brown, Commanding General, Madigan Army Medical Center/Northwest Health Service Support Activity

Brig. Gen. Reginald G. Clemmons, Assistant Division Commander (Maneuvers), 1st Infantry Division, U.S. Army Europe and 7th Army

Brig. Gen. Billy R. Cooper, Commander, Joint Rear Area Coordinator, U.S. Central Command

Brig. Gen. James E. Donald, Assistant Division Commander (Operation), 25th Infantry Division (Light)

Brig. Gen. Robert A. Harding, Director for Operations, Defense Intelligence Agency

Brig. Gen. Mack C. Hill, Assistant Surgeon General for Force Management/Chief Medical Service Corps, Office of the Surgeon General, U.S. Army

Brig. Gen. Russel L. Honore, Assistant Division Commander (Support), 1st Cavalry Division

Brig. Gen. Alan D. Johnson, Director of Plans, J-5, U.S. Space Command

Brig. Gen. Samuel L. Kindred, Deputy Commanding General, U.S. Army Recruiting Command (West)

Brig. Gen. Robert L. Nabors, Commanding General/Deputy Chief of Staff, Information Management, 5th Signal Command, U.S. Army Europe and 7th Army

Brig. Gen. Hawthorne L. Proctor, Commander, Defense Personnel Support Center, Defense Logistics Agency

Brig. Gen. William H. Russ, Deputy Director, Chief Information Office/Deputy Commander, Army Signal Command

Brig. Gen. Bettye H. Simmons, Command Surgeon, U.S. Army Forces Command/Chief, Army Nurse Corps

Brig. Gen. Earl M. Simms, Adjutant General/Commanding General, Physical Disability Agency

Brig. Gen. William A. Ward, Assistant Division Commander (Support), 82nd Airborne Division

AIR FORCE

Gen. Lloyd Newton, Director, Air Education Training Command

Lt. Gen. Lester Lyles, Director, Ballistic Missile Defense Office

Maj. Gen. Russell Davis, Vice-Chief, Air National Guard Bureau

Maj. Gen. John Hopper, Vice-Director for Logistics, Joint Chiefs of Staff

Brig. Gen. Frank Anderson, Deputy Assistant Secretary for Contracting

Brig. Gen. Claude Bolton, Director of Acquirements, Air Force Matériel Command

Brig. Gen. Leonard Randolph, Commander, 60th Medical Group, Air Mobility Command

Brig. Gen. Mary Saunders, Director of Transportation, Air Force Headquarters

Brig. Gen. William Stevens, Assistant Deputy for International Affairs, Office of the Secretary of the Air Force

Brig. Gen. Francis Taylor, Commander, Air Force Office of Special Investigation

NAVY

Admiral J. Paul Reason, Commander in Chief, U.S. Atlantic Fleet

Rear Admiral David Lawrence Brewer III, Commander, Amphibious Group THREE

Rear Admiral (Lower Half) Osie "V" Combs Jr., Vice Commander, Space and Naval Warfare Systems Command

Rear Admiral (Lower Half) Alberto Diaz Jr., Medical Officer to the Marine Corps, Medical Corps

Rear Admiral (Lower Half) Lillian Elaine Fishburne, Chief of Naval Operations, Code N6

Rear Admiral Macea Eugene Fussell, Chief of Staff, Chief of Naval Operations and Medical Corps, U.S. Naval Reserve

Rear Admiral (Lower Half) Michael Lynn Holmes, Commanding Officer, Patrol Squadron THREE ZERO

Rear Admiral Gene Roger Kendall, Director, Surface Warfare Manpower and Training Requirements Branch, Office of the Chief of Naval Operations

Rear Admiral Edward Moore Jr., Associate Director for Plans, Policy, and Operations, Office of the Chief of Naval Operations

Rear Admiral (Selectee) Larry Lafayette Poe, U.S. Naval Reserve

MARINE CORPS

Maj. Gen. Charles F. Bolden Jr., Deputy Commanding General, First Marine Expeditionary Force, Marine Forces Pacific

Maj. Gen. Leo V. Williams III, Commanding General, Marine Corps Reserve Support Command

Brig. Gen. Arnold Fields, Commander, Forward Headquarters Element/Inspector General, U.S. Central Command

Brig. Gen. Clifford L. Stanley, Director of Public Affairs, Marine Corps Headquarters

TRAINING FOR LEADERSHIP

Black enrollment at the U.S. military academies increased steadily during the last half of the 20th century. For example, at the U.S. Military Academy at West Point, enrollment rose dramatically since 1969, as the following chart indicates, largely due to an overall expansion in the cadet corps from 2,500 to 4,400 (although this was reduced to 4,000 in 1995).

	Number of African Americans entered	Number of African Americans graduated
1900–1949	26	10
1950–1959	32	24
1960–1969	52	37
1970–1979	458	269
1980–1989	845	596[*]

[*]Best estimate of the number who graduated by June of 1989.
The academy did not admit women until 1976, so the first class to graduate with women was 1980. In 1988, 13 African American women were admitted; 6 graduated. In 1998, 17 African American women were admitted; 13 graduated. The current statistics for the entering class of 2002 is 113 African Americans admitted (96 males and 17 females). This represents 9.6% of the entire class.

VETERANS ORGANIZATIONS

American Veterans Committee
6309 Bannockburn Drive
Bethesda, MD 20817
301-320-6490
Maintains a long-standing civil-rights program and previously monitored the integration of the armed forces; currently focuses on identifying and rectifying discrimination in the military.

Black Revolutionary War Patriots Foundation
1612 K Street, NW, Suite 1104
Washington, DC 20006
202-452-1776
Raises funds for the establishment of a national memorial to African Americans who fought in the Revolutionary War.

Black Veterans for Social Justice
686 Fulton Street
Brooklyn, NY 11217
718-935-1116
Aids veterans in obtaining benefits and proper treatment; provides educational assistance and training; offers social services.

National Association for Black Veterans
3929 N. Humboldt
Milwaukee, WI 53211
414-332-3931
Represents the interests of African American veterans to the Veterans Affairs Department; provides social services; conducts workshops on posttraumatic stress disorder and other conditions affecting veterans.

Organization of African-American Veterans
P.O. Box 873
Ft. Huachuca, AZ 86513
602-458-7475
Promotes the physical, mental, economic, and social well-being of black veterans; works to obtain compensation and benefits.

369th Veterans Association
369th Regiment Armory
One 369th Plaza
New York, NY 10037
212-281-3308
Includes veterans of World War I, World War II, Korea, and Vietnam; provides a variety of services, including scholarships, aid to hospitals, senior-citizens centers, athletic programs, and housing; sponsors annual Martin Luther King, Jr., Memorial Parade on Fifth Avenue.

Tuskegee Airmen, Inc.
65 Cadillac Square, #3200
Detroit, MI 20036
313-965-8858
Provides educational and social services; commemorates the achievements of these African American airmen in World War II; holds annual reunions.

NOTABLE MILITARY FIGURES

Attucks, Crispus (1750?–1770).   Though he was never a U.S. soldier, Attucks is recognized as the first man to lose his life fighting for the cause of American independence and thus deserves his status as a military figure. Born into slavery in Framingham, Massachusetts, Attucks escaped and went to Boston, where he found work as a seafarer and dockhand. On the night of March 5, 1770, Attucks led a group of dockers who began to harass the British sentry outside the State House on King Street. The incident escalated into a confrontation between British soldiers and a rock-throwing mob. When the British opened fire, Attucks was the first man to fall. The Boston Massacre, as it became known, served as a rallying point for American patriots, and Attucks was revered as a martyr to the cause. He was interred in the Old Granary Burial Ground, the final resting place of other Revolutionary War heroes.

Baker, Edward Lee, Jr. (1865–1913).   Born in Wyoming, Baker enlisted in the army in 1882 and served with both the 9th and the 10th Cavalry, attaining the rank of sergeant major in 1892. Serving in the Spanish-American War in 1898, Baker earned a Congressional Medal of Honor for braving heavy fire to save the life of a comrade during the assault on San Juan Hill. Promoted to captain after the war and given command of the Negro 49th Infantry, Baker led his 100-man unit to an unprecedented record of efficiency and discipline. He retired from the army in 1910 and spent his last years in California.

Bolden, Charles F., Jr. (1946–).   Born in South Carolina, Bolden graduated from the U.S. Naval Academy in 1968, accepted a commission in the Marine Corps, and qualified as a naval aviator in 1970. During the Vietnam War, he flew more than 100 combat missions as an A-6A *Intruder* pilot and won the Distinguished Flying Cross. While serving in a variety of assignments during the 1970s, Bolden also obtained an M.S. degree from the University of Southern California and qualified as a naval test pilot. He was chosen by NASA as an astronaut candidate in 1980 and flew four missions in space between 1986 and 1994—the final mission, on the space shuttle *Discovery*, was the first joint U.S.-Russian space venture. After retiring as an astronaut, Bolden spent a year as deputy commandant of the Naval Academy. In 1997, he became deputy commanding general of the 1st Marine Expeditionary Force.

Brown, Jesse Leroy (1926–1950).   A native of Mississippi, Brown joined the Naval Reserve in 1947 and began flight training at Pensacola, Florida. In 1948, he became the first African American to qualify as a naval aviator. Assigned to the aircraft carrier USS *Leyte*, he flew 20 combat missions during the first months of the Korean conflict. Brown was killed in action on December 4, 1950. He was posthumously awarded the Distinguished Flying Cross, and in 1973 the navy named a destroyer escort in his honor.

Cailloux, André (1820?–1863).   A man of numerous accomplishments and a leader of free black society in New Orleans, Cailloux helped raise the 440-man Native Guard Regiment at the outbreak of the Civil War and offered to defend the Confederacy. When Union forces captured New Orleans in April 1862, Cailloux's unit was incorporated into the Union Army as the 1st Louisiana Regiment. Originally used as support troops, the 1st Regiment and the rest of the Corps d'Afrique got their chance to fight in the May 1863 assault on Fort Hudson. The black troops made six assaults on the fort, suffering heavy losses. During the final assault, Cailloux was killed by an artillery shell as he led his men in a charge. He was given a hero's burial in New Orleans and became a symbol of African American military achievements.

Carney, William H. (1840–1908).   Though Carney was born into slavery in Virginia, his father purchased the family's freedom in 1856, and the Carneys then moved to Massachusetts. In 1863, William Carney enlisted in the 54th Massachusetts Infantry and attained the rank of sergeant. During the 54th's assault on Fort Wagner in July, Carney rescued the regimental banner when the standard-bearer was hit; despite being wounded himself, he led his men to the ramparts of the fort before withering fire forced them to fall back. Carney's heroism earned him the Congressional Medal of Honor, the first ever awarded to a black soldier. Due to the effects of his wounds, Carney was discharged from the army in 1864. He worked as a mail carrier in New Bedford, Massachusetts, for the next 32 years and then accepted a post at the State House in Boston. Upon his death, the flag at the State House flew at half mast.

Davis, Benjamin O., Jr. (1912–).   After attending Western Reserve University and the University of Chicago, Davis entered the U.S. Military Academy in 1932. Four years later, he graduated 35th in a class of 276. He then served in the infantry for five years before transferring to the Army Air Corps. Assigned to Tuskegee, Alabama, for flight training, Davis was one of the first six African American flight cadets to qualify for active duty. He commanded the 99th Pursuit Squadron until the fall of 1943, when he returned to the United States to train three additional squadrons of African American pilots. He then took command of the 332nd Fighter Group for the duration of the war. In the course of World War II, Davis flew 60 combat missions and earned the Silver Star and other decorations. After the war, Davis served in a number of important command positions, heading the 12th Air Force and United Nations Command in Korea. He retired in 1970 with the rank of lieutenant general.

Davis, Benjamin O., Sr. (1877–1970).   After graduating from Howard University, Davis enlisted in the army during the Spanish-American War. In 1899 he became a lieutenant in the 9th Cavalry and rose to the rank of colonel by 1930, a rare achievement for an African American in that era. He also taught military science at Wilberforce and Tuskegee universities and served as military attaché to Liberia. In 1940, Davis was promoted to brigadier general, becoming the first African American to attain that rank. He retired from active duty in 1941 but was reactivated when the United States entered World War II. During the war, he served as special advisor to the commander of the European Theater of Operations. He then took the post of assistant to the inspector general of the army before retiring for good in 1948. Davis's many decorations included the Bronze Star, the Distinguished Service Medal, and the croix de guerre.

Flipper, Henry Ossian (1856?–1940).   A student at Atlanta University during the Reconstruction era, Flipper became the first African American cadet at the U.S. Military Academy in 1873. Ostracized by the other cadets throughout his four years at West Point, he graduated 50th in a class of 76. As a lieutenant in the 10th Cavalry, he served first at Fort Sill, Oklahoma, and then at a succession of posts in Texas. Flipper was dismissed from the army in 1882 after being court-martialed on a charge of embezzlement—he maintained that the charges arose from his practice of going horseback riding with a white woman. Flipper remained in the West after leaving the army and achieved considerable success as a miner, engineer, and surveyor. Though Flipper's efforts to clear his military record were unsuccessful during his lifetime, the army exonerated him fully in 1976. The following year, the U.S. Military Academy marked the centennial of Flipper's graduation by unveiling a bust in his honor.

Gravely, Samuel Lee, Jr. (1922–).   Gravely left college to enlist in the navy at the start of World War II and served as an ensign aboard the submarine chaser USS *PC-1268*. He remained in the navy after the war and served aboard the cruiser USS *Toledo* during the Korean conflict. In 1962, Gravely was given command of USS *Falgout*, a destroyer escort. It was the first time an African American attained command over a combat ship in modern times. In 1971, Gravely became the first African American admiral; he became a vice admiral in 1971 and served as commander of the Third Fleet for the next seven years. Before retirement, he also served as director of the Defense Communications Agency. A veteran of three wars, Gravely holds numerous awards and decorations.

James, Daniel, Jr. (1920–1978).   Known as "Chappie," James trained as a pilot at Tuskegee in 1943. During the Korean conflict, he flew 101 combat missions and rose steadily through the ranks of the air force. In 1970 he became a brigadier general and took command of the 72nd Flying Training Wing. James won promotion to lieutenant general in 1973, and two years later, when he was chosen to head the North American Defense Command, he became the first African American four-star general.

Johnson, Hazel W. (1927–).   After training as a nurse at Harlem Hospital in New York, Johnson enlisted in the army in 1955. By 1960 she attained the rank of lieutenant in the Nursing Corps and also continued her studies in nursing and education, obtaining a doctorate from Catholic University. In 1979, Johnson assumed command of the Army Nurse Corps and became the first African American woman to attain the rank of brigadier general. She retired from the army in 1983 and later joined the faculty of George Mason University.

Johnson, Henry (1897?–1929).   A resident of Albany, New York, Johnson enlisted in the 15th New York National Guard when the United States entered World War I in 1917. When Johnson's unit (renamed the 369th Infantry) entered the war zone, he held the rank of sergeant. On May 13, 1918, Johnson and another soldier, Private Needham Roberts, were guarding a bridge near the Aisne River when they were attacked by a 32-man German patrol. The two men held their own until they ran out of ammunition, whereupon Roberts was captured. Johnson then assaulted the Germans with a knife and the butt of his pistol; though seriously wounded, he managed to drive the Germans back and rescue Roberts. Both men were awarded the croix de guerre, and Johnson got a hero's welcome when he returned to Albany in 1919. Still recovering from his wounds, he received many offers of financial aid. None of these ever materialized, however, and he died in poverty in Washington, D.C.

Miller, Dorie (1919–1943).   A Texas sharecropper's son, Miller enlisted in the navy at age 19. He was assigned to the battleship *Arizona* as a messman (the only naval rank then open to African Americans) and was on duty when Japanese planes attacked Pearl Harbor on December 7, 1941. Though he had never been trained for combat and could have jumped over the side, Miller remained onboard throughout the attack. After locating the wounded captain and removing him from the line of fire, Miller took charge of a machine gun and shot down four Japanese planes. His heroism earned him a Navy Cross and a promotion to messman first class. During the war, Miller served on the aircraft carrier USS *Liscome Bay*. On November 24, 1943, the *Liscome Bay* was sunk by a Japanese submarine off Makin Island in the Pacific, and Miller was among those who went down with the ship.

Poor, Salem (1758–?).   Born free in Massachusetts, Salem enlisted in a militia company at the outbreak of the American Revolution. He fought at the Battle of Bunker Hill in 1775 and reputedly shot a high-ranking British officer, Lt. Col. James Abercrombie. After the battle, a group of white officers petitioned the Massachusetts legislature to provide a financial reward for Poor, but there is no indication that he actually received it. He also served with General Washington at Valley Forge and White Plains.

Powell, Colin L. (1937–   ).   The son of West Indian immigrants, Powell grew up in the Bronx and graduated from the City College of New York in 1958, where he was a cadet colonel in the Reserve Officers Training Corps. Powell accepted a commission in the army upon graduation; during the 1960s, he served two tours of duty in Vietnam as a combat officer, earning a Purple Heart and a Bronze Star. In 1971, Powell obtained an M.B.A. from Georgetown University, and the following year he gained political experience as a White House Fellow. Returning to active duty, he rose rapidly through the officer ranks, becoming a brigade commander with the 101st Airborne Division in 1976 and assistant division commander of the 4th Infantry Division in 1981. During the Reagan Administration, Powell served as military assistant to the secretary of defense and became national security advisor in 1988. In 1989, President Bush appointed Powell as the first African American chairman of the Joint Chiefs of Staff. In that capacity, Powell oversaw U.S. operations in the Persian Gulf War in 1991 and became a national hero. He retired from the army with four-star rank in 1993. In 1995, he published an autobiography, *My American Journey* (Random House), and briefly considered running for president.

Salem, Peter (1750–1816).   Salem was born into slavery in Massachusetts but was manumitted so that he could serve in the militia. He took part in the defense of Concord Bridge in April 1775 and fought with the 5th Massachusetts Regiment at Bunker Hill. Salem also fought at Saratoga in 1777 and at Stony Point in 1779. After the war, Salem built a cabin near Leicester, Massachusetts, and earned his living as a cane weaver. He died in the poorhouse in Framingham, where the citizens later built a monument in his honor (in 1882).

Savary, Joseph (?–1822).   Born in Haiti, Savary came to New Orleans in 1809 with a reputation as an accomplished soldier. In the years before the War of 1812, he may have been a privateer in the employ of the Lafitte brothers. In 1814, when Andrew Jackson decided to recruit additional black troops, Savary organized the 2nd Battalion of the Free Men of Color, staffing the unit almost entirely with immigrants from Haiti. Many traditions credit Savary with shooting the British commander, General Pakenham, during the Battle of New Orleans. Jackson warmly praised Savary for his military leadership, but the two men later had a falling-out, probably based on the issue of mistreatment endured by the black troops. In 1816, Savary took a number of his men to Galveston, Texas, where he rejoined the Lafittes and took part in military actions that hastened the end of Spanish rule in Mexico and South America.

SOURCES FOR ADDITIONAL INFORMATION

Bowers, William T., William M. Hammond, and George McGarrigle. *Black Soldier, White Army: The 24th Infantry Regiment in Korea.* Washington, DC: Center of Military History, 1996.

Buchanan, A. Russell. *Black Americans in World War II.* Santa Barbara and Oxford: Clio Books, 1977.

Butler, John S. *Inequality in the Military: The Black Experience*. Washington, DC: Century Twenty-One Publishing, 1980.

Converse, Elliott V., et al. *The Exclusion of Black Soldiers from the Medal of Honor in World War II: The Study Commissioned by the United States Army to Investigate Racial Bias*. Jefferson, NC: McFarland, 1997.

Davis, Benjamin O., Jr. *Benjamin O. Davis, Jr., American: An Autobiography*. Washington, DC: Smithsonian Institution Press, 1991.

Donaldson, Gary. *The History of African Americans in the Military: Double V*. Malabar, FL: Krieger, 1991.

Fowler, Arlen L. *The Black Infantry in the West, 1869–1891*. Norman: University of Oklahoma Press, 1996.

Higginson, Thomas Wentworth. *Army Life in a Black Regiment*. New York: Penguin, 1869, (reprint) 1997.

Holway, John B. *Red Tails, Black Wings: The Men of America's Black Air Force*. Las Cruces, NM: Yucca Tree, 1997.

Kelly, Mary Pat. *Proudly We Served: The Men of the USS Mason*. Annapolis, MD: Naval Institute Press, 1995.

Lanning, Michael Lee. *The African-American Soldier: From Crispus Attucks to Colin Powell*. Secaucus, NJ: Birch Lane, 1997.

Leckie, William H. *The Buffalo Soldiers: A Narrative of the Negro Cavalry in the West*. Norman: University of Oklahoma Press, 1967.

Lee, Irvin H. *Negro Medal of Honor Men*. New York: Dodd, Mead, 1967.

Lee, Ulysses G. *The Employment of Negro Troops: U.S. Army and World War II*. Washington, DC: Office of the Chief of Military History, 1966.

McGuire, Philip, ed. *Taps for a Jim Crow Army: Letters from Black Soldiers in World War II*. Lexington: University Press of Kentucky, 1993.

Mershon, Sherie, and Steven L. Schlossman. *Foxholes and Color Lines: Desegregating the U.S. Armed Forces*. Baltimore: Johns Hopkins University Press, 1998.

Moore, Brenda L. *To Serve My Country, To Serve My Race: The Story of the Only African American WACs Stationed Overseas during World War II*. New York: New York University Press, 1996.

Morden, Bettie J. *The Women's Army Corps, 1945–1978*, Army Historical Series (ed., John W. Elsberg). Washington, DC: Center of Military History, United States Army, 1992.

Moskos, Charles C., and John S. Butler. *All That We Can Be: Black Leadership and Racial Integration the Army Way*. New York: Basic Books, 1996.

Nalty, Bernard C. *Strength for the Fight: A History of Black Americans in the Military*. New York: Free Press, 1986.

———, and Morris J. MacGregor, eds. *Blacks in the Military: Essential Documents*. Wilmington, DE: Scholarly Resources, 1986.

Powell, Colin L. *My American Journey: An Autobiography*. New York: Random House, 1995.

Putney, Martha S. *When the Nation Was in Need: Blacks in the Women's Army Corps during World War II*. Metuchen, NJ: Scarecrow Press, 1992.

Terry, Wallace. *Bloods: An Oral History of Vietnam by Black Veterans*. New York: Random House, 1984.

Truxton-Moebs, Thomas. *Black Soldiers–Black Sailors–Black Ink: Research Guide on African-Americans in U.S. Military History, 1526–1900*. Moebs Publishing, 1994.

Wilson, Joseph Thomas. *The Black Phalanx*. New York: Arno, 1890, (reprint) 1968.

Wilson, Ruth Danenhower. *Jim Crow Joins Up: A Study of Negroes in the Armed Forces of the United States*. New York: W. J. Clark, 1944.

Young, Warren L. *Minorities and the Military*. Westport, CT: Greenwood Press, 1982.

12

The Law

HISTORIC LEGAL CASES

1842

Prigg v. Pennsylvania   The Supreme Court struck down a Pennsylvania antikidnapping statute, voiding the conviction of a slave catcher who had captured a fugitive slave residing in the state. With this decision, the Court established that the right of slaveholders to retrieve escaped slaves could not be curtailed by state law.

1850

Strader v. Graham   The Supreme Court ruled that each state had the right to determine the status of slaves within its jurisdiction.

1857

Dred Scott v. Sanford   In refusing to free a slave who was residing on free soil, the Supreme Court ruled that African Americans did not have the rights of U.S. citizens. The Court thus upheld the right of slave owners to recapture fugitives throughout the nation. By also denying Congress the authority to outlaw slavery in the territories, the *Dred Scott* ruling made further compromise on the issue of slavery impossible.

1873

Slaughterhouse Cases   The Supreme Court ruled that the Fourteenth Amendment, which was designed to extend various legal and civil rights to former slaves, did not supersede the principle of federalism. In other words, the federal government could no longer discriminate against African Americans, but state governments were free to do so. Because most civil rights, including voting rights, fell under state citizenship, this decision allowed Southern states to continue to deprive black citizens of equal rights.

1876

United States v. Cruikshank   The Supreme Court ruled that the Fifteenth Amendment, designed to grant male former slaves the right to vote, did not guarantee them the absolute right to vote but only the general right not to be discriminated against. This meant that state governments were not obliged to protect black voters from the terrorist tactics of the Ku Klux Klan and other groups. This decision played a significant role in bringing Southern Reconstruction to an end.

1880

Neal v. Delaware   The Supreme Court ruled that a jury commissioner had violated the constitutional rights of a black defendant by excluding African Americans from the jury deciding his case.

1883

Civil Rights Cases   Hearing a group of five cases, the Supreme Court decreed that the 1875 Civil Rights Act, which prohibited racial discrimination in hotels and other public accommodations, was unconstitutional; in the Court's view, the Thirteenth and Fourteenth Amendments did not give Congress the power to outlaw discrimination in public accommodations.

1890

Re Green   The Supreme Court conferred the control of elections upon state officials, further weakening the position of black voters.

Ferguson v. Gies   The Michigan Supreme Court ruled that the owner of a restaurant could not maintain a whites-only section and restrict African American patrons to a separate seating area; the case served as a precedent for a number of civil rights cases during the 20th century.

1896

Plessy v. Ferguson   In this landmark case that paved the way for legal segregation, the Supreme Court upheld a Louisiana law creating separate railway carriages for black passengers; the Court held that the Fourteenth Amendment was not designed to enforce "a co-mingling of the two races upon terms unsatisfactory to either" and that the provision of "separate but equal facilities" was within the power of the states.

1917

Buchanan v. Warley   The Supreme Court overturned a Louisville, Kentucky, law that prevented blacks and whites from residing on the same block.

1927

Nixon v. Herndon   The Court struck down a Texas law that barred African Americans from voting in Democratic primary elections.

1932

Nixon v. Condon   The Court struck down a Texas law designed to circumvent *Nixon v. Herndon* by allowing the Democratic executive committee to set up its own rules on voting qualifications for primaries.

Powell v. Alabama   The Court ruled in the Scottsboro Boys case that African Americans had equal rights to adequate legal representation.

1935

Hollins v. Oklahoma   In upholding a state-court reversal of the death penalty against a convicted black rapist, the Supreme Court confirmed that the exclusion of black jurors is a violation of the Fourteenth Amendment.

1938

Missouri ex rel. Lloyd Gaines v. Canada   Applying the doctrine of separate but equal facilities, the Court upheld Gaines's petition for admission to the law school at the State University of Missouri, on the grounds that the state had not established an alternative facility for African Americans.

1939

Lane v. Wilson   The Court declared that an Oklahoma statute requiring all new voters to register within a 12-day period was in conflict with the Fifteenth Amendment.

1944

Smith v. Allwright   The Court overturned a previous decision (*Grovey v. Townsend*) that had allowed the Texas Democratic Party to limit its membership to whites; the Court ruled that political parties operate as agencies of the state when they choose candidates and cannot exclude members of a particular group from participating in the process.

Steele v. Louisville & Nashville Railroad   The Supreme Court directed a white labor union (the bargaining agent for all railway firefighters under the 1934 Railway Labor Act) to fairly represent African American firefighters who were excluded from the union.

1946

Morgan v. Commonwealth of Virginia   The Supreme Court overturned the conviction of a woman who refused to move to the back of a Greyhound bus during an interstate trip; the Court ruled that the state's segregation law could not apply to interstate travel.

1948

Sipuel v. Board of Regents of the University of Oklahoma   Applying the principles laid down in the 1938 *Gaines* decision, the Court ruled that Ada Lois Sipuel be admitted to the University of Oklahoma Law School; the ruling was based on the state's failure to provide an equivalent all-black facility.

Shelley v. Kraemer   The Supreme Court ruled that restrictive covenants designed to exclude black property owners from all-white areas could not be enforced by state courts.

1950

Sweatt v. Painter   The Court directed that Herman M. Sweatt be admitted to the University of Texas Law School because the state law school for black students was far from equal in quality. This was a major step in the process of abandoning *Plessy v. Ferguson*.

1952

District of Columbia v. John R. Thompson   The Supreme Court ruled that a restaurant owner violated federal law by refusing to serve African American patrons.

1954

Brown v. Board of Education of Topeka   In a landmark decision, the Supreme Court overturned *Plessy v. Ferguson*, ruling 9-0 that segregated schools were "inherently unequal" and thus deprived African American children of equal protection under the laws, as guaranteed by the Fourteenth Amendment. In the following year, the Court instructed federal district courts to supervise the desegregation of schools "with all deliberate speed."

1955

Flemming v. South Carolina Electric and Gas Co.   The U.S. Court of Appeals in Richmond, Virginia, ruled that segregation on interstate buses was unconstitutional.

Mayor and City Council of Baltimore v. Dawson   The Supreme Court ruled that Baltimore could not enforce segregation in public beaches and bathhouses.

1956

Frazier v. University of North Carolina   The Supreme Court upheld a lower-court ruling that African Americans could not be excluded from institutions of higher learning on the basis of skin color.

Gayle v. Browder   The Supreme Court upheld a federal district-court ruling barring segregation on public buses in Birmingham, Alabama; the lower-court ruling had brought the Birmingham bus boycott to a successful conclusion.

1958

Cooper v. Aaron   Responding to a suit brought by the Justice Department, the Supreme Court blocked an attempt by the state of Arkansas to circumvent the *Brown* decision by exempting white students from attending integrated public schools.

1964

Katzenbach v. McClung and Heart of Atlanta Motel v. United States   In separate cases decided on the same day, the Supreme Court upheld major provisions of the Civil Rights Act of 1964, which forbade racial discrimination in employment and outlawed segregation in public accommodations.

1966

South Carolina v. Katzenbach   The Supreme Court dismissed a suit brought by the state against the U.S. attorney general, seeking to bar him from enforcing the Voting Rights Act of 1965, which prohibited altogether the use of "tests or devices" (the most common being discriminatory literacy tests) as a prerequisite to voting.

1967

Loving v. Virginia   By refusing to void the marriage of an interracial Virginia couple who married in Washington, D.C., the Supreme Court paved the way for the nullification of various state antimiscegenation laws.

1969

Allen v. State Board of Elections   The Supreme Court banned all regulations, whether obvious or subtle, that worked to deny citizens the right to vote because of race; in doing so, the Court stated that the Voting Rights Act of 1965 "should be given the broadest possible scope."

1971

North Carolina State Board of Education v. Swann and Swann v. Charlotte Mecklenburg Board of Education   The Supreme Court upheld the use of busing to overcome the effects of segregation in public schools.

Griggs v. Duke Power Co.   The Supreme Court ruled that the company could not employ intelligence tests and diploma requirements to restrict the employment opportunities of African Americans; the Court found that the requirements had no bearing on job performance and were designed to maintain a pattern of discrimination.

1973

Georgia v. United States   The Court upheld a provision of the Voting Rights Act of 1965, requiring that all states with a history of voting-rights violations receive approval from the U.S. attorney general for any proposed change in voting procedures.

White v. Regester   The Court disallowed a Texas redistricting scheme designed to prevent blacks from being elected to public office.

1977

Castanda v. Partida   The Supreme Court upheld the use of statistical data to show that members of a minority group (in this case, Mexican Americans) had been excluded from jury service; the ruling established that statistics could be applied to the entire spectrum of civil rights cases.

1978

Regents of University of California v. Allan Bakke   The Court ruled that numerical quota systems designed to increase the admission of black students were unconstitutional.

1980

City of Mobile, Alabama v. Wiley L. Bolden et al.   The Court ruled that Mobile's practice of electing city commissioners at large violated the constitutional rights of black citizens. Mobile was directed to revamp its government so that a mayor and city council would be elected from single-member districts, thereby enabling African American voters to have an impact on the outcome.

1983

Bob Joncs University v. IRS   The Court ruled unconstitutional a long-standing IRS policy that denied tax-exempt status to any university practicing racial discrimination.

1984

Allen v. Wright   The Supreme Court denied a challenge to the *Bob Jones* decision made by black parents. In one part of its ruling, the Court maintained that denial of tax-exempt status would not necessarily induce schools to abandon segregation.

Firefighters Local Union No. 1784 v. Stotts   The Supreme Court ruled that African American firefighters in Memphis, Tennessee, could not be exempt from layoffs solely because they were hired on the basis of affirmative action; seniority rules would have to apply.

1985

Meritor Savings Bank FSB v. Vinson   Responding to the complaint of Michelle Vinson, a black teller who charged sexual harassment by a white supervisor, the Supreme Court ruled that federal civil rights laws apply to sexual harassment in the workplace.

1986

Thornburgh v. Gingles   The Court struck down a North Carolina redistricting plan that had the effect of diluting black voting strength.

Wygant v. Jackson Board of Education   The Supreme Court rejected the affirmative-action plan of a Michigan school board on the grounds that its goals were too vague.

Local No. 93, International Association of Firefighters v. City of Cleveland   The Supreme Court dismissed the union's challenge to Cleveland's affirmative-action program, ruling that lower courts had broad discretion in the approval of such plans.

1987

Watson v. Fort Worth Bank & Trust   The Supreme Court upheld a discrimination complaint by an African American employee who was repeatedly denied promotion. The Court held that it was not necessary for a plaintiff to prove that there was an intentional policy of discrimination to demonstrate that discrimination had occurred.

McKleskey v. Kemp   The Supreme Court upheld the imposition of the death penalty in a Georgia case, even though the plaintiff presented a statistical analysis of 2,000 murder cases showing a disproportion of death sentences meted out to black defendants convicted of killing whites.

United States v. Paradise   The Supreme Court approved the use of court-ordered racial hiring quotas in the Alabama Department of Highways, where a consistent pattern of discrimination had been demonstrated.

Johnson v. Transportation Agency, Santa Clara County, California   The Supreme Court ruled that any employer—not only those with a history of discrimination—could legally institute programs to ensure a racially balanced workforce.

1989

Martin v. Wilks   The Court upheld a plan by the city of Birmingham, Alabama, to hire black firefighters as a means of correcting past policies of discrimination; the suit had been challenged by white firefighters, who claimed that the agreement violated their civil rights.

City of Richmond v. J. A. Croson   The Supreme Court ruled that the Constitution limits the power of states and localities to set aside a percentage of business for minority contractors; in the wake of the ruling, Atlanta and other cities abolished their minority set-aside programs.

1991

Chison v. Roemer and Houston Lawyers v. Texas Attorney General   The Supreme Court ruled that the Voting Rights Act of 1965 extended to judicial elections.

Hater v. Melo   In a case arising from the firing of 18 workers by the Pennsylvania auditor general, the Supreme Court ruled that state officials who violated the civil rights of individuals could be sued for monetary damages and obliged to pay out of their own pockets.

1992

Presley v. Etowah County Commission and Mack v. Russell County Commission   The Supreme Court ruled that the state of Alabama did not need federal approval to diminish the authority of county commissioners. (The state had taken this action after a number of African Americans won election to previously all-white county commissions.) This was the first instance in which the Court took a narrow view of the Voting Rights Act of 1965; it marked a clear retreat from the principles established in *Allen v. State Board of Elections* (1969).

1993

St. Mary's Honor Center v. Hicks   In a significant departure from previous judicial decisions, the Supreme Court ruled that workers must provide direct evidence of discrimination in order to qualify for protection under civil rights laws; it would no longer be sufficient simply to indicate a pattern of unequal treatment for whites and minorities. The ruling would make it far more difficult for individuals to bring suits because few, if any, employers would explicitly state that they were practicing discrimination.

Shaw v. Reno   The Supreme Court ruled that irregularly shaped congressional districts could be challenged on constitutional grounds.

1996

Bush v. Vera and Shaw v. Hunt   The Supreme Court struck down majority black and Hispanic congressional districts in Texas and North Carolina, claiming that race had played too great a role in the determination of the boundaries. The suits had been brought by white voters after a number of black candidates won seats in Congress during the 1992 elections, doubling the size of the Congressional Black Caucus.

Hopwood v. Texas   The U.S. Court of Appeals (Fifth Circuit) ruled that the university could not use race in any way as a factor governing admissions. As a result of the ruling, enrollment in the University of Texas Law School declined from 31 African American and 42 Hispanic students in 1996–97 to 3 African American and 20 Hispanic students in 1997–98; similar effects also prevailed in California, where the governor chose to implement the *Hopwood* ruling.

CRIME AND JUSTICE: STATISTICAL OVERVIEW

LYNCHING AND OTHER HATE CRIMES: INSTRUMENTS OF TERROR

By the late 19th and early 20th centuries, the practice of *lynching* (execution by mob action without legal sanction) had became a weapon of intimidation used by whites against blacks, as well as against some whites who supported civil rights. Black people, including some women, have been lynched for a variety of "offenses," including owning property, voting, testifying in court against a white person, or otherwise failing to express deference to whites. Lynching was particularly widespread after the Civil War, when former supporters of the Confederacy were struggling to maintain control of the South.

Table 12.1 Lynchings, by Race and Year, 1882–1962

Year	Whites	Blacks	Total	Year	Whites	Blacks	Total
1882	64	49	113	1908	8	89	97
1883	77	53	130	1909	13	69	82
1884	160	51	211	1910	9	67	76
1885	110	74	184	1911	7	60	67
1886	64	74	138	1912	2	61	63
1887	50	70	120	1913	1	51	52
1888	68	69	137	1914	4	51	55
1889	76	94	170	1915	13	56	69
1890	11	85	96	1916	4	50	54
1891	71	113	184	1917	2	36	38
1892	69	161	230	1918	4	60	64
1893	34	118	152	1919	7	76	83
1894	58	134	192	1920	8	53	61
1895	66	113	179	1921	5	59	64
1896	45	78	123	1922	6	51	57
1897	35	123	158	1923	4	29	33
1898	19	101	120	1924	0	16	16
1899	21	85	106	1925	0	17	17
1900	9	106	115	1926	7	23	30
1901	25	105	130	1927	0	16	16
1902	7	85	92	1928	1	10	11
1903	15	84	99	1929	3	7	10
1904	7	76	83	1930	1	20	21
1905	5	57	62	1931	1	12	13
1906	3	62	65	1932	2	6	8
1907	2	58	60	1933	4	24	28

Table 12.1 (continued)

Year	Whites	Blacks	Total	Year	Whites	Blacks	Total
1934	0	15	15	1949	0	3	3
1935	2	18	20	1950	1	1	2
1936	0	8	8	1951	0	1	1
1937	0	8	8	1952	0	0	0
1938	0	6	6	1953	0	0	0
1939	1	2	3	1954	0	0	0
1940	1	4	5	1955	0	3	3
1941	0	4	4	1956	0	0	0
1942	0	6	6	1957	1	0	1
1943	0	3	3	1958	0	0	0
1944	0	2	2	1959	0	1	0
1945	0	1	1	1960	0	0	0
1946	0	6	6	1961	0	1	1
1947	0	1	1	1962	0	0	0
1948	1	1	2	Total	1,294	3,442	4,736

Source: Negro Almanac, p. 368.

Table 12.2 Lynchings, by State and Race, 1882–1962

State	Whites	Blacks	Total	State	Whites	Blacks	Total
Alabama	48	299	347	New Jersey	0	1	1
Arizona	31	0	31	New Mexico	33	3	36
Arkansas	58	226	284	New York	1	1	2
California	41	2	43	North Carolina	15	85	100
Colorado	66	2	68	North Dakota	13	3	16
Delaware	0	1	1	Ohio	10	16	26
Florida	25	257	282	Oklahoma	82	40	122
Georgia	39	491	530	Oregon	20	1	21
Idaho	20	0	20	Pennsylvania	2	6	8
Illinois	15	19	34	South Carolina	4	156	160
Indiana	33	14	47	South Dakota	27	0	27
Iowa	17	2	19	Tennessee	47	204	251
Kansas	35	19	54	Texas	141	352	493
Kentucky	63	142	205	Utah	6	2	8
Louisiana	56	335	391	Vermont	1	0	1
Maryland	2	27	29	Virginia	17	83	100
Michigan	7	1	8	Washington	25	1	26
Minnesota	5	4	9	West Virginia	20	28	48
Mississippi	40	538	578	Wisconsin	6	0	6
Missouri	53	69	122	Wyoming	30	5	35
Montana	82	2	84	Total	1,294	3,442	4,736
Nebraska	52	5	57				
Nevada	6	0	6				

Source: Negro Almanac, p. 365.

HATE CRIMES

Also known as "bias crimes," *hate crimes* are unlawful acts—from vandalism to murder—motivated by hostility toward the victim as a member of a group. According to FBI statistics for hate crimes in 1995 (limited to those crimes committed by reason of race, religion, national origin, or sexual orientation), there were a total of 7,947 incidents, 61 percent motivated by racial bias: 2,988 hate crimes were directed against African Americans, 1,226 against whites. Most of the incidents involved vandalism, destruction of property, and intimidation, though there were 20 murders. Of 8,433 known offenders, 4,991 (59%) were white, and 2,253 (27%) were black.

ALABAMA JUSTICE

On June 6, 1997, a member of the Ku Klux Klan was executed for the 1981 murder of a black teenager, Michael Donald, in Mobile. It was the first execution for a white-on-black crime in the state since 1913. (In 1987, a wrongful-death suit brought by Donald's mother resulted in a $7 million judgment that bankrupted the United Klans of America.)

IMPRISONMENT OF AFRICAN AMERICANS

Table 12.3 Persons Arrested, by Charge and Race, 1994 (thousands)

Offense Charged	Arrests		
	Total	Black	% Black
TOTAL	11,880	3,712	31.2
SERIOUS CRIMES	2,388	866	36.3
Murder and nonnegligent manslaughter	19	10	56.4
Forcible rape	30	12	41.7
Robbery	147	89	60.8
Aggravated assault	450	176	39.2
Burglary	321	98	30.7
Larceny/theft	1,239	409	33.0
Motor vehicle theft	166	67	40.1
Arson	17	4	23.0
ALL OTHER NONSERIOUS CRIMES			
Other assaults	993	343	34.6
Forgery and counterfeiting	93	32	34.4
Fraud	331	121	36.5
Embezzlement	12	4	32.8
Stolen property—buying, receiving, possessing	135	55	40.5
Vandalism	260	59	22.8
Weapons; carrying, possessing, etc.	213	88	41.1
Prostitution and commercialized vice	87	31	35.6
Sex offenses (except forcible rape and prostitution)	82	18	21.6
Drug-abuse violations	1,120	430	38.4
Gambling	16	7	45.7
Offenses against family and children	91	30	32.7
Driving under the influence	1,067	108	10.1
Liquor laws	427	58	13.5

Table 12.3 (continued)

Offense Charged	Arrests		
	Total	Black	% Black
Drunkenness	572	96	16.8
Disorderly conduct	602	199	33.1
Vagrancy	21	9	40.4
All other offenses (except traffic)	3,050	1,093	35.8
Suspicion	11	6	49.5
Curfew and loitering law violations	107	22	20.7
Runaways	202	38	19.0

Source: Statistical Abstract of the U.S., No. 323.

Note: Represents arrests, not charges, reported by 10,693 agencies with a total 1994 population of 208 million as estimated by FBI.

Table 12.4 Homicide Victims, by Race and Sex, 1970 to 1993

Year	Total[1]	Homicide Victims				Total[1]	Homicide Rate[2]			
		White		Black			White		Black	
		Male	Female	Male	Female		Male	Female	Male	Female
1970	16,848	5,865	1,938	7,265	1,569	8.3	6.8	2.1	67.6	13.3
1980	24,278	10,381	3,177	8,385	1,898	10.7	10.9	3.2	66.6	13.5
1981	23,646	9,941	3,125	8,312	1,825	10.3	10.4	3.1	64.8	12.7
1982	22,358	9,260	3,179	7,730	1,743	9.6	9.6	3.1	59.1	12.0
1983	20,191	8,355	2,880	6,822	1,672	8.6	8.6	2.8	51.4	11.3
1984	19,796	8,171	2,956	6,563	1,677	8.4	8.3	2.9	48.7	11.2
1985	19,893	8,122	3,041	6,616	1,666	8.3	8.2	2.9	48.4	11.0
1986	21,731	8,567	3,123	7,634	1,861	9.0	8.6	3.0	55.0	12.1
1987	21,103	7,979	3,149	7,518	1,969	8.7	7.9	3.0	53.3	12.6
1988	22,032	7,994	3,072	8,314	2,089	9.0	7.9	2.9	58.0	13.2
1989	22,909	8,337	2,971	8,888	2,074	9.2	8.2	2.8	61.1	12.9
1990	24,932	9,147	3,006	9,981	2,163	10.0	9.0	2.8	69.2	13.5
1991	26,513	9,581	3,204	10,628	2,330	10.5	9.3	3.0	72.0	14.2
1992	25,488	9,456	3,012	10,131	2,187	10.0	9.1	2.8	67.5	13.1
1993	26,009	9,054	3,232	10,640	2,297	10.1	8.6	3.0	69.7	13.6

[1] Includes races not shown separately.

[2] Rate based on enumerated population figures as of April 1 for 1970, 1980, and 1990; July 1 estimates for other years.

Source: U.S. National Center for Health Statistics, *Vital Statistics of the United States,* annual, and unpublished data.

Note: Rates per 100,000 resident population in specified group. Excludes deaths to nonresidents of United States. Beginning in 1980, deaths are classified according to the ninth revision of the *International Classification of Diseases;* for earlier years, classified according to revision in use at the time. See also *Historical Statistics, Colonial Times to 1970,* series H-971–978.

Table 12.5 Jail Inmates, by Race and
Detention Status, 1978 to 1994

Year	Total Inmates[1]	Black
1978	158,394	65,104
1985	256,615	102,646
1988	343,569	141,979
1989	395,553	185,910
1990	405,320	174,335
1991	426,479	187,618
1992	444,584	195,156
1993	459,804	203,463
1994	490,442	206,278

[1] For 1988 and 1990–1994 includes 31,356;
38,675; 43,138; 52,235; 66,249; and 93,058
persons, respectively, of unknown race not
shown separately.
Note: Excludes federal and state prisons or
other correctional institutions; institutions exclusively for juveniles; state-operated jails in
Alaska, Connecticut, Delaware, Hawaii, Rhode
Island, and Vermont; and other facilities that
retain persons for less than 48 hours. For 1978
and 1988, data based on National Jail Census;
for other years, based on sample survey and
subject to sampling variability.
Source: U.S. Bureau of Justice Statistics, *Profile
of Jail Inmates, 1978 and 1989; Jail Inmates*, annual; and *1988 Census of Local Jails*.

INCARCERATION RATES

A 1997 study by the Sentencing Project shows a rising disparity between the numbers of incarcer-
ated blacks and those of whites: In 1994, there were 7.66 African Americans in federal and state
prisons for every white, up from a ratio of 6.88 to 1 in 1988. African Americans make up 51 percent of the 1.1 million inmates nationwide, and on any given day, 1 of every 3 African American
men in their 20s is under the control of the criminal-justice system—in prison, on probation, or on
parole.

DRUG CONVICTIONS

According to a 1995 study by the Sentencing Project, African Americans compose 13 percent of monthly drug users in the United States. Yet they account for 35 percent of arrests for drug possession, 55 percent of drug-related convictions, and 74 percent of the drug-related prison sentences handed out. Between 1986 and 1991, the number of African American women in state prisons for drug offenses rose by 828 percent.

COCAINE AND THE LAW

In 1986, amid rising concerns about violence accompanying a crack-cocaine epidemic, Congress mandated a 100 : 1 ratio for sentencing in cases of cocaine possession with intent to distribute. According to the formula, an individual apprehended with 5 grams of crack cocaine received the same five-year sentence as someone apprehended with 500 grams of powdered cocaine. Because the vast majority of crack-cocaine users are black, this policy weighed heavily on African Americans, who represent 84.5 percent of those convicted of crack possession. Thus, many low-level black crack offenders are serving longer sentences than whites who were high-level traffickers in powdered cocaine. In 1997, the Federal Sentencing Commission, the U.S. attorney general, the White House drug-policy advisor, and the Congressional Black Caucus all recommended a reduction of the sentencing ratio to 10 : 1 or 5 : 1.

RACE AND THE DEATH PENALTY

Of the 3,122 inmates on death row in 1997, 1,439 (48%) were white, and 1,272 (41%) were black; African Americans represented 39 percent of the 328 prisoners executed between 1976 and 1997, whereas whites represented 56 percent. Whites convicted of murdering whites accounted for 58 percent of death-row inmates. Blacks convicted of murdering whites composed 23 percent, and 12 percent of the condemned prisoners were blacks convicted of killing blacks. (Of the prisoners on death row in 1997, only 49 were women.) A 1995 Gallup poll indicated that 81 percent of whites interviewed favored the death penalty, compared with 58 percent of African Americans. A 1998 U.N. Human Rights Commission report on executions criticized the preponderance of whites in the U.S. judicial system and stated that race, ethnic origin, and economic status were important factors in determining who does—and who does not—receive a death sentence in the United States. The U.S. government rejected the report, claiming the study was "seriously flawed."

I t is the poor and members of minority groups who are least able to voice their complaints against capital punishment. Their impotence leaves them victims of a sanction that the wealthier, better-represented, just-as-guilty person can escape. So long as the capital sanction is used only against the forlorn, easily forgotten members of society, legislators are content to maintain the status quo.

Thurgood Marshall, concurring opinion in *Furman v. Georgia* (1972)

Table 12.6 Prisoners Executed under Civil Authority, 1930 to 1994

Year or period	Total[1]	White	Black	Executed for Murder			Executed for Rape			Executed, Other Offenses[2]		
				Total[1]	White	Black	Total[1]	White	Black	Total[1]	White	Black
All years	4,116	1,907	2,165	3,591	1,820	1,734	455	48	405	70	39	31
1930 to 1939	1,667	827	816	1,514	803	687	125	10	115	28	14	14
1940 to 1949	1,284	490	781	1,064	458	595	200	19	179	20	13	7
1950 to 1959	717	336	376	601	316	280	102	13	89	14	7	7
1960 to 1967	191	98	93	155	87	68	28	6	22	8	5	3
1968 to 1976	—	—	—	—	—	—	—	—	—	—	—	—
1977 to 1982	6	5	1	6	5	1	—	—	—	—	—	—
1983	5	4	1	5	4	1	—	—	—	—	—	—
1984	21	13	8	21	13	8	—	—	—	—	—	—
1985	18	11	7	18	11	7	—	—	—	—	—	—
1986	18	11	7	18	11	7	—	—	—	—	—	—
1987	25	13	12	25	13	12	—	—	—	—	—	—
1988	11	6	5	11	6	5	—	—	—	—	—	—
1989	16	8	8	16	8	8	—	—	—	—	—	—
1990	23	16	7	23	16	7	—	—	—	—	—	—
1991	14	7	7	14	7	7	—	—	—	—	—	—
1992	31	19	11	31	19	11	—	—	—	—	—	—
1993	38	23	14	38	23	14	—	—	—	—	—	—
1994	31	20	11	31	20	11	—	—	—	—	—	—

— Represents zero.

[1] Includes races other than white or black.

[2] Includes 25 armed robbery, 20 kidnapping, 11 burglary, 8 espionage (6 in 1942 and 2 in 1953), and 6 aggravated assault.

Source: Through 1978, U.S. Law Enforcement Assistance Administration; thereafter, U.S. Bureau of Justice Statistics, Correctional Populations in the United States, annual.

Note: Excludes executions by military authorities.

AFRICAN AMERICANS IN THE FEDERAL JUDICIARY: 1997

(Source: Alliance for Justice.)

SUPREME COURT

Clarence Thomas—10/18/91 (Bush)

DISTRICT OF COLUMBIA CIRCUIT
CIRCUIT JUDGES

Harry Edwards (Chief Judge)—2/20/80 (Carter)
Judith Rogers—3/10/94 (Clinton)

DISTRICT JUDGES

Norma Holloway Johnson—5/12/80 (Carter)
John Garrett Penn—3/23/79 (Carter)
Emmett Sullivan—6/15/94 (Clinton)

FIRST CIRCUIT (MAINE, MASSACHUSETTS, NEW HAMPSHIRE, RHODE ISLAND, PUERTO RICO)
CIRCUIT JUDGES

None

DISTRICT JUDGES

Reginald Lindsay—11/20/93 (Clinton)—Massachusetts

SECOND CIRCUIT (CONNECTICUT, NEW YORK, VERMONT)
CIRCUIT JUDGES

Amalya Lyle Kearse—6/21/79 (Carter)—New York

DISTRICT JUDGES

Deborah Batts—5/6/94 (Clinton)—Southern New York
Sterling Johnson—6/28/91 (Bush)—Eastern New York (Brooklyn)
Barrington Parker Jr.—9/14/94 (Clinton)—Southern New York
Alvin Thompson—10/7/94 (Clinton)—Connecticut

SENIOR JUDGE, U.S. DISTRICT COURT

Constance Baker Motley—8/30/66 (Johnson)—Southern New York

THIRD CIRCUIT (DELAWARE, NEW JERSEY, PENNSYLVANIA, U.S. VIRGIN ISLANDS)
CIRCUIT JUDGES

Timothy Lewis—10/8/92 (Bush)—Pennsylvania
Theodore McKee—6/15/94 (Clinton)—Pennsylvania

DISTRICT JUDGES

Raymond Finch—5/6/94 (Clinton)—U.S. Virgin Islands (St. Thomas)
James T. Giles—11/27/79 (Carter)—Eastern Pennsylvania
Joseph Greenaway—7/16/96 (Clinton)—New Jersey
Herbert J. Hutton—8/12/88 (Reagan)—Eastern Pennsylvania
Curtis Joyner—4/8/92 (Bush)—Eastern Pennsylvania
Gary Lancaster—11/20/93 (Clinton)—Western Pennsylvania
Anne E. Thompson—11/2/79 (Carter)—New Jersey
William Walls—10/7/94 (Clinton)—New Jersey

FOURTH CIRCUIT (MARYLAND, NORTH CAROLINA, SOUTH CAROLINA, VIRGINIA, WEST VIRGINIA)
CIRCUIT JUDGES

None

DISTRICT JUDGES

James Beaty Jr.—10/7/94 (Clinton)—Central North Carolina
Andre Davis—8/11/95 (Clinton)—Maryland
Raymond Jackson—11/20/93 (Clinton)—Eastern Virginia
James Spencer—10/14/86 (Reagan)—Eastern Virginia
Alexander Williams—8/17/94 (Clinton)—Maryland

FIFTH CIRCUIT (LOUISIANA, MISSISSIPPI, TEXAS)
CIRCUIT JUDGES

Carl Stewart—5/6/94 (Clinton)—Louisiana

DISTRICT JUDGES

Vanessa Gilmore—6/15/94 (Clinton)—Southern Texas
Kenneth Hoyt—4/1/88 (Reagan)—Southern Texas
Henry Wingate—10/17/85 (Reagan)—Southern Mississippi

SIXTH CIRCUIT (KENTUCKY, MICHIGAN, OHIO, TENNESSEE)
CIRCUIT JUDGES

R. Guy Cole—12/22/95 (Clinton)—Southern Ohio

DISTRICT JUDGES

Curtis Collier—5/8/95 (Clinton)—Eastern Tennessee
Bernice B. Donald—12/22/95 (Clinton)—Western Tennessee
Benjamin Gibson (Chief Judge)—9/26/79 (Carter)—Western Michigan
Denise Page-Hood—6/15/94 (Clinton)—Eastern Michigan
Solomon Oliver Jr.—5/6/94 (Clinton)—Northern Ohio
George White—5/23/80 (Carter)—Northern Ohio

SENIOR JUDGE, U.S. COURT OF APPEALS

Nathaniel R. Jones—10/15/79 (Carter)—Ohio

SEVENTH CIRCUIT (ILLINOIS, INDIANA, WISCONSIN)
CIRCUIT JUDGES

None

DISTRICT JUDGES

David Coar—10/7/94 (Clinton)—Northern Illinois
Blanche Manning—8/9/94 (Clinton)—Northern Illinois

Joe McDade—11/21/91 (Bush)—Central Illinois

Ann Williams—4/4/85 (Reagan)—Northern Illinois

EIGHTH CIRCUIT (ARKANSAS, IOWA, MINNESOTA, MISSOURI, NEBRASKA, NORTH DAKOTA, SOUTH DAKOTA)
CIRCUIT JUDGES

Theodore McMillan—9/23/78 (Carter)—Eastern Missouri

DISTRICT JUDGES

Michael Davis—3/25/94 (Clinton)—Minnesota

Fernando Gaitan—7/18/91 (Bush)—Western Missouri

George Howard Jr.—9/30/80 (Carter)—Arkansas

Carol Jackson—8/12/92 (Bush)—Eastern Missouri

Charles Shaw—11/20/93 (Clinton)—Eastern Missouri

NINTH CIRCUIT (ARIZONA, CALIFORNIA, MONTANA, NEVADA, OREGON, WASHINGTON, ALASKA, HAWAII, GUAM, NORTHERN MARIANA ISLANDS)
CIRCUIT JUDGES

None

DISTRICT JUDGES

Saundra Brown Armstrong—6/18/91 (Bush)—Northern California

Franklin Burgess—3/15/94 (Clinton)—Western Washington

Garland Burrell—2/27/92 (Bush)—Eastern California

Audrey Collins—5/6/94 (Clinton)—Central California

Ancer Haggerty—3/25/94 (Clinton)—Oregon

Terry Hatter Jr.—12/20/79 (Carter)—Central California

Thelton Henderson (Chief Judge)—6/30/80 (Carter)—Northern California

Napoleon Jones—9/14/94 (Clinton)—Southern California

Consuelo Bland Marshall—9/30/80 (Carter)—Central California

James Ware—9/28/90 (Bush)—Northern California

TENTH CIRCUIT (COLORADO, KANSAS, NEW MEXICO, OKLAHOMA, UTAH, WYOMING)
CIRCUIT JUDGES

None

DISTRICT JUDGES

Wiley Daniel—6/30/95 (Clinton)—Colorado
Vicki Miles-LaGrange—10/7/94 (Clinton)—Western Oklahoma

ELEVENTH CIRCUIT (ALABAMA, FLORIDA, GEORGIA)
CIRCUIT JUDGES

Joseph Hatchett—7/13/79 (Carter)—Northern Florida

DISTRICT JUDGES

Henry Lee Adams—11/20/93 (Clinton)—Central Florida
U. W. Clemon—6/30/80 (Carter)—Northern Alabama
Clarence Cooper—5/6/94 (Clinton)—Northern Georgia
Wilkie Ferguson—11/20/93 (Clinton)—Southern Florida
Donald Graham—9/12/90 (Bush)—Southern Florida
W. Louis Sands—5/6/94 (Clinton)—Central Georgia
Myron Thompson (Chief Judge)—9/29/80 (Carter)—Central Alabama

U.S. CLAIMS COURT

Reginald Gibson—12/10/82 (Reagan)—Washington, D.C.

LEGAL ORGANIZATIONS

Alabama Black Lawyers Association
3505 23rd Street
Birmingham, AL 35207
205-254-0608

Alliance of Black Women Attorneys
Legal Aid Bureau
714 E. Pratt Street
Baltimore, MD 21202
301-539-5340

Alliance for Justice
200 P Street, NW, Suite 712
Washington, DC 20036
202-822-6070
National coalition dedicated to ensuring access to
    justice for all. Works to strengthen public-
    interest community and build the next
    generation of advocates.

American Bar Association
Commission on Minorities in the Profession
750 N. Lake Shore Drive
Chicago, IL 60611
312-988-5000

American Civil Liberties Union
1400 20th Street, NW, Suite 119
Washington, DC 20036
202-457-0800
Champions the rights set forth in the Bill of
    Rights of the U.S. Constitution through
    litigation, advocacy, and public education.

American Civil Liberties Union—New York
    Chapter
125 Broad Street, 17th Floor
New York, NY 10004
212-344-3005
See the preceding description of the organization's
    mission.

Association of Black Women Attorneys
134 W. 32nd Street
New York, NY 10001
212-815-0478
National networking and advocacy organization.

California Association of Black Lawyers
3580 Wilshire Boulevard, Suite 1920
Los Angeles, CA 90010
213-387-6628

Center for Constitutional Rights
666 Broadway, 7th Floor
New York, NY 10012
212-614-6464
Works "to halt and reverse the steady erosion of
    civil liberties in the U.S." Programs include the
    Ella Baker Student Program, the Movement
    Support Network, and the Voting Rights
    Project.

Charles Houston Bar Association
1901 Harrison Street, No. 901
Oakland, CA 94612
415-834-7897
An official bar association of the State Bar of
    California since 1975, this organization
    provides a forum for African American lawyers
    and works to protect the legal rights of African
    Americans through litigation.

Lawyers' Committee for Civil Rights Under Law
National Office
1450 G Street, NW, Suite 400
Washington, DC 20005
202-662-8600
Provides legal assistance to poor and minority
    groups in eight major cities through local
    committees of private lawyers. National office
    takes on reform efforts in such areas as voting
    rights and housing discrimination.

Massachusetts Black Lawyers Association
P.O. Box 2411
Boston, MA 02208
617-722-2860

Minnesota Minority Lawyers Association
P.O. Box 2754, Loop Station
Minneapolis, MN 55402

NAACP Legal Defense and Education Fund
99 Hudson Street, 16th Floor
New York, NY 10021
212-310-9000

Works to provide and support litigation on behalf of blacks, other racial minorities, and women by representing both individuals and civil rights groups in cases involving discrimination.

National Association of Blacks in Criminal Justice
North Carolina Central University
Criminal Justice Building, Room 106
P.O. Box 19758
Durham, NC 27707
919-683-1801

National Bar Association
1225 11th Street, NW
Washington, DC 20001
202-842-3900
Internet: http://www.melanet.com/nba
Composed of minority (predominantly black) attorneys, judges, law students, and law faculty; addresses the interests of members and the communities they serve. Affiliated with 12 regional and 76 local groups.

National Bar Association—Women Lawyers Division
1211 Connecticut Avenue, Suite 702
Washington, DC 20036
202-291-1979
Forum for women lawyers, law students, and others to address issues unique to women in the legal profession, promote professional growth, and encourage community service.

National Black Law Student Association
1225 11th Street, NW
Washington, DC 20001
Black law students united to meet the needs of black people within their profession and to work for the black community in general.

National Conference of Black Lawyers
116 W. 111th Street
New York, NY 10026
212-864-4000
Attorneys throughout the United States and Canada united to provide legal services, public education, and research in the service of black and poor communities.

National Prison Project of the ACLU Foundation
1875 Connecticut Avenue, NW, Suite 410
Washington, DC 20009
202-234-4830
Provides inmate litigation in class-action suits.

North Carolina Association of Black Lawyers
New Bold Station
1200 Murchison Road
Lafayetteville, NC 28301
919-486-1142

The Sentencing Project
918 F Street, NW, Suite 501
Washington, DC 20004
202-628-0871
Internet: http://www.sproject.com
Provides technical research on alternative sentencing and public education about alternatives to incarceration.

South Carolina Black Lawyers Association
P.O. Box 8417
Columbia, SC 29202

Wisconsin Association of Minority Attorneys
230 Westwells
Milwaukee, WI 53202
414-271-5888

NOTABLE LAWYERS, JUDGES, AND LEGAL SCHOLARS

Allen, Macon B. (1816–1894).   A native of Indiana, Allen moved to Portland, Maine, where he became a prosperous businessperson. He was admitted to the Maine bar in 1845, becoming the first African American officially licensed to practice law. Two years later, Allen moved to Boston and was the first African American admitted to the Massachusetts bar. After the Civil War, Allen took up residence in Charleston, South Carolina. There, he formed a law firm in partnership with fellow African Americans William J. Whipper and Robert Brown Elliott, both of whom were members of the state legislature. (Elliott later served in the U.S. Congress.) In 1873, Allen was elected a judge of the South Carolina Interior

Court, becoming one of the first black judges in the nation. After completing one term, he resumed his private law practice and played a prominent role in local politics.

Anderson, Violette (1882–?).   Born in England, Anderson came to the United States as a child and was educated in Chicago, earning a law degree from the Chicago Law School in 1920. She was the first African American woman admitted to the Illinois bar and the first woman prosecutor in Chicago (1922–1923). In 1926, Anderson was admitted to practice before the U.S. Supreme Court, becoming the first African American woman to gain that distinction.

Bell, Derrick Albert (1930–   ).   A native of Pittsburgh, Bell earned his law degree from the University of Pittsburgh in 1957. He worked as an attorney for the U.S. Department of Justice (1957–1959) and for the NAACP Legal Defense and Education Fund (1960–1966). Bell joined the faculty at Harvard Law School in 1969 and became its first tenured black professor in 1971. After serving as dean of the law school at the University of Oregon from 1980 to 1986, he returned to his tenured post at Harvard. He later took an unpaid leave of absence to protest Harvard's hiring policies and was dismissed in 1992 when he exceeded his two-year maximum leave. He has been a visiting professor of law at New York University ever since. Known as a forceful and outspoken champion of racial justice, Bell is the author of *Race, Racism, and American Law* (1980) and *We Are Not Saved: The Elusive Quest for Racial Justice* (1987).

Bolin, Jane Matilda (1908–   ).   Bolin earned a law degree from Yale in 1931 and practiced law in New York City until 1937, when she was appointed assistant corporation counsel. Two years later, Mayor Fiorello La Guardia appointed Bolin to the Domestic Relations Court (now the Family Court), making her the first African American female judge in the nation. She remained on the bench for 40 years, taking an active interest in a number of social-service organizations. After retiring, Bolin worked as a volunteer reading teacher in the New York public schools and then accepted a post with the New York Board of Regents.

Cobb, James Adlai (1876–1958).   After graduating from Howard University Law School in 1899, Cobb began to practice law in Washington, D.C. From 1907 to 1915, he served as a special assistant in the Justice Department and gained a national reputation for prosecuting cases under the Pure Food and Drugs Act of 1906. Cobb joined the faculty at Howard in 1916. The following year he was associate counsel before the Supreme Court in the case of *Buchanan v. Warley*. He later served in the same capacity in *Nixon v. Herndon* and *Nixon v. Condon*. In 1926, Cobb was appointed a judge of the Municipal Court of the District of Columbia. He served until 1935, when President Franklin D. Roosevelt, noting that Cobb was a Republican, chose not to reappoint him; more than 100 lawyers and judges protested in vain. Upon leaving the bench, Cobb became a senior partner in Washington's leading African American law firm: Cobb, Howard, and Hayes.

Guinier, Lani (1950–   ).   A 1974 Yale University Law School graduate, Guinier worked as a law clerk, a referee in juvenile court, and a special assistant in the Justice Department before joining the NAACP Legal Defense and Education Fund in 1981, where she worked until 1989, when she accepted a teaching position at the University of Pennsylvania Law School. Guinier gained national recognition in 1993 when President Bill Clinton chose her as head of the Justice Department's civil rights division. When controversy arose, Clinton withdrew his nomination. Author of *The Tyranny of the Majority: Fundamental Fairness in a Representative Democracy* (1994), Guinier is currently a tenured law professor at the University of Pennsylvania.

Hastie, William Henry (1904–1976).   After graduating from Harvard Law School, Hastie joined the faculty of Howard University. In 1933, he joined the firm of Houston & Houston in handling civil rights cases for the NAACP and also served as assistant solicitor in the Department of the Interior (1933–1937). In 1937, Hastie became the first African American appointee to the federal bench when he was named district judge for the U.S. Virgin Islands. He resigned his judgeship in 1939 to join the faculty of Howard University's School of Law.

THE SCOTTSBORO CASE

In 1931, nine young black men—the youngest was age 13—were arrested in Scottsboro, Alabama, and charged with raping two white women on a freight train. When the nine were sentenced to death, the verdict touched off a storm of protest that swept the nation. With the aid of the NAACP, the case was appealed to the Supreme Court, which ordered a new trial on the grounds that the defendants had not had adequate counsel. Upon retrial, each of the defendants was convicted anew and sentenced to 99 years in prison. Marches and protests on behalf of the Scottsboro Boys continued throughout the 1930s. By 1950, all had been paroled or freed on appeal.

Higginbotham, A. Leon, Jr. (1928–1998).   A graduate of Yale Law School, Higginbotham served as an assistant district attorney in Philadelphia and a member of the Pennsylvania Human Rights Commission during the early 1950s. From 1954 to 1962, he was a partner in the firm of Norris, Green, Harris & Higginbotham. He served on the Federal Trade Commission from 1962 to 1964, when President Lyndon Johnson named him a federal district-court judge. In 1978, Higginbotham was named to the U.S. Court of Appeals (Third Circuit, Pennsylvania) by President Jimmy Carter. He retired from the bench in 1993 to join the faculty at Harvard Law School. An influential commentator on legal issues affecting African Americans, he has published more than 100 articles; his books include *In the Matter of Color* (1978) and *Shades of Freedom* (1996).

Houston, Charles Hamilton (1895–1950).   After service in World War I, Houston attended Harvard Law School. He then practiced law with his father and William Hastie from 1933 to 1950. In 1935, Houston argued the case of *Hollins v. Oklahoma* before the Supreme Court and won a reversal of the death sentence for a black man convicted of rape, on the grounds that African Americans had been excluded from the jury. At this time, Houston became full-time legal counsel to the NAACP. In this capacity he worked with Thurgood Marshall and others to prepare an all-out legal assault on segregation in the United States. Houston argued several key discrimination cases before the Supreme Court, including *Missouri ex rel. Gaines v. Canada* (1938) and *Steele v. Louisville & Nashville Railroad* (1944). He was also a long-time member of the faculty at Howard University Law School, helping to train a new generation of civil rights lawyers.

Jones, Nathaniel R. (1926–   ).   Jones received his law degree from Youngstown University in 1956 and subsequently served as a U.S. attorney for the Northern District of Ohio. From 1966 to 1969, he was executive director of the Fair Employment Practices Commission in the city of Youngstown and also served as counsel to the 1967 Kerner Commission investigating the causes of urban rioting. As general counsel to the NAACP (1969–1979), he played a pivotal role in promoting school desegregation in the North. In 1979, Jones was named to the U.S. Court of Appeals for the Sixth Circuit of Ohio.

PERCENTAGE OF AFRICAN AMERICANS IN LEGAL PRACTICE

In 1995, African Americans represented 3.6 percent of all lawyers and judges in the United States, up from 2.7 percent in 1983. According to statistics compiled by the United Negro College Fund, 43.8 percent of African American law school graduates enter private practice; 21.2 percent work in government; and 14.3 percent work in business and industry. (Surveys of white law school graduates indicate 57.4% in private practice, 12% in government, and 13.5% in business and industry.)

Jones, Scipio Africanus (1863?–1943).   Jones began to study law while teaching at an Arkansas public school and was admitted to the state bar in 1899. In 1915, he was elected a special judge of the Municipal Court in Little Rock. As an attorney, Jones was a steadfast champion of African American rights. His most notable effort was the defense of 12 blacks sentenced to death (after a trial lasting less than an hour) for their role in a 1919 race riot in Elaine, Arkansas. Jones prepared the legal brief for the defendants' appeal to the U.S. Supreme Court, which overturned the convictions in 1923 (*Moore v. Dempsey*).

Marshall, Thurgood (1908–1993).   Born in Baltimore, Marshall attended Lincoln University and Howard University Law School, where he studied with Charles Houston and graduated first in his class in 1933. After leaving Howard, Marshall entered private practice in Baltimore. In 1936, he began working for the NAACP, and two years later, he took charge of all the organization's civil rights cases. Marshall became director of the Legal Defense and Education Fund in 1950 and directed the assault on school segregation that resulted in the historic *Brown v. Board of Education* decision in 1954. During his career at the NAACP, Marshall argued 32 cases before the Supreme Court, winning 29. In 1961, President John Kennedy appointed Marshall to the U.S. Court of Appeals for the Second Circuit of New York. Six years later, Marshall became the first African American to serve as a justice of the U.S. Supreme Court. He served until 1991, when declining health caused him to retire.

> I nstead of making us copy out stuff on the blackboard after school when we misbehaved, our teacher sent us down into the basement to learn parts of the Constitution. I made my way through every paragraph.
>
> Thurgood Marshall, *Columbia Oral History Interview* (1989)

Motley, Constance Baker (1921–   ).   Upon her graduation from Columbia University Law School in 1946, Motley immediately joined the legal staff of the NAACP. Working closely with Thurgood Marshall and other attorneys, she played a leading role in the legal fight against segregation and successfully argued nine cases before the Supreme Court. Her best-known achievement came in 1962, when she secured a court order directing the admission of James Meredith to the University of Mississippi. In 1964, Motley

Lawyers George E. C. Hayes, Thurgood Marshall, and James M. Nabrit celebrate victory in the landmark Brown v. Board of Education of Topeka, *1954.*

won election to the New York State Senate, becoming the first African American woman to serve in that body. The following year, she ran successfully for the post of Manhattan borough president. In 1966, President Kennedy appointed Motley a federal district judge, making her the first African American woman to serve on the federal judiciary.

Rock, John Sweat (1825–1866).   Born free in New Jersey, Rock began his professional career as a schoolteacher. In 1850, he obtained a medical degree from the American Medical College in Philadelphia and practiced both medicine and dentistry. He became a staunch abolitionist during the 1850s and gradually abandoned his medical practice to study law and become a full-time antislavery lecturer. In the years leading up to the Civil War, Rock emerged as one of the nation's leading advocates for equal rights. In 1865, he became the first African American admitted to practice law before the U.S. Supreme Court, but he died of tuberculosis before he had the opportunity to argue a case. (The first African American actually to argue a case before the Court was Samuel R. Lowery, in 1880.)

Straker, David Augustus (1842–1908).   Born and raised in Barbados, Straker came to the United States in 1868 to assist in the education of freed former slaves. While teaching school in Louisville, Kentucky, he entered Howard University Law School and received his law degree in 1871. In 1875, Straker moved to South Carolina and became a partner in a law firm. After serving in the state legislature, Straker became dean of the newly created law school at Allen University and gained wide recognition for his innovative defense ("transitory insanity") of a black defendant in an 1883 murder trial. Straker moved to Detroit in 1887 and began a successful law practice. His greatest achievement during this time was the equal accommodations case of *Ferguson v. Gies*, which he argued successfully before the Michigan Supreme Court (in 1890). In addition to his legal activities, Straker was a prolific author and an influential advocate for the political rights of African Americans.

CRITICAL RACE THEORY

During the 1990s, a number of African American legal scholars developed the view that the U.S. legal system, created by a society that held black Americans in bondage, can never be race-neutral. Proponents of critical race theory argue that the system's inbuilt bias can be corrected by giving as much value to the experience and perceptions of blacks as to traditional evidentiary criteria. Many views associated with critical race theory have aroused controversy, such as the suggestion that African American jurors take political action by acquitting black defendants in nonviolent drug cases, even if the evidence points to guilt. (Arguments underpinning critical race theory are contained in a collection edited by Kimberlé Crenshaw; Daniel Farber and Suzanna Sherry's *Beyond All Reason* offers counterarguments—see "Sources for Additional Information.")

SOURCES FOR ADDITIONAL INFORMATION

Bedau, Hugo A., ed. *The Death Penalty in America: Current Controversies*. New York: Oxford University Press, 1997.

Cook, Anthony. *Law, Race, and Social Theory*. Boston: New England School of Law, 1991.

Crenshaw, Kimberlé, ed. *Critical Race Theory: The Writings That Formed the Movement*. New York: Free Press, 1995.

Farber, Daniel A., and Suzanna Sherry. *Beyond All Reason: The Radical Assault on Truth in American Law*. New York: Oxford University Press, 1997.

Finkelman, Paul, ed. *Race, Law, and American History, 1700–1990: The African-American Experience*, 10 vols. New York: Garland, 1991–1992.

Higginbotham, A. Leon, Jr. *In the Matter of Color: Race and the American Legal System*. New York: Oxford University Press, 1978.

———. *Shades of Freedom: Racial Politics and Presumptions of the American Legal Process*. New York: Oxford University Press, 1996.

Kennedy, Randall. *Race, Crime, and the Law*. New York: Pantheon, 1997.

Kluger, Richard. *Simple Justice: The History of* Brown v. Board of Education *and Black America's Struggle for Equality*, 2 vols. New York: Knopf, 1975.

Kull, Andrew. *The Color-Blind Constitution*. Cambridge, MA: Harvard University Press, 1992.

McNeill, Genna Rae. *Groundwork: Charles Hamilton Houston and the Struggle for Civil Rights*. Philadelphia: University of Pennsylvania Press, 1983.

Miller, Loren. *The Petitioners: The Story of the Supreme Court of the United States and the Negro*. New York: Pantheon, 1966.

Nieli, Russel, ed. *Racial Preference and Racial Justice: The New Affirmative Action Controversy*. Washington, DC: Ethics and Public Policy Center, 1991.

Peltason, J. W. *Fifty-Eight Lonely Men: Southern Federal Judges and School Desegregation*. Urbana: University of Illinois Press, 1961.

Urofsky, Melvin I. *A Conflict of Rights: The Supreme Court and Affirmative Action*. New York: Scribners, 1991.

Wilkerson, J. Harvie. *From Brown to Bakke: The Supreme Court and School Integration*. New York: Oxford University Press, 1979.

Zangrando, Robert L. *The NAACP Crusade against Lynching, 1909–1950*. Philadelphia: Temple University Press, 1980.

13

Literature and Language

LITERARY MOVEMENTS

LITERARY BEGINNINGS

During the colonial and early national eras (roughly 1740–1820), black American authors focused on three major themes: freedom for those enslaved, the necessity of equal rights for members of all groups, and the importance of education. (Education was an especially urgent concern because most enslaved African Americans were denied formal instruction in reading and writing.) These authors made use of all the available literary forms, including poetry, narrative, journalistic essays, and letters. One of the earliest forums for black literary expression was *Freedom's Journal,* founded in 1827 by John Russwurm and Samuel Cornish. Striking the keynote for the generations of writers to come, the editors of *Freedom's Journal* declared in their first issue, "We wish to plead our own cause. Too long have others spoken for us. Too long has the public been deceived by misrepresentations, in things which concern us dearly."

ANTISLAVERY WORKS

Growing nationwide resistance to slavery went hand in hand with an outpouring of African American writing. By 1860, there were 18 African American newspapers throughout the United States, and their pages carried a wide variety of works. The most distinctive writings of this period were the narratives of those who had escaped from slavery. In these works, the authors described the hardships they had endured in slavery and the adventures that had befallen them as they made their way to freedom. Among the most widely read works in this genre were the narratives of Frederick Douglass, William Wells Brown, Harriet A. Jacobs, Henry Bibb, J. D. Green, Charles Ball, Moses Roper, and Lunsford Lane. The slave narratives were customarily advertised in the abolitionist press and sold at antislavery meetings. In many cases the fugitives related their stories to white abolitionists, who wrote the narratives in their own words, according to the literary conventions of the day.

THE RECONSTRUCTION ERA

Following the abolition of slavery, African American literature was powerfully influenced by a series of important developments: the rapid growth of educational facilities for African Americans, the emergence of a sizable African American middle class with a vigorous interest in literature, and the founding of African American periodicals and literary societies. No longer preoccupied by the overriding issue of slavery, African American writers explored their position in American society and confronted the evils of racism in a new—and in many ways more difficult—context. In the quest to define a new and positive identity, many African American writers explored their heritage, making use of folklore and oral tradition. Prominent examples of this approach were the works of Paul Laurence Dunbar and of Charles Chesnutt, the first African American writers to achieve a truly national audience. Of equal significance were the first efforts—by George Washington Williams and others—to write comprehensive histories of African Americans in the United States.

THE HARLEM RENAISSANCE

Also known as the New Negro Movement and the Negro Renaissance, the Harlem Renaissance flourished from about the mid-1910s to the mid-1930s. It resulted from a wide variety of influences: the emergence of bold new cultural leaders such as W. E. B. Du Bois and Alain Locke, the migration of African Americans from the rural South to the cities of the North, and the self-confidence emanating from African American veterans of World War I. As a broad cultural movement, the Harlem Renaissance encompassed all the creative arts and included a lively social scene that ranged from spontaneous block parties to A'Lelia Walker's glittering soirees. Recognition of the Harlem Renaissance as a formal literary movement began in 1925 with the publication of Alain Locke's anthology *The New Negro*, which presented works by the rising generation of African American authors. The Harlem Renaissance writers followed their literary forebears by celebrating black culture and racial identity, but they wrote with a new sense of political urgency and an unprecedented interest in psychology, sexuality, and personal revelation. Two leading African American journals, the NAACP's *Crisis* and the National Urban League's *Opportunity*, played a major role in the Harlem Renaissance, providing a large readership and offering financial incentives such as the annual *Opportunity* Awards. Though the advent of the Great Depression in 1930 marked the beginning of the end for the Harlem Renaissance, many of its leading lights—such as Langston Hughes and Zora Neale Hurston—went on to achieve great distinction in American letters.

> We younger Negro artists . . . intend to express our individual dark-skinned selves without fear or shame. If white people are pleased, we are glad. If they are not, it doesn't matter. We know we are beautiful. And ugly too.
>
> Langston Hughes, *The Nation* (June 23, 1926)

MIDCENTURY

As the 20th century progressed, African American authors continued to reveal the harsh realities of black life across America. Their naturalistic novels of the 1940s and 1950s brought an unstinting gaze to bear on the lives of rural and urban blacks, documenting the social and economic hardships they endured. Richard Wright's *Native Son* (1940), a story of a boy raised in a Chicago slum and driven to murder, established a benchmark for contemporary writers with its visceral depiction of emotion and circumstance. Ralph Ellison's naturalistic masterpiece *Invisible Man* (1952) also detailed the life of a young black male disfranchised by his society. Chester Himes, who began writing while in prison, detailed the prejudice faced by young black laborers in a defense plant in *If He Hollers Let Him Go* (1945) and in labor unions in *The Lonely Crusade* (1947). Later, his detective stories, filled with graphic language and violence, became popular. The youngest writer of this group, James Baldwin, wrote about both racism and homosexuality. He fictionalized his Harlem youth and strict religious upbringing in *Go Tell It on the Mountain* (1953) and explored many sophisticated issues of race and sexuality in the novels *Giovanni's Room* (1956) and *Another Country* (1962). Baldwin, like several other African American writers of his generation, became an expatriate and chose to live abroad as a response to racism in America. He returned in the 1960s and through his speeches, appearances, and criticism became a spokesman of the civil rights movement.

THE MODERN ERA

The late 20th century witnessed the full flowering of African American literature, as writers delved into every existing genre and sometimes created new forms of their own. Under the influence of the civil rights movement and the growing resonance of black nationalism, African American writers often adopted a defiant aesthetic stance that mirrored African American political efforts. The most cohesive literary initiative was the Black Arts Movement, which developed during the early 1960s and inspired new developments in art, music, and dance, as well as literature. Led by Amiri Baraka, Larry Neal, Ed Bullins, and others, the writers of the Black Arts Movement rejected assimilation into white culture, celebrated their African heritage, and looked on literature as a weapon in the black-liberation struggle. The influence of the Black Arts Movement was enhanced by the appearance of nationally distributed magazines such as *Negro Digest*, *Black Worker*, *Freedomways*, *Liberator*, and *Black Dialogue*. By affirming the intrinsic power and integrity of the black experience, the Black Arts Movement inspired many African Americans to express themselves in poetry and prose for the first time.

By the end of the 1960s, African American writers were gaining an unprecedented acceptance among mainstream literary critics and the reading public at large. As a result, African American literature branched out in many new directions that continued to flourish for the rest of the 20th century. Female writers with a highly developed feminist consciousness—Toni Morrison, Alice Walker, Audre Lourde, Gloria Naylor, Ntozake Shange, Paule Marshall, and many others—formed a distinctive current in African American literature. Other important developments have been an intensive investigation of history, particularly slavery; experimentation with African American traditions and vernacular; and the use of autobiography to illuminate political and philosophical issues. At the threshold of the 21st century, African American literature exhibits an unprecedented variety, without any dilution of its distinctive power and identity. Terry McMillan's works *Waiting to Exhale* and *How Stella Got Her Groove Back* have been both national best-sellers and major motion pictures. Other popular and critically praised contemporary authors include Bebe Moore Campbell, Sapphire, Walter Mosley, John Edgar Wideman, Charles Johnson, and A. J. Vervelle.

MAJOR LITERARY WORKS

The following works are listed in chronological order of their appearance in print.

- "Bars Fight" (1746). The first known work in English by an African American author. Lucy Terry's poem narrates an attack by Native Americans on white settlers in Deerfield, Massachusetts (the term *bars* was used in colonial times as a synonym for "meadows").
- *A Narrative of the Uncommon Sufferings, and Surprising Deliverance of Briton Hammon, A Negro Man—Servant to General Winslow* (1760). Hammon's tale of captivity by both the Cherokees and the British is regarded as the first African American autobiography and the first slave narrative.
- *Poems on Various Subjects, Religious and Moral* (1773), by Phillis Wheatley. The first book published by an African American in North America, Wheatley's volume includes 37 poems that encompass a wide range of subjects, including the art of poetry, literary patronage, religious faith, and the desire for freedom.
- *The Interesting Narrative of the Life of Olaudah Equiano or Gustavus Vassa the African* (1789). Olaudah Equiano's stirring account of his life in both Africa and the New World was one of the most important antislavery documents of the day, running to 17 editions in Britain and the United States by 1827.

- *Narrative of the Life of Frederick Douglass*. Published in 1845, the first of Douglass's three autobiographies sold 5,000 copies in four months and 30,000 copies overall by 1850. The book did much to arouse Northern feelings against slavery and also encouraged other African Americans, such as Harriet Jacobs and William Wells Brown, to write their own life stories. Douglass's achievement was all the more important because he told his story in his own words, breaking with the common practice of using a white amanuensis.
- *Three Years in Europe, or Places I Have Seen and People I Have Met* (1852). Written by the multifaceted William Wells Brown, this volume is the first known travel book by an African American.
- *Clotel, or the President's Daughter: A Narrative of Slave Life in the United States* (1853). Once again, William Wells Brown broke new ground, becoming the first African American to publish a full-length novel. The heroine of the story is the daughter of Thomas Jefferson and his African American lover, Currer. (In 1998, genetic testing proved that Jefferson did have African American descendants.) After Currer and her children are sold to a Virginia slave owner, Clotel undergoes many hardships and eventually escapes; although she meets a tragic end, her own daughter survives and begins a new life in England. Brown later revised the novel twice, and new editions were published in 1864 and 1867.
- *Our Nig, or Sketches of a Free Black in a Two Story White House, North, Showing that Slavery's Shadows Fall Even There* (1859). Harriet Wilson's novel was the first full-length work of fiction by an African American woman.
- *History of the Negro Race in America from 1619 to 1880*. Published in 1883 by George Washington Williams, this was the first comprehensive history of African Americans.
- *Iola Leroy, or Shadows Uplifted*. Frances Ellen Watkins Harper's 1892 novel is the story of a well-to-do mulatto woman who passes for white until she is identified as an African American and enslaved; after emancipation, she becomes a teacher and battles for equal rights. Popular in its own day, *Iola Leroy* is highly regarded as an important work because of its fully realized characters and its concern with the major racial and gender issues of the 1890s.
- *Lyrics of Lowly Life* (1896). Paul Laurence Dunbar's first commercially published book was also the most popular volume of poetry by an African American before the Harlem Renaissance. The poems in the volume were equally divided between those written in standard English (such as "Frederick Douglass," "Ode to Ethiopia," and "Columbian Ode") and those written in dialect ("When Malindy Sings," "A Banjo Song," "An Ante-Bellum Sermon," and others).
- *The House Behind the Cedars* (1900). Charles Chesnutt's first novel was also the first African American novel to be offered by a major publishing house (Houghton Mifflin). Chesnutt tells the story of John and Rena Walden, the children of a white father and a mulatto mother, and the consequences of their decision to live as whites in the South.
- *The Souls of Black Folk*. Published in 1903, W. E. B. Du Bois's collection of 14 prose pieces introduced the concept of "double-consciousness" among African Americans and predicted that racism would be the greatest problem of the 20th century. The book, which exerted enormous influence within the African American community, also illuminates Du Bois's own intellectual and emotional life.
- *Autobiography of an Ex-Colored Man* (1912). James Weldon Johnson's novel was the first fictional treatment of Du Bois's concept of double-consciousness. Its hero, the product of an interracial love affair, experiences life on both sides of the color line and decides, with agonizing psychological consequences, to pass for white. The book was published anonymously, and Johnson did not acknowledge his authorship until 1927.
- "The Negro Speaks of Rivers" (1921). Langston Hughes was only 19 when this poem appeared in *Crisis*, the first national magazine to publish his work. Though it contains only 13 lines, the poem has become one of the emblematic works of African American literature, evoking both the anguish and the majesty of the black experience.
- *The New Negro* (1925). Alain Locke's anthology contained works by most of the leading writers of the Harlem Renaissance. The book was divided into two parts: The first was devoted to fiction, poetry, and essays on the creative arts; the second consisted of essays on social and political topics.

A *rt must discover and reveal the beauty which prejudice and caricature have overlaid.*

Alain Locke, "The Legacy of Ancestral Arts" in *The New Negro* (1925)

- *Home to Harlem* (1928). Claude McKay's first novel, describing the urban adventures of a railroad cook named Jake Brown, was the first novel by an African American to make the best-seller lists in New York City. However, *Home to Harlem* was bitterly condemned by many African Americans. McKay's critics objected to his emphasis on the pleasure-seeking aspects of Harlem life and charged him with reinforcing racist stereotypes.
- *Their Eyes Were Watching God* (1937). Reportedly written in only seven weeks, this novel is widely regarded as Zora Neale Hurston's masterpiece. In addition to depicting the spiritual development of a woman who has been previously dependent on the men in her life, the novel provides a rich portrait of Eatonville, Florida, Hurston's childhood home.
- *Native Son* (1940). Richard Wright's unsparing portrait of Bigger Thomas, an oppressed and ultimately violent resident of Chicago's black ghetto, catapulted Wright into the front ranks of American writers. *Native Son* was the first work by an African American to be offered by the Book-of-the-Month Club.
- *Annie Allen* (1949). Gwendolyn Brooks's second volume of poetry won the first Pulitzer Prize ever awarded to an African American author. Telling an apparently simple story by the means of complex poetic techniques, *Allen* follows Annie from girlhood to womanhood in Chicago.
- *Invisible Man* (1952). Ralph Ellison's novel marked a new era in African American literature by breaking with the strict realism that had previously governed the fiction of black authors. Employing folklore, musical idioms, and an array of literary symbols, Ellison interprets the African American experience through the fictional memoirs of an anonymous narrator, the "invisible man."
- *Go Tell It on the Mountain* (1953). This novel, regarded as James Baldwin's finest, relates the story of Harlem's Grimes family and illuminates Baldwin's own personal development.
- *Raisin in the Sun* (produced on Broadway in 1959). Lorraine Hansberry's portrait of an African American family captured the currents of thought and feeling sweeping the black community during the civil rights era. It became an instant classic of the American stage and has been translated into more than 30 languages.
- *Brown Girl, Brownstones* (1959). Paule Marshall's coming-of-age novel, set in Brooklyn, broke new ground by exploring mother-daughter relationships and the experiences of West Indians in New York. Marshall is credited with paving the way for later African American writers whose works express a decidedly feminist viewpoint.
- *Dutchman*. One of the seminal works of the Black Arts Movement, Amiri Baraka's hard-hitting drama was produced off-Broadway in 1964 (when he was still known as LeRoi Jones). In portraying the grisly fate of an assimilated African American man who gets involved with a white woman, Baraka gave voice to the growing impulse for black self-determination.
- *Autobiography of Malcolm X* (1965). A collaboration between Malcolm X and Alex Haley, this work detailed an extraordinary personal odyssey and shone a harsh light on racism in the United States. In the years since Malcolm's death, his autobiography has achieved the status of a unique American testament.
- *Autobiography of Miss Jane Pittman* (1971). Louisiana-born author Ernest Gaines narrated the history of the black population of the South from the point of view of a 110-year-old woman. Both a popular and a critical triumph, the novel was turned into a film soon after its publication.
- *Roots: The Saga of an American Family* (1976). Alex Haley's book, combining historical research with fictional narrative techniques, was as much a cultural as a literary phenomenon. By tracing his family history back through seven generations to an African ancestor named Kunta Kinte, Haley reestablished a link that had been violently broken by the onslaught of the slave trade. Its message was amplified by a 12-hour, record-breaking TV miniseries that aired to millions in 1977. *Roots* inspired African Americans, educated whites about slavery, and spurred members of all ethnic groups to investigate their

own genealogies. Touted for both its creativity and its scholarship, *Roots* met with some negative criticism from book reviewers who claimed that Haley blurred the line between fiction and nonfiction in his work in order to enhance its narrative.

- *Song of Solomon* (1977). This novel announced Toni Morrison's arrival as a major 20th-century novelist. In telling the complex story of Milkman Dead, Morrison blended history, folklore, magic, allegory, and linguistic inventiveness in a way that dazzled both readers and critics.
- *The Color Purple* (1982). In the first epistolary novel by an African American woman, Alice Walker tells the story of Celie, a young girl who suffers repeated abuse at the hands of men before finding a measure of self-fulfillment. Walker was harshly criticized for her sexual frankness and her perceived indictment of African American men, but *The Color Purple* deeply moved countless readers and established Walker as a powerful voice for women's rights.
- *Fences*. August Wilson's Pulitzer Prize–winning drama was first performed in 1983 and opened on Broadway in 1987. In telling the story of Troy Maxson, a former baseball player determined to shield his children from the racism that thwarted his own career, Wilson presented a classic dilemma experienced by African Americans. Critics hailed *Fences* as a milestone in American theater and placed Wilson in the front rank of modern dramatists.
- *A Lesson Before Dying*. Ernest J. Gaines's 1993 novel, set in rural Louisiana during the 1940s, tells the story of a young teacher who reluctantly agrees to tutor an uneducated young prisoner awaiting execution—in the process, both men are unexpectedly transformed. The book earned Gaines a National Book Critics Circle Award.
- *The Wedding*. Published in 1995, this is the long-awaited second novel by Dorothy West, the last survivor of the illustrious Harlem Renaissance literary circle, who died in 1998. Illuminating the rarefied world of an African American resort colony on Martha's Vineyard, West explores a distinguished family's painful history.

WINNERS OF MAJOR LITERARY PRIZES

NOBEL PRIZE

1992   Derek Walcott (St. Lucia)
1993   Toni Morrison (United States)

PULITZER PRIZE
DRAMA

1970   Charles Gordone, *No Place to Be Somebody*
1982   Charles Fuller, *A Soldier's Play*
1987   August Wilson, *Fences*
1990   August Wilson, *The Piano Lesson*

FICTION

1978   James A. McPherson, *Elbow Room*
1983   Alice Walker, *The Color Purple*
1988   Toni Morrison, *Beloved*

POETRY

1950   Gwendolyn Brooks, *Annie Allen*

1987   Rita Dove, *Thomas and Beulah*

SPECIAL CITATION

1977   Alex Haley, *Roots*

NATIONAL BOOK AWARD

1957   Ralph Ellison, *Invisible Man* (Fiction)

1983   Gloria Naylor, *The Women of Brewster Place* (First Novel)

Joyce Carol Thomas, *Marked by Fire* (Children's Literature)

Alice Walker, *The Color Purple* (Fiction)

1990   Charles Johnson, *Middle Passage* (Fiction)

1991   Melissa Fay Green, *Praying for Sheetrock* (Nonfiction)

Orlando Patterson, *Freedom* (Nonfiction)

1993   Edward P. Jones, *Lost in the City* (Fiction)

1995   Gwendolyn Brooks (Medal for Distinguished Contribution to American Letters)

AMERICAN ACADEMY AND INSTITUTE OF ARTS AND LETTERS AWARD FOR LITERATURE

1946   Gwendolyn Brooks and Langston Hughes

1956   James Baldwin

1961   John A. Williams

1970   James A. McPherson

1971   Charles Gordone

1972   Michael S. Harper

1974   Henry Van Dyke

1978   Lerone Bennett Jr. and Toni Morrison

1987   Ernest J. Gaines

1992   August Wilson

NATIONAL BOOK CRITICS CIRCLE AWARD

1990   Shelby Steele, *The Content of Our Character* (General Nonfiction)

1993   Ernest J. Gaines, *A Lesson Before Dying* (Fiction)

CORETTA SCOTT KING BOOK AWARD

(For works with particular educational and inspirational value)

1970   Lillie Patterson, *Dr. Martin Luther King*

1971   Charlemae Rollins, *Black Troubador: Langston Hughes*

1972   Elton Fax, *Seventeen Black Artists*

1973   Alfred Duckett, *I Never Had It Made: The Autobiography of Jackie Robinson* (coauthor)

1974   Sharon Bell Mathis, *Ray Charles*

1975   Dorothy Robinson, *The Legend of Africania*

1976   Pearl Bailey, *Duey's Tale*

1977   James Haskins, *The Story of Stevie Wonder*

1978   Eloise Greenfield, *African Dream*

1979   Ossie Davis, *Escape to Freedom: A Play about Young Frederick Douglass*

1980   Walter Dean Myers, *The Young Landlords*

1981   Sidney Poitier, *This Life*

1982   Mildred D. Taylor, *Let the Circle Be Unbroken*

1983   Virginia Hamilton, *Sweet Whispers, Brother Rush*

1984   Lucille Clifton, *Everett Anderson's Goodbye*

1985   Walter Dean Myers, *Motown and Didi: A Love Story*

1986   Virginia Hamilton, *The People Could Fly: American Black Folktales*

1987   Mildred Pitts Walter, *Justin and the Best Biscuits in the World*

1988   Mildred D. Taylor, *The Friendship*

1989   Walter Dean Myers, *Fallen Angels*

1990   Patricia and Fredrick McKissack, *A Long Journey: The Story of the Pullman Porter*

1991   Mildred D. Taylor, *The Road to Memphis*

1992   Walter Dean Myers, *African American Struggle for Freedom*

1993   Patricia McKissack, *The Dark Thirty: Southern Tales of the Supernatural*

1994   Angela Johnson, *Toning the Sweep*

1995   Patricia and Fredrick McKissack, *Christmas in the Big House, Christmas in the Quarters*

1996   Virginia Hamilton, *Her Stories: African American Folktales, Fairy Tales, and True Tales*

1997   Walter Dean Myers, *Slam*

1998   Sharon Draper, *Forged by Fire*

BOOKS FOR YOUNG READERS

(Selected by the New York Public Library and *Publishers Weekly*)

PICTURE BOOKS

African Dream, by Eloise Greenfield (John Day, 1977)

Always My Dad, by Sharon Dennis Wyeth (Knopf, 1995)

Boundless Grace, by Mary Hoffman (Dial, 1995)

The Children's Book of Kwanzaa, by Dolores Johnson (Simon & Schuster/Alladin, 1997)

The Gifts of Kwanzaa, by Synthia Saint James (Whitman, 1997)

Just Us Women, by Jeannette Caines (HarperCollins, 1995)

Minty: A Story of Young Harriet Tubman, by Alan Schroeder (Dial, 1996)

Mirandy and Brother Wind, by Patricia McKissack (Knopf, 1988)

The Patchwork Quilt, by Valerie Flournoy (Dial, 1985)

The Sunday Outing, by Gloria Pinkney (Dial, 1994)

Tar Beach, by Faith Ringgold (Crown, 1991)

Uncle Jed's Barbershop, by Margaree King Mitchell (Simon & Schuster, 1993)

When Joe Louis Won the Title, by Belinda Rochelle (Houghton Mifflin, 1994)

POETRY AND SONG

The Block: Poems, by Langston Hughes, collage by Romare Bearden (Viking, 1995)

Brown Angels: An Album of Pictures and Verse, by Walter Dean Myers (HarperCollins, 1993)

Brown Honey in Broomwheat Tea: Poems, by Joyce Carol Thomas (HarperCollins, 1993)

Climbing Jacob's Ladder: Heroes of the Bible in African American Spirituals, by John Langstaff (Macmillan, 1991)

The Creation, by James Weldon Johnson (Holiday House, 1994)

The Dream Keeper and Other Poems, by Langston Hughes (Knopf, 1994)

Everett Anderson's Year, by Lucille Clifton (Holt, 1992)

In Daddy's Arms I Am Tall: African Americans Celebrating Fathers, by Javaka Steptoe (Lee & Low, 1997)

Knoxville, Tennessee, by Nikki Giovanni (Scholastic, 1994)

Lift Every Voice and Sing, by James Weldon Johnson (Walker, 1993)

Meet Danitra Brown, by Nikki Grimes (Lothrop, Lee & Shepard, 1995)

Pass It On: African American Poetry for Children, by Wade and Cheryl Hudson (Scholastic, 1993)

Soul Looks Back in Wonder, by Maya Angelou (Dial, 1993)

FOLKLORE

The Dark Thirty: Southern Tales of the Supernatural, by Patricia McKissack (Knopf, 1992)

The Faithful Friend, by Robert D. San Souci (Simon & Schuster, 1995)

John Henry, by Julius Lester (Dial, 1994)

The Last Tales of Uncle Remus, by Julius Lester (Dial, 1994)

When Birds Could Talk and Bats Could Sing: The Adventures of Bruh Sparrow, Sis Wren, and Their Friends, by Virginia Hamilton (Blue Sky, 1996)

STORIES

The Friends, by Rosa Guy (Holt, Rinehart & Winston, 1973)

I Hadn't Meant to Tell You This, by Jacqueline Woodson (Delacorte, 1994)

Justin and the Best Biscuits in the World, by Mildred Pitts Walter (Bullseye, 1991)

Letters from a Slave Girl, by Mary E. Lyons (Scribners, 1992)

Oren Bell, by Barbara Hood Burgess (Delacorte, 1991)

The Slave Dancer, by Paula Fox (ABC-Clio, 1988)

The Stories Julian Tells, by Ann Cameron (Pantheon, 1981)

Toning the Sweep, by Angela Johnson (Orchard, 1993)

The Watsons Go to Birmingham—1963, by Christopher Paul Curtis (Bantam Doubleday Dell, 1997)

The Well, by Mildred D. Taylor (Dial, 1995)

Yolonda's Genius, by Carol Fenner (McElderry, 1995)

NONFICTION

Alvin Ailey, by Andrea Davis Pinkney (Hyperion, 1993)

Christmas in the Big House, Christmas in the Quarters, by Patricia and Fredrick McKissack (Scholastic, 1994)

Cornrows, by Camille Yarbrough (Coward, McCann & Geoghegan, 1979)

Dear Benjamin Banneker, by Andrea Davis Pinkney (Harcourt Brace, 1994)

The Freedom Rides: Journey for Justice, by James Haskins (Hyperion, 1995)

Freedom's Children: Young Civil Rights Activists Tell Their Own Stories, by Ellen Levine (Avon, 1993)

The Great Migration: An American Story, by Jacob Lawrence (HarperCollins, 1993)

Happy Birthday, Martin Luther King, Jr., by Jean Marzollo (Scholastic, 1993)

I Have a Dream, by Martin Luther King, Jr. (Scholastic, 1997)

Jackie Robinson and the Story of All-Black Baseball, by Jim O'Connor (Random House, 1989)

Many Thousands Gone: African Americans from Slavery to Freedom, by Virginia Hamilton (Knopf, 1996)

The March on Washington, by James Haskins (HarperCollins, 1993)

Now Is Your Time! by Walter Dean Myers (HarperCollins, 1991)

Oh, Freedom! Kids Talk about the Civil Rights Movement with the People Who Made It Happen, by Casey Kin and Linda Barrett Osborne (Knopf, 1997)

Undying Glory: The Story of the Massachusetts 54th Regiment, by Clinton Cox (Scholastic, 1991)

Wilma Unlimited: How Wilma Rudolph Became the World's Fastest Woman, by Kathleen Krull (Harcourt Brace, 1996)

AFRICAN AMERICAN BOOKSTORES

CALIFORNIA

African Book Mart
2440 Durant Avenue
Berkeley, CA 94704
510-843-3088

Antiquarian Bookshop
3995 S. Western Avenue
Los Angeles, CA 90062
213-296-1633

Black and Latino Multicultural Book Center
23 N. Mentor Avenue
Pasadena, CA 91006
818-792-0117

Eso Won Books
3655 S. LaBrea Avenue
Los Angeles, CA 90016
213-294-0324

Iron Wood Corner
462 Tooten Place

Pasadena, CA 91103
626-398-5539
www.choicemail.com/iwc

Marcus Books
1712 Filmore Street
San Francisco, CA 94115
415-346-4222

COLORADO

African Child Bookstore
3415 E. Colfax Avenue
Denver, CO 80206
303-399-7206

Hue-Man Experience Bookstore
911 Park Avenue, W
Denver, CO 80205
303-293-2665

DISTRICT OF COLUMBIA

JMA Enterprises, Inc.
218 46th Street, NE
Washington, DC 20019
202-398-3787

FLORIDA

African-American Bookstore
3600 W. Broward Boulevard
Fort Lauderdale, FL 33312
954-584-0460

African-American Heritage Book
515 Northwood Road
West Palm Beach, FL 33407
407-835-3551

Afro-American Awakening Book
1710 45th Street
West Palm Beach, FL 33407
407-848-3224

Afro-In Books & Things
5575 N.W. Seventh Avenue
Miami, FL 33127
305-756-6107

GEORGIA

Shrine of the Black Madonna
946 Gordon Street, SW
Atlanta, GA 30310
404-752-6125

ILLINOIS

African American Book Center
7524 Cottage Grove Avenue
Chicago, IL 60621
312-651-9101

Afrika North Bookstore
$4629\frac{1}{2}$ N. Broadway
Chicago, IL 60640
312-907-0005

Afrocentric Books
234 S. Wabash Avenue
Chicago, IL 60604
312-939-1956

DuSable Museum Gift Shop/Bookstore
740 E. 56th Place
Chicago, IL 60637
312-947-0600

INDIANA

Afrikan-American Book Source
3490 Village Court
Gary, IN 46408
291-981-2133

LOUISIANA

Afro-American Book Stop
7166 Crowder Boulevard
New Orleans, LA 70127
504-246-6288

Authentic Book Distributors
P.O. Box 52916
Baton Rouge, LA 70892
504-356-0076

MARYLAND

African American Books Plus
8640 McGilford Road
Columbia, MD 21045
410-730-0779

Pyramid Bookstore
3500 East-West Highway
Hyattsville, MD 20782
301-559-5200

MASSACHUSETTS

African American Books
892 State Street
Springfield, MA 01109
413-781-2233

Afro-American Book Source
P.O. Box 851
Boston, MA 02120
617-445-9209

Savanna Books
858 Massachusetts Avenue
Cambridge, MA 02139
617-868-3423

MISSOURI

Progressive Books
6265 Delmar Boulevard
St. Louis, MO 63130
314-721-1344

NEW YORK

A & B Books
149 Lawrence Street
Brooklyn, NY 11201
718-596-0872

African University Book Store
1661 Amsterdam Avenue

New York, NY 10031
212-281-8650

Liberation Bookstore
421 Malcolm X Boulevard
New York, NY 10037
212-281-4615

Nkiru Books
76 Saint Marks Avenue
Brooklyn, NY 11217
718-783-6306

Positive Images Unlimited Bookstore
137-07 Bedell Street
Rochdale Village, NY 11434
718-949-2535

NORTH CAROLINA

Afro-Centric Connections Book Dealers
116 E. Walnut Street
Goldsboro, NC 27530
919-731-4404

OHIO

The African Book Shelf
13240 Euclid Avenue
Cleveland, OH 44112
216-681-6511

African & Islamic Books Plus
3752 Lee Road
Cleveland, OH 44128
216-561-5000

Afrikids
108 William Howard Taft Road
Cincinnati, OH 45219
513-569-8286

PENNSYLVANIA

Hakim's Bookstore
210 S. 52nd Street

Philadelphia, PA 19139
215-474-9495

SOUTH CAROLINA

TDIR Books
6920 N. Main Street
Columbia, SC 29203
803-754-4922
www.tdirbooks.com

TENNESSEE

Simpsons Books & Things
4699 Saint Elmo Avenue

Memphis, TN 38128
901-371-9812
http://38.244.128.30/simpson

TEXAS

Amistad Bookplace
P.O. Box 729
Prairie View, TX 77446
409-857-9101

Black Images Book Bazaar
142 Wynnewood Village
Dallas, TX 75224
214-943-0142

PUBLISHERS AND LITERARY ORGANIZATIONS

African American Books and Publishing
2313 W. Lafayette Avenue
Baltimore, MD 21216
410-945-8429

African American Family Press
170 W. 74th Street
New York, NY 10023
800-297-5577

African American Publications
1225 General Mercer Road
Washington Crossing, PA 18977
215-321-7742

African American Reference Guide, Inc.
1083 Allenwood Drive
Plainfield, NJ 07061
908-755-0655

African American Writers Guild
4108 Arkansas Avenue, NW
Washington, DC 20011
202-722-2760

African Heritage Literature Society
7676 New Hampshire Avenue

Hyattsville, MD 20780
301-445-7616

African Latino Press
1213 Kalamazoo Avenue
Grand Rapids, MI 49507
616-241-4600

Africana Publishing
160 Broadway
New York, NY 10038
212-374-1313

Afro-American Publishing Company, Inc.
407 E. 25th Street, Suite 600
Chicago, IL 60616
312-791-1611

Amistad Press, Inc.
1271 Avenue of the Americas
New York, NY 10020
212-522-7282

Ashley Publishing Company, Inc.
4600 W. Commercial Boulevard
Fort Lauderdale, FL 33319
954-739-2221

Black Registry Publishing Company
1223 Rosewood Avenue
Austin, TX 78702
512-476-0082

Black Writers Guild
P.O. Box 29351
Oakland, CA 94604
510-569-8298

Blind Beggar Press (Lamplight Editions)
P.O. Box 437
Bronx, NY 10467
914-683-6792

Broadside Press
P.O. Box 04257
Detroit, MI 48204
313-934-1231

Career Communications Group
729 E. Pratt Street, Suite 504
Baltimore, MD 21202
410-244-7101

Duncan & Duncan, Inc.
2809 Pulaski Highway
Edgewood, MD 21040
410-538-5759

Fordham Distribution
487 S. U.S. Highway One
Ormond Beach, FL 32174
904-672-6993

Horn of Africa
P.O. Box 803
Summit, NJ 07901
201-273-1515

Howard University Press
1240 Randolph Street, NE
Washington, DC 20008
202-806-4935

JMA Enterprises, Inc.
218 46th Street, NE
Washington, DC 20019
202-298-3787

Juju Publishing Company
1310 Harden Street
Columbia, SC 22902
803-799-5252

Lotus Press
P.O. Box 21607
Detroit, MI 48221
313-861-1280

The Majority Press
P.O. Box 538
Dover, MA 02030
508-655-5636

Mind Productions and Associates, Inc.
P.O. Box 11221
Tallahassee, FL 32302
904-222-5331

National Baptist Publishing Board
6717 Centennial Boulevard
Nashville, TN 37209
615-350-8000

Path Press
53 W. Jackson Boulevard
Chicago, IL 60604
312-663-0167

Red Sea Press
15 Industry Court
Trenton, NJ 08638
609-771-1666

Renaissance Publications
1516 Fifth Avenue
Pittsburgh, PA 15219
412-391-8208

Shoptalk Publications, Inc.
8825 S. Greenwood
Chicago, IL 60619
312-978-6400

Third World Press
7822 S. Dobson
Chicago, IL 60619
312-651-0700

Urban Research Press, Inc.
840 E. 87th Street
Chicago, IL 60619
312-994-7200

Vincom, Inc.
P.O. Box 702400

Tulsa, OK 74170
918-254-1276

World Institute of Black Communications, Inc.
463 Seventh Avenue
New York, NY 10018

LANGUAGE IN AFRICA AND THE AMERICAS

AFRICAN LANGUAGES

Africa has an extraordinarily rich linguistic heritage, with approximately 1,500 distinct languages spoken on the continent. Linguists have grouped this vast array into four major phyla and several families. These are listed here, along with the most widely spoken languages belonging to each. Languages widely spoken by African migrants to the New World are indicated in boldface type.

Phylum	Family	Language
Khoisan	Khoikhoi	Nandi, Nama, Korana, Griqua
	San	!Kung, //aikwe, /nu//en
Nilo-Saharan	Eastern Sudanic	Nuer, Karamojong
	Central Sudanic	Bongo, Mangebutu, Madi
	Saharan	Kanuri, Teda, Zaghawa
	Songhai	Songhai
Afro-Asiatic	Semitic	Arabic, Amharic, Tigrinya
	Berber	Tuareg, Kabyle, Jerba
	Cushitic	Beja, Somali, Iraqw
	Chadic	**Hausa**, Logone, Fali
Niger-Congo	Kwa	Akan, **Ewe, Yoruba, Kru, Bini, Ga, Igbo, Twi**
	Mande	**Soninke, Bambara, Vai, Mende, Susu, Kpelle, Malinke (Mandinka)**
	Voltaic	**Dogon, Senufo,** Mossi
	Atlantic	**Wolof, Fulfulde, Serer, Temne**
	Bantu	**Luganda, Kimbundu, Kongo, Kikongo, Umbundu,** Xhosa, **Tshiluba,** Swahili, Zulu
	Adamawa	Zande, Mbum, Kotoko
	Benue-Congo	**Efik, Ibibio**

CREOLE LANGUAGES

Throughout the New World, African Americans developed distinctive forms of communication that were long regarded as corruptions of European languages. In this view, deviations from standard grammar and vocabulary indicated the "backwardness" of black populations in the diaspora. In recent years, however, scholars have uncovered linguistic patterns that point to a far different conclusion. It is now understood that Africans and African Americans created their own linguistic hybrids—known collectively as *creole languages*—by combining European forms with African grammar, syntax, and vocabulary. As late as the 1960s, Maureen Warner Lewis of the University of the West Indies encountered individuals in Trinidad and Jamaica who spoke Yoruba, Kikongo, Hausa, and other African languages. Comparing Yoruba with Trinidadian English, she found numerous parallels, a few examples of which are indicated here.

Yoruba: *Enia ni.*
Literal translation: Human being he is.
Trinidadian English: *He is people.* (He deserves consideration.)

Yoruba: *Ohunkohun.*
Literal: Thing + connective + thing.
Trinidadian. *T'ing and t'ing.* (And so on and so forth.)

Yoruba: *Ki l'o se e?*
Literal: What is it does/grieves you?
Trinidadian: *What do you?*

Yoruba: *Mo je tan.*
Literal: I ate finish.
Trinidadian: *I done eat.*

Yoruba: *Fi omi si igi.*
Literal: Put water to plant.
Trinidadian: *Put water to the plant.*

Yoruba: *So oro buruku.*
Literal: Speak word bad.
Trinidadian: *Bad-talk.* (Speak ill of someone.)

In addition, nearly identical grammatical structures are found in different creole languages. Thus, the Haitian creole phrase *mwe malad* finds its parallel in the Jamaican phrase *mi sick* (I'm ill); *mwe va kuri* in *mi wi run* (I will run); *mwe pote yo ale* in *mi carry dem go* (I took them away); *se kuri li ap kuri* in *a run im a run* (he is really running).

In the United States, the most distinctive creole is the Gullah language spoken on the barrier islands and communities of the Georgia and South Carolina coasts. Gullah is essentially a blend of 17th- and 18th-century English with various African languages belonging to the Atlantic, Mande, Kwa, and Bantu families. (The term *Gullah* itself is probably derived from *Ngola*, an ethnic group in central Africa.) Scholars have linked thousands of items from Gullah—personal names, words, grammatical structures, and stories—directly to Africa. One grammatical example among many is the absence of differentiation in the gender of pronouns, a trait shared by Gullah and Tshiluba.

Tshiluba: *Yeye wakalela muana.*
Literal: He (or she) has a child.
Gullah: *E hab a chile.*

Tshiluba: *Yeye mmukaji mubi.*
Literal: She (or he) is a bad woman.
Gullah: *Him a bad ooman.*

Tshiluba: *Yeye udi muana wa bakaji.*
Literal: She (or he) is a girl child.
Gullah: *Him's a gal.*

Gullah also exhibits strong links with Caribbean English. A number of Gullah words—for example, *big eye* (greedy), *bad mouth, buckra* (poor white), *hoppin John, day-clean* (dawn), and *hoe cake*—are also common in Barbados.

BLACK ENGLISH

The subject of African American speech patterns in the United States has aroused a good deal of academic and political controversy. Many linguists maintain that Black English (also known as Ebonics), is a bona fide African-derived creole language, while others classify Black English as a variation of Standard American English. Debates about the relevance of Black English to the educational process have occasionally drawn major attention from the news media, evoking strong feelings on both sides of the issue. There can be little disagreement, however, about the massive debt that contemporary English owes to African Americans. In addition to staples of African American slang that have been universally adopted (e.g., "telling it like it is," "going through changes," "doing your thing"), Standard American English is replete with words that can be traced back to Africa. In *The African Heritage of American English,* Joseph E. Holloway and Winifred K. Vass have identified scores of such terms. Some prime examples include:

bogus: Hausa *boko, boko-boko* (deceit, fraud)

booboo: Bantu *mbubu* (stupid, blundering act; error, blunder)

boogie (-woogie): Bantu *mbuki-mvuki* (to take off in dance performance)

bug: Mandinka *baga* (to offend, annoy, harm someone); Wolof *bugal* (to annoy, worry)

dirt: Akan *dôte* (earth, soil)

hep, hip: Wolof *hepi, hipi* (to open one's eyes, to be aware of what is going on)

hullaballoo: Bantu *huala balualua* (literally, when those that are coming arrive—the noise and uproar of greeting)

jazz: Bantu *jaja* (to make dance)

jiffy: Bantu *tshipi* (short, in a moment)

jive: Wolof *jev, jew* (to talk about someone in the person's absence—hence, misleading or insincere talk)

juke: Wolof *dzug* (to misbehave)

kook, kooky: Bantu *kuku* (dolt, blockhead)

moolah: Bantu *mulambo* (receipts, tax money)

okay: Mandinka *o-ke*, Dogon *o-kay*, Fulfulde *eeyi kay*, Wolof *waw ke*, among other examples from West Africa, meaning "yes, indeed." Holloway and Vass indicate that *oh ki* as an affirmation was recorded as being in use by black Jamaicans in 1816, 20 years before *okay* became common in New England.

palooka: Bantu *paluka* (to have a fit, spasm, or convulsion)

phony: Mandinka *fani, foni* (false, valueless; to tell a lie)

tote: Kikongo *tota* (to pick up)

yackety-yack: Bantu *yakula-yakula* (gabbing, chattering)

NOTABLE AFRICAN AMERICAN WRITERS

Angelou, Maya (1928–). Writer noted for her autobiographical narratives, which include *I Know Why the Caged Bird Sings* (1970), *Gather Together in My Name* (1974), *The Heart of a Woman* (1981), and *All God's Children Need Traveling Shoes* (1986). Angelou's recitation of her specially composed poem, "On the Pulse of Morning," was one of the high points of President Bill Clinton's inauguration in 1993.

Attaway, William (1911–1986).   Highly regarded for portrayals of African American life during the Great Migration. Attaway wrote two novels—*Let Me Breathe Thunder* (1939) and *Blood on the Forge* (1941)—a number of books about music, and scripts for both radio and television.

Baldwin, James (1924–1987).   The successor to Richard Wright as the most powerful voice in African American literature. Baldwin confronted the issues of racism, religion, and sexuality in his novels and essays. Among his major novels are *Go Tell It on the Mountain* (1953), *Giovanni's Room* (1956), and *Another Country* (1962). His leading nonfiction works—*Notes of a Native Son* (1955) and *The Fire Next Time* (1962)—are searing personal indictments of racism in the United States.

Bambara, Toni Cade (1939–1995).   A writer whose work was deeply influenced by her commitment to feminism and her experiences as a social worker, political activist, and community organizer. Her major short stories are collected in *Gorilla, My Love* (1972) and *The Sea Birds Are Still Alive* (1977). Bambara's major novel, *The Salt Eaters*, won an American Book Award in 1981.

Baraka, Amiri (1934–   ).   A major figure in New York's East Village avant-garde scene and in the Black Arts Movement. Baraka first made his mark as LeRoi Jones in the 1960s with off-Broadway plays such as *Dutchman*, *The Slave*, and *The Toilet*. His commitment to political radicalism and black nationalism is reflected in poetry volumes such as *It's Nation Time* (1970), *Hard Facts* (1975), and *Daggers and Javelins* (1984).

Bell, James Madison (1826–1902).   Known for long narrative poems recounting the history of his times, from slavery through Reconstruction. Trained as a plasterer in Cincinnati, Bell was a staunch abolitionist and a supporter of John Brown. Bell's works include *A Poem Entitled the Day and the War* (1864), *An Anniversary Poem Entitled the Progress of Liberty* (1866), *A Poem Entitled the Triumph of Liberty* (1870), and *Poetical Works* (1901).

Bennett, Gwendolyn (1902–1981).   A significant figure in the Harlem Renaissance. Bennett excelled both as a graphic artist and as a poet. Her best-known poems, produced between 1923 and 1928, include "Heritage," "To Usward," "Wedding Day," and "Ebony Flute."

Bibb, Henry (1815–1854).   Best known for his *Narrative of the Life and Adventures of Henry Bibb, An American Slave*, published in 1849. Born into slavery in Kentucky, Bibb escaped to Canada and played an active role in the abolition movement as editor of a newspaper, *The Voice of the Fugitive*.

Bonner, Marita (1899–1971).   First achieved recognition with a pair of essays, "On Being Young—A Woman—and Colored" (1925) and "The Young Blood Hungers" (1928). Bonner also explored the urban landscape in plays such as *The Purple Flower* (1928) and in short stories, which included "The Hands" (1925), "Nothing New" (1928), "Tin Can" (1934), and "The Whipping" (1939).

Bontemps, Arna Wendell (1902–1973).   Writer whose career extended from the Harlem Renaissance into the 1970s, known for novels such as *Black Thunder: Gabriel's Revolt—Virginia 1800* (1936), *Sad-Faced Boy* (1937), and *Drums at Dusk* (1939). Bontemps also wrote children's books and edited anthologies of African American poetry and folklore.

Bradley, David (1950–   ).   Pennsylvania-born novelist. Bradley is noted for *South Street* (1975), a depiction of life in the Philadelphia ghetto, and for *The Chaneysville Incident* (1981), a major historical novel exploring the theme of resistance during slavery days.

Brooks, Gwendolyn (1917–   ).   The first African American writer to win a Pulitzer Prize, awarded in 1950 for her book of poems *Annie Allen*. Notably, Brooks has customarily placed her work with African American publishing houses. Other major works by Brooks include *A Street in Bronzeville* (1945), her first book of poems; *Maud Martha* (1953), a novel; and *Bronzeville Boys and Girls* (1956), a children's book.

Brown, William Wells (1814–1884).   A leading abolitionist who escaped from bondage at age 20. Brown was also an original and multifaceted writer who is regarded as the first African American to achieve national distinction in belles lettres. In addition to writing his classic autobiography, *Narrative of William W. Brown, A Fugitive Slave, Written by Himself* (1847), Brown is credited with writing the first travel book by an African American (*Three Years in Europe*, 1852) and the first African American novel (*Clotel, or the President's Daughter*, 1853). Brown also wrote a pair of historical works: *The Black Man: His Antecedents, His Genius, and His Achievements* (1863) and *The Negro in the American Rebellion* (1867).

Bullins, Ed (1953–   ).   One of the leading exponents of the Black Arts Movement in the theater. Bullins is known for plays that expose the harsh realities of African American urban life; his major works include *Clara's Ole Man* (1965), *Goin' a Buffalo* (1968), *Home Boy* (1976), and *Dr. Geechee and the Blood Junkies* (1991).

Butler, Octavia (1947–   ).   Science-fiction writer known for her explorations of slavery and its cultural implications. Butler's major works include *Patternmaster* (1976), *Kindred* (1979), *In Clay's Ark* (1984), and *The Parable of the Sower* (1993). Butler also won a MacArthur Fellowship.

Campbell, James Edwin (1867–1895).   Especially noted for the skillful poems he wrote in the Gullah language of South Carolina. After teaching at African American schools in West Virginia and South Carolina, Campbell joined the staff of the Chicago *Times-Herald* in 1891. Though he died of pneumonia at age 28, Campbell produced two collections of poetry: *Driftings and Gleanings* (1887) and *Echoes from the Cabin and Elsewhere* (1895).

Chesnutt, Charles Waddell (1858–1932).   The leading African American fiction writer of his generation. While working as a court reporter in Cleveland, he published two collections of short stories in 1899: *The Conjure Woman* and *The Wife of His Youth and Other Stories of the Color Line*. Subsequently devoting himself to writing full-time, Chesnutt produced three novels that examined such topics as passing, interracial marriage, and race relations in the South: *The House behind the Cedars* (1900), *The Marrow of Tradition* (1901), and *The Colonel's Dream* (1905). Chesnutt's work brought the evils of racism to the attention of a national audience.

Corrothers, James D. (1869–1917).   Journalist and autobiographer. Born in Michigan, Corrothers worked as a successful journalist in Chicago before becoming a minister in the A.M.E. Church. His best-known work is *The Black Cat Club* (1902), a collection of his popular newspaper sketches about African American life. Corrothers also published an autobiography, *In Spite of the Handicap* (1916).

Craft, William (c. 1826–1900).   Memoirist. After he and his wife, Ellen, made a dramatic escape from slavery in Georgia, Craft wrote *Running a Thousand Miles for Freedom* (1860).

Cullen, Countee (1903–1946).   One of the major figures of the Harlem Renaissance. Cullen produced three volumes of poetry while still a student at New York University in the mid-1920s. Collections of his poetry include *Color* (1925), *Copper Sun* (1927), *The Ballad of the Brown Girl* (1927), and *The Black Christ and Other Poems* (1929).

Danner, Margaret Esse (1915–1984).   Pioneering poet noted for incorporating African and Caribbean themes into her work as early as the 1940s. Collections of her work include *To Flower* (1962), *Poem Counterpoem* (1966), *Impressions of African Art Forms* (1968), and *Iron Lace* (1968).

Davis, Frank Marshall (1905–1987).   Poet and journalist who did groundbreaking work on black contributions to American culture. His often impassioned poetry is collected in *Black Man's Verse* (1935), *I Am the American Negro* (1937), *Through Sepia Eyes* (1938), and *47ᵗʰ Street: Poems* (1948).

Douglass, Frederick   (See Chapter 2, "Slavery and Freedom.")

Dove, Rita (1952–   ).   Poet laureate for the United States from 1993 to 1995. Dove's major verse collections include *The Yellow House on the Corner* (1980), *Museum* (1983), and *Thomas and Beulah* (1986; winner of the 1987 Pulitzer Prize). Dove has also published *Fifth Sunday* (1985), a collection of short stories, and *Through the Ivory Tower* (1992), a novel.

Dunbar, Paul Laurence (1872–1906).   Acclaimed poet of the late 19th and early 20th centuries. Though an outstanding student at his Dayton, Ohio, high school, Dunbar was obliged to work as an elevator operator after graduation. Writing whenever he could, he published poems in major U.S. literary magazines such as the *Century* and *Atlantic Monthly* and gained a nationwide audience. His 11 published collections of poetry include *Lyrics of Lowly Life* (1896), *When Malindy Sings* (1903), and *Lyrics of Sunshine and Shadow* (1905). Dunbar also wrote novels, including *Folks from Dixie* (1898) and *The Sport of the Gods* (1902).

Dunbar-Nelson, Alice Moore (1875–1935).   Published two volumes of stories during the 1890s: *Violets and Other Tales* (1895) and *The Goodness of St. Roque and Other Stories* (1899). During the Harlem Renaissance, she published poems in *Crisis* and *Opportunity*; her diary was published in 1984 under the title *Give Us Each Day* (edited by Gloria T. Hull).

Ellison, Ralph (1914–1994).   Influential writer who created a stylistic revolution in African American fiction with *Invisible Man* (1952) and who devoted much of his time and energy to teaching. Additional works include two volumes of essays, *Shadow and Act* (1964) and *Going to the Territory* (1986), and a second, unfinished novel, edited posthumously, *Juneteenth*.

Equiano, Olaudah (See Chapter 2, "Slavery and Freedom.")

Fauset, Jesse Redmon (1882–1961).   Literary editor of *Crisis* from 1919 to 1926. As a writer, Fauset is best known for four novels exploring African American identity through the situation of light-skinned individuals: *There Is Confusion* (1924), *Plum Bun* (1929), *The Chinaberry Tree* (1931), and *Comedy: American Style* (1933).

Fisher, Rudolph (1897–1943).   Physician-author best known for chronicling the 1920s social scene in *The Walls of Jericho* (1928). Fisher also wrote noted short stories, including "The City of Refuge," "High Yaller," and "The Conjure Man Dies."

Fuller, Charles H., Jr. (1939–   ).   Playwright whose work has been closely associated with Douglas Turner Ward's Negro Ensemble Company. Fuller's major works include *The Brownsville Raid* (1976), *Zooman and the Sign* (1979), and *A Soldier's Play* (winner of a 1982 Pulitzer Prize).

Gaines, Ernest J. (1933–   ).   Noted for novels and stories exploring race relations in his native Louisiana. Gaines's major works include *The Autobiography of Miss Jane Pittman* (1971), *In My Father's House* (1978), *A Gathering of Old Men* (1984), and *A Lesson before Dying* (1993). Gaines has steadily achieved the status of a major American writer.

Giovanni, Nikki (1943–   ).   Influential poet who emerged as a leading voice of the Black Arts Movement with her *Black Feeling, Black Talk* (1968) and *Black Judgment* (1969). Her subsequent volumes of poetry evince a more introspective tone, reflecting her experiences as a single mother, but these works continue to confront social and political issues. Her volumes include *My House* (1972), *The Women and the Men* (1975), and *Those Who Ride the Night Winds* (1983). Giovanni has also written several volumes of poetry for children.

Gordone, Charles (1925–1995).   Pulitzer Prize–winning playwright who began his career in the theater as an actor and wrote in order to earn money. In addition to the acclaimed *No Place to Be Somebody* (1969), Gordone's dramas include *Baba Chops* (1975) and *Anabiosis* (1979).

Graham, Shirley (1896–1977).   Writer and composer. Graham's works include plays such as *Elijah's Raven* (1941), a number of books for young readers, a historical novel about Frederick Douglass (*Your Most Humble Servant*, 1949), and a novel of South Africa (*Zulu Heart*, 1974).

Green, J. D. (1813–?).   Author of a slave narrative. Green escaped from slavery in Maryland in 1848 and lived in Canada and England. His autobiography, *Narrative of the Life of J. D. Green, a Runaway Slave* (1864), is notable for its portrayal of the subterfuges Green confesses to employing against whites and blacks alike.

Griggs, Sutton E. (1872–1933).   Born in Texas, Griggs became a Baptist minister and turned to writing in order to combat racist stereotypes. His novels, which depict talented African Americans fighting for equality, include *Imperium in Imperio* (1899), *Overshadowed* (1901), and *The Hindered Hand* (1905).

Grimké, Angelina Weld (1880–1958).   Poet, dramatist, and short-story writer who contributed to the leading periodicals of the Harlem Renaissance. Grimké's best-known works include *Rachel* (1916, a social protest play) and "The Closing Door" (a short story dealing with lynching and infanticide).

Haley, Alex (1921–1992).   The award-winning author of *Roots* (1976). Haley began his writing career as a journalist and first achieved prominence through his collaboration on *The Autobiography of Malcolm X* (1965). Following the spectacular success of *Roots*, he published a second novel, *A Different Kind of Christmas*, in 1988.

Hammon, Briton (1700s).   Autobiographer. All that is known about Hammon's life is contained in his 1760 autobiography, *A Narrative of the Uncommon Sufferings, and Surprising Deliverance of Briton Hammon, A Negro Man—Servant to General Winslow*. The 14-page work, published in Boston, recounts Hammon's adventures when he was shipwrecked in 1747, captured by Native Americans, and imprisoned by the Spanish in Cuba before being reunited with General Winslow.

Hammon, Jupiter (1711–c. 1806).   A poet and essayist. Hammon lived on a plantation in Oyster Bay, Long Island, and worked in a business owned by the Lloyd family. Hammon's first published poem, "An Evening Thought, Salvation, by Christ, with Penitential Cries" (1760), is regarded as the first formal literary work by an African American.

Hansberry, Lorraine (1930–1965).   Award-winning dramatist. Hansberry captured the spirit of the civil rights movement in her *Raisin in the Sun* (1959), an enduring classic of the American stage. Hansberry's second play, *The Sign in Sidney Brustein's Window*, opened in 1964. After Hansberry's premature death from cancer, her husband, Robert Nemiroff, adapted some of her other writings into a successful dramatic work, *To Be Young, Gifted, and Black* (1968).

Harper, Frances Ellen Watkins (1825–1911).   Prolific writer of fiction and nonfiction, poetry and prose. Born free in Maryland, Harper became a college professor and antislavery activist, while contributing to a number of journals. Among her best-known works are "The Two Offers" (1859), believed to be the first African American short story; *Moses, a Story of the Nile* (1868), a dramatic epic; and *Iola Leroy* (1892), a novel.

Hayden, Robert (1913–1980).   Regarded as one of the most technically gifted African American poets of all time. Hayden first achieved prominence during the 1930s, and his published volumes of poetry include *Heart-Shape in the Dust* (1940), *The Lion and the Archer* (1948), *A Ballad of Remembrance* (1962), *Angle of Ascent* (1975), and *Collected Poems* (1985).

Himes, Chester (1909–1984).   Best known for his hard-boiled detective novels featuring Grave Digger Jones and Coffin Ed Johnson. Himes has also been acclaimed for his incisive portrayal of Harlem and other African American communities. Himes's major works include *If He Hollers Let Him Go* (1945), *The Third Generation* (1947), *The Real Cool Killers* (1959), *Cotton Comes to Harlem* (1965). He also recalled his often turbulent life in *The Quality of Hurt* (1972) and *My Life of Absurdity* (1976).

Horton, George Moses (c. 1797–c. 1883).   Known as the Colored Bard of North Carolina. Horton wrote more than 150 poems on a variety of themes. Despite the restrictions imposed on him by enslavement, Horton became a celebrated figure. His poems were published in three collections: *The Hope of Liberty, Containing a Number of Poetical Pieces* (1829), *The Poetical Works* (1845), and *Naked Genius* (1865). After emancipation, Horton moved to Philadelphia.

Portrait of the legendary Langston Hughes, 1930.

Hughes, Langston (1902–1967).   One of the giants of American literature and a master of many genres. His poetry collections include *The Weary Blues* (1926), *Fine Clothes to the Jew* (1927), *Montage of a Dream Deferred* (1951), and *The Panther and the Lash* (1967). As a playwright, Hughes is noted for *Mulatto* (1935), *Little Ham* (1936), *Tambourines to Glory* (1963) and *Jericho–Jim Crow* (1964). His fiction includes the novel *Not without Laughter* (1930) and the short-story collection *The Ways of White Folks* (1934). Hughes's popular columns for the *Chicago Defender* were collected in *Simple Speaks His Mind* (1950) and four subsequent volumes.

Hurston, Zora Neale (1891–1960).   A leading figure of the Harlem Renaissance, increasingly recognized as a major 20th-century American writer. Best known for her novels *Jonah's Gourd Vine* (1934) and *Their Eyes Were Watching God* (1937), Hurston also wrote an autobiography, *Dust Tracks on a Road* (1942), and a pioneering study of African American folklore, *Mules and Men* (1935).

Jacobs, Harriet A. (c. 1813–1897).   Autobiographer. Jacobs escaped from slavery in North Carolina in 1835. Her *Incidents in the Life of a Slave Girl* (1861) is regarded as the outstanding autobiography of an African American woman in the antebellum period.

Johnson, Amelia E. (1858–1922).   Born in Toronto, Johnson moved to Boston in the 1870s. She is best known for her three novels: *Clarence and Corinne, or God's Way* (1890), *The Hazeley Family* (1894), and *Martina Meriden, or What Is My Motive?* (1901). Though she dealt with social problems, Johnson did not specifically confront racial issues, concentrating instead on the affirmation of Christian principles.

Johnson, Charles R. (1948–   ).   Multitalented artist known for a complex aesthetic system that blends philosophy, folklore, and fiction. Johnson's major fictional works include *Faith and the Good Thing* (1964),

Oxherding Tale (1982), and *Middle Passage* (1986). A successful graphic artist and the holder of a Ph.D. in philosophy, Johnson has also published a volume of criticism, *Being and Race: Black Writing Since 1970* (1988).

Johnson, Fenton (1888–1958).   A progenitor of the Harlem Renaissance who founded several literary magazines. Johnson published three volumes of poetry: *A Little Dreaming* (1913), *Visions of the Dark* (1915), and *Songs of the Soil* (1916). His short stories were collected as *Tales of Darkest America* (1920).

Johnson, Georgia Douglas (1880–1966).   Leader of the literary expression of the Harlem Renaissance as it was reflected in Washington, D.C. Although best known for her poetry, collected in four volumes—*The Heart of a Woman* (1918), *Bronze* (1922), *Autumn Love Song* (1928), and *Share My World* (1962)— Johnson also wrote a number of plays, including *Blue Blood* (1926) and *Plumes* (1927).

Johnson, James Weldon (1871–1938).   Multitalented artist who excelled in many fields, including music, journalism, law, and diplomacy. Johnson's most notable literary creations were the novel *Autobiography of an Ex-Colored Man* (1912); *God's Trombones, Seven Negro Sermons in Verse* (1927); and *Black Manhattan* (1930), a classic account of African American contributions to urban culture. Johnson also edited a volume of African American poetry and two volumes of spirituals.

Jones, Gayl (1949–   ).   Writer and critic noted for her concern with the value of African American oral traditions. Jones's major works include the novels *Corregidora* (1975) and *Eva's Man* (1976); a short-story collection, *White Rat* (1977); and three volumes of poetry, *Song for Anninho* (1981), *The Hermit Woman* (1983), and *Xaque and Other Poems* (1985).

Kelley, Emma Dunham (1800s).   Novelist. Though little is known of Kelley's life, two of her novels survive: *Megda* (1891) and *Four Girls at Cottage City* (1895). Both works follow a group of girls from adolescence to adulthood and confirm the importance of Christian principles.

Kelley, William Melvin (1937–   ).   Novelist and short-story writer noted for his sardonic examination of racial attitudes in the United States. Kelley's best-known works include *A Different Drummer* (1962), *A Drop of Patience* (1965), *dem* (1967), and *Dunford Travels Everywheres* (1970).

Killens, John Oliver (1916–1987).   Novelist known for confronting racism during the civil rights era, in such works as *Youngblood* (1954) and *'Sippi* (1967). A subsequent novel, *The Cotillion, or One Good Bull Is Half the Herd* (1971), takes a satiric look at competing currents of thought within the black community.

Kincaid, Jamaica (1949–   ).   Novelist and commentator. Born in Antigua, Kinkaid came to the United States at age 17 and first made her reputation with a series of short stories in the *New Yorker*. In addition to the story collection *At the Bottom of the River* (1983), she has published the novels *Annie John* (1985) and *The Autobiography of My Mother* (1996), and a nonfiction book on Antigua, *A Small Place* (1988).

Larsen, Nella (1891–1964).   Leading novelist of the Harlem Renaissance. Larsen's novels *Quicksand* (1928) and *Passing* (1929) are noted for their exploration of the situation of African American women in modern society.

Lester, Julius (1939–   ).   Activist, broadcaster, and writer known for his independent and sometimes controversial views. Lester first came to public attention in 1968 with his *Look Out, Whitey! Black Power's Gon' Get Your Mama*. Lester has since written in a wide variety of genres, including poetry (*Who I Am*, 1974), autobiography (*All Is Well*, 1976), and folklore (*The Tales of Uncle Remus*, 1987).

Locke, Alain (1885–1954).   Leading figure in the Harlem Renaissance and one of the major influences on the development of African American culture. Locke edited *The New Negro* (1925) and several other important anthologies. His own books include *Negro Art: Past and Present* (1936), *The Negro and His Music* (1936), and *The Negro in Art* (1940).

Lorde, Audre (1934–1992).   Self-described "black feminist lesbian mother poet." Lorde's major works include *The First Cities* (1968), *Cables to Rage* (1970), *Coal* (1976), and *The Black Unicorn* (1978). Lorde also wrote two accounts of her battle with cancer: *The Cancer Journals* (1980) and *A Burst of Light* (1988).

Marrant, John (1755–1791).   Memoirist. Though born free in New York, Marrant traveled to the South, where he was first captured by the Cherokees and then by the British, who forced him to serve as a sailor during the Revolutionary War. His account of his adventures, *A Narrative of the Lord's Wonderful Dealings with John Marrant, A Black,* was published in 1785 and achieved great success in Europe and the United States. In the later part of his life, Marrant served as a missionary in Canada; he published his *Journal* in 1790.

Marshall, Paule (1929–   ).   Brooklyn-born writer whose work reflects her West Indian ancestry. Marshall's major works include *Brown Girl, Brownstones* (1959); *Soul Clap Hands and Sing* (1961); *The Chosen Place, the Timeless People* (1969); *Praisesong for the Widow* (1983); and *Daughters* (1991).

Matthews, Victoria Earle (1861–1907).   Well-known journalist. Born in Georgia, Matthews educated herself while working as a domestic in New York City. Later, she was a correspondent for African American papers such as the *Boston Advocate* and the *New York Globe.* She is best known for her essay "The Value of Race Literature" (1895) and her novella *Aunt Lindy* (1893). She also edited *Black Belt Diamonds* (1898), a collection of Booker T. Washington's speeches.

McKay, Claude (1890–1948).   Jamaican-born poet and novelist of the Harlem Renaissance. McKay published two volumes of poetry, *Songs of Jamaica* and *Constab Ballads,* in 1912 before immigrating to the United States. McKay's best-known novel, *Home to Harlem,* was published in 1928. Later novels include *Banjo* (1929), *Gingertown* (1932), and *Banana Bottom* (1933).

McMillan, Terry (1951–   ).   Best-selling novelist. McMillan explores family and romantic relationships in such works as *Mama* (1987), *Disappearing Acts* (1989), *Waiting to Exhale* (1992), and *How Stella Got Her Groove Back* (1996).

McPherson, James Alan (1943–   ).   Short-story writer and essayist concerned with themes such as identity and diversity. Following the appearance of *Elbow Room* (1977), his Pulitzer Prize–winning collection of stories, McPherson has concentrated on writing personal and political essays.

Miller, May (1899–1995).   Poet and playwright who first achieved prominence during the 1920s with plays on historical and political themes. Some of her plays were set in Africa (*Samory*) and in Haiti (*Christophe's Daughters*). Miller concentrated on poetry after the 1940s: Her collections include *Into the Clearing* (1959) and *Dust of Uncertain Journey* (1975).

Morrison, Toni (1931–   ).   First African American woman to win the Nobel Prize in Literature. As a longtime editor at Random House, Morrison was also instrumental in developing the careers of Gayl Jones, Toni Cade Bambara, and other writers. Morrison's major novels include *Sula* (1973), *Song of Solomon* (1977), *Tar Baby* (1981), *Beloved* (1987), *Jazz* (1992) and *Paradise* (1998). Morrison has also published a book of criticism, *Playing in the Dark: Whiteness and the Literary Imagination* (1992).

Mosley, Walter (1952–   ).   Los Angeles–based writer of detective fiction best known for his Easy Rawlins series. Mosley's major works include *Devil in a Blue Dress* (1990), *A Red Death* (1991), *White Butterfly* (1992), and *Black Betty* (1994).

Murray, Albert (1916–   ).   Novelist, essayist, and critic known for exploring the cultural and literary importance of blues and jazz. Murray's nonfiction works include *The Omni-Americans* (1970), *South to a Very Old Place* (1971), *The Hero and the Blues* (1973), and *Stomping the Blues* (1976). Murray has also published three highly regarded novels: *Train Whistle Guitar* (1974), *The Spyglass Tree* (1991), and *The Seven-League Boots* (1996).

Naylor, Gloria (1950–   ).   Mississippi-born novelist known for her wide range of subject matter and narrative technique. Naylor's major works include *The Women of Brewster Place* (1982), *Linden Hills* (1985), *Mama Day* (1988), and *Bailey's Cafe* (1992).

Nell, William C. (1816–1874).   Journalist and historian. Born free in Boston, Nell contributed to the *Liberator* and the *North Star*, aided other African American writers, and fought for desegregation of Boston's schools. As a writer, he is best known for historical works such as *The Colored Patriots of the American Revolution* (1855).

Parks, Suzan-Lori (1963–   ).   Award-winning playwright known for her poetic style and experimentation with language. Parks's major works include *Imperceptible Mutabilities in the Third Kingdom* (1989), *Devotees in the Garden of Love* (1991), *The America Play* (1992), and *The Death of the Last Black Man in the Whole Entire World* (1992).

Payne, Daniel A. (1811–1893).   Poet, memoirist, and historian. Born in South Carolina, Payne was a minister of the African Methodist Episcopal Church, a theologian, and the first black president of a college (Wilberforce University, 1863–1879) in the United States. He was also a dedicated writer whose works include *The Pleasures and Other Miscellaneous Poems* (1850), *Recollections of Seventy Years* (1888), and *History of the African Methodist Episcopal Church* (1891).

Pennington, James W. C. (1807–1870).   Memoirist and historian. Born into slavery in Maryland, Pennington escaped in 1828 and moved to Long Island, where he obtained an education and plunged into antislavery work. His first book, a guide for teachers, was entitled *A Text Book of the Origin and History . . . of Colored People* (1841). Pennington later wrote an account of his experiences, *The Fugitive Blacksmith*, which appeared in 1849.

Petry, Ann (1908–1997).   Novelist noted for urban realism. Petry first achieved prominence with *The Street* (1946). Her other works of fiction include *The Narrows* (1953) and *Miss Muriel and Other Stories* (1971).

Ray, Henrietta Cordelia (c. 1849–1916).   Poet and biographer. A graduate of the City College of New York, Ray taught at an African American school before launching her literary career. She is best known for two verse collections, *Sonnets* (1893) and *Poems* (1910), and (in collaboration with her sister Florence) a biography of her father, *Sketches of the Life of Rev. Charles E. Ray* (1887). Her poem "Commemoration Ode" was read at the unveiling of the Freedmen's Monument in Washington, D.C., in 1876.

Reason, Charles L. (1818–1893).   Poet and essayist. Born in New York to West Indian parents, Reason spent his life as a teacher at a number of African American schools and a champion of equal rights. He contributed essays and poems to a variety of journals; his best-known poems include "The Spirit Voice" (1841) and "Freedom" (1846).

Reed, Ishmael (1938–   ).   One of the most distinctive voices in American literature. Reed is known for developing the aesthetic of "neohoodooism," a celebration of the many traditions, African and other, making up the artistic culture of the New World. Reed's major fictional works include *The Free-Lance Pallbearers* (1967), *Mumbo Jumbo* (1972), and *Flight to Canada* (1976). His essay collections include *Shrovetide in Old New Orleans* (1978) and *Airing Dirty Laundry* (1993).

Richardson, Willis (1889–1977).   First African American playwright to have a nonmusical production on Broadway (*The Chip Woman's Fortune*, 1923). Richardson's other plays, focusing on the everyday lives of African Americans, include *The Deacon's Awakening* (1920); *Broken Banjo, A Folk Tragedy* (1925); and *The Bootblack Lover* (1926). As a playwright and a director, Richardson had a major influence on African American theater groups, both professional and amateur.

Sanchez, Sonia (1934–   ).   Poet and playwright closely identified with the militancy of the Black Arts Movement. This style pervaded her early poetry collections such as *Homecoming* (1969) and *We a BaddDDD People* (1970) and her plays such as *The Bronx Is Next* (1968) and *Sister Sonja* (1969). Sanchez's later works often have a more personal and introspective focus, including *I've Been a Woman: New and Selected Poems* (1981), *Homegirls and Handgrenades* (1984), and *Under a Soprano Sky* (1987).

Schomburg, Arthur A. (1874–1938).   Historian and bibliographer who emigrated to the United States from Puerto Rico in 1891 and dedicated his life to collecting materials on black culture. Schomburg contributed numerous articles to *Crisis, Opportunity, Negro World*, and other periodicals. Schomburg's private collection became the basis of the New York Public Library's Schomburg Center for Research in Black Culture.

Shadd, Mary Ann (1823–1893).   Journalist and newspaper founder. Born in Delaware, Shadd was educated in Pennsylvania and went on to become a teacher. After emigrating to Canada in 1850 she began her literary career. In 1850, Shadd published *Notes on Canada West*, a pamphlet that encouraged other African Americans to move to Canada. She also cofounded an abolitionist newspaper, the *Provincial Freeman*, in 1853, performing as both editor and contributor. After the Civil War, Shadd returned to the United States and worked as a teacher, lawyer, and women's suffrage advocate.

Shange, Ntozake (1948–   ).   Multifaceted writer known for her experimental techniques and exploration of themes concerning women of all backgrounds. In addition to her award-winning 1974 play, *for colored girls who have considered suicide / when the rainbow is enuf*, she has written *From Okra to Greens* (1978), *Mother Courage and Her Children* (1980), *Daddy Says* (1989), and other dramas. Shange's poetry collections include *Nappy Edges* (1978) and *Ridin' the Moon in Texas* (1989). Her prose work has been collected in volumes that include *Sassafras: A Novella* (1977), *A Daughter's Geography* (1983), *See No Evil: Prefaces Essays and Accounts* (1984), and *Besty Brown* (1985).

Smith, Venture (c. 1729–1805).   Author of a slave narrative. Born in West Africa, Smith came to the United States at age eight and spent the next 28 years earning enough money to buy his own freedom, along with that of his wife and three children. He dictated his life story to an amanuensis (said to be Elisha Niles, a Connecticut schoolmaster), and it was published in 1789 as *A Narrative of the Life and Adventures of Venture, a Native of Africa*.

Terry, Lucy (c. 1730–1821).   Poet and orator. Born in Africa, Terry was kidnapped in her youth and transported to New England. In 1756, she married Obijah Prince (who purchased her freedom) and moved to Vermont, where they raised six children. Though Terry wrote the poem "Bars Fight" when she was 16, it was not published until 1855, and during her lifetime she was known mainly as an inspiring orator and a champion of African American rights.

Thurman, Wallace (1902–1934).   Revolutionary force within the Harlem Renaissance who criticized established writers and founded the experimental journal *Fire!!* in 1926. His novels, which often deal with controversial themes, include *The Blacker the Berry* (1929) and *Infants of the Spring* (1932).

Toomer, Jean (1894–1967).   Poet, dramatist, and novelist best known for *Cane* (1923). Toomer's later works include *Essentials* (1931) and *The Blue Meridian* (1936).

Vashon, George B. (1824–1878).   Poet and essayist. Born in Pennsylvania, Vashon graduated from Oberlin College in 1844. During the early part of his career, he practiced law in New York and spent three years teaching in Haiti. He then became a school principal in Pittsburgh and began contributing essays and poems to a number of periodicals. His best-known work is "Vincent Ogé" (1854), an epic poem on the Haitian Revolution.

Walker, Alice (1944–   ).   Poet and novelist noted for her concern with the lives of African and African American women and her involvement in human-rights issues in the United States and Africa. Walker's major novels include *The Strange Life of Grange Copeland* (1970), *Meridian* (1976), *The Color Purple* (1982), *The Temple of My Familiar* (1989), and *Possessing the Secret of Joy* (1992). Walker's work was long neglected, but the success of *The Color Purple* catapulted her into the front rank of American writers.

Walker, Margaret (1915–1998).   Writer and educator who began her career in the 1930s. Walker achieved recognition in 1966 with the publication of *Jubilee*, a historical novel drawing on the oral history of her own family. Her poetry collections include *For My People* (1942), *Prophets for a New Day* (1970), and *October Journey* (1973).

Walrond, Eric (1898–1966).   British Guiana–born writer who made his most notable contribution with the short-story collection *Tropic Death* (1926). This collection explores themes of migration and cultural displacement within the black diaspora. As an editor, Walrond also played a leading role in African American publications such as *Negro World* and *Opportunity*.

Ward, Theodore (1902–1983).   Playwright who achieved critical acclaim with *Big White Fog* (1938) and *Our Lan'* (1941). These plays tackled subjects such as black nationalism, anti-Semitism, communism, racism, and color prejudice within the African American community. Ward's other works include *Deliver the Goods* (1942), *John Brown* (1950), and *Candle in the Wind* (1967).

West, Dorothy (1907–1998).   Fiction writer, journalist, and editor who contributed to many African American publications during the Harlem Renaissance. West published her first novel, *The Living Is Easy*, in 1948. West's second novel, *The Wedding*, was published to critical acclaim in 1995, along with *The Richer, the Poorer*, a collection of stories and other short pieces.

Wheatley, Phillis (c. 1753–1784).   Poet. Born in Senegambia, Wheatley was taken into captivity as a child and transported to Boston, where she became a servant. She began publishing poetry at age 14, and her first volume, *Poems on Various Subjects, Religious and Moral*, in 1773, made her a celebrity in England and the colonies. She soon achieved her freedom and married, but she struggled to support her three children and died in poverty at age 31.

Whitfield, James Monroe (1822–1871).   Poet and essayist. Born in New Hampshire, Whitfield spent his life working as a barber in New York and California. A proponent of African colonization, he contributed essays and poems to the *North Star* and other publications, expressing his anger over racial discrimination. His shorter poetry, collected in *America and Other Poems* (1853), is marked by great technical sophistication. In 1867, Whitfield published a 400-line epic simply entitled *Poem*, in which he surveys American history in often caustic terms.

Whitman, Albery Allson (1851–1901).   Poet. Born into slavery in Kentucky, Whitman worked at a variety of jobs before becoming a minister and a poet. While following the poetic forms established by the 19th-century Romantic poets, he explored contemporary personal and racial issues. Whitman's longer poems are generally considered his best; they include *Leelah Misled* (1873), *Not Yet a Man, and Yet a Man* (1877), and *The Rape of Florida* (1884).

Wideman, John Edgar (1941–   ).   Wide-ranging writer whose works explore the many facets of African American history and culture. Wideman's major novels include *Hurry Home* (1970), *Hiding Place* (1981), *Sent for You Yesterday* (1983), and *Philadelphia Fire* (1990). Wideman's shorter fiction has been collected in *Damballah* (1981) and *All Stories Are True* (1992).

Williams, George Washington (1849–1891).   Historian of African Americans up to and during Reconstruction. A Civil War veteran, Baptist minister, and Ohio State legislator, Williams wrote the first comprehensive history of African Americans, *History of the Negro Race in America from 1619 to 1880*. Published in 1883, Williams's work was notable for its use of newspaper accounts and primary sources, and it influenced the writing of history books during the late 19th and early 20th centuries. In 1887, Williams produced a second book, *History of the Negro Troops in the War of the Rebellion*.

Williams, John A. (1925–   ).   Prolific fiction writer noted for his unsparing examination of racial injustice and his concern with understanding history. Of his 11 novels, the best known is *The Man Who Cried I Am* (1967). His others include *Sissie* (1963), *Captain Blackman* (1972), *!Click Song* (1982), and *The Berhama Account* (1985). In 1963, Williams traveled across the United States on a magazine assignment and recorded his experiences in *This Is My Country Too* (1965).

Williams, Sherley Anne (1944–   ).   A major figure in the endeavor to develop a black aesthetic, as expressed in scholarly works such as *Give Birth to Brightness: A Thematic Study in Neo-Black Literature* (1972). As a creative writer, Williams has focused on the lives of women, notably in the novel *Dessa Rose* (1986), the children's picture book *Working Cotton* (1992), and two collections of poetry, *Peacock Poems* (1975) and *Someone Sweet Angel Chile* (1982).

Wilson, August (1945–).   One of the leading playwrights of the modern American stage and the only African American writer to win the Pulitzer Prize twice. Wilson's best-known works include *Ma Rainey's Black Bottom* (1982), *Joe Turner's Come and Gone* (1984), *Fences* (1986), *The Piano Lesson* (1986), and *Two Trains Running* (1989).

Wilson, Harriet E. (c. 1827–?).   The first African American female novelist. Wilson was born in New Hampshire. Abandoned by her husband, she wrote the novel *Our Nig* in 1859, hoping to earn enough money to reclaim her son, who had been taken in by another family. Wilson's status as a pioneer of African American literature remained obscure until 1984, when scholarly research confirmed her contribution.

Woodson, Carter G. (1875–1950).   Founder of the Association for the Study of Negro Life (1915) and the *Journal of Negro History* (1916) and originator of Negro History Week (later Black History Month). Woodson ranks with W. E. B. Du Bois and Alain Locke as a driving force in 20th-century African American culture. Woodson's major works include *The Education of the Negro Prior to 1861* (1915), *The History of the Negro Church* (1921), *The Negro in Our History* (1922), *Negro Orators and Their Orations* (1925), and *The African Background Outlined* (1936).

Wright, Richard (1908–1960).   Groundbreaking novelist who achieved international stature after the publication of *Native Son* in 1940. Wright's other influential works include the short-story collection *Uncle Tom's Children* (1938) and his autobiography *Black Boy* (1945, republished posthumously in 1977 with additional material as *American Hunger*). Wright's nonfiction works, written after he moved to Paris, include *Black Power* (1954), *The Color Curtain* (1955), *Pagan Spain* (1956), and *White Man, Listen* (1957).

NOTABLE CONTEMPORARY AFRICAN AND CARIBBEAN WRITERS

Achebe, Chinua (1930–).   Nigeria. Novelist. *Things Fall Apart* (1958); *Arrow of God* (1964); *A Man of the People* (1966); *Anthills of the Savannah* (1987).

Aidoo, Ama Ata (1942–).   Ghana. Poet, playwright, and fiction writer. *Someone Talking to Sometime* (1985); *The Eagle and the Chicken and Other Stories* (1986); *Birds and Other Poems* (1987).

Anthony, Michael (1932–).   Trinidad. Fiction writer. *Green Days by the River* (1967); *Cricket in the Road and Other Stories* (1973); *All That Glitters* (1981).

Armah, Ayi Kwei (1939–).   Ghana. Novelist and short-story writer. *Why Are We So Blest?* (1972); *Two Thousand Seasons* (1973); *The Beautyful Ones Are Not Yet Born* (1968).

Awoonor, Kofi (1935–).   Ghana. Poet. *Rediscovery and Other Poems* (1964); *Guardians of the Sacred Word* (1974); *Until the Morning After* (1987).

Bâ, Mariama (1929–1981).   Senegal. French-language novelist. *So Long a Letter* (1979); *Scarlet Song* (1981).

Badian, Seydou (1928–).   Mali. French-language novelist. *Under the Storm* (1967); *The Death of Chaka* (1968); *The Blood of the Masks* (1976).

Bebey, Francis (1929–).   Cameroon. French-language fiction writer. *Embarrassment and Company* (1968); *The Ashanti Doll* (1973); *King Albert* (1976).

Bennett, Louise (1919–).   Jamaica. Poet. *Jamaica Labrish* (1966); *Selected Poems* (1983).

Beti, Mongo (1932–).   Cameroon. French-language novelist. *The Poor Christ of Bomba* (1956); *Remember Ruben* (1974); *The Revenge of Guillaime Ismaël Dzewatama* (1984).

Brathwaite, Edward Kamau (1930–). Barbados. Poet and fiction writer. *The Arrivants: A Trilogy* (1973); *Days and Nights* (1975); *Middle Passages* (1992).

Brodber, Erna (1940–). Jamaica. Poet and novelist. *Jane and Louisa Will Soon Come Home* (1980); *Myal* (1988).

Brutus, Dennis (1924–). South Africa. Poet. *Sirens, Knuckles, Boots* (1963); *Poems from Algiers* (1970); *Stubborn Hope* (1978).

Césaire, Aimé (1913–). Martinique. French-language poet and essayist; longtime mayor of Fort-de-France. *Notebook on a Return to My Native Land* (1939); *Discourse on Colonialism* (1950); *The Tragedy of King Christophe* (1963); *A Season in the Congo* (1966); *Collected Poetry* (1983).

Chamoiseau, Patrick (1953–). Martinique. Novelist writing in French and Creole. *Manman Dlo vs. the Fairy Carabosse* (1982); *Past Childhood* (1990); *Texaco* (1992).

Cheny-Coker, Syl (1945–). Sierra Leone. Poet. *Concerto for an Exile* (1973); *The Graveyard Also Has Teeth* (1980); *The Blood in the Desert's Eyes* (1990).

Clarke, Austin C. (1934–). Barbados. Fiction writer. *Amongst Thistles and Thorns* (1965); *Growing Up Stupid under the Union Jack* (1980); *Proud Empires* (1986).

Cliff, Michelle (1946–). Jamaica. Fiction writer. *Claiming an Identity They Taught Me to Despise* (1980); *Abeng* (1984); *Bodies of Water* (1990).

Collins, Merle (1950–). Grenada. Fiction writer. *Because the Dawn Breaks!* (1985); *Angel* (1987).

Condé, Maryse (1937–). Guadeloupe. Novelist and essayist. *God Gave It to Us* (1973); *Ségou: The Walls of Earth* (1984); *The Last Magi Kings* (1992).

Damas, Léon-Gontran (1912–). French Guiana. Poet. *Pigments* (1937); *Graffiti* (1952); *Black Label* (1956).

Depestre, René (1926–). Haiti. Poet. *Journal of a Sea Creature* (1965); *For the Revolution: For Poetry* (1974); *Hadriana in All My Dreams* (1988).

Edgell, Zee (1941–). Belize. Novelist. *Beka Lamb* (1982); *In Times Like These* (1991).

Gilroy, Beryl (1924–). Guyana. Novelist. *Frangipani House* (1986); *Boy-Sandwich* (1989); *Stedman and Joanna* (1991).

Glissant, Edouard (1928–). Martinique. Novelist, playwright, and poet. *The Indies* (1956); *Foul Death* (1975); *Caribbean Discourse* (1989).

Goodison, Lorna (1947–). Jamaica. Poet. *Tamarind Season* (1980); *I Am Becoming My Mother* (1986); *Selected Poems* (1992).

Harris, Wilson (1921–). Guyana. Novelist and essayist. *Palace of the Peacock* (1960); *Ascent to Omai* (1970); *The Infinite Rehearsal* (1987).

Head, Bessie (1937–1986). South Africa. Fiction writer. *The Collector of Treasure and Other Botswana Village Tales* (1977); *A Bewitched Crossroad* (1984); *A Woman Alone: Autobiographical Writings* (1990).

Hearne, John (1926–). Jamaica. Novelist. *The Autumn Equinox* (1959); *Land of the Living* (1961); *The Sure Salvation* (1981).

Heath, Roy A. K. (1926–). Guyana. Novelist. *A Man Come Home* (1974); *One Generation* (1981); *Shadows Round the Moon* (1990).

James, C. L. R. (1901–1989). Trinidad. Fiction writer, historian, and autobiographer. *Minty Alley* (1936); *The Black Jacobins* (1938); *Beyond a Boundary* (1963).

Juminer, Bertène (1927–).   French Guiana. Novelist. *On the Threshold of a New Cry* (1963); *Bozambo's Revenge* (1969); *Heirs to the Peninsula* (1981).

Labou Tonsi, Sony (1947–).   Congo. French-language novelist. *Life and a Half* (1979); *The State of Shame* (1981); *The Antipeople* (1983).

Lamming, George (1927–).   Barbados. Novelist. *The Emigrants* (1954); *The Pleasures of Exile* (1960); *Natives of My Person* (1972).

Laye, Camara (1928–).   Guinea. French-language novelist and memoirist. *The Dark Child* (1954); *The Radience of the King* (1956); *A Dream of Africa* (1968).

Lovelace, Earl (1935– .   Trinidad. Novelist and playwright. *The Dragon Can't Dance* (1979); *The Wine of Astonishment* (1982); *Jestina's Calypso and Other Plays* (1984).

Maillu, David (1939–).   Kenya. Novelist. *Unfit for Human Consumption* (1973); *After 4:30* (1974); *The Equatorial Assignment* (1980).

Mais, Roger (1905–1955).   Jamaica. Poet, playwright, fiction writer. *The Hills Were Joyful Together* (1953); *Brother Man* (1954); *Black Lightning* (1955).

Marechera, Dambudzo (1952–1987).   Zimbabwe. Poet and short-story writer. *The House of Hunger* (1978); *Black Sunlight* (1980); *Mindblast, or the Definitive Buddy* (1984).

Maximin, Daniel (1947–).   Guadeloupe. French-language novelist. *Lone Sun* (1981); *Sulfur Mines* (1987).

Métellus, Jean (1937–).   Haiti. Poet and novelist. *Jacmel at Dusk* (1981); *Anancona* (1986); *The Revolutionaries* (1989).

Munonye, John (1929–).   Nigeria. Novelist. *Obi* (1969); *A Dancer of Fortune* (1974); *Bridge to a Wedding* (1978).

Mwangi, Meja (1948–).   Kenya. Novelist. *Kill Me Quick* (1973); *Going Down River Road* (1976); *Striving for the Wind* (1990).

Nwapa, Flora (1931–1993).   Nigeria. Fiction writer. *Efuru* (1966); *This Is Lagos and Other Stories* (1971); *Cassava Song and Rice Song* (1986).

Ogot, Grace (1930–).   Kenya. Novelist and short-story writer. *Land without Thunder* (1968); *The Other Woman: Selected Short Stories* (1976); *Ber Wat* (1981).

Okri, Ben (1959–).   Nigeria. Fiction writer. *The Landscapes Within* (1981); *The Famished Road* (1991); *Songs of Enchantment* (1993).

Phelps, Anthony (1928–).   Haiti. Poet. *Bursts of Silence* (1962); *Minus the Infinite* (1973); *The Caribbean Ram* (1980).

Phillips, Caryl (1958–).   St. Kitts. Novelist and short-story writer. *The Final Passage* (1975); *Cambridge* (1992); *Crossing the River* (1994).

Reid, V. S. (1913–1987).   Jamaica. Novelist. *New Day* (1949); *The Young Warriors* (1967); *Nanny-Town* (1983).

Salkey, Andrew (1928–).   Jamaica. Poet and fiction writer. *Stories from the Caribbean* (1968); *Hurricane* (1977); *Anancy, Traveller* (1988).

Sembène, Ousmane (1923–).   Senegal. Fiction writer and filmmaker. *God's Bits of Wood* (1960); *Tribal Scars and Other Stories* (1975); *Xala* (1976).

Senghor, Léopold Sédar (1906–   ).   Senegal. Poet; president of Senegal, 1960–1980. *Shadow Songs* (1945); *Songs for Naëtt* (1949); *Ethiopics* (1956); *Selected Poems* (1964).

Senior, Olive (1941–   ).   Jamaica. Fiction writer. *Talking of Trees* (1985); *Summer Lightning and Other Stories* (1986); *Arrival of the Snake-Woman* (1989).

Soyinka, Wole (1934–   ).   Nigeria. Playwright, novelist, essayist, and memoirist. Nobel Prize for Literature, 1986. *Death and the King's Horsemen* (1975); *Aké: The Years of Childhood* (1981); *A Play of Giants* (1984).

Tutuola, Amos (1920–1997).   Nigeria. Novelist. *The Palm-Wine Drinkard* (1952); *The Brave African Huntress* (1958); *Feather Woman of the Jungle* (1962).

Walcott, Derek (1930–   ).   St. Lucia. Poet and dramatist. Nobel Prize for Literature, 1992. *Dream on Monkey Mountain and Other Plays* (1970); *The Fortunate Traveler* (1981); *Omeros* (1990).

SOURCES FOR ADDITIONAL INFORMATION

Alleyne, Mervin C. "A Linguistic Perspective on the Caribbean." In Mintz, Sidney, ed. *Caribbean Contours*. Baltimore: Johns Hopkins University Press, 1985.

Allsopp, Richard. *Dictionary of Caribbean English Usage*. New York: Oxford University Press, 1996.

Andrews, William L., Frances Smith Foster, and Trudier Harris, eds. *The Oxford Companion to African American Literature*. New York: Oxford University Press, 1996.

Collier-Thomas, Bettye, ed. *A Treasury of African-American Christmas Stories*. New York: Holt, 1997.

Davis, Arthur, Saunders J. Redding, and Joyce Ann Joyce, eds. *The New Cavalcade: African American Writing from 1760 to the Present*, rev. ed., 2 vols. Washington, DC: Howard University Press, 1991–1992.

Gates, Henry Louis, Jr., and Nelly Y. McKay, eds. *The Norton Anthology of African American Literature*. New York: Norton, 1996.

Greenberg, Joseph. *Languages of Africa*. Bloomington: Indiana University Press, 1966.

Holloway, Joseph E., and Winifred K. Vaas. *The African Heritage of American English*. Urbana: University of Illinois Press, 1993.

Lewis, David Levering, ed. *The Harlem Renaissance Reader*. New York: Viking, 1994.

——— . *When Harlem Was in Vogue*. New York: Knopf, 1981.

Lewis, Maureen Warner. "The African Impact on Language and Literature in the Caribbean." In Margaret E. Crahan and Franklin W. Knight, eds., *Africa and the Caribbean: The Legacies of a Link*. Baltimore: Johns Hopkins University Press, 1979.

Major, Clarence. *Juba to Jive: The Dictionary of African-American Slang*. New York: Penguin, 1994.

Popkin, Michael, ed. *Modern Black Writers*. New York: Ungar, 1978.

Serafin, Steven R. *Modern Black Writers: Supplement*. New York: Continuum, 1995.

Watson, Steven. *The Harlem Renaissance*. New York: Pantheon, 1995.

14
Music

MAJOR AFRICAN AMERICAN MUSICAL FORMS

Black music arrived in North America with the first Africans who landed in Virginia, the Carolinas, and Georgia in the 17th and 18th centuries. These men and women brought with them tonal instruments such as the banjo and drums, the conga and the bongos. African rhythmical and tonal expression mixed with European instrumentation and harmonies to create new musical forms: spirituals, blues, jazz, gospel, rhythm and blues, rock 'n' roll, rap, soul, funk, and disco. Here, in rough chronological order, is a survey of these distinctly African American musical forms.

SPIRITUALS

Spirituals are African American religious folk songs. Their roots go back to the days of slavery, when European American church music was infused with African American rhythmic complexity, call-and-response choruses, and lyrical expression related to the condition of slavery. Music associated with the white revivalist and evangelical movements of the 19th century is thought to have been especially influential in the growth of spirituals. Spirituals convey a wide range of emotions, from melancholy to jubilation. The texts are often related to biblical passages; because the singers frequently improvised as they went along, there may be hundreds of different versions of each song. In *The Souls of Black Folk*, W. E. B. Du Bois enumerated a group of 10 "master songs" exemplifying the spiritual tradition: "The Coming of John," "Nobody Knows the Trouble I've Seen," "Glory, Hallelujah," "Swing Low, Sweet Chariot," "Roll, Jordan, Roll," "Been A-Listening," "My Lord, What a Morning! When the Stars Begin to Fall," "My Way's Cloudy," "Wrestlin' Jacob, the Day Is A-Breaking," and "Steal Away."

> The negro folk song—the rhythmic cry of the slave—stands today not simply as the sole American music, but as the most beautiful expression of human experience born this side of the seas.
>
> W. E. B. Du Bois, *The Souls of Black Folk* (1903)

GOSPEL

Gospel music is one of the most distinctive creations of African American culture. It is solidly rooted in traditional African music, sharing such features as the call-and-response interplay between singer and chorus, and is a direct outgrowth of the spiritual (see the preceding description). From around 1900 to the 1920s, gospel songs slowly began to emerge from spirituals as a separate musical style. One change was that some congregations employed written melodies that were designed to be sung in harmony, and they also incorporated musical instruments. During the 1920s, leading black preachers began to make recordings of their services, many of which included gospel singing. By the same token, gospel singers began listening to jazz and blues recordings, absorbing new musical techniques from secular performers. This blending of styles enabled gospel to become a wholly distinctive art form, and gospel singers were soon performing at secular concerts, as well as in church. Among those who achieved wide recognition from the late 1920s to the 1950s were the Reverend Gary Davis, Sister Rosetta Tharpe, the Soul Stirrers, Marion Williams, and Mahalia Jackson. The rousing gospel style has left its mark on many forms of popular music, powerfully influencing rhythm and blues, soul, and rock, as well as African styles such as *mbube*.

BLUES

The blues, which evolved from *field hollers* (work songs sung in the fields), ballads, church music, and other sources (which may have included folk music popular among Southern whites), was created by African Americans in the South during the years after the Civil War. The blues shares some important features with traditional African music, such as the use of *blue notes* (flatted, off-pitch notes) often substituted for third or seventh notes of the European diatonic scale, and the call-and-response interplay between the singer and an accompanying instrument. (See "A Glossary of Black Music" later in this chapter.)

As blues music developed, it featured several distinctive variants. The Piedmont style of the Carolinas and Virginia, as exemplified by Blind Willie McTell, tended to be more tuneful than the rough, haunting Mississippi Delta blues style played by musicians such as Son House and Robert Johnson. Further west, in Texas, a more hard-driving style was being developed by musicians such as Blind Lemon Jefferson, Leadbelly, and T-Bone Walker.

The first blues records were cut during the 1920s by powerhouse performers such as Bessie Smith and Ma Rainey. As more and more African Americans moved to the North during the 1940s and 1950s, an urban blues style developed, often featuring a driving beat, drums, and electric guitars. Leading the way in this blues revolution were Muddy Waters, Howlin' Wolf, Willie Dixon, T-Bone Walker, and B. B. King. During the 1950s, blues influenced the development of jazz, soul music, rhythm and blues, and rock 'n' roll.

JAZZ

Jazz is the major African American musical form and the outstanding U.S. contribution in the realm of music. Jazz grew out of the blues, and many early jazz players were also blues musicians. The first African American jazz bands were formed in New Orleans during the 1890s and centered in the red-light district known as Storyville. When Storyville was closed down in 1917 on orders from the U.S. Navy, the jazz bands went north to Chicago and other cities. Originally, jazz musicians played together throughout each piece, with the three lead instruments (cornet or trumpet, clarinet, and trombone) improvising on a melody while the rhythm section laid down the beat. During the 1920s, cornetist/trumpeter Louis Armstrong expanded the possibilities of jazz by performing dazzling solos, often playing against or behind the beat.

By the late 1920s, Kansas City, New York, and Los Angeles had joined Chicago as leading jazz centers. The small New Orleans–style ensembles gave way to "big bands" that typically had 15 members. Led by Duke Ellington, Count Basie, Fletcher Henderson, and others, these bands played a style of jazz known as *swing*; though they continued to feature outstanding soloists, the swing bands favored carefully orchestrated, highly rhythmic music over improvisation.

During the late 1930s, musicians in Kansas City and New York began to chafe at the restrictions of big-band music and experimented with new forms. By the mid-1940s, *bebop* arose to challenge the dominance of swing. Bebop musicians—with Dizzy Gillespie, Charlie Parker, and Thelonious Monk in the vanguard—reestablished the primacy of the small combo and brought improvisation to new heights. The hallmarks of their style were the rapid, complex chord changes they inserted into standard songs, using the original melody as a springboard for daring harmonic inventions.

Though widely condemned at first, bebop (and its main offshoot, hard-bop) became the dominant jazz style of the 1950s and 1960s. At this point, jazz musicians were taking their art in a variety of new directions. The major innovations were *free jazz,* pioneered by Ornette Coleman and others, and Miles Davis's efforts to combine jazz and rock, an endeavor that led to the style known as *fusion.* During the 1980s, Wynton Marsalis and other musicians spearheaded a revival of more traditional styles, giving jazz fans and musicians an extraordinary range of choices.

> The memory of things gone is important to a jazz musician. Things like old folks singing in the moonlight in the back yard on a hot night, or something said long ago.
>
> Louis Armstrong, quoted in the *New Yorker*

RHYTHM AND BLUES

Rhythm and blues, also known as R&B, is a catchall phrase used to describe several styles of music produced by African American musicians and intended mainly for an African American audience. The term came into vogue during the 1940s as an alternative to the term *race music.* At this time, the main practitioners of R&B were small combos that often added jazz and blues elements to the popular songs of the day. The presence of a strong dance rhythm distinguished the work of R&B artists from the styles played by blues and jazz musicians. Rhythm and blues also had a distinctly urban style, reflecting the desire of many young African Americans to distance themselves from the rural associations of the traditional blues. Successful performers emerging from this tradition included the saxophonist and band leader Louis Jordan and "blues shouters" such as Big Joe Turner, La Vern Baker, Ruth Brown, Big Mama Thornton, and Wynonie Harris.

One of the most important features of R&B was the development of groups singing the close harmony style that came to be known as "doo-wop"—Sonny Til and the Orioles led the way, enjoying a nationwide R&B hit with "It's Too Soon to Know" in 1948. As rock 'n' roll became popular during the 1950s—largely the result of white singers covering songs by R&B performers—little distinction was made between rock 'n' roll and R&B. At this point, leading African American R&B performers such as Chuck Berry and Fats Domino were considered rock 'n' roll stars, sharing the same niche as white musicians such as Bill Haley and Elvis Presley. With the emergence of the Motown phenomenon and the Memphis soul sound during the 1960s (music exemplified by The Supremes, The Temptations, Aretha Franklin, Otis Redding, and other soul groups and singers), however, it was once again possible to distinguish a uniquely African American music style by calling it R&B. That distinction continues to be made, even though many African American R&B stars have enjoyed enormous success with general rock 'n' roll audiences. The 1960s, '70s, and '80s also saw the development of new styles of R&B, including funk and disco.

CALYPSO AND REGGAE

A music with its origins in the Caribbean rather than the continental United States, calypso, known originally as "kaiso," began in Port-of-Spain, Trinidad, in the early part of the 20th century. Combining Trinidadian folk traditions with dance music from nearby Venezuela, calypso became commercially popular in the 1920s and 1930s and was popularized in the United States by Harry Belafonte in the 1950s.

Reggae, which originated in Jamaica in the late 1960s, evolved from two earlier Jamaican musical forms—ska and rocksteady—that were influenced by calypso. *Ska* was a fast-paced Jamaican dance music from the late 1950s, which began as a mix of North American R&B and a form of Jamaican calypso called *mento*. Eventually, under the influence of American soul music of the 1960s, Jamaican musicians slowed the beat of ska. This in turn created a style known as *rocksteady*, which soon turned into reggae.

The distinctive features of reggae include the addition of the Rastafarian drumming tradition known as *nyabingi* and use of the guitar as a rhythm instrument while the bass carries the melody. Reggae songs often feature lyrics of political protest. Its words often highlight Rastafarian political and social goals, and a Black Power consciousness in which the late Ethiopian emperor Haile Selassie is viewed as a prophet of black pride and dignity. Bob Marley, Toots Maytall, Burning Spear, and Peter Tosh were the stars of reggae in the 1970s and 1980s.

RAP AND HIP-HOP

Rap, which originated in African American communities during the late 1970s, was inspired by Jamaican innovators such as Lee "Scratch" Perry, who had been mixing reggae rhythm tracks (dubbing) and talking over the music (toasting) for a number of years. In the United States, the pioneers of rap were the "spinners," deejays working in discos around the Bronx. The spinners were adept at manipulating turntables to produce imaginative sound combinations from the recordings of James Brown, Sly and the Family Stone, and other leading African American musicians. The spinners were soon joined by rappers who talked, rhymed, and chanted over the beat. The first recognized rap record was "Rapper's Delight," made in 1979 by the Sugar Hill Gang. Selling more than 2 million copies, "Rapper's Delight" paved the way for a rap music boom—gradually, major labels began distributing rap records, and rappers were garnering Grammy Awards. By the mid-1980s, rap had developed a number of distinct styles, including the hard-hitting "gangsta" rap (exemplified by Schooly D, Ice Cube, Ice-T, and Snoop Doggy Dogg) and jazz-rap. The term *hip-hop*, usually used interchangeably with *rap*, originally referred to the backing provided by spinners and production crews. It is also used to define the black, urban subculture from which rap had emerged, the original and major subcomponents of which were break dancing, rap, graffiti art, and "b-boy" clothing.

A GLOSSARY OF BLACK MUSIC

Afro-beat: West African dance music with strong African American influences, epitomized by Fela Anikulapo Kuti of Nigeria.

balafon: xylophone-like West African instrument containing 17–19 keys mounted above a series of gourds.

benga: Kenyan music originating with the Luo people during the 1970s, combining traditional lyre music with pronounced bass lines; *benga* songs are performed mainly in Swahili.

 he common root, of course, comes out of Africa. That's the pulse. The African pulse. It's all the way back from what they first recognized as the old slave chants, up through the blues, the jazz, and up through the rock. And the avant-garde. And it's all got the African pulse.

Duke Ellington, quoted in *Jazz Anecdotes* (1990)

berimbau: Brazilian instrument consisting of a single string suspended over a gourd; played with both melodic and percussive techniques, the berimbau was brought to Brazil from central Africa.

blue notes: off-pitch, or "flatted," notes derived from African music; blues and jazz musicians often substitute blue notes for the third and seventh (and sometimes the fifth) notes of the European diatonic scale.

boogie-woogie: highly rhythmic, driving blues piano music, possibly derived from ragtime and featuring a distinctive left-hand walking bass accompaniment.

call-and-response: traditional African musical device in which one instrument or singer responds to another; common in African American work songs, gospel music, blues, and jazz.

chord change: the technique of replacing the original chord in a melody with one or more related chords, creating a new harmonic structure; typically, skilled jazz musicians may improvise two to three chord changes within a given measure (legendary saxophonist John Coltrane was able to insert four).

cross-rhythms: essential technique of African music whereby singers or musicians superimpose contrasting rhythms over a ground beat; typically a pattern of two, four, or eight beats per time unit will run alongside a pattern of three or six beats, producing a complex interplay. Cross-rhythms—often misidentified as European-style syncopation, which merely stresses the weak beat over the strong beat—are common in both ragtime and jazz.

cubop: blend of Afro-Cuban rhythms and African American jazz that flourished during the 1940s, notably in the collaboration among Dizzy Gillespie, Mario Bauzá, and Chano Pozo.

dancehall: a rap-based offshoot of reggae that became popular in Jamaica and the United States during the 1990s.

Dixieland: early 20th-century New Orleans jazz style that enjoyed a revival in the 1940s; traditional Dixieland repertoire pieces were first recorded by Sidney Bechet, Jelly Roll Morton, Jimmie Noone, and others.

doo-wop: rhythm-and-blues harmony style popular during the 1950s and 1960s, so-called because it used phonetic syllables (such as a "doo-wop" sound) in place of words; African American doo-wop masters included the Five Satins, the Moonglows, the Penguins, the Cadillacs, and the Flamingos.

dub: style created by Jamaican recording engineers and studio musicians, who created endless variations on a given piece of music by dropping different tracks in and out.

field hollers: verbal form of musical expression dating back to slavery days, when African Americans working at various tasks would exchange calls and shouts; hollers might simply consist of phonetic syllables, or they might be improvised songs.

free jazz: avant-garde style pioneered by Ornette Coleman, Charlie Mingus, and Cecil Taylor during the 1960s; characterized by a shift from the set forms and complex chord progressions of bebop to "freer" compositions and a greater variety of timbres.

funk: brass- and bass-driven dance music with complex rhythms that developed during the 1960s and formed the basis of later African American styles such as hip-hop and rap; major exponents of funk include James Brown, Sly and the Family Stone, and George Clinton's Parliament/Funkadelic.

griot (djeli): a bard and storyteller in West African Mande-speaking societies; the most important *griots* preserve important oral traditions, recounting historical events in epic form.

highlife: Nigerian music that combines dance-band motifs from Ghana with Nigerian drum and guitar traditions; popular throughout Anglophone West Africa in the 1960s and 1970s.

jit: Zimbabwean dance music featuring percussion and vocals, originating from traditional musical forms of the Shona people; popularized by the Bhundu Boys during the 1980s.

jive: a style of dance music combining blues and boogie-woogie, which became popular during the 1940s; a precursor of rhythm and blues, it features a lively beat and raucous lyrics; also known as jump.

juju: guitar-based music of Nigeria with roots in Yoruba traditions; arising during the 1940s, *juju* has been elaborated by the addition of drums, electric guitars, and other instruments. Major practitioners have included Ebenezer Obey, I. K. Dairo, and King Sunny Ade.

kalimba: a type of African thumb piano used to augment the bass rhythm in Jamaican *mento* music.

kora: a 21-string instrument similar to both the harp and the lute, the *kora* is the chosen instrument of the griot and plays a major role in the musical life of Gambia, Senegal, Mali, and Guinea.

makossa: dance music of Cameroon, which draws on *soukous, highlife,* and Congolese rumba, employing horns, guitar, bass, drums, and piano; popularized in Europe and North America by Manu Dibango.

mbalax: Senegalese percussion music exemplified by Youssou N'Dour and others; created during the late 1970s by N'Dour's Star Band, *mbalax* incorporates a number of Wolof drumming traditions.

mbaqanga: South African township music that originated among black miners; combines traditional Zulu music and *mbube* with influences from jazz and other African American forms.

mbube: South African choral music influenced by African American gospel singing; popularized by Miriam Makeba during the 1960s, *mbube* was the first South African township music to be recorded.

mento: Jamaican form of calypso popular during the 1940s and 1950s; a precursor of *ska* and reggae.

Motown sound: 1960s style popularized by Motown Records, combining gospel and rhythm and blues. In addition to founder Berry Gordy, the main architects of the Motown sound were the Holland-Dozier-Holland songwriting team (Eddie and Brian Holland, Lamont Dozier), who penned 28 top 10 hits between 1963 and 1966.

MPB (Música Popular Brasileira):   music following the bossa nova tradition (*bossa nova* was a mixture of Brazilian samba and American jazz) and featuring songs with heavy social and political content, exemplified by Milton Nascimento and others.

New Orleans jazz: early 20th-century style played chiefly by small ensembles consisting of trumpet or cornet, trombone, clarinet, bass, drums, and guitar; these groups featured a repertoire of rags, marches, and blues. This style was exemplified by such 1920s groups as King Oliver's Creole Jazz Band and Louis Armstrong's Hot Fives and Hot Sevens.

ragtime: complex piano style showing the influence of African cross-rhythms, exemplified by the compositions of Scott Joplin; later developed into the stride piano style.

rara: Haitian music associated with annual pre-Lenten carnivals.

rocksteady: Jamaican style that evolved when *ska* musicians slowed their tempos, absorbing influences from North American soul music and other sources; precursor of reggae.

scat: a jazz singing style in which the singer duplicates in vocal phrases the musical passages of the supporting band.

soca: Trinidadian music style that arose in the 1970s when calypso musicians began using trap drums to duplicate rhythms derived from local folk religions and North American funk.

soukous: Congolese dance music combining local elements with Afro-Cuban and other Caribbean rhythms, as well as North American country-and-western music.

soul: African American music style that grew out of rhythm and blues in the 1960s, combining gospel-style singing with secular subject matter and funk-style rhythms; soul reached its peak in the 1970s in the art of Aretha Franklin, James Brown, and others.

stride: piano style derived from ragtime; highly embellished and generally characterized by fast tempos and a "striding" left hand that alternates between low bass notes and higher chords; exemplified by James P. Johnson, Willie "the Lion" Smith, and others.

steel drum: concave metal percussion instrument (or "pan") invented in Trinidad and designed to produce a variety of tones when struck with a rubber mallet.

taarab: East African string-band music; sung in Swahili, it combines Indo-Egyptian melodies, African percussion, and Latin beats; typically performed at weddings.

wassoulou: music that originated in Mali, West Africa, during the early 1960s, combining traditional call-and-response motifs with North American funk rhythms.

GRAMMY AWARD WINNERS

Since the National Academy of Recording Arts and Sciences began the Grammy Awards in 1958, African American artists have received more than 600 Grammies. African American winners for Album of the Year and Record of the Year are listed here.

ALBUM OF THE YEAR

1973   *Innervisions*—Stevie Wonder

1974   *Fulfillingness' First Finale*—Stevie Wonder

1976   *Songs in the Key of Life*—Stevie Wonder

1983   *Thriller*—Michael Jackson

1984   *Can't Slow Down*—Lionel Richie

1990   *Back on the Block*—Quincy Jones

1991   *Unforgettable with Love*—Natalie Cole, with Nat "King" Cole

1993   *The Bodyguard*—Whitney Houston

1995   *Kiss from a Rose*—Seal

1998   *The Miseducation of Lauryn Hill*—Lauryn Hill

RECORD OF THE YEAR

1967   "Up, Up and Away"—Fifth Dimension

1969   "Aquarius/Let the Sunshine In"—Fifth Dimension

1972   "The First Time Ever I Saw Your Face"—Roberta Flack

1973   "Killing Me Softly with His Song"—Roberta Flack

1976   "The Masquerade"—George Benson

1983   "Beat It"—Michael Jackson

1984   "What's Love Got to Do with It?"—Tina Turner

1985   "We Are the World"—Quincy Jones, producer

1988   "Don't Worry, Be Happy"—Bobby McFerrin

1991   "Unforgettable"—Natalie Cole, with Nat "King" Cole

1993   "I Will Always Love You"—Whitney Houston

1995   "Kiss from a Rose"—Seal

1998   "Change the World"—Eric Clapton and Kenneth "Babyface" Edmonds

NUMBER-ONE ALBUMS

The following albums reached number one on *Billboard* magazine's charts.

1956   *Calypso*—Harry Belafonte

1957   *Love Is the Thing*—Nat "King" Cole

1958   *Johnny's Greatest Hits*—Johnny Mathis

1962   *Modern Sounds in Country and Western Music*—Ray Charles

1963   *Little Stevie Wonder/The 12-Year-Old Genius*—Stevie Wonder

1964   *Hello, Dolly!*—Louis Armstrong

1966   *The Supremes A'Go-Go*—The Supremes

1967   *Diana Ross and The Supremes Greatest Hits*—The Supremes

1968   *Electric Ladyland*—Jimi Hendrix Experience

1969   *TCB*—Diana Ross and The Supremes with The Temptations

1971   *Shaft*—Isaac Hayes
        There's a Riot Goin' On—Sly and the Family Stone

1972   *First Take*—Roberta Flack
        Superfly—Curtis Mayfield

1973   *The World Is a Ghetto*—War
        Lady Sings the Blues—Diana Ross

1974   *Fulfillingness' First Finale*—Stevie Wonder
        Can't Get Enough—Barry White

1975   *That's the Way of the World*—Earth, Wind & Fire
        The Heat Is On—Isley Brothers

1976   *Gratitude*—Earth, Wind & Fire
        Breezin'—George Benson
        Songs in the Key of Life—Stevie Wonder

1978   *Live and More*—Donna Summer

1979   *Bad Girls*—Donna Summer

1980   *On the Radio—Greatest Hits, Vols. I & II*—Donna Summer

1983   *Thriller*—Michael Jackson
        Can't Slow Down—Lionel Richie

1984   *Purple Rain*—Prince and the Revolution

1985   *We Are the World*—USA for Africa
        Around the World in a Day—Prince and the Revolution

1986   *Whitney Houston*—Whitney Houston
        Control—Janet Jackson
        Winner in You—Patti LaBelle
        Dancing on the Ceiling—Lionel Richie

1987   *Whitney*—Whitney Houston
        Bad—Michael Jackson

1988   *Tracy Chapman*—Tracy Chapman
        Givin You the Best That I Got—Anita Baker

1989   *Don't Be Cruel*—Bobby Brown
        Loc-ed After Dark—Tone-Loc
        Batman—Prince
        Janet Jackson's Rhythm Nation 1814—Janet Jackson

1990   *Please Hammer Don't Hurt 'Em*—M. C. Hammer

1991   *EFIL4ZAGGIN*—N.W.A.
        Unforgettable—Natalie Cole, with Nat "King" Cole
        Dangerous—Michael Jackson

1992   *Totally Krossed Out*—Kriss Kross
        The Predator—Ice Cube
        The Bodyguard—Whitney Houston

1993   *janet*—Janet Jackson
        Black Sunday—Cypress Hill
        Doggstyle—Snoop Doggy Dogg

1994   *Toni Braxton*—Toni Braxton
        II—Boyz II Men

1995   *Me Against the World*—2Pac (Tupac Shakur)
        HIStory: Past, Present and Future, Book 1—Michael Jackson

E. 1999 Eternal—Bone Thugs-N-Harmony
Dogg Food—Tha Dogg Pound
R. Kelly—R. Kelly

1996   *It Was Written*—Nas
The Score—Fugees

1997   *Life After Death*—The Notorious B.I.G.
No Way Out—Puff Daddy and the Family
Live—Erykah Badu
R U Still Down? (Remember Me)—2Pac (Tupac Shakur)

RECORD HOLDERS

African American artists whose albums spent the most weeks at number one Michael Jackson (49), Whitney Houston (45), Harry Belafonte (31), Prince (33). Jackson is third on the all-time list, trailing only the Beatles (122) and Elvis Presley (64).

STAYING POWER

Of the top 10 albums with the longest tenure at number one on the charts, five are by African American artists:

*Thriller** (Michael Jackson)—37 weeks

Calypso (Harry Belafonte)—31 weeks

Purple Rain (Prince)—24 weeks

Please Hammer Don't Hurt 'Em (M. C. Hammer)—21 weeks

The Bodyguard (Whitney Houston)—20 weeks

Thriller is second only to the soundtrack from *West Side Story*, which topped the charts for 54 weeks in 1962–1963.

MUSICAL ORGANIZATIONS AND SOCIETIES

African Heritage Center for Dance and Music
4018 Minnesota Avenue, NE
Washington, DC 20019
202-399-5252
Multicultural center for training in West African music.

Bessie Smith Society
c/o Prof. Michael Roth
Franklin and Marshall College
Lancaster, PA 17604
717-291-3915

Black Arts Music Society
P.O. Box 3214

Jackson, MS 39207
601-354-1049
Books jazz concerts, among other activities.

Black Music Archives
8615 Central Park Avenue
Skokie, IL 60076
312-663-1600

Black Music Association
c/o Louise West
1775 Broadway, 7th Floor
New York, NY 10019
212-307-1459

Works with schools, sponsors seminars to preserve the heritage of black music worldwide.

Black Rock Coalition
P.O. Box 1054, Cooper Station
New York, NY 10276
212-713-5097

Boys Choir of Harlem
127 W. 127th Street
New York, NY 10027
212-749-1717

Center for Black Music Research
Columbia College
600 S. Michigan Avenue
Chicago, IL 60605
312-663-1600

Charlie Parker Memorial Foundation
Academy of the Arts
4605 The Paseo
Kansas City, MO 64110
816-924-2200
Preserves jazz heritage through studies, performances, and workshops; offers youth study programs.

Gospel Music Association
P.O. Box 23201
Nashville, TN 37202
615-242-0303

Gospel Music Workshop of America
3908 W. Warren Street
Detroit, MI 48208
313-898-2340

Indiana University–Bloomington
Afro-American Arts Institute
109 N. Jordan Avenue
Bloomington, IN 47405
812-855-9501
Sponsors research and maintains three performance groups.

International Rhythm & Blues Association
P.O. Box 1625

Chicago, IL 60616
312-326-5270

Motown Museum and Historical Foundation
2648 W. Grand Boulevard
Detroit, MI 48208
313-867-0991

Mutual Musicians Foundation
1823 Highland Street
Kansas City, MO 64108
816-421-9297
Preserves the heritage of Kansas City jazz.

National Association of Negro Musicians
P.O. Box S-011
237 E. 115th Street
Chicago, IL 60628
312-779-1325

National Black Music Caucus
Music Educators National Conference
c/o D. Willis Patterson
University of Michigan
Ann Arbor, MI 48109
313-764-0586
Fosters the study and promotion of black music in education.

National Black Music Foundation
902 42nd Avenue, N
Nashville, TN 37209
615-321-3319
Promotes music, publishes catalogs and newsletters.

New York Philharmonic Music Assistance Fund
Avery Fisher Hall
10 Lincoln Center Plaza
New York, NY 10023
212-875-5737
Provides scholarships for students of African descent to study at conservatories and university music departments; orchestral instruments only (no piano).

Scott Joplin Foundation of Sedalia
113 E. Fourth Street
Sedalia, MO 65301
Sponsors concerts and educational programs.

University of Mississippi   University, MS 38677
John Davis Williams Library   601-323-7753
Music Library/Blues Archive—Farley Hall

NOTABLE AFRICAN AMERICAN AND AFRICAN MUSICIANS AND GROUPS

Note: Recordings listed under performers' names do not constitute a complete discography; rather, they indicate best-known or most popular songs, albums, or pieces.

Addy, Obo (1936– ; *highlife*).   Ghanaian vocalist and percussionist. Descended from a long line of Ghanaian musicians, he apprenticed in *highlife* clubs in the 1950s. Under the patronage of President Kwame Nkrumah, Addy traveled widely, playing traditional music in the villages. *The Rhythm of Which a Chief Walks Gracefully* (Earthbeat, 1994).

Ade, King Sunny (1946– ; *juju*).   Nigerian guitarist and vocalist, leading exponent of *juju* music. As leader of the African Beats, Ade has introduced new techniques into *juju,* including Hawaiian guitars, synthesizers, and reggae-style dub effects. *Juju Music* (Mango, 1982); *Aura* (Mango, 1984).

Allen, Geri (1957– ; jazz).   Influenced by Thelonious Monk and others, Allen is one the major pianists to emerge from the 1980s jazz renaissance. *Live at the Village Vanguard* (DIW, 1989); *Maroons* (Blue Note, 1992).

Anderson, Marian (1897–1993; classical and spiritual).   Contralto whose rich voice and quiet courage were an inspiration to generations of aspiring black concert singers. Barred from opera in the United States in the 1930s, she sang spirituals, arias, and oratorios, achieving a wide following in Europe. On Easter Sunday 1939—after the Daughters of the American Revolution had refused to let her perform in their concert hall—Anderson sang for 75,000 listeners at the Lincoln Memorial and for millions more on radio. On January 7, 1955, Anderson became the first African American to sing at the Metropolitan Opera, performing the role of Ulrica in Verdi's *Un Ballo in Maschera.*

Armatrading, Joan (1950– ; reggae, folk, rock).   A singer born in St. Kitts and raised in England, Armatrading rose to stardom in the 1970s with a blend of folk, reggae, soul, and rock. *The Very Best of Joan Armatrading* (A&M, 1991).

Armstrong, Louis (1901–1971; jazz).   Trumpeter and cornetist. A major force in the shaping of jazz, Armstrong made his first great contributions during the 1920s, first as a member of Joe "King" Oliver's Creole Jazz Band and then as the leader of his own bands, notably the Hot Fives. In the 1930s he began making historic recordings for Decca. *The Hot Fives, Vol. I* (Columbia, 1988); *The Hot Fives and Hot Sevens, Vol. II* (Columbia, 1988); *The Hot Fives and Hot Sevens, Vol. III* (Columbia, 1989); *St. Louis Blues* (Columbia, 1991); *Louis Armstrong and King Oliver* (Milestone, 1992).

Baker, Josephine.   (See Chapter 15, "Performing Arts.")

Bambaataa, Afrika [Kevin Donovan] (1960– ; rap).   Bronx-born deejay who founded the rap crews Jazzy 5 and SoulSonicForce, whose *Planet Rock* was a hit album in 1982. Bambaataa later worked with James Brown, John Lydon, and other artists. *Planet Rock* (Tommy Boy, 1986).

Banton, Buju [Mark Myrie] (1974– ; reggae).   Jamaican *dancehall* star who made his mark at age 19 with "Bogle" and "Love Me Browning/Love Black Woman." After he became a Rasta, Banton's songs showed increasing social awareness, championing the cause of the poor and condemning violence and sexual exploitation. His album *'Til Shiloh* changed the direction of *dancehall* by using a studio band in place of synthesized and computer-generated music. *Voice of Jamaica* (Mercury, 1993); *'Til Shiloh* (Loose Cannon, 1995).

Basie, William "Count" (1904–1984; jazz).   Pianist, bandleader, and composer who achieved fame during the big-band era of the 1930s and remained popular for 40 years, despite radical changes in public taste. Among his most popular compositions is "One O'Clock Jump," the signature tune of the Basie band. *The Essence of Count Basie* (Columbia Legacy, 1991); *The Complete Decca Recordings* (Decca/GRP, 1992).

Bebey, Francis (1929– ; *makossa*).   Cameroonian singer-songwriter and music historian who combines Latin American music, Western pop, and classical motifs with African forms. *Nandolo: 1962–1994* (Original Music, 1997).

Bechet, Sidney (1897–1959; jazz).   One of the first great jazz soloists and one of the most influential soprano saxophonists. *Sidney Bechet, 1932–43: The Bluebird Sessions* (BMG); *Brussels World's Fair Concert* (Vogue, 1958).

Belafonte, Harold George "Harry."   (See Chapter 15, "Performing Arts.")

Benson, George (1943– ; jazz, pop).   Guitarist and singer who began playing the ukulele on the streets of Pittsburgh at age eight years. Like West Montgomery and Nat "King" Cole, his greatest influences, he is both commercially successful and widely admired by fellow musicians. *Compact Jazz: George Benson* (Verve, 1967–1968); *The George Benson Collection* (Warner Bros., 1981).

Berry, Charles Edward Anderson "Chuck" (1926– ; rock, R&B).   Trend-setting vocalist and guitarist whose list of rock 'n' roll anthems includes "Maybelline," "Roll Over Beethoven," "Johnny B. Goode," and "Sweet Little Sixteen." *Chuck Berry's Golden Decade* (Chess, 1967); *The Chess Box* (Chess/MCA, 1988).

Black Uhuru (reggae).   Formed in Kingston, Jamaica, in 1974. Known for intense political consciousness and tight harmonies, Black Uhuru has worked with reggae's finest musicians, including Lee "Scratch" Perry and Sly and Robbie. *Liberation: The Island Anthology* (Island, 1993).

Blake, Eubie (1883–1983; jazz, pop).   Composer and pianist who ranks as one of the greatest exponents of ragtime. In partnership with Noble Sissle, Blake produced the music for the landmark musical *Shuffle Along* and numerous other shows. At age 95, Blake performed in *Eubie!* the hit Broadway musical created around his music. *The 86 Years of Eubie Blake* (Columbia, 1969).

Bland, Bobby "Blue" (1930– ; blues).   Vocalist who began his career in Memphis, performing with B. B. King and other musicians, and had a substantial influence on the development of soul music. *The Best of Bobby Bland, Vols. 1 & 2* (MCA, 1974).

Bland, James A.   (See Chapter 15, "Performing Arts.")

Blanton, Jimmy (1918–1942; jazz).   The first of the great bassists, Blanton played his instrument like a horn, improvising melodies and rapid, complex passages. Discovered by Duke Ellington in 1939, he became a major member of the Ellington band and influenced Oscar Pettiford, Ray Brown, and Charles Mingus. *The Indispensable Duke Ellington* (RCA, 1940).

Bledsoe, Jules.   (See Chapter 15, "Performing Arts.")

Boukman Eksperyans (*rara*). Haitian band formed by Thedore Beaubrun in 1988. Noted for creating Voudo Adjae, a new form of dance music that mixes religious drumming and the Haitian carnival and parade music known as *rara*. The band's progressive political stance has made Boukman a prominent feature of the Haitian scene in the 1990s. *Voudou Adjae* (Mango, 1991); *Kalfou Danjere* (Mango, 1992).

Boyz II Men (rap, R&B).   Formed in Philadelphia in 1988, this hip-hop/harmony quartet became an overnight sensation in 1991. Their hit single "End of the Road" stayed at number one on the pop chart for 12 weeks in a row, breaking the record previously held by Elvis Presley. *Cooleyhighharmony* (Motown, 1991); *II* (Motown, 1994).

Braxton, Anthony (1945– ; classical and avant-garde jazz).   Composer and wind player involved with Chicago's Association for the Advancement of Creative Musicians during the 1960s. A MacArthur Fellowship recipient, he recorded the first solo album for alto sax, *For Alto; Composition No. 107* (Arista, 1968).

Brown, Charles (1922– ; R&B, blues).   Texas-born, California-based pianist and singer. Brown recorded his first hit, "Driftin' Blues," with Johnny Moore and the Three Blazers in 1945. Soon he struck out on a solo career and racked up a number of hits—including "Merry Christmas, Baby," "Get Your Kicks on Route 66," and "I Cried Last Night"—on the R&B charts in the late 1940s and 1950s. Brown's sound exerted a major influence on the young Ray Charles. *One More for the Road* (Blue Side, 1986).

Brown, Clarence "Gatemouth" (1924– ; blues).   Louisiana guitarist and vocalist who combined blues and country styles, leading two bands—one black, one white—during the 1950s. Brown's influence on Albert Collins, Johnny Copeland, and Johnny "Guitar" Watson was instrumental in the development of Texas blues. *The Original Peacock Recordings* (Rounder, 1984).

Brown, James (1928– ; soul).   Legendary vocalist and entertainer known as the Godfather of Soul and the Hardest-Working Man in Show Business. After starting as a gospel singer, Brown emerged as a superstar in the 1960s with hits such as "Papa's Got a Brand New Bag," "I Got You (I Feel Good)," and "Say It Loud, I'm Black and I'm Proud." *Live at the Apollo, Vols. 1 & 2* (Rhino, 1963, 1968); *Solid Gold* (1977); *Doin' It to Death* (Polydor, 1984); *Star Time* (Polydor, 1991).

Brown, Ray (1926– ; jazz).   Bassist who played with Dizzy Gillespie, Charlie Parker, Max Roach, and Bud Powell after arriving in New York in 1945. Still active in the 1990s, he has played with a new generation of rising stars. *Bam Bam Bam* (Concord, 1988); *Don't Get Sassy* (Telarc, 1994).

Bumbry, Grace (1937– ; classical).   Outstanding mezzo-soprano who was the first African American to perform at the Wagner Bayreuth Festival, making a sensational debut as Venus in the 1961 production of *Tannhäuser*. Bumbry made her debut at the Metropolitan Opera in 1974 and has sung at all the world's leading opera houses.

Burleigh, Henry Thacker "Harry" (1866–1945; classical).   Singer and composer who studied with Antonin Dvořák at the National Conservatory of Music in New York. His early arrangements and performances of African American spirituals are credited with inspiring Dvořák to incorporate elements of spirituals into his *New World Symphony* and *American Quartet*. Burleigh's most famous arrangement is perhaps "Deep River," from *Jubilee Songs of the USA* (1916).

Burning Spear [Winston Rodney] (1945– ; reggae).   Employing a spare, haunting vocal style, Burning Spear focuses on the legacy of slavery and advocates the cause of peace and justice. "Marcus Garvey" and "Slavery Days" are among his classic singles. *Marcus Garvey* (Island, 1975); *Harder than the Best* (Island, 1979); *The World Should Know* (Heartbeat, 1993).

Caesar, Shirley (1938– ; gospel).   Singer of traditional gospel shout. Born in Durham, North Carolina, she started out with the Caravans in the 1960s, going solo in 1966. *Just a Word* (Sony, 1996); *Rejoice* (Myrrh, 1997).

Carter, Benny (1907– ; jazz).   Alto saxophonist and trumpeter who began his career in the late 1920s and remained active into the 1990s. *Urbane Sessions* (Verve, 1952); *The King* (Pablo, 1976); *Songbook* (Music Masters, 1995).

Carter, Betty (1930–1998; jazz).   Vocalist noted for strikingly complex arrangements. Performed with Charlie Parker as a teenager and joined Lionel Hampton's band in 1948. *The Audience with Betty Carter* (Verve, 1979).

Carter, Ron (1937– ; jazz).   Bassist noted for rigorous technique and fluid timekeeping. Member of the second Miles Davis Quintet (1963–1968). As sideman, he is featured on more than a thousand recordings and has also recorded classical music. *Pastels* (Milestone, 1976); *Patrio and Parfait* (Milestone, 1980); *Ron Carter Meets Bach* (Blue Note, 1992).

Catlett, Sid (1910–1951; jazz).   Drummer known for his impeccable timekeeping and his innovative use of the snare drum. Widely considered the preeminent drummer of the swing era, Catlett played with most of the leading bands of the day. *Masters of Jazz, Vols. 1–3* (Rhino, 1996).

Chambers, Paul (1935–1969; jazz).   Perhaps *the* bassist of the mid-1950s and 1960s, Chambers was a member of the first Miles Davis Quintet (1955–1963) and the Wynton Kelly Trio (1963–1966). *Paul Chambers Stars* (Jazz View, 1960).

Charles, Ray [Ray Charles Robinson] (1930–   ; R&B, soul, country).   Pioneering vocalist and pianist who is credited with creating soul music by blending elements of gospel, jazz, blues, and country music. He is blind. Charles enjoyed his first national hit in 1955 with "I've Got a Woman" and followed up with "What'd I Say," "Georgia on My Mind," "Hit the Road, Jack," and many more. The winner of more than a dozen Grammy Awards, Charles was awarded the National Medal of the Arts in 1993. *Genius + Soul = Jazz* (1961); *Ray Charles* (Time Life, 1991); *The Birth of Soul* (Atlantic, 1991); *Genius and Soul—The 50ᵗʰ Anniversary Collection* (Rhino, 1997).

Cherry, Don (1936–1995; jazz).   Trumpeter. A product of the fertile 1940s West Coast jazz scene, Cherry made influential recordings with Ornette Coleman in the 1950s. In the 1970s, he lived in Europe and the Middle East, studying indigenous music forms. *Complete Communion* (Blue Note, 1965).

Christian, Charlie (1916–1942; jazz).   Guitarist. Credited as a co-inventor of bebop, Christian began recording with Benny Goodman's band shortly before his untimely death. He established the electric guitar as a modern jazz instrument, producing unprecedented tonalities. *Live Sessions at Minton's Playhouse* (Jazz Anthology, 1941); *The Genius of the Electric Guitar* (Columbia, 1987).

Cleveland, (Reverend) James (1932–1991; gospel).   Singer and choirmaster who came to prominence during the 1950s by incorporating jazz and pop techniques into gospel; had a powerful influence on later performers such as Andrae Crouch and Edwin Hawkins. *Peace Be Still* (Savoy, 1963); *James Cleveland Sings with the World's Greatest Choirs* (Savoy, 1980); *Touch Me* (Savoy, 1990).

Cliff, Jimmy [James Chambers] (1948–   ; reggae).   One of the first reggae stars to achieve a following outside of Jamaica. Best known for the 1972 film *The Harder They Come* and its soundtrack album. *Hanging Fire: The Best of Jimmy Cliff* (Mango, 1988).

Cole, Nat "King" (1917–1965; jazz).   Outstanding pianist who led the King Cole Trio before embarking on a solo vocal career. From the 1950s until his death, Cole was one of the most successful performers in the United States, with 86 singles and 17 albums reaching the top 40. He was also the first African American to host a radio show (1948). *Jumpin' at Capitol: The Best of the Nat King Cole Trio* (Capitol, 1992); *The Nat King Cole Story* (Capitol, 1991).

Coleman, Ornette (1930–   ; jazz).   Groundbreaking tenor saxophonist influential in the development of free jazz. His technique features abrupt tempo changes and complex phrasing. *The Shape of Jazz to Come* (Atlantic, 1960); *Free Jazz* (Atlantic, 1960).

Collins, Albert (1932–1993; blues).   Texas blues guitarist and singer known as the Iceman because of the eerie chill of his high-pitched guitar sound. Widely admired by both blues and rock musicians, he sat in on recordings issued by a wide variety of artists. *Truckin' With Albert Collins* (1969); *Ice Pickin'* (Alligator, 1978); *The Complete Imperial Recordings* (EMI, 1991).

Coltrane, John (1926–1967; jazz).   Legendary tenor saxophonist who began by playing with Dizzy Gillespie, Miles Davis, and Thelonious Monk in the 1950s. Coltrane's greatest work was done in the 1960s with his own quartet, when he created new dimensions in the sound of jazz. A diligent student of music theory, Coltrane experimented with techniques previously limited to classical music, such as polytonality. *Giant Steps* (Atlantic, 1960); *A Love Supreme* (Impulse, 1964); *The Best of John Coltrane* (Atlantic, 1970).

Cook, Will Marion (1869–1944; classical).   Versatile composer and conductor who bridged classical and popular forms. Trained as a violinist in New York and Berlin, Cook turned to conducting in 1890 and performed at the Chicago World's Fair in 1893. His classical compositions included art songs, choral works, and operas. Cook also enjoyed great success as a composer of popular musicals, most notably *Clorindy—The Origin of the Cakewalk* (1898) and the various shows starring the comedy team of Williams and Walker.

Cooke, Sam (1935–1964; R&B, soul, gospel).   Singer-songwriter who was a major gospel performer (with the Soul Stirrers) before turning to soul and R&B. His classic hits include "You Send Me," "Only Sixteen," and "Bring It on Home to Me" Cooke was one of the first African American artists to establish his own record label, music publishing firm, and management company. *The Best of Sam Cooke* (RCA, 1962; 1965); *Sam Cooke with the Soul Stirrers* (Specialty, 1991).

Copeland, Johnny "Texas Twister" (1937–1997; blues).   Singer and guitarist influenced by T-Bone Walker. Copeland formed his own band in the 1950s, then spent two decades playing around Houston before moving to New York City in 1975. On a 10-city tour of West Africa in 1982, he made one of the first recordings by an American blues musician in Africa, *Bringing It All Back Home* (Rounder); *Copeland Special* (Rounder, 1981).

Cray, Robert (1953– ; blues).   Blending Memphis soul with Texas blues, Cray emerged as one the blues standard-bearers of the 1980s. *Bad Influence* (High Tone, 1983); *Midnight Stroll* (Mercury, 1990).

Crouch, Andrae (1950– ; gospel).   Innovative pianist and singer known for infusing pop-music techniques into traditional gospel music, bringing him substantial crossover success. *Andrae Crouch and the Disciples* (Light, 1978); *Don't Give Up* (Warner Bros., 1981); *Mercy* (Qwest, 1994).

Davis, Anthony (1951– ; classical, jazz).   Composer and pianist who gained recognition as a piano virtuoso in the early 1970s after graduating from Yale. Influenced by classical, jazz, popular, and world music, Davis composed the opera X: *The Life and Times of Malcolm*, which premiered in 1986.

Davis, Miles (1926–1991; jazz).   A fiery genius with a uniquely understated and soulful trumpet style, Davis charted new directions in jazz from the 1950s through the 1980s. At various times he experimented with postbop, classical, cool jazz, and fusion styles. Davis's various ensembles were among the greatest in jazz history, and his *Kind of Blue* album is rated by many fans and critics the finest jazz recording ever made. *Milestones* (Columbia, 1958); *Kind of Blue* (Columbia, 1959); *Sketches of Spain* (Columbia, 1960); *Nefertiti* (Columbia, 1967); *Bitches Brew* (Columbia, 1969); *Tutu* (Warner Bros., 1986).

Davis, Sammy, Jr.   (See Chapter 15, "Performing Arts.")

De la Soul (rap).   Formed in 1985 in Amityville, New York, this trio started a new rap trend with a lighter beat and musical experimentation that included tight harmonies and inventive lyrics. *3 Feet High and Rising* (Tommy Boy, 1989); *De la Soul Is Dead* (Tommy Boy, 1991).

De Priest, James (1936– ; classical).   Conductor who studied at the Philadelphia Conservatory (1959–1961) and won first prize at the Dimitri Mitropolous International Competition in 1964. De Priest served as assistant conductor of the New York Philharmonic under Leonard Bernstein in 1965 and conducted Marian Anderson's farewell concert in Philadelphia. (De Priest is Anderson's nephew.) After moving to Europe in 1967, he conducted the Rotterdam, Cleveland, and Los Angeles Philharmonic orchestras. From 1971 to 1975, De Priest was associate and principal guest conductor of the National Symphony Orchestra. He has been the music director of the Oregon Symphony since 1980.

Dibala, Diblo (1954– ; zouk).   Zairean zouk guitarist. A recognized virtuoso at age 15, Dibala is in great demand as a studio musician, both at home and in France. *Super Soukous* (Shanachie, 1989).

Dibango, Manu (1934– ; makossa).   Cameroonian saxophonist and bandleader who introduced North Americans to African pop styles, notably through his 1972 hit recording "Soul Makossa." In recent years, Dibango has worked with jazz, funk, and rap musicians in Europe, the Caribbean, and the United States. *Soul Makossa* (Atlantic, 1972).

Diddley, Bo [Elias Bates] (1928– ; R&B, rock).   Guitarist and vocalist whose songs have been covered by numerous rockers. Made an immediate impact in 1955, when his single "Bo Diddley" topped the R&B charts. *Bo Diddley* (1958); *The Chess Box* (MCA, 1990).

Dixon, Charles Dean (1915–1976; classical).   Conductor trained at Columbia University and the Juilliard School of Music. Made his conducting debut at Town Hall in 1937. In 1941, Dixon became the first African American to conduct Arturo Toscanini's NBC Symphony Orchestra. Dixon subsequently conducted the New York Philharmonic, the Philadelphia Orchestra, and the Boston Symphony. In 1949 he moved to Europe, where he remained active as conductor or guest conductor of the Gothenburg, Frankfurt Radio, and BBC Symphony orchestras.

Dixon, Willie (1915–1992; blues).   Chicago-based songwriter, bandleader, arranger, and producer who held important positions at Chess Records in the 1950s and 1960s. As a songwriter, his credits include "Little Red Rooster," "Back Door Man," "I Just Want to Make Love to You," and a host of other classics. *The Chess Box* (1988).

Dolphy, Eric (1928–1964; jazz).   Innovative and influential flutist and clarinetist. Among his many achievements, Dolphy established the bass clarinet as a solo instrument with his celebrated rendition of Billie Holiday's "God Bless the Child." *Far Cry* (Original Jazz Classics, 1960); *Out to Lunch!* (Blue Note, 1964); *Eric Dolphy in Europe, Vol. 1* (Prestige, 1989).

Domino, Antoine "Fats" (1929– ; R&B, rock).   Singer-songwriter who parlayed his boogie-woogie R&B style into 23 gold singles, including "Blueberry Hill," "Ain't That a Shame," and "Whole Lotta Loving." Among the pioneering rock 'n' roll stars, Domino is second only to Elvis Presley in total record sales. *They Call Me the Fat Man: The Legendary Imperial Recordings* (EMI, 1991).

Dr. Dre [Andre Young] (1965– ; rap).   Dr. Dre became involved in rap in South-Central Los Angeles in the early 1980s. In 1986, Dre formed the influential "gangsta" rap group N.W.A. (standing for Niggaz With Attitude) with the rappers Ice Cube and Eazy-E. N.W.A. broke up in 1991, and Dre began a solo career as a rapper and producer. He pioneered a brand of rap called G-Funk (for gangsta-funk) that borrowed a heavy, slow-rolling bass from 1970s funk music. Dre's style influenced a new generation of rappers such as Snoop Doggy Dogg, Warren G, and 2-Pac (Tupac Shakur). *Straight Outta Compton* (Ruthless, 1988); *The Chronic* (Death Row, 1992); *Dr. Dre Presents . . . The Aftermath* (Aftermath, 1997).

The Drifters (soul, rock).   Formed in 1953 in New York City; leaders in the creation of soul, combining gospel-style music with secular material. Featuring lead singers such as Clyde McPhatter, Ben E. King, and Rudy Lewis, the Drifters produced a steady stream of R&B classics that included "There Goes My Baby," "Save the Last Dance for Me," "This Magic Moment," "Up on the Roof," "On Broadway," and "Under the Boardwalk." *The Drifters' Golden Hits* (Atlantic, 1968).

El Din, Hamza (c. 1940– ; Sudanese folk).   Sudanese lutenist. Master of the *oud*, a traditional fretless lute prominent in the Middle East and North Africa, Hamza El Din was introduced to American audiences by Bob Dylan and the Grateful Dead. *Escalay: The Water Wheel-Oud Music of Nubia* (Nonesuch, 1968).

Eldridge, Roy (1911–1989; jazz).   The dominant trumpeter of the 1930s and 1940s, Eldridge achieved the height of his fame as a soloist with Gene Krupa's band. He was renowned for blending power, imagination, and technique, and he had a profound influence on Dizzy Gillespie and other trumpeters of the bebop era. During the 1980s, Eldridge began performing as a vocalist. *Roy and Diz* (Clef, 1954); *Tour de Force* (Verve, 1957).

Ellington, Arthur Kennedy "Duke" (1899–1974; jazz, classical).   A composer and big-band leader equally at home in the Cotton Club and Carnegie Hall, Ellington ranks as one of America's musical giants. His more than 2,000 compositions include "Mood Indigo," "Sophisticated Lady," "Don't Get Around Much Anymore," and "Black and Tan Fantasy." *The Essence of Duke Ellington* (Columbia/Legacy, 1991).

"Mood Indigo" was one of over two thousand compositions by Duke Ellington.

Estes, Simon (1938– ; classical).   Bass-baritone who began his operatic career in Germany, singing with companies in Berlin, Lübeck, and Hamburg. In 1966 he won the silver medal in the Tchaikovsky Vocal Competition in Moscow. Estes subsequently performed with numerous opera companies in Europe and the United States and made his Metropolitan Opera debut in 1982. He has also given numerous recitals and performed with major symphony orchestras.

FISK JUBILEE SINGERS

The world-famous Fisk Jubilee Singers occupy a unique place in African American musical history. The original group of 11 men and women was organized at Fisk University in Nashville in 1867, with the aim of raising funds for the newly created black university. The Fisk Jubilee Singers began performing at churches and religious conventions throughout Ohio, offering a mix of religious and secular material and introducing African American spirituals to European American audiences. Though the group initially met with harsh prejudice, they enjoyed increasing success after 1870, touring New England and singing for President Grant in the White House. The Fisk Jubilee Singers' earnings enabled the university to complete its first permanent building, Jubilee Hall, in 1875, and to graduate its first class.

Fitzgerald, Ella (1918–1996; jazz).   Vocalist admired by musicians as diverse as Charlie Parker and Dietrich Fischer-Dieskau for her range, swing, and agility. Began with Chick Webb during the swing era and performed with Louis Armstrong, Count Basie, Duke Ellington, and Oscar Peterson. Her classic

Songbooks series on Verve—celebrating Ellington, Porter, Rodgers and Hart, Gershwin, Kern, and other composers—is a matchless treasury of American popular music. *The Best of Ella Fitzgerald* (MCA, 1973); *The Best of Ella Fitzgerald, Vol. 2* (MCA, 1977).

Franklin, Aretha (1942–   ; soul, R&B, gospel).   Memphis-born singer who dominated the charts in the 1960s and 1970s with a dynamic style that blended gospel, R&B, jazz, and pop. With hits such as "Chain of Fools," "Respect," and "You Make Me Feel Like a Natural Woman," Franklin has had more million-selling records than any other woman in music history. *The Queen of Soul* (Rhino/Atlantic, 1992).

Franklin, Kirk (1970–   ; gospel, R&B).   Texas-born gospel and R&B singer and musician. A musical prodigy, Franklin was leading the adult choir of Dallas's Mt. Rose Baptist Church when he was 11. Franklin rebelled from his church upbringing during his teen years but returned following the accidental shooting death of a friend. He formed a 17-member choir, the Family, in 1991. His debut album, *Kirk Franklin and the Family*, stayed on the gospel charts for 100 weeks before it crossed over to the R&B charts, becoming the first gospel album to sell a million copies. *Kirk Franklin and the Family* (Interscope, 1993), *Whatcha Lookin' 4* (Interscope, 1996).

Fugees (rap).   Haitian trio (Lauryn Hill, Wyclef Jean, and Prakazrel Michel) blending pop, rap, and reggae. Their second album, *The Score*, sold more than 4 million copies in the four months following its release. *Blunted on Reality* (Ruffhouse, 1994); *The Score* (Ruffhouse, 1996).

Gardner, Newport (1746–1852; classical).   African-born musician who was the first African American to write music in the European tradition. Enslaved and brought to Rhode Island at age 14, Gardner began writing music only four years later. In 1791 he purchased his freedom and that of his family and opened a singing school in Newport. Most of his music has apparently been lost, but the text of his choral piece "Promise Anthem" survives.

Gaye, Marvin (1939–1984; soul).   One of the mainstays of the Motown sound, Gaye maintained his popularity over three decades with hits such as "I Heard It through the Grapevine" and "Your Precious Love." *What's Going On* (Tamla, 1971); *Anthology* (PGD/Motown, 1974).

Gillespie, John Birks "Dizzy" (1917–1993; jazz).   Trumpeter and composer credited—along with Charlie Parker and Thelonious Monk—with creating bebop. A dazzling trumpet virtuoso and a bravura performer, Gillespie was—despite his reputation for clowning—an astute businessperson and a nurturer of other musicians. During the 1970s and 1980s, he toured the world and served as the elder statesman of jazz. *Shaw 'Nuff* (Musicraft, 1946); *Dizziest* (RCA, 1987); *Compact Jazz 1954–1964* (Mercury, 1987).

MAKING HISTORY

On May 15, 1953, the disbanded Dizzy Gillespie Quintet—Gillespie (trumpet), Charlie Parker (alto saxophone), Bud Powell (piano), Max Roach (drums), and Charlie Mingus (sitting in for Ray Brown on bass)—was reunited for a concert at Massey Hall in Toronto, Canada. Playing "Salt Peanuts," "A Night in Tunisia," and other bebop classics, the five jazz legends electrified a packed house. Jazz fans have since labeled the performance "the greatest jazz concert ever" (*The Quintet: Jazz at Massey Hall*, Fantasy, 1989).

Gilpin, Charles Sidney.   (See Chapter 15, "Performing Arts.")

Gordon, Dexter (1923–1990; jazz).   Tenor saxophonist known for his resounding tone and dynamic attack. One of the first tenors to play bebop, Gordon had a profound influence on Sonny Rollins and John Coltrane. Relatively ignored during much of his career, Gordon achieved recognition during the 1970s and gave a memorable performance in the 1985 film *Round Midnight*. *Dexter Calling* (Blue Note, 1961); *Go* (Blue Note, 1962); *The Other Side of Round Midnight* (Blue Note, 1986).

Grandmaster Flash and the Furious Five (rap).   Formed in the Bronx in 1977, the leading deejay-rap team of the early 1980s. Grandmaster Flash (Josep Saddler, born in Barbados in 1958) pioneered techniques that became cornerstones of the rapper's art. *Message from Beat Street: The Best of Grandmaster Flash, Melle Mel, and the Furious Five* (Rhino, 1994).

Green, Al (1946– ; soul, gospel).   Inheriting the mantle of Sam Cooke and Otis Redding, Green sold more than 20 million records during the 1970s. He entered the ministry in 1976 but has continued to record on occasion. *Call Me* (1973); *One in a Million* (Word/Epic, 1991) *Anthology* (EMI, 1997).

Greenfield, Elizabeth Taylor (c. 1819–1876; classical).   The first African American concert singer. Known as the Black Swan, Greenfield made her professional debut in Buffalo, New York, in 1851. After touring the United States and Canada, Greenfield gave a command performance before Britain's Queen Victoria in 1853. She made her New York debut the same year; when African Americans were barred from attending the performance at Metropolitan Hall, she sang for them in a separate performance at the Broadway Tabernacle. Greenfield organized her own opera company, the Black Swan Opera Troupe, during the 1860s.

Hall, Juanita.   (See Chapter 15, "Performing Arts.")

Hammer [Stanley Kirk Burrell] (1963– ; rap).   Born in Oakland, Hammer was a hit on the West Coast before exploding onto the national scene in 1990 with his 10-million-selling debut album. Though his second album was less successful, Hammer made an unforgettable impression with his elaborate stage performances. *Please Hammer Don't Hurt 'Em* (Capitol, 1990); *Too Legit to Quit* (Capitol, 1991).

Hampton, Lionel (1909– ; jazz).   Vibraphonist who came to prominence during the swing era and performed well into his 80s. Hampton's skill and verve made the vibraphone an essential part of the jazz repertoire. *Compact Jazz: Lionel Hampton* (Verve, 1955); *Hamp: The Legendary Decca Recordings* (GRP, 1996).

Hancock, Herbie (1940– ; jazz).   Versatile composer and pianist who made his concert debut with the Chicago Symphony Orchestra in a Mozart piano concerto at age 11. Hancock artfully combines an impressionistic harmonic palette with elements of straight-ahead jazz and blues. *Maiden Voyage* (Blue Note, 1965); *VSOP Quintet* (Columbia, 1977).

Handy, William Christopher "W. C." (1873–1958; blues).   Alabama-born composer, cornetist, and bandleader who was among the first to publish blues compositions. Classics such as "Memphis Blues" (1912), "St. Louis Blues" (1914), and "Beale Street Blues" (1917) earned him the nickname Father of the Blues, which was also the title of his 1941 autobiography.

Hawkins, Coleman (1904–1969; jazz).   The first prominent tenor saxophonist in jazz history. Hawkins laid the groundwork for modern tenor playing during the 1920s and 1930s, exploring chord changes more fully than any previous musician. His 1939 recording of "Body and Soul" established him as the most innovative musician in jazz. *The Hawk Flies High* (Original Jazz Classics, 1957).

Hawkins, Edwin (1943– ; gospel).   Singer and choirmaster who formed the Edwin Hawkins Singers in 1969. The group's rendition of "Oh Happy Day" was a top 10 hit. Hawkins is considered the standard-bearer of traditional gospel. *Oh Happy Day* (Buddah, 1969); *The Best of the Edwin Hawkins Singers* (Savoy, 1985).

Hayes, Isaac (1938– ; soul, R&B).   As a vocalist, keyboard player, arranger, and producer, Hayes was a driving force in both Memphis soul and early disco. He was the first African American composer to win an Academy Award, gaining the honor in 1971 for his *Shaft* soundtrack. *Hot Buttered Soul* (Stax, 1969); *Best of Isaac Hayes, Vols. 1 & 2* (Stax, 1986).

Henderson, Fletcher (1897–1952; jazz).   Bandleader, arranger, pianist. As a bandleader, Henderson pioneered strict orchestral arrangement with free improvisation. In 1923, he formed a band that later served as a showcase for Louis Armstrong, Coleman Hawkins, and Benny Carter. As arranger for the Benny

Goodman Orchestra in the 1930s, Henderson profoundly influenced big-band music. *Fletcher Henderson: His Best Recordings 1921–1941* (Best of Jazz, 1995).

Hendrix, Jimi (1942–1970; rock, blues).   Guitar magician and one-of-a-kind performer whose legend continues to grow. Hendrix set the standard for rock guitar in the late 1960s. He pioneered the use of distortion and feedback in rock 'n' roll and developed a wide following that crossed racial boundaries. *The Essential Jimi Hendrix* (Reprise, 1989).

Hinderas, Natalie (1927– ; classical).   Pianist who gave her first recital at age 8 and performed the Grieg Piano Concert in Cleveland when she was only 12. A specialist in the works of William Grant Still, George Walker, and other African American classical composers, Hinderas has also recorded a strikingly "African" version of the *John Cage Sonatas and Etudes for Prepared Piano* as well as *Piano Music by Africa-America* (Composers Recordings).

Hines, Earl "Fatha" (1903–1983; jazz).   Pianist and bandleader who first gained notice playing with Louis Armstrong (1928–1933). Hines's early solos, noted for great textural variety, marked the turning point from ragtime to jazz piano. *Earl Hines (1928–1932)* (Classics); *Tour de Force* (Black Lion, 1972).

Hinton, Milt (1910– ; jazz).   Starting out in Chicago in the 1920s and 1930s, Hinton was the premier bassist in jazz until the advent of Jimmy Blanton. *Old Man Time* (Chiaroscuro, 1989).

Holiday, Billie (1915–1959; jazz).   Hailed by many as the greatest jazz singer of all time, Holiday transformed familiar songs with impeccable jazz phrasing and intensely personal interpretations. *The Complete Billie Holiday on Verve (1946–1959)* (1992); *The Quintessential Billie Holiday, Vols. 1–9* (Columbia, 1987–1991); *The Complete Decca Recordings* (GRP, 1991).

Hooker, John Lee (1920– ; blues).   Deep-voiced Mississippi singer/guitarist who enjoyed a hit with his first recording, "Boogie Chillun" (1948). Hooker's spare but relentless electric guitar style has had a major influence on rock 'n' roll; he has recorded with Van Morrison, Canned Heat, and Bonnie Raitt, as well as Miles Davis. *John Lee Hooker Plays and Sings the Blues* (Chess, 1961); *Alone* (Tomato, 1989); *The Ultimate Collection: 1948–1990* (Rhino, 1991).

Hopkins, Sam "Lightnin'" (1912–1982; blues).   Texas country-blues classicist known for his call-and-response pattern of voice and guitar work. Though he did not begin performing until middle age, Hopkins made more recordings than any other traditional blues artist. *Lightnin' Hopkins* (Smithsonian/Folkways, 1959); *Texas Blues* (Arhoolie, 1989); *The Complete Prestige/Bluesville Recordings* (Prestige, 1991).

Horne, Lena.   (See Chapter 15, "Performing Arts.")

House, Eddie "Son" (1902–1988; blues).   Growing up in the Mississippi Delta, House came under the influence of Charley Patton, and in turn influenced both Robert Johnson and Muddy Waters. House enjoyed a major revival after the 1960s. *Son House* (Arhoolie, 1979); *Delta Blues: The Original Library of Congress Sessions Field Recordings, 1941–1942* (Biograph, 1991).

Houston, Whitney (1963– ; R&B, soul).   Singer who began performing at age 15 and signed a recording contract at age 19. Since then, she has consistently topped both the pop and the R&B charts, turning out hits such as "Saving All My Love for You," "Didn't We Almost Have It All," and "So Emotional." *Whitney Houston* (Arista, 1985); *Whitney* (Arista, 1987); *I'm Your Baby Tonight* (Arista, 1990).

Howlin' Wolf [Chester Arthur Burnett] (1910–1976; blues).   Harmonica-playing Chicago blues musician whose electric blues style helped shape rock 'n' roll. He began broadcasting on radio in the late 1940s and made his first recordings during the early 1950s. *Howlin' Wolf* (Chess, 1959); *Howlin' Wolf Rides Again* (Virgin, 1993).

Ibrahim, Abdullah (1934– ; jazz, South African traditional).   South African pianist noted for his unique blend of African rhythms and traditional jazz. *African Piano* (Japo, 1969); *Echoes from Africa* (Enja, 1979); *Water from an Ancient Well* (Blackhawk, 1985); *African River* (Enja, 1989).

Ice Cube [O'Shea Jackson] (c. 1969– ; rap).   Raised in South-Central Los Angeles, Ice Cube was one of the pioneers of gangsta rap. He has also acted in films such as *Boyz N the Hood*. *AmeriKKKa's Most Wanted* (Priority, 1990); *The Predator* (Priority, 1992).

Ice-T [Tracy Marrow] (1958– ; rap).   Los Angeles rapper and actor who aroused nationwide controversy with the song "Cop Killer." Ice-T has appeared in several films, as well as on the TV series *Players*. *O.G. Original Gangster* (Sire, 1989); *The Classic Collection* (Rhino, 1993).

Jackson, Mahalia (1911–1972; gospel).   The most popular of all gospel singers, noted for her bluesy, expressive contralto and intensely moving interpretations. *How I Got Over* (Columbia, 1976); *Gospels, Spirituals and Hymns* (Columbia, 1991).

Jackson, Michael (1958– ; soul, rock).   Singer and dancer who made his debut as a member of the Jackson Five, went solo in the 1970s, and was anointed the King of Pop after the success of *Thriller*, the first album in history to top both the pop and the R&B charts. *Off The Wall* (Epic, 1979); *Thriller* (Epic, 1982); *Bad* (Epic, 1987); *Dangerous* (Epic, 1991).

Jackson, Milt "Bags" (1923– ; jazz).   Leading vibraphonist noted for his powerful attack and heavy use of vibrato. Jackson was a major force in the Modern Jazz Quartet (with John Lewis, Percy Heath, and Connie Kay) during the group's peak years. *Milt Jackson* (Blue Note, 1948–1952); *Bags and Trane* (1959); *The Big 3* (Pablo, 1975).

James, Elmore (1918–1963; blues).   Slide guitarist who enjoyed a prolific recording career in Chicago from the 1950s until his death. James had a powerful influence on the 1960s British blues guitarists and others. *Red Hot Blues* (Quicksilver, 1982); *The Complete Fire and Enjoy Sessions* (Collectables, 1989); *The Complete Elmore James* (Capricorn/Warner Bros., 1992).

James, Etta (1938– ; blues, R&B).   Vocalist who had her first R&B hit ("Roll with Me, Henry") in 1955 and proved her staying power in 1994, when she won a Grammy Award for her jazz vocals on "Mystery Lady." *The Sweetest Peaches: The Chess Years, Vols. 1 & 2 (1960–1975)* (Chess, 1988); *Mystery Lady: Songs of Billie Holiday* (Private Music, 1994).

Jarrett, Keith (1945– ; jazz, classical).   Composer, pianist, organist, and harpsichordist who has become an outspoken critic of commercialism in jazz. Jarrett played with Art Blakey, Charles Lloyd, and Miles Davis before forming his own combos. He has also recorded classical music, including Bach's *Well-Tempered Clavier*. *Expectations* (Columbia, 1971); *Vienna Concert* (ECM, 1991); *Bye Bye Blackbird* (ECM, 1993).

Jawara, Jali Musa (1961– ; *griot*).   Guinean guitarist, harpist, and vocalist. Singer of traditional Mandinka *griot* music. *Yasimika* (Hannibal, 1991).

Jefferson, Blind Lemon (c. 1897–c. 1930; blues).   Among the first great Texas blues guitarists. Between 1926 and 1929, he recorded both classic country blues laments and sharp satires. *Blind Lemon Jefferson* (Milestone, 1974); *King of the Country Blues* (Yazoo, 1989).

Johnson, Blind Willie (1900–1950; blues).   Father of Texas gospel blues. Between 1927 and 1930, Johnson recorded his best-known work, including the haunting "Dark Was the Night, Cold Was the Ground." *The Complete Blind Willie Johnson* (Columbia, 1993).

Johnson, J. J. (1924– ; jazz).   Trombonist, composer, and arranger who emerged from the once-thriving Indianapolis jazz scene. Johnson was the first slide trombonist to master the fast-paced complexities of bebop, a feat many had considered beyond the capacities of the instrument. *The Eminent Jay Jay Johnson, Vols. 1 & 2* (Blue Note, 1953–1955).

Johnson, James P. (1894–1955; jazz).   One of the dominant figures in the development of stride piano during the 1920s. Growing up in the Northeast, Johnson, was heavily exposed to European music, and his playing was marked by a fuller, more orchestral style that set him apart from most other jazz pianists. *Snowy*

Morning Blues (GRP, 1930); *Original James P. Johnson* (Smithsonian/Folkways, 1947); *Runnin' Wild* (Tradition, 1997).

Johnson, Lonnie (1889–1970; blues).   Vocalist and instrumentalist hailed as the founding father of modern blues guitar. Starting out in New Orleans, he played with Louis Armstrong's Hot Five and made his first recordings in 1925. *Steppin' on the Blues* (Columbia, 1990).

Johnson, Robert (1911–1938; blues).   A master of the Delta blues style who sometimes claimed that he learned to play the guitar from the devil himself. Johnson has had a profound influence on both modern blues and rock 'n' roll. His entire recorded legacy consists of 29 songs recorded in four days near the end of his short life. *The Complete Recordings* (Columbia, 1989).

Jones, Elvin (1927–   ; jazz).   Drummer who reached his peak with the John Coltrane Quartet in the early 1960s, when his contributions advanced the role of the rhythm section in African American music. *Elvin* (Riverside, 1961–1962); *And Then Again* (Atlantic, 1965); *Reunited* (Blackhawk, 1986).

Jones, Jo (1911–1985; jazz).   Influential swing-era drummer who played with Count Basie's band from 1935 to 1948. Jones influenced later drummers by minimizing the use of the bass drum and keeping time on the top cymbal, making it possible to do more with the rest of the drum kit. *Main Man* (Pablo, 1976).

Jones, Joseph Rudolph "Philly Joe" (1923–1985; jazz).   Drummer known for his work with Dexter Gordon and Miles Davis, especially Davis's legendary 1956–1958 Prestige recordings. *Philly Joe's Beat* (Atlantic, 1960); *Philly Mignon* (Galaxy, 1977).

Jones, Quincy (1933–   ; jazz).   Multifaceted musician who played trumpet with Lionel Hampton and Count Basie in the 1940s. Jones later turned to mass media and pop music, scoring films, writing themes for TV shows, and producing records for George Benson, Michael Jackson, and other artists. As of 1997, Jones had been nominated for a record 96 Grammy Awards, winning 27. He is also a successful entrepreneur with business interests in all the media, including Qwest Records and *Vibe* magazine. *Quintessence* (MCA/Impulse, 1961); *Smackwater Jack* (A&M, 1971); *Compact Jazz: Quincy Jones* (Phillips/Polygram, 1989).

Jones, Sisieretta (1868–1933; classical).   Dramatic soprano born in Virginia and educated in Rhode Island, where she studied voice at the Providence Academy of Music. Jones made her debut in New York in 1888, toured extensively in the United States, the West Indies, and Europe, and performed for President Harrison at the White House in 1892. Journalists began calling Jones "the black Patti," a reference to the renowned Italian soprano Adelina Patti. (Jones disliked the nickname, but her manager insisted on using it.) Barred from performing at the Metropolitan Opera, Jones sang operatic arias on the musical stage, appearing in Bob Cole's *Oriental America* in 1893. She then began to tour with a troupe named Black Patti's Troubadors, continuing to expand her operatic repertoire until her retirement in 1916.

Joplin, Scott (1868–1917; classical, ragtime).   Best known for his dazzling piano rags, Joplin was trained as a classical musician and was a longtime teacher of piano and composition at George R. Smith College for Negroes in Sedalia, Missouri. He enjoyed popular success at the turn of the 20th century with "Maple Leaf Rag" and other pieces. Joplin's greatest work, the opera *Treemonisha*, was given a full production only in 1972, after the Joplin-inspired soundtrack of *The Sting* earned him a new generation of admirers.

Kay, Ulysses (1917–1994; classical).   Composer who was trained at Rochester, Yale, and Columbia universities and studied in Rome on a Fulbright Fellowship. Kay's major compositions include *Choral Triptych, Six Dances, Fantasy Variations,* and *Sinfonia in E*.

Keita, Salif (1949–   ; *wassoulou*).   Paris-based singer from Mali noted for his soaring, high-pitched vocal lines, combining traditional African music with jazz and rock. Keita has recorded with King Sunny Ade, Youssou N'Dour, Wayne Shorter, Carlos Santana, and other musicians. *Amen* (Mango, 1991); *The Mansa of Mali . . . A Retrospective* (Mango, 1994).

King, Albert [Albert Nelson] (1923–1992; blues).   Guitarist who exerted an influence on both Jimi Hendrix and Eric Clapton. Best known for the recordings he made in Memphis for Stax Records, beginning in the 1960s. *The Best of Albert King* (Stax/Fantasy, 1989).

King Curtis [Curtis Ousley] (1934–1971; R&B, jazz).   Alto, soprano, and tenor saxophonist. Part of an intense north Texas musical scene that included peers such as Ornette Coleman and David "Fathead" Newman, Curtis began playing the sax in Fort Worth, Texas, at age 12. An extraordinarily expressive and fluid sax player, King Curtis defined the R&B sax sound of the 1960s through his own solo work and as a session player with such greats as Aretha Franklin. *The Best of King Curtis* (Capitol, 1996).

King, Freddy (1934–1976; blues).   Guitarist and singer. Born in Texas, King moved with his family to Chicago when he was 16. Getting a start in Chicago clubs under the tutelage of Howlin' Wolf and Muddy Waters, King worked with a mix of Texas country blues and the more citified Chicago sound of the 1950s. By the early 1960s, King had developed his own style, which featured innovative use of sustained notes and a driving instrumental line. His hits included "Hideaway," "Have You Ever Loved a Woman?" and "Tore Down," among others. He was a major influence on English rockers of the 1960s such as Eric Clapton, Jimmie Page, and Jeff Beck. *The Best of Freddy King* (Shelter, 1975), *Takin' Care of Business* (Charlie, 1985).

King, Riley "B. B." (1925–   ; blues).   A former Memphis disc jockey, King taught himself guitar in 1945, combining the influences of Django Reinhardt, Charlie Christian, Lonnie Johnson, and Blind Lemon Jefferson into his own inimitable style. An indefatigable performer, he became world famous during the 1960s and has carried the blues to Russia and South America. King has also given many concerts in prisons and has set up a foundation for inmate rehabilitation. *Live at the Apollo* (GRP, 1991); *The Best of B. B. King* (Flair/WEA, 1991).

Konte, Alhaji Bai (1920–1983; *griot*).   Gambian master of traditional *kora* music. *Kora Melodies: Music from Gambia* (Rounder, 1979); *Simbomba* (Red House, 1979).

Kuti, Fela Anikulapo (1938–1997; Afro-beat).   Nigerian singer and bandleader usually known simply as Fela. Fela virtually invented the style known as Afro-beat, combining jazz and funk with traditional African music. A steadfast opponent of political dictatorship, Fela was known for his subversive lyrics and provocative performing style. Jailed more than a dozen times by the authorities, he was idolized by the Nigerian public and by musicians across Africa. *Fela's London Scene* (Makossa, 1970); *Original Sufferhead* (Shanachie, 1991).

Ladysmith Black Mambazo (*mbaqanga*). Formed in Ladysmith, South Africa, in 1964. A cappella choir known primarily for performing *mbaqanga* music. After releasing 28 albums in South Africa, LBM achieved an international following when the choir took part in Paul Simon's *Graceland* album and tour (1986–1987). *Best of Ladysmith Black Mambazo* (Shanachie, 1992).

Leadbelly [Huddie William Ledbetter] (c. 1885–1949; blues).   Guitarist, singer. An unrivaled master of the 12-string guitar, Leadbelly tapped into some of the oldest African American musical traditions, and he played a major role in the national revival of blues music. Discovered by music scholars while serving a prison term for attempted murder, he embodied the legend of the hard-living, long-suffering blues musician. *Leadbelly's Last Sessions, Vols. 1 & 2* (Folkways, 1953); *Midnight Special* (Rounder, 1991).

Lewis, Henry (1932–1996; classical).   The first African American to be the resident conductor of a major symphony orchestra, taking over the New Jersey Symphony in 1968. Lewis was also the first African American to conduct at the Metropolitan Opera, making his debut with *La Bohème* in 1972. A guest conductor with many orchestras, he also founded the Los Angeles Chamber Orchestra.

Little Richard [Richard Penniman] (1932–   ; R&B, rock).   Singer and pianist who has personified the energy and exuberance of rock 'n' roll since the 1950s. His indispensable hits include "Tutti Frutti," "Long Tall Sally," and "Good Golly, Miss Molly." *18 Greatest Hits* (Rhino, 1985); *The Specialty Sessions* (Specialty, 1990).

Little Walter [Marion Walter Jacobs] (1930–1968; blues).   Pioneer in the development of the blues harmonica style and longtime associate of Muddy Waters, both in Mississippi and in Chicago. *The Essential Little Walter* (Chess, 1993).

L. L. Cool J [James Smith] (1968– ; rap).   L. L. Cool J was one of the artists who defined the "East Coast" rap sound. His first songs, "I Need a Beat" (1984) and "I Can't Live Without My Radio" (1985), made him a star and made his record label, Def Jam, a powerhouse in rap. His initial style was streetwise, but not particularly political, and it celebrated partying and, with his ballads, romance. He later moved from rap to a synthesis that embraced mainstream pop music, and he starred as an actor in the television series *In the House*. *Radio* (Def Jam, 1985); *Bigger and Deffer* (Def Jam, 1986); *Mr. Smith* (Def Jam, 1995).

Lymon, Frankie, and the Teenagers (R&B, rock).   Formed in New York City in 1955, when Frankie Lymon was 13, the group had an immediate hit with "Why Do Fools Fall in Love?" Lymon, who died in 1968, was America's first African American teen idol. *Best of Frankie Lymon and the Teenagers* (Rhino, 1989).

Makeba, Miriam (1934– ; *mbube*).   South African singer who introduced African music to Western audiences; her recording of "The Lion Sleeps Tonight" popularized South Africa's *mbube* music. *An Evening with Miriam Makeba and Harry Belafonte* (RCA, 1965); *The Best of Miriam Makeba* (Castle, 1994).

Mapfumo, Thomas (1945– ; *jit*, pop).   Zimbabwean guitarist who became a national hero during the resistance to white minority rule in the 1970s. *Chimurenga Singles* (Shanachie, 1984).

Marley, Robert Nesta "Bob" (1945–1981; reggae).   Singer and songwriter who created an international audience for reggae as leader of the Wailers (with Peter Tosh and Bunny Wailer). "No Woman, No Cry," "I Shot the Sheriff," "One Love," "Buffalo Soldier," and a host of other Marley songs have taken their place among the classics of popular music. A spiritual visionary and social prophet, Marley set the standard for all others to follow. *Legend: The Best of Bob Marley and the Wailers* (Tuff Gong, 1984); *Natural Mystic: The Legend Lives On* (Tuff Gong, 1995).

Marsalis, Wynton (1961– ; jazz, classical).   Classical and jazz trumpeter, composer. In 1984, he became the first musician to win Grammys for classical and jazz performances in a single year. His composition *Blood on the Fields* was the first jazz piece to win the Pulitzer Prize for Music (1997). *Wynton Marsalis* (Columbia, 1981); *Black Codes* (Columbia, 1985); *Thick in the South* (Columbia, 1991).

Martha and the Vandellas (soul).   Formed in Detroit in 1962, Martha and the Vandellas vied with The Supremes as Motown's top female stars. Led by lead singer Martha Reeves, the Vandellas reached their peak with "Heat Wave" (1963) and "Dancing in the Street" (1964). *Martha Reeves and the Vandellas Anthology* (Motown, 1974).

Masekela, Hugh (1939– ; jazz, Afro-pop).   South African trumpeter and flugelhorn player who has worked throughout the world with a host of musicians, playing pop, jazz, R&B, and Afro-pop. *Home Is Where the Music Is* (Blue Thumb, 1972).

Mayfield, Curtis (1942– ; soul).   Chicago-based singer, songwriter, and producer best known for the sound track of the 1972 film *Superfly*. As a soloist and member of the Impressions, he scored repeatedly with songs such as "It's All Right," "People Get Ready," and "For Your Precious Love." *Curtis Mayfield: His Early Years with the Impressions* (ABC, 1973); *Take It to the Streets* (Curtom, 1990).

Maynor, Dorothy (1910–1996; classical).   Opera singer and educator who mastered more than a hundred roles during the 1930s and 1940s but was unable to perform in opera houses because of racism. In 1963, Maynor founded the Harlem School for the Arts, where youngsters were given instruction in the fine and performing arts, regardless of their ability to pay.

McBride, Christian (1973– ; jazz).   One of many prodigies to revitalize the jazz scene since the 1980s and 1990s, he is commonly considered the best of the young bassists. Admired for his intonation and note choice, he is already featured on more than 70 recording sessions. *Gettin' to It* (Verve, 1995).

McTell, Willie Samuel "Blind Willie" (1901–1959; blues).   Master of the Piedmont blues style; renowned for his renditions of "Broke Down Engine Blues," "Georgia Rag," "Stomp Down Rider," and other songs. *The Complete Blind Willie McTell* (Columbia, 1994).

Mighty Clouds of Joy (gospel).   Formed in Los Angeles during the late 1950s, this group has combined traditional gospel with pop and soul styles. *Live and Direct: The Very Best of the Mighty Clouds of Joy* (Epic, 1978).

Mills, Florence.   (See Chapter 15, "Performing Arts.")

Mingus, Charles (1922–1979; jazz).   Bassist who experimented with new fingerings and complex chordal progressions during the 1950s. The bass, which had functioned primarily as rhythmic support, became a leading melodic instrument in Mingus's hands; he introduced audiences to the beauty and flexibility of the instrument. Mingus also founded the influential Jazz Workshop. *Pithecanthropus Erectus* (Atlantic, 1956); *Mingus Ah Um* (Columbia, 1959).

Monk, Thelonious Sphere (1917–1982; jazz).   Pianist and composer. A bebop innovator, Monk lived in a rhythmically and harmonically unique sound world. Among his classic compositions are "Pannonica," "In Walked Bud," "Tinkle Tinkle," and "Crepuscule with Nellie." *Brilliant Corners* (Riverside, 1987); *The Genius of Modern Music, Vols. 1 & 2* (Blue Note, 1989); *Complete Riverside Recordings* (Original Jazz Classics, 1988).

Morton, Jelly Roll [Ferdinand Joseph La Menthe] (1890–1941; jazz).   Composer and pianist. A seminal figure in early jazz, he introduced sophisticated harmonies and arrangements to what was considered the "bordello music" of New Orleans's Storyville section. Among his most notable compositions are "King Porter Stomp," "Jelly Roll Blues," and "The Crave." *Jelly Roll Morton, Vols. I–V* (JSP, 1926–1930); *The Alan Lomax Library of Congress Recordings, Vols. I–VIII* (Classic Jazz Masters, 1938).

MOTOWN

The most successful black-owned record company in history, Motown Records was founded in Detroit in 1959 by Berry Gordy Jr., who had previously enjoyed success as a producer, songwriter, and music publisher. Working out of a modest frame house at 2648 West Grand Boulevard (prophetically christened Hitsville, U.S.A.), Gordy assembled a roster of performers that eventually included The Marvelettes, The Supremes, The Four Tops, Smokey Robinson and the Miracles, Martha and the Vandellas, Marvin Gaye, Mary Wells, Al Green, The Temptations, Stevie Wonder, The Jackson Five, and others. During the decade of the 1960s, Motown produced 79 top 10 singles, a feat matched by no other record company. Building on his spectacular success, Gordy took Motown into areas previously off-limits to African American companies, such as film and television production. Gordy sold Motown Records to MCA in 1988, though he still retains a half-interest in Jobete, the publishing company owning all the classic Motown songs. He has played a major role in the creation and development of the Motown Museum, housed in Hitsville, U.S.A.

Nascimento, Milton (1942– ; jazz, pop).   Brazilian singer-songwriter who has been combining jazz and pop styles since the late 1960s, creating nearly 30 albums. *Sentimela* (Verve, 1990); *Minas* (A&M, 1995).

Navarro, Theodore "Fats" (1923–1950; jazz).   Trumpeter known for his beautiful tone and lightning-fast technique. Though his career was cut short by heroin, Navarro is regarded as one of the founders of modern jazz trumpet technique, and he was widely admired by other musicians. *The Complete Blue Note and Capitol Recordings of Fats Navarro and Tadd Dameron* (Blue Note, 1995).

N'Dour, Youssou (1959– ; *mbalax*, Afro-pop).   Senegalese Afro-pop pioneer noted for mixing traditional African music with pop strings and jazz-derived chord changes; as leader of the Star Band, N'Dour created the musical style known as *mbalax*. *The Lion* (Columbia, 1990); *The Guide* (Columbia, 1994).

Noone, Jimmie (1895–1944; jazz).   One of the great clarinetists of the 1920s, Noone was renowned for his fluidity and technical proficiency. His playing bridged the transition from New Orleans–style jazz to swing. *The Complete Recordings, Vol. 1* (Affinity, 1926–1930); *Apex Blues* (Decca, 1928–1930); *Jimmie Noone* (Best of Jazz, 1996).

Norman, Jessye (1945– ; classical).   World-renowned soprano who made her debut in Europe in 1969, singing at the Deutsche Oper, La Scala, the Salzburg Festival, and other venues. Norman made her U.S. debut at the Hollywood Bowl in 1972. Among her many distinctions are honorary music degrees from Howard and Cambridge, the Grande Prix du Disque (1983), the Woman of the Arts Award (1992), and a Kennedy Center Lifetime Achievement Award (1997).

N.W.A. [Niggaz With Attitude].   Formed in Los Angeles in 1986 by Dr. Dre (Andre Young), Ice Cube (O'Shea Jackson), and the rapper known as Eazy E, N.W.A. was the pioneering "gangsta" rap group of the 1980s. Unlike earlier rappers, who frequently offered cautionary tales about inner-city life, N.W.A. celebrated the amoral life of the street gang. This gangsta sound, as imagined by N.W.A., brought collagelike sound snippets over a funky bass and drum beat. The group broke up in 1992. *Straight Outta Compton* (Ruthless, 1988), *EFIL4ZAGGIN* (Ruthless, 1991).

Olatunji, Babatunde (1929– ; *juju*).   Nigerian percussionist who came to the United States during the early 1960s as a medical student. Among the first African musicians to make an impact on American musical tastes, Olatunji's influence is celebrated by John Coltrane's "Tunji." *Drums of Passion: Invocation* (Rykodisc, 1988); *Drums of Passion: The Beat* (Rykodisc, 1989).

Oliver, Joe "King" (1885–1938; jazz).   Cornetist. New Orleans–born jazz giant who formed the Creole Jazz Band in Chicago in 1919, making historic recordings with Louis Armstrong in 1923. Later organized the Dixie Syncopators. *Jazzy Wonderland* (Keyboards, 1996).

Parker, Charlie "Yardbird" (1920–1955; jazz).   Alto saxophonist. With Dizzy Gillespie, a co-inventor of bebop and one of the seminal influences in all of jazz. His unique method of improvising chord changes, developed during the late 1930s, created a new era in the art of the saxophone. *Bird: The Complete Charlie Parker on Verve* (Verve, 1988); *The Legendary Dial Masters, Vols. I & II* (Stash, 1989).

Patton, Charley (1891–1934; blues).   One of the founding fathers of the Delta blues, Patton is renowned for his bottleneck (slide) guitar technique. His rhythmic and structural innovations are said to bear traces of West African drumming. *Founder of the Delta Blues: 1929–1934* (Yazoo, 1991).

Pendergrass, Teddy (1950– ; soul, R&B). Vocalist who began his career with Harold Melvin and the Blue Notes; went solo in 1976, releasing four platinum-selling albums in the late 1970s and early 1980s. *Greatest Hits: Love Language* (Asylum, 1984).

Perry, Lee "Scratch" (1940– ; reggae).   Singer, songwriter, producer, and music entrepreneur who pioneered the technique of dubbing. In addition to performing and recording with his own band, the Upsetters, Perry played a major role in the development of the Wailers and produced records for numerous other reggae musicians. *Arkology* (Island, 1997).

Pettiford, Oscar (1922–1960; jazz).   Bassist and cellist who replaced Jimmy Blanton in Duke Ellington's orchestra. Pettiford recorded with Coleman Hawkins, Ben Webster, and Earl Hines in the 1940s and is credited with elevating the cello to the front ranks of jazz solo instruments. *The New Oscar Pettiford Sextet* (Original Jazz Classics, 1956–1957); *Deep Passion* (Impulse, 1957).

Pine, Courtney (1964– ; jazz).   Tenor and soprano saxophonist, bass clarinetist. Born in London of Jamaican ancestry, Pine founded a big band, the Jazz Warriors, in 1985. He also leads a smaller ensemble, The World's First Saxophone Posse. *Journey to the Urge Within* (Island, 1986); *Out of Many, One People* (Island, 1987).

The Platters (R&B, rock).   Formed in Los Angeles in 1953, the Platters were at their peak from 1955 to 1960, topping the charts with "My Prayer," "Smoke Gets in Your Eyes," and "Twilight Time." *The Very Best of the Platters* (Mercury, 1991).

Powell, Bud (1924–1966; jazz).   Brilliant, mercurial pianist who radically influenced the vocabulary of jazz piano, bridging the swing and bebop eras. His own compositions include "Un Poco Loco" and "Dance of the Infidels." *The Genius of Bud Powell* (Verve, 1950–1951); *The Amazing Bud Powell, Vols. 1–3* (Blue Note, 1949–1956).

Pratt, Awadagin (1967– ; classical).   Pianist with a big sound and remarkable facility in fast, intricate passages. Pratt graduated from the Peabody Conservatory with concentrations in piano, violin, and conducting. In 1992, he won the prestigious Naumburg International Piano Competition.

Price, Leontyne (1927– ; classical).   Lyric soprano who was one of opera's reigning superstars for more than a quarter century. The first African American to sing an operatic role on television, she gained national acclaim in NBC-TV's 1955 production of *Tosca*. Price made her debut at the Metropolitan Opera in *Il Trovatore* in 1961, and in 1966 she created the role of Cleopatra in Barber's *Antony and Cleopatra*, inaugurating the new Metropolitan Opera House at Lincoln Center.

Prince [Prince Rogers Nelson] (1958– ; rock, R&B).   Singer-songwriter, guitarist, vocalist, and keyboarder who emerged during the late 1970s. In the 1980s, Prince produced a seemingly endless string of albums and singles fusing funk and rock. *Dirty Mind* (Warner Bros., 1980); *Purple Rain* (Warner Bros., 1984); *Black Album* (Warner Bros., 1987).

Professor Longhair [Henry Roeland Byrd] (1918–1980; blues, R&B).   Pianist and singer. A self-taught pianist, Professor Longhair created a style of New Orleans piano playing that merged Cuban rumba, urban R&B, and New Orleans parade music, and influenced such rock and R&B performers as Ray Charles, Fats Domino, and Allen Toussaint. His hits included "She Ain't Got No Hair," "Big Chief," and "Tipitina." *Professor Longhair: New Orleans Piano, Vols. 1–2* (Atlantic, 1972); *Crawfish Fiesta* (Alligator, 1980).

Public Enemy (rap).   Formed in 1982 in Garden City, New York. With Chuck D (Carlton Ridenhour) and Flavor Flav (William Drayton) vocalizing over the innovative musical mix of the Bomb Squad, Public Enemy emerged as the top rap group of the late 1980s and early 1990s. The group's work was distinguished by a hard beat and a black-nationalist point of view. *Yo! Bum Rush the Show* (Def Jam, 1987); *Fear of a Black Planet* (Def Jam, 1990).

Queen Latifah [Dana Owens] (1970– ; rap).   One of the pioneering female rappers, Queen Latifah established a feminist hip-hop attitude with "Ladies First" (1989). She parlayed her success into a variety of business endeavors and also branched out into acting, starring in the TV sitcom *Living Single*. *All Hail the Queen* (Tommy Boy, 1989); *Nature of a Sista'* (Tommy Boy, 1991); *Black Reign* (Motown, 1993).

Rainey, Ma [Gertrude Pridgett] (1886–1939; blues).   The first African American to sing the blues professionally (1902), Rainey traveled the country with the Rabbit Foot Minstrels. She was also one of the first blues artists to make a commercial recording. *Ma Rainey* (Milestone, 1974); *Ma Rainey's Black Bottom* (Yazoo, 1990).

Rawls, Lou (1935– ; R&B, soul).   Chicago-born singer who began turning out million-selling albums in the 1960s. In addition to his numerous concert dates and TV appearances, Rawls is noted for his annual telethon benefiting the United Negro College Fund. *Greatest Hits* (Curb, 1990).

RECORD COMPANIES

African Americans entered the recording business in 1921, when Harry Pace established the Pace Phonograph Company. Pace quickly sold over half a million records on the Black Swan label, enjoying a major hit with Ethel Waters's "Down Homes Blues/Oh Daddy." Three other African

American labels—Black Patti, Sunshine, and Meritt—also began operations during the decade. However, these companies were soon bought by the leading white firms or forced out of business, and none survived the onset of the Great Depression. African American record companies did not emerge again until the late 1940s and early 1950s. The new labels included Vee Jay and J.O.B. in Chicago, Peacock in Houston, and Red Robin/Fury/Everlast in New York: All enjoyed a degree of success releasing R&B and gospel records, paving the way for the advent of Motown in 1959. In 1970, Motown's Holland-Dozier-Holland songwriting team founded Invictus/Hot Wax, and the following year Kenny Gamble and Leon Huff started Philadelphia International Records (PIR), which produced 30 million-selling singles in a five-year period. In the 1980s, Prince founded the Paisley Park studio and record label; Curtis Mayfield revived his Curtom label (first established during the late 1960s); and Quincy Jones created Qwest. At the same time, the emergence of rap led to the formation of several important black companies, including Sugar Hill, Def Jam, Jive, Cold Chillin', Bad Boy, Delicious Vinyl, and No Limit.

Redding, Otis (1941–1967; soul).   Soul balladeer who earned his place in music history with "I've Been Loving You Too Long," "(Sittin' on) The Dock of the Bay," and other hits, before dying in a plane crash. *Otis Blue* (Atlantic, 1965); *The Otis Redding Story* (Atlantic, 1987).

Richie, Lionel (1950– ; soul).   Alabama-born singer and songwriter who began his career at age 18, with the Commodores and went solo in the early 1980s, producing a pair of number-one albums—*Can't Slow Down* (Motown, 1983) and *Dancing on the Ceiling* (Motown, 1986).

Roach, Max (1924– ; jazz).   Drummer who played in gospel groups as a child. Roach is credited with redefining the role of the drums during the bebop period. *Freedom Now Suite* (Columbia, 1960); *Birth and Rebirth* (Black Saint, 1978); *To the Max* (Blue Moon, 1991).

Roberts, Marcus (1963– ; jazz).   Exceptional young pianist who first gained prominence playing with Wynton Marsalis. His wide-ranging repertoire includes standards, classic jazz compositions, and his own compositions, which include "Preach, Reverend, Preach," and "Snowy Morning Blues." *Alone with Three Giants* (BMG, 1991); *If I Could Be with You* (BMG, 1993).

Robeson, Paul.   (See Chapter 15, "Performing Arts.")

Robinson, William "Smokey" (1940– ; soul).   Singer-songwriter who started out with Motown as the lead singer of the Miracles, formed in 1957. In addition to writing "Shop Around" and 26 other top 40 hits with the Miracles, Robinson penned "My Girl" and "The Way You Do the Things You Do" for the Temptations. Over the years, dozens of leading artists have covered his songs. *Anthology* (Motown, 1986); *Quiet Storm* (Motown, 1991).

Rollins, Theodore Walter "Sonny" (1930– ; jazz).   Tenor saxophonist noted for playing short, widely spaced figures in a uniquely deep, gravelly tone. His playing style has been influenced by both swing and bebop. *Sonny Rollins with the Modern Jazz Quartet* (Prestige, 1953); *Saxophone Colossus* (Prestige, 1956).

Ross, Diana (1944– ; soul, rock).   Singer and actress who starred with The Supremes during the 1960s and went solo in 1970. Her popular record albums include *Touch Me in the Morning* (1973), *Diana* (1980), and *Silk Electric* (1982). As a film actress, Ross was hailed for her portrayal of Billie Holiday in the 1972 film *Lady Sings the Blues*. *Diana Ross Anthology* (Motown, 1983).

Run-D.M.C. (rap).   Formed in 1981 in Queens, New York. Run (Joseph Simmons), D.M.C. (Darryl McDaniel), and Jam Master Jay (Jason Mizell) took hip-hop into the commercial mainstream with "It's Like That" (1983) and a string of later hit singles. *Together Forever: Greatest Hits: 1983–1991* (Profile, 1991).

Salt-n-Pepa (rap).   Formed in 1985 in Queens, New York. Cheryl "Salt" James, Sandy "Pepa" Denton, and Pamela Greene were the first female rappers to cross over to the pop charts. In 1988, Greene left the group, and Deidre "Spinderella" Roper took her place. *Hot, Cool and Vicious* (Next Plateau, 1986); *Blacks' Magic* (Next Plateau, 1990).

Sangaré, Oumou (1966– ; *wassoulou*).   Malian vocalist who is the leading practitioner of *wassoulou* music. Her lyrics often address the situation of women in modern West African society. *Moussolou* (World Circuit, 1989); *Ko Sira* (World Circuit, 1993).

Scott-Heron, Gil (1949– ; rap).   Writer-singer who anticipated rap with recorded poetry backed by jazz and funk instrumentals, most notably in "The Revolution Will Not Be Televised" (1974) and "Johannesburg" (1975). *The Best of Gil Scott-Heron* (Arista, 1991).

Seals, Son (1942– ; blues).   Guitarist who learned the blues in his native Arkansas and moved to Chicago, where he played with Albert King in the late 1960s. *The Son Seals Blues Band* (Alligator, 1973); *Midnight Son* (Alligator, 1977); *Live and Burning* (Alligator, 1978).

Shorter, Wayne (1933– ; jazz).   Tenor and soprano saxophonist profoundly influenced by John Coltrane, though his style is more lyrical than Coltrane's. Beginning with Art Blakey's Jazz Messengers in the late 1950s, Shorter was a key member of the second Miles Davis Quintet and then moved on to the fusion group Weather Report. *The Vee Jay Years* (Charly, 1959–1960); *Speak No Evil* (Blue Note, 1964); *Adams Apple* (Blue Note, 1966).

Silver, Horace (1928– ; jazz).   Composer and pianist whose blend of gospel, blues, bebop, soul, and Latin elements—in standards such as "Lonely Woman"—has been widely influential. *Song for My Father* (Blue Note, 1964).

Skatalites (*highlife*, reggae).   Formed in Kingston, Jamaica, in 1963. The leading exponents of *ska*, the Skatalites established their reputation with hits such as "Ball o' Fire," "Independent Anniversary Ska," and "Dick Tracy" *Legendary Skatalites* (Top Ranking, 1975); *Skavoovee* (Shanachie, 1993).

Sly and Robbie (reggae).   Formed in Kingston, Jamaica, in 1975. Bassist Sly Dunbar (1952–) and drummer Robbie Shakespeare (1953–) formed reggae's top rhythm section, backing Black Uhuru, Jimmy Cliff, and other artists, many of whom they produced on their own label, Taxi Productions. *Sly and Robbie Present Taxi* (Mango, 1981); *Rhythm Killers* (Island, 1987).

Smith, Bessie (1894–1937; blues).   Singer known as the Empress of the Blues. Smith blended rural traditions, spirituals, and jazz into an unmistakable and widely imitated blues style. Her 1923 recording of "Downhearted Blues/Gulf Coast Blues" sold 780,000 copies in six months and became the first million-seller by an African American artist. In all, Smith recorded more than 160 songs, many of which she wrote or cowrote. *The Complete Recordings, Vols. 1 & 2* (Columbia, 1991).

Smith, Willie "the Lion" (1897–1973; jazz).   Leading stride pianist who earned his nickname as a combat soldier in World War I. A stylish figure during the Harlem Renaissance, Smith had a profound influence on Duke Ellington. *Willie "the Lion" Smith 1925–1937* (Classics, 1937); *Porks and Beans* (Black Lion, 1996).

The Soul Stirrers (gospel).   Gospel quartet formed in Trinity, Texas, in 1927. Moving to Chicago soon after their formation, this influential group was the first to abandon the traditional repertoire (jubilees and old spirituals) for new gospel music. The Soul Stirrers were also the first quartet to have a second lead, an innovation that freed the first lead to do extensive solos. Still active. *Soul Stirrers* (Specialty, 1995).

Still, William Grant (1895–1978; classical).   The first African American composer to have his work performed by a major symphony orchestra (*Afro-American Symphony*, performed by the Rochester Philharmonic in 1931). Still was also the first African American to conduct a major symphony orchestra, leading the Los Angeles Philharmonic in a program of his works in 1936. His opera *Troubled Island* was performed by the New York City Opera in 1949, another first for an African American composer. Other major works by Still include *The Peaceful Land, Song of a New Race, Darker America*, and *Pages from Negro History*.

Strayhorn, Billy "Sweet Pea" (1915–1967; jazz).   Composer, arranger, and pianist who collaborated with Duke Ellington for a quarter century. Strayhorn classics include "Lush Life," "Take the A Train," and "Blood Count." *Lush Life: The Music of Billy Strayhorn* (recorded by Joe Henderson et al., Verve, 1992).

The Sugar Hill Gang (rap).   Formed in New York City in 1977. Selling 2 million copies of their debut album, the trio of Master Gee, Wonder Mike, and Big Bank Hank transformed rap from a party routine to a major pop-music genre. *Rapper's Delight* (Sugarhill, 1979); *The 8th Wonder* (Sugarhill, 1981).

Sun Ra [Herman Blount] (1914–1993; jazz).   Organ, piano, and synthesizer. A flamboyant innovator who claimed to be a native of Saturn, Sun Ra influenced rock and R&B musicians, as well as jazz players. As leader of the Sun Ra Arkestra, Sun Ra contributed heavily to the jazz revival of the 1980s. *Jazz in Silhouette* (Evidence, 1958); *The Solar Myth Approach* (Affinity, 1970–1971).

The Supremes (soul).   Formed in Detroit in 1959. Diana Ross, Nona Hendryx, and Florence Ballard were the mainstays of the Motown empire in the 1960s, producing 12 number-one singles, including "Where Did Our Love Go?", "Stop! In the Name of Love," "You Can't Hurry Love," and "You Keep Me Hanging On." The group underwent a number of personnel changes, including Ballard's departure in 1967 and Ross's in 1970. When The Supremes gave their farewell performance in 1977, the trio consisted of Susaye Green, Mary Wilson, and Scherrie Payne. *Diana Ross and the Supremes Greatest Hits, Vols. 1 & 2* (Motown, 1967); *Anthology* (Motown, 1974).

Take 6 (gospel).   A cappella group formed in Hunstville, Alabama, in 1987. Known for their complex jazz-based arrangements of standards and original compositions. *Take 6* (Reprise, 1988); *So Much 2 Say* (Reprise, 1990).

Tatum, Art (1909–1956; jazz).   Pianist who left Ohio for New York in 1932 and achieved international fame by the middle of the decade. Endowed with musical inventiveness and phenomenal technique, he inspired awe in both jazz and classical pianists. Tatum's most famous recorded solos include "Tea for Two," "Sweet Lorraine," and "Get Happy." *Art Tatum Solo Masterpieces* (Pablo, 1953–1956); *Classic Early Solos (1934–1937)* (GRP, 1991).

Taylor, Cecil (1929– ; jazz).   Pianist. A leader of the free-jazz movement during the late 1950s, Taylor has emerged as a musician who defies categorization. Winner of a MacArthur Foundation "genius" award, Taylor now creates complex, free-ranging piano works that draw from jazz and classical traditions. *Unit Structures* (Blue Note, 1966); *Silent Tongues* (Black Lion, 1975); *Air above Mountains* (Enja, 1992).

The Temptations (soul).   Formed in Detroit in 1961, the Temptations were the top male vocal group of the 1960s and early 1970s, with timeless hits such as "My Girl" and "Papa Was a Rollin' Stone." *The Temptations Greatest Hits, Vols. 1 & 2* (Motown, 1988).

Tharpe, Rosetta "Sister" (1921–1973; gospel).   Singer and guitarist who was largely responsible for bringing gospel music into the mainstream, performing at the Cotton Club (1938), Carnegie Hall (1938), and the Apollo Theater (1943). Tharpe was also the first gospel singer to sign with a major record company (Decca) and the first to tour Europe. Her guitar playing was heavily influenced by jazz and blues styles. *Complete Recorded Works, Vols. 1 & 2* (Document, 1996).

Toots and the Maytals (reggae).   Formed in 1962 in Kingston, Jamaica. Frederick "Toots" Hibbert created his unique brand of reggae by imbuing his songs with a gospel-like fervor. Among the group's best-known hits are "Pressure Drop," "Sailin' On," and "Country Road." *The Best of Toots and the Maytals* (Island, 1979).

Tosh, Peter [Winston Hubert MacIntosh] (1944–1987; reggae).   In addition to his work with the Wailers, Tosh had an outstanding solo career, creating hits such as "I'm the Toughest" and "400 Years." Notably outspoken in political matters, he was murdered in his home in 1987. *Legalize It* (Columbia, 1976); *Honorary Citizen* (Columbia Legacy, 1997).

Touré, Ali Farka (1939–   ; *griot*).   Malian guitarist and vocalist who has recorded with Taj Mahal, Ry Cooder, and the Chieftains. *Ali Farka Touré* (Mango, 1988); *Talking Timbuktu* (World Circuit, 1994).

2-Pac [Tupac Shakur] (1971–1996; rap).   2-Pac symbolized the promise and danger of "gangsta" rap. Brought up largely on the East Coast, 2-Pac moved with his mother to California in 1988. In California, 2-Pac got into the rap scene as a dancer and roadie for the group Digital Underground. He soon went solo, and his first record, "2Pacalypse Now" (1992), garnered critical raves and commercial success. 2-Pac followed in the gangsta style of NWA (see previous description in this listing), with bass-heavy rhythm lines and lyrics about the raw side of ghetto life. He found himself in more or less continual legal trouble from 1992 and served eight months in a New York prison in 1995 for sexual assault on a female fan. In September 1996, he was murdered in Las Vegas, Nevada. *2Pacalypse Now* (Jive, 1992), *Me Against the World* (Jive, 1995), *All Eyez on Me* (Death Row, 1996).

Turner, Big Joe (1911–1985; blues).   Kansas City blues singer who built on boogie-woogie rhythms to create the style known as "blues shouting" during the 1930s and 1940s. A series of classic Turner songs—"Shake, Rattle & Roll," "Flip, Flop, and Fly," "Corrina, Corrina," to name a few—became R&B hits during the early 1950s, and Turner kept on touring until the 1980s. *The Boss of the Blues* (1956); *Big Joe Turner Memorial Album: Rhythm & Blues Years* (Atlantic, 1986).

Turner, Tina (1938–   ; R&B; rock).   Singer who spent her early career with the Ike and Tina Turner Revue, then went solo in 1976 and became an international star. *Proud Mary: The Best of Ike & Tina Turner* (EMI, 1991); *Tina: The Collected Recordings, Sixties to Nineties* (Capitol, 1994).

Tyner, McCoy (1938–   ; jazz).   Pianist with a dynamic and fluid style, best known for his work with the John Coltrane Quartet in the early 1960s. As a soloist and composer, Tyner has continued to be a seminal influence; his own compositions include "Blues on the Corner," "Contemplation," and "Rio." *The Real McCoy* (Blue Note, 1967); *Revelations* (Blue Note, 1989); *Things Ain't What They Used to Be* (Blue Note, 1990).

Vandross, Luther (1951–   ; R&B, soul).   Singer and songwriter who began his career by singing on commercials and backing other artists. Vandross broke out with his number-one R&B single "Never Too Much" in 1981 and has since produced a string of chart-toppers, including "Stop to Love," "Here and Now," and "The Best Things in Life Are Free." *Never Too Much* (Epic, 1981); *Any Love* (Epic, 1988); *Never Let Me Go* (LV/Epic, 1993).

Vasconcelos, Naná (1945–   ; Brazilian traditional, jazz).   Brazilian percussionist known for his virtuosity on the *berimbau* and other traditional Brazilian instruments. *Saudades* (ECM, 1979); *Bush Dance* (Antilles, 1986); *Storytelling* (Hemisphere, 1995).

Vaughan, Sarah (1924–1990; jazz).   Singer discovered in 1942 during Amateur Night at the Apollo. Celebrated for her complex bebop phrasing and impeccable scat singing, Vaughan made her first recording in 1944 and remained active in the jazz scene until her death. *Sarah Vaughan with Clifford Brown* (EmArcy, 1954); *After Hours* (Roulette, 1961); *Crazy and Mixed Up* (Pablo, 1982).

Wailer, Bunny [Neville O'Reilly Livingston] (1947–   ; reggae).   Due to his reluctance to leave Jamaica, Wailer is less well known abroad than his late bandmates Bob Marley and Peter Tosh, but his buoyant tenor voice and spiritual intensity place him in the front rank of reggae artists. *Blackheart Man* (Island, 1976); *Time Will Tell: A Tribute to Bob Marley* (Shanachie, 1990).

Walker, Aaron Thibeaux "T-Bone" (1910–1975; blues).   Texas blues guitarist who started out at age 13 under the influence of "Blind Lemon" Jefferson and Lonnie Johnson. When Walker began recording in 1929, he pioneered the use of the electric guitar, creating a legacy that influenced both jazz and rock 'n' roll. *The Complete Imperial Recordings, 1950–1954* (EMI, 1991).

Walker, George (1922–   ; classical).   Composer of more than 70 published works, including overtures, sinfonias, concertos, sonatas, string quartets, cantatas, and sacred works. Walker trained at the Curtis

Institute of Music, made his debut as a pianist at New York's Town Hall in 1945, and later performed with the Philadelphia Orchestra under Eugene Ormandy. He has taught composition at a number of universities, including Johns Hopkins and Rutgers. In 1996, Walker became the first African American to win the Pulitzer Prize in Composition; he was honored for *Lilacs*, a setting for soprano and orchestra of Walt Whitman's classic poem "When Lilacs Last in the Dooryard Bloomed."

Waller, Thomas "Fats" (1904–1943; jazz).   Pianist, organist, singer, and songwriter. A protégé of James P. Johnson, Waller began recording in the 1930s and made hundreds of records in the course of a relatively short career. As a pianist, he remained close to the ragtime tradition. He is now best known for his numerous compositions, which include "Honeysuckle Rose," "Black and Blue," and "Ain't Misbehavin'." *The Complete Fats Waller, Vols. 1–4* (Bluebird, 1981–1987).

Warfield, William (1920– ; classical).   Baritone who trained at the Eastman School of Music and the University of Rochester. Warfield made his recital debut at Town Hall in 1950 and then toured Australia. In addition to his numerous concert appearances, Warfield has been acclaimed for his performances in the film version of *Show Boat* and in various productions of *Porgy and Bess*.

Washington, Dinah [Ruth Lee Jones] (1924–1963; blues).   Starting out as a gospel singer, Washington switched to secular music in 1942 and excelled in both jazz and blues. Hits such as "What a Diff'rence a Day Makes" and "Baby Get Lost" made her the top African American female singer of the 1950s. *The Complete Dinah Washington on Mercury, Vols. 1–7, 1946–1961* (Mercury, 1987–1989).

Waters, Muddy [McKinley Morganfield] (1915–1983; blues).   Guitarist and singer whose early style was formed under the influence of Robert Johnson and Son House. When Waters moved to Chicago in 1943, he adopted the amplified electric guitar and transformed the Mississippi Delta blues into a distinctive urban sound. Waters's classics such as "Honey Bee," "I Just Wanna Make Love to You," and "I'm Ready" have inspired countless blues and rock musicians. *The Complete Plantation Recordings; The Chess Box* (MCA, 1989); *The Best of Muddy Waters* (MCA, 1985).

Watts, André (1945– ; classical).   Pianist who performed with the Philadelphia Orchestra at age 9 and performed with Leonard Bernstein and the New York Philharmonic at age 16. In the course of his distinguished concert career, Watts has been awarded the Lincoln Center Medallion (1972) and the Gold Medal of the National Society of Arts and Letters (1982).

Webster, Ben (1909–1973; jazz).   This Kansas City native was one of a triumvirate of swing-era tenor saxophonists, which also included Coleman Hawkins and Lester Young. Webster played a leading role in the development of Duke Ellington's band in the early 1940s; his talents were highlighted in numbers such as "Perdido," "Cotton Tail," and "C-Jam Blues." *Soulville* (Verve, 1953–1957); *Meet You at the Fair* (Impulse, 1964).

Williams, Tony (1945– ; jazz).   As a member of the second Miles Davis Quintet, Williams established himself as the leader of a new generation of drummers. He later formed his own band, The Tony Williams Lifetime. *Lifetime* (Blue Note, 1964); *Tokyo Live* (Blue Note, 1992).

Williamson, John Lee "Sonny Boy" (1914–1948; blues).   The original and lesser known of the two Delta blues musicians who shared the same name. Sonny Boy Williamson I is credited with elevating the harmonica to lead-instrument status. As a songwriter, he is best known for "Good Morning Little Schoolgirl." *Blues in the Mississippi Night* (Rykodisc, 1990).

Williamson, "Sonny Boy" [Rice Miller] (c. 1899–1965; blues).   The author of "One Way Out," "Bye Bye Bird," and other blues standards, Williamson appropriated the name of his harmonica rival while starring on the first live blues radio program, *King Biscuit Time*. After moving to Chicago in the 1950s, he played with Muddy Waters and recorded hits such as "All My Love in Vain." *The Essential Sonny Boy Williamson* (MCA/Chess, 1993).

Wilson, Cassandra (1955–   ; jazz).   Vocalist who emerged during the 1980s jazz revival. Gifted with a rich, supple contralto voice, Williams has increasingly expanded her range of material. *Blue Light Till Dawn* (Blue Note, 1993); *New Moon Daughter* (Blue Note, 1997).

Wilson, Jackie (1934–   ; R&B, soul, rock).   One of the top vocalists of the 1950s and 1960s, Wilson enjoyed a string of hits that included "Lonely Teardrops," "To Be Loved," and "You Better Know It." *The Very Best of Jackie Wilson* (Rhino, 1994).

The Winans (gospel).   Detroit-based family quartet (David Jr., Michael, Marvin, and Carvin) formed in 1980. The Winans are known for their "funky" gospel style, which incorporates guitars, electric keyboards, bass, and saxophones. Two additional Winan siblings, BeBe and CeCe, are also enjoying successful solo gospel careers. *Let My People Go* (Warner Brothers, 1985); *Best of the Winans* (Light, 1995).

Wonder, Stevie [Stevland Judkins Morris] (1950–   ; soul, rock).   Vocalist and master of many instruments who began recording with Motown at age 10. He is blind. His music has become increasingly complex over the years, combining elements from all the major black music forms. *Talking Book* (Motown, 1972); *Looking Back* (Motown, 1978); *Journey through the Secret Life of Plants* (Motown, 1979).

Young, Lester "Pres" (1909–1959; jazz).   Tenor saxophonist. Young first gained recognition as a member of Count Basie's band in the mid-1930s and began to work in small-group settings during the 1940s. Acknowledged as the "president" of all the tenor players during the swing era, he later adapted his style to the rise of bebop. *Complete Aladdin Sessions* (1942–1948); *The Complete Lester Young on Keynote* (Mercury, 1944); *Pres and Teddy and Oscar* (Verve, 1956).

SOURCES FOR ADDITIONAL INFORMATION

Appleby, David P. *Music of Brazil*. Austin: University of Texas Press, 1983.

Bebey, Francis. *African Music: A People's Art*, translated by Josephine Bennett. Westport, CT: Lawrence Hill, 1975.

Collier, John Lincoln. *The Making of Jazz: A Comprehensive History*. New York: Delta, 1978.

Cusic, Don. *The Sound of Light: A History of Gospel Music*. Bowling Green, OH: Bowling Green State University Press, 1990.

Gillett, Charlie. *The Sound of the City: The Rise of Rock and Roll*, rev. ed. London: Souvenir Press, 1983.

Jones, LeRoi (a.k.a. Amiri Baraka). *Blues People*. New York: Morrow, 1963.

Kernfeld, Barry, ed. *The New Grove Dictionary of Jazz*. New York: Macmillan, 1988.

Merlis, Bob, and Davin Seay. *Heart & Soul: A Celebration of Black Music Style in America*. New York: Stewart, Tabori & Chang, 1997.

Morgan, Thomas, and William Barlow. *From Cakewalks to Concert Halls: An Illustrated History of African-American Music*. Washington, DC: Elliot & Clark, 1992.

Nelson, Havelock, and Michael A. Gonzales. *Bring the Noise: A Guide to Rap Music and Hip-Hop Culture*. New York: Harmony, 1991.

Oliver, Paul. *The New Grove Gospel, Blues and Jazz with Spirituals and Ragtime*. New York: Norton, 1986.

———. *Savannah Syncopators: African Retention in the Blues*. New York: Stein and Day, 1970.

Potash, Chris. *Reggae, Rasta, Revolution: Jamaican Music from Ska to Dub*. New York: Schirmer, 1997.

Romanowksi, Patricia, and Holly George-Warren, eds. *The New Rolling Stone Encyclopedia of Rock & Roll.* New York: Fireside, 1995.

Santoro, Gene. *Stir It Up: Musical Stews from Roots to Jazz.* New York: Oxford University Press, 1997.

Southern, Eileen. *The Music of Black Americans*, 3rd ed. New York: Norton, 1997.

———. *Biographical Dictionary of Afro-American and African Musicians.* Westport, CT: Greenwood, 1982.

Story, Rosalyn. *And So I Sing: African American Divas of Opera and Concert.* New York: Amistad, 1990.

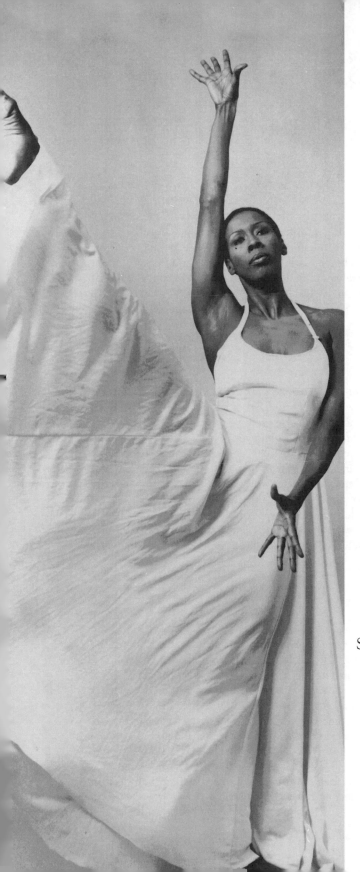

15
Performing Arts

MILESTONES IN AFRICAN AMERICAN THEATER

AFRICAN GROVE THEATRE

African American participation in the organized theater dates back to 1821, when free blacks in New York City established the African Grove Theatre at Mercer and Bleecker Streets. The company presented *Othello, Hamlet,* and other works by Shakespeare, as well as *The Drama of King Shotaway,* the first dramatic work by an African American to be produced on the stage. (Written by the African Grove's director—a West Indian named Brown whose first name is now a matter of conjecture—the play depicted the black Carib revolt on the island of St. Vincent during the 1790s.) The African Grove Theatre was closed by the police in 1823, allegedly because of disturbances on the premises. Among its other contributions, the African Grove Theatre launched the career of the renowned Shakespearean actor Ira Aldridge, who went on to great success in Europe.

MINSTREL SHOWS

As early as the 1820s, mainly white performers in blackface portrayed African Americans on the stage in minstrel shows. The minstrel show was an early form of vaudeville that featured a series of singers, dancers, and comedians in short skits. The premise of the minstrel show was that it purported to show the world through African American eyes.

Although the minstrel shows perpetuated gross racial stereotypes, African Americans themselves began performing as minstrels after the Civil War, using the popular medium as a way of getting into show business. Charles Hicks organized the first all-black company, the Georgia Minstrels, in 1865; under a variety of names, the group enjoyed considerable success at home and abroad over the next two decades. Despite the harm done by minstrelsy to the image of the African American, minstrel shows provided black performers with essential experience in all aspects of show business, including composing, choreography, and management.

THE EMERGENCE OF THE BLACK THEATER

African American theater made a great leap forward in 1890, when Sam T. Jack organized the *Creole Show,* a revue built around 16 African American female dancers. Organized along the lines of a minstrel show but devoid of any derogatory content, the *Creole Show* ran for six seasons in Chicago and New York, including a yearlong run at the Chicago World's Fair in 1893. John W. Isham, the white advance agent for the *Creole Show,* made his own mark as a producer in 1896 with *Oriental America,* the first Broadway show with an African American cast.

In 1898, Bob Cole created the musical comedy *A Trip to Coontown,* which (despite its title) made a complete break from the minstrel tradition. The first production completely organized by African Americans, *A Trip to Coontown* was also the first to have a recognizable plot and a credible cast of characters. It spawned a host of successful African American productions on Broadway. These included the Bert Williams–George Walker vehicles *In Dahomey* (1903), *In Abyssinia* (1906), and *Bandana Land* (1907), and a pair of operettas created by Bob Cole and J. Rosamond Johnson—*The Shoo-Fly Regiment* (1906) and *The Red Moon* (1908).

THEATER IN HARLEM

Because of the declining health (and eventual deaths in 1911) of Robert Cole and George Walker, and because of Bert Williams's switch to vaudeville, black performers were absent from the Broadway stage between 1910 and 1917. Also, Harlem, where the black population had begun to grow significantly, was becoming the favored area for black theater production. For the first time in New York, African American performers appeared before black audiences, thereby allowing the performers a far wider range of expression. (Chicago's Pekin Theatre, which opened in 1907, had previously established a mainly African American clientele.)

Two Harlem theaters—the Lincoln (135th Street and Lenox Avenue, opened 1910) and the Lafayette (132nd Street and Seventh Avenue, opened 1912)—developed their own stock companies. The first major production was the Lafayette's *Darktown Follies* (1913), which also attracted white audiences from downtown, beginning a trend that continued throughout the 1920s. Other noteworthy productions by the Lafayette Players included *Madame X*, *The Servant in the House*, *On Trial*, *The Love of Choo Chin*, and *Within the Law*.

Among the major events of this period was the 1917 appearance of the Colored Players at Madison Square Garden in three dramatic one-act plays (by a white playwright, Ridgely Torrance) dealing with African American themes: *The Rider of Dreams*, *Granny Maumee*, and *Simon the Cyrenian*. According to James Weldon Johnson, "It was the first time anywhere in the United States for Negro actors in the dramatic theatre to command the serious attention of the critics and of the general press and public."

THE HARLEM RENAISSANCE

During the Harlem Renaissance era (1920–1930), African American musicals returned to the Broadway stage. The team of Eubie Blake and Noble Sissle, who produced *Shuffle Along* in 1921 and followed up with *Chocolate Dandies* in 1924, led the resurgence. Other notable musicals of the decade included *Dixie to Broadway* (1925), *Africana* and *Rang Tang* (1927), *Keep Shuffling* (1928), *Blackbirds of 1928* and *Hot Chocolates* (1929). In the realm of serious drama, the Ethiopian Art Players (which included a number of actors previously from the Lafayette Players) made their Broadway debut in 1923. These players enacted a variety of works, including Oscar Wilde's *Salome*, William Shakespeare's *Comedy of Errors*, and *The Chip Woman's Fortune*, an original work by Willis Richardson, the first black playwright to have a nonmusical play on Broadway. Another serious black drama was Em Jo Basshe's *Earth*, produced by the New Playwrights in 1927. The period also featured a number of plays by white dramatists, which focused on African American themes and provided opportunities for black actors and actresses: *The Emperor Jones* (1920) and *All God's Chillun' Got Wings* (1924) by Eugene O'Neill; *In Abraham's Bosom* by Paul Green (1926); *Porgy* by Dorothy and Du Bose Heyward (1927); *Show Boat* by Oscar Hammerstein II (1927); and *Green Pastures* by Marc Connelly (1930).

THE GREAT DEPRESSION AND THE FEDERAL THEATER PROJECT

The onset of the Great Depression took a severe toll on independent black theaters. The situation did not improve until 1935, when the (Franklin) Roosevelt Administration launched the Federal Theater Project (FTP), which employed a total of 13,000 men and women during its four years of operation. The FTP's Negro Unit operated in 22 cities and employed more than 850 African Americans, many new to the theater. In New York, the Negro Unit's efforts were centered in the Lafayette Theater, which launched its first FTP production with Frank Wilson's *Talk Together Chillun* and followed with his *Conjur Man Dies*. The Lafayette came to be highly regarded for the quality of its costume, lighting, and carpentry departments, as well as the professionalism of its backstage crew and house staff. In Chicago, the FTP enjoyed success with Theodore Ward's *Big White Fog* and *The Swing Mikado,* and adaptation of the popular Gilbert and Sullivan operetta.

The political currents of the era gave rise to a number of independent productions: These included *Stevedore,* an exploration of racial conflict on the waterfront of a Southern city, and *They Shall Not Die,* a commentary on the Scottsboro case. In addition, the great African American writer Langston Hughes founded three theaters devoted to the production of his own and others' plays: the Harlem Suitcase Theater, the Negro Art Theatre in Chicago, and the Skyloft Players in Los Angeles. Hughes's play *Mulatto,* in which the illegitimate son of a plantation owner demands his birthright, enjoyed a substantial run on Broadway in 1935.

AMERICAN NEGRO THEATER

In 1940, Abram Hill and Frederick O'Neal founded the American Negro Theater (ANT) in order to fill the gap created by the demise of the FTP. The ANT was founded as a cooperative, with all members sharing in the expenses and the profits—members who worked in non-ANT productions agreed to contribute 2 percent of their earnings to ANT. By 1942, Hill and O'Neal were able to establish the ANT Theater in the 135th Street branch of the New York Public Library. In all, ANT produced 19 plays, 12 of them original works.

ANT enjoyed its greatest success with *Anna Lucasta,* adapted from a Philip Yordan play about a Polish American family. After moving to Broadway, *Anna Lucasta* played for 957 performances, still a record for a serious African American drama. However, only a few of the actors from the Harlem company took part in the Broadway run, causing friction within the company. After 1945, ANT also became less community oriented and produced only works by established playwrights. Though the company disbanded by 1949, it served as the training ground for a new generation of outstanding African American performers, including Ruby Dee, Sidney Poitier, and Harry Belafonte.

BLACK ARTS MOVEMENT

By the 1950s, serious African American dramas had won acceptance in the mainstream theater, most notably in the case of Louis Peterson's *Take a Giant Step* (1953) and Lorraine Hansberry's *Raisin in the Sun* (1959). By the 1960s, a new generation of African American artists—in a host of disciplines—focused on the affirmation of a distinct racial and cultural identity, with strong overtones of black nationalism and political radicalism. In the theater, the Black Arts Movement was most prominently represented by the New Lafayette Theatre (directed by Robert Macbeth) and by Douglas Turner Ward's Negro Ensemble Company.

In other regions of the country, the movement manifested itself in theater groups such as the Free Southern Theater (Jackson, Mississippi), Black Arts South (New Orleans), the Ebony Talent Theater and KUUMBA (Chicago), Black Arts/West (San Francisco), the Black House Theater (Oakland), and Concept-East Theater (Detroit). Theaters associated with the Black Arts Movement presented groundbreaking works by Amiri Baraka (formerly LeRoi Jones), Ed Bullins, Charles Fuller, Douglas Turner Ward, Lonnie Elder, Adrienne Kennedy, and others. In the opinion of most commentators, the Black Arts Movement as a distinct cultural phenomenon began to ebb in the mid-1970s, after creating a new era in African American cultural history.

1980s AND 1990s—A PLURALITY OF VOICES

In the 1980s and 1990s, no single movement or ideology emerged to capture the spirit of the era in the way the Black Arts Movement did in the 1960s and 1970s. Instead, African American playwrights have written about a variety of topics, as the venues in which their work is performed become increasingly diverse and mainstream.

A good example of this new accessibility can be seen in the career of playwright and director George Wolfe. In his own plays, Wolfe has dealt with black identity (*Up for Grabs*) and satirized stereotypical views about African Americans (even those views held by African Americans themselves, as in his *The Colored Museum*). By the mid-1980s, Wolfe's plays were being produced at the New York Public Theater, a major off-Broadway venue. By 1990, Wolfe had become director of the Public Theater, where he has continued that organization's tradition of showing innovative work by playwrights and actors of all racial and ethnic groups. He has also helped revive interest in black dance, specifically tap dance, with his production of Savion Glover's *Bring in 'da Noise, Bring in 'da Funk*, for which Wolfe won a Tony Award for directing in 1996. Wolfe has also directed other productions, such as *Angels in America*, a play about gay life in the United States in the 1980s, the subject of which is not specifically African American.

August Wilson and Anna Deavere Smith are two other notable playwrights of this fin de siècle era. In plays such as *Fences* (1987) and *The Piano Lesson* (1990), Wilson has explored how racism, social change, and family histories collide in black families. In her plays, Smith examines the complexities of racial identity and the ways in which members of different racial and ethnic groups understand, and misunderstand, one another. This theme is especially apparent in her *Twilight: Los Angeles, 1992*, a look at some of the individuals caught up in the drama immediately before, during, and after the Los Angeles riot of 1992.

MILESTONES IN AFRICAN AMERICAN DANCE

TRADITIONAL AFRICAN DANCES IN THE AMERICAS

Dance has been important socially and ceremonially in the lives of African peoples. In Africa, dignitaries have been welcomed to villages and capitals by dance ceremonies, and ordinary villagers have danced to the accompaniment of traditional drums, flutes, marimbas, and stringed instruments. Often the musicians have sung about heroes, mythical events, and deities as the villagers danced. These dance forms were carried by African slaves to the Americas, where the forms survived in areas containing proportionately large concentrations of African Americans.

BATUQUE (SAMBA)

An Afro-Brazilian dance, the *batuque* (also known as the samba) had its roots in the Congo-Angola region of Africa. In colonial Brazil, the dance derived its name from the *batuques*, Sunday gatherings in which Africans celebrated their ancestral traditions. The *batuque* was performed in 2/4 time at a lively tempo, and singing, hand clapping, drumming, or other percussion sounds (made by striking pieces of wood or iron) often accompanied it. Typically, one to three soloists would lead the performance, dancing within a circle of spectators. In time the *batuque* developed two separate traditions: a more syncopated version that prevailed in the countryside, and an urban variation featuring a less varied beat. By the 1920s the urban version, centered in the Afro-Brazilian neighborhoods of Rio de Janeiro, had established itself as the standard samba. During the 1930s, an assimilated form of this urban samba became a popular ballroom dance throughout the Americas. The original tradition survives today in Rio de Janeiro. The samba is the centerpiece of Rio's annual Carnival, in which a large number of *escolas de samba* (samba schools) compete for supremacy.

BUCK DANCE

Popular in the American South, the buck dance was similar to the *chica* (see the subsequent description). During the 19th century, the buck dance was combined with the pigeon wing (described later) to create the classic tap-dance step known as the buck and wing.

CAKEWALK

The cakewalk originated in the American South. In slavery days, the cakewalk was often a means of mocking the pretentious refinement of slave owners and their families. When adapted for the stage, the cakewalk (with contestants often vying for a cake) evolved into a series of high-stepping movements executed with the head held high and the body tilted slightly backward. The famous black show business team of Williams and Walker made the cakewalk popular in 1896, during their engagement at Koster and Bial's in New York, and it soon became the rage of high society. The dance also took Europe by storm after *In Dahomey* (starring Williams and Walker) opened in London in 1903.

CALENDA

Popular throughout the West Indies, the *calenda* was performed by two parallel lines of dancers, one male and one female. Following the musical direction of a drummer, the two lines would initially approach to within two or three feet of one another and then draw back. Finally, the dancers would come together until their thighs collided; in some variations, the dancers would lock arms and pirouette while continuing to strike thighs.

CHICA

Probably of Congolese origin, the *chica* was prevalent throughout the Windward Islands and Santo Domingo. The dance was primarily performed by a female dancer, who would move only the lower half of her body while holding the ends of a kerchief or the sides of her skirt. Sometimes a male dancer would approach her and mirror her movements.

CONGA

Afro-Cuban in origin, the conga had its roots in the *congadas*, assemblies in which Africans on plantations would elect kings, queens, and other officials to govern the internal affairs of the community. Some *congadas* featured royal processions and ceremonies in which courtiers and subjects would parade before the king and queen, duplicating traditional practices observed in the various African kingdoms. Transplanted to the cities, the conga developed into a street procession celebrated during festivals and carnivals. Participants would move to a 2/4-march rhythm, accenting every second beat. This traditional conga was considerably smoother than the exaggerated "1-2-3-kick" routine of the modern ballroom version.

JONKONNU (JOHN CANOE)

The *Jonkonnu* dates back to slavery days, when costumed dancers would appear around Christmastime throughout the West Indies. This dance follows traditions that may have originated among Ewe-speaking peoples of West Africa, whose word for "sorcerer" is *dzonkonu*. Typically, a group of female dancers (often wearing animal masks) would be led by a man brandishing a wooden sword and wearing an elaborate headdress (known as a *Jonkonnu*) in the form of a model house. The dancers would move in time to the music of a drum known as a *gumbé*. The *Jonkonnu* tradition is still very much alive: Christmas festivals throughout the West Indies feature *Gombey* (*gumbé*) drummers and dancers costumed as the Cowhead, the Horsehead, the Veiled King and Queen, and other supernatural creatures.

JUBA

The *juba* (based on the African *giouba*) was a competitive dance in which participants would demonstrate all their skills, moving in a counterclockwise circle and rhythmically shuffling their feet. Typically, a woman would begin the dance and then draw a male partner from the group of onlookers. Once he joined the dance, the man would try to equal or exceed the woman's feats. Eventually, one of the pair would admit to being outdanced and drop out, whereupon a new challenger would come forward. The spectators would keep time by clapping, stamping their feet, or slapping their thighs ("patting *juba*").

PIGEON WING

Dancers performing the pigeon wing in the South would imitate the movements of the bird, flapping their arms and legs in the air while holding their necks rigid.

RUMBA

Originating in Afro-Cuban festivals, the rumba was danced in 2/4 time, with emphasis on movement of the body rather than the feet. It was accompanied by complex cross-rhythms created by drums and other percussion instruments. In a less authentic form, the rumba became a popular ballroom dance throughout the Americas during the 1930s.

STAGE DANCE

Because African Americans were largely excluded from classical dance during the 19th and early 20th centuries, they concentrated instead on tap dance and show dancing. Tap dance (also known as jazz dance) traces its origins back to the early colonial era, when enslaved Africans had extensive social contact with Irish and Scottish indentured servants. Eventually, the

African-derived *juba* style, which emphasized relatively flat-footed rhythmic movement, combined with the techniques of European jigs and clog dances, which featured hopping, stomping, and precise heel-and-toe work.

Following the lead of William Henry Lane (Master Juba) in the 1840s, African American performers began to define tap dance as an art form, introducing a variety of new steps and employing many of the same percussive syncopations that also underlay the development of jazz. Early tap dancers often danced on boards or wore clogs, hobnailed boots, and hollow-soled shoes; when dancing in soft shoes, they frequently used sand or a similar substance to create a rhythmic sound. During the late 19th century, tap dancing became a standard feature of black musicals such as the *Creole Show*. Performers such as Williams and Walker, Bill "Bojangles" Robinson, and John Bubbles further popularized the art in the early 20th century. Apart from a period of decline during the 1950s and 1960s, tap dance has remained a vital part of modern culture. As of 1997, 42 U.S. cities and 12 foreign countries (including South Africa) observed Tap Dance Day (May 25, Bill Robinson's birthday) by staging celebrations led by local tap-dance groups.

Another expression of African American dance can be found in musicals presented by African American companies in the early part of the 20th century. Bert Williams and George Walker were not only expert actors, but dancers, too, as they demonstrated in their musicals *In Abyssinia* and *In Dahomey*. The Charleston, one of the favorite popular dances of the 1920s, was first introduced in another musical, *Liza*, in 1922.

The first African American classical dance performances were presented in the 1930s. Unlike the classical pieces performed by segregated white companies, these performances were largely based on African and African American dance traditions. The first major black classical dance company was Hemsley Winfield's New Negro Art Theater Dance Group, which began performing in New York during the early 1930s. Winfield's 1931 New York production, *The First Negro Concert in America*, presented dances based on African themes.

In 1934, Eugene Von Grona created a dance troupe by running an ad for aspiring dancers in the *Amsterdam News*; Von Grona's American Negro Ballet made its debut three years later at Harlem's Lafayette Theater. Also in 1934, the Sierra Leone émigré dancer Asadata Dafora presented *Kyunkor*, a program of African dance, in New York. These programs influenced the next wave of African American dancers and choreographers: people such as Katherine Dunham and Pearl Primus, whose modern-dance troupes were popular from the 1940s through the 1960s.

BALLET AND MODERN DANCE

Two of the early pioneers in modern dance and ballet were Katherine Dunham and Pearl Primus. Interestingly, both were trained in anthropology before they became dancers and choreographers. Dunham's company, founded in the late 1930s, performed modern-dance styles that were based on interpretations of African American folk dances. Primus choreographed and danced in many works at various venues during the 1940s and 1950s. Dunham's company folded in the 1960s, but she continued teaching and choreographing. Primus also later worked as a dance teacher, first in Liberia, then back in New York.

> We weren't pushing Black is beautiful. We just showed it.
>
> Katherine Dunham, quoted in *American Visions* (1987)

The Los Angeles–based first Negro Classic Ballet began performing in 1948 and moved to New York in 1956, when it merged with the newly created New York Negro Ballet. The combined company enjoyed critical acclaim—notably during a 1957 tour of the British Isles—but dissolved in 1960 due to lack of funding. A similar fate befell Aubrey Hitchens's Negro Dance Theater, which performed from 1953 to 1955. Though short-lived, these pioneering companies provided training for a number of outstanding African American dancers, many of whom went on to successful careers with European companies: Among them were Sylvester Campbell (Netherlands National Ballet), Gene Sagan (Marseilles Ballet), Roland Fraser (Cologne Ballet), and Raven Wilkenson (Ballets Russes de Monte Carlo).

Opportunities for African American dancers in the United States began to increase with the growth of the civil rights movement and the advent of the Black Arts Movement. Growing pride in African American identity and heritage helped inspire the creation of groups such as the Alvin Ailey American Dance Theater, the Dayton Contemporary Dance Company (Ohio), Dance Theater of Harlem, Philadelphia Dance Company, Garth Fagan's Bucket Dance (Rochester, New York), the Cleo Parker Robinson Dance Ensemble (Denver), and the Joel Hall Dancers (Chicago). In the ensuing years, these companies and others have provided unprecedented opportunities for African American dancers and choreographers, as well as making unique contributions to American dance.

BROADWAY'S FIRST BLACK DRAMA

When the Ethiopian Art Theatre presented *The Chip Woman's Fortune* at the Frazee Theatre on May 17, 1923, it was the first performance of a nonmusical play by an African American author on Broadway. Written by Willis Richardson (1899–1977), *The Chip Woman's Fortune* explores the dilemma of a humble woman who has amassed some hard-earned savings to help her jailed son; in the course of the play, she receives an appeal for help from her suddenly unemployed landlord and his invalid wife, and she must make a heartbreaking choice. Though well received by the critics, the play could not surmount the unfavorable reaction to its two companion pieces, *Salome* and *A Comedy of Errors*, and the entire production closed after a brief run. Richardson went on to a distinguished career as a playwright, director, and educator.

THE CHITLIN CIRCUIT

During the 1920s, many shows directed at African American audiences were presented through the Theater Owners Booking Association (TOBA), which served more than 80 theaters in Philadelphia, Chicago, and cities throughout the South and the Midwest. Though it provided opportunities for many African American performers and theater workers, TOBA was often condemned for paying performers poorly. Because of its tendency to present low-quality material, TOBA was also nicknamed the Chitlin Circuit. TOBA was largely defunct by 1930, but touring African American theatrical companies have remained in existence. They continue to perform for black audiences in community-based theaters, presenting plays with immediately recognizable characters and situations, such as *My Grandmother Prayed for Me*, *Mama I Want to Sing*, and *Beauty Shop*. The role of these productions in African American culture has been assessed by Henry Louis Gates Jr. in "The Chitlin Circuit" (*New Yorker*, February 3, 1997).

VOODOO MACBETH

On April 14, 1936, the Lafayette Theater was the scene of dazzling opening-night excitement as the Federal Theater Project's Negro Unit presented its all-black version of Shakespeare's *Macbeth*. Set in 19th-century Haiti with a cast of 100 (95 of them amateurs recruited from the community), the production starred Jack Carter as Macbeth, Edna Thomas as Lady Macbeth, and Canada Lee as Banquo. (It also marked the directorial debut of 20-year-old Orson Welles.) The three witches were cast as voodoo priestesses, and a group of drummers from Sierra Leone helped create an evocative atmosphere. *Macbeth* ran to sold-out houses for 10 weeks at the Lafayette (ticket prices ranged from (15 to 40 cents), moved to Broadway for another 10 weeks, and then toured the Northeast and the Midwest. The success of the production inspired similar efforts by other Negro Unit companies, such as a production of Aristophanes's *Lysistrata* in Seattle.

UPTOWN AT THE APOLLO

The Apollo Theater, the legendary African American performing-arts venue, opened in 1913 at 253 West 125th Street. Originally known as Hurtig and Seamon's Music Hall, it presented white burlesque and vaudeville acts to white audiences. The theater changed its name to the Apollo in 1933 and soon began showcasing jazz bands led by Duke Ellington, Lionel Hampton, Count Basie, and other greats. The Apollo's famous Amateur Night began at this time, enabling aspiring artists to perform for demanding audiences every Wednesday from 11:00 P.M. until midnight. Though many contestants were booed off the stage, future stars such as Ella Fitzgerald, Sarah Vaughan, and Pearl Bailey launched their careers with Amateur Night triumphs. As rhythm and blues replaced jazz during the 1950s, the Apollo presented James Brown, Sam Cooke, Jackie Wilson, and other favorites. Though the Apollo's financial fortunes began to waver during the 1970s, it was declared a National Historic Landmark in 1983 and underwent a $22 million renovation in 1988. In 1991, the theater achieved a new level of stability when it was taken over by a nonprofit community-based organization and became the focal point of 125th Street's economic development project.

"HIP-HOP UNDER THE BIG TOP"

Established in Atlanta in 1994, the UniverSoul Circus is the first all-black circus in more than a hundred years. Performing in a 2,000-seat tent to the accompaniment of rap, soul, R&B, and gospel music, UniverSoul aims to celebrate African American culture, as well as to entertain. In addition to ringmaster Cal Dupree (co-owner with Cedric Walker), the acts include the King Charles Unicycle Troop, a contortionist, a magician, trapeze artists, and Denise Payne, the first African American female clown. Audiences have been known to take part by singing and clapping in time to the music, and there is often a dance party in the ring after the performance.

TONY AWARD WINNERS

ACTOR (DRAMATIC)

1969   James Earl Jones, *The Great White Hope*

1975   John Kani, *Sizwe Banze Is Dead;* Winston Ntshona, *The Island*

1987   James Earl Jones, *Fences*

SUPPORTING OR FEATURED ACTOR (DRAMATIC)

1982   Zakes Mokae, *Master Harold . . . and the Boys*

1992   Laurence Fishburne, *Two Trains Running*

1994   Jeffrey Wright, *Angels in America*

ACTOR (MUSICAL)

1970   Cleavon Little, *Purlie*

1973   Ben Vereen, *Pippin*

1982   Ben Harvey, *Dreamgirls*

1992   Gregory Hines, *Jelly's Last Jam*

SUPPORTING OR FEATURED ACTOR (MUSICAL)

1954   Harry Belafonte, *Almanac*

1975   Ted Rose, *The Wiz*

1981   Hinton Battle, *Sophisticated Ladies*

1982   Cleavant Derricks, *Dreamgirls*

1983   Charles "Honi" Coles, *My One and Only*

1984   Hinton Battle, *The Tap Dance Kid*

1991   Hinton Battle, *Miss Saigon*

SUPPORTING OR FEATURED ACTRESS (DRAMATIC)

1977   Trazana Beverley, *for colored girls who have considered suicide/when the rainbow is enuf*

1987   Mary Alice, *Fences*

1988   L. Scott Caldwell, *Joe Turner's Come and Gone*

ACTRESS (MUSICAL)

1962   Diahann Carroll, *No Strings*

1968   Leslie Uggams, *Hallelujah, Baby*

1974   Virginia Capers, *Raisin*

1982   Jennifer Holliday, *Dreamgirls*

1989   Ruth Brown, *Black and Blue*

SUPPORTING OR FEATURED ACTRESS (MUSICAL)

1950   Juanita Hall, *South Pacific*

1968   Lillian Hayman, *Hallelujah, Baby*

1970   Melba Moore, *Purlie*

1975   Dee Dee Bridgewater, *The Wiz*

1977   Delores Hall, *Your Arms Too Short to Box with God*

1978   Nell Carter, *Ain't Misbehavin'*

1992   Tonya Pinkins, *Jelly's Last Jam*

1996   Ann Duquesnay, *Bring in 'da Noise, Bring in 'da Funk*

DIRECTOR (DRAMA)

1987   Lloyd Richards, *Fences*

1993   George C. Wolfe, *Angels in America*

DIRECTOR (MUSICAL)

1975   Geoffrey Holder, *The Wiz*

1996   George C. Wolfe, *Bring in 'da Noise, Bring in 'da Funk*

LONGEST-RUNNING PRODUCTIONS

A number of productions created by African American artists or featuring African American performers have enjoyed significant runs on the Broadway and the off-Broadway stages. The leaders (with year of opening and number of performances) are listed as follows:

BROADWAY

The Wiz (1975)	1,672
Ain't Misbehavin' (1978)	1,604
Dreamgirls (1981)	1,521
Bring in 'da Noise, Bring in 'da Funk (1996)	1,131
Don't Bother Me, I Can't Cope (1972)	1,065
Anna Lucasta (1944)	957
Raisin (1973)	847
Sophisticated Ladies (1981)	767
Bubbling Brown Sugar (1976)	766
for colored girls . . . (1976)	742
Purlie (1970)	688
*Sarafina!*** (1988)	597
Jelly's Last Jam (1992)	569
Jamaica (1957)	558
Green Pastures (1930)	557
Raisin in the Sun (1959)	538
Fences (1987)	526
Blackbirds of 1928 (1928)	518
Shuffle Along (1921)	504
Carmen Jones (1943)	502
Eubie! (1978)	439
Your Arms Too Short to Box with God (1976)	429
Mulatto (1935)	373

** South African production.

OFF-BROADWAY

The Blacks (Les Noirs) (1961)	1,408
One Mo' Time (1979)	1,372
A Soldier's Story (1981)	481
River Niger (1973)	400
To Be Young, Gifted and Black (1969)	380
Dutchman (1964)	366
No Place to Be Somebody (1969)	312

MILESTONES IN FILM AND TELEVISION

NOTABLE FILMS FEATURING AFRICAN AMERICANS AND AFRICANS
UNITED STATES

The Autobiography of Miss Jane Pittman (TV, 1974).   Directed by John Korty. Starring Cicely Tyson, Michael Murphy, Thalmus Rasulala, Rod Perry, Josephine Premise, Joel Fluellen, Valerie O'Dell, Odetta, Barbara Chaney, and Richard Dysart. The life story of a woman who lived from slavery days into the civil rights era. Based on the novel by Ernest J. Gaines. Tyson won an Emmy Award for Best Actress, and the film itself won nine Emmys, including Best Director, Best Screenplay, and Best Special Program.

Boyz N the Hood (1991).   Directed and written by John Singleton. Starring Laurence Fishburne, Cuba Gooding Jr., Ice Cube, Morris Chestnut, Angela Bassett, Nia Long, and Tyra Ferrell. A trio of young men grow up amid the violence of South-Central Los Angeles and end up taking very different paths. Singleton was only 23 when he made this film and was nominated for Academy Awards for writing and direction. *Boyz* won the 1991 NAACP Image Awards for Best Picture and Best Screenplay and inspired a new wave of African American films.

Carmen Jones (1954).   Directed by Otto Preminger. Starring Dorothy Dandridge, Harry Belafonte, Pearl Bailey, Roy Glenn, Diahann Carroll, Brock Peters. Adapted from Bizet's opera by Oscar Hammerstein II. Dandridge plays the femme fatale role of Carmen, although her singing was dubbed by opera star Marilyn Horne. An electrifying performance by Dandridge in a role that should have established her as a major star.

Cooley High (1975).   Directed by Michael Schultz; written by Eric Monte. Starring Glynn Turman, Lawrence Hilton-Jacobs, Garrett Morris, Cynthia Davis, Christine Jones, Lynn Caridine, Norman Gibson, Sheran Smith, Corin Rogers, Maurice Leon Havis, and Joseph Carter Wilson. High school friends lose their innocence as they discover love, danger, and tragedy in 1960s Chicago.

Countdown at Kusini (1976).   Directed by Ossie Davis, who stars. Also starring Greg Morris, Ruby Dee, Tom Aldredge, Michael Ebert, Thomas Baptiste, Jab Adu, Yomi Cbileye, and Funso Adeolu. A musician becomes involved in the liberation of an African nation. Financed by the Delta Sigma Theta sorority. Cowritten by Al Freeman Jr. and producer Ladi Ladebo.

Cry, the Beloved Country (1951).   Directed by Zoltan Korda. Starring Canada Lee, Charles Carson, Sidney Poitier, Geoffrey Keen, Joyce Carey, Charles McCrae, Ribbon Dhalmini, Michael Godliffe, Lionel Ngakane, Edric Connor, Albertina Temba, and Vivien Clinton. A black South African preacher travels from his country home to the big city to find his sister; aided by a cynical white minister, he confronts the evils of racism. Written by Alan Paton and based on his best-selling novel, the film was remade in 1995 with James Earl Jones and Richard Harris in the lead roles.

Daughters of the Dust (1991).   Written and directed by Julie Dash. Starring Cora Lee Day, Kaycee Moore, Alva Rodgers, Adisa Anderson, and Barbara O. This dazzling Dash debut film is set in 1902 in the

Sea Islands off the coast of Carolina, where the Gullah people retain many of their ancestors' African traditions. Matriarch Nana Peazant welcomes her two urbanized daughters back home as the family gathers for a final reunion before moving to the mainland. Nana, who opposes the move, shares the family history and legends in hopes of keeping her children from leaving. *Daughters of the Dust* won the award for Best Cinematography at the 1991 Sundance Film Festival. Partially in Gullah dialect with English subtitles.

Do the Right Thing (1989).   Directed by Spike Lee. Starring Danny Aiello, Ossie Davis, Ruby Dee, Richard Edson, and John Turturro. A look at life in a black Brooklyn neighborhood centers on a white-owned pizza parlor. Miscommunications and misperceptions abound, eventually leading to violence on a hot summer day.

Ethnic Notions (1987).   Produced and directed by Marlon Riggs; narrated by Esther Rolle. Examining the ways in which racism is deeply interwoven into American popular culture, this documentary analyzes stereotypes from antebellum times to the present. Winner of an Emmy Award.

Hair Piece: A Film for Nappyheaded People (1982).   Written, produced, and directed by Ayoka Chenzira. This animated satire confronts myths, prejudice, and attitudes about the politics of hair texture and care in the black community.

Hollywood Shuffle (1987).   Written, produced, and directed by Robert Townsend, who also acts. Starring Keenen Ivory Wayans, Anne-Marie Johnson, Helen Martin, Paul Mooney, and Craigus R. Johnson. Townsend's self-financed debut film presents a struggling actor's satirical take on images, stereotypes, and opportunities (or the lack thereof) in the Hollywood film industry.

The Learning Tree (1969).   Written and directed by Gordon Parks, Sr., based on his book. A visually gorgeous, heartwarming coming-of-age tale of an African American youth growing up in 1920s Kansas. *The Learning Tree* was among the first films selected for the National Film Registry of the Library of Congress, which recognizes works that are "culturally, historically, or aesthetically significant."

Malcolm X (1992).   Written and directed by Spike Lee, who also acts. Starring Denzel Washington, Angela Bassett, Al Freeman Jr., Delroy Lindo, Albert Hall, and Kate Vernon. Lee's epic film biography pays tribute to America's most controversial spiritual leader and political activist. Washington's performance in the title role earned him an Academy Award nomination.

Mississippi Masala (1991).   Directed by Mira Nair. Starring Denzel Washington, Sarita Choudhury, Charles S. Dutton, and Roshan Seth. The delightful film explores forbidden romance and cultural tensions as a beautiful East Indian woman falls for a hard-working black Mississippian.

Nothing but a Man (1964).   Directed by Michael Roemer. Starring Ivan Dixon, Abbey Lincoln, Gloria Foster, Yaphet Kotto, and Julius Harris. Musical score by Motown's Holland-Dozier-Holland songwriting team. The life of a happy-go-lucky Southern railroad worker begins to change when he falls in love with a minister's daughter. Sent packing by the woman's father, the young man begins to confront his past—which includes an alcoholic father and a casual affair that produced a child—and finally resolves to take charge of his own destiny. This highly acclaimed film won the San Giorgio Prize at the 1964 Venice Film Festival.

Purple Rain (1984).   Directed by Albert Magnoli. Starring Prince, Appolonia Kotero, Clarence Williams III, Morris Day, Olga Karlatos, Jerome Benton, Des Dickerson, Billy Sparks, Brenda Bennett, and Jill Jones. This film, which made Prince a mainstream phenomenon, explores a young musician's struggles to make it in show business and to create a personal life better than that of his dysfunctional parents.

Shaft (1971).   Directed by Gordon Parks Sr. Starring Richard Roundtree, Moses Gunn, Sherry Brewer, Gwenn Mitchell, Christopher St. John, Drew Bundini Brown, Arnold Johnson, Buddy Butler, and Charles Cioffi. One of the most popular of the 1970s "blaxploitation" films, this movie tells the story of a tough private detective hired to find a crime boss's kidnapped daughter. Isaac Hayes won an Oscar for his musical score.

She's Gotta Have It (1986).   Written and directed by Spike Lee, who also acts. Starring Tracy Camilla Johns, John Canada Terrell, Tommy Redmond Hicks, Joie Lee, and Raye Dowell. A free-spirited, artistic Brooklyn woman is pressured to choose among her three very different lovers. Lee's first feature film presents a very distinctive view of African American life, culture, and sexuality.

A Soldier's Story (1984).   Directed by Norman Jewison. Starring Howard E. Rollins Jr., Adolph Caesar, Denzel Washington, Art Evans, Larry Riley, and Patti LaBelle. In 1944, a military lawyer is sent to a Louisiana army base to investigate the murder of an unpopular sergeant. Adapted by Charles Fuller and based on his Pulitzer Prize–winning play.

Sounder (1972).   Directed by Martin Ritt. Starring Cicely Tyson, Paul Winfield, Kevin Hooks, Janet MacLachlan, Taj Mahal, Eric Hooks, and Carmen Mathews. This drama, set in the 1930s, tells the moving story of a Louisiana sharecropper who is imprisoned for stealing food; in his absence, his wife holds the family together. Written by the noted playwright Lonne Elder III, based on a novel.

Sparkle (1976).   Directed by Sam O'Steen. Starring Philip Michael Thomas, Irene Cara, Lonette McKee, Tony King, Dwan Smith, Mary Alice, Dorian Harewood, Beatrice Winde, Armelia McQueen, and Paul Lambert. The growing pains, triumphs, and tragedies of three sisters who form a singing group, with a musical score by Curtis Mayfield.

Stormy Weather (1943).   Directed by Andrew L. Stone. Starring Lena Horne, Bill "Bojangles" Robinson, Fats Waller, Dooley Wilson, The Nicholas Brothers, Cab Calloway, Katherine Dunham and her Dance Troupe, Ada Brown, Nicodemus Stewart, Babe Wallace, Ernest Whitman, and Mae F. Johnson. Filled with exceptional singing and dancing, this film tells the story of a glamorous singer who sacrifices love for the sake of her career.

Sweet Sweetback's Baad Asssss Song (1971).   Written, produced, and directed by Melvin Van Peebles, who also acts. Starring Simon Chuckster, Hubert Scales, Rhetta Hughes, Mario Van Peebles, Megan Van Peebles, and John Amos. African American community residents aid and abet a Los Angeles sex-show performer after he shoots a policeman, and the fugitive himself gradually becomes politically aware. Brutally frank in its examination of racism, sexual exploitation, and the lives of ordinary African Americans, the once-controversial film has since become a classic.

Waiting to Exhale (1995).   Directed by Forest Whitaker. Starring Angela Bassett, Whitney Houston, Loretta Devine, and Lela Rochon. Based on Terry McMillan's blockbuster novel—she cowrote the screenplay and was an executive producer—the film follows four exceptional African American women as they search for love, selfhood, and the meaning of togetherness.

Watermelon Man (1970).   Directed by Melvin Van Peebles. Starring Godfrey Cambridge, Estelle Parsons, D'Urville Martin, and Mantan Moreland. A white insurance salesman awakens to find that he has turned black. Van Peebles also wrote the musical score.

INTERNATIONAL

Black Orpheus/Orfeu Negro (1959, France, Brazil).   Directed by Marcel Camus. Starring Breno Mello, Marpessa Dawn, and Lourdes De Oliveira. An Afro-Brazilian version of the tragic Greek myth of Orpheus and Eurydice, set in the sensual whirl of Brazilian Carnival. Includes electrifying sequences of samba dancing. In Portuguese with subtitles. Winner of the 1959 Academy Award for Best Foreign Film.

The Harder They Come (1973, Jamaica).   Directed by Perry Henzell. Starring Jimmy Cliff, Carl Bradshaw, and Janet Barkley. A poor Jamaican country boy, frustrated while trying to become a singer, turns outlaw. This cult favorite has a brilliant soundtrack and unsparingly depicts the contrasting wealth and poverty of Jamaican society.

Rockers (1978, Jamaica).   Directed by Theodoros Bafaloukos. Starring Gregory Isaccs, Robbie Shakespeare, and others. A drummer rallies his Rastafarian brethren to hunt for his stolen motorcycle, and the men discover the intricacies of friendship, loyalty, and self-knowledge; exceptional soundtrack.

Sarafina! (1992, South Africa).   Directed by James Roodt. Starring Whoopi Goldberg, Leleti Khumalo, Miriam Makeba, and John Kani. This adaptation of the hit Broadway musical tells the story of a beloved schoolteacher who presents her students with ideas and truths not sanctioned by the apartheid regime.

Sugar Cane Alley (1984, France).   Written and directed by Euzhan Palcy. Starring Garry Cadenat and Darling Legitimus. Set in Martinique in the 1930s. With his grandmother's help, a young boy wins a scholarship, which allows him to escape a life of poverty and ignorance. Palcy's debut feature film, it is stunningly beautiful and emotionally powerful.

Xala (1974, Senegal).   Directed by Ousmane Sembène. Starring Tierno Leye, Seune Samb, Younouss Syee, Miriam Niang, Dieynaba Niang, and Fatim Diagne. A wealthy businessman takes a very young woman as his third wife and is cursed with impotence by his other wives.

AFRICAN AMERICAN ACADEMY AWARD WINNERS

1939   Best Supporting Actress: Hattie McDaniel, *Gone with the Wind*

1963   Best Leading Actor: Sidney Poitier, *Lilies of the Field*

1982   Best Supporting Actor: Louis Gossett Jr., *An Officer and a Gentleman*

1989   Best Supporting Actor: Denzel Washington, *Glory*

1990   Best Supporting Actress: Whoopi Goldberg, *Ghost*

1996   Best Supporting Actor: Cuba Gooding Jr., *Jerry Maguire*

NOTABLE TELEVISION SERIES FEATURING AFRICAN AMERICANS

The Arsenio Hall Show. This syndicated show, which aired from 1989 to 1994, was the first major late-night talk show hosted by an African American. Hall brought a youthful, urban flavor to the airwaves while giving major exposure to African American entertainers, sports figures, and celebrities.

Beulah. This ABC situation comedy aired from 1950 to 1953 and was the first show to feature an African American in a title role. Centering on the character of Beulah, the popular maid who began as a supporting character on radio's Fibber McGee and Molly in 1944, the show was a hit with viewers. The former blues singer and stage performer Ethel Waters created the TV character, followed by Louise Beavers. Percy Harris played Beulah's beau, and Butterfly McQueen (of *Gone with the Wind* fame) played Beulah's best friend. Beulah finally went off the air when Ms. Beavers decided to leave the show.

The Cosby Show. Touted as "the show that saved NBC," this gentle sitcom was the number-one TV show during the mid-1980s. It featured the upscale Huxtable family of New York, with actor/comedian Bill Cosby as the wise patriarch and Phylicia Rashad as his wife. Like the real-life Cosbys, the Huxtables had five children—four girls and a boy—and shared a home full of laughter, love, music, and art. *The Cosby Show* appealed to viewers of all ethnic groups and presented a portrait of African American family life that was both upbeat and believable.

A Different World. A spin-off of the top-rated *Cosby Show*, this sitcom featured Denise Huxtable (Lisa Bonet) at the fictional historically black Hillman College. After a slow start, the show was revamped and went on to become a huge hit. Exterior scenes were shot at Spelman and Morehouse colleges in Atlanta, and the producers often consulted with faculty, staff, and students at those and other black colleges to ensure the show's authenticity.

The Flip Wilson Show. This show aired from 1970 to 1974 on NBC, putting comedian Flip Wilson on the map as the first African American performer to achieve major popularity as host of his own variety hour. *The Flip Wilson Show* was the first successful black TV series of the 1970s and the first successful black variety series in the history of TV. During its first two seasons, the show ranked second in the ratings among all programs. Wilson's old-style ethnic characters aroused some controversy in the African American community, with critics arguing that the show represented a throwback to *Amos 'n' Andy* or minstrel humor.

Frank's Place. This CBS sitcom aired from 1987 to 1988, with *WKRP in Cincinnati* veteran Tim Reid and his wife, Daphne Maxwell Reid. The show offered a mellow, offbeat look at a spicy mix of eccentric characters in a small Creole restaurant in New Orleans. Though the TV critics loved *Frank's Place*, the network had trouble developing a coherent marketing strategy—just as African Americans were beginning to tune in, the show was canceled due to poor ratings.

Gabriel's Fire. This moody, introspective drama aired from 1990 to 1992 on ABC. The renowned actor James Earl Jones was cast as Gabriel Bird, a bitter ex-cop imprisoned for life after shooting his white police partner to stop the man from killing an innocent mother and child. A sympathetic white female takes an interest in Bird's case and helps spring him from prison, after which she convinces him to join her firm as an investigator. Madge Sinclair starred as Empress Josephine, Bird's close friend and love interest, and Dylan Walsh and Richard Crenna rounded out the cast. *Gabriel's Fire* was well received by critics, but the network felt that audiences were not warming to its complex emotional atmosphere. In 1991, the show was renamed *Pros & Cons* and given a more upbeat tone, which did not appeal to either critics or viewers.

Get Christie Love! Airing on ABC during the 1974–1975 season, this short-lived phenomenon featured Teresa Graves as a karate-kicking member of the Los Angeles Police Department and the first black female cop on TV. Graves, an alumna of Rowan and Martin's *Laugh-In*, brought a new image of African American womanhood to the small screen.

In Living Color. This hugely successful comedy/variety show aired from 1990 to 1994, bringing recognition—and African American audiences—to the Fox network. The brainchild of Keenen Ivory Wayans, with a dynamic ensemble cast featuring Kim, Damon, Marlon, and Shawn Wayans and a slew of other young talents, *In Living Color* featured biting satirical parodies of movies, TV series, commercials, celebrities, black stereotypes, and people in the news.

Julia. Airing on NBC from 1968 to 1971, this was the first TV series starring an African American woman since *Beulah*. It was also the first time an African American woman starred in her own comedy series in a prestigious role—that is, not as a maid or a secondary character. Actress Diahann Carroll played a widowed nurse (and the mother of a charming young son) who worked for a benevolent (but cranky) white doctor. Though the show did well in the ratings, it was criticized for placing black characters into an antiseptic, white, middle-class environment when issues such as civil rights, Black Power, student unrest, and urban rioting were making headlines in the real world.

Living Single. Airing on the Fox network since 1993, *Living Single* is the first TV series conceived, written, and produced by an African American woman (Yvette Lee Bowser). This urban sitcom features a quartet of female friends (Queen Latifah, Kim Coles, Kim Fields Freeman, and Erica Alexander). T. C. Carson and John Henton play the women's male neighbors, friends, and love interests. When Fox announced that it was canceling the show in 1997, viewers protested in such numbers that network officials granted *Living Single* a reprieve.

Room 222. Filmed on location at Los Angeles High School (with many real-life students as extras), this hit ran from 1969 to 1974 on ABC. One of the first attempts to deal with the problems of young black and white Americans coming of age together, the show struck a chord during a politically restless era and won several awards. Stars Lloyd Haynes, Denise Nichols, Michael Constantine, Eric Laneuville, and Karen Valentine portrayed teachers who tackled tough issues such as prejudice, drugs, and dropouts. The show was also significant in that Haynes and Nichols, both African Americans, were portrayed as substantial characters.

EMMY AWARD WINNERS

OUTSTANDING COMEDY SERIES

1985   *The Cosby Show*
1990   *In Living Color* (Keenen Ivory Wayans, creator and producer)

OUTSTANDING LEAD ACTOR IN A DRAMA SERIES

1966   Bill Cosby, *I Spy*
1967   Bill Cosby, *I Spy*
1991   James Earl Jones, *Gabriel's Fire*
1998   Andre Braugher, *Homicide: Life on the Street*

OUTSTANDING SUPPORTING ACTOR IN A COMEDY, VARIETY, OR MUSIC SERIES

1979   Robert Guillaume, *Soap*
1985   Robert Guillaume, *Benson*

OUTSTANDING SUPPORTING ACTOR IN A MINISERIES OR SPECIAL

1991   James Earl Jones, *Heatwave*

OUTSTANDING LEAD ACTRESS IN A COMEDY SERIES

1981   Isabel Sanford, *The Jeffersons*

OUTSTANDING SUPPORTING ACTRESS IN A DRAMA SERIES

1984   Alfre Woodard, *Hill Street Blues*
1991   Madge Sinclair, *Gabriel's Fire*
1993   Mary Alice, *I'll Fly Away*

OUTSTANDING GUEST PERFORMER IN A DRAMA SERIES

1987   Alfre Woodard, *L.A. Law*
1993   Laurence Fishburne, *Tribeca*

OUTSTANDING SUPPORTING ACTRESS IN A MINISERIES OR SPECIAL

1991   Ruby Dee, *Decoration Day*
1994   Cicely Tyson, *Oldest Living Confederate Widow Tells All*

OUTSTANDING LEAD ACTRESS IN A COMEDY OR DRAMA SPECIAL

1974   Cicely Tyson, *The Autobiography of Miss Jane Pittman*

1997   Alfre Woodard, *Miss Evers' Boys*

OUTSTANDING LEAD ACTRESS IN A MINISERIES OR SPECIAL

1991   Lynn Whitfield, *The Josephine Baker Story*

OUTSTANDING DIRECTING IN A DRAMA SERIES

1986   Georg Stanford Brown, *Cagney and Lacey*

1990   Thomas Carter, *Equal Justice*

1991   Thomas Carter, *Equal Justice*

1992   Eric Laneuville, *I'll Fly Away*

OUTSTANDING VARIETY, MUSIC, OR COMEDY SPECIAL

1969   *The Bill Cosby Special*

1997   Chris Rock, *Bring the Pain*

PERFORMING-ARTS ORGANIZATIONS

African-American Drama Company of California
195 Ney Street
San Francisco, CA 94112
415-333-2232

African American Performing Arts
1332 Morris Road, SE
Washington, DC 20020
202-610-1571

African Continuum Theater Coalition
410 Eighth Street, NW
Washington, DC 20004
202-783-6547

African Heritage Center for African Dance and
    Music
4018 Minnesota Avenue, NE
Washington, DC 20019
202-399-5252

Afrikan American Studio Theater Company
3944 Chalmers Street

Detroit, MI 48215
313-885-5222

Afrikan Poetry Theater
176-03 Jamaica Avenue
Jamaica, NY 11432
718-532-3312

Afro-American Children's Theater
345 N. College Street
Charlotte, NC 28202
704-372-7410

Afro-One Dance, Drama, and Drum Theater
Park Plaza Mall, Route 130 South
Willingboro, NJ 08046
609-871-8340

Alliance for Community Theaters
P.O. Box 50575
New Orleans, LA 70150
504-595-8411

Alvin Ailey American Dance Theater
Dance Theater Foundation, Inc.
211 W. 61st Street, 3rd Floor
New York, NY 10023
212-767-0590

Andrew Cacho African Drummers and Dancers
P.O. Box 15282
Washington, DC 20003
202-889-0350

Artists Doing Business Worldwide
874 Brooklyn Avenue
Brooklyn, NY 11206
718-693-1274

Audience Development Committee
P.O. Box 30, Manhattanville Station
New York, NY 10027
212-368-9606

Ballethnic Dance Company/Ballethnic Academy
of Dance
P.O. Box 7749
Atlanta, GA 30357
404-762-1416

Billie Holiday Theater
1368 Fulton Street
Brooklyn, NY 11216
718-636-0919

Black Actors Network
1680 Vine Street
Los Angeles, CA 90028
213-962-4408

Black Awareness in Television
13217 Livernois
Detroit, MI 48238
313-931-3427

Black Ensemble Theater
4520 N. Beacon Street
Chicago, IL 60640
312-769-4451

Black Experience Ensemble
5 Homestead Avenue
Albany, NY 12203
518-457-5651

Black Repertory Company
634 N. Grand, 10th Floor, Suite F
St. Louis, MO 63103
314-534-3807

Black Spectrum Theater Company
Roy Wilkins Park of Southern Queens
119th Avenue and Merrick Boulevard
Jamaica, NY 11434
718-723-1800

Black Theater Troupe
333 E. Portland Street
Phoenix, AZ 85004
602-258-8128

Charles Moore Dance Theater
1043 President Street
Brooklyn, NY 11225
718-587-1122

Chicago City Theater Company/Joel Hall Dancers
1511 West Berwyn Avenue
Chicago, IL 60640
312-587-1122

Collective of Black Artists (COBA)
159 Essex Street
Toronto, Canada M6G 1T6
416-588-7327

Crossroads Theater Company
7 Livingston Avenue
New Brunswick, NJ 09801
908-249-5581

Dance Theater of Harlem
466 W. 152nd Street
New York, NY 10031
212-690-2800

EDEN Theatrical Workshop
1570 Gilpin Street
Denver, CO 80218
303-321-2320

Emmy Gifford Children's Theater
3504 Center Street
Omaha, NE 68105
402-345-4849

Frederick Douglass Creative Arts Center
270 W. 96th Street
New York, NY 10025
212-864-3375

Gateway Dance Theater
1225 Stephenson Way
Des Moines, IA 50314
515-282-8696

Harambee Dance Ensemble
3026 57th Avenue
Oakland, CA 94605
510-532-8558

Harlem School of the Arts
645 St. Nicholas Avenue
New York, NY 10030
212-926-4100

Harmonie Park Playhouse and Actors Laboratory
250 E. Grand River, 5th Floor
Detroit, MI 48226
313-965-2480

Hedzoleh African Dance Troupe
2630 Smithfield Drive
Madison, WI 53718
608-274-9769

Henry Street Settlement's Art Center
466 Grand Street
New York, NY 10002
212-598-0400

Homowa Foundation for African Arts and Culture
2915 NE 15th Avenue
Portland, OR 97212
503-288-3025

Indiana University–Bloomington
Afro-American Arts Institute
109 N. Jordan Avenue
Bloomington, IN 47405
812-855-9501

Inner City Cultural Center
Langston Hughes Memorial Library
c/o The Ivar Theatre
1605 N. Ivar Street

Los Angeles, CA 90028
213-962-2102

Jomandi Productions
1444 Mayson Street, NE
Atlanta, GA 30324
404-876-6346

Just Us Theater Company
P.O. Box 42271
Atlanta, GA 30311
404-753-2399

Karamu House
2355 E. 89th Street
Cleveland, OH 44106
216-795-7070

Ko-Thi Dance Company
P.O. Box 1093
Milwaukee, WI 53201
414-442-6844

Macon County Fine Arts Manifesto
104 Frazier Street
Tuskegee, AL 36083
205-727-3029

McCree Theater and Performing Arts Center
115 E. Pierson Road
Flint, MI 48505
313-232-1665

Memphis Black Arts Alliance
P.O. Box 40854
Memphis, TN 38174
901-274-8134

National Black Theater Institute
2033 Fifth Avenue
New York, NY 10035
212-722-3800

National Black Touring Circuit
417 Convent Avenue
New York, NY 10031
212-283-0974

National Center for Afro-American Artists
122 Elm Hill Avenue
Dorchester, MA 02121
617-422-8820

Negro Ensemble Company
1600 Broadway
New York, NY 10019
212-582-5860

New Freedom Theater
1346 N. Broad Street
Philadelphia, PA 19121
215-765-2793

North Carolina Black Repertory Company
610 Coliseum Drive
Winston-Salem, NC 27106
919-723-7907

Oakland Ensemble Theater
1428 Alice Street, Suite 306
Oakland, CA 94612
510-763-7774

Pin Points Traveling Theater
4353 Du Bois Place, SE

Washington, DC 20019
202-582-0002

Sign of the Times Cultural Arts Center
605 56th Street, NE
Washington, DC 20019
202-399-3400

TABS Center
2226 Westnedge Avenue
Kalamazoo, MI 49008
616-342-1382

Theatre North
P.O. Box 6255
Tulsa, OK 74148
918-587-8937

Wayne County Minority Performing Arts Series
P.O. Box 181
Alton, NY 14413
315-483-4092

ACHIEVERS IN THE PERFORMING ARTS

Ailey, Alvin (1931–1991).   Dancer and choreographer. When Ailey founded the Alvin Ailey American Dance Theater (AAADT) in 1958, he added a new dimension to the artistic interpretation of the African American experience. His first major work, *Blues Suite* (1958), explored African American life in the South; his classic *Revelations* (1960) explored African American spiritual life through the lens of his own Baptist upbringing. In addition to the many works he created for AAADT, Ailey choreographed Samuel Barber's opera *Antony and Cleopatra* (1966), Leonard Bernstein's *Mass* (1971), and jazz dance sequences for the 1976 American Bicentennial celebration. Under Ailey's guidance, AAADT grew to be one of the premier modern-dance troupes and has performed throughout the world. Among other distinctions, it was the first modern-dance troupe to perform in the former Soviet Union. Ailey received the NAACP's Spingarn Medal in 1976 and was honored at the Kennedy Center in 1988.

Aldridge, Ira Frederick (c. 1807–1867).   Actor. Aldridge gained acting experience in New York's African Grove Theatre as a youth and went to England in 1824. He opened at the Royal Coburg, London, in 1825, in *The Revolt of Surinam, or A Slave's Revenge*. His first starring role was in *The Death of Christophe, King of Hayti*. One of the most acclaimed Shakespearean actors of his day, Aldridge gained enormous popularity throughout Europe in the roles of Othello, Macbeth, Shylock, Lear, and Richard III. His honors included an army commission from the government of Haiti, membership in the Prussian Academy of Arts and Sciences, and Austria's Grand Cross of the Order of Leopold. In 1928, when the Shakespeare Memorial Theatre was under construction at Stratford-on-Avon, England, African Americans led by James Weldon Johnson raised a thousand dollars to endow an Ira Aldridge Memorial Chair in the facility.

Allen, Debbie (1950–   ).   Actress, singer, dancer, and director. Allen began in the chorus of *Purlie* in 1972 and had her first featured role in *Raisin* (1973). She went on to gain acclaim for her performances in *Ain't Misbehavin'* (1979) and the revival of *West Side Story* (1980), which earned her a Drama Desk Award and a Tony nomination. In 1982, Allen appeared in the film *Ragtime* and starred in the TV series *Fame*, for which she also choreographed the dance sequences. Allen subsequently directed numerous episodes of *Fame* and was the director for the TV series *A Different World*. She had her own TV special during the 1988–1989 season and also produced the 1997 film *Amistad*.

Baker, Josephine (1906–1975).   Singer, dancer, and actress. Baker began her career as a chorus girl in *Shuffle Along* in 1923. She had a major dancing role in *La Revue Nègre*, an American production that opened in Paris in 1925. Baker left the show to create the role of the "Dark Star" at the Follies Bergère and became an overnight sensation. In addition to her stage work at the Follies and the Casino de Paris, she appeared in a number of films, including *Zouzou* (1934) and *La Créole* (1934). Baker retired from the stage in 1956 and devoted herself to the care of a multiracial group of orphans she had adopted over the years.

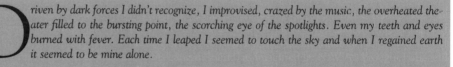

riven by dark forces I didn't recognize, I improvised, crazed by the music, the overheated theater filled to the bursting point, the scorching eye of the spotlights. Even my teeth and eyes burned with fever. Each time I leaped I seemed to touch the sky and when I regained earth it seemed to be mine alone.

Josephine Baker, recalling her 1925 performance in *La Revue Nègre*

Bates, Clayton "Peg Leg" (1907–1998).   Tap dancer. Bates began dancing at age 5 but lost his leg in a cotton-mill accident when he was 12. Equipped with a wooden leg, he resumed his career three years later, appearing in minstrel shows, carnivals, and vaudeville. In the 1930s, Bates was a featured performer in Harlem nightclubs and at the Cotton Club, and he also appeared on the white vaudeville circuits with Bill "Bojangles" Robinson, Bing Crosby, and Gene Kelly. In 1952, Bates bought property in the Catskill Mountains and opened the Peg Leg Bates Country Club, which ranked as the largest black-owned resort in the nation into the 1980s.

Beatty, Talley (1923–).   Dancer and choreographer. Beatty danced with Katherine Dunham's troupe from 1937 to 1943 while also branching out into films and Broadway. In 1952 he formed his own company. His major works of the 1950s and 1960s were often thematically related to the civil rights movement, notably *The Route of the Phoebe Snow* (1959), *Come and Get the Beauty of It Hot* (1960), *Montgomery Variations* (1967), and *Black Belt* (1969). Beatty works created for other ballet companies include *Stack Up* (1983), *Blues Shift* (1984), and *Ellingtonia* (1994). Beatty has also worked on Broadway, providing the choreography for such shows as *Your Arms Too Short to Box with God*.

Belafonte, Harold George "Harry" (1927–).   Singer and actor. Belafonte joined New York's American Negro Theater in 1948 but turned to singing when he found that racial stereotyping limited the roles available to him. His success as a singer opened opportunities in Hollywood and on Broadway, where he won a 1954 Tony Award for *Almanac* and starred with Marge and Gower Champion in *Three for Tonight* (1954). Having spent part of his childhood in Jamaica, Belafonte was familiar with calypso songs, and he began performing them during the mid-1950s. His 1956 album *Calypso* created a calypso craze in the United States and became the first solo album to sell more than a million copies. In 1960, Belafonte became the first African American to star in a TV special. Committed to the civil rights movement, he refused to appear in the South until segregation was legally abolished. Though he continues to perform, Belafonte has increasingly devoted his energies to causes such as human rights and famine relief in Africa. He was appointed goodwill ambassador for UNICEF in 1986, and in 1990 he served as chair of the committee welcoming Nelson Mandela to the United States.

Bland, James A. (1854–1911).   Composer and minstrel entertainer. Bland was a student at Howard University when he learned to play the banjo and became a performer. In the 1870s he began touring with the Georgia Minstrels, the first successful all-black company. He published his best-known song, "Carry

Me Back to Old Virginny," in 1879; another Bland composition, "Oh Dem Golden Slippers," sold 100,000 copies by 1880. In 1881, Bland went to England with the Minstrel Carnival of Genuine Colored Minstrels, a 65-performer group. He remained in Europe until 1901, mainly as a solo performer. Known as the Idol of the Music Halls, Bland toured the European continent and gave a command performance for Queen Victoria and the Prince of Wales.

Bledsoe, Jules (1898–1943).   Singer and actor. Gifted with a rich baritone voice, Bledsoe made his concert debut at Aeolian Hall, New York City, in 1924, followed by a tour of 13 states. His first dramatic role was in *Deep River* (1926), the first U.S. opera with a multiracial cast. He also starred in Paul Green's *In Abraham's Bosom* (1926) and sang in the premiere of James Weldon Johnson's *Creation* (1927). Bledsoe won the role of Jo in *Show Boat* (1927) and created the interpretation of "Old Man River," which he sang an estimated 18,000 times during his lifetime. His 1929 performance as Amonasro in *Aida* was the first appearance of an African American in grand opera opposite a white singer.

Bubbles, John [John William Sublett] (1902–1986).   Tap dancer. At age seven, Bubbles teamed with Ford "Buck" Washington to form the vaudeville act Buck and Bubbles, which achieved enormous popularity throughout the 1920s and 1930s. Bubbles also starred as Sportin' Life in the 1935 production of *Porgy and Bess*. After Washington's death in 1955, Bubbles stopped performing for a time, but he began dancing in nightclubs during the mid-1960s. In 1979, he appeared in the Lincoln Center special *Black Broadway*, and the following year the American Guild of Variety Artists presented him with its Lifetime Achievement Award.

Carroll, Vinette (c. 1922–   ).   Director, actress, and playwright. Carroll achieved renown as an actress in off-Broadway productions such as *Caesar and Cleopatra* (1955), *The Octoroon* (1961), and *Moon on a Rainbow Shawl* (1962), for which she won an Obie Award. She was one of the first African American women to direct on Broadway, where her credits include *Black Nativity* (1962), *Don't Bother Me, I Can't Cope* (1961), and *Your Arms Too Short to Box with God* (1975). In 1986, Carroll founded the Vinette Carroll Repertory Company in Fort Lauderdale, Florida.

Cole, Bob (1863?–1911).   Composer, musician, singer, dancer, and actor. Cole began his career as playwright/manager of Al Worth's Museum for the All-Star Company, the first African American stock company. He wrote the music for the minstrel show *Black Patti's Troubadors* (1893) and (with Billy Johnson) created *A Trip to Coontown* (1898), the first black full-length musical comedy and a milestone in the presentation of African American characters on the stage. Cole also wrote numerous songs for Broadway shows. Along with J. Rosamond Johnson, Cole created and acted in *The Shoo-Fly Regiment* (1906), which was the first show to present romantic love between black characters outside the minstrel context.

Coles, Charles "Honi" (1911–1992).   Tap dancer. Coles went to New York City in 1931 as a member of the Three Millers and was soon hailed as having the "fastest feet in show business." After World War II, he teamed with Charles "Cholly" Atkins. The duo of Coles and Atkins appeared with the leading bands of the day, including those of Cab Calloway, Count Basie, Duke Ellington, and Lionel Hampton. Tap went out of fashion during the 1950s and 1960s, but Coles was again in demand during the 1970s, dancing on Broadway in *Bubbling Brown Sugar* (1976), performing with the Joffrey Ballet (1978), and appearing in films and TV shows. He won Tony and Drama Desk Awards for choreography in *My One and Only* (1983) and was awarded the National Medal of Arts in 1991.

Dafora, Asadata (1890–1965).   Dancer and choreographer. Born in Sierra Leone, Dafora was the great-grandson of a former slave who had returned to Africa from Nova Scotia. Dafora moved to Europe in 1910 and arrived in New York City in 1929. In that year, he founded Shogola Oloba, an African dance ensemble, the members of which he recruited from the National African Union, a New York social club. In 1935, the company was incorporated into the Federal Theater Project and became known as the African Dance Troupe. In addition to appearing in the renowned FTP production of *Macbeth*, the company was best known for performing Dafora's works, which included *Zoonga*, *Kykunkor*, and *Zunguru*. Dafora returned to Sierra Leone in 1960, leaving the African Dance Troupe under the direction of Esther Rolle.

Davis, Charles Rudolph "Chuck" (1937–).   Dancer and choreographer. Born in North Carolina, Davis was educated at Howard University. Angered by the biased portrayal of African Americans in the mass media during the 1950s, he began studying African dance to achieve a new cultural perspective. After training with a number of African American choreographers in New York, he formed the Chuck Davis Dance Company in 1968. Davis soon emerged as the leading exponent of African dance in the United States. He augmented his knowledge by making annual trips to Senegal, Guinea, Ivory Coast, and other nations, studying with local dance masters. In 1977, Davis organized the Dance Africa festival, which is held annually at the Brooklyn Academy of Music. He moved back to North Carolina in 1980, founding the African American Dance Ensemble in Durham.

Davis, Ossie (1917–).   Actor, playwright, and director. Davis began his stage career with a role in *Jeb* (1946) and subsequently appeared in *No Time for Sergeants*, *Raisin in the Sun*, and *Jamaica*. In 1961, Davis's satire on Southern racism, *Purlie Victorious*, was produced on Broadway, with Davis and his wife, Ruby Dee, in the lead roles. Davis went on to play numerous roles in films and television; as a director, his credits have included *Cotton Comes to Harlem* and *Black Girl*. Deeply committed to the civil rights movement from its earliest days, Davis has consistently spoken out on social and political issues. In order to advance the participation of African Americans in the arts, Davis and Dee founded the Institute of New Cinema Artists and the Recording Industry Training Program.

Davis, Sammy, Jr. (1925–1990).   Actor, comedian, dancer, and singer. Davis began performing at age four, appearing in vaudeville as a member of the Will Mastin Trio, which achieved growing popularity throughout the 1930s and 1940s. During the early 1950s, Davis gradually embarked on a solo career and emerged as one of the superstars of American show business. In addition to a number of film roles, he appeared on Broadway in *Mr. Wonderful* (1956), *Golden Boy* (1964), and *Sammy on Broadway* (1974). Davis used his celebrity status to promote humanitarian causes, staging a number of benefits for civil rights organizations and groups trying to promote amity between African Americans and Jews. (He converted to Judaism following a near-fatal auto accident in 1954.) Davis received the NAACP's Spingarn Medal in 1968 and was honored at the Kennedy Center in 1987.

Dee, Ruby (1923–).   Actress, author, and journalist. Dee made her Broadway debut in 1942. Four years later, she appeared in *Jeb* alongside Ossie Davis, whom she married in 1948. She made her film debut as Rachel Robinson in *The Jackie Robinson Story* (1950). In 1965, Dee joined the American Shakespeare Festival and was the first African American actress to perform in major roles with the company. She won an Obie Award in 1971 for her performance in *Bozeman and Lena* and a 1974 Drama Desk Award for *Wedding Band*. As a writer, Dee has consistently championed civil rights efforts, and in 1970 the National Urban League honored her with the Frederick Douglass Award for her work in this area. In 1975, Dee and Davis received a special award from Actors Equity for "outstanding contributions both in the performing arts and in society at large." In 1990, Dee starred in and wrote the script for the American Playhouse production *Zora Is My Name*, based on the life and work of the great African American writer Zora Neale Hurston.

DeLavallade, Carmen (1931–).   Dancer and choreographer. DeLavallade joined the Lester Horton Dance Theater in 1949 and appeared as a principal dancer from 1950 to 1954. From 1955 to 1956, she was a prima ballerina at the Metropolitan Opera. She later danced with the Alvin Ailey American Dance Theater and other companies in works created by her husband, Geoffrey Holder, most notably *Come Sunday*. DeLavallade has also appeared on the off-Broadway stage, on TV, and in film, and she was a choreographer and performer-in-residence at the Yale School of Drama from 1970 to 1980. During the 1990s,

DeLavallade performed in works by Bill T. Jones and others and choreographed dance sequences for the Metropolitan Opera.

Destiné, Jean-Leon (1927–).   Dancer and choreographer. Born in Haiti, Destiné began studying dance with Lina Mathon-Blanchet, founder of the first Haitian dance company dedicated to folk traditions. He moved to New York City with Blanchet's troupe in the early 1940s and joined Katherine Dunham's company in 1946, making his mark as the possessed boy in Dunham's *Shango*. In 1949, he formed the Destiné Afro-Haitian Dance Company, basing his work on African, French, and Haitian dances. The company was soon touring the world, and the Haitian government named Destiné cultural attaché to the United States. He has taught dance for a number of years at New York University, UCLA, and the New York Dance Group Studio.

Dove, Ulysses (1947–).   Dancer and choreographer. After beginning with Merce Cunningham, Dove joined the Alvin Ailey American Dance Theater in 1973 and quickly became a principal dancer. His first choreographic work, *Inside,* was performed in 1980. Dove then began working as a freelance choreographer, creating pieces for companies such as the Basel Ballet, the Dutch National Ballet, American Ballet Theater, and the New York City Ballet. His major works include *Night Shade* (1982), *Bad Blood* (1984), *Vespers* (1986), and *Episodes* (1987).

Dunham, Katherine (1910–).   Dancer and choreographer. Trained as an anthropologist, Dunham spent a number of years doing research in the Caribbean and in Brazil. Exposure to both regions' rituals and dances inspired her to create her own dance company during the 1930s. As a choreographer, Dunham fused traditional African and African American dance movements with the techniques of the Broadway stage, creating a unique synthesis. Her first major work, *L'Ag'Ya* (1938), was based on a folktale from Martinique.

     Dunham achieved a breakthrough in 1939, when her company played a 10-week engagement in New York, performing Dunham's *Tropics and Le Jazz Hot: From Haiti to Harlem.* During the late 1940s, the Katherine Dunham Dance Company toured the world, appearing in Latin America and Europe, as well as the United States. In 1945, Dunham founded the Dunham School of Dance and Theater, training a new generation of African American performers. During the 1960s, she became the first African American to choreograph dances at the Metropolitan Opera. Other major works by Dunham include *Haitian Suite (II)* (1941), *Bal Negre* (1946), *Spirituals* (1951), *Afrique du Nord* (1953), and *Anabacoa* (1963). Dunham's achievements were recognized in a gala at Washington, D.C.'s, Kennedy Center in 1983, and the Alvin Ailey American Dance Company featured her works in its 1987–1988 repertory.

Gilpin, Charles Sidney (1878–1930).   Singer and actor. Born in Richmond, Virginia, Gilpin began his career in 1896 with Brown's Big Spectacular Log Cabin Company, a minstrel show, and he joined Williams and Walker's Abyssinia Company in 1903. Four years later, Gilpin moved on to the Pekin Stock Company of Chicago (1907), the first legitimate theater operated by African Americans. At the Pekin, he starred in *The Mayor of Dixie* (1907). Moving to New York in 1915, Gilpin played lead roles with the Lafayette Theater Company in Harlem. He made his Broadway debut as a preacher in *Abraham Lincoln* (1919) and achieved stardom in *The Emperor Jones* (1920). In 1921, the Drama League cited Gilpin as one of the top 10 contributors to the American theater.

Glover, Savion (1973–).   Dancer and choreographer. Born in Newark, New Jersey, Glover was a prodigy drum student who switched to dance after he attended a tap-dance workshop by veteran performers Lon Chaney and Chuck Green. Soon, Glover began studying dance in New York City. By the time he was 11 years old, he had taken the lead role in the Broadway production of *The Tap Dance Kid.* In short order he danced and acted in two other hit Broadway plays, *Black and Blue* and *Jelly's Last Jam.* Glover's biggest hit and greatest critical success came with a play that he created in collaboration with George Wolfe, *Bring in 'da Noise, Bring in 'da Funk.* In 1996, the play won him a Tony Award for best choreographer, as well as a Tony nomination for best actor in a musical.

Hall, Juanita (1901–1968).   Singer. Born in Keyport, New Jersey, Hall studied voice at New York's prestigious Juilliard School of Music. In 1928, she won her first major stage role, appearing in *Show Boat*. She then worked with the Hall Johnson Choir (1931–1936) and led the WPA Chorus in New York from 1936 to 1941. Hall then organized the Juanita Hall Choir and performed on the radio with Kate Smith, Rudy Vallee, and others. She appeared in several Broadway shows, including *The Pirate* (1942), *St. Louis Woman* (1945), and *Street Scene* (1947). Hall's best-known Broadway role was Bloody Mary in *South Pacific* (1949), for which she won the 1950 Tony Award as best supporting actress. Throughout the 1950s, Hall sang in nightclubs and gave concerts around the country.

Hines, Gregory (1946–   ).   Tap dancer, actor, musician, and songwriter. Hines began dancing at age five. For the next 15 years he and his older brother, Maurice Jr., performed as the Hines Kids; their father, Maurice Sr., joined them in 1964, when the popular act—which incorporated all the great African American tap traditions—became known as Hines, Hines, and Dad. After leaving the act in the early 1970s for a stint as a musician and songwriter, Hines began appearing on Broadway, dancing in *Eubie* (1978), *Comin' Uptown* (1979), and *Sophisticated Ladies* (1980–1981), earning three Tony nominations along the way. He made several films during the 1980s, including *Cotton Club* (1984) and *Tap* (1989), and he also appeared in the 1989 Central Park production of Shakespeare's *Twelfth Night*. Hines's performance as Jelly Roll Morton in *Jelly's Last Jam* earned him a Tony Award in 1992. In 1997, his prime-time sitcom, *The Gregory Hines Show*, debuted on ABC-TV.

Holder, Geoffrey (1930–   ).   Actor, dancer, choreographer, and director. Born in Trinidad, Holder began dancing at age seven with the Holder Dance Company, directed by his brother Boscoe. He became director of the company in 1947 and remained at the helm until 1954, when he moved to New York City. Distinguished by a slender 6'6" frame, Holder made his Broadway debut as Samedi, a Haitian conjuror, in *House of Flowers* (1954), alongside Carmen DeLavallade (his future wife) and Alvin Ailey. He danced at the Metropolitan Opera in 1955–1956 and toured with his own troupe, Geoffrey Holder and Company, until 1960. Holder soon branched out into choreography, combining African and European elements in works such as *Bele* and *Prodigal Prince*. During the 1960s, he appeared in films and also made some highly popular TV commercials. In 1976, Holder won two Tony Awards for his work in *The Wiz*, one for directing and a second for costume design. He also directed and choreographed the 1978 musical *Timbuktu*. In recent years, the multitalented Holder has turned his energies to painting and writing, with comparable success.

Horne, Lena (1917–   ).   Singer and actress. Horne first appeared on the stage when she was 6 years old and became a member of the chorus line at the Cotton Club at age 16. As her career developed, she was among the first African Americans to sing at upscale venues such as the Fairmont in San Francisco and the Empire Room at the Waldorf-Astoria. She began recording in 1936, and in 1941 became the first African American to sign a contract with a major Hollywood studio. Though she made a number of films, Horne was frustrated by Hollywood's racial stereotyping, and during the 1950s her progressive political views and interracial marriage caused her to be blacklisted for a time. In the end, she overcame all obstacles and established herself as one of the luminaries of American show business. Her Broadway appearances have included *Jamaica* (1957) and *Lena Horne: The Lady and Her Music* (1974). In 1984, Horne was honored at the Kennedy Center for her contributions to American culture.

Jamison, Judith (1944–   ).   Dancer and choreographer. Jamison's career has been identified with the Alvin Ailey American Dance Theater, which she joined in 1965. She has starred in numerous Ailey ballets, including *Cry*, *Maskela Language*, *Choral Dances*, and *Revelations*. She has also appeared as a guest artist with the American Ballet Theatre, the Vienna State Opera, and the Munich State Opera, as well as dancing on Broadway in *Sophisticated Ladies* (1980). Jamison left the Ailey company in 1980 and has since achieved renown as a choreographer and director of her own group, the Jamison Project. Her dance pieces include *Divining* (1984), *Forgotten Time* (1989), and *Hymn* (1993).

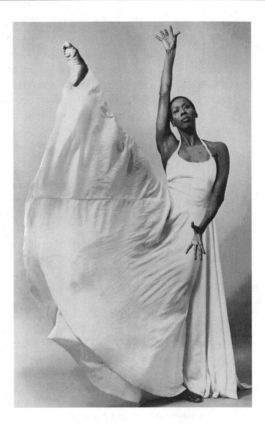

Dancer and choreographer Judith Jamison.

Johnson, J. Rosamond (1873–1954).   Composer, actor, and director. Johnson made his singing debut in Boston in 1894, and three years later he made his acting debut in the first African American play on Broadway, *In Oriental America* (1897). While pursuing his performing career, he also served as the choirmaster of a Baptist church in Jacksonville, Florida, and was supervisor of music for the Jacksonville public schools (1896–1908). Johnson also founded the New York Music School Settlement for Colored People, which was located in Harlem. As a performer, Johnson played leading roles in plays such as *Porgy* (1935), *Mamba's Daughters* (1939), and *Cabin in the Sky* (1940). Often collaborating with Bob Cole and his older brother, James Weldon Johnson, he wrote more than 160 songs for Broadway musicals between 1897 and 1940. Johnson is also noted for cowriting (with his brother) "Lift Every Voice and Sing" (1990), often called the "Black National Anthem."

Jones, Bill T. (1952–).   Dancer, choreographer, and director. Jones built his reputation during the 1970s, dancing in collaboration with Arnie Zane, and the two men founded the Bill T. Jones/Arnie Zane Company in the 1980s. Jones is known as a postmodernist who performs only in his own works and those of his collaborators. Among his best-known pieces are *Negroes for Sale* (1972); *Stories, Steps, and Stomps* (1978); *Monkey Run Road* (1979); *How to Walk an Elephant* (1985); and *War between the States* (1993). In the 1990s, he began choreographing and directing musical works such as Michael Tippetts's *New Year* and Kurt Weill's *Lost in the Stars*. In 1993, Jones received a MacArthur Foundation "genius" award.

Jones, James Earl (1931–).   Actor. Jones began his illustrious acting career by appearing in such plays as *Wedding in Japan* (1957), *Sunrise at Campobello* (1958), *The Blacks* (1960), and *The Blood Knot* (1964). His breakthrough came in 1968, when he portrayed Jack Johnson in *The Great White Hope*, a performance that won him a Tony Award in 1969. Jones was catapulted into the front ranks of American actors, appearing in *King Lear, Of Mice and Men, Hedda Gabler, Othello,* and a one-man show in which he portrayed Paul Robeson. In 1987, Jones won a second Tony for his performance as Troy Maxson in August Wilson's *Fences.* Beginning with *Dr. Strangelove* in 1964, he has appeared in numerous films and television programs, and his unmistakable voice has been heard in countless voice-overs.

Lane, William Henry (c. 1825–c. 1852).   Tap dancer. Lane began performing with white minstrel players as a youth, and by 1844 he was being hailed as the champion minstrel dancer of the Northeast. Known as Master Juba, he was the first African American to tour with the all-white Ethiopian Minstrels. During the late 1840s he enjoyed great success in England, profoundly influencing European music hall and circus traditions. Lane is considered the most influential performer in 19th-century American dance. He is credited with laying the groundwork for modern tap dancing by combining traditional African American dance styles with European jig and clog dances.

Lee, Canada [Leonard Corneliou Canagata] (1907–1952).   Actor. Born in New York City, Lee studied violin with J. Rosamond Johnson and performed in Aeolian Hall while still in his teens. At age 14, he ran away from home and became a jockey. He then turned to boxing, winning 175 of 200 professional bouts. Lee began acting in 1934 while leading his own band. He won acclaim as Banquo in Orson Welles's 1936 production of *Macbeth* at the Lafayette Theater in Harlem. Lee's most renowned role was as Bigger Thomas in *Native Son* (1941). Other notable stage appearances included *Across the Board Tomorrow Morning* (1942) and *South Pacific* (1949). As a film actor, Lee appeared in *Lifeboat* (1944), *The Tempest* (1945), and *Body and Soul* (1947), among other films.

Micheaux, Oscar (1884–1951).   Writer and film producer. Born in rural Illinois, Micheaux left home at age 17 and worked as a Pullman porter before settling down as a farmer in South Dakota. He eventually began writing fiction and energetically promoted his works in person throughout African American communities in the West. In 1918, a newly created black film company in Nebraska offered to film one of Micheaux's books, *The Homesteader.* They refused to let him direct the film, however, so he raised funds from his readers and formed his own company, the New York–based Oscar Micheaux Corporation. Beginning with *The Homesteader* in 1919, Micheaux produced nearly 30 films in 20 years. Many were melodramatic and commercialized, but all sought to present a positive image of African Americans to black audiences. At least one Micheaux film, *Birthright* (1924), was a serious examination of race relations in the South, and *Body and Soul,* another 1924 vehicle, marked the screen debut of Paul Robeson. In 1931, Micheaux released *The Exile,* the first talking picture by an African American company. Micheaux's last film, *The Wind from Nowhere,* premiered in a Broadway movie house in 1948. Though the film was a commercial failure, Micheaux's influence was already evident in the gradual improvement of the African American image in Hollywood films.

Mills, Florence (1895–1927).   Singer and dancer. Mills began her performing career in 1901 (at age six) and broke into vaudeville with her sisters Olivia and Maude (the Mills Trio) in 1910. After embarking on a solo career, she won fame in 1921 in *Shuffle Along* at the 63rd Street Music Hall in New York City. She then starred in *Plantation Revue* (1922), *Dixie to Broadway* (1924), and *Blackbirds of 1926,* earning international acclaim in Paris and London. After Mills died of complications from a ruptured appendix, more than 100,000 admirers attended her Harlem funeral.

Mitchell, Arthur (1934–   ).   Dancer and choreographer. Mitchell began studying ballet with George Balanchine in 1952 and joined the New York City Ballet in 1955. He was among the first Americans to work with a white classical dance company in the United States, and television networks refused to broadcast programs in which Mitchell partnered with white ballerinas. Despite this atmosphere of prejudice, Mitchell quickly became a principal dancer with the company, making his mark in Balanchine classics such as *Agon* and *A Midsummer Night's Dream.* Mitchell remained with the City Ballet until 1968, when he and Karel Shook founded the pioneering Dance Theater of Harlem (DTH), with the aim of providing opportunities for African American dancers. DTH made its official debut at the Guggenheim Museum in 1971 and had its first full-length season in 1974. Under Mitchell's unflagging guidance, the company has remained a consistent source of excitement and excellence on the classical dance scene, maintaining its vision and creative edge despite financial pressures and a 1997 dancers' strike.

BLACKS IN BALLET

An informal 1997 *New York Times* survey of 10 major U.S. ballet companies revealed that of 495 company members (excluding apprentices and trainees), only 23 (4.6%) were African American. At the time, there were only two African American classically oriented dance companies—Dance Theater of Harlem and Ballethnic. Since then, however, a number of ballet companies have been making efforts to interest youngsters from African American communities; in 1997, the New York City Ballet included four African American dancers, and the company's repertory included works by two black choreographers: John Alleyne and Ulysses Dove.

Moore, Charles (1928–1986).   Dancer and choreographer. Moore studied ballet, modern dance, and African dance with Jean-Leon Destiné, Pearl Primus, and Katherine Dunham. He became a versatile and popular performer during the 1950s and 1960s, appearing in a number of Broadway musicals. At the same time, he began teaching Dunham's techniques to students at New York colleges, schools, and youth centers. In 1972–1973, Moore founded both the Charles Moore Center for Ethnic Studies and the troupe known as Dances and Drums of Africa, which toured the world during the 1970s and 1980s. Moore's dance works—which include *Bundao*, *Maiden's Stick Dance*, and *African Congo*—are based on extensive research into African dance, costumes, and music.

Nicholas, Fayard (1917–) **and Harold** (1924–).   Dancers. Renowned for their innovation, daring, and acrobatic skill, the Nicholas Brothers set the standard for all the tap dancers who followed them. They performed on Broadway in *Babes in Arms* (1937), toured the world from Africa to Europe, and appeared in numerous films, including *The Big Broadcast of 1936* (1936), *Down Argentine Way* (1940), and *The Pirate* (1948). Though they were denied the recognition accorded white dancers such as Fred Astaire and Gene Kelly, the Nicholas Brothers continued to work throughout the 1960s and 1970s, appearing in numerous TV shows; Fayard Nicholas also won a Tony Award for choreographing *Black and Blue*. In 1991, the Nicholas Brothers received a Lifetime Achievement Award at the Kennedy Center.

Poitier, Sidney (1927–).   Actor and director. Born in Miami and raised in the Bahamas, Poitier served in the U.S. Army Medical Corps during World War II and then led the life of a struggling young actor in New York City. After suppressing his West Indian accent, he was able to find work with Abram Hill's American Negro Theater (ANT). After appearing on Broadway in *Lysistrata* (1946) and *Anna Lucasta* (1948), Poitier broke into films with a part in *No Way Out* (1950). He was soon playing leading roles in films that included *Cry, the Beloved Country* (1951), *Blackboard Jungle* (1955), and *Something of Value* (1957). In 1958, Poitier's performance in *The Defiant Ones* earned him an Oscar nomination and a New York Film Critics Award for Best Actor. In 1963, Poitier became the first African American to win an Academy Award for Best Actor, winning the Oscar for *Lilies of the Field*. In addition to starring in films, Poitier also turned to directing; his credits include *Buck and the Preacher* (1972), *Uptown Saturday Night* (1974), *Stir Crazy* (1980), and *Fast Forward* (1985). Poitier has also taken an active role in many humanitarian causes; in recognition of his efforts, the NAACP chose him to receive its first Thurgood Marshall Lifetime Achievement Award in 1993.

Pomare, Eleo (1937–).   Dancer and choreographer. Born in New York, Pomare spent his childhood in Colombia and Panama before returning to attend the New York High School of Performing Arts. By 1958 he was directing his own company and creating works for other companies in the United States and abroad. He is known for interpreting visual and literary works in dance and for exploring social and political issues. His major works include *Missa Luba* (1965), *Blues for the Jungle* (1966), and *Las Desenamoradas*

(1967). In 1967, Pomare founded Dancemobile, a program providing free dance performances to New York City neighborhoods.

Primus, Pearl (1919–1994).   Dancer and choreographer. Born in Trinidad, Primus began performing in New York in 1943 and formed her own dance company in 1946. During the 1950s she traveled widely in Africa and the Caribbean, studying indigenous dance techniques and performing works that drew on diverse African and African American traditions. Among her major pieces are *Fanga* (1959) and *Michael, Row Your Boat Ashore* (1978). In 1990, Primus became chair of the Five Colleges consortium in Massachusetts, and the following year she was honored with the National Medal of Arts.

Richards, Lloyd (1919–   ).   Director. After beginning his stage career as an actor, Richards achieved renown as a director in 1959 with Lorraine Hansberry's classic *Raisin in the Sun,* for which he won a New York Drama Critics Circle Award. In 1969 he took the helm of the Eugene O'Neill Theater in Waterford, Connecticut, and nurtured the talents of numerous young playwrights and actors. Richards has directed nearly all of August Wilson's best-known works, winning a Tony Award in 1987 for his staging of Wilson's *Fences.* He also served as dean of the Yale Drama School from 1969 to 1991. Upon Richards's retirement, Yale established an endowed professorship in his name, the first time an African American had been so honored by the university.

Robeson, Paul (1898–1976).   Actor and singer. After distinguishing himself as a scholar-athlete at Rutgers University and attending Columbia Law School, Robeson practiced law in New York. Frustrated by racial barriers, he gave up law for the stage. Robeson had his first success off-Broadway in *The Emperor Jones* (1923) and followed with another bravura performance in *All God's Chillun Got Wings* (1925). In 1925, Robeson began singing African American spirituals in recital, drawing rave reviews in New York and London. He appeared in the London production of *Show Boat* in 1928 and joined the New York production in 1930. Among his other memorable Broadway roles during this time were *Othello* (1930), *The Hairy Ape* (1931), and *Stevedore* (1933), and his film work included *King Solomon's Mines* (1935) and *Show Boat* (1936). The NAACP awarded Robeson its Spingarn Medal in 1945. During the anticommunist hysteria that followed World War II, Robeson's long-time friendship with African freedom fighters and his support for leftist causes brought persecution from the U.S. government, and his passport was confiscated in 1950. Embittered by this treatment, Robeson gave a farewell concert at Carnegie Hall in 1958 and took up residence in the Soviet Union. He returned to the United States in 1963, announced his retirement as a performer, and lived quietly in Philadelphia until his death.

> M y father was a slave and my people died to build this country and I'm going to stay right here and have a part of it, just like you. And no fascist-minded people like you will drive me from it. Is that clear?
>
> Paul Robeson, testifying before the House Un-American Activities Committee (June 12, 1956)

Robinson, Luther [Bill "Bojangles"] (1878–1949).   Dancer and choreographer. Born in Richmond, Virginia, Robinson studied minstrel dancing in his youth and developed a unique personal style as a street dancer. He became a headline vaudeville performer in the 1910s, billed as the Dark Cloud of Joy and the King of the Tap Dancers. During the early 1920s he performed in Europe, returning home to star in *Blackbirds of 1928* (1928) and *Brown Buddies* (1930). His film appearances included *The Little Colonel* (1935) and *Rebecca of Sunnybrook Farm* (1938). Robinson has been credited with inventing the staircase dance and with transforming African American folk dancing into a new art form. In 1989, Congress declared May 25, Robinson's birthday, National Tap Dance Day.

Smith, Anna Deavere (1950–).   Actress and playwright. Renowned for her ability to inhabit a wide array of characters, Smith has created a series of one-woman shows, including *On the Road* (1983), *Fires in the Mirror* (1991), and *Piano* (1992). She has won Obie and Drama Desk Awards and has received two Tony nominations. Smith is also a professor of arts and drama at Stanford University.

Walker, George (1873–1911).   Comedian, dancer, singer, actor, and producer. Walker began his career performing in medicine shows and formed a legendary partnership with Bert Williams in 1895. Williams and Walker appeared (with their own repertory company) in *Clorindy* (1899), *In Dahomey* (1902), *In Abyssinia* (1908), *Bandana Land* (1908), and other musicals, becoming the first African American entertainment team to achieve international fame. Walker played the flamboyant man-about-town, contrasting with Williams's portrayal of the wry, long-suffering working man.

Ward, Douglas Turner (1930–).   Actor and playwright. In 1956, Ward made his debut in an off-Broadway production of *The Iceman Cometh*. He soon began writing, and his plays *Happy Ending* and *Day of Absence* were produced off-Broadway in 1965, earning him an Obie Award for acting and a Drama Desk–Vernon Rice Award for writing. Ward founded the Negro Ensemble Company (NEC) in 1968. In addition to mounting renowned productions such as Joseph Walker's *River Niger* (1973) and Charles Fuller's *A Soldier's Story* (1981), NEC has also performed several works by Ward, including *The Reckoning* (1969), *Brotherhood* (1970), and *The Redeemer* (1979).

Williams, Bert (1873–1922).   Entertainer. Williams began to perform in cafés and bars after attending school in San Francisco. He performed with George Walker from 1895 until 1907, when Walker had to retire due to poor health. As a solo performer, Williams triumphed in the annual *Ziegfield Follies* throughout the 1910s, opening the way for African American performers in vaudeville. He later appeared in two shows built around his talents: *Broadway Brevities* (1920) and *Under the Bamboo Tree* (1922). Despite his stardom and large fees, Williams was often forced to stay in run-down, segregated hotels while touring, and he was known to be a deeply melancholy man.

Wilson, August (1945–).   Playwright. A Pittsburgh native, Wilson began writing poetry and short stories after dropping out of high school at age 15. In the late 1960s, he cofounded (with Rob Penny, another playwright) the Black Horizon theater company in one of Pittsburgh's black neighborhoods, the Hill. Wilson's work at this time drew on what he has called the "angry, didactic, . . . pushing outward" spirit of 1960s black nationalism. By the early 1980s, Wilson had honed his work so that it was based much more on an inward examination of his characters, rather than on overt political rhetoric and consciousness raising. His first big success came with *Ma Rainey's Black Bottom*, a play that he submitted to the National Playwrights Conference in 1981, which ended up on Broadway three years later. He followed this with *Fences* (1987), the story of Troy, a fallible hero who alternately overprotects and dominates his family. Wilson has won Pulitzer Prizes for playwriting for *Fences* (1987) and *The Piano Lesson* (1990).

Wolfe, George C. (1954–).   Playwright and director. Wolfe first achieved renown as a writer when his play *Paradise* was produced off-Broadway in 1985, followed by an acclaimed production of his *The Colored Museum* at the New York Public Theater in 1986. He became an artistic associate at the Public Theater in 1990, directing *Spunk*, *The Caucasian Chalk Circle*, and other works. In 1990, Wolfe wrote the book for *Jelly's Last Jam* and directed the Los Angeles production of the play, which moved to Broadway in 1992. Wolfe won a Tony Award in 1993 for directing *Angels in America* on Broadway and also succeeded Joseph Papp as the Public Theater's producer. In 1996, he won a second Tony for his direction of *Bring in 'da Noise, Bring in 'da Funk*, which he helped to create.

SOURCES FOR ADDITIONAL INFORMATION

Adamczyk, Alice J. *Black Dance: An Annotated Bibliography*. New York: Garland, 1990.

Banham, Martin, Erroll Hill, and George Woodyard, eds. *The Cambridge Guide to African and Caribbean Theater*. Cambridge, England: Cambridge University Press, 1994.

Browning, Barbara. *Samba: Resistance in Motion*. Bloomington: Indiana University Press, 1995.

Duberman, Martin Bauml. *Paul Robeson*. New York: Knopf, 1989.

Emery, Lynne Fauley. *Black Dance in the United States from 1619 to 1970*. Palo Alto, CA: National Books, 1972.

Frank, Rusty. *Tap! The Greatest Tap Dance Stars and Their Stories, 1900–1955*. New York: Morrow, 1990.

Gray, John. *Black Theatre and Performance: A PanAfrican Bibliography*. Westport, CT: Greenwood, 1990.

Haskins, James. *Black Dance in America: A History through Its People*. New York: Crowell, 1990.

Hill, Errol, ed. *The Theater of Black Americans: A Collection of Critical Essays*. Englewood Cliffs, NJ: Prentice-Hall, 1979.

Johnson, James Weldon. *Black Manhattan*. New York: Da Capo, 1930, (reprint) 1996.

Mapp, Edward. *Directory of Blacks in the Performing Arts*, 2nd ed. Metuchen, NJ: Scarecrow, 1990.

Salzman, Jack, David Lionel Smith, and Cornel West, eds. *Encyclopedia of African-American Culture and History*, 5 vols. New York: Simon & Schuster, 1996.

Sanders, Leslie C. *The Development of Black Theater in America*. Baton Rouge: Louisiana State University Press, 1988.

Stearns, Marshall, and Jean Stearns. *Jazz Dance: The Story of American Vernacular Dance*. New York: Schirmer, 1964.

Thorpe, Edward. *Black Dance*. Woodstock, NY: Overlook, 1990.

Welsh-Asante, Kariamu. *African Dance: An Artistic, Historical, and Philosophical Inquiry*. Trenton, NJ: Africa World Press, 1996.

Williams, Mance. *Black Theater in the 1960s and 1970s*. Westport, CT: Greenwood, 1985.

Woll, Allen. *Black Musical Theatre: From "Coontown" to "Dreamgirls."* Baton Rouge: Louisiana State University Press, 1989.

———. *Dictionary of the Black Theatre*. Westport, CT: Greenwood, 1983.

16

Fine and
Applied Arts

AFRICAN ARTS AND CRAFTS IN THE AMERICAS

ARCHITECTURE

The single-story shotgun house, a familiar sight throughout the deep South, is an adaptation of African architecture. The first shotgun houses were built in New Orleans, Louisiana, around 1810, after more than 6,000 Haitians—two thirds of them slaves and free people of color—emigrated to the city. Many of these newcomers worked in the building trades as carpenters and masons. The rectangular, gable-roofed design of the shotgun house, and the practice of placing the entrance at the narrow end, followed the plan of houses in southern Haiti and ultimately derived from architectural styles popular in Congo-Angola and other parts of Central Africa.

The design of many larger plantations in Louisiana were also based on African homes, primarily from Senegal, which were designed to stay cool in summer. Art historians have also detected a Yoruba influence in the slave-built single house in Charleston, South Carolina. Indeed, the contributions of both enslaved and freed builders is present in plantation homes all over the South, including Thomas Jefferson's home at Monticello; the Melrose Plantation, Natchitoches, Louisiana; various homes in the town of Williamsburg, Virginia; and many others elsewhere. In these projects and others, African Americans served as artisans, carpenters, brick makers, stonecutters, and skilled builders. In addition to homes, black builders and architects in both the North and the South have created courthouses, churches, convents, and even a synagogue (Newport, Rhode Island).

BASKETRY

Coiled baskets, similar to rice fanners found in West and Central Africa, first appeared in South Carolina around 1690. They were made by tying grasses and reeds into tight bundles and then coiling the bundles to form wide trays. By the 1930s, these baskets were being sold by craftspeople at roadside stands along Highway 17 in Mount Pleasant, South Carolina, located at the southern end of the Sea Islands chain. As a result, the basketmaking craft spread throughout the deep South, but connoisseurs maintain that the finest baskets are still made in the South Carolina low country.

"FOLK" OR "OUTSIDER" ART

Echoing styles and techniques that arrived with enslaved African craftspeople in the 19th century, some early 20th-century artists began to use available materials and unschooled methods in painting and sculpture, which formed a distinct style of art referred to as "folk" or "outsider" art. Though their work is highly individual in appearance, these artists are distinguished by their lack of academy training and, more importantly, by their being labeled as "outside" traditional (read, "white") aesthetic categories. Though set apart artificially, these artists draw deeply on spiritual sources—including religion, dreams, or inner visions—not unlike the sources of some mainstream movements such as surrealism or expressionism, though differing greatly in style and approach. The visual representation of signs, symbols, or objects in highly personal yet profound arrangements speaks of their connection to mysticism, which has roots in various African traditions.

These self-taught artists include David Butler, John Dunkley, Minnie Evans, James Hampton, Bessie Harvey, Mr. Imagination, John Landry Sr., David Philpot, Elijah Pierce, Moses Tolliver, William Traylor, Inez Walker, and Derek Webster. Visually, their work is highly symbolic and strikingly graphic. Surreal fantasy-scapes or assemblages of materials, enigmatic yet pure and direct in line and form and bold in color, are the hallmarks of their art.

GRAVE DECORATION

In many parts of Africa, mourners have long decorated graves with a variety of objects: articles used by the deceased, broken pottery, bits of glass, and carved wooden figures with religious significance. This tradition has continued in the Americas throughout many generations; in the United States, offerings have included dishes of food and a wide variety of household objects. Many mourners have also fashioned gravestones and wooden markers.

At times, this practice has been raised to a considerable art. During the first half of the 20th century, Cyrus Bowens of Georgia carved a number of abstract human figures out of wood as grave markers for members of his family: The most remarkable is a slender, curving form reaching a height of 13 feet. In more recent years, outstanding contributions to the art of grave decoration have been made by Henry Dorsey of Kentucky, who works in stone.

IRONWORK

Drawing on the ancient iron-making traditions of Africa, numerous Africans and African Americans were employed as blacksmiths and foundry workers in America. Some of these early artisans produced works of art, as well as useful objects. For example, a late-18th-century wrought-iron statue discovered on the site of former slave dwellings in Alexandria, Virginia, shows clear affinities with similar work done by Mande blacksmiths in West Africa. In the realm of decorative arts, scholars believe that 18th- and 19th-century black ironsmiths were largely responsible for the intricate wrought-iron work (balconies, gates, grilles, locks, lamp brackets, etc.) that can still be seen in sections of Charleston and New Orleans. In Charleston, the African American ironworking tradition was continued during the 20th century by artists such as Philip Simmons, its leading practitioner, who learned his craft from a former slave. His work was part of the International Exhibition of Folk Art at the Smithsonian Institution in 1976.

MUSICAL INSTRUMENTS

The art of carving tree trunks into mortars for pounding rice was transported from Africa to South Carolina and Georgia. These mortars did double duty as drums and were used to accompany rice-husking songs. The oldest extant traditional drum crafted by African Americans has been dated back to the end of the 17th century; made in Virginia of cedar and deerskin, it followed a design common among the Akan-speaking peoples of present-day Ghana. The most original African American contribution to instrument making was the banjo. The earliest African American banjos consisted of a homemade calabash (a bowl-shaped vessel common throughout Africa), a fretless neck, an animal-skin head, and gut strings. This instrument closely paralleled a number of traditional African models, and etymologists have traced the word *banjo* to the *mbanza*, a stringed instrument common in Angola. (Because the banjo became a staple of white minstrel shows that burlesqued African Americans, many black musicians abandoned the instrument during the 19th century.)

POTTERY

African American pottery traditions are centered in the Edgefield District of western South Carolina, where as many as 150 black potters were employed making jars during the 19th century. Much of their work followed Anglo-American models, but distinctive decorative works have also been found, such as a series of 5-inch-tall jugs that incorporate human faces and show stylistic resemblances to jugs from Central Africa. Other vessels with stirrup handles and canted spouts are similar to the so-called monkey jugs still being made by black potters in the West Indies.

TEXTILES

Africans are as renowned for textile making as for ironworking, and many of these traditions survived in America. Leading examples include the quilts made by Harriet Powers of Georgia in the late 19th century, two of which survive. Their panels illustrate scenes from the Bible, and the human and animal figures closely resemble those found in the celebrated appliqué cloths made by the Fon peoples of Dahomey (present-day Benin). So-called strip quilts made by African Americans throughout the South follow the West African practice of creating a large textile from narrow strips of other textiles, each strip having a distinct pattern and color scheme. Some of the most striking examples of this art have been produced by the Saramacca artists of Surinam, who have been remarkably successful in preserving their African heritage.

WOOD CARVING

The crafting of decorated walking sticks has long been one of the primary forms of African American wood carving. The most prized example of this art is a walking stick created by Henry Gudgell, a multitalented Missouri artisan, around 1863. The carvings on the stick include geometric figures, a coiled serpent, a lizard, a tortoise, a branch with a single leaf, and a man whose arms embrace the shaft of the stick. Twentieth-century carvers who have produced similarly ornate walking sticks include David Philpot of Chicago, Howard Miller and William Howard of Georgia, and Leon Rucker, Lester Willis, and Sulton Rogers of Mississippi.

MILESTONES IN THE FINE ARTS

EIGHTEENTH CENTURY

African American involvement in the fine arts dates back at least to 1724, when the enslaved artisans Pompey and Caesar Fleet, employed by a Boston print shop, created woodcuts for sheet music and books. During the 18th century, African Americans were rarely given credit for artisanry and artistic work. However, it is known that a Rhode Island man named Neptune Thurston excelled at painting, and the Bostonian Scipio Moorhead is acknowledged as the creator of a well-known portrait of the African American poet Phillis Wheatley.

NINETEENTH CENTURY

During this era, African American artists began to emerge from anonymity, and many—such as Edmonia Lewis, Edward Bannister, Henry Ossawa Tanner, and Robert Duncanson—gained considerable reputations. Almost all studied in Europe at some point in their careers; as a result, their work invariably followed European styles, even when they depicted African American life. In 1997, a painting by H. O. Tanner became the first by an African American to hang permanently in the White House.

HARLEM RENAISSANCE

A truly distinctive African American style in painting and sculpture began to emerge during the 1920s. Inspired by a growing sense of cultural identity, African Americans began incorporating African motifs into their work. The work of these artists gained nationwide exposure through the efforts of the Harmon Foundation. Created by a white real-estate developer in 1922, the foundation offered awards to African American artists and organized traveling exhibitions of their work. Among the artists who achieved prominence during this period were Aaron Douglas, Sargent Johnson, Lois M. Jones, Archibald J. Motley, William Henry Johnson, Palmer Hayden, Richmond Barthé, and Hale Woodruff.

THE NEW DEAL AND THE HARLEM ARTISTS GUILD

Between 1935 and 1939, the Works Progress Administration (WPA), a federal agency established under the New Deal, funded artistic projects that paid participants $15 to $90 a month. In New York, African American artists formed the Harlem Artists Guild in 1935 to ensure that they were treated fairly under the WPA. Leaders of the group included Aaron Douglas, Augusta Savage, Charles Alston, and Selma Burke. Many of the projects sponsored by the WPA involved the painting of murals on the walls of public buildings: Enduring classics from this era included murals in the lobby of Harlem Hospital by Alston and by Savage, as well as Aaron Douglas's murals for the Countee Cullen Branch of the New York Public Library (now in the Schomburg Center Collection).

Coming out of the Harlem Renaissance tradition were muralist Jacob Lawrence and sculptor/printmaker Elizabeth Catlett-Mora. Lawrence attained early fame for the WPA, producing large-scale, highly graphic works of social commentary. It was during 1939 to 1941 that Lawrence completed many of his best-known works, notably the extensive series of images chronicling the life of Toussaint L'Ouverture (Louverture), the Great Migration, and the Harlem scene. African American artists were also active in Chicago, where the Southside Community Art Center nurtured outstanding talents such as Charles White, Eldzier Cortor, Margaret Burroughs, and Gordon Parks. In Cleveland, Hughie Lee-Smith and others got their start in art programs sponsored by Karamu House.

THE MODERNIST MOVEMENT

Following the end of World War II, a number of African American artists began moving away from the social realism that had dominated the art scene of the 1930s. Leading the way in explorations of abstraction and expressionism were Norman Lewis and brothers Beauford and Joseph Delaney. At the same time, a significant number of African American artists chose to live and work in Europe.

CIVIL RIGHTS AND THE BLACK ARTS MOVEMENT

The civil rights movement had a powerful impact on African American visual artists, inspiring countless works that pointedly explored political and cultural issues. Among those playing a prominent role in these developments was Romare Bearden, who was instrumental in founding the artists' group Spiral (1964–1965) and the Cinque Gallery; both projects were dedicated to promoting political awareness and improving opportunities for black artists. Later in the 1960s, the Black Arts Movement intensified this new spirit, which emphasized self-determination and brought art home to the African American community. In a number of eastern and midwestern cities, black artists painted huge outdoor murals celebrating civil rights leaders and black nationalists. The most striking example of this art was the *Wall of Respect* at the intersection of 43rd Street and Langley Avenue in Chicago. In New York, a group of African American artists formed AfriCobra (African Commune of Bad Relevant Artists), concentrating on vivid and straightforward forms of expression that would be accessible to all members of the community. By the 1980s, the intensely political focus of the Black Arts Movement had subsided. Since that time, African American artists have maintained a keen social consciousness, drawing on the insights of previous generations, but they have also explored the full range of styles and techniques available to contemporary artists.

> **M**odern art has borrowed heavily from Negro sculpture . . . the fine surface qualities of the sculpture, the vitality of the work, and the unsurpassed ability of the artist to create such significant forms. Of great importance has been the fact that the African would distort his figure, if by doing so he could achieve a more expressive form. This is one of the cardinal principles of the modern artist.
>
> Romare Bearden, "The Negro and Modern Art" (*Opportunity*, 1934)

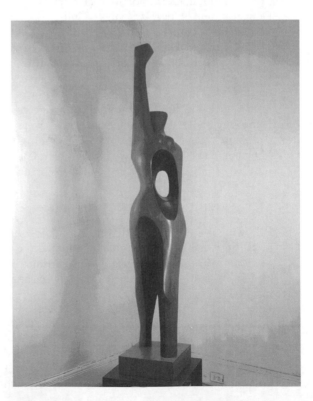

Elizabeth Catlett, Homage to My Young Black Sisters, 1968, *red cedar, 68 × 12 × 12".*

AFRO-BRAZILIAN ARTS

During the colonial era in Brazil, many of the country's leading artists and artisans were mulattos and free blacks. They erected magnificent rococo churches, created religious murals and statues, and crafted most of the ironwork that adorns Brazil's great cities. The most renowned of all was the sculptor and architect Antônio Francisco Lisbôa (1738–1814), known popularly as Aleijandinho (the Little Cripple). Aleijandinho' greatest surviving works are four churches in the province of Minas Gerais, which epitomize the Brazilian rococo style: São Francisco in Ouro Prêto, São João de Rei and Nossa Senhora do Carmo in Sabará, and Bom Jesus de Matosinhos in Congonhos. To adorn Bom Jesus de Matosinhos, Aleijandinho carved 66 life-size wooden figures depicting the Stations of the Cross and 12 soapstone statues of Old Testament prophets. Afflicted by a disease that may have been leprosy or syphilis, he lost his toes and the use of his hands but continued to work—assistants carried him to the worksite and strapped his chisel and mallet to the gnarled stumps of his hands.

LOCATION OF SELECTED MAJOR ARTWORKS

(Note: In most cases, the works indicated here represent only a small fraction of each institution's total holdings in African American art.)

AMISTAD RESEARCH CENTER, TULANE UNIVERSITY, NEW ORLEANS, LA

- Elizabeth Catlett-Mora—*Survivor; Target*
- Aaron Douglas—*Triboro Bridge*
- William Henry Johnson—*Honeymooners*
- Jacob Lawrence—*Toussaint L'Ouverture* series
- Gregory Ridley Jr.—*Seated Figure*
- Ellis Wilson—*Haitian Funeral Procession; Shore Leave*

CINCINNATI ART MUSEUM, CINCINNATI, OH

- Robert S. Duncanson—*Blue Hole, Little Miami River; The Rising Mist; Sunset on the New England Coast;* murals from the Nicholas Longworth House

CLEVELAND MUSEUM OF ART, CLEVELAND, OH

- Meta Vaux Warrick Fuller—sculptures

HAMPTON UNIVERSITY MUSEUM, HAMPTON, VA

- John Biggers—*Climbing Higher Mountains*
- Malvin Gray Johnson—*Negro Masks*
- Archibald J. Motley Jr.—*Black Belt*
- Charles White—*Contribution of the Negro to American Democracy*
- Hale A. Woodruff—*Returning Home*

HOWARD UNIVERSITY GALLERY OF ART, WASHINGTON, DC

- Robert S. Duncanson—*Landscape with Classical Ruins, Recollections of Italy*
- Lois Mailou Jones—*Jennie*
- Edmonia Lewis—*Forever Free; The Old Indian Arrowmaker and His Daughter*
- Archibald J. Motley Jr.—*Barbecue; The Liar; Saturday Night*
- Annie E. Walker—*La Parisienne*
- Charles White—*Awaiting His Return*
- Ellis Wilson—*Fishermen's Wives*

JOSEPH HIRSCHHORN MUSEUM AND SCULPTURE GALLERY, SMITHSONIAN INSTITUTION, WASHINGTON, DC

- William Edmonson—*Mary and Martha*
- Jacob Lawrence—*The Cabinetmaker; This Is Harlem*
- Horace Pippin—*Holy Mountain III*
- Alma W. Thomas—*Blue Asteroid; Joe Summerford's Still Life Study; Watusi; Hard Edge*

METROPOLITAN MUSEUM OF ART, NEW YORK, NY

- Richmond Barthé—*The Boxer*
- Hale A. Woodruff—*Torso No. 1*

MILWAUKEE ART MUSEUM

- Henry Ossawa Tanner—*Moonlight Hebron*

MUSEUM OF AFRICAN AMERICAN ART, LOS ANGELES, CA

- Palmer C. Hayden—*The Baptizing Day; The Blues Singer; John Henry* series; *No Easy Riders*

MUSEUM OF MODERN ART, NEW YORK, NY

- Elizabeth Catlett-Mora—*Malcolm X Speaks for Us*
- Jacob Lawrence—*Migration* series

NATIONAL MUSEUM OF AMERICAN ART, SMITHSONIAN INSTITUTION, WASHINGTON, DC

- Edward M. Bannister—*In Morton Park, Newport, R.I., Looking South; Dorchester, Massachusetts; Moon over a Harbor; Oak Trees; Landscape with a Man on a Horse; Approaching Storm; Sunset*
- Elizabeth Catlett-Mora—*Sharecropper*
- Palmer C. Hayden—*Fétiche et Fleurs; The Janitor Paints a Picture*
- Malvin Gray Johnson—*Self-Portrait*
- William Henry Johnson—*City Gates, Kairouan; Fruit Trees and Mountains; Going to Church; Jacobia Hotel; Lessons in a Soldier's Life; Minnie; Mom and Dad; Mount Calvary; Sun Setting, Denmark; Under Fire*
- Lois Mailou Jones—*Les Fétiches*

- Edmonia Lewis—*Hagar in the Wilderness*
- Henry Ossawa Tanner—*Angels Appearing before the Shepherds*
- Alma W. Thomas—*Light Blue Nursery; Grassy Melodic Chant; Red Azaleas Singing and Dancing Rock and Roll Music; Snoopy—Early Sun Display on Earth; Wind and Crepe Myrtle Concerto*
- James W. Washington Jr.—*Young Queen of Ethiopia*
- James Lesesne Wells—*The Temptation of Eve*
- Ellis Wilson—*Field Workers*

NELSON-ATKINS MUSEUM, KANSAS CITY, MO

- Henry O. Tanner—*The Young Sabot Maker*

NEWARK MUSEUM, NEWARK, NJ

- Beauford Delaney—*Portrait of a Man*
- William Edmonson—*Jack Johnson; Mother and Child; The Preacher; Two Birds*

OAKLAND MUSEUM, OAKLAND, CA

- Grafton T. Brown—*Mount Tacoma; Grand Canyon of the Yellowstone from Hayden Point*
- Sargent Johnson—*Lenox Avenue; Singing Saints*
- William Henry Johnson—*Street Musicians*

PENNSYLVANIA ACADEMY OF FINE ARTS, PHILADELPHIA, PA

- Horace Pippin—*John Brown Going to His Hanging*
- Henry Ossawa Tanner—*Nicodemus Visiting Jesus; West Chester Courthouse*

PHILADELPHIA MUSEUM OF ART, PHILADELPHIA, PA

- Horace Pippin—*Christian Brinton; The End of the War: Starting Home*
- Henry Ossawa Tanner—*The Annunciation*

PHILLIPS COLLECTION, WASHINGTON, DC

- Jacob Lawrence—*Migrants* series
- Horace Pippin—*The Domino Players*

SAN FRANCISCO MUSEUM OF MODERN ART, SAN FRANCISCO, CA

- Sargent Johnson—*Chester; Copper Mask; Elizabeth Gee; Forever Free*

SCHOMBURG CENTER FOR RESEARCH IN BLACK CULTURE, NEW YORK, NY

- Richmond Barthé—*Booker T. Washington*
- Aaron Douglas—*Aspects of Negro Life: From Slavery to Reconstruction*
- Meta Warrick Fuller—*Ethiopia Awakening*
- Malvin Gray Johnson—*Soldier*
- Archibald J. Motley Jr.—*Dans la Rue; Jockey Club, Paris*
- Augusta Savage—*Gamin; James Weldon Johnson; The Pugilist*

STUDIO MUSEUM IN HARLEM, NEW YORK, NY

- Romar Bearden—*Conjur Woman;* several other works
- Elizabeth Catlett—several works
- Norman Lewis—several works

WHITNEY MUSEUM OF AMERICAN ART, NEW YORK, NY

- Charles H. Alston—*The Family*
- Richmond Barthé—*African Dancer; Blackberry Woman*

JAMAICAN ART

Beginning in the 1920s, self-taught Jamaican artists such as John Dunkley, Kapo, David Miller Sr., Gaston Tabois, and Sidney McLaren began producing outstanding works that transcended the island's folk-art tradition. An organized fine-arts movement began in Jamaica during the nationalistic revival of the 1930s. At that time the Institute of Jamaica, led by H. D. Molesworth and Edna Manley, took the lead in nurturing artists such as Alvin Marriott, David Pottinger, and Carl Abrahams. The Jamaican School of Arts and Crafts, founded with government funding in 1950, provided scholarships for artists to study in Europe: Taking advantage of this opportunity were Gloria Escoffery, Albert Huie, Ralph Campbell, and others. During the 1960s, the Jamaican Contemporary Artists' Association and the Olympia International Arts Center in Kingston nurtured a new generation of artists, which included Karl and Seya Parboosingh, Barrington Watson, Milton Harley, Alexander Cooper, and Eugene Hyde. Artists achieving prominence during the 1980s and 1990s have included David Boxer, Eric Cadien, Laura Facey Cooper, Winston Patrick, and Norma Rodney Harrack. Though their styles range from realism to abstraction, almost all have remained profoundly rooted in Jamaican life and culture.

HAITIAN ART

Though Haiti has a long tradition of folk and religious art, a formal arts movement did not begin until 1944, when DeWitt Peters opened the Centre d'Art in Port-au-Prince. The center attracted a host of talented artists, led by the *houngan* (Vaudou priest) Hector Hippolyte; this "first generation" of Haitian artists also included Philomé Obin, Rigaud Benoit, Castera Bazile, and Wilson Bigaud. The success of these artists inspired the creation of numerous art schools in Port-au-Prince and Cap Haitien. Obin and Bigaud painted murals in Holy Trinity Cathedral. Virtually without exception, the artists of Haiti have drawn their inspiration from the country's landscape, everyday life, and religious traditions. (Especially renowned as a religious painter is André Pierre, who has painted many scenes inspired by Vaudou beliefs.) Renowned for its passion, exuberance, and bold use of form and color, Haitian art has become increasingly popular with art enthusiasts and collectors. The following is a list of outstanding 20th-century Haitian artists. Their work, and that of other Haitian artists, can be viewed at www.medalia.net, the Art of Haiti website.

Montas Antoine—painter
Castera Bazile—painter
Rigaud Benoit—painter
Wilson Bigaud—painter
André Blaise—painter
Byron Bourmand—painter
Murat Brierre—sculptor
Wilner Chérizol—painter
G. E. Ducasse—painter
Jean-Baptiste Edger—painter

René Exumé—painter
Enguérrand Gourgue—
  painter
Hector Hippolyte—painter
Jean-Baptiste Jean—painter
Ulrick Jean—painter
Jasmin Joseph—sculptor
Raymond Lafaille—painter
Wesner Laforest—painter
Georges Liautaud—sculptor

Seresier Louisjuste—sculptor
Philomé Obin—painter
Raymond Olivier—painter
Gérard Paul—painter
André Pierre—painter
Micius Stéphane—painter
Gérard Valcin—painter
Eddy Valmont—painter

GALLERIES AND MUSEUMS SPECIALIZING IN AFRICAN AND AFRICAN AMERICAN ART

See also "Museums and Historic Sites" on page 137.

CALIFORNIA

African American Art Gallery
4208 N. Freeway Boulevard, #4
Sacramento, CA 95834
916-568-1238

African American Artists Gallery
428 E. Manchester Boulevard
Inglewood, CA 90301
310-412-1773

African Art Design
310 E. 12th Street
Los Angeles, CA 90000
213-747-5638

African Arts and Crafts Center
411 Divisadero Street
San Francisco, CA 94117
415-252-0199

African Connection Arts and Crafts
7204 Melrose Avenue
Los Angeles, CA 90046
213-965-8628

African Connexion
468 Main Street
Ferndale, CA 95536
707-786-9211

African Gallery
2233 Grand Canal Boulevard
Stockton, CA 95207
209-951-0291

Black Art Gallery
2251 Florin Road
Sacramento, CA 95822
916-395-1690

Black Art Production Co.
1732 103rd Avenue
Oakland, CA 94601
510-568-1135

Black Gallery
107 Santa Barbara Plaza
Los Angeles, CA 90008
213-294-9024

Museum of African American Art
4005 Crenshaw Boulevard
Los Angeles, CA 90008
213-294-7071

DISTRICT OF COLUMBIA

Sign of the Times Cultural Workshop and Gallery
605 56th Street, NE
Washington, DC 20019
202-399-3400

FLORIDA

African American Caribbean Cultural Center
1601 S. Andrews Avenue
Fort Lauderdale, FL 33316
305-467-4056

Afrikan Culture Gallery
4065 L. B. McLeod Road
Orlando, FL 32811
407-245-1171

Gallery Antiqua
5138 Biscayne Boulevard
Miami, FL 33137
305-759-5355

GEORGIA

Hammonds House Galleries
503 Peeples Street, SW
Atlanta, GA 30310
404-752-8730

McIntosh Gallery
One Virginia Hill
587 Virginia Avenue
Atlanta, GA 30306
404-892-4023

IDAHO

African Fine Arts
601 Sun Valley Road
Ketchum, ID 83340
208-726-3144

ILLINOIS

African American Images, Inc.
1909 W. 95th Street
Chicago, IL 60643
312-445-0322

INDIANA

African Art & More
6101 N. Keystone Avenue
Indianapolis, IN 46220
317-466-0036

LOUISIANA

The African American Art Gallery
1796 Rosiere Street
New Orleans, LA 70119
504-245-4036

MAINE

African Imports and New England Arts
1 Union Street
Portland, ME 04101
207-772-9505

MASSACHUSETTS

African Heritage Gallery
930 Main Street
Worcester, MA 01610
508-752-1199

African Traditional Art
1132 Massachusetts Avenue
Cambridge, MA 02138
617-661-8282

Cousens-Rose Gallery
Circuit Avenue
Oak Bluffs
Martha's Vineyard, MA 02568

Liz Harris Gallery
54 Burroughs Street
Boston, MA 02130
617-338-1315

Wendell Street Gallery
17 Wendell Street
Cambridge, MA 02138
617-864-9294

MICHIGAN

Black Arts and Cultural Center
225 Parsons Street
Kalamazoo, MI 49007
616-349-1035

G. R. N'namdi Gallery
161 Townsend Street
Birmingham, MI 48009
248-642-2700

Your Heritage House
110 E. Ferry Street
Detroit, MI 48202
313-871-1667

NEVADA

African American Cultural Arts
1048 W. Owens Avenue
Las Vegas, NV 89106
702-646-1520

NEW YORK

African Art Source
127 W. 26th Street
New York, NY 10001
212-645-6526

African Gallery at the Courtyard
223 Katonah Avenue
Katonah, NY 10536
914-232-9511

African Gallery at the Depot
8 Depot Plaza
Scarsdale, NY 10583
914-725-2727

African Trader Art Gallery
317 W. 78th Street
New York, NY 10024
212-724-3114

Afro Arts Cultural Center
2192 Adam Clayton Powell, Jr., Boulevard
New York, NY 10027
212-996-3333

Cinque Gallery
560 Broadway
New York, NY 10012
212-966-3464

Community Folk Art Gallery
2223 Genessee Street
Syracuse, NY 13210
315-424-8487

Grinnell Fine Art Collections
800 Riverside Drive, Suite 5E
New York, NY 10032
212-927-7941

Hatch-Billops Collection
491 Broadway
New York, NY 10012
212-966-3231

June Kelly Gallery
591 Broadway, 3rd Floor
New York, NY 10012
212-226-1660

Studio Museum in Harlem
114 W. 125th Street
New York, NY 10027
212-864-4500

NORTH CAROLINA

African American Art
202 Four Seasons Town Center
Greensboro, NC 27401
910-292-3209

African-American Atelier
Greensboro Cultural Center
200 N. Davie Street
Greensboro, NC 27411
910-333-6885

AM Studio
1610 E. 14th Street
Winston-Salem, NC 27105
336-725-4959

Biggers Arts Sales Traveling Gallery
1404 N. Oakwood Street
Gastonia, NC 28052
704-867-4525

H. C. Taylor Gallery
North Carolina A & T State University
Greensboro, NC 27411
910-334-7784

Huff's Art Studio
2846 Patterson Avenue
Winston-Salem, NC 27105
336-724-7581

Selma Burke Gallery
Winston-Salem State University
Winston-Salem, NC 27110
336-750-2458

OHIO

Karamu House
2355 E. 89th Street
Cleveland, OH 44106
216-795-7070

OKLAHOMA

Sanamu African Gallery
Kirkpatrick Museum Complex
Oklahoma City, OK 73105
405-427-7529

PENNSYLVANIA

Africamerica Festival
2247 N. Broad Street
Philadelphia, PA 19132
215-232-2900

African American Heritage, Inc.
4601 Market Street
Philadelphia, PA 19132
215-748-7817

SOUTH CAROLINA

African American Gallery
43 John Street
Charleston, SC 29403
803-722-8224

TENNESSEE

African American Art Gallery
114 Carr Street

Knoxville, TN 37919
423-584-1320

The University Galleries
Fisk University
1000 D. B. Todd Boulevard
Nashville, TN 37208
615-329-8543

TEXAS

African Art Connection
3400 Montrose Boulevard
Houston, TX 77006
213-529-8266

African Artifacts Imports
5501 Davis Boulevard
Fort Worth, TX 76180
817-581-6358

Black Art Gallery
5408 Alameda Road
Houston, TX 77004
713-529-7900

VIRGINIA

African Art—Gallerie Lataj
1203 King Street
Alexandria, VA 22314
703-549-0508

WISCONSIN

African-American Art Gallery
3528 W. Villard Avenue
Milwaukee, WI 53209
414-536-644

AFRICAN AMERICAN ARTISTS ORGANIZATIONS

African American Artists Alliance of Chicago
1805 E. 71st Stree
Chicago, IL 60637
312-288-5100

African American Culture and Arts Network
501 W. 145th Street
New York, NY 10031
212-749-4408

Black Arts Alliance
1157 Navasota Street
Austin, TX 78702
512-477-9660

Black Cultural Arts Coalition
141 N.E. Third Avenue
Miami, FL 33010
305-379-6025

Caribbean Cultural Center
408 W. 58th Street
New York, NY 10012
212-307-7420

International Agency for Minority
Artists Affairs, Inc.
147 W. 42nd Street
New York, NY 10036
212-873-5040

Minority Arts Resource Council
1421 W. Girard Avenue
Philadelphia, PA 19130
215-236-2688

National Center of Afro-American Artists
300 Walnut Avenue
Boston, MA 02119
617-442-8614

National Conference of Artists
P.O. Box 1287 MCS
Dayton, OH 45407
513-381-0645

Research Institute of African and African
Diaspora Arts
12 Morley Street
Roxbury, MA 02119
617-427-8325

Studio Museum in Harlem
144 W. 125th Street
New York, NY 10027
212-864-4500

"Where We At" Black Women Artists
1452 Bedford Avenue
Brooklyn, NY 11216
718-398-3871

NOTABLE AFRICAN AMERICAN ARTISTS

Abele, Julian Francis (1881–1950). Architect and painter. First African American to have an impact on the design of large buildings in the United States, though his role was usually concealed; known for modernizing classical forms; long-time partner in Philadelphia firm of Horace Trumbauer Associates, which he headed from 1938 to 1950. Major designs include the Free Library and Museum of Art, Philadelphia; Widener Library, Harvard University; and much of the Duke University campus.

Allen, Tina (1957–). Sculptor. Noted for works memorializing outstanding African Americans, including A. Philip Randolph and Marcus Garvey.

Alston, Charles (1907–1972). Painter, sculptor, muralist. Works include murals on the façade of Harlem Hospital; *Black Man and Black Woman—U.S.A.* (1967); *Blues Song* (1958); *Farm Boy* (c. 1942); *Walking* (1958).

Andrews, Benny (1930–   ).   Painter known for collages and murals. Works often depict scenes of African American life based on his early life in rural Georgia. Works include *American Gothic* (1971); *Champion* (1968); *The Family* (1965).

Bannister, Edward Mitchell (1828–1901).   Painter. Paintings distinguished by their celebration of nature, most notably in peaceful pastoral scenes. Bannister also cofounded the Providence Art Club, which later became the Rhode Island School of Design. Works include *After the Storm* (1875); *Driving Home the Cows* (1881); *Sabin Point, Narragansett Bay* (1875); *Sad Memories* (1882).

Barthé, Richmond (1901–1989).   Sculptor. First black sculptor elected (1945) to the American Academy of Arts and Letters. African and African American themes predominate in his work. Sculptures include *African Dancer* (1934); *Blackberry Woman* (1932); *Booker T. Washington* (1946); *The Boxer* (1942); *Henry O. Tanner* (1928); *West Indian Girl* (1930).

Basquiat, Jean-Michel (1960–1988).   Painter of Haitian and Puerto Rican descent. First achieved notoriety by spray-painting graffiti on New York City buildings. A retrospective of his art was presented by the Whitney Museum in 1992 to 1993. Works include *CPRKR (in honor of Charlie Parker); Flexible; Hollywoods Africans; Self-Portrait as a Heel #3; Untitled (History of Black People).* (All were painted in the 1980s.)

Bearden, Romare (1914–1988).   Painter. Known for his modernist paintings and innovative collages depicting aspects of the African American experience and the life of the urban black community; cofounder of Spiral and of the Cinque Gallery. One-person show at the Museum of Modern Art in 1971. Works include *Black Manhattan* (1969); *He Is Arisen* (1945); *Showtime!* (1974); *Summertime* (1967); *The Train* (1975).

Biggers, John (1924–   ).   Painter. Known for combining realism and expressionism; later paintings show the influence of African art. Works include *The Contributions of Negro Women to American Life and Education* (1953); *Jubilee* (1957); *Mother and Child* (1960).

Billops, Camille (1933–   ).   Sculptor. Known for her work in ceramics; also excels as a filmmaker, book illustrator, and jewelry designer. Major pieces include *Black Suffering Jesus and Yellow Man* (1976); *Tenure* (1973).

Blackburn, Robert (1921–   ).   Printmaker. Prints distinguished by powerful images of African Americans; founded the Printmaking Workshop (1949), a mecca for minority artists. Works include *Boy with Green Head* (1948); *The Toiler* (1938).

Blayton-Taylor, Betty (1937–   ).   Painter and sculptor. Active as a teacher and administrator, as well as an artist; created the Children's Art Carnival in Harlem and helped found the Studio Museum in Harlem. Works include *Childhood's End* (1967); *Concentrated Energies* (1970); *I Am Me* (1968).

Bond, James Max (1935–   ).   Architect. Graduated from Harvard, then began working and teaching in Ghana; dean of the School of Architecture and Environmental Studies at City College of New York since 1985. Designs include the Martin Luther King, Jr., Center for Nonviolent Social Change, Atlanta, Georgia; the Studio Museum in Harlem.

Bowling, Frank (1936–   ).   Painter. Born in Guyana; won grand prize at the first World Festival of Negro Art in Dakar, Senegal, in 1966. Works include *Mel Edwards Decides* (1969); *Where Is Lucienne?* (1970); *Whoosh* (1974).

Braxton, William E. (1878–1932).   Painter. Regarded as the first African American expressionist painter. Works include *Figural Study; Wife of Arthur Schomburg* (1900).

Burke, Selma (1900–   ).   Sculptor. Studied in Paris with Aristide Maillol during the 1930s; founded the Selma Burke Art Center in Pittsburgh. First African American artist whose work appeared on a U.S. coin—her bronze plaque depicting Franklin D. Roosevelt (1943) having been used for the 10-cent piece. Works include *Falling Angel* (1977); *Grief* (1945); *Jim* (1939); *Mother and Child* (1968); *Peace* (1972).

Burroughs, Margaret (1917–). Painter and sculptor. Multifaceted artist who was also a leader in founding artist groups and in fostering art education. Works include *Black Queen; Mexican Landscape; Two Girls.*

Catlett-Mora, Elizabeth (1919–). Sculptor and painter. Combines realism and abstraction; has been deeply influenced by the civil rights movement; employs themes from Mexican culture, as well as African American life. Sculptures include *Black Unity* (1968); *The Black Woman Speaks* (1970); *Dance* (1970); *Homage to My Young Black Sisters* (1968); *Malcolm X Speaks for Us* (1969); *Sharecropper* (1976); *Target* (1970).

Chandler, Dana (1941–). Muralist. Known for creating large, striking murals of social protest throughout Boston. Works include *Fred Hampton's Door* (1970); *Death of Uncle Tom* (1968); *Knowledge Is Power, Stay in School* (1972).

Chase-Riboud, Barbara (1939–). Sculptor. Paris-based sculptor who has exhibited throughout the world; blends African motifs with European, Asian, and Middle Eastern themes; also known for novels and essays, notably *Sally Hemings.* Major artworks include *The Bulls* (1958); *Monuments to Malcolm X* (1969); *Zanziber* (1972).

Clark, Edward (1926–). Painter. Known for "shaped" paintings in which the figures extend beyond the boundaries of the canvas; often works with ellipses. Works include *Earth Zone* (1978); *Paris Rose* (1970).

Colescott, Robert (1925–). Painter. Employs satire and parody to attack racial stereotypes, often replacing whites with blacks in famous American and European paintings. United States representative to the 47th Venice Biennale, 1997. Works include *Colored TV* (1977); *George Washington Carver Crossing the Delaware* (1975); *Natural Rhythm* (1975).

Conwill, Houston (1947–). Installation artist. Expresses his African American heritage through ritual objects assembled in art environments and installations. Works include *Edison Tale* (1976–1977); *Juju Installation* (1977).

Cortor, Eldzier (1915–). Painter noted for elongated nudes hailed as both sensual and surreal. Works include *Americana* (1947); *Southern Gate* (1945).

Crichlow, Ernest (1914–). Painter and illustrator of Barbadian ancestry. Known for his depictions of children and family groups, often reflecting underlying social issues; has illustrated numerous children's books with African American themes. Works include *The Domestic* (1960); *Lend Me Your Hand; The White Fence* (1967); *Young Boy* (1960).

Cruz, Emilio (1938–). Painter. Known for his bold experiments with the human figure. Works include *Browner Drownin Secret Blue* (1972); *Figure Composition 6* (1964).

DeCarava, Roy (1919–). Photographer. Noted for his portraits and explorations of urban life, including an extensive record of major jazz musicians. Collaborated with Langston Hughes to produce *The Sweet Flypaper of Life* (1955), a literary and visual tribute to Harlem.

Delaney, Beauford (1910–1979). Painter. Known for his portrayals of New York life and portraits of leading personalities of the 1930s; moved to Paris during the 1950s. Works include *Greene Street* (1951); *Yaddo* (1952).

Delaney, Joseph (1904–1991). Painter. Did much of his work on the sidewalks of New York; known for his street scenes and portraits. Works include *Albert Ammons* (1943); *Penn Station at Wartime* (1943); *V-J Day Times Square* (1945).

Douglas, Aaron (1899–1979). Painter/muralist. First achieved recognition as an illustrator and ranked as one of the leading artists of the Harlem Renaissance. Illustrated the books of renowned African American writers, such as Countee Cullen, Alain Locke, and Langston Hughes. Works include the *Aspects* *of Negro Life* (1934) series and the murals in the Countee Cullen Branch of the New York Public Library (104 W. 136th Street).

Dowell, John (1941–   ).   Painter. Influenced by East Asian art forms; created the Visual Arts Ensemble (1976), an instrumental group that interprets his work musically. Paintings include *It Can't Be Possessed* (1973); *To Dance Yesterday's Dreams* (1977).

Duncanson, Robert (1817–1872).   Painter. Duncanson's work included landscapes, portraits, and murals. Known as a Cincinnati artist, he was the first African American artist to win recognition as a studio painter. Works include *Blue Hole, Flood Waters, Little Miami River* (1851); *Landscape with Classical Ruins, Recollections of Italy* (1854); *View of Cincinnati, Ohio, from Covington, Kentucky* (1851).

Edmonson, William (1882–1951).   Sculptor and tombstone artist. Self-taught artist who began as a stonecutter; renowned for transcending the traditional line between folk art and fine art; portraits are noted for their masklike quality, and animal figures often echo African and African American folktales. First African American to have a solo exhibition at the Museum of Modern Art, New York. Works include *Horse; Jack Johnson; Mary and Martha* (1930); *Mother and Child; The Preacher* (1937); *Two Birds* (1973).

Edwards, Melvin (1937–   ).   Sculptor. Expresses African American themes in a modernist idiom. Works include *August, the Squared Fire* (1965); *Double Circles* (1968); *Homage to My Father and the Spirit* (1969).

Fax, Elton (1909–1993).   Illustrator. Known for his depiction of African themes; also a distinguished writer. Works include *Ethiopia Old and New* (1970); *Steelworker* (1939).

Fuller, Meta Vaux Warrick (1877–1968).   Sculptor. Studied with Auguste Rodin in Paris. Works include *The Awakening of Ethiopia* (1914); *John* (1899); *The Talking Skull* (1937); *The Wretched* (1930).

Gilliam, Sam (1933–   ).   Painter. Known for his technique of hanging brightly pigmented canvases in startling combinations. Works include *Carousel Change* (1970); *Mazda* (1970); *Watercolor 4* (1969).

Hammons, David (1939–   ).   Painter and sculptor. Early works incorporate the American flag in various contexts; later works employ natural substances and found objects, including his own hair, to convey a strong political message. Works include *America the Beautiful* (1968); *Injustice Case* (1970); *Pray for America* (1969).

Harper, William (1873–1910).   Painter. Born in Canada, Harper traveled widely across the United States and Europe and was living in Mexico City at the time of his death. His work was widely exhibited and reviewed, especially after his death. Works include *Afternoon at Montigny* (1905); *Landscape* (1906); *The Sunlit Wall: Brittany* (1904).

Hathaway, Isaac (1871–?).   Sculptor and ceramist. Works include busts of Frederick Douglass, Booker T. Washington, and Paul Laurence Dunbar.

Hayden, Palmer C. (1893–1973).   Painter. Noted for landscapes, street scenes, and portrayals of African American life (often with a sharp edge of social commentary and political protest). Works include *The Janitor Who Paints* (1937); the *John Henry* series (1940–1947).

Hunt, Richard (1935–   ).   Sculptor. Often explores spatial concepts; some works resemble trees, horns, and other inanimate objects. Works include *The Chase* (1965); *Linear Spatial Theme* (1962); *Man on a Vehicular Construction* (1956).

Jackson, May Howard (1877–1931).   Sculptor. Best known for her busts of prominent individuals; later work includes sculptures on African American themes, such as *Head of a Negro Child* (1916).

Johnson, Daniel (1938–   ).   Sculptor. Creates painted wooden sculptures, including *Big Red* (1963); *Death of Tarzan* (1970); *Yesterday* (1963).

Johnson, Malvin Gray (1896–1934).   Painter. Among the first African American artists to assimilate the techniques of cubism. Works include *Picking Beans* (1935); *Self-Portrait* (1934); *Southern Landscape* (1934).

Johnson, Sargent (1888–1967).   Sculptor. Strongly influenced by African artistic traditions; strived to capture the "natural beauty and dignity" of African Americans in his art. Works include *Chester* (1929); *Copper Mask* (1929); *Elizabeth Gee* (1925); *Esther* (1926); *Forever Free* (1936); *Lenox Avenue* (1938); *Sammy* (1927).

Johnson, William Henry (1901–1970).   Painter. Experimented with many forms of modernist painting, ranging from realistic studies of African American life to abstract expressionism. Works include *City Gates, Kairouan* (1932); *Fruit Trees and Mountains* (c. 1936–1938); *Going to Church*; *Jesus and the Three Marys* (c. 1939); *Mom and Dad* (1944); *Street Musicians*; *Under Fire* (c. 1941–1942).

Johnston, Joshua (c. 1765–1830).   Painter. The first African American to be recognized as a major artist in the United States. Based in Baltimore, he specialized in portrait painting. Works include *Benjamin Franklin Yoe and Son, Benjamin F., Jr.* (c. 1810); *In the Garden* (1805); *Portrait of a Cleric* (c. 1805–1810).

Jones, Lois Mailou (1905–).   Painter. Began working as textile designer and fashion illustrator before moving to oils and watercolors; themes have included scenes from Africa and the Caribbean. Works include *Les Fétiches* (1938); *Old Street in Montmartre* (1948); *Ubi Girl from Tai Region, Nigeria* (1972).

Joseph, Ronald (1910–1992).   Painter. Regarded as the leading African American abstractionist of his generation. Works include *Card Players* (1945); *Introspect* (1937).

Lankford, John Anderson (1874–1946).   Architect. Opened the first African American architectural office (Washington, D.C., 1897); designed the Pythian Building in Washington, D.C. (1901), the first large office building in the United States designed by a black architect. Designs included St. John's Church, Norfolk, Virginia; A.M.E. Church of Cape Town, South Africa; Haven Methodist Episcopal Church, Washington, D.C., Palmer Hall, Alabama A&M University; Chappelle Administration Building, Allen University.

Lawrence, Jacob (1917–).   Painter. Influential modernist whose works depict African American history; best known for creating narratives on a series of panels. Major restrospective of his art was presented by the Seattle Museum in 1986. Leading works include *The Cabinetmaker* (1957); *The Life of Harriet Tubman* (1939–1940); *The Life of Toussaint L'Ouverture* (1939); *The Negro Migration Northward in the World War* (1940–1941); *Parade* (1960); *Street Orator* (1936).

Lee-Smith, Hughie (1915–).   Painter. Has worked in both realist and surrealist modes, often portraying human figures in bleak, stylized settings; uses allegory to explore social issues. Works include *Boy with Tire* (1955); *Impedimenta* (1958).

Lewis, Edmonia (1845–1890).   Sculptor. Recognized as the first major African American female artist in the United States, Lewis was educated at Oberlin College and also studied art in Rome. Her sculptures exemplify the neoclassical style of the 19th century. Works include *Forever Free* (1867); *Hagar in the Wilderness* (1875); *Henry Wadsworth Longfellow* (1879); *An Old Indian Arrowmaker and His Daughter* (1872).

Lewis, Norman (1909–1979).   Painter. Began as a social realist and gravitated to abstract expressionism. Works include *Arrival and Departure, 1963* (1963); *The Yellow Hat* (1936).

Mayhew, Richard (1924–).   Painter. Works in oil. Works include *Hilltop* (1963); *Time* (1969); *West* (1965).

McCullough, Geraldine (1922–).   Sculptor. Works include *Black Knight on a Unicorn* (1965); *Confrontation* (1969); *Phoenix* (1969).

Miller, Earl (1930–).   Abstract painter. Often works in acrylics. Works include *Accordian Flyer* (1963); *Stellar* (1976); *Tone Poems with Two Blue Squares* (c. 1978).

Motley, Archibald J., Jr. (1891–1980).   Painter. Noted for his vivid portrayals of life in the African American community. Works include *Black Belt—Harlem* (1934); *Blues* (1929); *Chicken Shack* (1936); *Jockey Club, Paris* (1929); *The Octoroon Girl* (1929); *Parisian Scene* (1929); *Saturday Night.*

Overstreet, Joseph (1934–   ).   Painter. Work includes abstract canvases employing African and Asian color patterns. Works include *Indian Sun* (1969); *Justice, Faith, Hope and Peace* (1968); *The New Jemima* (1964).

Parks, Gordon, Sr. (1912–   ).   Photographer and multitalented artist. First made his reputation as a photographer and was the first African American to cover assignments for magazines such as *Life* and *Vogue.* Also did memorable work for the Farm Security Administration and the Office of War Information during the 1940s. Published collections include *Born Black* (1971); *Flavio* (1978); *Gordon Parks: A Poet and His Camera* (1968); *Gordon Parks: Whispers of Intimate Things* (1975).

Pindell, Howardena (1943–   ).   Painter. Known for use of collage; more recent works have explored the subject of memory. Works include *East-West*; *Inflation*; *Lake Lilies for Kim*; *Memory Tes*; *Waterfall*; *You Have a Friend at Chase.*

Pippin, Horace (1888–1946).   Painter. Self-taught artist frequently compared with Henri Rousseau. Especially renowned for scenes of World War I, in which Pippin served as an infantry soldier. Works include *The Domino Players* (1943); *The End of the War: Starting Home* (1933); *John Brown Goes to His Hanging* (c. 1942); *The Milkman of Goshen, N.Y.* (1945); *Chester Court House* (1940).

Porter, James Amos (1905–1970).   Painter. Known for portraits incorporating African and Caribbean themes, inspired by the bold colors of the fauves; chaired the Department of Art at Howard University from 1953 to 1970 and wrote the classic art history book, *Modern Negro Art* (1943). Works include *The Haitian Market Woman* (1947); *On a Cuban Bus* (1946); *Tempest—World of the Niger* (1964); *Woman Holding a Jug* (1933).

Puryear, Martin (1937–   ).   Sculptor. Explores the boundaries of abstraction with wall-mounted works, quasi-architectural constructions, and large-scale three-dimensional pieces. Works include *Bask* (1976); *Some Tales* (1975–1978).

Ringgold, Faith (1934–   ).   Expressionist painter, author, and illustrator. Known for use of powerful symbols to explore the situations of women and of African Americans. Techniques range from three-dimensional assemblage boxes to story quilts that function as visual narratives. Works include *The Flag Is Bleeding* (1967); *Flag for the Moon: Die Nigger* (1969).

Saar, Alison (1956–   ).   Sculptor/painter/installation artist. A member of an artistic family, Saar is best known for her rough-hewn wooden figural sculptures, brightly painted and artfully installed. Drawing inspiration from the past, including African, American, and European art, she intuitively interprets her subjects in the present. Works include *Diva* (1988); *Dying Slave* (1989); *Love Potion #9* (1988); *Sweet Thang* (1983).

Saar, Bettye (1926–   ).   Painter and sculptor. Known for montages composed of photographs, flowers, and material objects. Works include *Africa* (1968); *The Vision of El Cremo* (1970).

Saunders, Raymond (1934–   ).   Painter. Known for densely layered paintings and collages employing found objects and symbolic fragments. Works include *An American Dream* (1967); *Celery Root* (1975); *Jack Johnson* (1971); *Valentine* (1978).

Savage, Augusta (1900–1962).   Sculptor. First black member of the National Association of Women Painters and Sculptors (1934). Works include *Gamin* (c. 1929); *James Weldon Johnson* (1940); *Lift Every Voice and Sing* (1939; created for the 1939 World's Fair); *Marcus Garvey* (1972).

Scott, William Edouard (1884–1964).   Painter and muralist. Studied with Henry Ossawa Tanner. Noted for neoclassical style and depictions of life in Haiti, where he visited in the early 1930s. Works include *Blind Sister Mary* (c. 1931); *Haitian Man* (c. 1931).

Simpson, Lorna (1960–).   Photographer and conceptual artist. Works include *Guarded Conditions; Outline; Untitled ("prefer/refuse/decide")*.

Sklarek, Norma Merrick (1928–).   Architect. First African American woman licensed as an architect in the United States (1954) and the first to become a fellow of the American Institute of Architects (1966). Projects include the U.S. Embassy in Tokyo; City Hall in San Bernardino, California; Terminal One, Los Angeles International Airport.

Sleet, Moneta (1926–).   Photographer. A major photojournalist of the civil rights era and staffer of *Ebony* magazine; traveled the world photographing celebrities and heads of state, as well as ordinary people. In 1969, Sleet became the first African American winner of the Pulitzer Prize for photography for his picture of Coretta Scott King comforting her daughter at the funeral of Martin Luther King Jr. A retrospective of his work was organized by the New York Public Library in 1986.

Smith, Marvin (1910–) **and Morgan** (1910–1993).   Photographers known for their extensive recording of Harlem life during the 1930s and 1940s. More than 2,000 of their photographs reside in the collection of the Schomburg Center for Research in Black Culture. Their work appeared in numerous African American publications, as well as in Claude McKay's *Harlem Metropolis, 1940*.

Smith, Vincent (1929–).   Painter. Multifaceted canvases have reflected African culture, jazz themes, and Harlem family life. Works include *The Black Family* (1974); *Sharecropper's Shack* (1968).

Stout, Renee (1958–).   Sculptor. Born in Junction City, Kansas, and educated at Carnegie Mellon University. Disliking the cold, impersonal cityscapes of Boston and Washington, D.C., in which she lived, Stout turned toward her inner spiritual self to find sources of artistic expression. The world of spiritualism and vodun imagery led her to African art. She began to make assemblages from boxes, hair, and found objects that look like ritual figures, often incorporating old sepia photographs. Works include *Fetish #1* (1987); *Fetish #2* (1988).

Tandy, Vertner Woodson, Sr. (1885–1949).   Architect. First African American architect licensed by New York State. Major designs include St. Philip's Episcopal Church and Old Rectory in Harlem; Presbyterian Hospital, Puerto Rico; Abraham Lincoln Houses, Bronx, New York; Madame C. J. Walker's mansion, Villa Lewaro, Irvington-on-Hudson, New York.

Tanner, Henry Ossawa (1859–1937).   Painter. Early paintings often depicted black themes, but religious themes predominated after Tanner settled in Paris during the 1890s. Won the Medal of Honor at the Paris Exposition of 1900, among other awards. Major retrospectives of his work were exhibited by the M. H. de Young Memorial Museum, San Francisco (1992) and the Nelson-Atkins Museum, Kansas City, Missouri (1995). He is the first African American artist in the White House permanent collection (1997). Works include *Angels Appearing before the Wise Men* (c. 1910); *The Annunciation* (1898); *The Banjo Lesson* (1893); *Daniel in the Lions' Den* (1896); *Disciples on the Sea of Galilee* (undated); *Flight into Egypt* (1898).

Thompson, Robert Louis "Bob" (1937–1966).   Painter. Known for depicting flat figures in hallucinatory scenes that often illustrate oral traditions. Works include *Ascension to the Heavens* (1964); *The Dentist* (1963); *Expulsion and Nativity* (1964); *Tree; Untitled Diptych* (1960).

Traylor, Bill (1854–1949).   Painter. Former slave and sharecropper; began drawing on pieces of cardboard and the backs of posters and did not exhibit his work until 1940. Traylor's abstract images of people and animals in everyday settings combine innovative technique with shrewd observation. Works, all painted between 1939 and 1947, include *Airplane Sighting; Black Jug; He Smells a Cow; Man in Blue House with Rooster; Treeing Dog; Turkeys*.

Van Der Zee, James (1886–1983).   Photographer. Began chronicling Harlem in 1916, working out of a studio on 135th Street. Van Der Zee's multifaceted works were featured in the 1969 Metropolitan Museum exhibition "Harlem on My Mind."

Walker, Kara (1970–). Collage artist. Known for cut-paper silhouettes depicting the African American experience, often with startling and sexually explicit imagery. Works include *Girl; Gone: An Historical Romance of the Civil War as It Occurred between the Dusky Thighs of One Young Negress and Her Heart; I'll Be a Monkey's Uncle; Jockey.*

Warbourg, Eugene (1825–1867).   Sculptor. Based in New Orleans, trained as a stonemason before turning to sculpture. Lived and worked in Paris after 1852. Works include *John Young Mason; Le Pecheur; Le Premier Baiser.*

Waring, Laura Wheeling (1887–1948).   Painter noted for classical, dignified portraits. Works include *James Weldon Johnson* (1945); *Mother and Daughter* (c. 1925); *W. E. Burghardt Du Bois* (1945).

Webb, Clifton (1950–).   Painter and sculptor. Known for exploring the intersection of African, African American, and Native American forms. Works include *A Closer Connection; Landscape; The Raft.*

Weems, Carrie Mae (1953–).   Painter, photographer, and filmmaker. Has studied African American folklore, as well as art. Works include *Ain't Jokin'; Black Woman with Chicken; Colored People; Family Pictures and Stories; High Yella Girl; Mirror, Mirror.*

White, Charles (1918–1979).   Painter. Began to concentrate on black-and-white drawings in the 1950s; often depicted the travails of African Americans and their contributions to society. Works include *Contributions of the Negro to American Democracy* (1943); *Frederick Douglass* (1950); *Homage to Langston Hughes* (1942); *J'Accuse No. 5* (1966).

Whitten, Jack (1939–).   Painter. Best known for 1970s "energy fields," which presented stylized urban images and scientific and technical metaphors. Works include *First Frame* (1971); *Sigma I* (1978).

Williams, Paul Revere (1894–1980).   Architect. Licensed in 1915; started his own firm in 1923; became the first African American fellow of the American Institute of Architects in 1926. Designed more than 3,000 buildings and 400 homes, including residences for Cary Grant, Frank Sinatra, Bill "Bojangles" Robinson, and other performers. Designs include Los Angeles County Airport, Palm Springs Tennis Club, Saks Fifth Avenue of Beverly Hills.

Williams, William Thomas (1942–).   Painter. Abstract canvases exhibit motion and conflict through the use of bold colors and stark lines; his most recent works have moved away from formalism toward a more personal perspective. Works include *Buttermilk* (1971–1972); *Elbert Jackson L.A.M.F. Part II* (1969).

Wilson, Ellis (1899–1977).   Painter. Known as a chronicler of African American history. Works include *Field Workers* (1967); *Fisherwoman* (1968); *Funeral Procession* (1940); *Shore Leave* (1971); *To Market* (1971).

Wilson, John (1922–).   Painter, printmaker, and sculptor. Paintings and prints draw on the tradition of the great Mexican muralists, often addressing social problems and African American life. Began working as a sculptor in the 1980s. Works include *Black Soldier* (c. 1943); *Child Praying* (1968); *Roxbury Landscape* (1960); *Trabajador* (1973).

Woodruff, Hale (1900–1980).   Painter and muralist. Known for a wide range of modernist styles, including cubism and abstraction. Works include *The Amistad Murals* (1939; at Talladega College); *The Art of the Negro* (1977; murals at Atlanta University); *The Cardplayers* (1928–1929); *Medieval Chartres* (1928); *Returning Home* (1935); *Torso No. 2* (1971).

Yarde, Richard (1939–).   Painter. Has exhibited at the Boston Museum of Fine Arts, the Wadsworth Atheneum, and the Studio Museum in Harlem, among others. Works include *Parlor* (1976); *Sweet Daddy Graxe* (1977).

SOURCES FOR ADDITIONAL INFORMATION

African American Art: 20th Century Masterworks, IV. New York: Michael Rosenfeld Gallery, 1997.

Bearden, Romare, and Harry Henderson. *A History of African-American Artists from 1792 to the Present*. New York: Pantheon, 1993.

Bearing Witness: Contemporary Works by African American Women Artists. New York: Spelman College/Rizzoli, 1996.

Black Art Ancestral Legacy: The African Impulse in African-American Art. Dallas, TX: Dallas Museum of Art, 1989.

Davis, Lenwood G., and Janet L. Sims. *Black Artists in the United States: An Annotated Bibliography of Books, Articles, and Dissertations on Black Artists, 1779–1979*. Westport, CT: Greenwood Press, 1980.

Directory of People of Color in the Visual Arts. New York: College Art Association, 1993.

Fine, Elsa Honig. *The Afro-American Artist: A Search for Identity*. New York: Holt, Rinehart & Winston, 1973.

Ferris, William, ed. *Afro-American Folk Art and Crafts*. Boston: G. K. Hall, 1983.

Gillon, Werner. *A Short History of African Art*. New York: Penguin, 1984.

Hall, Robert L. *Gathered Visions: Selected Works by African American Women Artists*. Washington, DC: Anacostia Museum, Smithsonian Institution, 1992.

Igoe, Lynn Moody. *250 Years of Afro-American Art: An Annotated Bibliography*. New Providence, NJ: R. R. Bowker, 1981.

Lewis, Samella S. *African American Art and Artists*. Berkeley: University of California Press, 1994.

McElroy, Guy C., Richard J. Powell, and Sharon F. Patton; introduction by David C. Driskell. *African American Artists, 1880–1987: Selections from the Evans-Tibbs Collection*. Washington, DC: Smithsonian Institution Traveling Exhibition Service, in association with University of Washington Press, Seattle, 1989.

Patton, Sharon F. *African-American Art*. New York: Oxford University Press, 1988.

Perry, Regenia. *Free within Ourselves: African-American Artists in the Collection of the National Museum of American Art*. San Francisco: National Museum of American Art in Association with Pomegranate Artbooks, 1992.

Powell, Richard. *Black Art and Culture in the 20th Century*. New York: Thames and Hudson, 1997.

Powell, Richard, and David A. Bailey. *Rhapsodies in Black: Art of the Harlem Renaissance*. Berkeley: University of California Press, 1997.

Price, Richard, and Sally Price. *Afro-American Arts of the Suriname Rain Forest*. Berkeley: University of California Press, 1980.

Rodman, Selden. *Where Art Is Joy: Haitian Art—The First Forty Years*. New York: Ruggles & de Latour, 1988.

Staats, Florence J. *African Americans and the Visual Arts: A Resource Guide to Books, Articles, and Dissertations, 1900–1990*. Rosendale, NY: Arts and Communications Network, 1990.

Straw, Petrine Archer, and Kim Robinson. *Jamaican Art*. Kingston, Jamaica: Kingston Publishers, 1990.

Thomison, Dennis. *The Black Artist in America: An Index to Reproductions*. Metuchen, NJ: Scarecrow, 1991.

Thompson, Robert Farris. *Flash of the Spirit: African and Afro-American Art and Philosophy*. New York: Vintage, 1983.

Travis, Jack. *African-American Architects in Current Practice*. Princeton, NJ: Princeton Architectural Press, 1991.

Vlach, John Michael. *The Afro-American Tradition in Decorative Arts*. Cleveland: Cleveland Museum of Art, 1978.

Vlach, John Michael. *By the Work of Their Hands: Studies in Afro-American Folk Life*. Charlottesville: University Press of Virginia, 1991.

Wardlaw, Alvia. *Black Art: Ancestral Legacy—The African Impulse in African American Art*. New York: Abrams, 1990.

Willis-Thomas, Deborah. *An Illustrated Bio-Bibliography of Black Photographers, 1940–1988*. New York: Garland, 1988.

17

The Media

All the following media organizations either are black owned or publish or broadcast content that is predominantly targeted at a black audience.

TELEVISION STATIONS AND NETWORKS

CALIFORNIA

KMTP-TV Channel 32
Minority Television Project & Company
1504 Bryant Street
San Francisco, CA 94103
(415) 777-3232

KNTV-TV
Granite Broadcasting
645 Park Avenue
San Jose, CA 95110
(408) 286-1111

KSBW-TV
238 John Street
Salinas, CA 93901
(408) 758-8888

KSEE-TV Channel 24
KSEE-TV, Inc.
5035 E. McKinley Avenue
Fresno, CA 93726
(209) 454-2424

COLORADO

KTVJ-TV
Roberts Broadcasting Company
2100 Downing Street
Denver, CO 80202
(303) 832-1414

DISTRICT OF COLUMBIA

Black Entertainment Television (BET)
1899 Ninth Street, NE
Washington, DC 20018
(202) 608-2300

WHMM-TV Channel 32
Howard University Television
2222 Fourth Street, NW
Washington, DC 20059
(202) 806-3200

FLORIDA

WBSF-TV
Black Star Communications of Florida, Inc.
4450-L Enterprise Court
Melbourne, FL 32934
(407) 254-4343

ILLINOIS

WEEK-TV Channel 25
Granite Broadcasting, Inc.
2907 Springfield Road
E. Peoria, IL 61611
(309) 698-2525

WJYS-TV Channel 62
Jovon Broadcasting, Inc.
18600 Oak Park Avenue
Tinley Park, IL 60477
(708) 633-0001

INDIANA

WPTA-TV
Granite Broadcasting, Inc.
3401 Butler Road
Fort Wayne, IN 46808
(219) 483-0584

LOUISIANA

WNOL-TV Channel 38
Quincy Jones Broadcasting, Inc.
1661 Canal Street
New Orleans, LA 70112
(504) 525-3838

MAINE

WVII-TV Channel 7
Seaway Communications
371 Target Industrial Circle
Bangor, ME 04401
(207) 945-6457

MICHIGAN

WBSX-TV Channel 31
Blackstar Communications
P.O. Box 2267
Ann Arbor, MI 48106
(313) 973-7900

WLAJ-TV Channel 53
Lansing 53, Inc.
5815 S. Pennsylvania Avenue
Lansing, MI 48909
(517) 394-5300

MINNESOTA

KBJR-TV Channel 9
Granite Broadcasting Corp.
230 E. Superior Street
Duluth, MN 55802
(218) 727-8484

MISSISSIPPI

WGCB TV-30
4608 Skyland Drive
Meridian, MS 39301
(601) 485-3030

WLBT-TV Channel 3
TV-3, Inc.

715 S. Jefferson Street
Jackson, MS 39202
(601) 948-3333

MISSOURI

WHSL-TV Channel 46
Roberts Broadcasting, Inc.
1408 N. Kings Highway
St. Louis, MO 53113
(314) 367-4600

NEW YORK

WKBW-TV
Granite Broadcasting Corp.
7 Broadcast Plaza
Buffalo, NY 14202
(716) 845-6100

WTVH-TV Channel 5
WTVH, Inc.
980 James Street
Syracuse, NY 13203
(315) 425-5555

OREGON

KBSP-TV
Blackstar Communications
4928 Indian School Road, NE
Salem, OR 97305
(503) 390-2202

SOUTH CAROLINA

WRDW-TV
1301 Georgia Avenue
N. Augusta, SC 29841
(803) 278-1212

TEXAS

KTRE-TV
TV-3, Inc.

P.O. Box 729
Lufkin, TX 75902
(409) 853-5873

VIRGINIA

WJCB-TV
2700 Washington Avenue, 4th Floor
Newport News, VA 23607
(804) 247-0049

WISCONSIN

WJFW-TV
Seaway Communications
Box 858, S. Oneida Avenue
Rhinelander, WI 54501
(715) 369-4700

WJJA-TV
P.O. Box 92
Oakcreek, WI 53154
(414) 764-4953

TV FIRSTS

The first African American to host a network television show was the Trinidad-born singer and pianist Hazel Scott. The *Hazel Scott Show* premiered on the Dumont network in July 1950 and remained on the air until the end of September. The show's cancellation was due in part to accusations that Scott was a Communist sympathizer. A second and equally short-lived variety program hosted by a black performer was *The Billy Daniels Show*, which aired on ABC for two months in late 1952. The first performer to achieve a solid foothold was Nat "King" Cole, whose half-hour weekly variety show debuted on NBC in November 1956. The *Nat King Cole Show*, featuring Cole's inimitable vocals and guests such as Count Basie and Mahalia Jackson, is now considered a classic of 1950s TV. At the time, however, big-name sponsors were not prepared to identify their products with an African American star, and the show was canceled after 50 weeks.

ROOTS

On January 23, 1977, television history was made when ABC presented the first episode of *Roots*, the pioneering miniseries based on Alex Haley's best-selling book. Over the course of eight consecutive evenings, 130 million Americans tuned in to watch LeVar Burton, Louis Gossett Jr., Leslie Uggams, Ben Vereen, and Cicely Tyson star in the dramatic saga of Kunta Kinte and his American descendants. The final episode of *Roots* achieved a 51.1 percent Nielsen rating, the highest ever up to that point.

LONGEST RUN

The longest-running, black-oriented TV show to date has been *The Jeffersons*, starring Sherman Hemsley and Isabel Sanford. A spin-off of *All in the Family*, *The Jeffersons* premiered on CBS in 1975 and lasted until 1985, ranking as the 24th highest-rated TV show of all time.

BROADCAST GROUPS AND RADIO STATIONS

BROADCAST GROUPS

American Urban Radio Networks
463 Seventh Avenue
New York, NY 10018
(212) 714-1000

Inner-City Broadcasting Corporation
801 Second Avenue
New York, NY 10017
(212) 663-3344

National Black Network Broadcasting
   Corporation
463 Seventh Avenue, 6th Floor

New York, NY 10018
(212) 714-1000

Sheridan Broadcasting Corporation
411 Seventh Avenue, #1500
Pittsburgh, PA 15219
(412) 281-6747

Willis Broadcasting Corporation
1645 Church Street, #400
Norfolk, VA 23510
(804) 622-4600

FIRST ON THE AIR

The first black-owned broadcasting operation was the Harlem Broadcasting Corporation, which operated out of studios at 125th Street and Lenox Avenue. The company leased airtime from WRNY and began airing its programs in 1929. The first station completely owned by African Americans was WERD in Atlanta, which was acquired by J. B. Blayton Jr. in 1950.

NEW SOUNDS

The first radio station to have a completely black-oriented format was WDIA in Memphis, which began its new programming in 1949. Though white owned, the station hired Nat D. Williams, the first African American disk jockey in the South, and under his guidance, WDIA became a center for live broadcasts of blues bands and the airing of early rhythm-and-blues recordings. Following Williams's breakthrough, a number of other African American deejays—led by Maurice "Hot Rod" Hulbert in Baltimore, Martha Jean "The Queen" Stienburg in Detroit, and Jack "The Rapper" Gibson in Atlanta—paved the way in changing America's musical tastes. By the mid-1950s, more than 400 radio stations were airing black-oriented music programs.

RADIO STATIONS

ALABAMA

WAGG-AM & WENN-FM
P.O. Box 697
Birmingham, AL 33201
(205) 741-9244

WAPZ-AM
Route 6, P.O. Box 43

Wetumpka, AL 36092
(205) 567-2251

WATV-AM
P.O. Box 39054
Birmingham, AL 35208
(205) 780-2014

WAVE-AM
1408 Third Avenue, W
Birmingham, AL 35208
(205) 786-9293

WAYE-AM
386 Lomb Avenue, SW
Birmingham, AL 35211
(205) 786-9293

WBIL-AM & -FM
P.O. Box 666
Tuskegee, AL 36083
(205) 727-2100

WEUP-AM
P.O. Box 1198
Huntsville, AL 35814
(205) 837-9387

WGOK-AM
P.O. Box 1425
Mobile, AL 36633
(205) 432-8661

WJLD-AM
1449 Spaulding Ishkooda Road
Birmingham, AL 35211
(205) 942-1776

WMGJ-AM
815 Tuscaloosa Avenue
Gadsden, AL 35901
(205) 546-4434

WOOF-AM
P.O. Box 1427
Dothan, AL 36302

WORJ-AM
P.O. Box 1259
Ozark, AL 36360

WOXR-AM
Drawer E
Talladega, AL 35160
(205) 362-9041

WQIM-FM
P.O. Box 604
Prattsville, AL 36067
(205) 365-0390

WRAG-AM
P.O. Box 71
Carrollton, AL 35447
(205) 367-8136

WSLY-FM
P.O. Box 400-B
York, AL 36925
(205) 392-4787

WTQX-AM
1 Valley Creek Circle
Selma, AL 36701
(205) 872-1570

WTSK-AM
142 Skyland Boulevard
Tuscaloosa, AL 35405
(205) 345-7200

WXAL-AM
Highway 80 E
Drawer X
Demolis, AL 36732
(205) 289-1400

WXVI-AM
P.O. Box 4280
Montgomery, AL 36104
(205) 263-3459

WZMG-AM
P.O. Box 2329
Opelika, AL 36803
(205) 745-4656

WZZA-AM
1570 Woodmont Drive
Tuscumbia, AL 35674
(205) 381-1862

ARKANSAS

KAKJ-FM
Highway 1 North
Marianna, AR 72360
(800) 475-1053

KCAT-AM
P.O. Box 8808

Pine Bluff, AR 71611
(501) 534-5000

KCLT-FM
307 Hwy 49
P.O. Box 2870
West Helena, AR 72390
(501) 572-9506

KLRT-AM & KMZX-FM
200 Arch Street
Little Rock, AR 72201
(501) 376-1063

KSNE-FM
Highway 65
Marshall, AR 72650
(501) 448-5800

KXAR-AM
P.O. Box 320
Hope, AR 71801
(501) 777-3601

KYDE-AM
P.O. Box 5086
Pine Bluff, AR 71611
(501) 534-0300

KYFX-FM
610 Plaza West Building
Little Rock, AR 72205
(501) 666-9499

CALIFORNIA

KACE-FM
161 N. LaBrea Avenue
Inglewood, CA 90301
(213) 330-3100

KBLX-AM & -FM
601 Ashby Avenue
Berkeley, CA 94710
(510) 848-7713

KCKC-AM & KAEV-FM
740 W. Fourth Street
San Bernardino, CA 92410
(909) 384-1039

KDIA-AM
100 Swan Way
Oakland, CA 94621
(510) 633-2548

KEST-AM
185 Berry Street, #6500, Building 2
San Francisco, CA 94107
(415) 978-5378

KFOX-FM
13 W. Torrance Boulevard
Redondo Beach, CA 90217
(213) 374-9796

KGFJ-AM
1100 S. La Brea Avenue
Los Angeles, CA 90019
(213) 930-9090

KGGI-FM
2001 Iowa Avenue, #200
Riverside, CA 92507
(714) 684-1991

KJLH-FM
3847 Crenshaw Boulevard
Los Angeles, CA 90008
(213) 299-5960

KJOP-AM
15279 Hanford Armoba Road
LeMoore, CA 93245
(209) 584-5242

KKBT-FM
7635 Yucca Street
Hollywood, CA 90028
(213) 466-9566

KKGO-FM
P.O. Box 250028
Los Angeles, CA 90025
(310) 478-5540

KMAX-FM
3844 E. Foothill Boulevard
Pasadena, CA 91107
(213) 681-2486

KMJC-AM
4875 N. Harbor Drive
San Diego, CA 92106-2304
(619) 224-1556

KOJJ-FM
165 N. D Street, Suite 3
East Porterville, CA 93257
(209) 782-1005

KPOO-FM
P.O. Box 11008
San Francisco, CA 94101
(415) 346-5373

KRGO-FM
P.O. Box 129
Fowler, CA 93625
(209) 834-5337

KRML-AM
P.O. Box 22440
Carmel, CA 93922
(408) 624-6431

KSBW-TV
238 John Street
Salinas, CA 93901
(408) 758-8888

KSDS-FM
1313 12th Avenue
San Diego, CA 92101
(619) 234-1062

KUOR-AM
1200 E. Colton Avenue
Redlands, CA 92374
(909) 792-0721

KVTO-AM
55 Hawthorne Street, Suite 900
San Francisco, CA 94105
(415) 284-1029

COLORADO

KDHT-FM
9351 Grant Street, Suite 550
Thornton, CO 80229
(303) 252-1090

KDKO-AM
2559 Welton Street
Denver, CO 80205
(303) 295-1225

KEPC-FM
5675 S. Academy Boulevard
Colorado Springs, CO 80906
(719) 540-7489

CONNECTICUT

WKND-AM
544 Windsor Avenue
Windsor, CT 06095
(203) 688-6221

WNHC-AM
112 Washington Avenue
New Haven, CT 06473
(203) 234-1340

WYBC-FM
165 Elm Street
New Haven, CT 06520
(203) 432-4118

DISTRICT OF COLUMBIA

WHUR-FM
Howard University
529 Bryant Street, NW
Washington, DC 20059
(202) 806-3500

WJYE-FM
5321 First Place, NE
Washington, DC 20011
(202) 722-1000

WKYS-FM & WOL-AM
4001 Nebraska Avenue, NW
Washington, DC 20016
(202) 686-9300

WMMJ-FM & WOL-AM
400 H Street, NE
Washington, DC 20002
(202) 675-4800

WPFW-FM
701 H Street, NW
Washington, DC 20016
(202) 783-3100

WUST-AM
815 V Street, NW
Washington, DC 20001
(202) 462-0011

WYCB-AM
National Press Building
529 14th Street, NW, #228
Washington, DC 20045
(202) 737-6400

FLORIDA

WANM-AM
300 W. Tennessee Street
Tallahassee, FL 32301
(904) 222-1070

WAPN-FM
1508 State Avenue
Holly Hill, FL 32017
(904) 677-4272

WAVS-AM
4124 S.W. 64th Avenue
Davie, FL 33314
(305) 584-1170

WCGL-AM
4035 Atlantic Boulevard
Jacksonville, FL 32207
(904) 399-0606

WEDR-FM
P.O. Box 551748
Opalocka, FL 33055
(305) 623-7711

WEXY-AM
412 W. Oakland Park Boulevard
Fort Lauderdale, FL 33111-1712
(305) 561-1520

WHJX-AM
10592 E. Balmoral Circle, #1

Jacksonville, FL 32218
(904) 696-1015

WJHM-FM
37 Skyline Drive, #4200
Lake Mary, FL 32746
(407) 333-0072

WJIV-FM
3279 Sherwood Road
Punta Gorda, FL 33980
(813) 624-5000

WLIT-AM
3033 Rivera Drive, #200
Naples, FL 33940-4134
(803) 248-9040

WPOM-AM
6667 42nd Terrace, N
West Palm Beach, FL 33407
(407) 844-6200

WPUL-AM
2598 S. Nova Road
Daytona Beach, FL 32119
(904) 767-1131

WRBD-AM
4431 Rock Island Road
Fort Lauderdale, FL 33139
(305) 731-4800

WRFA-AM
800 S.E. Eighth Avenue
Largo, FL 34649
(813) 581-7800

WRXB-AM
1700 34th Street, S
St. Petersburg, FL 33711
(813) 327-9792

WSVE-FM
4343 Spring Grove Road
Jacksonville, FL 32209
(904) 269-3693

WSWN-AM
P.O. Box 1505

Belle Glade, FL 33430
(407) 996-2063

WTMP-AM
5207 Washington Boulevard
Tampa, FL 33619
(813) 626-4108

WTOT-AM
P.O. Box 469
Marianna, FL 32446
(904) 482-3046

WTWB-AM
P.O. Box 7
Auburndale, FL 33823
(813) 967-1570

WYFX-AM
400 Gulf Stream Boulevard
Delray Beach, FL 33444
(407) 737-1040

WZAZ-AM
2611 Werd Radio Drive
Jacksonville, FL 32204
(904) 389-1111

GEORGIA

WAOK-AM & WFYE-FM
120 Ralph McGill Boulevard, #1000
Atlanta, GA 30365
(404) 898-8900

WBKZ-AM
548 Hawthorn Avenue
Athens, GA 30606
(706) 548-8800

WFAV-FM
P.O. Box 460
Cordele, GA 31015
(912) 273-1404

WFXA-AM & -FM
P.O. Box 1584
Augusta, GA 30903
(803) 279-2330

WFXM-FM
369 Second Street
Macon, GA 31208
(912) 742-2505

WGML-AM
P.O. Box 615
Huntsville, GA 31313
(912) 368-3399

WGOV-AM
P.O. Box 1207
Valdosta, GA 31603
(912) 242-4513

WGUN-AM
2901 Mountain Industrial Boulevard
Tucker, GA 30084-3073
(404) 491-1010

WHCJ-FM
P.O. Box 31404
Savannah, GA 31402
(912) 356-2399

WHGH-AM
P.O. Box 2218
Thomasville, GA 31799
(912) 228-4124

WHKN-FM
P.O. Box 346
Statesboro, GA 30458
(912) 489-2086

WIBB-AM
369 Second Street
Macon, GA 31208
(912) 742-2505

WIGO-AM
1532 Howell Mill Road
Atlanta, GA 30318
(404) 352-3943

WJGA-FM
100 Brownlee Road
Jackson, GA 30233
(404) 775-3151

WJIZ-FM
506 W. Oglethorpe Boulevard
Albany, GA 31701
(912) 436-0112

WJYZ-AM
2700 N. Slappey Boulevard
Albany, GA 31707
(912) 436-0112

WKIG-AM
226 E. Bolton Street
Glenville, GA 30427
(912) 654-3580

WKZK-AM
P.O. Box 1454
Augusta, GA 30903
(706) 738-9191

WLOV-AM & -FM
833 Berkshire Drive
Washington, GA 30673
(706) 678-2125

WPGA-AM
Drawer 980
Perry, GA 31069
(912) 982-2980

WQVE-FM
P.O. Box 434
Camilla, GA 31730
(912) 294-0010

WRDW-AM & -FM
1480 Eisenhower Drive
Augusta, GA 30907
(404) 667-8001

WROM-AM
P.O. Box 5031
Rome, GA 30162
(706) 234-7171

WSAI-AM
206 E. Factors Walk
Savannah, GA 31401
(912) 947-1450

WSNT-AM & -FM
P.O. Box 150
Sandersville, GA 31082
(912) 552-5182

WTHB-AM
P.O. Box 1584
Augusta, GA 30903
(706) 279-2330

WTJH-AM
2146 Dudson Drive
East Point, GA 30364
(404) 344-2233

WUWU-AM & WKKN-FM
P.O. Box 4606
Cordele, GA 31015
(912) 276-0306

WVEE-FM
120 Ralph McGill Boulevard, #1000
Atlanta, GA 30605
(404) 549-1470

WXAG-AM
2145 S. Milledge Avenue
Athens, GA 30605
(404) 549-1470

WXKO-AM & WKXK-FM
P.O. Box 1150
Fort Valley, GA 31030
(912) 825-5547

WXRS-AM
P.O. Box 1590
Swainsboro, GA 30401
(912) 237-1590

WYZE-AM
11 11th Boulevard, SE
Atlanta, GA 30312
(404) 622-7802

ILLINOIS

WBCP-AM
P.O. Box 1023

Champaign, IL 61820
(217) 359-1580

WBEE-AM
15700 Campbell Avenue
Harvey, IL 60426
(708) 331-7840

WBGE-FM
516 W. Main Street
Peoria, IL 61606
(309) 686-9292

WCFJ-AM
1000 Lincoln Highway
Ford Heights, IL 60411
(708) 758-8600

WESL-AM
149 S. Eighth Street
East St. Louis, IL 62201
(618) 271-1490

WGCI-FM
332 S. Michigan Avenue, #600
Chicago, IL 60614
(312) 984-1400

WJPC-AM & WLNR-FM
820 S. Michigan Avenue
Chicago, IL 60605
(312) 247-6200

WLUV-FM
2272 Elmwood Street
Rockford, IL 61103
(815) 877-9588

WPNA-AM
408 S. Oak Park Avenue
Oak Park, IL 60302
(708) 524-9762

WSBC-AM
4949 W. Belmont Avenue
Chicago, IL 60641
(312) 282-9722

WSDR-AM & WZZT-FM
3101 Freeport Road

Sterling, IL 61081
(815) 625-3400

WVAZ-FM
800 S. Wells Street, #250
Chicago, IL 60607
(312) 360-9000

WVON-AM
3350 S. Kedzie Avenue
Chicago, IL 60623
(312) 247-6200

WXKO-FM
P.O. Box 465
Pama, IL 62557
(217) 562-3949

INDIANA

WLTH-AM
3669 Broadway
Gary, IN 46402
(219) 884-9409

WPZZ-FM
645 Industrial Drive
Franklin, IN 46131
(317) 736-4040

WSLM-FM
P.O. Box 385
Salem, IN 47167
(812) 833-5750

WUBU-FM
3371 Cleveland Road Extension
Southbend, IN 46628
(219) 271-9333

WWCA-AM
487 Broadway, #207
Gary, IN 46402
(219) 886-9171

IOWA

KBBG-FM
527-2 Cottage Street

Waterloo, IA 50703
(319) 234-1441

KIGC-FM
William Penn College
N. Market and Trueblood Avenues
Oskaloosa, IA 52577
(515) 673-1095

KTFC-FM
P.O. Box 102-A
Sioux City, IA 51106
(712) 252-4621

KANSAS

KEYN-FM
2829 Salina Avenue
Wichita, KS 67402
(316) 838-7744

KQAM-AM
2829 Salina Avenue
Wichita, KS 67204
(316) 838-7744

KTPK-FM
3003 S.W. Van Buren
Topeka, KS 66611
(913) 267-2300

KENTUCKY

WCKU-FM
651 Perimeter Drive, #102
Lexington, KY 40517
(606) 269-9540

WLLV-AM
515 S. Third Street
Louisville, KY 40202
(502) 581-1240

WLOU-AM
2549 S. Third Street
Louisville, KY 40208
(502) 636-3535

WQKS-AM
905 S. Main Street
Hopkinsville, KY 42240
(502) 886-1480

WRLV-AM
P.O. Box 550
Salyersville, KY 41465
(606) 349-6125

WTCV-AM
P.O. Box 685
Greenup, KY 41144
(606) 473-7377

LOUISIANA

KBCE-FM
P.O. Box 69
Boyce, LA 71409
(318) 793-4003

KFXZ-FM
3225 Ambassador Caffery Parkway
Lafayette, LA 70506-7214
(318) 898-1112

KGRM-FM
Drawer K
Grambling, LA 71245
(318) 247-2344

KJCB-AM
413 Jefferson Street
Lafayette, LA 70501
(318) 233-4262

KLBG-AM
107 Bolton Avenue
Alexandria, LA 71301
(318) 442-2070

KOKA-AM
P.O. Box 103
Shreveport, LA 71161
(318) 222-3122

KQLX-FM
7707 Waco Street

Baton Rouge, LA 70806
(504) 926-1106

KRUS-AM
P.O. Box 430
Ruston, LA 71273
(318) 255-2530

KTRY-AM & -FM
P.O. Box 1075
Bastrop, LA 71220
(318) 281-3656

KXLA-AM
P.O. Box 990
Rayville, LA 71269
(318) 728-6990

KYEA-FM
516 Martin Street
West Monroe, LA 71291
(318) 322-1491

KZZM-AM
311 Alamo Street
Lake Charles, LA 70601
(318) 436-7277

WBOK-AM
1639 Gentilly Boulevard
New Orleans, LA 70119
(504) 943-4600

WQUE-AM & -FM
1440 Canal Street, #800
New Orleans, LA 70112
(504) 581-1280

WTKL-AM
2777 Rosedale Road
Port Allen, LA 70767
(504) 383-4920

WWOZ-FM
P.O. Box 51840
New Orleans, LA 70151
(504) 568-1239

WXOK-AM
7707 Waco Drive

New Orleans, LA 70806
(504) 927-7060

WYLD-AM & -FM
2228 Gravier Avenue
New Orleans, LA 70119
(504) 882-1945

MARYLAND

WANN-AM
P.O. Box 631
Annapolis, MD 21404
(301) 269-0700

WBGR-AM
3000 Druid Park Drive
Baltimore, MD 21215
(410) 367-7733

WERQ-AM & -FM
1111 Park Avenue
Baltimore, MD 21201
(410) 332-8200

WESM-FM
University of Maryland, Eastern Shore
Backbone Road
Princess Anne, MD 21853
(301) 651-2816

WJDY-AM
1633 N. Division Street
Salisbury, MD 21801
(301) 742-5191

WWIN-AM & -FM
200 S. President Street, 6th Floor
Baltimore, MD 21202
(410) 332-8200

WWZZ-FM
5217 Auth Road
Marlow Heights, MD 20746
(301) 899-3014

WXTR-FM
5210 Auth Road
Marlow Heights, MD 20746
(301) 899-3014

MASSACHUSETTS

WEIB-FM
6 Wilken Drive
Longmeadow, MA 01106
(413) 567-7644

WILD-AM
90 Warren Street
Boston, MA 02119
(617) 427-2222

WLVG-AM
670 Cummins Way
Boston, MA 02126-3243
(617) 576-2895

WUNB-FM
University of Massachusetts
Boston Harbor Campus
Boston, MA 02125
(617) 929-7919

MICHIGAN

WCHB-AM
32790 Henry Ruff Road
Inkster, MI 48141
(313) 278-1440

WCXT-FM
220 Polk Road
Hart, MI 49420
(616) 873-7129

WDZR-FM
850 Stephenson Highway, Suite 405
Troy, MI 48083
(810) 589-7900

WDZZ-FM
1830 Genessee Tower
Flint, MI 48503
(313) 767-0130

WFLT-AM
5317 S. Averill Street
Flint, MI 48506
(313) 239-5733

WGPR-FM
3146 Jefferson Avenue, E
Detroit, MI 48207
(313) 259-8862

WGVU-FM
301 W. Fulton Street
Grand Rapids, MI 49504-6495
(616) 771-6666

WJLB-FM
645 Griswold Street, #633
Detroit, MI 48226
(313) 965-2000

WJZZ-FM
2994 E. Grand Boulevard
Detroit, MI 48202
(313) 871-0591

WKSG-FM
850 Stephenson Highway
Troy, MI 48083
(313) 792-6600

WKWM-AM
P.O. Box 828
Kentwood, MI 49508
(616) 676-1237

WLTZ-FM
126 N. Franklin Street, #514
Saginaw, MI 48607
(517) 754-1071

WMTG-AM
P.O. Box 1310
Dearborn, MI 48126
(313) 846-8500

WNMC-FM
1701 E. Front Street
Traverse City, MI 49684
(616) 922-1091

WOWE-FM
100 S. Main Street
Vassar, MI 48768
(517) 823-3399

WQBH-AM
Penobscot Building, #2056
Detroit, MI 48226
(313) 965-4500

WXLA-AM
101 Northcrest Road, #4
Lansing, MI 48906
(517) 484-9600

MISSISSIPPI

WACR-FM
1919 14th Avenue, N
Columbus, MS 39713
(601) 328-1050

WALT-AM
P.O. Box 5797
Meridian, MS 39301
(601) 693-2661

WAML-AM
P.O. Box 367
Laurel, MS 39440
(601) 425-4285

WBAD-FM
P.O. Box 4426
Greenville, MS 38704
(601) 335-9265

WBFL-1190
1000 Blue Meadow Road
Bay St. Louis, MS 39520
(601) 467-1190

WESY-AM
P.O. Box 5804
Greenville, MS 38704
(601) 385-9405

WGNL-FM
503 Ione Street
Greenwood, MS 38930
(601) 453-1646

WJMG-FM & WORV-AM
1204 Grave Line Street
Hattiesburg, MS 39401
(601) 544-1941

WKKY-FM
P.O. Box 1919
McComb, MS 39648
(601) 475-4108

WKRA-FM
P.O. Box 298
Holly Springs, MS 39635
(601) 252-1110

WKXG-AM
P.O. Box 1686
Greenwood, MS 38930
(601) 453-2174

WKXI-AM
P.O. Box 9446
Jackson, MS 39206
(601) 957-1300

WLTD-FM
Drawer N
Lexington, MS 39095
(601) 834-2295

WMIS-AM
20 E. Franklin Street
Natchez, MS 39120
(601) 442-2522

WMLC-AM
P.O. Box 949
Monticello, MS 39654
(601) 587-7997

WNBN-AM
1290 Hawkins Crossing Road
Meridian, MS 39301
(601) 483-7930

WOAD-AM
P.O. Box 10387
Jackson, MS 39289
(601) 948-1515

WOKJ-AM
1350 Lynch Street
Jackson, MS 39203
(601) 948-1515

WQFX-AM & -FM
P.O. Box 789
Gulfport, MS 39502
(601) 863-3626

WQIS-AM
P.O. Box 151
Laurel, MS 39441
(601) 425-1491

WRDC-AM
114 T. M. Jones Highway
Boyle, MS 38730
(601) 843-1400

WRJH-FM
P.O. Box 145
Brandon, MS 39043
(601) 825-5045

WRKN-AM
P.O. Box 145
Brandon, MS 39043
(601) 825-5045

WTYJ-FM
20 E. Franklin Street
Natchez, MS 39120
(601) 442-2522

MISSOURI

KATZ-AM & -FM
1139 Olive Street
St. Louis, MO 63101
(314) 241-6000

KCXL-AM
2420 E. Linwood Boulevard, #10
Kansas City, MO 64110
(816) 333-2583

KIRL-AM
3713 Highway 94 North
St. Charles, MO 63301
(314) 946-6600

KMJM-FM
P.O. Box 4888
St. Louis, MO 63108
(314) 361-1108

KPRT-AM & KPRS-FM
11131 Colorado Avenue
Kansas City, MO 64137
(816) 763-2040

KSTL-AM
814 N. Third Street
St. Louis, MO 63102
(314) 621-5785

NEBRASKA

KBWH-FM
5829 N. 60th Street
Omaha, NE 68104
(402) 571-3714

NEVADA

KCEP-FM
330 W. Washington Avenue
Las Vegas, NV 89106
(702) 648-4218

NEW JERSEY

WIMG-AM
1737 Princeton Avenue
Lawrenceville, NJ 08648
(609) 278-1944

WNJR-AM
1 Riverfront Plaza, #345
Newark, NJ 07102
(201) 642-8000

WTTH-FM & WNBC-FM
2922 Atlantic Avenue, #201
Atlantic City, NJ 08401
(609) 348-4040

WUSS-AM
P.O. Box 7539
Atlantic City, NJ 08401
(609) 345-7134

NEW YORK

WBLK-FM
712 Main Street, #112
Buffalo, NY 14202
(716) 852-5955

WBLS-FM
3 Park Avenue
New York, NY 10016
(212) 545-1075

WDKX-FM
683 Main Street
Rochester, NY 14605
(716) 262-2050

WGNY-AM & -FM
P.O. Box 2307
Newburgh, NY 12550
(914) 561-2131

WLIB-AM (Caribbean focus)
3 Park Avenue
New York, NY 10016
(212) 447-1000

WPNR-FM
c/o Utica College
Burnstone Road
Utica, NY 13502
(315) 792-3069

WRKS-FM
1440 Broadway
New York, NY 10018
(212) 642-4300

WUFO-AM
89 La Salle Avenue
Buffalo, NY 14214
(716) 834-1080

WWRL-AM
40-30 58th Street

Woodside, NY 11377
(718) 335-1600

NORTH CAROLINA

WAAA-AM
4950 Indiana Avenue
P.O. Box 11197
Winston-Salem, NC 27116
(336) 767-0430

WARR-AM
P.O. Box 577
Warrenton, NC 27589
(252) 257-2121

WBMS-AM
310 Princeton Street
Wilmington, NC 28404
(910) 763-4633

WBXB-FM
P.O. Box O
Edenton, NC 27932
(252) 482-2224

WCLY-AM
647 Maywood Avenue
Raleigh, NC 27603
(919) 821-1550

WCPS-AM
3403 Main Street
Tarboro, NC 27886
(252) 823-2191

WDJB-FM
P.O. Box 509
Windsor, NC 27983
(252) 794-3131

WDKS-FM
P.O. Box 2008
Fayetteville, NC 28302
(919) 484-2107

WDUR-AM
P.O. Box 650
Durham, NC 27702
(919) 596-2000

WEAL-AM
1060 Coatewood Avenue
Greensboro, NC 27405
(919) 272-5121

WEED-AM & WRSV-FM
P.O. Box 2666
Rocky Mount, NC 27802
(252) 443-5976

WEGG-AM
P.O. Box 608
Rose Hill, NC 28458
(919) 289-2031

WGIV-AM
520 Highway 20 North
Concord, NC 28025
(701) 342-2644

WGSP-AM
4209 F. Stuart Andrew Boulevard
Charlotte, NC 28217
(704) 527-9477

WGTM-AM
P.O. Box 3837
Wilson, NC 27893
(919) 243-2188

WIDU-AM
Drawer 2247
Fayetteville, NC 28302
(919) 483-6611

WIZS-AM
P.O. Box 1299
Henderson, NC 27536
(919) 492-3001

WKJA-AM
P.O. Box 591
Bellhaven, NC 27810
(919) 964-9290

WLLE-AM
649 Maywood Avenue
Raleigh, NC 27603
(919) 833-3874

WMQX-AM
93 Salem Valley Road
Box 593
Winston-Salem, NC 27102
(919) 723-9393

WOKN-AM
522 E. Martin Street
Raleigh, NC 27601
(919) 833-3874

WOKN-FM
P.O. Box 2006
Goldsboro, NC 27530
(919) 734-4213

WOOW-AM
304 Evans Street
Greensville, NC 27834
(919) 757-0365

WPEG-FM
520 Highway 29 North
Concord, NC 28025
(704) 333-0131

WRVS-FM
1704 Weeksville Drive
Elizabeth City, NC 27909
(252) 335-3517

WSMX-AM
P.O. Box 16049
Winston-Salem, NC 27115
(919) 761-1545

WSRC-AM
P.O. Box 1331
Durham, NC 27702
(919) 477-7999

WTNC-AM
P.O. Box 1920
Thomasville, NC 27360
(919) 472-0790

WVOE-AM
Route 3, P.O. Box 328
Chadbourn, NC 28431
(919) 654-5621

WWLE-AM
5106 Wrightsville Avenue
Wilmington, NC 28403
(919) 791-9083

OHIO

WABQ-AM
8000 Euclid Avenue
Cleveland, OH 44103
(216) 231-8005

WBBY-FM
P.O. Box 14
Westerville, OH 43081
(614) 891-1829

WBGU-FM
Bowling Green State University
31 W. Hale
Bowling Green, OH 43403
(419) 372-8800

WCER-AM
4537 22nd Street, NW
Canton, OH 44708
(216) 478-6666

WCIN-AM
106 Glenwood Avenue
Cincinnati, OH 45217
(513) 281-7180

WCKX-FM
510 E. Mount Street
Columbus, OH 43215
(614) 464-0020

WDAO-AM
4309 W. Third Street
Dayton, OH 45417
(513) 263-9326

WIZF-FM
7030 Reading Road, #316

Cincinnati, OH 45237
(513) 351-5900

WJMO-AM & -FM
11821 Euclid Avenue
Cleveland, OH 44106
(216) 795-1212

WJTB-AM
105 Lake Avenue
Elyria, OH 44035
(216) 327-1833

WMMX-AM
P.O. Box 1110
Fairborn, OH 45324
(513) 878-9000

WNOP-AM
1518 Dalton Avenue
Cincinnati, OH 45214
(513) 241-9667

WNRB-AM
P.O. Box 625
Niles, OH 44446
(216) 652-0106

WSLN-FM
Ohio Wesleyan University
40 Slocum Hall
Delaware, OH 43015
(614) 369-4431

WVKO-AM
4401 Carriage Hill Lane
Columbus, OH 43220
(614) 451-2191

WVOI-AM
6695 Jackman Road
Toledo, OH 43613
(419) 243-7052

WZAK-FM
1729 Superior Avenue
Cleveland, OH 44114
(216) 621-9300

OKLAHOMA

KPRW-AM
4045 N.W. 64th Street
Oklahoma City, OK 74063
(918) 245-0254

KTOW-FM
886 W. 21st Street
Sand Springs, OK 74063
(918) 245-0524

KXOJ-AM
P.O. Box 1250
Sapulpa, OK 74067
(918) 224-2620

PENNSYLVANIA

WADV-AM
P.O. Box 940
Lebanon, PA 17042
(717) 273-2611

WAMO-AM & -FM
411 Seventh Avenue, #1500
Pittsburgh, PA 15219
(412) 471-2181

WCDL-AM
43 Seventh Avenue
Carbondale, PA 18407
(717) 282-2770

WCXJ-AM
7138 Kelly Street
Pittsburgh, PA 15208
(412) 243-3050

WDAS-AM & -FM
Belmont Avenue and Edgely Drive
Philadelphia, PA 19131
(215) 878-2000

WHAT-AM
2471 N. 54th Street
Philadelphia, PA 19131
(215) 581-5161

WIMG-AM
P.O. Box 436
Washington Crossing, PA 18977
(215) 321-1300

WJSM-FM
P.O. Box 87
Martinsburg, PA 16662
(814) 793-2188

WLIU-FM
c/o Office of Student Activities
Lincoln University
Lincoln, PA 19352
(215) 932-8300

WPLW-AM
201 Ewing Avenue
Pittsburgh, PA 15205
(412) 922-0550

WPRP-FM & WVAM-AM
2727 W. Albert Drive
Altoona, PA 16602
(814) 944-9456

WURD-AM
5301 Tacony Street
P.O. Box 233
Philadelphia, PA 19137
(215) 533-8900

WUSL-FM
440 Domino Lane
Philadelphia, PA 18128
(215) 483-8900

WYJZ-AM
411 Seventh Avenue, Suite 1500
Pittsburgh, PA 15219
(412) 471-2181

SOUTH CAROLINA

WASC-AM
P.O. Box 3686
Spartanburg, SC 29304
(803) 585-1530

WBSC-AM
Drawer 629
Bennettsville, SC 29512
(803) 479-7121

WCIG-FM
P.O. Box 1005
Mullins, SC 29574
(803) 464-9252

WGSW-AM
2410 Kateway Road
Greenwood, SC 29646
(803 223-5945

WHYZ-AM
P.O. Box 4309
Greenville, SC 29608
(803) 246-1441

WKQB-AM
P.O. Box 10164
Charleston, SC 29411
(803) 744-1779

WMCJ-AM
314 Rembert Dennis Boulevard
Monks Corner, SC 29461
(803) 761-6010

WOIC-AM
P.O. Box 565
Columbia, SC 29202
(803) 796-9975

WPAL-AM
1717 Wappo Road
Charleston, SC 29417
(803) 763-6330

WQIZ-AM
P.O. Box 10164
Charleston, SC 29411
(803) 744-1779

WQKI-AM
P.O. Box 777

St. Matthews, SC 29135
(803) 874-2777

WRDW-TV
1301 Georgia Avenue
North Augusta, SC 29841
(803) 278-1212

WSSB-FM
P.O. Box 1915
Orangeburg, SC 29117
(803) 536-8196

WSSC-AM
P.O. Box 1468
Sumter, SC 29150
(803) 778-2355

WTGH-AM
1303 State Street
Cayce, SC 29033
(803) 796-9533

WVBX-AM
Drawer W
Georgetown, SC 29442
(803) 546-5141

WVGB-AM
806 Monston Street
Beaufort, SC 29902
(803) 524-4700

WWKT-FM
P.O. Box 525
Kingstree, SC 29556
(803) 392-2361

WWWZ-AM
WWWZ-FM
2045 Spaulding Drive
North Charleston, SC 29418
(803) 308-9300

WYNN-AM & -FM
P.O. Box F-14
Florence, SC 29501
(803) 662-6364

TENNESSEE

KFTH-FM
2265 Central Avenue
Memphis, TN 38104
(901) 375-9324

WABD-AM
P.O. Box 2249
Clarksville, TN 37042
(615) 431-4984

WBOL-AM & WOJG-FM
P.O. Box 191
Bolivar, TN 38008
(901) 658-3690

WDIA-AM
112 Union Avenue
Memphis, TN 38103
(901) 529-4300

WFKX-FM
P.O. Box 2763
Jackson, TN 38302
(901) 427-9616

WHRK-FM
112 Union Avenue
Memphis, TN 38103
(901) 529-4300

WLOK-AM
P.O. Box 69
Memphis, TN 38101
(901) 526-9565

WMDB-AM
3051 Stokers Lane
Nashville, TN 37218
(615) 255-2876

WNAH-AM
44 Music Square, E
Nashville, TN 37203
(615) 254-7611

WNOO-AM
108 Hendricks Street
Chattanooga, TN 37406
(615) 894-1023

WQQK-FM
P.O. Box 8085
Nashville, TN 37207
(615) 227-1470

WTBG-FM
P.O. Box 198
Brownsville, TN 38012
(901) 772-3700

WVOL-AM
P.O. Box 8085
Nashville, TN 37207
(615) 227-1470

TEXAS

KADO-AM
303 W. Broad Street
Texarkana, TX 75501
(214) 793-4671

KALO-FM
7700 Gulfway Street
Port Arthur, TX 77642
(409) 963-1276

KAZI-FM
4700 Loyola Lane, #104
Austin, TX 78723
(512) 926-0275

KBWC-FM
711 Wiley Avenue
Marshall, TX 74670
(214) 938-8341

KCOH-AM
5011 Almeda Street
Houston, TX 77004
(713) 522-1000

KEGG-AM
P.O. Box 600
Dangerfield, TX 75638
(903) 645-3928

KFKY-FM
2727 Inwood Road
Dallas, TX 77535
(214) 352-3975

KGBC-AM
P.O. Box 11138
Galveston, TX 77553
(409) 744-4567

KHEY-AM & -FM
2419 N. Piedras Street
El Paso, TX 79930
(915) 566-9301

KHNV-AM
P.O. Box 7116
Fort Worth, TX 76111
(817) 640-7900

KHRN-FM
219 N. Main Street, Suite 600
Bryan, TX 77803
(409) 779-3337

KKZR-FM
6161 Savoy Street, Suite 1100
Houston, TX 77036
(713) 260-3600

KSAQ-FM
217 Alamo Plaza, Suite 200
San Antonio, TX 78205
(512) 271-9600

KSII-AM
217 Alamo Plaza, Suite 100
San Antonio, TX 78205
(512) 271-9600

KSJL-FM
217 Alamo Plaza, Suite 200
San Antonio, TX 78205
(512) 271-9600

KWWJ-AM
4638 Decker Drive
Baytown, TX 77520
(713) 424-7000

KYOK-AM
3001 LaBranch Street
Houston, TX 77004
(713) 526-7131

KZEY-AM
P.O. Box 75712
Tyler, TX 75712
(214) 593-1744

UTAH

KDAB-FM
385 24th Street
Ogden, UT 84401
(801) 393-8611

VIRGINIA

WANT-AM
P.O. Box 6747
Richmond, VA 23230
(804) 353-9113

WARR-AM
553 Michigan Drive
Hampton, VA 23669-3899
(919) 257-2121

WCDX-FM
2809 Emergywood Parkway, 300
Richmond, VA 23294
(804) 672-9300

WCLM-AM
4719 Nine Mile Road
Richmond, VA 23223
(804) 236-0532

WFTH-AM
5021 Brooks Road, #100
Richmond, VA 23227
(804) 262-8624

WGCV-AM
10600 Jefferson Davis Highway

Richmond, VA 23237
(804) 275-1234

WHOV-FM
Hampton University
Hampton, VA 23668
(804) 727-5407

WILA-AM
P.O. Box 3444
Danville, VA 24543
(804) 792-2133

WKBY-AM
P.O. Box 105A
Chatham, VA 24531
(804) 432-8108

WMYK-FM & WPCE-AM
645 Church Street, #400
Norfolk, VA 23510
(804) 622-4600

WOWI-FM
645 Church Street, #201
Norfolk, VA 23510
(804) 625-5800

WPAK-AM
800 Old Plank Road
Farmville, VA 23901
(804) 392-8114

WPLZ-FM
P.O. Box 1510
Petersburg, VA 23805
(804) 672-9300

WRBN-AM & WREJ-AM
6001 Wilkinson Road
Richmond, VA 23227
(804) 264-1540

WTJZ-AM
553 Michigan Drive
Hampton, VA 23669
(804) 723-1270

WTOY-AM
2614 Cove Road, NW
Roanoke, VA 24017
(703) 362-9558

WZAM-AM
168 Business Park Road
Virginia Beach, VA 23462
(804) 473-1194

WASHINGTON

KKFX-AM
2815 Second Avenue, #500
Seattle, WA 98121
(206) 728-1250

KLUJ-AM
P.O. Box 513
Walla Walla, WA 99362
(509) 529-8000

KRIZ-AM
P.O. Box 22462
Seattle, WA 98122
(206) 251-5151

WISCONSIN

WAWA-AM
12800 W. Bluemond Road
Elm Grove, WI 53122
(414) 785-1021

WBJX-AM & WKKV-FM
2400 S. 102nd Street, Suite 230
West Allis, WI 53227
(414) 321-1007

WGLB-AM
900 E. Green Bay Road
Saukille, WI 53080
(414) 284-2666

WLUM-FM
2500 N. Mayfair Road, #390
Milwaukee, WI 53226-1409
(414) 771-1021

WMCS-AM & WMVP-AM
4222 W. Capitol Drive, #1290

Milwaukee, WI 53216
(414) 444-1290

WNOV-AM
3815 N. Teutonia Avenue
Milwaukee, WI 53206
(414) 449-9668

WSUN-FM
P.O. Box 219
Keuwaunee, WI 54216
(414) 388-4852

WYMS-FM
5225 W. Violet Street
Milwaukee, WI 53208
(414) 475-8389

U.S. VIRGIN ISLANDS

WSTA-AM
Box 1340
St. Thomas, VI 00804
(809) 774-1340

WSTX-AM & -FM
P.O. Box 3279
Christiansted, St. Croix VI 00822
(809) 773-0490

WTBN-FM
Havensight Executive Tower, Suite 1033, No. 19
Charlotte Amalie, VI 00802
(809) 776-2610

MAGAZINES

About . . . Time
283 Genessee Street
Rochester, NY 14661
(716) 235-7150
Circulation: 189,500

African American Heritage
8443 S. Crenshaw Boulevard, #103
Inglewood, CA 90305
(213) 752-3706
Circulation: 25,000

American Visions: The Magazine of Afro-American Culture
1156 15th Street, NW, Suite 615
Washington, DC 20005
(202) 296-9593
Circulation: 125,000

BET Weekend
Black Entertainment Television
1900 W. Place, NE
Washington, DC 20018
(202) 608-2000
Circulation: 1.2 million

Black Careers
Project Magazine Inc.
P.O. Box 8214

Philadelphia, PA 19101-8214
(215) 387-1600
Circulation: 400,000

Black Child
Heritage Publishing Group
P.O. Box 12048
Atlanta, GA 30355
(404) 350-7877
Circulation: 25,500

The Black Collegian: The Career & Self-Development Magazine for African American Students
Black Collegiate Services, Inc.
140 Carondelet Street
New Orleans, LA 70130
(504) 523-0154
Circulation: 120,000

Black Elegance: Lifestyles of Today's Black Women
475 Park Avenue, S
New York, NY 10016
(212) 689-2830
Circulation: 302,500

Black Employment and Education Magazine
Hamdani Communications, Inc.
2625 Piedmont Road, Building 56, Suite 282

Atlanta, GA 30324
(404) 469-4891
Circulation: 175,000

Black Enterprise
130 Fifth Avenue
New York, NY 10011
(212) 242-8000
Circulation: 307,000

Black Family
Kent Enterprises, Inc.
11800 Sunrise Valley Drive, #320
Reston, VA 22091
(703) 860-1343
Circulation: 225,000

Black Issues in Higher Education
10520 Warwick Avenue, Suite B-8
Fairfax, VA 22030-3136
(703) 385-2981
Circulation: 4,000

The Black Scholar
P.O. Box 2869
Oakland, CA 94609
(510) 547-6633
Circulation: 10,000

*Callaloo: A Journal of Afro-American and African
  Arts & Letters*
Johns Hopkins University Press
2715 N. Charles Street
Baltimore, MD 21218
(410) 516-6983
Circulation: 1,200

Career Focus (Circulation: 250,000)
College Preview (Circulation: 600,000)
Direct Aim (Circulation: 500,000)
First Opportunity (Circulation: 500,000)
Collegiate and professional magazines for young
  African Americans and Hispanics
Communications Publishing Group
3100 Broadway, Suite 225
Kansas City, MO 64111
(816) 960-1988

Class Magazine
R-E John Sandy Communications
900 Broadway, 8th Floor

New York, NY 10003
(212) 677-3055
Circulation: 208,845

The Crisis: Magazine of the NAACP
National Association for the Advancement of
  Colored People
4805 Mt. Hope Drive
Baltimore, MD 21215
(410) 358-8900
Circulation: 400,000

Dollars and Sense
1610 E. 79th Street
Chicago, IL 60649
(312) 375-6800
Circulation: 286,000

Ebony (Circulation: 1.8 million)
Ebony Man (Circulation: 200,000)
Johnson Publishing
820 S. Michigan Avenue
Chicago, IL 60605-2190
(312) 322-9250

Emerge: Black America's Newsmagazine
Black Entertainment Television
1900 W. Place, NE
Washington, DC 20018
(202) 608-2000
Circulation: 211,155

Essence
1500 Broadway
New York, NY 10036
(212) 642-0600
Circulation: 1 million

Everybody's: The Caribbean-American Magazine
1630 Nostrand Avenue
Brooklyn, NY 11226
(718) 941-1879
Circulation: 250,000

The Final Call
734 W. 79th Street
Chicago, IL 60620
(312) 602-1230
Circulation: 105,000

Fresh
P.O. Box 91878
Los Angeles, CA 90009
(818) 885-6800
Circulation: 100,000

HealthQuest: The Publication of Black Wellness
200 Highpoint Drive, Suite 215
Chalfont, PA 18914
(215) 822-7935
Circulation: 500,000

*Heart and Soul: Health & Fitness for African-
    American Women*
33 E. Minor Street
Emmaus, PA 18098
(610) 967-5171
Circulation: 125,000

Hype Hair
Try It Yourself Hair
(publications alternate monthly)
63 Grand Avenue, Suite 230
River Edge, NJ 07661
(201) 487-6124
Circulation: 225,000

Interrace
Heritage Publishing Group
P.O. Box 12048
Atlanta, GA 30355
(404) 350-7877
Circulation: 25,000

Jazz Times
Glenn Sabini, Publisher
8737 Colesville Road, 5th Floor
Silver Spring, MD 20910
(301) 588-4114
Circulation: 90,000

Jet
Johnson Publishing
820 S. Michigan Avenue
Chicago, IL 60605-2190
(312) 322-9250
Circulation: 800,000

Journal of the National Medical Association
6900 Grove Road
Thorofare, NJ 08086

(609) 848-1000
Circulation: 30,000

*Living Blues: Covering the African-American Blues
    Tradition*
Center for the Study of Southern Culture
University of Mississippi
Hill Hall, Room 301
University, MS 38677
(601) 232-5742
Circulation: 30,000

*Message: A Christian Magazine of Contemporary
    Issues*
55 Oak Ridge Drive
Hagerstown, MD 21740
(301) 791-7000
Circulation: 102,000

Minorities and Women in Business
Venture X, Inc.
P.O. Drawer 210
Burlington, NC 27216
(919) 229-1462
Circulation: 85,000

Minority Business Entrepreneur
925 N. Market Street
Inglewood, CA 90302
(310) 673-9398
Circulation: 26,851

Negro History Bulletin
The Association for the Study of Afro-American
    Life and History
1407 14th Street, NW
Washington, DC 20005-3704
(202) 667-2822
Circulation: 10,000

The NSBE Bridge (Circulation: 100,000)
The NSBE Magazine (Circulation: 23,000)
The National Society of Black Engineers
1454 Duke Street
Alexandria, VA 22314
(703) 549-2207

Players
Players International Publications
8060 Melrose Avenue
Los Angeles, CA 90046

(213) 653-8060
Circulation: 175,000

QBR: The Black Book Review
625 Broadway, 10th Floor
New York, NY 10017
(212) 475-1010
Circulation: 35,000

Right On!
Lexington Library, Inc.
355 Lexington Avenue
New York, NY 10017
(212) 973-3200
Circulation: 350,000

Savoir Faire
Shop Talk
Visions in Black
Shoptalk Publications, Inc.
8825 S. Greenwood
Chicago, IL 60614-7044
(312) 939-8600
Circulation (total): 70,000

Sister 2 Sister: Giving it to Ya Straight, No Chaser!
930 Annapolis Road, Suite 205
Lanham, MD 20706
(301) 306-0100
Circulation: 100,000

SISTERS
National Council of Negro Women, Inc.
1667 K Street, NW, Suite 700
Washington, DC 20006

(202) 659-0006
Circulation: 100,000

Sophisticate's Black Hairstyles and Care Guide
Associated Publications, Inc.
1165 N. Clark Street, #607
Chicago, IL 60610
(312) 266-8680
Circulation: 182,250

The Source
215 Park Avenue, S., 11th Floor
New York, NY 10003
(212) 283-8700
Circulation: 367,000

Upscale
Upscale Communications
600 Bronner Brothers Way
Atlanta, GA 30310
(404) 658-7467
Circulation: 200,000

U.S. Black Engineers
The Career Communications Group, Inc.
729 E. Pratt Street, Suite 504
Baltimore, MD 21298-6669
(410) 244-7101
Circulation: 15,000

Vibe
205 Lexington Avenue
New York, NY 10016
(212) 522-7092
Circulation: 482,000

NEWSPAPERS

ALABAMA

Birmingham Times
P.O. Box 10501
Birmingham, AL 35204
(205) 251-5158
Circulation: 21,000

Birmingham World
312 N. 17th Street
Birmingham, AL 35203

(205) 251-6253
Circulation: 13,000

Green County Democrat
P.O. Box 598
Euraw, AL 35462
(205) 372-3373
Circulation: 2,810

Inner City News
P.O. Box 1545

Mobile, AL 36633-1545
(205) 452-9329
Circulation: 8,000

Mobile Beacon
P.O. Box 1407
Mobile, AL 36617
(205) 479-0629
Circulation: 5,000

Montgomery-Tuskegee Times
P.O. Box 9133
Montgomery, AL 36108
(205) 264-7149
Circulation: 10,000

News Times
156 S. Broad Street
Mobile, AL 36602
(205) 432-0356
Circulation: 5,150

Shoals News Leader
P.O. Box 427
Florence, AL 35631
(205) 766-5542
Circulation: 10,000

Speakin' Out News
P.O. Box 2826
Huntsville, AL 35804
(205) 551-1020
Circulation: 20,105

ARIZONA

Arizona Informant
1746 E. Madison Street, #2
Phoenix, AZ 85034
(602) 257-9300
Circulation: 10,000

ARKANSAS

Arkansas State Press
P.O. Box 164037
Little Rock, AR 72216
(501) 371-9991
Circulation: 5,000

CALIFORNIA

Bakersfield News Observer
1219 20th Street
Bakersfield, CA 93301
(805) 324-9466
Circulation: 21,009

Berkeley Tri-City Post
P.O. Box 1350
Oakland, CA 94612
(510) 763-1120
Circulation: 20,000

Black Voice News
P.O. Box 1581
Riverside, CA 92502
(714) 682-6070
Circulation: 7,500

California Advocate
452 Fresno Street
Fresno, CA 93706
(209) 268-0941
Circulation: 22,500

California Voice (Sundays in Oakland) and
California Sun-Report (Thursdays in San Francisco)
    (Circulation 160,435)
Metro Reporter Group (Circulation: 108,895)
Sun-Reporter (Circulation: 11,249)
1366 Turk Street
San Francisco, CA 94115
(617) 671-1000

Carson Bulletin
P.O. Box 4248
Compton, CA 90224
(213) 774-0018
Circulation: 18,000

Central Star/Journal (Circulation: 39,900)
Compton/Carson Wave (Circulation: 38,200)
Culver City/Westchester Star (Circulation: 33,750)
Inglewood/Hawthorne Wave (Circulation: 44,075)
Mesa Tribune Wave (Circulation: 30,100)
Southwest Topics/Sun Wave (Circulation: 30,000)
Central News-Wave Publications
2621 W. 54th Street
Los Angeles, CA 90043
(213) 290-3000

Compton Bulletin
Rapid Publishing
P.O. Box 4248
Compton, CA 90224
(213) 774-0018
Circulation: 22,000

Compton Metropolitan Gazette
First-Line Publishers
17939 Chatsworth Street, Suite 429
Granada Hills, CA 91344
(818) 782-8695
Circulation: 60,000

Firestone Park News & Southeast News Press
   (Circulation: 24,000)
Herald Dispatch (Circulation: 35,000)
Watts Star Review (Circulation: 30,000)
P.O. Box 1927A
Los Angeles, CA 90019
(213) 291-9486

Inglewood Tribune (Circulation: 10,000)
Lynnwood Journal (Circulation: 15,000)
P.O. Box 4248
Compton, CA 90244
(213) 774-0018

Long Beach Express (Circulation: 60,000)
Los Angeles Metropolitan Gazette (Circulation:
   60,000)
Pasadena Gazette (Circulation: 60,000)
14621 Titus Street, Suite 228
Van Nuys, CA 91402
(818) 782-8695

Los Angeles Sentinel
3800 Crenshaw Boulevard
Los Angeles, CA 90008
(213) 299-3800
Circulation: 20,000

New Bayview
Double Rock Press
1624 Oakdale Avenue
P.O. Box 24477
San Francisco, CA 94124-0477
(310) 282-7894
Circulation: 12,000

Oakland Tri-City Post
P.O. Box 1350
Oakland, CA 94612
(510) 763-1120
Circulation: 62,496

Precinct Reporter
1677 W. Baseline Street
San Bernardino, CA 92411
(714) 889-0597
Circulation: 55,000

Richmond Post
P.O. Box 1350
Oakland, CA 94612
(510) 763-1120
Circulation: 13,661

Sacramento Observer
3540 Fourth Avenue
Sacramento, CA 95817
(916) 452-4781
Circulation: 49,876

San Diego Voice & Viewpoint
1729 N. Euclid Avenue
San Diego, CA 92105
(619) 266-2233
Circulation: 22,000

San Francisco Gazette Express
14621 Titus Street, #228
Van Nuys, CA 91402
(818) 782-8695
Circulation: 60,000

San Francisco New Bayview Newspaper
4401 Third Street
San Francisco, CA 94124
(415) 695-0713
Circulation: 10,000

San Francisco Post
P.O. Box 1350
Oakland, CA 94612
(510) 763-1120
Circulation: 18,289

Seaside Post–News Sentinel
P.O. Box 670

Seaside, CA 93955
(408) 394-6632
Circulation: 10,120

Wilmington Beacon
P.O. Box 4248
Compton, CA 90224
(213) 774-0018
Circulation: 10,000

COLORADO

Denver Weekly News
P.O. Box 569
Denver, CO 80201
(303) 839-5800
Circulation: 17,500

CONNECTICUT

Hartford Inquirer
P.O. Box 1260
Hartford, CT 06143
(203) 522-1462
Circulation: 125,000

Inner-City
2 Eld Street
New Haven, CT 06511
(203) 773-0688
Circulation: 25,000

DELAWARE

The Defender
1702 Locust Street
Wilmington, DE 19802
(302) 656-3252
Circulation: 15,300

DISTRICT OF COLUMBIA

Capital Spotlight
National Press Building
529 14th NW, #202

Washington, DC 20045
(202) 745-7858
Circulation: 60,000

Washington Informer
3117 Martin Luther King, Jr. Avenue, SE
Washington, DC 20032
(202) 561-4100
Circulation: 27,000

Washington News Observer
811 Florida Avenue, NW
Washington, DC 20032
(202) 232-3060
Circulation: 20,000

FLORIDA

Broward Times
1001 W. Cyprus Creek Road, #111
Fort Lauderdale, FL 33309
(305) 351-9070
Circulation: 22,500

Bulletin
P.O. Box 2650
Sarasota, FL 34230
(813) 953-3990
Circulation: 16,500

Capital Outlook
P.O. Box 1335
Tallahassee, FL 32301
(904) 681-1852
Circulation: 14,500

Daytona Beach Times
427 S. Martin Luther King, Jr. Boulevard
Daytona Beach, FL 32114
(904) 253-0321
Circulation: 15,000

Florida Sentinel-Bulletin
P.O. Box 363
Tampa, FL 33601
(813) 248-1921
Circulation: 22,434

Florida Sun Review
P.O. Box 2348
Orlando, FL 32802
(407) 423-1156
Circulation: 16,500

Fort Pierce Chronicle
1527 Avenue D
Fort Pierce, FL 33450
(407) 416-7093
Circulation: 10,500

Jacksonville Advocate
6172 Pettiford Drive
Jacksonville, FL 32209
(904) 764-4740
Circulation: 31,624

Miami Times
900 N.W. 54th Street
Miami, FL 33127
(305) 757-1147
Circulation: 22,000

News Reporter
1610 N. Howard Avenue
Tampa, FL 33607
(813) 254-2608
Circulation: 9,694

Orlando Times
4403 Vineland Road, #B-5
Orlando, FL 32811
(407) 841-3052
Circulation: 10,000

Pensacola Voice
213 E. Yonge Street
Pensacola, FL 32503
(904) 434-6963
Circulation: 36,255

Weekly Challenger
2500 Ninth Street, #C
St. Petersburg, FL 33705
(813) 896-2922
Circulation: 22,920

Westside Gazette
P.O. Box 5304

Fort Lauderdale, FL 33310
(813) 523-5115
Circulation: 37,000

GEORGIA

Atlanta Daily World
145 Auburn Avenue, NE
Atlanta, GA 30335
(404) 659-1110
Circulation: 30,000

Atlanta Inquirer
P.O. Box 92367
Atlanta, GA 30314
(404) 523-6086
Circulation: 61,082

Atlanta Tribune
875 Old Roswell Road, #C-100
Roswell, GA 30076
(404) 487-0501
Circulation: 30,000

Atlanta Voice
P.O. Box 2123
Atlanta, GA 30312
(404) 524-6426
Circulation: 133,000

Augusta Focus
P.O. Box 1282
Augusta, GA 30903
(706) 724-7855
Circulation: 21,000

Columbus Times
P.O. Box 2845
Columbus, GA 31993
(404) 304-2404
Circulation: 20,000

Fort Valley Herald
P.O. Box 899
Ft. Valley, GA 31030
(912) 825-7000
Circulation: 5,000

Herald
P.O. Box 486

Savannah, GA 31402
(912) 232-0450
Circulation: 8,000

Metro County Courier
P.O. Box 2385
Augusta, GA 30903
(706) 724-6556
Circulation: 21,560

Savannah Tribune
P.O. Box 2066
Savannah, GA 31402
(912) 233-6128
Circulation: 8,000

ILLINOIS

Chicago Crusader
6429 S. Martin Luther King, Jr. Drive
Chicago, IL 60637
(312) 752-2500
Circulation: 68,052

Chicago Independent Bulletin
2037 W. 95th Street
Chicago, IL 60616
(312) 225-2400
Circulation: 62,000

Chicago Metro News
3437 S. Indiana Avenue
Chicago, IL 60616-3840
(312) 842-5950
Circulation: 84,500

Chicago Shoreland News
11740 S. Elizabeth
Chicago, IL 60643
(312) 568-7091
Circulation: 38,000

Chicago South Shore Scene
P.O. Box 49007
Chicago, IL 60649
(312) 363-0441
Circulation: 20,000

Chicago Weekend (Circulation: 21,300)
Hyde Park Citizen (Circulation: 15,000)

South End Citizen (Circulation: 17,087)
South Suburban Citizen (Circulation: 18,500)
412 E. 87th Street
Chicago, IL 60619
(312) 487-7700

Chicago Westside Journal
16618 S. Hermitage
Markham, IL 60426
(708) 333-2210
Circulation: 47,000

East St. Louis Monitor
1501 State Street
Box 2137
East Saint Louis, IL 62205
(618) 271-0468
Circulation: 22,500

Muslim Journal
910 W. Van Buren
Chicago, IL 60607
(312) 243-7600
Circulation: 16,000

Observer
6040 S. Harper Street
Chicago, IL 6637
(312) 288-5840
Circulation: 30,000

South Suburban Standard
615 S. Halsted Street
Chicago Heights, IL 60411
(312) 755-5021
Circulation: 25,000

Tri-City Journal
8 S. Michigan Avenue, #1111
Chicago, IL 60603
(312) 346-8123
Circulation: 50,000

INDIANA

Frost Illustrated
3121 S. Calhoun Street
Fort Wayne, IN 46807-1901
(219) 745-0552
Circulation: 2,011

Gary American
2268 Broadway
Gary, IN 46407
(219) 883-4903
Circulation: 11,000

Gary Info
P.O. Box M-587
Gary, IN 46401-0587
(219) 882-5591
Circulation: 21,055

Gary New Crusader
1549 Broadway
Gary, IN 46407
(219) 885-4359
Circulation: 34,689

Indiana Herald
2170 N. Illinois Street
Indianapolis, IN 46202
(317) 923-8291
Circulation: 20,000

Indianapolis Recorder
P.O. Box 18267
Indianapolis, IN 46218
(317) 924-5143
Circulation: 12,000

KENTUCKY

Louisville Defender
P.O. Box 2557
Louisville, KY 40210
(502) 772-2591
Circulation: 9,000

Suspension Press
P.O. Box 2064
Covington, KY 41012
(606) 431-6786
Circulation: 40,200

LOUISIANA

Alexandria News Weekly
P.O. Box 608
Alexandria, LA 71301

(318) 443-7664
Circulation: 5,000

Baton Rouge Community Leader
1010 North Boulevard
Baton Rouge, LA 70802
(504) 343-0544
Circulation: 21,700

Baton Rouge Weekly Press
1384 Swan Street
Baton Rouge, LA 70807
(504) 775-2002
Circulation: 7,500

The Louisiana Weekly
1001 Howard Avenue, #2600
New Orleans, LA 70113
(504) 524-5563
Circulation: 8,000

New Orleans Black Data
P.O. Box 51933
New Orleans, LA 70151
(504) 522-1418
Circulation: 10,000

Shreveport Sun
P.O. Box 38357
Shreveport, LA 71133
(318) 631-6222
Circulation: 3,819

MARYLAND

Afro-American (Circulation: 13,385; every
   Wednesday)
Richmond Afro-American (Circulation: 42,777)
Washington Afro-American (Circulation: 5,500)
628 N. Eutaw Street
Baltimore, MD 21201
(301) 728-8200

MASSACHUSETTS

Bay State Banner
925 Washington Street
Dorchester, MA 02124

(617) 288-4900
Circulation: 10,838

Boston Greater News
P.O. Box 497
Roxbury, MA 02119-0004
(617) 445-7063
Circulation: 12,300

MICHIGAN

Blazer News
P.O. Box 806
Jackson, MI 49204
(517) 787-0450
Circulation: 10,000

Ecorse Telegram
4122 10th Street
Ecorse, MI 48229
(313) 928-2955
Circulation: 12,000

Grand Rapid Times
2061 Eastern Avenue, SW
Grand Rapids, MI 49501
(616) 245-8737
Circulation: 6,000

Michigan Chronicle
427 Ledyard Street
Detroit, MI 48201
(313) 963-5522
Circulation: 48,686

Michigan Citizen
12541 Second Street
Highland Park, MI 48203
(313) 869-0033
Circulation: 41,520

Michigan Sentinel
27350 Southfield Road, #127
Lathrup Village, MI 48076
(313) 559-1010
Circulation: 18,000

MINNESOTA

Minneapolis Spokesman
3744 Fourth Avenue, S
Minneapolis, MN 55409
(612) 827-4021
Circulation: 6,762

St. Paul Recorder
590 Endicott Avenue
St. Paul, MN 55407
(612) 827-4021
Circulation: 2,295

MISSISSIPPI

Jackson Advocate
P.O. Box 3708
Jackson, MS 39207
(601) 948-4122
Circulation: 23,000

Mississippi Memo Digest
P.O. Box 5782
Meridian, MS 39301
(601) 693-2372
Circulation: 3,000

MISSOURI

Evening Whirl
P.O. Box 5088
Nagel Station
St. Louis, MO 63115
Circulation: 40,000

Kansas City American
4144 Lindell Boulevard
St. Louis, MO 63108
(314) 533-8000
Circulation: 65,500

Kansas City Call
P.O. Box 410477
Kansas City, MO 64141
(816) 842-3804
Circulation: 35,000

Kansas City Globe
P.O. Box 090410
Kansas City, MO 64109
(816) 531-5253
Circulation: 30,000

St. Louis Argus
4595 Martin Luther King, Jr. Drive
St. Louis, MO 63113
(314) 531-1323
Circulation: 33,000

St. Louis Metro Sentinel
2900 N. Market Street
St. Louis, MO 63106
(314) 531-2101
Circulation: 24,338

NEVADA

Las Vegas Sentinel-Voice
1201 S. Eastern Avenue
Las Vegas, NV 89104
(702) 383-4030
Circulation: 5,000

NEW JERSEY

New Jersey Afro-American
P.O. Box 22162
Newark, NJ 07103
(201) 242-5364
Circulation: 20,000

New Jersey Greater News
1188 Raymond Boulevard, #178
Newark, NJ 07102
(201) 643-3364
Circulation: 50,000

NEW YORK

Amsterdam News
2340 Frederick Douglass Boulevard
New York, NY 10027
(212) 932-7400
Circulation: 45,000

Big Red News
Smith Haj Enterprises
155 Water Street, 4th Floor
Brooklyn, NY 11201
(718) 852-6001
Circulation: 53,766

Black American
310 Lenox Avenue, #304
New York, NY 10027
(212) 564-5110
Circulation: 352,650

Buffalo Challenger
1303 Fillmore Avenue
Buffalo, NY 14211
(716) 897-0442
Circulation: 11,190

Buffalo Criterion
623–625 William Street
Buffalo, NY 14206
(716) 882-9570
Circulation: 10,000

City Sun
GPO 560
Brooklyn, NY 11202
(708) 624-5959
Circulation: 20,000

Communicade
67 Elba Street
Rochester, NY 14615
(716) 235-6695
Circulation: 3,000

Hudson Valley Black Press
P.O. Box 2160
Newburgh, NY 12550
(914) 562-1313
Circulation: 42,500

Jamaica Shopping & Entertainment Guide
164-11 89th Avenue, Suite 190
Jamaica, NY 11432
(718) 591-7777
Circulation: 30,000

New York Beacon
15 E. 40th Street, #402
New York, NY 10016
(212) 213-8585
Circulation: 63,750

New York Carib News
15 W. 39th Street
New York, NY 10018
(212) 944-1991
Circulation: 71,500

New York Voice
75-43 Parsons Boulevard
Flushing, NY 11366
(718) 591-6600
Circulation: 90,000

Westchester County Press
P.O. Box 152
White Plains, NY 10602
(914) 684-0006
Circulation: 12,500

NORTH CAROLINA

Carolina Peacemaker
P.O. Box 20853
Greensboro, NC 27420
(919) 274-6210
Circulation: 8,600

Carolinian
P.O. Box 25308
Raleigh, NC 27601
(919) 834-5558
Circulation: 12,500

Charlotte Post
1531 Camden Road
Charlotte, NC 28203
(704) 376-0496
Circulation: 10,000

Iredell County News
P.O. Box 407
Statesville, NC 28677
(919) 873-1054
Circulation: 2,500

Wilmington Journal
P.O. Box 1618
Wilmington, NC 28402
(919) 762-5502
Circulation: 8,600

Winston-Salem Chronicle
617 N. Liberty Street
Winston-Salem, NC 27102
(919) 722-8624
Circulation: 10,523

OHIO

Akron Reporter
P.O. Box 2042
Akron, OH 44309
(216) 773-4196
Circulation: 17,000

Buckeye Review
626 Belmont Avenue
Youngstown, OH 44502
(216) 743-2250
Circulation: 3,000

Call & Post
P.O. Box 6237
Cleveland, OH 44106
(216) 791-7600
Circulation: 31,782

Cincinnati Herald
836 Lincoln Avenue
Cincinnati, OH 45206
(513) 221-5440
Circulation: 24,500

Toledo Journal
P.O. Box 2536
Toledo, OH 43616
(419) 472-4521
Circulation: 19,000

OKLAHOMA

Black Chronicle
P.O. Box 17498

Oklahoma City, OK 73136
(405) 424-4695
Circulation: 30,017

Oklahoma Eagle
P.O. Box 3267
Tulsa, OK 74101
(918) 582-7124
Circulation: 15,000

OREGON

Portland Observer
P.O. Box 3137
Portland, OR 97208
(503) 288-0033
Circulation: 25,000

The Skanner
P.O. Box 5455
Portland, OR 97228-5455
(503) 278-3562
Circulation: 30,000

PENNSYLVANIA

The Leader
2923 W. Cheltenham Avenue
Philadelphia, PA 19150
(215) 885-4111
Circulation: 29,000

New Pittsburgh Courier
315 E. Carson Street
Pittsburgh, PA 15219
(412) 481-8302
Circulation: 18,343

Philadelphia New Observer
1930 Chestnut Street, #900
Philadelphia, PA 19103
(215) 665-8400
Circulation: 8,000

Philadelphia Tribune
522 S. 16th Street
Philadelphia, PA 19146

(215) 893-4050
Circulation: 33,890

SOUTH CAROLINA

Charleston Black Times (Circulation: 10,893)
Columbia Black News (Circulation: 22,834)
Florence Black Sun (Circulation: 6,704)
Greenville Black Star (Circulation: 9,110)
Orangeburg Black Star Voice (Circulation: 7,403)
Rock Hills Black View (Circulation: 5,091)
Sumpter Black Post (Circulation: 5,355)
1310 Harden Street
Columbia, SC 29204
(803) 799-5252

Charleston Chronicle
P.O. Box 2548
Charleston, SC 29403
(803) 723-2785
Circulation: 6,000

Coastal Times
2106 Mount Pleasant Street, #1
Charleston, SC 29403
(803) 273-5318
Circulation: 29,830

View South News
P.O. Box 1849
Orangeburg, SC 29116
(803) 531-1662
Circulation: 5,000

TENNESSEE

Memphis Silver Star News
3144 Park Avenue
Memphis, TN 38111
(901) 452-8828
Circulation: 25,000

Memphis Tri-State Defender
124 E. Calhoun Avenue
Memphis, TN 38101
(901) 523-1818
Circulation: 9,096

TEXAS

Dallas Examiner
424 Centre Street
Dallas, TX 75208
(214) 948-9175
Circulation: 20,000

Dallas Post Tribune
2726 S. Beckley Street
Dallas, TX 75224
(214) 946-7668
Circulation: 17,100

Dallas Weekly
3101 Martin Luther King Jr. Boulevard
Dallas, TX 74215
(214) 428-8958
Circulation: 20,300

Houston Defender
P.O. Box 8005
Houston, TX 77288
(713) 663-7716
Circulation: 27,014

Houston Forward Times
P.O. Box 8346
Houston, TX 77004
(713) 526-4727
Circulation: 51,627

Houston Informer
P.O. Box 3086
Houston, TX 77253
(713) 527-8261
Circulation: 23,000

Houston Sun
1520 Isabella Street
Houston, TX 77004
(713) 524-4474
Circulation: 80,000

San Antonio Register
P.O. Box 1598
San Antonio, TX 78296
(210) 222-1721
Circulation: 7,800

Southwest Digest
902 E. 28th Street
Lubbock, TX 79404
(806) 762-3612
Circulation: 4,000

Villager
1223-A Rosewood Court
Austin, TX 78702
(512) 476-0082
Circulation: 6,000

Waco Messenger
P.O. Box 287
Waco, TX 76703
(817) 799-6911
Circulation: 3,000

VIRGINIA

New Journal & Guide
362 Campostella Road
Norfolk, VA 23523
(804) 543-6531
Circulation: 25,000

Tribune
P.O. Box 6021
Roanoke, VA 24017
(703) 343-0326
Circulation: 5,600

WASHINGTON

Facts
P.O. Box 22015
Seattle, WA 98122
(206) 324-0552
Circulation: 40,270

Northwest Dispatch
P.O. Box 5637
Tacoma, WA 98405
(206) 272-7587
Circulation: 15,000

Seattle Medium
2600 S. Jackson Avenue
Seattle, WA 98144
(206) 323-3070
Circulation: 13,500

Tacoma True Citizen
2600 S. Jackson Street
Seattle, WA 98144
(206) 627-1103
Circulation: 13,500

WEST VIRGINIA

West Virginia Beacon Digest
P.O. Box 981
Charleston, WV 25324
(304) 342-4600
Circulation: 35,861

WISCONSIN

Milwaukee Community Journal
3612 N. Martin Luther King Drive
Milwaukee, WI 53212
(414) 265-5300
Circulation: 9,500

Milwaukee Courier (Circulation: 15,000)
Milwaukee Star (Circulation: 5,000)
2431 W. Hopkins Street
Milwaukee, WI 53206
(414) 449-4860

Milwaukee Times
2216 N. Martin Luther King Drive
Milwaukee, WI 53212
(414) 263-5088
Circulation: 15,000

 FREEDOM'S JOURNAL

The first African American newspaper in the United States was *Freedom's Journal*, which first published in New York City on March 16, 1827. Founded by John Russwurm and Samuel Cornish, *Freedom's Journal* set out to combat the negative portrayals of African Americans in the New York newspapers. The paper carried a wide-ranging selection of news articles, feature stories, literary pieces, and social announcements. In addition to advocating the abolition of slavery, *Freedom's Journal* also championed the rights of free blacks in the North and publicized the accomplishments of blacks around the world. The paper continued to appear until 1829.

 GOING ABROAD

The first African American foreign correspondent was Jamaica-born Joel Augustus Rogers, who was employed by the black-owned *Pittsburgh Courier*. In October 1935, the *Courier* dispatched Rogers to Ethiopia to report on the Italian-Ethiopian War. Rogers remained on assignment in Africa until the spring of 1936.

 BREAKING BARRIERS

African American journalists gained access to White House press conferences only in 1944, when Harry S. McAlpin became White House correspondent for the Negro Newspaper Publishers Association and the *Atlanta Daily World*, the nation's first black-owned daily paper. McAlpin attended his first press conference, presided over by President Franklin Roosevelt, on February 8. Three years later—largely through the efforts of Congressional Representative Adam Clayton Powell Jr.—African American reporters were admitted to the Congressional Press Galleries for the first time.

MEDIA ORGANIZATIONS

Amalgamated Publishers Inc.
45 W. 45th Street, Suite 500
New York, NY 10036
(212) 869-5220

Black Awareness in Television
13217 Livernois Avenue
Detroit, MI 48238
(313) 931-3427

Black Filmmaker Foundation
Tribeca Film Center
375 Greenwich Street, #600
New York, NY 10013
(212) 941-3944

Black Religious Broadcasters
2416 Orcutt Avenue
Newport News, VA 23607
(804) 380-6118

Black Women in Publishing
c/o Phelps-Stokes Fund Affiliate
10 E. 87th Street
New York, NY 10128
(212) 772-5951

Capital Press Club
P.O. Box 19403
Washington, DC 20036
(301) 933-3863

Foundation for Minority Interests in Media
(FMIM)
825 Seventh Avenue, 4th Floor
New York, NY 10019
(212) 456-1992

Minorities in Cable and New Technologies
1900 E. 78th Street
Chicago, IL 60617
(312) 721-7500

National Alliance of Third World Journalists
P.O. Box 43208
Washington, DC 20010
(202) 462-8197

National Association of Black College
    Broadcasters (NABCB)
P.O. Box 3191
Atlanta, GA 30302
(404) 523-6136

National Association of Black Journalists
3100 Taliaferro Hall
University of Maryland
College Park, MD 20742-7717
(301) 405-8500
www.nabj.org

National Association of Black Owned
    Broadcasters (NABOB)
1333 New Hampshire Avenue, NW, Suite 1000
Washington, DC 20036
(202) 463-8970

National Association of Broadcasters (NAB)
1771 N Street, NW
Washington, DC 20036-2891
(202) 429-5496

National Association of Media Women, Inc.
213-16 126th Avenue
Laurelton, NY 11413
(718) 712-4544

National Association of Minority Media
    Executives (NAMME)
5746 Union Mill Road, Box 310
Clifton, VA 20124
(888) 968-7658

National Black Media Coalition
38 New York Avenue, NE
Washington, DC 20002
(202) 387-8155

National Black Programming Consortium, Inc.
929 Harrison Avenue, #104
Columbus, OH 43215
(614) 299-5355

National Black Public Relations Society of
    America
6565 Sunset Boulevard, #301
Los Angeles, CA 90028
(213) 466-8221

National Conference of Editorial Writers
6223 Executive Boulevard
Rockville, MD 20852
(301) 984-3015

National Newspaper Publishers Association
3200 13th Street, NW
Washington, DC 20045
(202) 588-8764

National TV Art Association
2100 N.E. 52nd Street
Oklahoma City, OK 73711
(405) 427-5461

Young Black Programmers Coalition
P.O. Box 11243
Jackson, MS 39213
(601) 634-5775

NOTABLE MEDIA FIGURES

Abbott, Robert Sengstacke (1870–1940).   Born in Georgia, Abbott studied at Claflin University and Hampton Institute and earned a law degree from Kent College of Law in Chicago. After practicing law in Indiana and Kansas, he returned to Chicago and founded the *Chicago Defender* in 1905, with the aim of fighting segregation, lynching, and racism. Having no capital, Abbott used the kitchen of his lodging house as an office, depended on friends for news articles and columns, and sold the four-page paper from door to door. Despite heavy competition from established black papers such as the *Broad Ax*, the *Idea*, and the *Conservator*, Abbott's paper found a readership throughout the Midwest, the West, and the South.

When the Great Migration began during World War I, the *Defender* mounted a campaign, "The Great Northern Drive," to attract African Americans from the South. By 1917, the *Defender*'s circulation stood at 230,000. The paper considered itself the voice of the African American community, fighting for black rights and helping new arrivals find work and adjust to urban life. The *Defender* also played a role in the development of African American literature as the home of Langston Hughes's classic columns reporting the opinions of the fictional Jesse B. Semple, popularly known as "Simple." In addition to serving as president of the Robert Abbott Publishing Company, Abbott was deeply involved in community and church affairs. Upon his death, his nephew John H. Sengstacke (1913–1997) took over the direction of the paper.

Bradley, Edward R. (1941–   ).   Born in Philadelphia, Bradley graduated from Cheyney State College in Cheyney, Pennsylvania. He began his media career as a disk jockey and news reporter for WDAS radio in Philadelphia and WCBS radio in New York City. In 1971, Bradley became a stringer in CBS's Paris bureau. After a stint in Saigon, he was transferred to Washington, D.C., in 1974. Bradley then became an anchor for CBS *Sunday Night News* and principal correspondent for CBS *Reports*. In 1981, he replaced Dan Rather as a correspondent for *60 Minutes*. In 1992, Bradley became the host of *Street Stories* on CBS News. He has won seven Emmy Awards, two Alfred I. du Pont Columbia University Awards, a George Foster Peabody Broadcasting Award, a George Polk Award, and an NCAA (National Collegiate Athletic Association) Anniversary Award.

Brown, William Anthony "Tony" (1933–   ).   Born in Charleston, West Virginia, Brown earned a B.A. and an M.A. from Wayne State University in Detroit and went to work as a drama critic at the *Detroit Courier*. He became involved in the civil rights movement, helping to organize the 1963 March to Freedom in Detroit. After promotion to city editor at the *Courier*, he delved into television programming and production at WTVS, the Detroit PBS station. There he produced *C.P.T.* (colored people's time), the station's first series for African Americans. In 1970, Brown became executive producer and host of the PBS program *Black Journal*. In 1977 the show was renamed *Tony Brown's Journal* and ranks as the longest-running nationally syndicated minority-affairs program. Brown founded the Howard University School of Communications and served as dean from 1971 until 1974. In 1985, he organized the Council for the Economic Development of Black Americans and developed the Buy Freedom Network, which promotes black-owned businesses around the country. Brown is a syndicated newspaper columnist, a commentator for National Public Radio, and the president of Tony Brown Productions in New York City.

Clayton, Xernona Brewster (1930–).   Born in Muskogee, Oklahoma, Clayton earned a B.S. from Tennessee State University. She then became a newspaper columnist for the *Atlanta Voice*, taught public school in Chicago and Los Angeles, worked in photography and fashion modeling, and then joined WAGA-TV in Atlanta. In 1968, when Clayton became host of WAGA's *Xernona Clayton Show*, she made history as the first African American woman to have her own television show in the South. A dedicated community activist, Clayton has been corporate vice president for urban affairs at the Turner Broadcasting System in Atlanta since 1988.

Cosby, William Henry, Jr. "Bill" (1937–).   Born in Germantown, Pennsylvania, Cosby enrolled at Temple University, where he excelled in track and field but ultimately dropped out to pursue a career as a stand-up comic. He began working in network television during the 1960s, and in 1965 he began to costar with Robert Culp in *I Spy*, becoming the first African American to star in a dramatic series on TV. The success of the series led to a host of TV projects for Cosby, aimed at both adult and juvenile audiences. Having blazed the trail, he made special efforts to find opportunities for other African American actors and technicians. At the same time, he resumed his education, finally earning his B.A. from Temple in 1976, along with a master's degree and a doctorate in education from the University of Massachusetts at Amherst. Cosby's stardom reached new heights with the advent of *The Cosby Show* in 1984. The success of the series—added to Cosby's earnings from concerts, Grammy-winning comedy record albums, and corporate sponsorship—made him one of the world's wealthiest individuals. Cosby and his wife, Camille, have made major donations to a variety of African American institutions, most notably a record $20 million gift to Spelman College.

Fortune, T. Thomas (1856–1928).   One of the leading African American journalists of the post–Civil War era, Fortune was born in Florida and educated at Howard University. Before reaching age 30, he completed two major scholarly works: *Black and White: Land, Labor and Politics in the South* and *The Negro in Politics*. In 1878, Fortune took a job as a printer for the *New York Sun* and soon moved up to the editorial staff. He also served as editor of the *Globe*. In 1883, Fortune founded the *New York Age*, which became the leading black journal of opinion in America. A forceful advocate of equal rights, Fortune was an early crusader against segregated schools and made the term *Afro-American* a popular substitute for *Negro* in New York newspapers. In 1890, he established the Afro-American League, a precursor of the NAACP. After selling the *Age* in 1907, Fortune was an editorial writer for several African American newspapers, and in 1923, he replaced Marcus Garvey as editor of the *Negro World.*

Goode, Malvin Russell (1908–).   A native of White Plains, Virginia, Goode worked in the Pittsburgh steel mills during high school and while attending the University of Pittsburgh. He continued to work in the mills for five years after graduating from college. During the 1930s, Goode became director of the Centre Avenue YMCA and led a campaign to end discrimination in the Pittsburgh branches of the YMCA. After serving with the Pittsburgh Housing Authority, he joined the *Pittsburgh Courier* in 1948. The following year he began a career in radio news. In 1952, Goode became news director at WHOD radio. For six years he worked alongside his sister, Mary Dee, creating the only brother-sister duo in radio. Goode was the first African American member of the National Association of Radio and TV News Directors. In 1962 he joined ABC-TV, becoming the first African American network TV reporter.

Graves, Earl G. (1935–).   Born in Brooklyn, Graves developed a successful lawn-care business during his junior year at Morgan State University. After graduation in 1958 he served in the U.S. Army and then became a narcotics agent for the U.S. Department of Justice. In 1965, Graves joined the staff of New York Senator Robert Kennedy, as a specialist in economic and urban affairs. After Kennedy's assassination in 1968, Graves began working as a management consultant and conceived the idea of publishing a magazine on African American business affairs. With backing from the Chase Manhattan Bank, Graves published the first issue of *Black Enterprise* in 1970. The magazine has become a major force in providing business, career, and financial information for African Americans and anchors Earl Graves Ltd., which now includes publishing and marketing ventures. In 1997, Graves shared his business knowledge and personal experiences in the book *How to Succeed in Business without Being White*.

Gumbel, Bryant Charles (1948–).   Born in New Orleans and raised in Chicago, Gumbel graduated from Bates College in Lewiston, Maine. He then joined *Black Sports* magazine as a freelance writer, quickly moving up to staff writer and then editor-in-chief. In 1972, Gumbel became the weekend sportscaster for KNBC in Los Angeles; before long he was the station's weeknight sportscaster and finally sports director. He joined NBC in 1975 as a sports announcer, and in 1982 he became the first African American cohost of a major television news show, *The Today Show*. Gumbel remained a fixture on NBC's popular morning program until 1996, when he left to pursue other interests. In 1997, Gumbel signed a five-year contract with CBS to work on a variety of projects, which included hosting the TV news magazine *Public Eye*. His brother Greg has also enjoyed a successful career as a sports announcer with ESPN and NBC.

Hunter-Gault, Charlayne (1942–).   Born in South Carolina, Hunter-Gault made history in 1961 by integrating the University of Georgia, along with fellow student Hamilton Homes. After graduation, she won a Russell Sage Fellowship for graduate work at Washington University. Hunter-Gault then joined the staff of *Trans-Action* magazine and anchored the evening news at WRC-TV in Washington, D.C. In 1968, she became a metropolitan reporter for the *New York Times*, specializing in coverage of the urban black community. Hunter-Gault joined the *MacNeil/Lehrer Report* in 1978 as a correspondent and became its national correspondent in 1983. She has also been published in *The New York Times Magazine, Saturday Review, The New York Times Book Review, Essence*, and *Vogue*, and she is the author of *In My Place* (1992), a memoir about her experiences at the University of Georgia. Her numerous awards include two Emmys and a Peabody Award for excellence in broadcast journalism, and she also won the 1986 Journalist of the Year Award from the National Association of Black Journalists. In 1997, she moved to South Africa as chief of National Public Radio's African Bureau.

Johnson, John H. (1918–).   Born in Arkansas, Johnson eventually moved to Chicago, where he studied at the University of Chicago and the Northwestern School of Commerce. While producing the internal newsletter for the Supreme Liberty Life Insurance Company, he developed his own publishing ideas. In 1942, Johnson founded *Negro Digest* and followed up with *Ebony* in 1945. *Ebony* was the first African American publication to carry advertisements for general consumer merchandise. Building on his success, Johnson subsequently added *Jet, Ebony Man*, and *Ebony Jr.* to his roster of magazines. In 1987, *Black Enterprise* magazine named Johnson Businessman of the Decade. Today, Johnson Publishing Company is the strongest and most successful black publishing company in the United States. A versatile entrepreneur, Johnson has branched out into other areas besides publishing: He is also chair and CEO of his former employer, the Supreme Liberty Life Insurance Company, chair of WJPC-AM radio in Chicago, and president of Fashion Fair Cosmetics.

Johnson, Robert L. (1946–).   Born in Mississippi, Johnson was educated at the University of Illinois and the Woodrow Wilson School at Princeton. He began his TV career with the Corporation for Public Broadcasting and moved on to the National Cable Television Association as vice president for governmental relations. Envisioning a cable TV channel for African Americans, Johnson founded Black Entertainment Television (BET) in 1980 with $15,000 of his own money and $500,000 in backing from the Colorado Cable Company. Today, BET is in millions of homes, and BET Holdings publishes *Emerge* and *BET Weekend* magazines. In 1991, BET became the first black-owned company listed on the New York Stock Exchange. Johnson has also founded BET SoundStage, a restaurant/club in Largo, Maryland, which he envisions as the first of a nationwide chain.

Lee, Shelton Jackson "Spike" (1957–).   Born in Atlanta and raised in Brooklyn, Lee returned south to attend Morehouse College, where he earned a B.A. He then earned an M.F.A. in film production at New York University's Tisch School of the Arts. Lee created a new era in black cinema with his independently produced comedy, *She's Gotta Have It* (1986), which earned the Prix de Jeunesse Award at the Cannes Film Festival and brought him international acclaim. Lee then founded 40 Acres and a Mule Filmworks, based in the Fort Greene section of Brooklyn, and he created 10 feature films in as many years, including the critically acclaimed *Do the Right Thing* (1989) and *Malcolm X* (1992). At the same time, he has served as an executive producer; directed dozens of music videos for such artists as Curtis Mayfield, Michael Jackson, and Miles Davis; and made commercials for Nike and other companies, as well as for The College Fund/UNCF and American Express's Charge against Hunger. In 1997, Lee joined forces with the advertising giant DDB Needham to create Spike/DDB, a full-service advertising agency specializing in the urban/ethnic market. Lee's documentary, *Four Little Girls: Bombing of the 16*[th] *Street Baptist Church, Birmingham, Alabama,* aired on HBO in 1998 and was nominated for an Academy Award.

Maynard, Robert C. (1937–1993).   The Brooklyn-born son of a Barbadian immigrant, Maynard dropped out of high school at age 16 to become a writer in Greenwich Village. His journalism career began in 1961 at a daily newspaper in York, Pennsylvania, and in 1965, he received a Nieman Fellowship to study at Harvard University. After leaving Harvard, Maynard covered civil rights and urban unrest as a national correspondent for the *Washington Post.* He became the newspaper's ombudsman and later joined the staff of the editorial page. In 1979, Maynard took over as editor of the *Oakland Tribune,* which had been labeled "the second worst newspaper in the United States." He bought the paper in 1983, becoming the first African American to own a major metropolitan newspaper. Under the guidance of Maynard and his wife, Nancy, the *Oakland Tribune* has won hundreds of awards for editorial excellence, including a 1990 Pulitzer Prize for coverage of the Loma Prieta earthquake. The economic effects of the earthquake, combined with a nationwide recession, forced the Maynards to sell the *Tribune* in 1992. At the time, it had the most ethnically diverse newsroom of any major metropolitan newspaper in the United States. In 1977, Maynard cofounded the Institute for Journalism Education, a nonprofit corporation dedicated to expanding opportunities for minority journalists at the nation's newspapers; following his death, the organization was renamed the Robert C. Maynard Institute for Journalism Education.

Rodgers, Jonathan (1946–   ).   Rodgers earned his B.A. in journalism from the University of California at Berkeley and an M.A. in communications from Stanford University. Rodgers spent 20 years with the Columbia Broadcasting System, where he served as assistant news director for WMMB-TV, the Chicago CBS affiliate, and news director and station manager for KCBS-TV, the CBS affiliate in Los Angeles. He then became an executive producer for CBS News in New York, overseeing such programs as *CBS This Morning* and *CBS News Nightwatch.* Rodgers then served as vice president and general manager of WBBM-TV in Chicago, and in 1990 he was appointed head of CBS's television stations. In 1996, Rodgers was named president of the Discovery Networks, U.S., a unit of Discovery Communications, Inc., where he is responsible for all domestic business of Discovery Channel, The Learning Channel, Animal Planet, and Discovery digital services.

Taylor, Susan L. (1946–   ).   After beginning her career as an actress, Taylor founded Nequai Cosmetics and began freelance writing for *Essence* shortly after it was founded in 1970. In just a year, she was named *Essence*'s beauty editor, and a year later she was given responsibility for the fashion section, as well. In 1982, Taylor became editor-in-chief. During her tenure, *Essence* has achieved unprecedented success, becoming the only women's magazine to have a significant male readership and the only black-oriented magazine to have a significant white readership. Taylor was the host and executive producer of *Essence,* the country's first nationally syndicated black-oriented TV magazine show, which ran for four seasons in more than 60 U.S. markets and in several Caribbean and African countries. In 1993, Taylor was named senior vice president of Essence Communications, Inc. She has written two best-selling books, *In the Spirit: The Inspirational Writings of Susan L. Taylor* and *Lessons in Living.*

Winfrey, Oprah (1954–   ).   Born in Mississippi, Winfrey dropped out of Tennessee State University to do voice-overs and then weekend news reports on WVOL-AM radio in Nashville, becoming Nashville's first female and first black newscaster. At age 22, she became a weekend news anchor at WJZ-TV, the ABC affiliate in Baltimore. In 1977, Winfrey took over as the host of WJZ's morning talk show, *People Are Talking,* which beat *Donahue,* then the talk-show ratings champ, in the local ratings. She moved to Chicago in 1984 to host A.M. *Chicago,* a morning talk show at WLS-TV. That same year, Winfrey appeared as Sofia, a feisty wife and mother in the film adaptation of Alice Walker's prize-winning novel, *The*

Oprah Winfrey, one of the best-known media personalities in the world.

Color Purple, earning an Academy Award nomination for Best Supporting Actress. As A.M. *Chicago* gained national acclaim, it was syndicated to 138 stations nationwide as *The Oprah Winfrey Show.* Winfrey became the show's producer and purchased the production facility, which she named Harpo Productions. This made her the first African American and the third woman (after Mary Pickford and Lucille Ball) to own a major studio facility. Winfrey also produced a miniseries, *The Women of Brewster Place,* and went on to produce other works for television and film, including the film adaptation of Toni Morrison's award-winning *Beloved.* In 1987, she gave the commencement address and received her diploma from Tennessee State University. She has written *Make the Connection* (1996), *Journal of Daily Renewal* (1996), and other books. One of the most influential media figures and best-known personalities in the world, she is also a major philanthropist.

SOURCES FOR ADDITIONAL INFORMATION

Bogle, Donald. *Blacks in American Films and Television: An Illustrated Encyclopedia.* New York: Garland, 1988.

———. *Toms, Coons, Mulattoes, Mammies, and Bucks: An Interpretive History of Blacks in American Films,* rev. ed. New York: Continuum, 1989.

Brooks, Tim, and Earle Marsh. *The Complete Directory to Prime Time Network and Cable TV Shows.* New York: Ballantine, 1995.

Cripps, Thomas. *Black Film as Genre.* Bloomington: University of Indiana Press, 1978.

Dates, Jeannette L., and William Barlow. *Split Image: African Americans in the Mass Media*. Washington, DC: Howard University Press, 1990.

Hill, George. *Black Women in Television: An Illustrated History and Bibliography*. New York: Garland, 1990.

Leab, Daniel J. *From Sambo to Superspade: The Black Experience in Motion Pictures*. Boston: Houghton Mifflin, 1975.

MacDonald, J. Fred. *Blacks and White TV: Afro-Americans in White Television Since 1948*. Chicago: Nelson-Hall, 1983.

Pride, Armistead Scott. *History of the Black Press*. Washington, DC: Howard University Press, 1997.

Wolesley, Roland E. *The Black Press, USA*, 2nd ed. Ames: Iowa State University Press, 1990.

Woll, Allen L., and Randall M. Miller. *Ethnic and Racial Images in American Film and Television*. New York: Garland, 1987.

18

Sports

> I f contemporary black athletes' exploits are more well-known, few fully appreciate their true hard road to glory. Discrimination, vilification, incarceration, dissipation, ruination, and ultimate despair have dogged the steps of the mightiest of these heroes.
>
> Arthur Ashe, A Hard Road to Glory (1988)

BASEBALL

Baseball began as a game for white gentlemen in New York and New Jersey in the years before the Civil War. It quickly spread to other social classes, ethnic groups, and regions of the country, however, and by 1865, it had become a game for both black and white working men. Mixed-race teams, although not the norm, were not considered exceptional. Mixed-race play on the evolving professional teams came to a halt in 1867, however, when the National Association of Base Ball Players (NABBP) voted to exclude "any club which may be composed of one or more colored persons." The NABBP only lasted as a league for a few more years, but its successors carried on the ban informally. Even though many amateur and a very few professional teams in the North and West continued to be integrated into the 1880s, professional baseball continued to be a racially segregated enterprise until Jackie Robinson reintegrated the sport in 1947. To offer professional baseball to black players and fans, a number of leagues rose and fell between 1867 and 1947. They eventually coalesced into what became known as the Negro Leagues.

THE NEGRO LEAGUES
MILESTONES IN BLACK BASEBALL HISTORY

1867   In the first recorded game between two African American baseball teams, the Brooklyn Uniques host the Philadelphia Excelsiors (the visitors win, 37-24); the National Association of Base Ball Players (the first organized league in the United States) officially refuses to admit black or integrated teams.

1885   In Babylon, Long Island, New York, Frank P. Thompson organizes the first professional black team, the Cuban Giants. (Thompson is the headwaiter at the Argyle Hotel, and he reportedly recruits the men on his staff to play ball for the entertainment of the guests.)

1903   The Cuban X Giants, the best team of their day, win the Colored World Championship by defeating the Philadelphia Giants in a seven-game series.

1911   Rube Foster organizes the Chicago American Giants, the finest team in black baseball.

1920   Foster and other African American team owners meet in the Paseo YMCA in Kansas City and organize the Negro National League.

1923   The Eastern Colored League is formed as a rival to the Negro National League.

1924   The first Negro World Series is played between the Kansas City Monarchs and the Hilldale club (Kansas City wins, 5 games to 4); the series is played each year through 1927.

1931   The onset of the Great Depression, combined with the death of Rube Foster, causes the collapse of the black baseball leagues.

1933   Black baseball revives with the reorganization of the Negro National League under the leadership of Pittsburgh's Gus Greenlee; the first East-West All-Star Game is played in Chicago's Comiskey Park before 20,000 fans (the annual classic will draw 55,000 fans by the mid-1940s).

1937   The Negro American League begins operation, representing the Midwest, while the Negro National League represents the East.

1942   The Homestead Grays and the Kansas City Monarchs play the first World Series since 1927 (the Monarchs win in four straight games).

1948   The Negro National League disbands as the integration of the major leagues draws African American fans away from the Negro Leagues.

1960   The Negro American League disbands; a handful of teams, such as the Kansas City Monarchs and the Indianapolis Clowns, continue to barnstorm until the late 1960s.

NEGRO LEAGUES AND TEAMS

(Source: *Encyclopedia of African-American Culture and History*. Jack Salzman, ed. New York: Macmillan, 1996.)

NEGRO NATIONAL LEAGUE I (1920–1931)

Birmingham Black Barons (1925, 1927–1930)

Chicago American Giants (1920–1931)

Chicago Giants (1920–1921)

Cleveland Browns (1924)

Cleveland Cubs (1931)

Cleveland Elites (1926)

Cleveland Hornets (1927)

Cleveland Tate Stars (1922)

Columbus Buckeyes (1921)

Cuban Stars (1920, 1922)

Dayton Marcos (1920, 1926)

Detroit Stars (1920–1931)

Indianapolis ABCs (1920–1926, 1931)

Kansas City Monarchs (1920–1931)

Louisville White Sox (1931)

Memphis Red Sox (1924–1925, 1927–1930)

Milwaukee Bears (1923)

Nashville Elite Giants (1930)

Pittsburgh Keystones (1922)

St. Louis Giants (1920–1921)

Toledo Tigers (1923)

EASTERN COLORED LEAGUE (1923–1928)/AMERICAN NEGRO LEAGUE (1929)

Bacharach Giants [Atlantic City] (1923–1929)

Baltimore Black Sox (1923–1929)

Brooklyn Royal Giants (1923–1927)

Cuban Stars (East) (1923–1929)

Harrisburg Giants (1924–1927)

Hilldale [Philadelphia] (1923–1927)

Homestead [PA] Grays (1929)

Lincoln [NY] Giants (1923–1926, 1928–1929)

Newark Stars (1926)

Philadelphia Tigers (1928)

Washington Potomacs (1924)

NEGRO SOUTHERN LEAGUE (1932)

Cole's American Giants [Chicago]

Columbus [OH] Turfs

Indianapolis ABCs

Memphis Red Sox

Monroe Monarchs

Montgomery Grey Sox

Nashville Elite Giants

EAST-WEST LEAGUE (SPRING 1932)

Baltimore Black Sox

Cleveland Stars

Cuban Stars

Hilldale [Philadelphia]

Homestead [PA] Grays

Newark Browns

NEGRO NATIONAL LEAGUE II (1933–1948)

Bacharach Giants [Atlantic City] (1934)

Baltimore Black Sox (1933–1934)

Baltimore Elite Giants (1938–1948)

Brooklyn Eagles (1935)

Cleveland Giants (1933)

Cleveland Red Sox (1934)

Cole's American Giants [Chicago] (1933–1935)

Columbus Blue Birds (1933)

Columbus Elite Giants (1935)

Detroit Stars (1933)

Harrisburg–St. Louis Stars (1943)

Homestead Grays [DC] (1935–1948)

Nashville Elite Giants (1933–1934)

Newark Dodgers (1934–1935)

Newark Eagles (1936–1948)

New York Black Yankees (1936–1948)

New York Cubans (1935–1936, 1939–1948)

Philadelphia Stars (1934–1948)

Pittsburgh Crawfords (1933–1938)

Washington [DC] Black Senators (1938)

NEGRO AMERICAN LEAGUE (1937–1950)

Atlanta Black Crackers (1938)

Baltimore Elite Giants (1949–1950)

Birmingham Black Barons (1937–1938, 1940–1950)

Chicago American Giants (1937–1950)

Cincinnati Buckeyes (1942)

Cincinnati Tigers (1937)

Cleveland Bears (1939–1940)

Cleveland Buckeyes (1943–1948, 1950)

Detroit Stars (1937)

Houston Eagles (1949–1950)

Indianapolis ABCs (1938–1939)

Indianapolis Athletics (1937)

Indianapolis Clowns (1943–1950)

Indianapolis Crawfords (1940)

Jacksonville Red Caps (1938, 1941–1942)

Kansas City Monarchs (1937–1950)

Louisville Buckeyes (1949)

Memphis Red Sox (1937–1941, 1943–1950)

New York Cubans (1949–1950)

Philadelphia Stars (1949–1950)

St. Louis Stars (1937, 1939, 1941)

Toledo Crawfords (1939)

MEMORABLE TEAMS AND THEIR STARS

Atlanta Black Crackers (2 seasons).   Nat Peeples, Roy Welmaker, James "Red" Moore. The Black Crackers played most of their games in the South, sharing Atlanta's Ponce de Leon Park with the minor league team known as the White Crackers.

Baltimore Black Sox (10 seasons).   The Black Sox were famed for their infield of Jud "Boojum" Wilson (1B), Frank Warfield (2B), Oliver "Ghost" Marcelle (3B), and Sir Richard Lundy (SS). The four were known as the Million-Dollar Infield because sportswriters believed they would have commanded that much money if they had been white.

Baltimore Elite Giants (13 seasons).   The Giants pronounced their name "EE-leet" in traditional Southern fashion. During the 1940s, they groomed Joe Black, Jim Gilliam, and Roy Campanella for stardom with the Brooklyn Dodgers.

Birmingham Black Barons (26 seasons).   Lorenzo "Piper" Davis, Lloyd "Pepper" Bassett, Nat Rogers. Playing in Birmingham's historic Rickwood Field, the Barons were Negro American League champs in 1943, 1944, and 1948 (when their roster included a 17-year-old rookie named Willie Mays).

Brooklyn Royal Giants (21 seasons).   "Smokey" Joe Williams, "Cannonball" Dick Redding, Frank Wickware, John Henry "Pop" Lloyd, Charles "Chino" Smith. Boasting two of the greatest all-time pitchers in Williams and Redding, the Royal Giants were among the top teams of the World War I era.

Chicago American Giants (32 seasons).   Ted "Double Duty" Radcliffe, Willie Foster, Jimmie Crutchfield. Owned and managed by Rube Foster from 1911 to 1926, the American Giants were the finest Negro League team of the 1920s.

Cuban X Giants. Rube Foster, Pop Lloyd, Dan McClellan, Martin Dihigo, Grant "Home Run" Johnson. The X in the team's name was added to forestall legal action from Frank Thompson's original Cuban Giants, who often found other teams pirating their famous name.

Detroit Stars (15 seasons).   Norman "Turkey" Stearns, Bruce Petway, Pete Hill. During the 1940s, the Stars played their home games in Briggs Stadium when the Tigers were on the road.

Hilldale Giants (7 seasons).   Pop Lloyd, (William) Judy Johnson, Nip Winters. The Giants were the classiest team of the short-lived Eastern Colored League. They played out of Darby, a suburb of Philadelphia.

Homestead Grays (17 seasons).   Josh Gibson, James "Cool Papa" Bell, Walter "Buck" Leonard, William

Josh Gibson of the Homestead Grays of the Negro National League is considered one of the greatest hitters in baseball history.

"Judy" Johnson, Martin Dihigo, "Smokey" Joe Williams, Vic Harris, Luke Easter, Sam Bankhead. The Grays were the dominant team of the Negro National League. Dividing their home games between Pittsburgh's Forbes Field and Washington, D.C.'s, Griffith Stadium, they usually outdrew the lowly white Senators.

Indianapolis ABCs (11 seasons).   Oscar Charleston, Elwood "Bingo" De Moss, Ben Taylor, Raleigh "Biz" Mackey. The ABCs were named after their sponsor, the American Brewing Company. They enjoyed their best season in 1922, when they finished second in the Negro National League with a 46-33 record.

Indianapolis Clowns (17 seasons).   Buster Heywood, Woody Smallwood, Henry Aaron. Known for cutting up on the field, the Clowns at one time included the future Harlem Globetrotter Goose Tatum on their roster. After young Henry Aaron joined them, they won the Negro American League championship in 1952.

Kansas City Monarchs (37 seasons).   Satchel Paige, Willard Brown, Hilton Smith, Connie Johnson, Newt Allen, Ted Strong, Jesse Williams, Ernie Banks, Jackie Robinson. Baseball historians rate the Monarchs as one of the greatest teams in the history of the game.

Memphis Red Sox (32 seasons).   Dan Bankhead, Jehoise Heard, Marshall Bridges. The Red Sox had their best year in 1938, going 21-4 during the first half of the season. In later years, their roster included the future country-and-western star Charley Pride.

Newark Eagles (13 seasons).   Monte Irvin, Larry Doby, Don Newcomb, Ray Dandrige, Leon Day. The Eagles were the first baseball team owned and operated by a woman—the assertive Effa Manley often told her manager how to use his pitching staff.

New York Black Yankees (13 seasons).   George "Mule" Suttles, Clint Thomas, Barney Brown. The Black Yankees were jointly owned by the financier James "Soldier Boy" Semler and the dancing star Bill "Bojangles" Robinson. The team began playing out of Harlem but later shifted to Albany.

New York Cubans (14 seasons).   Martin Dihigo, Minnie Minoso. The Cubans won the Negro World Series in 1947, beating the Cleveland Buckeyes—their top pitcher was Luis Tiant, Sr., father of a future major-league star.

Philadelphia Stars (20 seasons).   Biz Mackey, Dick Lundy, Jud Wilson, "Slim" Jones, Harry "Suitcase" Simpson. The descendants of the Hilldale Giants, the Stars won the Negro National League pennant in 1934.

Pittsburgh Crawfords (7 seasons).   "Cool Papa" Bell, Josh Gibson, Oscar Charleston, Judy Johnson, Satchel Paige. Bankrolled by Gus Greenlee, a bootlegger and kingpin of a gambling "numbers" syndicate, the Crawfords were one of the top teams of the 1930s. They broke up when some of their stars, including Josh Gibson, opted to play in the Dominican Republic.

St. Louis Stars (12 seasons).   Willie Wells, Ted "Highpockets" Trent, George Giles. With two of the fastest players of all time in Wells and Giles, the Stars were world champions in 1928, 1930, and 1931.

NEGRO LEAGUES BATTING CHAMPIONS

Year	Player, Team	Average
NEGRO NATIONAL LEAGUE I		
1920	Cris Torriente, Chicago American Giants	.411
1921	Charles Blackwell, St. Louis	.448
1922	Heavy Johnson, Kansas City	.389
1923	Cris Torriente, Chicago American Giants	.412
1924	Dobie Moore, Kansas City	.453
1925	Edgar Wesley, Detroit	.416
1926	Mule Suttles, St. Louis	.418
1927	Red Parnell, Birmingham	.426

Year	Player, Team	Average
1928	Pythian Russ, Chicago American Giants	.406
1929	Mule Suttles, St. Louis	.372
1930	Willie Wells, St. Louis	.403
1931	Nat Rogers, Memphis	.424

EASTERN COLORED LEAGUE/AMERICAN NEGRO LEAGUE

Year	Player, Team	Average
1923	Jud Wilson, Baltimore	.373
1924	Pop Lloyd, Bacharach Giants	.433
1925	Oscar Charleston, Bacharach Giants	.445
1926	Robert Hudspeth, Lincoln Giants	.365
1927	Clarence Jenkins, Bacharach Giants	.398
1928	Pop Lloyd, Lincoln Giants	.564
1929	Chino Smith, Lincoln Giants	.454

NEGRO NATIONAL LEAGUE II

Year	Player, Team	Average
1933	Oscar Charleston, Pittsburgh	.372
1934	Jud Wilson, Homestead Grays	.361
1935	Turkey Stearns, Cole's American Giants	.430
1936	Lazaro Salazar, New York Cubans	.367
1937	Bill Wright, Homestead Grays	.410
1938	Ray Dandrige, Newark Eagles	.404
1939	Bill Wright, Baltimore Elite Giants	.402
1940	Buck Leonard, Homestead Grays	.383
1941	Monte Irvin, Newark Eagles	.463
1942	Willie Wells, Newark Eagles	.344
	Josh Gibson, Homestead Grays	.344
1943	Josh Gibson, Homestead Grays	.474
1944	Frank Austin, Philadelphia	.390
1945	Josh Gibson, Homestead Grays	.393
1946	Monte Irvin, Newark Eagles	.389
1947	Luis Marquez, Homestead Grays	.417
1948	Buck Leonard, Homestead Grays	.395

NEGRO AMERICAN LEAGUE

Year	Player, Team	Average
1937	Willard Brown, Kansas City	.371
1938	Willard Brown, Kansas City	.356
1939	Willard Brown, Kansas City	.336
1940	Chester Williams, Memphis	.473
1941	Lyman Bostock, Chicago American Giants	.488
1942	Ducky Davenport, Birmingham	.381
1943	Lester Lockett, Birmingham	.408
1944	Sam Jethroe, Cleveland Buckeyes	.353
1945	Sam Jethroe, Cleveland Buckeyes	.393
1946	Buck O'Neil, Kansas City	.350
1947	John Ritchie, Chicago American Giants	.381
1948	Artie Wilson, Birmingham	.402

Source: Encyclopedia of African-American Culture and History.

REMEMBERING THE GREATS

Approximately 2,600 players were on the rosters of the various black leagues throughout the history of the Negro Leagues. Their achievements are commemorated in the Negro Leagues Baseball Museum, located at 1601 E. 18th Street, Kansas City, MO 64108 (816-221-1920). The museum's website can be accessed at http://www.nlbm.com.

THE INTEGRATED MAJOR LEAGUES
BATTING CHAMPIONS

National League

Year	Player	Team	Average
1949	Jackie Robinson	Brooklyn	.342
1954	Willie Mays	New York	.345
1956	Henry Aaron	Milwaukee	.328
1959	Henry Aaron	Milwaukee	.355
1961	Roberto Clemente	Pittsburgh	.351
1962	Tommy Davis	Los Angeles	.346
1963	Tommy Davis	Los Angeles	.326
1964	Roberto Clemente	Pittsburgh	.339
1965	Roberto Clemente	Pittsburgh	.329
1967	Roberto Clemente	Pittsburgh	.357
1972	Billy Williams	Chicago	.333
1974	Ralph Garr	Atlanta	.353
1975	Bill Madlock	Chicago	.354
1976	Bill Madlock	Chicago	.339
1977	Dave Parker	Pittsburgh	.338
1978	Dave Parker	Pittsburgh	.334
1982	Bill Madlock	Pittsburgh	.341
1983	Al Oliver	Montreal	.331
1984	Tony Gwynn	San Diego	.351
1985	Willie McGee	St. Louis	.353
1986	Tim Raines	Montreal	.354
1987	Tony Gwynn	San Diego	.369
1988	Tony Gwynn	San Diego	.313
1989	Tony Gwynn	San Diego	.336
1990	Willie McGee	St. Louis	.335
1991	Terry Pendleton	Atlanta	.319
1992	Gary Sheffield	San Diego	.330
1994	Tony Gwynn	San Diego	.394
1995	Tony Gwynn	San Diego	.368
1996	Tony Gwynn	San Diego	.353
1997	Tony Gwynn	San Diego	.372

American League

Year	Player	Team	Average
1966	Frank Robinson	Baltimore	.316
1969	Rod Carew	Minnesota	.332
1970	Alex Johnson	California	.329
1972	Rod Carew	Minnesota	.318
1973	Rod Carew	Minnesota	.350
1974	Rod Carew	Minnesota	.364
1975	Rod Carew	Minnesota	.359
1977	Rod Carew	Minnesota	.388
1978	Rod Carew	Minnesota	.333
1982	Willie Wilson	Kansas City	.332
1989	Kirby Puckett	Minnesota	.339
1997	Frank Thomas	Chicago	.347

HOME RUN LEADERS

National League

Year	Player	Team	Total
1955	Willie Mays	New York	51
1957	Henry Aaron	Milwaukee	44
1958	Ernie Banks	Chicago	47
1960	Ernie Banks	Chicago	41
1962	Willie Mays	San Francisco	49
1963	Willie McCovey	San Francisco	44
1964	Willie Mays	San Francisco	47
1965	Willie Mays	San Francisco	52
1966	Henry Aaron	Atlanta	44
1967	Henry Aaron	Atlanta	39
1968	Willie McCovey	San Francisco	36
1969	Willie McCovey	San Francisco	45
1971	Willie Stargell	Pittsburgh	48
1973	Willie Stargell	Pittsburgh	44
1977	George Foster	Cincinnati	52
1978	George Foster	Cincinnati	40
1987	Andre Dawson	Chicago	49
1988	Darryl Strawberry	New York	39
1989	Kevin Mitchell	San Francisco	47
1992	Fred McGriff	San Diego	35
1993	Barry Bonds	San Francisco	46

American League

Year	Player	Team	Total
1952	Larry Doby	Cleveland	32
1954	Larry Doby	Cleveland	32
1966	Frank Robinson	Baltimore	49
1972	Dick Allen	Chicago	37
1973	Reggie Jackson	Oakland	32
1974	Dick Allen	Chicago	32
1975	Reggie Jackson	Oakland	36
	George Scott	Milwaukee	36
1977	Jim Rice	Boston	39
1978	Jim Rice	Boston	46
1980	Reggie Jackson	New York	41
	Ben Ogilvie	Milwaukee	41
1981	Eddie Murray	Baltimore	22
1982	Reggie Jackson	California	39
1986	Jesse Barfield	Toronto	40
1989	Fred McGriff	Toronto	36
1990	Cecil Fielder	Detroit	51
1991	Cecil Fielder	Detroit	44
1994	Ken Griffey Jr.	Seattle	40
1995	Albert Belle	Cleveland	50
1997	Ken Griffey Jr.	Seattle	56

Cy Young Award Winners

Year	Pitcher	W-L	ERA
1956	Don Newcomb, Brooklyn (NL)	27-7	3.06
1968	Bob Gibson, St. Louis (NL)	22-8	1.12
1970	Bob Gibson, St. Louis (NL)	23-7	3.12
1971	Vida Blue, Oakland (AL)	24-8	1.82
	Ferguson Jenkins, Chicago (NL)	24-13	2.77
1985	Dwight Gooden, New York (NL)	24-4	1.53

MOST VALUABLE PLAYERS

(Note: RBI = runs batted in; SB = stolen bases; HR = home runs; ERA = earned run average.)

National League

1949   Jackie Robinson, Brooklyn (.342, 124 RBI, 37 SB, 16 HR)

1951   Roy Campanella, Brooklyn (.325, 33 HR, 108 RBI)

1953   Roy Campanella, Brooklyn (.312, 41 HR, 142 RBI)

1954   Willie Mays, New York (.345, 41 HR, 110 RBI)

1955   Roy Campanella, Brooklyn (.318, 32 HR, 107 RBI)

1956   Don Newcomb, Brooklyn (27-7, 3.06 ERA)

1957   Henry Aaron, Milwaukee (.322, 44 HR, 132 RBI)

1958   Ernie Banks, Chicago (.313, 47 HR, 129 RBI)

1959   Ernie Banks, Chicago (.304, 45 HR, 143 RBI)

1961   Frank Robinson, Cincinnati (.323, 37 HR, 124 RBI)

1962   Maury Wills, Los Angeles (.299, 208 hits, 104 SB)

1965   Willie Mays, San Francisco (.317, 52 HR, 112 RBI)

1966   Roberto Clemente, Pittsburgh (.317, 29 HR, 119 RBI)

1968   Bob Gibson, St. Louis (22-9, 1.12 ERA)

1969   Willie McCovey, San Francisco (.320, 45 HR, 126 RBI)

1975   Joe Morgan, Cincinnati (.327, 17 HR, 94 RBI, 67 SB)

1976   Joe Morgan, Cincinnati (.320, 27 HR, 111 RBI, 60 SB)

1977   George Foster, Cincinnati (.320, 52 HR, 149 RBI)

1978   Dave Parker, Pittsburgh (.334, 30 HR, 117 RBI)

1979   Willie Stargell,* Pittsburgh (.281, 32 HR, 82 RBI)

1985   Willie McGee, St. Louis (.353, 10 HR, 82 RBI)

1987   Andre Dawson, Chicago (.287, 49 HR, 137 RBI)

1989   Kevin Mitchell, San Francisco (.291, 47 HR, 125 RBI)

1990   Barry Bonds, Pittsburgh (.301, 33 HR, 114 RBI)

*Shared award with Keith Hernandez.

1991   Terry Pendleton, Atlanta (.319, 23 HR, 86 RBI)

1992   Barry Bonds, San Francisco (.311, 34 HR, 103 RBI)

1993   Barry Bonds, San Francisco (.336, 46 HR, 123 RBI)

1995   Barry Larkin, Cincinnati (.319, 15 HR, 66 RBI, 51 SB)

American League

1963   Elston Howard, New York (.287, 28 HR, 85 RBI)

1966   Frank Robinson, Baltimore (.316, 44 HR, 121 RBI)

1971   Vida Blue, Oakland (24-8, 1.82 ERA)

1972   Dick Allen, Chicago (.308, 37 HR, 113 RBI)

1973   Reggie Jackson, Oakland (.293, 32 HR, 117 RBI)

1977   Rod Carew, Minnesota (.388, 239 hits, 100 RBI)

1978   Jim Rice, Boston (.315, 46 HR, 139 RBI)

1979   Don Baylor, California (.296, 36 HR, 139 RBI)

1987   George Bell, Toronto (.308, 47 HR, 134 RBI)

1990   Rickey Henderson, Oakland (.325, 28 HR, 119 RBI, 65 SB)

1993   Frank Thomas, Chicago (.317, 41 HR, 128 RBI)

1994   Frank Thomas, Chicago (.353, 38 HR, 101 RBI)

1995   Mo Vaughan, Boston (.300, 39 HR, 126 RBI)

1997   Ken Griffey Jr., Seattle (.304, 56 HR, 147 RBI)

ALL-TIME MAJOR LEAGUE LEADERS

Home runs: Henry Aaron—755

Runs batted in: Henry Aaron—2,297

Total bases: Henry Aaron—6,856

Stolen bases: Rickey Henderson—1,297[*]

Saves: Lee Smith—478

[*]Active player

I had to break that record [Babe Ruth's all-time home run total]. I had to do it for Jackie and my people and myself and for everybody who ever called me a nigger.

Henry Aaron

AFRICAN AMERICAN MEMBERS OF THE BASEBALL HALL OF FAME

Player	Position	Career	Year Inducted
Jackie Robinson	2B-3B	1947–1956	1962
Roy Campanella	C	1948–1957	1969
Leroy "Satchel" Paige[*]	P	1926–1950[**]	1971
Josh Gibson[*]	C	1930–1946	1972
Walter "Buck" Leonard[*]	1B	1933–1950	1972
Roberto Clemente	OF	1957–1972	1973
Monte Irvin[*]	OF	1938–1948[***]	1973
James "Cool Papa" Bell[*]	OF	1922–1946	1974
William "Judy" Johnson[*]	3B	1921–1938	1975
Oscar Charleston[*]	OF-1B-Mgr	1915–1950	1976
Ernie Banks	SS-1B	1953–1971	1977
Martin Dihigo[*]	P-OF	1923–1945	1977
Willie Mays	OF	1951–1973	1979
Andrew "Rube" Foster[*]	P-Mgr	1902–1926	1981
Bob Gibson	P	1959–1975	1981
Henry Aaron	OF	1954–1976	1982
Frank Robinson	OF	1956–1976	1982
Lou Brock	OF	1961–1979	1985
Willie McCovey	1B	1959–1980	1986
Ray Dandrige[*]	3B	1933–1949	1987
Billy Williams	1B-OF	1959–1976	1987
Willie Stargell	1B	1962–1982	1988
Joe Morgan	2B	1963–1984	1990
Rod Carew	1B	1967–1985	1991
Ferguson Jenkins	P	1965–1983	1991
Reggie Jackson	OF	1967–1987	1993
Leon Day[*]	P	1934–1950	1995
Bill Foster[*]	P-Mgr	1923–1937	1996
Willie Wells[*]	SS	1924–1949	1997

Note: Career dates indicate first and last appearance in the major leagues or the
Negro Leagues.
[*]Inducted as a member of the Negro Leagues.
[**]Paige also pitched in the major leagues from 1948 to 1965.
[***]Irvin also played in the major leagues from 1949 to 1956.

FIRST OF THE FIRST

Though Jackie Robinson is properly credited with breaking the color line in modern major-league
baseball by joining the Brooklyn Dodgers in 1947, he was not the first African American to play in
the major leagues. That distinction belongs to Moses Fleetwood "Fleet" Walker (1857–1924), a
college-educated catcher who was a member of the Toledo, Ohio, team when it joined the
American Association in 1884. Fleet's brother Weldy also joined Toledo during the 1884 season,
playing in a handful of games. During the next few years, at least half a dozen more African
Americans played in various professional baseball leagues. Resistance soon began to grow among
white players and baseball officials, however. The African Americans were squeezed out during the

1890s, and from the beginning of the 20th century until Robinson's advent in 1947, an unofficial but ironclad policy of segregation reigned in the major leagues.

ALL-STARS

On July 12, 1949, African Americans appeared in baseball's annual All-Star Game for the first time. Brooklyn's Jackie Robinson, Don Newcomb, and Roy Campanella were on the National League squad, while Cleveland's Larry Doby took the field for the American League. The American League won the game, 11-7.

TAKING THE HELM

In addition to being the only player in history to win the Most Valuable Player Award in both leagues, Frank Robinson made history again in 1975 when he became baseball's first African American manager, guiding the Cleveland Indians for two seasons. In 1981, Robinson was hired as manager of the San Francisco Giants, becoming the first black manager in the National League, as well.

BASKETBALL

PROFESSIONAL BLACK BASKETBALL

African Americans were excluded from the professional basketball leagues that sprang up during the 1920s and 1930s, but black teams were able to barnstorm against whites throughout the country. The finest of the African American squads was the Renaissance Big Five, familiarly known as the Harlem Rens. Created in 1923 by Robert J. Douglas (a native of St. Kitts), the Rens were based in Harlem's Renaissance Casino and Ballroom, located at 150 W. 138th Street. They often played during the intermissions between big-band performances. Most of the time, the Rens were on the road, playing both black and white teams all over the country. Led by Charles "Tarzan" Cooper, Bill Yancey, Casey Holt, Clarence Jenkins, Eyre Saitch, John Isaacs, and other stars, the Rens were the dominant team of the era and unquestionably one of the greatest of all time. They averaged more than 100 wins a year over a 20-year span and posted a 120-8 record for the 1932-33 season, winning 88 games in a row. The Rens encountered discrimination when they barnstormed and often had to fight their white opponents and the opponents' fans, who did not take kindly to being outplayed by African Americans. They were inducted into the Basketball Hall of Fame as a team in 1963.

The second-best team of the pre–World War II era, the Harlem Globetrotters, was actually based in Chicago, playing out of the Savoy Ballroom. The Globetrotters were tireless barnstormers during the 1930s, averaging more than 200 games a year. They normally outclassed their opponents by such a wide margin that they began clowning around to keep themselves interested. When their routines proved both popular and profitable, the Globetrotters began to emphasize showcraft over competition. They soon became a phenomenal worldwide attraction, featuring stars such as Goose Tatum, Meadowlark Lemon, and Marques Haynes. National Basketball Association (NBA) greats who started out with the Globetrotters included Nat "Sweetwater" Clifton, Connie Hawkins, and Wilt Chamberlain.

In the 1950s, the NBA abandoned its segregationist policies, and black players quickly joined and had a major impact on the league.

THE NATIONAL BASKETBALL ASSOCIATION
NBA SCORING LEADERS

Season	Player	Team	Average
1959–1960	Wilt Chamberlain	Philadelphia	37.9
1960–1961	Wilt Chamberlain	Philadelphia	38.4
1961–1962	Wilt Chamberlain	Philadelphia	50.4
1962–1963	Wilt Chamberlain	San Francisco	44.8
1963–1964	Wilt Chamberlain	San Francisco	36.5
1964–1965	Wilt Chamberlain	Philadelphia	34.7
1965–1966	Wilt Chamberlain	Philadelphia	33.5
1967–1968	Dave Bing	Detroit	27.1
1968–1969	Elvin Hayes	San Diego	28.4
1970–1971	Kareem Abdul-Jabbar	Milwaukee	31.7
1971–1972	Kareem Abdul-Jabbar	Milwaukee	34.8
1972–1973	Nate Archibald	Kansas City	34.0
1973–1974	Bob McAdoo	Buffalo	30.6
1974–1975	Bob McAdoo	Buffalo	34.5
1975–1976	Bob McAdoo	Buffalo	31.1
1977–1978	George Gervin	San Antonio	29.2
1978–1979	George Gervin	San Antonio	29.6
1979–1980	George Gervin	San Antonio	33.1
1980–1981	Adrian Dantley	Utah	30.7
1981–1982	George Gervin	San Antonio	32.3
1982–1983	Alex English	Denver	28.4
1983–1984	Adrian Dantley	Utah	30.6
1984–1985	Bernard King	New York	32.9
1985–1986	Dominique Wilkins	Atlanta	30.3
1986–1987	Michael Jordan	Chicago	37.1
1987–1988	Michael Jordan	Chicago	35.0
1988–1989	Michael Jordan	Chicago	32.5
1989–1990	Michael Jordan	Chicago	33.6
1990–1991	Michael Jordan	Chicago	31.5
1991–1992	Michael Jordan	Chicago	30.1
1992–1993	Michael Jordan	Chicago	32.6
1993–1994	David Robinson	San Antonio	29.8
1994–1995	Shaquille O'Neal	Orlando	29.3
1995–1996	Michael Jordan	Chicago	30.4
1996–1997	Michael Jordan	Chicago	29.6

NBA REBOUNDING LEADERS

Season	Player	Team	Rebounds
1955–1956	Maurice Stokes	Rochester	1,256
1957–1958	Bill Russell	Boston	1,564
1958–1959	Bill Russell	Boston	1,612
1959–1960	Wilt Chamberlain	Philadelphia	1,941
1960–1961	Wilt Chamberlain	Philadelphia	2,149
1961–1962	Wilt Chamberlain	Philadelphia	2,052

Season	Player	Team	Rebounds
1962–1963	Wilt Chamberlain	San Francisco	1,946
1963–1964	Bill Russell	Boston	1,930
1964–1965	Bill Russell	Boston	1,878
1965–1966	Wilt Chamberlain	Philadelphia	1,943
1966–1967	Wilt Chamberlain	Philadelphia	1,957
1967–1968	Wilt Chamberlain	Philadelphia	1,952
1968–1969	Wilt Chamberlain	Los Angeles	1,712
1969–1970	Elvin Hayes	San Diego	16.9[*]
1970–1971	Wilt Chamberlain	Los Angeles	18.2
1971–1972	Wilt Chamberlain	Los Angeles	19.2
1972–1973	Wilt Chamberlain	Los Angeles	18.6
1973–1974	Elvin Hayes	Washington, D.C.	18.1
1974–1975	Wes Unseld	Washington, D.C.	14.8
1975–1976	Kareem Abdul-Jabbar	Los Angeles	16.9
1977–1978	Len "Truck" Robinson	New Orleans	15.7
1978–1979	Moses Malone	Houston	17.6
1980–1981	Moses Malone	Houston	14.8
1981–1982	Moses Malone	Houston	14.7
1982–1983	Moses Malone	Philadelphia	15.3
1983–1984	Moses Malone	Philadelphia	13.4
1984–1985	Moses Malone	Philadelphia	13.1
1986–1987	Charles Barkley	Philadelphia	14.6
1987–1988	Michael Cage	LA Clippers	13.0
1988–1989	Hakeem Olajuwon	Houston	13.5
1989–1990	Hakeem Olajuwon	Houston	14.0
1990–1991	David Robinson	San Antonio	13.0
1991–1992	Dennis Rodman	Detroit	18.7
1992–1993	Dennis Rodman	Detroit	18.3
1993–1994	Dennis Rodman	San Antonio	17.3
1994–1995	Dennis Rodman	San Antonio	16.8
1995–1996	Dennis Rodman	Chicago	14.9
1996–1997	Dennis Rodman	Chicago	16.1

* Based on per-game average since 1969–1970.

NBA ASSISTS LEADERS

Season	Player	Team	Assists
1960–1961	Oscar Robertson	Cincinnati	690
1961–1962	Oscar Robertson	Cincinnati	899
1963–1964	Oscar Robertson	Cincinnati	868
1964–1965	Oscar Robertson	Cincinnati	861
1965–1966	Oscar Robertson	Cincinnati	847
1967–1968	Wilt Chamberlain	Philadelphia	702
1968–1969	Oscar Robertson	Cincinnati	772
1972–1973	Nate Archibald	KC-Omaha	11.4[*]
1974–1975	Kevin Porter	Washington, D.C.	8.0
1975–1976	Don "Slick" Watts	Seattle	8.1
1977–1978	Kevin Porter	NJ-Detroit	10.2
1978–1979	Kevin Porter	Detroit	13.4
1979–1980	Michael Ray Richardson	New York	10.1
1980–1981	Kevin Porter	Washington, D.C.	9.1

Year	Player	Team	Assists
1981–1982	Johnny Moore	San Antonio	9.6
1982–1983	Earvin "Magic" Johnson	Los Angeles	10.5
1983–1984	Earvin "Magic" Johnson	Los Angeles	13.1
1984–1985	Isaiah Thomas	Detroit	13.9
1985–1986	Earvin "Magic" Johnson	LA Lakers	12.6
1986–1987	Earvin "Magic" Johnson	LA Lakers	12.2
1996–1997	Mark Jackson	Indiana	11.4

*Based on per-game average since 1969–1970.

NBA MOST VALUABLE PLAYERS

Year	Player, Team	Year	Player, Team
1957–1958	Bill Russell, Boston	1978–1979	Moses Malone, Houston
1959–1960	Wilt Chamberlain, Philadelphia	1979–1980	Kareem Abdul-Jabbar, Los Angeles
1960–1961	Bill Russell, Boston	1980–1981	Julius Erving, Philadelphia
1961–1962	Bill Russell, Boston	1981–1982	Moses Malone, Houston
1962–1963	Bill Russell, Boston	1982–1983	Moses Malone, Philadelphia
1963–1964	Oscar Robertson, Cincinnati	1986–1987	Earvin "Magic" Johnson, Los Angeles
1964–1965	Bill Russell, Boston		
1965–1966	Wilt Chamberlain, Philadelphia	1987–1988	Michael Jordan, Chicago
1966–1967	Wilt Chamberlain, Philadelphia	1988–1989	Earvin "Magic" Johnson, Los Angeles
1967–1968	Wilt Chamberlain, Philadelphia		
1968–1969	Wes Unseld, Baltimore	1989–1990	Earvin "Magic" Johnson, Los Angeles
1969–1970	Willis Reed, New York	1990–1991	Michael Jordan, Chicago
1970–1971	Kareem Abdul-Jabbar, Milwaukee	1991–1992	Michael Jordan, Chicago
1971–1972	Kareem Abdul-Jabbar, Milwaukee	1992–1993	Charles Barkley, Phoenix
1973–1974	Kareem Abdul-Jabbar, Milwaukee	1993–1994	Hakeem Olajuwon, Houston
1974–1975	Bob McAdoo, Buffalo	1994–1995	David Robinson, San Antonio
1975–1976	Kareem Abdul-Jabbar, Los Angeles	1995–1996	Michael Jordan, Chicago
1976–1977	Kareem Abdul-Jabbar, Los Angeles	1996–1997	Karl Malone, Utah

ALL-TIME NBA LEADERS

Most points, career: Kareem Abdul-Jabbar—38,387

Most points, season: Wilt Chamberlain—4,029

Highest scoring average, career: Michael Jordan—31.5

Highest scoring average, season: Wilt Chamberlain—50.4

Most rebounds, career: Wilt Chamberlain—23,924

Most rebounds, season: Wilt Chamberlain—2,149

AFRICAN AMERICAN MEMBERS OF THE BASKETBALL HALL OF FAME

(by year of induction)

1963	New York Renaissance (team)
1971	Robert "Bobby" Douglass*
1974	Bill Russell
1976	Elgin Baylor
	Charles "Tarzan" Cooper
1978	Wilt Chamberlain
	John McClendon*
1979	Oscar Robertson
1981	Clarence "Bighouse" Gaines
	Hal Greer
	Willis Reed
1983	Sam Jones
1984	Nate Thurmond
1987	Walt Frazier
1988	Wes Unseld

1989	William "Pops" Gates
	K. C. Jones
	Len Wilkens
1990	Earl Monroe
	Dave Bing
	Elvin Hayes
1991	Nate Archibald
1992	Connie Hawkins
	Bob Lanier
	Lusia Harris Stewart
1993	Julius Erving
	Calvin Murphy
1995	Cheryl Miller
1996	George Gervin
	David Thompson
1997	Alex English

*coach

DOMINANCE

As of 1997, African Americans composed 80 percent of the players in the National Basketball Association, compared to 67 percent of the players in the National Football League and 17 percent of the players in major-league baseball.

(Source: Center for the Study of Sports in Society, Northeastern University.)

TRIPLE PLAY

After the NBA owners decided to integrate their league in 1950, three African Americans were drafted: Chuck Cooper (Boston Celtics), Nat "Sweetwater" Clifton (New York Knicks), and Earl Lloyd (Washington Capitols). Cooper was the first to sign a contract, and for that reason he is credited with being the first African American in the NBA. However, Lloyd was the first actually to play in an NBA game, taking the floor one day before Cooper and Clifton did.

FRONT-OFFICE PIONEER

The first African American to become a general manager in professional sports was Wayne Embry, who took the top job with the Milwaukee Bucks in 1972. A graduate of Miami University of Ohio, the burly Embry had been one of the NBA's premier centers and was named to the All-Star Team five times.

FOOTBALL

NATIONAL FOOTBALL LEAGUE (NFL) RUSHING LEADERS

Year	Player	Team	Yards (Average)
1950	Marion Motley	Cleveland	801 (5.8)
1952	Dan Towler	Los Angeles	894 (5.7)
1953	Joe Perry	San Francisco	1, 018 (5.3)
1954	Joe Perry	San Francisco	1,049 (6.1)
1957	Jim Brown	Cleveland	942 (4.7)
1958	Jim Brown	Cleveland	1,527 (5.9)
1959	Jim Brown	Cleveland	1,329 (4.6)
1960	Jim Brown	Cleveland	1,257 (5.8)
1961	Jim Brown	Cleveland	1,408 (4.6)
1963	Jim Brown	Cleveland	1,863 (6.4)
1964	Jim Brown	Cleveland	1,446 (5.2)
1965	Jim Brown	Cleveland	1,544 (5.3)
1966	Gayle Sayers	Chicago	1,231 (5.4)
1967	Leroy Kelley	Cleveland	1,205 (5.1)
1968	Leroy Kelley	Cleveland	1,239 (5.0)
1969	Gayle Sayers	Chicago	1,032 (4.4)
1970	Larry Brown	Washington, D.C.	1,125 (4.7)
1971	Floyd Little	Denver	1,133 (4.0)
1972	O. J. Simpson	Buffalo	1,251 (4.3)
1973	O. J. Simpson	Buffalo	2,003 (6.0)
1974	Otis Armstrong	Denver	1,407 (5.3)
1975	O. J. Simpson	Buffalo	1,817 (5.5)
1976	O. J. Simpson	Buffalo	1,503 (5.2)
1977	Walter Payton	Chicago	1,852 (5.5)
1978	Earl Campbell	Houston	1,450 (4.8)
1979	Earl Campbell	Houston	1,697 (4.6)
1980	Earl Campbell	Houston	1,934 (5.2)
1981	George Rogers	New Orleans	1,674 (4.4)
1982	Freeman McNeil	N.Y. Jets	786 (5.2)
1983	Eric Dickerson	L.A. Rams	1,808 (4.6)
1984	Eric Dickerson	L.A. Rams	2,105 (5.6)
1985	Marcus Allen	L.A. Raiders	1,759 (4.6)
1986	Eric Dickerson	L.A. Rams	1,821 (4.5)
1987	Charles White	L.A. Rams	1,374 (4.2)
1988	Eric Dickerson	Indianapolis	1,659 (4.3)
1989	Christian Okoye	Kansas City	1,480 (4.0)
1990	Barry Sanders	Detroit	1,304 (5.1)
1991	Emmitt Smith	Dallas	1,563 (4.3)
1992	Emmitt Smith	Dallas	1,713 (4.6)
1993	Emmitt Smith	Dallas	1,486 (5.3)
1994	Barry Sanders	Detroit	1,883 (5.7)
1995	Emmit Smith	Dallas	1,773 (4.7)
1996	Barry Sanders	Detroit	1,553 (5.1)
1997	Barry Sanders	Detroit	2,053 (6.1)

NFL RECEIVING LEADERS

Year	Player	Team	Number (Average)
1962	Bobby Mitchell	Washington, D.C.	72 (19.2)
1966	Charley Taylor	Washington, D.C.	72 (15.5)
1967	Charley Taylor	Washington, D.C.	70 (14.1)
1968	Clifton McNeil	San Francisco	71 (14.0)
1970	Dick Gordon	Chicago	71 (14.5)
1972	Harold Jackson	Philadelphia	62 (16.9)
1973	Harold Carmichael	Philadelphia	67 (16.7)
1974	Lydell Mitchell	Baltimore	72 (7.6)
1975	Chuck Foreman	Minnesota	73 (9.5)
1976	MacArthur Lane	Kansas City	66 (10.4)
1977	Lydell Mitchell	Baltimore	71 (8.7)
1978	Rickey Young	Minnesota	88 (8.0)
1979	Joe Washington	Baltimore	82 (9.1)
1980	Kellen Winslow	San Diego	89 (14.5)
1981	Kellen Winslow	San Diego	88 (12.2)
1984	Art Monk	Washington, D.C.	106 (12.9)
1985	Roger Craig	San Francisco	92 (11.0)
1987	J. T. Smith	St. Louis	91 (12.3)
1988	Al Toon	N.Y. Jets	93 (11.5)
1989	Sterling Sharpe	Green Bay	90 (15.8)
1990	Jerry Rice	San Francisco	100 (15.0)
1991	Haywood Jeffires	Houston	100 (11.8)
1992	Sterling Sharpe	Green Bay	108 (13.5)
1993	Sterling Sharpe	Green Bay	112 (11.4)
1994	Cris Carter	Minnesota	122 (10.3)
1995	Herman Moore	Detroit	123 (13.7)
1996	Jerry Rice	San Francisco	108 (11.6)
1997	Tim Brown	Oakland	104 (13.5)

ALL-TIME NFL LEADERS

Total yards gained: Walter Payton—21,803

Total rushing yards: Walter Payton—16,726

Touchdowns: Jerry Rice—166[*]

Total receptions: Jerry Rice—1,057[*]

Total receiving yards: Jerry Rice—16,455[*]

Quarterback sacks: Reggie White—176.5[*]

[*]Active player.

NFL MOST VALUABLE PLAYERS (MVPs)

1957	Jim Brown, Cleveland	1971	Alan Page, Minnesota
1965	Jim Brown, Cleveland	1972	Larry Brown, Washington, D.C.

1973	O. J. Simpson, Buffalo	1986	Lawrence Taylor, N.Y. Giants
1977	Walter Payton, Chicago	1991	Thurman Thomas, Buffalo
1979	Earl Campbell, Houston	1993	Emmitt Smith, Dallas
1985	Marcus Allen, L.A. Raiders	1997	Barry Sanders, Detroit*

*shared award.

AFRICAN AMERICAN MEMBERS OF THE PRO FOOTBALL HALL OF FAME

Year Inducted	Player	Position	Career Span
1967	Emlen Tunnell, N.Y. Giants	DB	1948–1961
1968	Marion Motley, Cleveland	RB	1946–1955
1969	Joe Perry, San Francisco	RB	1948–1962
1971	Jim Brown, Cleveland	RB	1957–1967
	Gene Upshaw, Oakland	OG	1957–1971
1972	Ollie Matson, St. Louis	RB	1952–1966
1973	Jim Parker, Baltimore	OT	1957–1967
1974	Dick "Night Train" Lane, Detroit	DB	1952–1965
1975	Roosevelt Brown, N.Y. Giants	OT	1953–1965
	Lenny Moore, Baltimore	WR-RB	1956–1967
1976	Len Ford, Detroit/Cleveland	DE	1948–1958
1977	Gayle Sayers, Chicago	RB	1965–1971
	Bill Willis, Cleveland	LB	1946–1953
1980	Herb Adderley, Dallas/Green Bay	DB	1961–1972
	David "Deacon" Jones, Los Angeles	DE	1961–1974
1981	Willie Davis, Cleveland/Green Bay	DE	1958–1969
1983	Bobby Bell, Kansas City	LB-DE	1963–1974
	Bobby Mitchell, Cleveland	WR-RB	1958–1968
	Paul Warfield, Cleveland/Miami	WR	1964–1974
1984	Willie Brown, Denver/Oakland	DB	1963–1978
	Charley Taylor, Washington, D.C.	WR	1964–1977
1985	O. J. Simpson, Buffalo	RB	1969–1979
1986	Ken Houston, Houston/Washington, D.C.	DB	1967–1980
	Willie Lanier, Kansas City	LB	1967–1977
1987	Joe Greene, Pittsburgh	DT	1969–1981
	John Henry Johnson, Detroit/Pittsburgh	RB	1954–1966
1988	Alan Page, Minnesota	DT	1967–1981
1989	Mel Blount, Pittsburgh	DB	1970–1983
	Art Shell, Oakland	OT	1968–1982
	Willie Wood, Green Bay	DB	1960–1971
1990	Buck Buchanan, Kansas City	DT	1963–1975
	Franco Harris, Pittsburgh	RB	1972–1984
1991	Earl Campbell, Houston/New Orleans	RB	1978–1985
1992	Lem Barney, Detroit	DB	1967–1977
	John Mackey, Baltimore	TE	1963–1972
1993	Larry Little, Miami	OG	1967–1980
	Walter Payton, Chicago	RB	1975–1987
1994	Tony Dorsett, Dallas	RB	1977–1988
	Jimmy Johnson, San Francisco	DB	1961–1976
	Leroy Kelley, Cleveland	RB	1964–1973

Year Inducted	Player	Position	Career Span
1995	Lee Roy Selmon, Tampa Bay	DE	1976–1984
1996	Charlie Joiner, San Diego	WR	1969–1986
	Mel Renfro, Dallas	DB	1964–1977
	Kellen Winslow, San Diego	TE	1979–1987
1997	Mike Haynes, New England/Oakland	DB	1976–1989

AFRICAN AMERICAN HEISMAN TROPHY WINNERS

1961	Ernie Davis, Syracuse University
1965	Michael Garrett, University of Southern California
1968	O. J. Simpson, University of Southern California
1972	Johnny Rodgers, University of Nebraska
1974	Archie Griffin, Ohio State University
1975	Archie Griffin, Ohio State University
1976	Tony Dorsett, University of Pittsburgh
1977	Earl Campbell, University of Texas
1978	Billy Sims, University of Oklahoma
1979	Charles White, University of Southern California
1980	George Rogers, University of South Carolina
1982	Herschel Walker, University of Georgia
1983	Mike Rozier, University of Nebraska
1985	Bo Jackson, Auburn University
1987	Tim Brown, University of Notre Dame
1988	Barry Sanders, Oklahoma State University
1989	Andre Ware, University of Houston
1991	Desmond Howard, University of Michigan
1992	Charlie Ward, Florida State University
1994	Rashaan Salaam, University of Colorado
1995	Eddie George, Ohio State University
1997	Charles Woodson, University of Michigan

PIGSKIN PIONEERS

One year before Jackie Robinson made his major league baseball debut, two African American football players broke the color line in modern professional sports. In 1946, the Cleveland Browns signed linebacker Bill Willis and fullback Marion Motley. Both men enjoyed exceptional NFL careers and are now in the Pro Football Hall of Fame.

LEADING THE WAY

On January 31, 1988, Doug Williams became the first African American quarterback to win a Super Bowl, leading the Washington [D.C.] Redskins to a 42-10 victory over Denver. Williams threw four touchdown passes in the game and was named Super Bowl MVP. In 1997, Williams was named to succeed the legendary Eddie Robinson as head football coach at Grambling University.

TACKLING JIM CROW

On October 11, 1947, when Harvard and Virginia squared off in Charlottesville, Harvard tackle Chester "Chet" Pierce became the first African American to play against a white university in the segregated South. Though many white spectators shouted racist insults at Pierce, there were no unpleasant incidents on the field apart from Virginia's 47-0 domination of the visitors. Pierce went on to become an eminent physician and was a professor of psychiatry at Harvard for nearly 30 years.

BOXING

NOTABLE AFRICAN AMERICAN BOXING CHAMPIONS

> For every point I'm given, I'll have earned two, because I'm a Negro.
>
> Jack Johnson, before his championship bout with Tommy Burns (1908)

HEAVYWEIGHTS

Jack Johnson (1908–1915)

Joe Louis (1937–1949)

Ezzard Charles (1949–1951)

Jersey Joe Walcott (1951–1952)

Floyd Patterson (1960–1962)

Sonny Liston (1962–1964)

Muhammad Ali (1964–1970, 1974–1978, 1978–1979)

Joe Frazier (1968–1970, 1970–1973)

Larry Holmes (1978–1980 [WBC], 1980–1985)

Mike Tyson (1987–1990)

Evander Holyfield (1996–   )

LIGHT HEAVYWEIGHTS

John Henry Lewis (1935–1938)

Archie Moore (1952–1962)

Harold Johnson (1962–1963)

Dick Tiger (1966–1968)
Bob Foster (1968–1974)
Michael Spinks (1983–1985)

MIDDLEWEIGHTS

Tiger Flowers (1926)
Sugar Ray Robinson (1951–1952, 1955–1957, 1958–1960)
Dick Tiger (1965–1966)
Emile Griffith (1966–1967, 1967–1968)
Marvin Hagler (1980–1987)

WELTERWEIGHTS

Joe "Barbados Demon" Walcott (1901–1904)
Aaron "Dixie Kid" Brown (1904–1905)
Henry Armstrong (1938–1940)
Sugar Ray Robinson (1946–1951)
Emile Griffith (1962–1963)
Sugar Ray Leonard (1979–1980, 1980–1982)
Pernell Whitaker (1993–1997 [WBC])

JUNIOR WELTERWEIGHTS

Aaron Pryor (1980–1983 [WBA], 1983–1985 [IBF])

LIGHTWEIGHTS

Joe Gans (1902–1904, 1906–1908)
Henry Armstrong (1938–1940)
Beau Jack (1942–1943 [NY], 1943–1944 [NY])
Bobcat Bob Montgomery (1943 [NY], 1944–1947 [NY])
Ike Williams (1947–1951)

JUNIOR LIGHTWEIGHTS

Kid Chocolate (1931–1933)
Sandy Saddler (1949–1950)

FEATHERWEIGHTS

George Dixon (1892–1897, 1898–1900)
Henry Armstrong (1937–1938)
Chalky Wright (1941–1942)
Sandy Saddler (1948–1949, 1950–1957)

FIRST CHAMPION

The first African American boxing champion in the United States is believed to be Tom Molineux, who was born into slavery in Virginia in 1784 but came to New York City as a free man at the age of 20. Molineux soon traveled to England, where he was trained by Bill Richmond, another expatriate African American boxer. After proving his skill abroad, Molineux gained a title bout with Tom Cribb, the world heavyweight champion. The legendary fight took place at Clapthall Common in Sussex on December 18, 1810. Molineux knocked Cribb out in the 28th round, but the English boxer's seconds jumped into the ring, and the referee allowed Cribb to recover and continue fighting. Realizing that he would not be allowed to win the match, a discouraged Molineux fought on but was defeated in 40 rounds.

BACKLASH

When Jack Johnson fought Jim Jeffries for the heavyweight championship in Reno, Nevada, on July 4, 1910, many of the spectators were heard shouting, "Kill the nigger." After Johnson defeated the "white hope," angry whites throughout the country retaliated by assaulting African Americans. The violence resulted in at least eight deaths and prompted many states and localities to ban the showing of the fight film.

TRACK AND FIELD

OLYMPIC GOLD MEDAL WINNERS
1924 (PARIS)

William DeHart Hubbard   long jump

1932 (LOS ANGELES)

Edward Gordon   long jump
Eddie Tolan   100-meter dash
                     200-meter dash

1936 (BERLIN)

Cornelius Johnson	high jump
Ralph Metcalfe	4 × 100-meter relay
Jesse Owens	100-meter dash
	200-meter dash
	long jump
	4 × 100-meter relay
Archie Williams	400-meter dash
John Woodruff	800-meter run

1948 (LONDON)

Women
Alice Coachman	high jump

Men
Harrison Dillard	100-meter dash
	4 × 100-meter relay
Norwood Ewell	4 × 100-meter relay
Wille Steele	long jump
Mal Whitfield	800-meter run
	4 × 100-meter relay
Lorenzo Wright	4 × 100-meter relay

1952 (HELSINKI)

Women
Mae Faggs	4 × 100-meter relay
Catherine Hardy	4 × 100-meter relay
Barbara Jones	4 × 100-meter relay

Men
Jerome Biffle	long jump
Harrison Dillard	110-meter hurdles
	4 × 100-meter relay
Andrew Stanfield	200-meter dash
	4 × 100-meter relay
Mal Whitfield	800-meter run

1956 (MELBOURNE)

Women
Mildred McDaniel	high jump

Men
Greg Bell	long jump
Lee Calhoun	110-meter hurdles

Milt Campbell	decathlon
Charles Dumas	high jump
Charles Jenkins	400-meter dash
	4 × 400-meter relay
Lou Jones	4 × 400-meter relay
Leamon King	4 × 100-meter relay
Ira Murchison	4 × 100-meter relay

1956 (ROME)

Women

Martha Hudson	4 × 100-meter relay
Barbara Jones	4 × 100-meter relay
Wilma Rudolph	100-meter dash
	200-meter dash
	4 × 100-meter relay
Lucinda Williams	4 × 100-meter relay

Men

Lee Calhoun	110-meter hurdles

1960 (ROME)

Men

Ralph Boston	long jump
Lee Calhoun	110-meter hurdles
Otis Davis	400-meter dash
	4 × 400-meter relay
Rafer Johnson	decathlon

1964 (TOKYO)

Women

Edith McGuire	200-meter dash
Wyomia Tyus	100-meter dash

Men

Henry Carr	200-meter dash
	4 × 400-meter relay
Paul Drayton	4 × 100-meter relay
Bob Hayes	100-meter dash
	4 × 100-meter relay
Hayes Jones	110-meter hurdles
Richard Stebbins	4 × 100-meter relay
Ulis Williams	4 × 400-meter relay

1968 (MEXICO CITY)

Women

Margaret Bailes	4 × 100-meter relay
Barbara Ferrell	4 × 100-meter relay
Madeline Manning	800-meter run
Mildred Netter	4 × 100-meter relay
Wyomia Tyus	100-meter dash
	4 × 100-meter relay

Men

Bob Beamon	long jump
Willie Davenport	110-meter hurdles
Lee Evans	400-meter dash
	4 × 400-meter relay
Ron Freeman	4 × 400-meter relay
Charles Green	4 × 100-meter relay
James Hines	100-meter dash
	4 × 100-meter relay
Larry James	4 × 400-meter relay
Vince Matthews	4 × 400-meter relay
Mel Pender	4 × 100-meter relay
Ronnie Smith	4 × 100-meter relay
Tommie Smith	200-meter dash

1972 (MUNICH)

Larry Black	4 × 100-meter relay
Eddie Hart	4 × 100-meter relay
Vince Matthews	400-meter dash
Rod Milburn	110-meter hurdles
Robert Taylor	4 × 100-meter relay
Gerald Tinker	4 × 100-meter relay
Randy Williams	long jump

1976 (MONTREAL)

Benny Brown	4 × 400-meter relay
Herman Frazier	4 × 400-meter relay
Harvey Glance	4 × 100-meter relay
Millard Hampton	4 × 100-meter relay
John Jones	4 × 100-meter relay
Edwin Moses	400-meter hurdles
Fred Newhouse	4 × 400-meter relay
Maxie Parks	4 × 400-meter relay
Steve Riddick	4 × 100-meter relay
Arnie Robinson	long jump

1984 (LOS ANGELES)

Women

Evelyn Ashford	100-meter dash
	4 × 100-meter relay
Jeanette Bolden	4 × 100-meter relay
Valerie Brisco-Hooks	200-meter dash
	400-meter dash
	4 × 400-meter relay
Alice Brown	4 × 100-meter relay
Chandra Cheeseborough	4 × 100-meter relay
	4 × 400-meter relay
Benita Fitzgerald-Brown	100-meter hurdles
Sherri Howard	4 × 400-meter relay
Lillie Leatherwood	4 × 400-meter relay

Men

Ray Armstead	4 × 400-meter relay
Alonzo Babers	400-meter dash
	4 × 400-meter relay
Ron Brown	4 × 100-meter relay
Sam Graddy	4 × 100-meter relay
Al Joyner	triple jump
Roger Kingdom	110-meter hurdles
Carl Lewis	100-meter dash
	200-meter dash
	long jump
	4 × 100-meter relay
Antonio McKay	4 × 400-meter relay
Edwin Moses	400-meter hurdles
Sunder Nix	4 × 400-meter relay
Calvin Smith	4 × 100-meter relay

1988 (SEOUL)

Women

Evelyn Ashford	4 × 100-meter relay
Alice Brown	4 × 100-meter relay
Sheila Echols	4 × 100-meter relay
Florence Griffith-Joyner	100-meter dash
	200-meter dash
	4 × 100-meter relay
Jackie Joyner-Kersee	heptathlon
	long jump

Men

Joe Deloach	200-meter dash
Danny Everett	4 × 400-meter relay
Robert Kingdom	110-meter hurdles

Carl Lewis	100-meter dash
	long jump
Steve Lewis	400-meter dash
	4 × 400-meter relay
Andre Phillips	400-meter hurdles
Butch Reynolds	4 × 400-meter relay

1992 (BARCELONA)

Women

Evelyn Ashford	4 × 100-meter relay
Gail Devers	100-meter dash
Carlette Guidry	4 × 100-meter relay
Esther Jones	4 × 100-meter relay
Jackie Joyner-Kersee	heptathlon
Gwen Torrence	200-meter dash
	4 × 100-meter relay

Men

Leroy Burrell	4 × 100-meter relay
Mike Conley	triple jump
Michael Johnson	4 × 400-meter relay
Carl Lewis	4 × 100-meter relay
	long jump
Steve Lewis	4 × 400-meter relay
Mike Marsh	200-meter dash
	4 × 100-meter relay
Dennis Mitchell	4 × 100-meter relay
Quincy Watts	400-meter dash
	4 × 400-meter relay
Andrew Yalmon	4 × 400-meter relay
Kevin Young	400-meter hurdles

1996 (ATLANTA)

Women

Gail Devers	100-meter dash
	4 × 100-meter relay
Chrystie Gaines	4 × 100-meter relay
Kim Graham	4 × 400-meter relay
Maicel Malone	4 × 400-meter relay
Jearl Miles	4 × 400-meter relay
Inger Miller	4 × 100-meter relay
Rochelle Stevens	4 × 400-meter relay
Gwen Torrence	4 × 100-meter relay

Men

| Derrick Adkins | 400-meter hurdles |
| Charles Austin | high jump |

Alvin Harrison	4 × 400-meter relay
Kenny Harrison	triple jump
Allen Johnson	110-meter hurdles
Michael Johnson	200-meter dash
	400-meter dash
Carl Lewis	long jump
Anthuan Maybank	4 × 400-meter relay
Derek Mills	4 × 400-meter relay
Dan O'Brien	decathlon
LaMont Smith	4 × 400-meter relay

WORLD RECORD HOLDERS

WOMEN

100-meter dash: Florence Griffith-Joyner—10.49 (7/16/1988)

200-meter dash: Florence Griffith-Joyner—21.34 (9/29/1988)

400-meter hurdles: Kim Batten—52.61 (8/11/1995)

heptathlon: Jackie Joyner-Kersee—7,291 points (9/23–24/1988)

MEN

200-meter dash: Michael Johnson—19.32 (8/1/1996)

400-meter dash: Butch Reynolds—43.29 (8/17/1988)

400-meter hurdles: Kevin Young—46.78 (8/6/1992)

4 × 100-meter relay: United States (Mike Marsh, Leroy Burrell, Dennis Mitchell, Carl Lewis)—37.40 (8/8/1992); United States (John Drummond, Andre Carson, Dennis Mitchell, Leroy Burrell)—37.40 (8/21/1993)

4 × 200-meter relay: Santa Monica Track Club (Mike Marsh, Leroy Burrell, Floyd Heard, Carl Lewis)—1:18.68 (4/17/1994)

4 × 400-meter relay: United States (Andrew Valmon, Quincy Watts, Butch Reynolds, Michael Johnson)—2:54.29 (8/22/1993)

long jump: Mike Powell—29-4$\frac{1}{2}$ (8/30/1991)

decathlon: Dan O'Brien—8,891 points (9/4–5/1992)

HORSE RACING

Considering the crucial role played by Africans and African Americans in the success of herding and ranching in the Americas (see Chapter 4), it is not surprising that black riders, grooms, and stable hands were instrumental in the growth of horse racing in the United States. When the first Kentucky Derby was held in 1875, 13 of the 14 jockeys involved were African Americans. The following African American jockeys rode their mounts (given in parentheses) to victory in the Kentucky Derby:

1875	Oliver Lewis (Aristides)	1891	Isaac Murphy (Kingman)
1877	William "Billy" Walker (Baden-Baden)	1892	Alonzo Clayton (Azra)
1880	George Lewis (Fonso)	1895	James "Soup" Perkins (Halma)
1882	Babe Hurd (Apollo)	1896	Willie Sims (Ben Brush)
1884	Isaac Murphy (Buchanan)	1898	Willie Sims (Plaudit)
1885	Erskine Henderson (Joe Cotton)	1901	Jimmy Winkfield (His Eminence)
1887	Isaac Lewis (Montrose)	1902	Jimmy Winkfield (Alan-a-Dale)
1890	Isaac Murphy (Riley)		

Isaac Murphy, hailed by James Weldon Johnson as "the most finished American horseman who ever rode a race," also won an astounding 49 of 51 races at Saratoga during the 1882 season. Another of the great black riders, Willie Sims, was the only non-English jockey to win a race in England. Sims was also the first to shorten his stirrups and lean forward over his mount's neck. As horse racing became big business in the early 20th century and top jockeys began earning as much as $20,000 a year, African Americans were systematically forced out of the profession. As Johnson wrote in 1930, "The same sort of thing might happen if the pay of Pullman porters was raised to three hundred dollars a month."

TENNIS (AMERICAN TENNIS ASSOCIATION)

The American Tennis Association (ATA) is the oldest continuously operating African American sports organization in the United States. The ATA was created in 1916 in Washington, D.C., and Baltimore, at a time when the United States Lawn Tennis Association (USLTA), the sport's governing body, barred African Americans from its tournaments. At the time of its founding, the ATA projected four major goals: to promote tennis among African Americans; to spur the formation of tennis clubs and the construction of courts; to develop junior players; and to foster the growth of local African American tennis associations.

The ATA held its first national championships in August 1917 at Baltimore's Druid Hill Park. Talley Holmes won the men's singles title, and Lucy Diggs Slowe was the women's champion. In the following years, the ATA developed a number of young players who went on to stardom at white universities. Among the top male players were Henry Graham, Richard Hudlin, Reginald Weir, Douglas Turner, and Gerald Norman. Outstanding women included Isadore Channels, Lulu Ballard, and Ora Washington. By 1951, the USLTA finally began to relax its discriminatory policies, agreeing to have the ATA nominate a number of African American players for national tournaments. Though all USLTA restrictions were lifted during the 1970s, the ATA continues to fulfill its mission. Arthur Ashe, Wimbledon men's single title winner in 1975, was one of the most distinguished ATA alumni at the end of the 20th century.

NOTABLE AFRICAN AMERICAN SPORTS FIGURES

Ali, Muhammad (1942–). Born Cassius Clay in Lexington, Kentucky, Ali achieved nationwide attention when he won the light-heavyweight boxing championship at the 1960 Olympics. Proclaiming himself "The Greatest," Ali stunned the sports world by knocking out Sonny Liston in 1964 and winning the world heavyweight championship. After adopting Islam and changing his name, he successfully defended his crown nine times between 1965 and 1967. However, after Ali condemned U.S. military actions in Vietnam and refused to enter the armed forces on religious grounds, boxing authorities stripped him of his title and banned him from fighting in the United States. The Supreme Court upheld Ali's position in 1970, and he returned to the ring after a three-and-a-half-year layoff. Though he had previously been a controversial figure, Ali's astounding 1974 upset of the fearsome George Foreman in Kinshasa, Zaire, made him a national hero. Having held the heavyweight title three separate times, Ali retired from the ring in 1981 with an overall record of 56-5, including 37 knockouts. His stature as an athletic legend was confirmed when he was chosen to light the ceremonial torch at the 1996 Olympic Games in Atlanta.

Ashe, Arthur Robert, Jr. (1943–1993).   Born in Richmond, Virginia, Ashe began to play tennis at the Richmond Racket Club, a facility created by the American Tennis Association. When Ashe was 16 the ATA nominated him to play in USLTA-sponsored national tournaments, and he won the Junior Indoor Singles title in both 1960 and 1961. After graduating from UCLA, Ashe became one of tennis's major stars, winning the U.S. men's singles championship in 1968, the Australian Open in 1970, and the Wimbledon title in 1975. He was the first African American to win these prestigious tournaments and the first named to the U.S. Davis Cup team. Ashe retired from tennis in 1979 after undergoing heart-bypass surgery but remained prominent as an author and humanitarian until his untimely death.

Brown, Jim (1936–   ).   A five-letter athlete at Manhasset High School in New York, Brown went on to Syracuse University, where he achieved All-American honors in both football and lacrosse. Signed by the Cleveland Browns in 1957, the powerful fullback quickly emerged as the most devastating runner in NFL history. During his 11 pro seasons, he ran for 12,312 yards and scored 106 touchdowns, both league records at the time of his retirement. After leaving football, Brown enjoyed a successful acting career and also founded the Black Economic Union to aid the creation of African American businesses. Named the Browns' honorary captain for life, Brown has remained active on the pro football scene and has spoken out on issues affecting African American players and coaches. During the 1990s he founded Amer-I-Can, an organization that has worked effectively with inner-city gang members in Los Angeles and Chicago.

Foster, Andrew "Rube" (1879–1930).   Born in Calvert, Texas, Foster began playing baseball at Tillotson College in 1897. He turned professional in 1900, pitching for a number of African American teams, including the Cuban X Giants and the Chicago Leland Giants. The best pitcher of his day, he earned his nickname when he outdueled the great white pitcher Rube Waddell in a barnstorming game. In 1911, Foster formed a partnership with a white businessperson, purchased a ballpark in Chicago, and created the Chicago American Giants. Combining his talents as a player, manager, and business owner, he masterminded the creation of the Negro National League in 1920. Foster oversaw the operations of the league until 1926, when he was diagnosed with mental illness and hospitalized. An imposing figure at 6 feet 4 inches and 240 pounds, Foster was renowned for his athletic ability, his magnetic personality, his gifts as a speaker and organizer, and his visionary determination.

Gibson, Althea (1927–   ).   Born in South Carolina, Gibson was raised in Harlem and learned to play tennis at the public courts on 152nd Street. After winning a Parks Department tournament in 1942, she began to receive professional coaching at Harlem's prestigious Cosmopolitan Tennis Club. Gibson soon began to dominate the African American tennis circuit, winning a string of girls' and women's singles titles during the late 1940s and early 1950s. In 1950, she became the first African American to play in the U.S. amateur championships at Forest Hills, and her performance opened the way for other African American players to enter USLTA events. Five years later, Gibson made history once again in Paris, winning the French Open and becoming the first African American to win a Grand Slam event. She reached the pinnacle of the tennis world in 1957 and 1958, winning two singles titles at Forest Hills, two more at Wimbledon, and pairing with Darlene Hard to win the 1957 Wimbledon doubles title. After retiring from competitive tennis, Gibson has worked as a teaching pro, become a standout golfer, performed as a professional singer, and served on the New Jersey State Athletic Commission.

Gibson, Josh (1911–1947).   Regarded as one of the greatest hitters in baseball history, Gibson worked in the Pittsburgh steel mills as a teenager and began playing professionally as a catcher with the Homestead

Grays in 1930. During his first full season (1931), he led the Negro National League in home runs and then spent five stellar years (1932–1936) with the Pittsburgh Crawfords. From 1937 on, Gibson divided his time between the Homestead Grays and various teams in the Caribbean. He played his final season in 1946, leading the league in doubles and home runs despite the effects of a brain tumor that was to prove fatal the following year. Baseball historians estimate that Gibson hit 823 home runs in 22 years. He is credited with some of the longest shots ever witnessed, including a 600-foot blast that sailed out of New York's Polo Grounds and landed on the elevated subway tracks across the street from the ballpark.

Johnson, John Arthur "Jack" (1878–1946).   Growing up in a rough section of Galveston, Texas, Johnson was a timid youngster who learned to use his fists at his mother's insistence. He began boxing seriously in 1899 and received a title shot nine years later. On December 26, 1908, Johnson knocked out Tommy Burns in Sidney, Australia, becoming the first black world heavyweight champion. He was an admirably active champion, successfully defending his title five times in 1909. Refusing to be humble about his prowess, Johnson incurred the wrath of whites by living in high style, driving fast cars, marrying and divorcing a white woman, and beating every "white hope" who challenged him. Finally, in 1913, federal authorities brought trumped-up legal charges against Johnson, who fled to Cuba. The boxing world still regarded him as a champion, and he defended his title twice in Paris and once in Buenos Aires before losing to Jess Willard in Havana on April 5, 1915. (Many boxing historians have speculated that Johnson threw the fight.) Johnson returned to the United States in 1920 and served a year in prison. After his release, he staged exhibitions, lectured, and wrote an autobiography, *Jack Johnson: In the Ring and Out* (1927).

Jordan, Michael (1963–   ).   Generally regarded as the greatest basketball player of all time, Jordan first came to national attention at the University of North Carolina, when he won the 1982 NCAA tournament for the Tar Heels with a last-second jump shot. He joined the Chicago Bulls for the 1984–1985 season, electrifying fans with his soaring dunks and becoming the NBA's Rookie of the Year. By the end of the 1997–98 season, Jordan had led his team to six NBA championships and won five MVP Awards and ten scoring titles. He has also achieved an international celebrity status rarely paralleled in athletic history.

Joyner-Kersee, Jackie (1962–   ).   Born in East St. Louis, Illinois, Joyner-Kersee attended UCLA on a basketball scholarship. In addition to starting on the basketball team all four years, she also won the NCAA heptathlon championship in 1982 and 1983. Despite a hamstring injury, Joyner-Kersee managed to win a silver medal in the heptathlon at the 1984 Olympics in Los Angeles. Joyner-Kersee became a dominant figure in 1987, winning the heptathlon and the long jump at the World Track and Field Championships in Rome—she was the first woman in history to win both a multisport event and an individual event at a major meet. She followed this success by taking the gold medal in the heptathlon at the 1988 Olympics, setting a world record for total points. She repeated as Olympic heptathlon champion at Barcelona in 1992, also winning the bronze medal in the long jump. Joyner-Kersee competed in her fourth set of Olympic games at Atlanta in 1996. Hampered by a variety of injuries, she won the bronze medal in the long jump but failed to medal in the heptathlon. Amid an outpouring of tributes from fellow athletes and fans, Joyner-Kersee announced her retirement from competition. She is generally regarded as the greatest female athlete of all time.

Lewis, Carl (1961–   ).   The son of two outstanding track athletes, Lewis grew up in Willingboro, New Jersey. A frail youngster, he was at first overshadowed by his athletic brothers and sisters, but a meeting with the legendary Jesse Owens inspired him to keep working. Lewis began to show his ability as a sprinter in high school and went on to star for the University of Houston and the Santa Monica Track Club. Lewis's brilliance was on full display at the 1984 Los Angeles Olympics, where he won gold medals in the 100-meter dash, 200-meter dash, long jump, and 4 × 100-meter relay. With this feat, Lewis became the second athlete in history to win four gold medals at a single Olympics, placing him alongside his idol Jesse Owens. Because of his intense dedication, Lewis was often perceived as arrogant and self-centered, but he ignored the criticism and continued to excel. He won two gold medals and a silver medal at Seoul in 1988 and two more gold medals at Barcelona in 1992. By 1996, Lewis had finally won over the public, and the decision to exclude him from the U.S. 4 × 100-meter relay team at Atlanta was highly unpopular. There seemed little chance of his earning another medal, but Lewis amazed everyone by winning the long jump and bringing his Olympic medals total to 10. No track athlete in the modern era has approached this feat.

Louis, Joe [Joseph Louis Barrow] (1914–1981).   The Alabama-born Louis moved to Detroit as a youngster and became an outstanding amateur boxer, winning 50 of 59 bouts before turning professional in 1934. After winning acclaim with victories over Primo Carnera and Max Baer, Louis then knocked out Jim Braddock on June 27, 1937, to win the heavyweight championship of the world. Combining quickness and power, Louis held the title for 12 years, dominating all challengers, while African Americans throughout the country cheered his every move. Perhaps the greatest moment of his career was his title defense against the German Max Schmeling, who had knocked out an overconfident, undertrained Louis in 1936. With Germany's Nazi regime boasting that an "inferior" black man could never defeat a member of the so-called Aryan race, Louis stepped into the ring on June 22, 1938, and demolished Schmeling in the first round. By the time Louis retired undefeated in 1949, the man known as the Brown Bomber had become one of the greatest figures in sports history. Louis returned to the ring briefly in 1950 to 1951 but retired for good after losses to future champions Ezzard Charles and Rocky Marciano. During his unparalleled career, he compiled a record of 68-3, with 54 knockouts.

Owens, James Cleveland "Jesse" (1913–1980).   Born in Alabama, Owens grew up in Cleveland. A star sprinter at East Technical High School, Owens moved on to Ohio State and proceeded to rewrite the record book in track and field. At the 1935 Big Ten Championships at Ann Arbor, Michigan, Owens put on an unbelievable display of athletic brilliance, breaking five world records and tying a sixth, all within the space of about 70 minutes. The following year, Owens traveled to Berlin for the Summer Olympics and captured an unprecedented four gold medals, setting new Olympic records in the 200-meter dash and the long jump. Though the Nazi dictator Adolf Hitler refused to present Owens with his medals, the German public cheered him deliriously. Owens returned to the United States a national hero, but the various business opportunities promised to him never materialized. During World War II, Owens supervised African American workers in Ford Motor Company's defense plants. He later went out on the lecture circuit and conducted track and field clinics in the United States and in a number of foreign countries. He was awarded the Presidential Medal of Freedom in 1976.

Paige, Leroy "Satchel" (1906–1982).   Born in Mobile, Alabama, Paige began his baseball career with the Mobile Tigers, a semipro club, in 1924. In 1926, he joined the Chattanooga Black Lookouts of the Negro Southern League and played for a number of other teams before joining the Pittsburgh Crawfords in 1932. Dominating hitters with his blazing fastball, the lanky Paige posted a 23-7 record in 1932 and improved to 31-4 the following year. The great Dizzy Dean of the St. Louis Cardinals, who often pitched against Paige in off-season exhibition games, said that Paige was the best pitcher he had ever seen. After a stint in the Dominican Republic and time off due to a sore arm, Paige joined the Kansas City Monarchs and led them to the Negro World Series in 1942 and 1946.

Paige had hoped to be the first African American in the major leagues and was frankly disappointed when his young teammate Jackie Robinson got the call in 1947; he later conceded that he could not have tolerated the abuse that Robinson had to endure. Paige got his chance in 1948, however, making his debut with the Cleveland Indians on his 42nd birthday before 78,383 fans at Municipal Stadium. He won six out of seven games during the second half of the season, helping the Indians win the American League pennant. Paige became the ageless wonder of baseball, winning 12 games for the St. Louis Browns at age 46, pitching effectively in the International League while in his 50s, and making a final appearance with the Kansas City Athletics at age 59. In 1971, the irrepressible Paige was the first Negro Leagues star inducted into the Baseball Hall of Fame.

Robinson, Edward Gay "Eddie" (1919–   ).   Born in Jackson, Mississippi, Robinson attended Leland College in Baker, Louisiana. Majoring in English, he also starred on the football team and served as a part-time coach. Graduating in 1941, he was immediately hired as head football coach and athletic director by the Louisiana Negro Normal and Industrial Institute (later Grambling State University) at a salary of $16 a week. Robinson guided his team to an 8-0 record during his first season and remained at Grambling for 56 more years. During his tenure, more than 200 Grambling players were drafted by NFL teams, the most of any U.S. college. Among the standout players who blossomed under Robinson's tutelage were Tank Younger, Buck Buchanan, Willie Davis, and Doug Williams. A living legend, Robinson coached his last home game at Grambling on November 15, 1997, saying good-bye in the stadium that bears his name.

Robinson, John Roosevelt "Jackie" (1919–1972).   Born in Georgia, Robinson grew up in Pasadena, California. Enrolling at UCLA in 1940, he emerged as the finest all-around athlete in the country, excelling in football, basketball, baseball, and track. After serving in the U.S. Army from 1942 to 1944, Robinson signed with the Kansas City Monarchs in the Negro American League. In 1945, Branch Rickey of the Brooklyn Dodgers offered Robinson a contract, provided that Robinson promised not to fight back against the abuse he would inevitably take as the first African American in the major leagues. Robinson accepted the conditions and spent the 1946 season with Brooklyn's top farm team, the Montreal Royals, leading the International League with a 0.349 average.

On April 15, 1947, Robinson changed the face of professional sports forever when he made his debut with the Brooklyn Dodgers at Ebbets Field. Throughout a year when he was subjected to vicious insults from rival players and fans, Robinson let his bat and glove do the talking—he batted .297 and won Rookie of the Year honors. The following year, he raised his average to .342 and was named National League MVP. Once established, Robinson was free to fight back, and opposing teams came to fear his retribution. Driven by a competitive fire rarely matched in sports history, Robinson was a daring base runner, a sure-handed fielder, and a supreme clutch hitter. He retired after the 1956 season with a .311 lifetime batting average and was elected to the Hall of Fame in 1961. As a successful businessperson, Robinson continued to fight for equal rights and harshly criticized organized baseball for failing to provide managerial and executive opportunities for African Americans. His legacy of achievement and social awareness is being carried on by the Jackie Robinson Foundation, which is overseen by his wife, Rachel.

Rudolph, Wilma Glodean (1940–).   Born in Tennessee, Rudolph contracted scarlet fever as a child and needed leg braces and special shoes until she was 11 years old. Determined to overcome the effects of her illness, she devoted herself to sports. By the time Rudolph reached Burt High School in Clarksville, she was a high-scoring basketball star and a peerless sprinter. Enrolling in Tennessee State University in 1957, Rudolph immediately began to dominate the women's track scene while setting her sights on the 1960 Olympics. At the Summer Olympic Games in Rome, she realized all her ambitions, becoming the first woman in history to win three gold medals in a single set of Olympics games: In addition to winning the 100-meter dash, Rudolph set an Olympic record in the 200-meter dash and anchored the U.S. 4 × 100-meter relay team in a world-record performance. In recognition of her achievements, United Press International named her Athlete of the Year for 1960. After receiving her degree from Tennessee State in 1963, Rudolph worked as a track coach and athletic consultant, devoting her efforts to youth groups around the country. In addition to creating the Wilma Rudolph Foundation, she has served on the Mayor's Youth Foundation in Chicago.

Russell, William Felton "Bill" (1934–).   Born in Louisiana, Russell grew up in Oakland, California. His basketball ability blossomed at the University of San Francisco; during his junior and senior years, the 6-foot-10-inch center became the premier player in college basketball, leading the Dons to two straight NCAA championships. Drafted by the Boston Celtics in 1957, Russell transformed the franchise into a dynasty that collected 10 NBA championships in 11 years. Never a prolific scorer, Russell dominated games with his rebounding and his shot blocking; he routinely controlled the boards at both ends and made it nearly impossible for opponents to drive the lane. During the course of his career, Russell won the MVP Award five times and retired with 21,721 rebounds, placing him second on the all-time list. Before the 1968-69 season, Russell was named the Celtics' player-coach, becoming the first African American to coach an NBA team. After leading the Celtics to yet another championship, the 35-year-old Russell retired as a player and also resigned his coaching position. He spent several years as a broadcaster and later coached both the Seattle SuperSonics and the Sacramento Kings. In 1988, Russell became the Kings' director of player personnel.

Woods, Eldrick "Tiger" (1975–   ).   Born in Cypress, California, Woods first swung a golf club when he was only six months old. He shot a 48 for nine holes at age three, and *Golf Digest* touted him as a future star when he was five. After winning the USGA Junior Championship in 1991, 1992, and 1993, Woods enrolled at Stanford University. He continued to dominate the amateur ranks, winning an unprecedented three successive U.S. amateur titles (1994, 1995, and 1996) as well as the 1996 NCAA championship. Woods left Stanford in the summer of 1996 to join the PGA Tour and quickly established his presence. Playing in eight tournaments, he finished in the top 10 on five occasions and won both the Las Vegas Invitational and the Walt Disney World Classic. In 1997, Woods broke through to the next level, winning the prestigious Masters Tournament by a record 12 strokes. The victory made him the first African American (and the first Asian American; his mother is Filipino) to win a major golf tournament. At age 21, he was also the youngest Masters champion of all time and the youngest golfer to win a major tournament since World War II. He won three more tour events during the year, ending as the first player to win more than $2 million in prize money. Woods's spectacular success earned him the PGA Player of the Year Award, and the Associated Press named him the Male Athlete of the Year for 1997.

SOURCES FOR ADDITIONAL INFORMATION

Ashe, Arthur. *A Hard Road to Glory: A History of the African-American Athlete,* 3 vols. New York: Amistad, 1993.

Chadwick, Bruce. *When the Game Was Black and White: The Illustrated History of Baseball's Negro Leagues.* New York: Abbeville, 1997.

Chalk, Ocania. *Black College Sports.* New York: Dodd, Mead, 1975.

Edwards, Harry. *The Revolt of the Black Athlete.* New York: Free Press, 1969.

George, Nelson. *Elevating the Game: Black Men and Basketball.* New York: HarperCollins, 1992.

Hoberman, George. *Darwin's Athletes: How Sport Has Damaged Black America and Preserved the Myth of Race.* Boston: Houghton Mifflin, 1997.

Holway, John B. *Black Diamonds: Life in the Negro Leagues from the Men Who Lived It.* New York: Stadium, 1991.

Lee, Spike, with Ralph Wiley. *Best Seat in the House: A Basketball Memoir.* New York: Crown, 1997.

Peterson, Robert. *Only the Ball Was White: A History of Legendary Black Players and All-Black Professional Teams.* New York: Oxford University Press, 1970.

Rampersad, Arnold. *Jackie Robinson: A Biography.* New York: Knopf, 1997.

Riley, James A. *The Biographical Encyclopedia of the Negro Leagues.* New York: Carroll & Graf, 1994.

Robinson, Jackie, with Alfred Duckett. *I Never Had It Made.* New York: Putnam, 1972.

Rust, Art. *Art Rust's Illustrated History of the Black Athlete.* Garden City, NY: Doubleday, 1985.

Shropshire, Kenneth. *In Black and White: Race and Sports in America.* New York: New York University Press, 1996.

Tygiel, Jules. *Baseball's Great Experiment: Jackie Robinson and His Legacy,* expanded ed. New York: Oxford University Press, 1997.

19
Resources

U.S. GOVERNMENT AGENCIES

U.S. Commission on Civil Rights
1121 Vermont Avenue, NW
Washington, DC 20425
202-523-5571

U.S. Commission on Civil Rights
Central Division
911 Walnut Street
Kansas City, MO 64106
816-426-5253
Territory: Alabama, Alaska, Iowa, Kansas,
   Louisiana, Mississippi, Missouri, Nebraska

U.S. Commission on Civil Rights
Eastern Region
624 Ninth Street, NW
Washington, DC 20425
202-376-7533
Territory: Connecticut, Delaware, District of
   Columbia, Maine, Maryland, Massachusetts,
   New Hampshire, New Jersey, New York,
   Pennsylvania, Rhode Island, Vermont, Virginia,
   West Virginia

U.S. Commission on Civil Rights
Midwestern Region
175 W. Jackson Street
Chicago, IL 60604
312-353-8311
Territory: Illinois, Indiana, Michigan, Minnesota,
   Ohio, Wisconsin

U.S. Commission on Civil Rights
Rocky Mountain Region
1700 Broadway
Denver, CO 80290
303-866-1040
Territory: Colorado, Montana, North Dakota,
   South Dakota, Utah, Wyoming

U.S. Commission on Civil Rights
Southern Region
101 Marietta Street
Atlanta, GA 30303
404-730-2476
Territory: Florida, Georgia, Kentucky, North
   Carolina, South Carolina, Tennessee

U.S. Commission on Civil Rights
Western Region
3660 Wilshire Boulevard
Los Angeles, CA 90010
213-894-3437
Territory: Arizona, California, Hawaii, Nevada,
   New Mexico, Oklahoma, Oregon, Texas,
   Washington

U.S. Department of Agriculture
Office of Advocacy and Enterprise
Equal Opportunity Services
14th Street and Independence Avenue, SW
1349 S. Agriculture Building
Washington, DC 20250
202-720-5681

U.S. Department of Commerce
Minority Business Development Agency
Herbert Clark Hoover Building
14th Street and Constitution Avenue, NW
Washington, DC 20230
202-482-5061

U.S. Department of Commerce
Office of Civil Rights
14th Street and Constitution Avenue, NW
Washington, DC 20230
202-482-0625

U.S. Department of Education
Assistant Secretary for Postsecondary Education
Historically Black Colleges and Universities
Seventh and D Streets, SW
Washington, DC 20202
202-708-8667

U.S. Department of Education
Office of the Secretary
Assistant Secretary for Civil Rights
330 C Street
Washington, DC 20202
202-205-5431

U.S. Department of Energy
Office of Minority Economic Impact

Forrestal Building
1000 Independence Avenue, SW
Washington, DC 20585
202-586-8383

U.S. Department of Health and Human Services
Administration for Children and Families
Office of Equal Opportunity and Civil Rights
370 L'Enfant Promenade, SW
Washington, DC 20447
202-401-4784

U.S. Department of Health and Human Services
Office for Civil Rights
Equal Employment Opportunity/Affirmative
    Action
330 Independence Avenue, SW
Washington, DC 20201
202-619-0585

U.S. Department of Health and Human Services
Public Health Service
Assistant Secretary for Health
Office of Minority Health
5515 Security Lane
Rockville, MD 20852
301-443-5084

U.S. Department of Housing and Urban
    Development
Assistant Secretary for Fair Housing and Equal
    Opportunity
451 Seventh Street, SW
Washington, DC 20410
202-708-4252

U.S. Department of the Interior
Policy, Management, and Budget
Office of the Assistant Secretary
Office of Equal Opportunity
1849 C Street, NW
Washington, DC 20240
202-208-5693

U.S. Department of Justice
Civil Rights Division
10th Street and Constitution Avenue
Washington, DC 20530
202-514-2151

U.S. Department of Labor
Office of Small Business and Minority Affairs
200 Constitution Avenue, NW
Washington, DC 20210
202-219-9148

U.S. Department of State
Bureau of Human Rights and Humanitarian
    Affairs
2201 C Street, NW
Washington, DC 20520
202-647-2126

U.S. Department of State
Office of the Secretary
Equal Employment Opportunity and Civil Rights
    Office
2201 C Street, NW
Washington, DC 20520
202-647-9294

U.S. Department of Transportation
Office of Civil Rights
400 Seventh Street, SW
Washington, DC 20590
202-366-4648

U.S. Environmental Protection Agency
Office of Civil Rights
National Black Employment Programs
401 M Street, SW
Washington, DC 20460
202-260-7495

U.S. Equal Employment Opportunity Commission
1801 L Street, NW
Washington, DC 20507
202-663-4001

U.S. General Accounting Office
Civil Rights Office
441 G Street, NW
Washington, DC 20548
202-512-6388

U.S. Information Agency
Bureau of Management
Office of Equal Employment Opportunity and
    Civil Rights
301 Fourth Street, SW
Washington, DC 20547
202-619-4700

U.S. National Aeronautics and Space
  Administration
Office of Equal Opportunity Programs
300 E Street, SW
Washington, DC 20546
202-358-2167

U.S. Office of Personnel Management
Office of Equal Employment Opportunity
1900 E Street, NW
Washington, DC 20415
202-606-2460

U.S. Small Business Administration
Minority Small Business and Capital Ownership
  Development
409 Third Street, SW
Washington, DC 20416
202-205-6410

U.S. Smithsonian Institution
Office of Equal Opportunity and Minority Affairs
915 L'Enfant Plaza, SW
Washington, DC 20560
202-287-3508

FOUNDATIONS AND SOCIAL-SERVICE ORGANIZATIONS

ARIZONA

Black Family and Child Services, Inc.
2323 N. Third Street
Phoenix, AZ 85004
602-256-2948

CALIFORNIA

African Community Health and Social Services
1212 Broadway
Oakland, CA 94612
510-839-7764

African Community Services of San Diego
7353 El Cajon Boulevard
San Diego, CA 91941
619-466-4364

African Refugee Center
6399 Wilshire Boulevard
Los Angeles, CA 90048
213-966-5537

Black Awareness Community Development
  Organization
4167 S. Normandie Avenue
Los Angeles, CA 90037
213-291-7188

Black Women's Resource Center
518 17th Street, Suite 202

Oakland, CA 94601
510-763-9501
Focuses on needs of African American women
  and youths; provides referrals, job counseling,
  networking, and other services.

DISTRICT OF COLUMBIA

A. Philip Randolph Institute
1444 I Street, NW
Washington, DC 20005
202-289-2774
Battles discrimination and prejudice in all walks of
  life; assists in employment and education; promotes community development; fosters cooperation between the labor movement and the
  African American community.

Children's Defense Fund
25 E Street, NW
Washington, DC 20001
202-628-8787
Acts as an advocate for the rights of children,
  with special emphasis on the rights of poor and
  minority children.

The Links, Inc.
1200 Massachusetts Avenue, NW
Washington, DC 20005
202-842-8686
Has 240 chapters in the United States, the
  Bahamas, and Europe; activities include services
  to the arts and to youths.

National Association of Neighborhoods
1651 Fuller Street, NW
Washington, DC 20009
202-332-7766
Represents 2,000 community groups nationwide; provides technical assistance, training, workshops, small-business development, and other services.

National Black Child Development Institute
1013 15th Street, NW
Washington, DC 20005
202-387-1281

National Council of Negro Women, Inc.
1211 Connecticut Avenue, NW
Washington, DC 20036
202-659-0006
Founded by Mary McLeod Bethune; operates through 214 local sections, providing programs to combat hunger and malnutrition; child-care and child-development programs; youth counseling; community leadership training; and other services.

GEORGIA

The Black Family Project
673 Beckwith Street, SW
Atlanta, GA 30314
404-880-0679

International Benevolent Society, Inc.
837 Fifth Avenue
P.O. Box 1276
Columbus, GA 31902
706-322-5671
Has 165 chapters in seven states; distributes scholarships to qualifying high-school seniors.

Modern Free and Accepted Masons of the World, Inc.
627 Fifth Avenue
Columbus, GA 31901
770-322-3326
Invests in businesses and provides employment opportunities for African Americans.

One Hundred Black Men of America
127 Peachtree Street, NE

Atlanta, GA 30309
404-532-3953
Provides economic and scholastic aid to the African American community.

ILLINOIS

African American National Charitable Trust
320 N. Michigan Avenue
Chicago, IL 60639
312-237-6600

LOUISIANA

African American Voters League
310 S. Broad Street
New Orleans, LA 70119
504-822-2890
Provides scholarships and a feed-the-needy program.

MARYLAND

Africa Cultural Center, Inc.
13815 Marianna Drive
Rockville, MD 20853
301-871-1397
Offers cultural and educational programs relating to Africa and the Caribbean; provides food and clothing to needy African families.

MICHIGAN

Ancient Egyptian Arabic Order
Nobles Mystic Shrine, Inc.
2211 Cass Avenue
Detroit, MI 48201
313-961-9148
Provides funds for hospitals, schools, and educational grants.

MISSOURI

Black Adoption and Foster Care Center
951 Jeannette Drive
St. Louis, MO 63130
314-863-1321

NEW YORK

The Africa Fund
198 Broadway
New York, NY 10038
212-962-1210
Provides financial, legal, educational, and medical assistance to needy Africans in the United States and elsewhere; conducts research and informs the American public about the needs of Africans.

African American Immigration Services, Inc.
1224 Sheepshead Bay Road
Brooklyn, NY 11235
718-743-5844

African Peoples Council, Inc.
6 Maiden Lane
New York, NY 10038
212-346-9863
Provides assistance for immigrants, including English language instruction and other services.

Arthur Ashe Foundation for the Defeat of AIDS, Inc.
120 Park Avenue
New York, NY 10016
212-922-0096

Associated Black Charities
105 E. 22nd Street
New York, NY 10010
212-777-6060
Services include child care and assistance to the elderly.

Interreligious Foundation for Community Organization
402 W. 145th Street
New York, NY 10031
212-926-5757

Ecumenical agency that coordinates church and community-action programs for social justice; offers community organizing and educational and other programs.

Jackie Robinson Foundation
80 Eighth Avenue
New York, NY 10011
212-675-1511
Provides approximately 100 scholarships yearly.

NORTH CAROLINA

Black Child Development Institute
1200 E. Market Street
Greensboro, NC 27401
910-230-2138
Provides tutorial and mentoring services.

Improved and Benevolent Protective Order of Elks of the World
P.O. Box 159
Winton, NC 27986
919-358-7661
Has contributed more than $2.5 million to scholarship funds for students of all ethnic backgrounds.

OREGON

Minority Youth Concerns Action
4732 N.E. Garfield
Portland, OR 97211
503-280-1050

WISCONSIN

African American Family Corporation
3940 N. 21st Street
Milwaukee, WI 53206
414-445-8481

LIBRARIES AND RESEARCH CENTERS

ALABAMA

Alabama A&M University
J. F. Drake Memorial Learning Resource Center
P.O. Box 489
Normal, AL 35762
205-851-5760
African American collection includes more than
3,000 items.

Alabama State University
University Library and Learning Resources
Archives and Special Collections
Levi Watkins Learning Center
915 S. Jackson Street
Montgomery, AL 36195
205-293-4106
Special collections include the Atlanta University
Black Culture Collection, the George W.
Carver Correspondence Collection, and the
Bibliography of Doctoral Research on the
Negro.

Bienville Historical Society
Center for Gulf Studies
606 Government Street
Mobile, AL 36602
205-457-5242
Holdings include colonial manuscripts and church
records.

Birmingham Public Library
Linn-Henley Library for Southern Historical
Research
Department of Archives and Manuscripts (205-
266-3645)
Tutweiler Collection of Southern History and
Literature (205-266-3655)
2100 Park Place
Birmingham, AL 35203
Holdings include microfilms and microforms on
civil rights in Alabama and books and manu-
scripts relating to slavery and Reconstruction.

Talladega College
Slavery Library
Historical Collections
627 W. Battle Street

Talladega, AL 35160
205-362-0206
Holdings include materials on the African
American church and on missions to African
nations.

Tuskegee University
Main Library
Tuskegee, AL 36088
205-727-8888
Holdings include the Booker T. Washington
Papers and the George Washington Carver
Papers; Tuskegee's Architecture Library (Wilcox
Building A) has materials on African American
architects and architecture.

ARKANSAS

University of Arkansas, Pine Bluff
John Brown Watson Memorial Library
N. University Boulevard
U.S. Highway 79
Pine Bluff, AR 71601
501-541-6825
Collections include the Paul Laurence Dunbar
Papers (on microfilm).

CALIFORNIA

African American Historical and Cultural Society
Library of San Francisco
762 Fulton Street
San Francisco, CA 94102
415-292-6172

Compton Community College Library
Black History Collection
1111 E. Artesia Boulevard
Compton, CA 90221
213-637-2660

County of Los Angeles Public Library
Black Resource Center
A. C. Bilbrew Library
150 E. El Segundo Boulevard
Los Angeles, CA 90061
213-538-3350

Oakland Public Library
125 14th Street
Oakland, CA 94612
510-273-3136
Holdings include the Schomburg Collection of
    Black Literature and History (in microform)
    and Negroes of New York, 1939 (WPA Writers
    Project, in microform).

University of California, Los Angeles
Department of Special Collections
University Research Library, Floor A
Los Angeles, CA 90024
310-825-4879
Holdings include material on African Americans
    in entertainment and literature.

DISTRICT OF COLUMBIA

Association for the Study of Afro-American Life
    and History
Carter G. Woodson Library
1407 14th Street, NW
Washington, DC 20005
Holdings include rare books on African
    Americans prior to 1865.

District of Columbia Public Library
Black Studies Division
Martin Luther King, Jr. Memorial Library
901 G Street, NW
Washington, DC 20001
202-272-1211

Howard University
Moorland-Spingarn Research Center
500 Howard Place
Washington, DC 20059
202-806-7260
Library Division and Manuscript Division hold-
    ings include the Ralph J. Bunche Oral History
    Collection (1960s civil rights activities) and the
    Rose McClendon Collection of Photographs of
    Celebrated Negroes by Carl Van Vechten.

Joint Center for Political and Economic Studies
Office of Information Resources
1301 Pennsylvania Avenue, NW

Washington, DC 20004
202-626-3530
Materials on African American elected officials
    and political participation; open by appoint-
    ment for reference use only.

Library of Congress
General Reading Rooms Division
Thomas Jefferson Building
Washington, DC 20540
202-707-5471
The library's vast holdings include extensive mate-
    rials on African American history and culture,
    including the American Memory Collection.

U.S. Commission on Civil Rights
National Civil Rights Clearinghouse Library
624 Ninth Street, NW
Washington, DC 20425
202-376-8110

GEORGIA

Atlanta-Fulton Public Library
Special Collections Department
1 Margaret Mitchell Square
Atlanta, GA 30303
404-730-1700
Holdings include materials on African American
    studies, genealogy, and Georgia history and lit-
    erature.

Black Women in Church and Society
Research/Resource Center
Interdenominational Theological Center
671 Beckwith Street, SW
Atlanta, GA 30314
404-527-7740

Clark Atlanta University Center
Robert W. Woodruff Library
Division of Archives and Special Collections
111 James P. Brawley Drive, SW
Atlanta, GA 30314
404-522-8980
Extensive collections of material on African
    American history, the civil rights movement,
    historically black colleges and universities, and
    other subjects.

Martin Luther King, Jr., Center for Nonviolent Social Change
King Library and Archives
449 Auburn Avenue, NE
Atlanta, GA 30312
404-524-1956
Holdings include over 1 million documents relating to the civil rights movement.

ILLINOIS

Chicago Public Library
Carter G. Woodson Regional Library
Vivian G. Harsh Research Collection of Afro-American History and Literature
9525 S. Halstead Street
Chicago, IL 60628
312-747-6910
Holdings include the Carl Sang Collection of Afro-American History and the Horace Revels Cayton Collection.

DuSable Museum of African American History, Library
740 E. 56th Place
Chicago, IL 60637
312-947-0600

INDIANA

Indiana University
Black Culture Center
109 N. Jordan Avenue
Bloomington, IN 47405
812-855-3237
Holdings include the Arno Press Collection (250 volumes) of classic works on African Americans, reprinted during the 1960s.

KANSAS

Kansas State University
Farrell Library
Minority Resource Research Center
Manhattan, KS 66506
913-532-7453
Collections include materials on African American history and literature.

LOUISIANA

Amistad Research Center
Library/Archives
Tulane University
6823 St. Charles Avenue
New Orleans, LA 70118
504-865-5535
With more than 8 million manuscript items, Amistad's collection of primary materials on African American history and culture is the largest in the United States; the center also houses the Aaron Douglas Art Collection and the Amistad Collection of African American Art.

MARYLAND

U.S. Navy
Naval Institute
Oral History Office
118 Maryland Avenue
Annapolis, MD 21402
410-268-6110
Collections include material on early African American naval officers.

MASSACHUSETTS

Boston University
Department of Special Collections
771 Commonwealth Avenue
Boston, MA 02215
617-353-3696
Holdings include 180 boxes of papers relating to Rev. Martin Luther King Jr.

Radcliffe College
Arthur and Elizabeth Schlesinger Library on the History of Women in America
10 Garden Street
Cambridge, MA 02138
617-495-8647
Holdings include the Black Women Oral History project.

University of Massachusetts Library
Special Collections and Archives

Amherst, MA 01003
413-545-2780
Collections include the papers of W. E. B. Du Bois.

MICHIGAN

Detroit Public Library
Music and Performing Arts Department
5201 Woodward Avenue
Detroit, MI 48202
Holdings include the E. Azalia Hackley Collection on African Americans in the performing arts.

MINNESOTA

Minneapolis Public Library and Information Center
Special Collections Department
300 Nicollet Mall
Minneapolis, MN 55401
612-372-6648
Holdings include the Huttner Abolition and Anti-Slavery Collection.

MISSISSIPPI

University of Mississippi
John Davis Williams Library
Music Library/Blues Archive
Farley Hall
University, MS 38677
601-232-7753
Holdings include the B. B. King Collection and the Living Blues Archival Collection.

MISSOURI

Lincoln University
Inman E. Page Library
Jefferson City, MO 65101
314-681-5512
Collections include proslavery and antislavery tracts and other historical materials from the pre– and post–Civil War periods.

U.S. National Park Service
George Washington Carver National Monument
P.O. Box 38
Diamond, MO 64840
417-325-4151
Library holdings include correspondence and artifacts relating to Carver's life and work.

NEW JERSEY

Newark Public Library
Humanities Division
5 Washington Street
Newark, NJ 07101
201-733-7820
Special collections on African American history, literature, and biography.

NEW YORK

African-American Institute
Africa Policy Information Center
833 United Nations Plaza
New York, NY 10017
212-949-5666
Special collections include clippings from U.S., European, and African publications, 1974 to present; holdings include 200 different journals.

Brooklyn Museum of Art
Art Reference Library
200 Eastern Parkway
Brooklyn, NY 11238
718-638-5000
Materials on African and African American art.

Caribbean Cultural Center
408 W. 58th Street
New York, NY 10019
212-307-7420
Library contains materials, including photographs and videotapes, relating to African influence on the culture of the Americas.

Center for Migration Studies
CMS Library
209 Flagg Place
Staten Island, NY 10304
718-351-8800

Columbia University
Oral History Research Office
Butler Library
P.O. Box 20
New York, NY 10027
212-854-2273

Cornell University
John Henrik Clarke Africana Library
310 Triphammer Road
Ithaca, NY 14850
607-255-5229
Holdings include the Civil Rights Microfilm
    Collection.

Hatch-Billops Collection
491 Broadway, 7th Floor
New York, NY 10012
212-966-3231
Holdings include more than 1,200 oral-history in-
    terviews relating to African Americans in the
    theater and visual arts.

New York Public Library
Countee Cullen Regional Branch Library
African-American Heritage Collection
104 W. 136th Street
New York, NY 10030
212-491-2070
Holdings include the James Weldon Johnson
    Collection of Children's Books on the Black
    Experience.

New York Public Library
The Research Libraries
Schomburg Center for Research in Black Culture
515 Malcolm X Boulevard
New York, NY 10037
212-491-2200
Holdings include the works of Harlem
    Renaissance authors and artists, recordings,
    photographs, an oral-history archive, and exten-
    sive materials on the Caribbean.

Queens Borough Public Library
History, Travel and Biography Division
89-11 Merrick Boulevard
Jamaica, NY 11432
718-990-0762

Holdings include the Carter G. Woodson
    Collection of Afro-American Culture and Life
    and the Schomburg Microfilm Collection.

Queens Borough Public Library
Langston Hughes Community Library and
    Cultural Center
102-09 Northern Boulevard
Corona, NY 11368
718-651-1100
Holdings include the Langston Hughes Collection
    (books by and about the author), the Black
    Heritage Reference Collection, and the
    Langston Hughes Music Collection.

State University of New York
Syracuse Educational Opportunity Center
Paul Robeson Library
100 New Street
Syracuse, NY 13202
315-472-0130
Holdings include the Frazier Library of Afro-
    American Books and the National Archives
    Collection of Afro-American Artists.

NORTH CAROLINA

Bennett College
Thomas F. Holgate Library
900 E. Washington
Campus Box M
Greensboro, NC 27401
919-273-4431
Holdings include the Afro-American Women's
    Collection.

North Carolina Central University
School of Library and Information Sciences
J. E. Shepard Library
Durham, NC 27707
919-560-5212
Holdings include the William Tucker Collection
    of children's literature by African American au-
    thors and illustrators and the Black Librarians'
    Collection.

OHIO

African American Museum, Library
1765 Crawford Road

The 135ᵗʰ Street Branch Library of The New York Public Library in the 1930s; it would later become the first home of the Schomburg Center.

Cleveland, OH 44106
216-791-1700
Special collections focus on music, aviation, theology, and the black church in Cleveland.

Cleveland Public Library
Fine Arts and Special Collections Department
325 Superior Avenue
Cleveland, OH 44114
216-623-2818
Holdings include materials on black names in America and African American religious beliefs in the South.

Oberlin College
Library Archives
420 Mudd Center
Oberlin, OH 44074
216-775-8014
Holdings include documents on the antislavery movement.

Ohio State University
Black Studies Library
1858 Neil Avenue Mall

Columbus, OH 43210
614-292-2393
Holdings include the W. E. B. Du Bois Papers, the Atlanta University Black Culture Collection, the Black Newpaper Collection, and the Papers of the NAACP.

Payne Theological Seminary
R. C. Ransom Memorial Library
P.O. Box 474
Wilberforce, OH 45384
513-376-2946
Holdings include materials on the history of the African Methodist Episcopal Church.

OKLAHOMA

Langston University
Melvin B. Tolson Black Heritage Center
Langston, OK 73050
405-466-3346
Holdings include the African Art Collection and the Langston University Archives.

PENNSYLVANIA

Cheyney University of Pennsylvania
Leslie Pinckney Hill Library
Special Collections
Cheyney, PA 19319
215-399-2491
Holdings include the Afro-American Collection
and the William Dorsey Collection of
Notebooks and Books on Afro-American
History.

Historical Society of Pennsylvania, Library
1300 Locust Street
Philadelphia, PA 19107
215-732-6201

Lincoln University
Langston Hughes Memorial Library
Lincoln University, PA 19352
215-932-8300
Holdings include rare antislavery pamphlets.

Temple University
Charles L. Blockson Afro-American Historical
    Collection
Sullivan Hall
Philadelphia, PA 19122
215-787-6632
Holdings include material on the history of
    African Americans in Pennsylvania and of the
    Underground Railroad.

University of Pittsburgh
Afro-American Library
Hillman Library, 1st Floor
Pittsburgh, PA 15260
412-648-7714
Holdings include slides of African American his-
    torical sites in Pennsylvania; microfilm versions
    of the Atlanta University Black Culture
    Collection, the W. E. B. Du Bois Papers, and
    the CORE Papers.

SOUTH CAROLINA

Avery Research Center for African American
    History and Culture
College of Charleston
125 Bull Street

Charleston, SC 29424
803-727-2009
Collections of personal papers, organizational
    records, photographs, recordings, art objects,
    and oral-history materials relating to African
    Americans in the Carolina low country; hold-
    ings also include the archives of the Avery
    Normal Institute, which trained African
    American teachers and professionals from 1868
    to 1957.

TENNESSEE

American Baptist Theological Seminary
T. L. Holcomb Library
1800 Baptist World Center Drive
Nashville, TN 37207
615-228-7877
Holdings include materials on the Bible, theology,
    and African American studies.

Center for Southern Folklore Archives
152 Beale Street
Memphis, TN 38103
901-525-3655
Holdings include the Reverend L. O. Taylor
    Collection, which documents Memphis's
    African American community from the 1920s
    to 1977.

Fisk University
Specials Collections Department
17 Jackson Street
Nashville, TN 37203
615-329-8846
Holdings include the Negro Collection, the
    Fiskiana Collection, and the Black Oral History
    Collection.

Meharry Medical College, Library
1005 D. B. Todd
Nashville, TN 37208
615-327-6728
Holdings include the Black Medical History
    Collection and the Meharry Archives.

Memphis State University
Special Collections
MSU Libraries
Memphis, TN 38152
901-678-2210

Holdings include documents relating to the assassination of Rev. Martin Luther King Jr.

TEXAS

Houston Public Library
Houston Metropolitan Research Center
500 McKinney Avenue
Houston, TX 77002
713-247-1661
Holdings include the Houston African-American Collection.

Prairie View A&M University
Special Collections/University Archives
John B. Coleman Library
Prairie View, TX 77446
409-857-3119
Holdings include the Black Heritage of the West Collection.

Texas Southern University
Heartman Collection
3100 Cleburne Street
Houston, TX 77004
713-527-7149
Holdings include the Barbara Jordan Archives, the Texas Southern University Archives, and the Jazz Archives.

U.S. National Park Service
Fort Davis National Historic Site
P.O. Box 1456
Fort Davis, TX 79734
915-426-3224
Library holdings include materials on the Buffalo Soldiers and on Lt. Henry Ossian Flipper.

VIRGINIA

Hampton University
William R. and Norma B. Harvey Library
30 Tyler Street
Hampton, VA 23668
804-727-5371
Holdings include the George Foster Peabody Collection of Negro History and Literature and the Hampton University Archives (4 million items).

U.S. National Park Service
Booker T. Washington National Monument
Route 3, P.O. Box 310
Hardy, VA 24101
703-721-2094
Library holdings include letters and documents relating to the Burroughs plantation, Washington's birthplace.

Virginia Union University
William J. Clark Library
Special Collections
1500 N. Lombardy Street
Richmond, VA 23220
804-257-5820
Holdings include materials on African American history in Richmond.

WASHINGTON

Seattle Public Library
Douglass-Truth Branch Library
2300 E. Yesley Way
Seattle, WA 98112
206-684-4704
Holdings include materials on African Americans in the Pacific Northwest and the portrayal of African Americans in children's literature.

WISCONSIN

Beloit College
Colonel Robert H. Morse Library
Black Information Center
731 College Street
Beloit, WI 53511
608-363-2487
Holdings include the Martin Luther King, Jr., Collection.

State Historical Society of Wisconsin
816 State Street
Madison, WI 53706
608-264-6534
Library holdings include the African American History Collection and publications by Phillis Wheatley, Harriet Jacobs, and other African American women.

INTERNET RESOURCES

BUSINESS

Black Enterprise Online
http://www.blackenterprise.com
Site includes rankings of the top African American companies, excerpts from articles in *Black Enterprise* magazine, classifieds, and numerous other features.

Virtual Africa Home Page
http://www.africa.com
Contains information about business in South Africa.

GENERAL INTEREST

African American Home Page
http://www.lainet.com/~joejones
Site includes artworks, online personals, recipes, information about fraternities and sororities, and links to other African American sites.

Afro-Diasporan Web Sites
http://www.artnoir.com/links.html
A truly all-purpose site containing links to 950 other sites, accessible through an alphabetical index; covers every conceivable topic.

Caribbean News Agency (CANA)
http://www.cananews.com
Site contains daily news stories and links to Caribbean newspapers and radio stations.

Everything Black
http://www.everythingblack.com
Site contains information on business, travel, the arts, sports, and history.

Internet Black Pages
http://www.blackpages.com
Listings of African American churches, businesses, schools, organizations, and events in New York, Boston, and Washington, D.C.

NetNoir: The Soul of Cyberspace
http://www.netnoir.com
Site contains information on business, careers, entertainment, personals, chat rooms, and other topics.

Universal Afrocentric Events Calendar
http://www.melanet.com.afro_today.html
A daily listing of events taking place in the diaspora.

Universal Black Pages
http://www.ubp.com
Site contains links to an events calendar, school and student organizations, and sites maintained by organizations in Africa and the Caribbean.

GOVERNMENT

Census Bureau Home Page
http://www.census.gov
Site contains a variety of statistics from the Census Bureau and links to other federal agencies.

Federal Web Locator
http://www.law.vill.edu.fed-agency/fedweb.new.html
Links to the legislative, judicial, and executive branches, including access to Supreme Court decisions; additional links to quasi-official organizations and nongovernment, federally related sites.

Fedstats
http://www.fedstats.gov
Links to 70 agencies.

HISTORY

African-American Journey
http://www.worldbook.com/features/blackhistory/index.html
Features on African American history compiled by the editors of *World Book Encyclopedia*.

The African-American Mosaic: A Library of Congress Resource Guide for the Study of Black History and Culture
http://www.lcweb.loc.gov/exhibits/african/afam001.html

African Burial Ground Archaeological Project
http://www.afrinet.net/halh.abg.html
An examination of the New York City historic site and its history; presentation includes an extensive list of frequently asked questions (FAQs).

Amistad
http://www.amistad.org
Site maintained by Amistad America, Inc., which is in the process of rebuilding the schooner *Amistad* at Mystic, Connecticut (projected completion date is 2000); site contains links to information about the *Amistad* case, including the text of the Supreme Court decision freeing the African rebels.

Historical Text Archive: African American History
http://www.msstate.edu/Archives/History/USA/Afro-Amer/afro.html

Martin Luther King, Jr., Directory
http://www.-leland.stanford.edu/group/King/index.html
Includes a biography, a chronology, articles about King, and access to the King papers. Maintained by the Martin Luther King, Jr., Center for Nonviolent Social Change and the Martin Luther King Papers Project at Stanford University.

Schomburg Center Home Page
http://gopher.nypl.org.research/sc.sc.htm
Site contains information about the Schomburg Center's resources, online exhibitions, and links to other sites.

Virtual Institute of Caribbean Studies
http://pw1.netcom.com/~hhenke/index.htm
Contains research papers on the Caribbean, an online forum, a newsletter, and links to other sites.

W. E. B. Du Bois Institute
http://www.web-dubois.fas.harvard.edu
Site is being combined with the home page of Harvard's Afro-American Studies Department; contains information on faculty and programs, as well as links.

LAW

National Bar Association (NBA)
http://www.nationalbar.org
Site maintained by the leading organization of African American attorneys; lists NBA chapters, events, membership information, and important articles; also contains links to Internet law sites.

National Organization of Black Law Enforcement Executives (NOBLE)
http://www.noblenatl.org
Site contains news about conferences, programs, membership, and publications.

LITERATURE

African-American Bookshelf
http://www.japhelps.com
Site contains reviews and online ordering.

African American Literature Book Club
http://www.aa/bc.com
Author and book profiles, book club resources.

Afro-in Books
http://www.afro-in-books.com
Reviews and online ordering.

American Black Book Writers Association
http://www.blackbookworld.com
Site includes literary news, information on writing resources, and guidance for authors seeking publishers.

Black Book Discounters
http://members.aol.com.BLACKBOOKS/
    index.html
Online ordering.

Cush City
http://cushcity.com
Online ordering.

Drum and Spear
http://drumandspear.com
Online ordering.

Eso Won Books
http://www.esowon.com
Online ordering.

Hue-Man Experience
http://www.hue-man.com
Online ordering.

IronWood Corner
http://www.choicemall.com/iwc
Online ordering.

Masterworks Books
http://master.com
Online ordering.

Mosaic Books
http://mosaicbooks.com
Reviews, articles, and links.

Quarterly Book Review
http://www.qbr.com
Sites contains reviews, features, articles, and other information.

What 2 Read
http://what2read.com
Reviews, articles, and online ordering.

MILITARY

African American Warriors
http://www.abest.com/~cklose/aawar.htm
Contains links to a number of sites covering all eras of African American military participation, from the American Revolution to Korea; also contains a bibliography of works on African American soldiers and regiments.

MUSIC

Afro-Caribbean Music
http://www.ina.fr/Music.index.en.html
Contains a database that can be searched by artist, country, style, and instrument.

All Music Guide Main Page
http://www.allmusic.com/amg/music_root.html
A truly comprehensive database that covers blues, jazz, gospel, R&B, and every other form of popular music; site also includes an extensive music glossary and a selection of essays on music.

Archives of African American Music and Culture
http://www.indiana.edu/~aamc/
Site contains information on the archives (maintained at Indiana University) and its exhibits; information (including interviews) with African Americans in classical music; and links to a variety of music and cultural sites, including the Black Film Center/Archive.

Black Music Archive
http://www.blackmusicarchive.co.uk
Database contains information on more than 10,000 albums.

SCIENCE

African Technology Forum
http://web.mit.edu/africantech.www
Contains information on science and technology in Africa, as well as articles from the quarterly journal *African Technology Forum*.

Faces in Science
http://www.lib.lsu.edu/lib/chem/display/faces.html
Site maintained by the Chemistry Department at Louisiana State University; contains biographies of African American scientists and statistics on African American science Ph.D.s.

SPORTS

Official Negro Leagues Site
http://www.majorleaguebaseball.com/nbl/index.sml
Site maintained by the Negro Leagues Baseball Museum; contains information on teams, players, Negro Leagues history, and Negro Leagues memorabilia.

TRAVEL AGENCIES

Africa Tours
210 Post Street
San Francisco, CA 94108
415-391-5788

African American Heritage Tours
240 W. Randolph Street
Chicago, IL 60606
312-443-9575

African American Tourism Coalition
2431 W. Hopkins Street
Milwaukee, WI 53206
414-449-4874

African American Tourism Council, Inc.
Indianapolis, IN 46268
317-876-0853

African American Tours
8029 Walnut Creek Lane
Charlotte, NC 28227
701-537-9411

African American Travel
7676 New Hampshire Avenue
Hyattsville, MD 20783
301-431-1162

African American Traveler
438 W. Cypress Street
Glendale, CA 91204
818-247-3697

African Caribbean Group Travel
1547 Ninth Street, NW
Washington, DC 20001
202-265-9488

African Division of Alken Group Tours
1661 Nostrand Avenue
Brooklyn, NY 11226
718-856-9100

African Express Travel and Tours
2932 Wilshire Boulevard
Santa Monica, CA 94115
310-828-4321

African Fantasy Travel Agent
161 Massachusetts Avenue
Boston, MA 02115
617-859-1877

African Tours and Travel
2170 Avenida de la Playa
La Jolla, CA 92092
619-454-9551

African Travel Association
3912 Prospect Avenue, E
Cleveland, OH 44115
216-431-6756

African Travel Bureau
610 228th Avenue
Redmond, WA 98052
206-868-4300

Black History Tours
1721 W. 85th Street
Chicago, IL 60620
312-233-8907

Greater New Orleans Black Tourism Network, Inc.

Louisiana Superdome
1520 Sugar Bowl Drive
New Orleans, LA 70112
504-523-5650

Rodgers Travel Services
50 SW Beal Parkway
Fort Walton Beach, FL 32548
800-853-1128

SOURCES FOR ADDITIONAL INFORMATION

Battle, Stafford L., and Rey O. Harris. *The African American Resource Guide to the Internet and Online Services.* New York: McGraw-Hill, 1997.

Biddle, Stanton F., ed. *The African-American Yellow Pages.* New York: Holt, 1996.

Bunkley, Crawford B., ed. *The African-American Network.* New York: Plume, 1996.

Crayton, Tabitha. *The African American Address Book.* New York: Perigee, 1996.

Van de Sande, Wendy, ed. *Black Americans Information Directory,* 3rd ed. Detroit: Gale, 1993.

Who's Who among Black Americans. Detroit: Gale, biennial.

Illustration Credits

Chapter 1, pages 1 and 12: *Brownies Book*, published by the NAACP

Chapter 2, pages 25 and 43: Courtesy of the Photographs and Prints Division, Schomburg Center for Research in Black Culture, The New York Public Library, Astor, Lenox and Tilden Foundations.

Chapter 3, pages 59 and 61: Library of Congress

Chapter 4, page 93: Robb Walsh, Austin, TX

Chapter 5, pages 121 and 127: Courtesy of the Robert N. Dennis Collection, Miriam & Ira D. Wallach Division of Art, Prints & Photographs, The New York Public Library, Astor, Lenox and Tilden Foundations.

Chapter 6, pages 147 and 152: Valentine Museum, Richmond, VA

Chapter 7, pages 173 and 179: Courtesy of the Photographs and Prints Division, Schomburg Center for Research in Black Culture, The New York Public Library, Astor, Lenox and Tilden Foundations; pages 197–198: Integrated Postsecondary Education Data Systems (IPEDS); page 199: National Postsecondary Student Aid Study: 1992/93; page 200: Baccalaureate and Beyond Longitudinal Study, First Follow-Up (B&B: 93/94); page 201: National Longitudinal Survey of Youth: Children 1986–1992, Females 1979–1992.

Chapter 8, pages 211 and 235: The Smithsonian Institution, National Museum of American History, Scurlock Studio

Chapter 9, pages 237 and 242: Courtesy of the Photographs and Prints Division, Schomburg Center for Research in Black Culture, The New York Public Library, Astor, Lenox and Tilden Foundations.

Chapter 10, pages 271 and 273: Courtesy of the Photographs and Prints Division, Schomburg Center for Research in Black Culture, The New York Public Library, Astor, Lenox and Tilden Foundations.

Chapter 11, pages 283 and 292: Leib Image Archives, York, PA

Chapter 12, pages 307 and 332: National Archives

Chapter 13, pages 335 and 357: Courtesy of the Photographs and Prints Division, Schomburg Center for Research in Black Culture, The New York Public Library, Astor, Lenox and Tilden Foundations.

Chapter 14, pages 367 and 384: Courtesy of Frank Driggs

Chapter 15, pages 403 and 430: Photo by Jack N. Mitchell/Courtesy of the Photographs and Prints Division, Schomburg Center for Research in Black Culture, The New York Public Library, Astor, Lenox and Tilden Foundations

Chapter 16, pages 437 and 442: Elizabeth Catlett/Licensed by VAGA, New York, NY

Chapter 17, pages 461 and 507: Sylvia Plachy, Richmond Hill, NY

Chapter 18, pages 509 and 513: National Baseball Library, Cooperstown, NY

Chapter 19, pages 545 and 556: Courtesy of the Photographs and Prints Division, Schomburg Center for Research in Black Culture, The New York Public Library, Astor, Lenox and Tilden Foundations.

Index

Page numbers in *italics* indicate tables.